Why Peace

Why Peace

Edited by Marc Guttman

This book is dedicated to the innocent victims,
and to the courageous dissenters and whistleblowers.

Contents

Foreword

That Necessary for
Evil to Triumph

Marc Guttman

Marc Guttman works as an emergency physician and is the editor of the book Why Liberty: Personal Journeys Toward Peace and Freedom. *He currently lives in Connecticut with his wife and children, and prefers to spend his time with them and playing outdoors.*

...The air was filled with dust and the building footprints were still smoking hot. The scene was framed by twisted beams and burnt and beaten buildings. Scattered atop the hills of metal and debris, rescue workers worked diligently to find survivors. Below us lay the ruined bodies of thousands of lost innocent victims, and we were helpless to do anything for them at that point....

Many individuals all around the world have learned that only by interacting peacefully can we achieve a more harmonious, prosperous, healthy, fair and tolerant society, that our lives on this planet can be far better. People universally oppose acts of aggression, theft, and fraud when committed by individuals. We accept the principle that the initiation of physical force against others is illegitimate, immoral, and may rightly be defended against. We for the most part also insist that organizations of individuals, such as corporations, also abide by this natural tenet.

When it comes to *state aggression*, however, especially that wrought by democratic governments, the perspective for many of us changes. Individuals too often excuse the state when it harms innocent individuals. This may be because they feel powerless to effect change or uninformed, preferring to defer to those more knowledgeable. They may possess cultivated feelings of nationalism and exceptionalism; expectations of benevolence and altruism in state officials; fears of attack, fostered by interventionist propaganda and complicit mainstream media; yearnings for conformity; or just a willingness to harm, burden or restrict others, in the expectation of benefit to ends and causes they themselves consider to be good ones. Thus, when our governments act as aggressors rather than protectors of human rights, many individuals remain silent.

This is an unfortunate root problem, since government actors are responsible for the greatest measure (by several orders of magnitude) of violence, coercion, and harm done to innocent individuals, both today and throughout human history. These state officials rule, by either might, divine right, or the consent of the governed. What's more, many government interventions, even those well-intentioned, lead to perverse incentives, which usually have a way of turning would-be cooperative participants into adversaries, as members of groups seeking unfair advantage for themselves and restrictions on others. Such aggression has unbalanced and disharmonized us in various ways. This state aggression is vastly important to everyone, as individuals around the planet are being impoverished, robbed, ripped off, maimed, and murdered.

The universal goal of the people in my profession is: *First Do No Harm*. As an emergency physician, my goal is to advise people on how to make the most appropriate medical decisions for themselves. The risk-benefit ratio of every diagnostic test and therapy is considered. I use my understanding of medicine to avoid harming my patients. Similarly, if we are going to commune by the use of government, then *First Do No Harm* needs to be our prime directive. We ought to use government power to protect the life and liberty of individuals, rather than as a weapon against the innocent.

Sometimes I think I'd prefer to be blissfully unaware and go on enjoying my pleasant life, without giving state intervention a second thought. Even if I had no empathy for the humans at home and abroad being violated, however, I know that inevitably the unchecked offenses done to me and my loved ones would exceed my tolerance. It's been rightly proclaimed that all that is necessary for the triumph of evil is that good men do nothing.

I feel as the civil disobedient Mohandas Gandhi did when he said, "If I seem to take part in politics, it is only because politics encircles us today like the coil of a snake, from which one cannot get out, no matter how much one tries. I wish therefore to wrestle with the snake." Historically as well as currently, dissenters have been bullied and silenced, and purposefully mischaracterized by interventionists with low tolerance for resistance. Since most public policies are coercive, it's right they be debated, and for dissenters and victims to voice their objections. May they be indefatigable in those objections, regardless of how they are treated. The policies most often detrimental and overreaching are foreign policy, military interventionism, and civil liberties infringements.

So many individuals with whom I interact are uninformed about much of governments' interventionism and its adverse effects. Maybe this is why such unjust violence is allowed to persist. This provides the impetus for this volume, and for my inviting knowledgeable individuals to contribute to it. After all, governments ultimately rule by the consent of the governed. If we really want to strike at the root and save humans from violent, aggressive force, allowing for greater peace and prosperity, we must withdraw our consent to it, and work actively against state violence.

Contributors from around the world—victims, witnesses, soldiers and military officers, former state officials, political prisoners, journalists, lawyers, civil disobedients, activists, economists, aid workers, epidemiologists, and others—have shared their personal experiences with military intervention and police state abuses, along with the understandings each has reached regarding the harms and adverse effects (both universal and individual) of such interventions. These diverse dissenters, from many corners of the world and different walks of life, explain here why they have embraced peace and believe non-intervention and human rights is preferable. Although they undoubtedly hold varying, perhaps even contradictory, opinions on some public policies (and you'll read and recognize some of them), what they share here are their objections to the most harmful ones. Some promote radical positions (radically peaceful) that are as worthy of consideration and discussion as they are thoughtful, intelligent, and perhaps even universally beneficial.

For me, my story was almost over before it began. In 1964, my father, knowing he would soon be drafted against his will into the US Army, decided to join the New York Army National Guard, in the hopes that this would keep him from being forced to go to Vietnam and fight a war he opposed. He was in the 105th field artillery of the 42nd infantry division (Rainbow Division) in New York City.

My father had no interest in soldiering. In fact, some of my fondest memories of childhood were begging him during family road trips to retell the hilarious stories of his mishaps during his military training. I loved the way he told these stories, always laughing and with a look that expressed some of the absurdity of his situation.

Let me share a few:

One Sunday at Camp Smith my father was sunning himself on a rock, rather than participating in worship, although the rule was if you didn't worship than you were supposed to be working. A sergeant approached him and said something along the lines of, "Guttman, why aren't you in religious services?" My father informed him that he was in fact a sun-worshiper and wished to be left to worship, to which he was told, "As you were." (Unfortunately, this dodge only worked the one time.)

On another occasion at Camp Drum my father answered a ringing phone he was walking past, "Camp Morgue ... You kill 'em, we chill 'em."

The incredulous voice on the other end of the line inquired angrily, "Do you know who this is?"

"No."

"This is Colonel _____," responded the commander of Camp Drum who would, my father thought, likely make his life truly miserable for his crack.

"Do you know who this is?" my frightened father responded with false bravado.

"No."

"Good!" and he hung up.

While shooting at Fort Dix, my father's arms were too short to achieve a correct cheek-to-stock weld with his rifle, so an officer gave him an ornately decorated award rifle of his own that was easier for Dad to handle. As he walked through the firing range, he felt the other men's eyes on him and his special gun. They assumed him to be an expert marksman, but he soon disappointed them in comical fashion. In a similar incident, my father's face mask was too big for his face while he was being exposed to some noxious gas. His face burning, he ran from the area. Blinded, he ripped off his mask and yelled, "Shit!" He heard an officer respond wryly, "Don't you mean 'Shit, Sir?'"

You can see my father wanted no part of being a soldier. He was assigned as company clerk, which was in fact a dangerous job in Vietnam, as clerks often needed to transport messages and often got killed. However, some tragic fateful events in Harlem changed his life ... and allowed for mine.

On July 16, 1964, a 15-year-old black boy, James Powell, alleged to be engaged in horseplay with friends in Harlem, was shot and killed by a New York City police officer, Lieutenant Thomas Gilligan. Gilligan alleged the boy had lunged at him with a knife. A planned peaceful civil rights rally that day quickly turned into a police-brutality protest, as news of the awful incident spread. Protestors marched on Harlem's 28th Police Precinct, demanding the dismissal and prosecution of Gilligan. Police charged the protestors, which incited violent retaliation from the crowd. For five days, there were scattered incidents of skirmishes between citizens and police officers. Meanwhile, some other civilians seized the opportunity to loot and vandalize.

The 42nd infantry was put on alert. Because of this incident and the expectation of more civil unrest, my father's division (which at the time was on yellow (standby) alert to go to Vietnam) had their mission changed. They were to remain in the States and be trained in riot control. My dad survived the Vietnam War, and never had to be in harm's way nor be ordered to harm others. He went on to become a very well-liked teacher in the Bronx, NY for 34 years, and he, along with my mother, a nurse, were shining examples to me and my brothers of good individuals who treated others well.

However, let's consider "riot" control. The men in my father's unit were trained to control individuals who were protesting, most often peacefully, against perceived injustices in government policies, one of which was the impression, though disputed, that black individuals were being drafted into the army at a disproportionate rate, compared to white individuals. It was later, on May 4, 1970 at Kent State, that Ohio National Guardsmen would fire 67 rounds at unarmed college students who were peacefully expressing their disapproval of the US invasion of Cambodia, killing four protestors and observers and wounding nine others, even paralyzing one of them.

While growing up, I was taught in school about tyrannical governments from long ago, the not-so-distant past, and the present—governments that aggressed against individuals in their own lands as well as abroad. I learned of the oppression and violence of European and Asian empires, of colonialism, of modern day European fascist governments, and of the Asian communist governments and the hundreds-of-millions of innocent individuals they murdered and incarcerated.

But at the same time I was also being taught, by way of countless examples, however spun and inaccurate, that Western democracies were exceptions to this. The colonists in North America, I learned, created the US federal government to protect their natural human rights and supposedly restrained it from "mischief"—from harming any individual in the world—with the "chains" of the Constitution. I was also taught that the US government, exclusively, was the greatest protector of justice and righteousness the world had known, as if human evolution had naturally led us to this safeguarding institution. Finally, I was taught that it was the responsibility of American citizens to share the wealth they create with the government, so it may maintain a massive military force. Furthermore, this super-power was not there just to protect Americans and any freedoms we were allowed to enjoy, but also to intervene overseas whenever necessary, to protect human rights from the intrusions of those other non-democratic states.

Perhaps thanks to the peace movement of the 1960s and '70s that I had also learned a bit about, I held some skepticism that US government militarism was always about justice, and never for such nefarious reasons and special interests as empire and corporatism. Over the years, I have come to understand that regardless of the true motivations of government actors, their interventions are most often unjust and harmful.

Going well beyond matters of defense—whether in the interest of aiding others, making resources available to themselves or protecting private industries' interests— countries adopt aggressive foreign policies, intervening with neither a moral justification nor any reasonable authority. Military interventions have caused the upheaval and destruction of the lives of so many millions of families. Studying world history makes it clear that aggression begets aggression and blowback. Despite popular arguments to the contrary, war nearly always impoverishes most everyone, except of course those trading in the war industry.

In the 4th grade (where ironically our teacher leaned heavily authoritarian in her interactions with us), we had a unit on civics. We students were encouraged to run for a few created classroom offices: judge, police officer, legislators, etc. I ran for police officer, and won the office. The classmates elected legislators then created laws that the students were expected to obey.

One law passed was that students were not allowed to talk when in line to exit the classroom at the end of the day. It's interesting that students would impose this restriction on themselves, but we were kids excited about playing our new game of making and enforcing laws. We were following our teacher's instructions. We were also mimicking the world in which we were being brought up, with our strict teacher and the restrictions we saw around us every day, both in and out of school. We were also finding out the truth: once individuals have power over others, they will often use it to restrain or burden them.

The 1971 Stanford Prison Experiment was a controversial study of the psychological effects of becoming a prisoner or prison guard. Student volunteers were assigned to play either of the two roles. The guards quickly began to display authoritarian behavior, and even harmed some of the prisoners. Many of the prisoners passively accepted this physical abuse, and some even readily followed orders by the guards to inflict punishment on other prisoners who attempted to stop it. Because of this, the experiment was abruptly terminated in just six days.

Although it seems silly to bring up here, my lesson has stuck, and it may be illustrative. Although the officers in my 4th grade class didn't follow the imposed rules themselves, I was eager to play, and cited two girls in my class for talking in line. Immediately, though, I felt uncomfortable and regretted it. The next day the girls had their trial, and I stood witness to my accusations.

I felt incredibly embarrassed, but lacked the courage to tell the "court" and the classroom that the girls, even though they had broken the new classroom law, had done nothing wrong and had neither harmed nor bothered anyone. The girls admitted their guilt and received some "fair" punishment, yet the injustice of it really bothered me at the time.

We all have grown accustomed to restrictions put in place by other humans. (I still cringe whenever my school-aged daughter asks me, "are we allowed?" when I suggest we do some fun activity.)

Two decades before the Stanford experiments, the Asch conformity studies, whose results were published in the 1950s, demonstrated the power of conformity in groups. Participants were asked to respond to questions about printed lines on cards presented by the experimenters with fairly obvious differences visible. At times, plants in the study would purposefully give incorrect answers when asked the questions. When more than two plants answered incorrectly, many of the unwitting other participants would conform, and also give the incorrect answer. This interesting study showed how people will go along with something obviously wrong, for the comfort of not standing against the consensus.

I was thirteen during the Iran-Contra hearings and had little idea of what was going on. I understood that officials in the Reagan administration were being investigated for illegal covert operations, somehow involving American hostages in Iran and conflict with anti-government forces in Central America. Several years later, I also learned of the context: the 1953 Iranian *coup d'état*, the overthrow of the democratically-elected government of Prime Minister Mohammad Mosaddegh (orchestrated by the intelligence agencies of the U.S. and U.K.), and the installation of Mohammad-Reza Shah Pahlavi as the leader of Iran. The Shah would of course then be friendly to US government interests (including those of U.S. oil companies), while running roughshod over Iranians and their rights. The 1979 Iranian Revolution then deposed the Shah and replaced the pro-Western royal dictatorship with the largely anti-Western Islamic Republic of Iran. The Iran Hostage Crisis would follow, rather naturally.

Meanwhile, I was faintly aware of U.S. military operations in Libya, Lebanon, Grenada, Honduras, Nicaragua, and Panama as they passed through the headlines and into history.

I remember the abundant yellow ribbons around neighborhood trees during the first Gulf War, *Operation Desert Storm*, and I accepted without much consideration that it was legitimate for the U.S. government to send U.S. soldiers to protect Kuwaitis from the Iraqi dictator, Saddam Hussein. I don't think I was aware at the time of the sanctions against Iraq that were initiated then, but I learned some years later of the many Iraqis who suffered horribly and unnecessarily, because of them, until the Iraq invasion in 2003.

Again, still a teenager when the U.S. government intervened during the warring in Bosnia, I did not educate myself to any significant degree about the conflict or the rationale for U.S. involvement, but I was resistant to U.S. efforts in nation-building.

For me, like most people, as an easy-going, younger adult, I took little interest in politics. I would much rather be backpacking or snowboarding than discussing public policy, let alone trying to convince anyone of anything. Government and politics had little to do with me, and I never thought to want anything to do with it. Little did I know....

My lessons really began when I was most free. At 21, I had graduated college, and was for the first time self-sufficient. Soon after my final exams, I traveled on a one-way ticket to Africa and solo-backpacked through a dozen countries for half a year. It was easy for me to feel liberated and inspired while hitchhiking through sub-Saharan Africa, where you can often pitch a tent right where you stand, or purchase meat from anyone on the street; on the ground, few rules seemed to exist. At least they didn't seem to exist for me, since I had no plans to prosper in Africa. Rather, I felt confident, self-aware, and excited. I enjoyed my experiences and the pleasant way and easy smiles of the Africans I met along the way.

Unfortunately, Africa is not a land of freedom in many important ways. For the most part, individual Africans have few rights to be defended against the might of government or the whims of local strongmen and bureaucrats. Many African countries have brutal histories of war, slavery, and oppression. Governments seem often an obstruction to people's prosperity. I was not savvy enough at the time to inquire about details, but I do remember talks with local people trying to get businesses going, and facing impenetrable bureaucracy, graft and bribery, as well as prohibitive costs and regulations.

A few times, I sensed a fear of government. I remember a Zimbabwean man grabbing my shoulder, alerting me not to move as President Robert Mugabe's motorcade rode past in Harare, because I would risk being shot at by his military. I was also not allowed to pass into Rwanda, because fleeing refugees were flooding in from warring Zaire. While hiking on the border between Zaire and Uganda, I was turned back by my local guide, because of evidence of violence in the area. I was later told that a nearby village had been burned in a civil-war-related incident.

It was during this time traveling—a time of seemingly endless leisure and adventure, free of the rigors and structure of school and study—that my mind unfastened, and I became starkly aware of it all. It occurred to me that for the first time I was having original, thoughtful ideas. I gained some perspective and learned a sense of the value of self-ownership and awareness. I also found a new interest in learning.

Once I got home, while talking with my older brother, Evan, I shared some of my budding ideas. He thought to introduce me to the writings of Harry Browne. Browne expertly explains why the non-aggression principle, peaceful voluntary interaction, is as universally beneficial with regard to public policy as it is in all other human relations. In reading his works, I learned a more detailed and even-handed story of U.S. history. This knowledge was enhanced by reading such revisionist historians as Thomas Woods, Thomas DiLorenzo, and others. I saw that the U.S. Constitution was not sufficient in binding the new government as many of the framers had intended, as it had not taken long for its members to impose the same oppressions as those of the thrown-off British Crown and Parliament.

These injustices would, unfortunately for so many, go much further. I realized that, in particular, not only were the bombings of civilians in Hiroshima and Nagasaki reprehensible acts, they were also unnecessary. Browne's writings also criticized the U.S. government's intrusive foreign policies and our numerous military bases overseas. They clearly explained why so many of those who were occupied objected. I came to understand the wrongs and harms of the U.S. government interventions in North America and overseas, actions I had once been taught were just, and necessary to human peace and prosperity.

One of the greatest benefits of my medical training and practice has been the vast amount of interaction I have had with individuals from all walks of life and cultures, as both patients and staff. Training in New York City and places far from there around the western US, including Alaska, as well as in India, has enhanced this exposure. This has only amplified my empathy for and connection to others.

Interspersed within my training and since, I have enjoyed other backpacking trips through North, Central, and South America, India, Nepal, Tibet, and the Iberian Peninsula in Europe. Perhaps, it was also my interaction with individuals in these places and other travelers along the way that has allowed me to appreciate the universal humanity of everyone everywhere, that Americans are no more exceptional, no better or worse, than other individuals across the globe, and that it makes little sense to conflate countries and the people who live there with their governments.

So, when individuals are killed by bombs halfway around the world, I feel no less sadness than when murderers flew planes into the Towers in lower Manhattan on September 11, 2001, and those buildings collapsed, and those innocent individuals died. It always surprises me how upset some individuals are and how indignant they become when their countrymen suffer, but how they can then be overwhelmingly indifferent to the suffering of others elsewhere. I appreciate the immoral equivalence of aggression, regardless of who initiates it, that too many people reject.

On 09/11, I was working in an emergency room in Harlem. As soon as the second plane hit, we went into our disaster/mass-casualty plan, while trying to suppress our own intense emotions. We were amped and focused for the next several hours. Unfortunately, there were not many walking wounded for us to treat, due to the overwhelming forces of impact, fire, and structure collapse that had killed everyone unable to escape the buildings. I spent that day caring for firemen, police-officers and some others who had inhaled dust. I made time to call my family, to let them know I was well, and to try consoling a scared friend whose husband, a fireman, had called her from Ground Zero. (Unlike many of his colleagues and friends, he was fortunate to survive, and we still have him with us.)

At the end of my thirteen-hour shift that evening, reluctant to use the subway system, I walked the 4 miles from Harlem to East 24th street, where I lived, and went to sleep immediately. The next morning, I walked to a nearby hospital, where I also worked, wearing my hospital credentials; along with other physicians, I rode an ambulance to Ground Zero to volunteer with the rescue effort.

The air was still filled with dust and the building footprints were still smoking hot. The scene was framed by twisted beams and burnt and beaten buildings. Scattered atop the hills of metal and debris, rescue workers worked diligently to find survivors. On our arrival, someone was found alive underground. I saw him or her carried on a backboard to an ambulance, and was enthusiastic that there was still help that could be provided.

Someone enlisted me to set up a breathing treatment station, to provide oxygen and nebulizer treatments to rescue workers suffering with bronchospasm. For a short time, someone asked me to mark on a diagram and tag where rescue workers had found body parts that were handed to me in dark plastic bags. Other than that, there was very little I was able to do to help.

That night, at a friend's apartment, I was finally able to see footage of the planes hitting the World Trade Center and hear eye-witness accounts. Over the next several weeks, I would read newspapers on the subway while commuting to work. They told the stories of victims and their loved ones. It was heart-breaking, and I would arrive at work each day teary-eyed and torn up.

It was an emotional time. The US President was making a case for national threats and a needed "War on Terrorism." I also read some very wise words, from Harry Browne, warning us against the danger of military interventions. Some other prominent libertarians were making the case for going after the individual accomplices to this criminal and murderous act; however, like Browne, they also rejected military mobilizations to Afghanistan.

I fully admit that I questioned my pretenses and debated with myself. National Defense is a legitimate function of government, and I wondered at the time whether military intervention might be the right path. I even contacted some military recruiters to talk about possible enrollment, wanting to do my part by taking care of soldiers overseas, once my emergency medicine training would be complete in a couple of years. (I later decided against this).

The explanations of George W. Bush and Colin Powell, about Iraq's alleged weapons of mass destruction and Saddam Hussein's possibly using them against innocents, concerned me. Hussein had already a decade earlier invaded Kuwait; might he harm more people now? I felt that if they could make a credible case of there being an immediate threat, then preemptive intervention might be appropriate. My good friend, John Calone, surprised by my contemplations, argued with me vehemently, pleading with me not to accept this farce, and his words got me re-oriented.

Of course, we know that a credible case for an imminent threat was never made, and no such weapons were found after the invasion. In the light of truth and clarity, it is clear that Iraq posed no threat, that the war on Iraqis has been offensive rather than defensive, and that the global War on Terror, which the government claims encompasses a global battlefield, has only been counterproductive, killing innocent individuals, and creating more new enemies. Insurgents trying to protect their homes and families are not terrorists. (What's more, John made the case that the US government has no moral authority to intervene, regardless of what weapons another government may produce or procure.)

Since 9-11 (which was itself a response to U.S. government military activities over several decades, according to the words of the alleged conspirators and the intelligence officers who analyzed them) the U.S. government has waged war on several fronts, vastly expanded the surveillance state at home, and infringed on many of our civil liberties, including incarcerating thousands of individuals without trial, even to this day. Like so many of my generation, this has been my time of greatest insight and awareness of U.S. government actions. Antiwar.com, and Antiwar Radio with Scott Horton and his terrific guests, have been the most helpful sources in enlightening me to the reality of world events.

I can understand how an individual might, out of fear, accept the government's argument for military interventions, and even preemptive wars. History, reason and knowledge refute these policies. The U.S. War on Terror on several fronts over the last decade was the final piece of the puzzle, causing me to deeply consider the morality, and reject the legitimacy of two centuries of interventionist US foreign policy.

During the US presidential campaign in 2008, there seemed to be no significant difference between Barack Obama and John McCain, on either domestic or foreign policy issues. Though I didn't vote for either of them, I had some hope that Obama might intervene less overseas were he to win. In the first few months of his presidency, Obama condemned torture and detention without due process, and talked less tough on the U.S. government's overseas ambitions. I conceded to some of my friends who had supported him that Obama was off to a good start.

Soon enough, though, his rhetoric proved hollow. President Obama's policies have been as harmful as his predecessor's were to individual rights and the security of ourselves, our soldiers, and the unfortunate communities overseas they harm. He has continued George Bush's policy of detaining prisoners without due process, and of extraditing our military prisoners to other governments to be tortured by them. He has supported extending the USA PATRIOT [*Uniting (and) Strengthening America (by) Providing Appropriate Tools Required (to) Intercept (and) Obstruct Terrorism*] Act of 2001; continued warrantless spying programs, secret prisons, and invasive Transportation Security Administration body searches; maintained the Military Commissions Act; and has even claimed an executive right to assassinate anyone in the world who he determines to be an enemy combatant. What's more, he has even executed that power. These policies infringe on our rights to due process and to be secure against unreasonable searches and seizures.

The US government continues to war in Iraq and to build large military bases there, guaranteeing our long-term occupation. Though the administration claims to be withdrawing from that country, the US military will still hold a strong presence there, as they increase forces in nearby countries. Obama has bombed Pakistanis and Yemenis, escalated the war in Afghanistan, engaged the U.S. military in Libya, even without congressional approval, and worsened the situation with Iran—misinforming the world that Iranians are working on a secret nuclear program, despite knowing Iran had already reported the program to International Atomic Energy Agency inspectors. It also appears we are on the verge of placing more sanctions on Iran's citizens, harming more innocent people and creating more enemies. That Obama won the Nobel Peace Prize suggests that George Orwell's doublespeak in *1984* is now real: "War is Peace."

According to the War Resisters League, current military spending makes up 36 percent of federal government spending. Another 18 percent they report is for veterans' benefits and interest payments on the national debt, which the League contends only exists because of our military spending.

Joseph Sobran was right, "War is just one more big government program," the biggest by far, as well as a massive industry. Contrary to claims in history textbooks, war creates no wealth. It is only destructive. Military planes, boats, tanks, bombs, trucks, guns, and bullets add nothing to our quality of life, not to forget the destroyed homes, buildings, streets, bridges, and the individuals lost and families ruined. War is the greatest and saddest waste of our resources.

Military spending is an opportunity-cost that detracts from our wealth. It is wealth that enables us to educate ourselves and our children, provide for our health care and safety, nourish ourselves with healthy foods, protect our environment, aid others, and engage in the activities in which we delight.

Being naturally tolerant and optimistic, I prefer not to be a detractor, but this evil will indeed continue to triumph if good men and women do nothing. A supposed Chinese curse says may you live in interesting times. Well, the 21st century has so far not disappointed with depressed economies, wars overseas, and authoritarianism and cronyism at home. But we can make these curses into blessings. There has already been a stiff shift in public opinion and conventional wisdom and massive grassroots movements to activism. Governments surely derive their power from the consent of the governed, and the governed lately (around the planet) are expressing their disapproval *en masse*. More and more individuals today understand and oppose state aggression.

Historically, though, thousands of brave citizens have refused to pay taxes, so as not to support what they believe are immoral actions by our government. Tax resistance has again increased in popularity over the last decade, with many protesting the American wars in Iraq, Afghanistan, Pakistan, Somalia, Yemen, and Libya.

Peace-activist heroes throughout history have participated in this type of civil disobedience. Henry David Thoreau was imprisoned for refusing to pay taxes as a protest against the American war on Mexico, as well as against slavery. Mohandas Gandhi's nonviolent protests included resistance to the British Salt Tax. He publicly boiled a pan of seawater, illegally producing salt. His action encouraged Indians to disobey the British authority and produce their own salt, rather than purchase it from the British monopoly and pay the excessive taxes. Tens-of-thousands of Indians were incarcerated. Britain's control of the colony weakened as their injustices were made more visible. Gandhi was following in the tradition of American revolutionaries like John Hancock, a successful merchant, big-time smuggler and tax protestor, and flamboyant signer of the Declaration of Independence.

My experience and study has led me to a position of non-intervention. For me, accepting the nonaggression principle, I believe that individuals and groups have the right to defend themselves from aggression. While at times defensive force may be necessary, I also believe that at times nonviolent disobedience and dissent, like that taught by Mohandas Gandhi and Martin Luther King Jr., can lead to more favorable results.

To many of us dissenters, positive ends are not justified, nor are they even achievable, by aggressive means. Most people could go along with governments intervening in cases of indisputable public goods. National security may be such a case, but it may not, for example, be gained at the expense of individuals' rights to due process and privacy.

In the end, is not the burden of proof on the proponents of an intrusive policy? They need prove that there is some incontrovertible public good being protected or provided, as good reason for their infringing on other humans. More than that, shouldn't we reject the government putting military personnel at risk in calamitous circumstances and asking them to engage in war, unless there is a clear-cut necessity?

Government is the only entity with a monopoly on relatively legitimate force, which is why it is prudent to be vigilant in our watchfulness and restraint. Not everyone accepts that governments consist of only disinterested parties endeavoring for peace and justice.

Ending government wars and protecting human rights are positions so basic, universal, and important to human wellness, fairness, peace and prosperity, most individuals will agree upon doing so, and on how we ought to unite to effect positive change. By ending aggression by states, we can stop this cycle of violence for future generations.

To help demonstrate the philosophy, morality, and universal benefits of peace, I have asked for the participation of intelligent individuals with particular insights in these matters, to share their experiences and knowledge with us. I have learned so much from the contributors to this volume. From Africa, from behind what was once the Iron Curtain, to Europe, the Middle East, Asia, and North, Central and South America... there are dozens of stories about why these diverse people came to a similar conclusion: *peace is best for all*. I expect you will find their stories as educational, illustrative, entertaining, insightful and inspiring as I have.

In the end, that is the most important goal of this endeavor: discovery, truth, and peace.

-    December 2011

For Ali Hussein
and my Grandson

Philip Giraldi

Philip Giraldi is a former counter-terrorism specialist for the United States Army and the Central Intelligence Agency who served twenty years in Italy, Germany, Turkey and Spain. He is a contributing editor to The American Conservative *and executive director of the Council for the National Interest. He writes regularly for* Antiwar.com.

I worked in the national-security establishment, for the CIA and Department of Defense, for over twenty years. I have always thought of myself as a realist in foreign policy, accepting that the United States must occasionally use its military power to maintain a *Pax Americana* that would benefit most nations. As a government insider and an army enlisted man during the Vietnam conflict, I understood perfectly well that the use of force by the United States had frequently been misguided, but I also believed that on balance it was better that my own country should function as *hegemon*, rather than some other less principled nation that might behave more ruthlessly.

As a realist, I accepted the invasion of Afghanistan in the wake of 9/11 and even took part in it, but I opposed the machinations that led to the war against Iraq. I understood perfectly well that no *casus belli* had been established; that the intelligence to justify the war had been fabricated or exaggerated; that Iraq was no threat to the United States; and that the White House appeared to be prepared to launch a war of aggression, without complying with the constitutional requirement that Congress be the only government authority that can declare war. When I realized that the march to war was inexorable, I began to write and speak against it, attending peace rallies for the first time in my life.

I predicted correctly that no good would come out of invading Iraq, and kept up my criticism of the conduct of the war and the evils that it had unleashed, including the use of torture and secret prisons. I also was concerned by the devastation inflicted on an essentially innocent Iraqi civilian population.

But my concerns continued to be realism-based and essentially conservative in nature. The war was costing too much, was killing large numbers of my fellow citizens, and would undoubtedly have a bad outcome. In my mind, it was a very serious policy mistake, possibly the worst mistake any administration had ever made in the foreign policy arena.

Then I saw the picture. It was April 29th, 2008. I remember the moment well. I had flipped open the *Washington Post* and there, on the front page, was a color photo of a two-year-old Iraqi boy named Ali Hussein, being pulled from the rubble of a house that had been destroyed by errant American missiles. The little boy was wearing shorts and a t-shirt and had on his feet flip-flops. His head was hanging back at an angle that told the viewer immediately that he was dead. That small boy looked remarkably like my little grandson, similarly attired, who was sitting beside me eating his cereal. When I gasped at the photo, my little guy looked up at me and grinned, wondering why grandpa was crying.

Four days later on May 3rd a letter by a Dunn Loring Virginia woman named Valerie Murphy was printed by the *Post*. Murphy complained that the Iraqi child victim photo should not have been run in the paper, because it would "stir up opposition to the war and feed anti-US sentiment." I suppose the newspaper thought it was being impartial in printing the woman's letter; I couldn't help but remember that the *Post* had generally been unwilling to cover anything antiwar, even ignoring a gathering of 300,000 protesters in Washington in 2005. Rereading the woman's complaint along with a comment on a website suggesting that the photo of the dead little boy had been staged, I thought to myself, "What kind of monsters have we become?" It was a turning point for me. The whole Iraq venture was not only a horrible mistake, it was wrong, dead wrong. Evil. My country had gone over to the dark side.

And in truth we had become monsters—bipartisan monsters, wrapped in the American flag. Bill Clinton's Secretary of State Madeleine Albright once said that killing 500,000 Iraqi children through sanctions was "worth it." She was neither removed from office nor even rebuked. She has never apologized. Every day, our current Democratic administration continues the policies of the preceding Republican administration, as it bombs and kills farmers in their fields, children in their schools, doctors and patients in hospitals, and wedding parties. It is the lifeless little Ali Hussein times one thousand. We kill using pilotless drones, helicopters, and airplanes flying so high in the sky that they are invisible to those on the ground.

The slaughter is strictly 21st-century high tech, death from the skies, bloodless, without looking into the eyes of those we are killing. We do it because our leaders tell us we need to kill to keep others from attacking us, but we all know it is a fraud. Does any American really believe that what is going on, in either Iraq or Afghanistan, has anything to do with genuine threats against the United States?

The more we kill the more we give cause to those who hate us, guaranteeing that the bloodshed will never end. Whatever our government does or does not do, we will undoubtedly leave Iraq and Afghanistan some day, and those two countries will quickly learn to live without us. One thing that is for sure is that there will be no friendly crowds as the last C-17 lifts off from Bagram Airbase, and we will only leave hatred behind us. Hatred and the dead, hundreds of thousands of dead.

These days, as the pattern of endless war seems to be seared into the DNA of all our leaders, be they Democrats or Republicans, I am locked in an endless struggle to make sense of something that defies all reason. As a veteran myself, I grieve particularly for our fellow countrymen who have given up their lives in service to their country over the past ten years. I remember well the young faces of my former Army comrades who died in Vietnam in a war that none of us understood, faces frozen in time from lives now lost forever. The numbers tell us that 4,439 Americans have died in Iraq and 1,491 in Afghanistan, with no end in sight and the death-rate in Afghanistan escalating dramatically. I carefully read the obituaries of soldiers and marines in the newspapers, men and women just like me who leave behind shattered families, who will never see their children grow, who will never have their dreams realized.

Dead Afghans and Iraqis are a huge and almost unimaginable human tragedy, but the Americans who have died are truly flesh of our flesh and blood of our blood. As John Donne put it, the dead are of us, so "Do not ask for whom the bell tolls, it tolls for thee." And they have died for nothing beyond shedding their blood—not to nourish the tree of liberty, but rather a garden of deceit planted by our politicians, elected leaders who have forgotten the cardinal rule that asking any American to die on foreign soil should be a last resort, not a "policy option." Ten years of the sacrifice of our children has not made us safer, has not made us better, and has only made much of the world hate us.

Ali Hussein and my grandson have made me determined to do better, to speak out more often and more loudly about the horror that has engulfed our nation. Americans need to unite to tell the Bushes, Clintons and Obamas that they will not have any more of our children for their wars. It is time for all of us to say to General Petraeus (as well as his enablers in Congress and the media), "Enough!" Every American should reflect on the men and women dying in Iraq and Afghanistan for nothing, lives thrown away.

Each of us should resolve to be selfish, thinking first of our grandchildren, sons and daughters and our friends and loved ones who might be consumed in the long war that the politicians and generals continue to embrace. There must not be one more senseless death, be it of an American, an Iraqi, an Afghan or an Iranian. Not one. I have made this demand for a restoration of decency to our politicians and, if they do not agree, I have urged that we do whatever it takes to remove them from office. They will undoubtedly be replaced by men and women only slightly better than they are, but if we repeat the lesson often enough they will eventually learn that the hell they have created will not endure. It cannot endure.

War: Not Anarchy,
but Shrinking Circles

Les Roberts

Les Roberts, PhD, holds has a Masters degree in Public Health from Tulane University and a Ph.D. in Environmental Engineering from Johns Hopkins University. He did a post-doctorate fellowship in epidemiology at the Centers for Disease Control and Prevention where he worked for four years. In 1994, he worked as an epidemiologist for the World Health Organization in Rwanda during their civil war. Les was Director of Health Policy at the International Rescue Committee from December 2000 until April of 2003. He had led over 50 surveys in 17 countries, mostly measuring mortality in times of war. In recent years he has taken part in studies to measure mortality in Democratic Republic of Congo, Iraq, Zimbabwe and Central African Republic. His present research is focused on developing methods to document the incidence of human rights violations. Les teaches at Columbia University's Program on Forced Migration and Health and lives in Central New York with his wife, Mary Grace.

In his book, *I Will Bear Witness: A Diary of the Nazi Years 1933-1941*, Victor Klemperer describes his shrinking world as a Jew in Germany surrounded by the rise of Nazism. A once-rich and full life, with outings and culture and educational opportunities shrunk little by little, until existence was reduced to hiding in one's home, focused on finding the next meal. The physical world outside stayed constant, but that lattice of communications and friends and activities that makes humanity something more than just proximal humans slowly disappeared. In the early stages of my career I worked with refugees from Mozambique. I did my dissertation research in a shanty town controlled by the Shining Path in Peru, but those were fundamentally peaceful settings with a palpable amount of stress added.

Thus, in 1993 when I was sent to Sarajevo by the Centers for Disease Control I had very little preparation or true understanding of just what the word "war" signified. Sarajevo was at the time surrounded by Serb forces who held almost all the high terrain. For months, hundreds of thousands of rounds of exploding weaponry had rained down on the city. A city that I had only seen on television as the host of a modern Olympics had been devastated. The residents had been reduced to living like rats, scurrying from safe haven to safe haven, trying to stay out of the sight of snipers. Almost all food was flown in by the international community, and most commercial and governmental activities had come to a halt. I have two extremely vivid memories of that six-week visit; both are visual expressions of how tiny the world of Sarajevo had become, and how the outside rules simply did not apply.

One day I was walking down the central avenue in the middle of town, and three young boys perhaps 10 or 12 years of age were walking about half a block ahead of me. There was a major crossroad where snipers on the hill above town could look down the cross-street and see people as they went by on the main avenue. At other cross-streets, concrete barriers had been erected to hide transiting pedestrians, but this street had remained open for traffic purposes. Everyone knew they had to sprint across this cross-street to avoid being picked-off by snipers. As the three lads arrived at the cross-street, they paused and got in the "to your mark" position as if starting a race. Two of the boys bolted, but the other paused until the others were almost across and then started running. A sniper shot at the third boy, and the bullet smacked concrete on the opposite side of the road, creating a little cloud of dust. As the third child reached his waiting mates on the other side and the dull report of the rifle arrived in our ears, he leapt in the air and gave each a high-five and burst into laughter. I do not know if the third lad hesitated to ensure he would have the thrill of being shot at, or if he had paused out of fear. Either way, their world, so inconceivably removed from the Europe of seatbelt laws and toy safety regulations that surrounded them, had somehow devolved to the point where a professionally trained killer attempting to shoot them had become sport. How could this be modern Europe?

My second lingering Sarajevo impression, while just as visual, probably arises from the statistical nature of my public-health training. During the summer of 1993, many, perhaps most of the children in Sarajevo had been sent away to live with relatives in safer areas. Thus, probably only 20 percent or less of the population were children during this siege. As my CDC colleague and I went around interviewing hospital, Red Crescent and other officials, many Bosnians attempted to horrify us with tales about what the Serb side had been doing. Among the litany of horrors that the interviewees described, two were particularly consistent: One, that the Serbs had bought German castration devices to use on Bosnian men; the other, that snipers would shoot children in the legs as bait, and then shoot others as they went to try and help them.

My colleague and I were highly skeptical of the rumors, and when we asked for specific episodes with dates and places, examples were never forthcoming. Then, toward the end of our stay, we walked into the surgical ward in Sarajevo's Kosovo Hospital, and saw that a huge fraction, probably a majority of the patients in the beds, were children who had been shot in the legs. My colleague and I just felt sick about our previous cynicism and skepticism. I simply did not have space in my imagination to allow the possibility that many—tens, perhaps hundreds of Serb soldiers—could bring themselves to shoot children as bait. This was because I did not understand that war allows that much isolation of thought and that much impunity. Thinking of this experience makes the recent arrest of Ratko Mladic, the general in charge of those snipers, all the more important. It shows that the norms of Europe shut out for that chapter of horror could not be kept out forever.

I spent a couple of months in both 2000 and 2001 conducting mortality surveys in the Eastern Democratic Republic of Congo. In some of the world's least developed terrain I rode motorbikes more than 1000 km, walked more than 500km, and bounced around in cars for distances far further. This physical struggle, this focus of my time and energy on the physical world, probably limited my ability to understand and interpret the data I was collecting. We recorded that like clockwork those communities that had been displaced experienced more death. In the Kalonge administrative area, where an estimated 90 percent of 59,000 people fled their homes over a three-month period, the mortality rate tripled after displacement from the already high rate. Most of these deaths were attributed by family members to malaria and diarrhea.

In another area on Lake Tanganyika, where most residents had fled their home for some period in the past year, 14 percent of the population had died over that period.

Children born since the 1998 invasion by Rwanda, Uganda, and Burundi had experienced a two-thirds chance of dying before the age of two. These are almost unheard-of mortality rates, reminiscent of WWII prisoner of war camps. As I traveled around the US speaking in public about this crisis, I tried to explain the link between violence and death by infectious diseases as being mediated by displacement. I argued that people displaced by violence and fear were dying because they were away from their water supply, slept out in the rain and cold, could not get medical care and perhaps ate little while displaced—all of which I still think is true.

But in 2002, we conducted a survey in the city of Kisangani, just months after withdrawing Rwandan forces and Congolese police had clashed over control of the diamond markets in that city. The Rwandan forces had attempted to install their proxies as they withdrew, and the Congolese police had attempted to usurp those proxies. Something on the order of 500 to 800 Congolese police were killed, and for months people in the city stayed in a heightened sense of fear as this power struggle sorted itself out. The ubiquitous bicycle taxis disappeared from the streets, and most shops remained closed for weeks. In the period during this flare-up, and for five months after, deaths in the civilian population rose by 80 percent, in spite of no similar pattern being seen elsewhere in the region. These folks had not been displaced. They were in their urban homes, with their usual water sources and still near a hospital. They had somehow experienced what Klemperer had in Germany 60 years before. They were dying of the stress, be that a psychological or social phenomena, induced by the political unrest.

Suddenly the processes leading to those infectious disease deaths I had reported in the past years were less clear. When people are displaced and hiding in the forest, they have psychological stress. They have less of a social circle. They can no longer ask an elder for advice, or have the traditional midwife help with the birth. In fact, in the population along Lake Tanganyika with that extraordinary mortality rate, there were 80 live births and eight maternal deaths (perhaps 200 times the regional norm) among the interviewees. Notes on the data forms by the interviewers suggested four of the eight maternal deaths happened while people were hiding in the bush. How does one separate the social components from the psychological and physical aspects of this misery?

This was really driven home for me in 2004 when I was helping measure the level of mortality in Iraq after the invasion. I was expecting that—as with Burundi, Sierra Leone, Rwanda, and all those other places where I had done mortality surveys of this kind—there would have been a dramatic rise in mortality among children and the elderly associated with a failing health system and diminishing resources. In fact, most of the post-invasion mortality rise was from violence, and the most dramatic non-violent rise was from traffic accidents as people rushed around in this insecure environment.

As I started probing people about how they kept their diabetic grandmothers and sick children alive, it was clear that, unlike the Congolese, they had kept their family structures and social connections intact in spite of the war. Cell phones and wealth and formal education made it so that everyone could find a doctor, even when the hospitals were closed. Everyone could find out about someone from the village who was coming from Baghdad that week and could bring more insulin for their grandmothers. Because everyone knew who was an engineer and who was a doctor, to some extent their services continued, in spite of there being no formal social service structures to support them.

The structure became the family and the clan—and, to a lesser extent, the religious sect. War had made the environment of Iraq unsafe, but social cohesion and social life still continued. In fact war in Kosovo and Bosnia had resulted in similarly little excess deaths from infectious diseases in spite of extreme levels of violence. Whether one wants to call this wealth or assets or being developed, some part of this resiliency—I suspect most of it—is the result of social assets, more than body fat or physical possessions. Perhaps what wealth and the connections to larger circles most brings is hope?

During the 2004 Iraq mortality survey, a very calm and measured 50-year-old physician who was working as an interviewer brought me a data form, stating that two children had died of fear. He insisted to me that this had been the case, and he was brought into the bedroom to see the bed upon which the two children were huddled when they had died. At the time of their death, it was dark, bombs were reportedly being dropped by the Americans on the town, and then one landed on the house next door. There was no damage in the room. Because I had asked for so many details on previous data forms, I think he half expected me not to believe him, or to at least question this story. Unfortunately, I found it completely believable, because I had encountered this twice before.

The last time had been in the town of Kalamie in the Congo, as planes dropped bombs on the town. That time it was two young twins. Each of the three times interviewers had recorded these fear-induced deaths, the story involved two small children alone, holding each other in times of fighting and erupting weapons. War is about shrinking circles of existence. And those small children, with their imaginations so vast and potential for fear so great, shrunk their worlds so small that everything important was reduced to that sibling they clenched. Somehow, once shrinking the world that small, a jarring percussive sensation or a deafening noise ratcheted-up the fear even further, and their world shrank too small to allow the beating of a heart. To me, the ultimate shrinking of one's support network seen with these children is the purest distillation of war.

Ten Years in a
North Korean Gulag

Kang Cheol Hwan

Kang Cheol Hwan is the Executive Director of North Korea Strategy Center in Seoul, Korea. Mr. Kang was once imprisoned in Yodok political prison camp in North Korea and received the Democracy Award from the National Endowment for Democracy (NED). He is the author of Aquariums of Pyongyang: Ten Years in the North Korean Gulag. *Mr. Kang also has a column in the* Chosun Daily *as a reporter specializing in North Korean issues.*

My name is Kang Cheol-Hwan. I was born in 1968 and spent my childhood days comfortably in Pyongyang, North Korea's capital. My family lived comfortably in relative luxury because my family was well-connected with the government. My grandfather was a successful businessman in Japan and had given North Korea his fortune when he returned from Japan. My grandmother was a staunch Party member in both countries but my family always lived under a cloud of suspicion for having lived in Japan.

In 1977, my entire family—including my father, uncle, grandmother and 7-year-old sister—was arrested and sent to Yodok prison camp. The only reason we were given was that my grandfather had supposedly committed an offense. To this day, I don't know what offense he had committed, but the North Korean government believes that politically deviant thoughts are hereditary, so my entire family was imprisoned. (Other former prisoners of Yodok also say that they also do not know the reasons for which they were imprisoned.)

Yodok prison camp is a business enterprise with gold mines, cornfields, and lodging operations, where prisoners of all ages labor endlessly. I was only nine years old, but my day would begin at 6:00 a.m. and it'd be filled with work. My work involved cultivating a cornfield, excavating clay, and carrying timber. I often walked for 12 miles with a log on my shoulder. Failure to accomplish the work quota would result in reduced food rations.

As a 10-year-old I was told to lift a 30-kg sack of earth (more than my own body weight) 30 times a day. If I slipped, I was beaten with sticks by my teachers. The work was too much for me, or for any child of my age. But I didn't dare complain. After the first ten rounds, my legs started shaking, my body was hurting and the skin on my shoulder was peeling off. I was close to collapsing, but the teachers were watching us and they beat us with sticks if we stopped. My education consisted of memorizing the sayings and speeches of Kim Il-sung, and even this limited education only lasted until I turned 15 years old.

Other than being a labor camp, Yodok is a place where inhumane acts are present in every aspect of daily life. Torture and beatings are routine and prisoners are treated worse than animals. Female prisoners who are pregnant undergo forced abortions; infanticide also exists. What goes on in Yodok is unimaginable and unthinkable to the average person. Even public executions occur, to execute people who attempted to escape. During these public executions, prisoners are forced to hurl rocks at the corpses, yelling, "Down with the traitors of the people!" Thirty percent of new prisoners die, unable to survive the horrific lifestyle.

Along with the rest of North Korea, food deficiency is a big concern as well. Prisoners eat anything that they can find, including earthworms. I remember rat meat was a delicacy and, to this day, I haven't tasted something as delicious as the rat meat that I ate in the darkest years of my life. Malnourishment was a common phenomenon among inmates. When I was 17 years old, I was less than 150 centimeters tall (4 feet, 9 inches), and weighed about 40 kilograms (88 pounds). Girls weren't taller than 145 centimeters (4 feet, 7 inches). Lacking the nutrition critical to healthy development in adolescent years and having unkempt hair, girls lacked feminine traits, as the identity and existence of all prisoners was reduced to being a mere body in a crowd of prisoners.

Yodok is one of the multiple prison camps in North Korea created by Kim Jong Il and his regime to control the North Korean people. Crimes for which you can go to a prison camp include: folding a piece of paper with Kim Il Sung's picture so that the crease falls on his face; eavesdropping on South Korean broadcasting; and watching South Korean videos. In addition to the atrocities that occur, the natural circumstances surrounding Yodok are dire as well. The average winter temperatures vary between 20 to 30 degrees below zero Celsius, and in most camps, there are no blankets. Sanitary conditions are horrible as well. There is one toilet for every 200 people, and no adequate access to medicine, which leads to diseases and infections left untreated. As an Amnesty International report puts it, "Hundreds of thousands of people exist with virtually no rights, treated essentially as slaves, in some of the worst circumstances we've documented in the last 50 years."

There are an estimated 200,000 prisoners in North Korea's network of political prison camps. The concept of human rights is nonexistent within and outside the prison camps and the people in North Korea live the bleakest lives void of any liberty.

After ten years, my family was released. Afterward, while living in North Korea, I owned an illegal radio receiver and listened to broadcasts from South Korea. In 1992, I defected to China by crossing the Yalu River, escaping both North Korean and Chinese authorities. I eventually made it to South Korea. Currently, there are over 20,000 North Korean defectors living in South Korea. Every day, North Koreans risk their lives to cross the Yalu River and the Tumen River seeking to escape into liberty.

The Two Koreas: One Oppressed & One Free

South Korea—a country that has experienced respectable economic development in the world—faces North Korea, the most oppressive and severe dictatorship regime in the world.

The North Korean government denies that political prisons even exist and, other than with satellite pictures, it is not possible to take an actual look into what the political camps look like. In addition to limiting information that exits the country, North Korea also currently maintains one of the most repressive information censorships in the world, and punishes its people on charges of treason by designating certain information (deemed ordinary in other states) as classified. Kim Jong Il's authoritarian regime has yet to collapse, despite a famine that cost millions of its citizens' lives, due to the state's complete control over the internal media and cutting access to outside information. Notably, the North Korea government regards its Department of People's Propaganda and

Incitement as the most important department in ensuring the security and survival of its system, precisely because propaganda and incitement play a vital role in keeping the status quo. As a result, North Korean people are cut off from outside information and exposed only to newspapers and television that blindly idolize and praise Kim Jong Il.

Factions in South Korea, however, though claiming to be the 'progressive left,' ignore groups in North Korea who fight against the dictatorship regime and seek freedom. Such factions also mistakenly believe that demanding the fall of the Kim Jong Il regime is the same as breaking peace and liberty.

Past South Korean presidents Kim Dae Joong and Roh Moo Hyun are well renowned for their struggles for human rights within South Korea, but have not taken any attitudes critical toward the North Korean regime. They have even created a questionable theory that resolving problems concerning public welfare through government-based economic support is the way to solve human right issues and freedom.

Thus, nowadays, groups in South Korea that have been negatively influenced by the Kim Jong Il regime are unable to voice their criticisms against the regime, due to their mistakes and multiple past connections to North Korea. These groups continuously urge for economic support to North Koreans, even though the Kim Jong Il regime has only used large-scale South Korean aid to develop nuclear weapons and missiles to strengthen its military.

The free world's mistaken choices that have lost their ethical discernment have lengthened the lives of dictatorships. As a result, freedom fighters in North Korea who hope for democracy under a dictatorship have lived through a period of darkness due to the pro-North Korean, anti-US policy supporting Kim Jong Il.

Democratization & Liberty: A Call to the International Community

As seen through the example of North and South Korea, the world is currently divided into free countries, countries in the process of liberalization, and dictatorships. Individuals in free developed countries do not seek to understand the pain and suffering of those living under dictatorship. People in these countries have forgotten that their own liberty and human rights have been established through the blood and tears of many.

Therefore, the corrupt powers that hurt freedom and democratization also exist in free democracies, and such powers collude with darker powers to extend the dictatorship regime of oppressive countries. People with corrupt morals in these free countries seek to understand and worry about the status of a country's dictator, before that of the people of the country who are dying from the oppression that exists within.

Nonetheless, as human rights activist Natan Sharansky writes in *The Case for Democracy,* human liberty is something basic, that all humans are entitled to, regardless of religion, culture, nationality or borders. He stresses that countries of any culture or ethnicity can undergo democratization.

Contrary to what was thought as impossible, both South Korea and Japan have undergone democratization, and it seems as though it will be difficult for even the great China to avoid the waves of democratization. Additionally, the recent Jasmine Revolution that swept through the Middle East has broken an old incorrect stereotype that democratization would be impossible due the religious nature of these Islam countries.

Perhaps the long dark period of Middle Eastern countries can be related to the neglect of free developed countries. The relationship between the Middle East and the West should be analyzed, not only through a religious aspect but also through freedom, democracy, and the systems of a dictatorial society.

People have been interested in leaders of the Middle East, and have attempted to understand Middle Eastern countries through them. People of such countries are repeatedly brainwashed and paralyzed by the oppression of the monarchic countries that use the Islam religion as a cloak to sustain the monarchic regime and support holy wars.

I believe that the reason these dictatorships have lasted for so long is the lack of effort on the part of free individuals in democratic countries to care about the people of such countries. People have not focused on the people of these countries, *their* lives, and what they're seeking.

Further information about my experiences in North Korea and Yodok Prison Camp can be found in my memoir, "Aquariums of Pyongyang: Ten Years in a North Korean Gulag."

For Now,
They Struggle

Dahlia Wasfi

Dahlia Wasfi was born in New York, NY and spent her early childhood in Saddam Hussein's Iraq, until she returned with her family to the United States in 1977. She graduated from Swarthmore College with a B.A. in Biology and from the University of Pennsylvania School of Medicine. In February/March of 2004, after years of separation, Dahlia visited Iraq to see her family in Basrah and Baghdad. She journeyed to Iraq again for a 3-month visit in 2006. This piece is excerpted from Dahlia's upcoming book, Liberate THIS. *Her website is* www.liberatethis.com.

"Dahlia, come here," my father called. The resignation in his voice told me that something was wrong.

On the east coast of the United States, it was 7 p.m., January 16, 1991. In Iraq—my father's birthplace—it was 3 a.m. the following day. I was upstairs in my parents' house in Delaware, during winter break of my sophomore year at Swarthmore College. When I heard his sad command, I tiptoed to the balcony overlooking the family room. I thought that if I stepped delicately enough, nothing would be disturbed when I reached my father. My efforts were futile. Peering over the railing, I saw him standing by the television.

"They started bombing," he said. The assault of Gulf War I had begun.

I looked down at my father over the banister with helpless despair. He stared at the television screen with helpless despair. I wanted to reach down into the TV and stop what was happening, maybe even stop time until I could figure out a solution. But I could only stand motionless, frozen at the balcony, trying to process what I was seeing. Even as I tell this story years later, my stomach churns as it did that day, for the hopelessness and helplessness of that moment. Fear and sadness instantly overcame me. My relatives were among the millions of Iraqis who had no say in their government's actions, but who would now pay dearly at the hands of the most powerful military in the world. I couldn't help my dad. I couldn't help my family.

Moments later, once the initial shock of the news passed, I found myself nervously humming. I soon realized the song was R.E.M.'s "It's the End of the World as We Know It." For me, it was.

My father was born and raised in Basra, Iraq. Graduating from Baghdad University, he earned a government scholarship to study in the United States. He completed his graduate studies at Georgetown University. While in DC, he met and married my mom, a nice Jewish girl from New York. Her parents had fled their homeland of Austria during Hitler's *Anschluss* and to the United States. Was it love at first sight? I don't know, but my sister was born in 1969, and I arrived in 1971. To pay back his scholarship from Iraq, my father taught at Basra University from 1972 to 1977. Thus, my early childhood was spent in both Iraq and the United States. For me, the bombing of Basra was equivalent to the bombing of Yonkers, New York. I had family in both places.

Upon returning to the Swarthmore College campus for the spring semester, I was dumbstruck by the mostly pro-war atmosphere. This militancy was in stark contrast to the peaceful traditions of its Quaker founders who had established the school in 1864. The Quakers, a Christian denomination also known as the Religious Society of Friends, are known as a peace church, because of their teachings' emphasis on pacifism. While Swarthmore no longer has any religious affiliation, it prides itself on being an institution that still reflects many Quaker values. As the current brochures describe, "Foremost among [these values] is a commitment to the common good and to the preparation of future leaders who will influence favorably a changing and complex world."[1]

However, in the early months of 1991, as far as I could tell, Swarthmore was a breeding ground for warmongers. Flags and pro-military banners hung from the dorms of Parrish Hall, the main building on campus. Their messages remain burned in my memory. On a white sheet, students had written, "By Air, By Sea, By Land: Bye-Bye, Iraq." Hanging from the next window: "U.S. Troops: Simply the Best." They made me cringe. The blatant disrespect for the lives of Iraqi victims was sickening to me. I thought, *what the hell is going on? Why didn't the best and brightest understand that war is unacceptable, no matter who is directing the tanks? Why was the anti-war sentiment drowned out at this supposedly 'liberal' institution?*

Internally, I condemned the hypocrisy of militancy on a campus that purported to reflect peaceful traditions. But the Swarthmore disconnect between image and reality was mirroring the hypocrisy that I despised within myself. I was living the American dream at one of the top—and among the most expensive—schools in the nation. Meanwhile, my government rained down terror in the form of cruise missiles on Iraqi families.

I had only vague pictures in my mind of a few of my relatives in Iraq. But I had very lucid and distinct memories of my childhood years spent there. The missiles that trailed across the Arabian night sky that January of 1991 fractured the calm over Iraq, as the war itself shattered my world and my memories to pieces. There was no question that the regime of Saddam Hussein was politically repressive. But now, Iraqis suffered under brutality from within and aerial bombardment from without. Iraqi families were under attack. My fellow students were celebrating. Yet, even though I had insights no one else could have, I said and did nothing for our victims. At the time, assimilation was a higher priority for me than speaking the truth. I reeked of selling out.

More than 100,000 Iraqis perished during the forty-two days of Gulf War I, but I was lucky. My blood relatives survived. The worst was yet to come, however, because U.S. and U.K. aerial assaults had purposely targeted Iraq's electricity plants, telecommunication centers, and water treatment facilities. These attacks were in direct violation of the Fourth Geneva Convention, relative to the protection of civilians in war.[2] In a matter of days, life for Iraqis became desperate. There was no potable water, no electricity, and—with economic sanctions in place—there soon would be no means of rebuilding.

On August 6, 1990, severe economic sanctions had been imposed on Iraq, four days after Iraqi troops entered Kuwait. (In sad irony, that date was the forty-five year anniversary of another Western targeting of a civilian population, the atomic bombing of Hiroshima, Japan.) All of Iraq's exports and imports were banned, in order to induce Iraqi withdrawal from Kuwait.[3] Though withdrawal was completed by the end of the 1991 Gulf War in April, those brutal sanctions had remained in place for years. Once stored resources were depleted, Iraqis had begun to starve. It was a stringent medical, cultural, intellectual, and nutritional embargo that victimized the already-suffering Iraqi people. I knew the direct correlation between my government's actions and human suffering. I did nothing.

Most of my cousins had been born after my immediate family left Iraq in 1977. I had never met them, and I had only faint memories of aunts and uncles, or of my paternal grandmother who had already passed away in 1979. I knew I had many relatives suffering under desperate conditions in Iraq, but I was emotionally, as well as geographically, distant from their pain. With English as my one and only language, I couldn't have spoken with them on the phone—even if U.S. and U.K. forces hadn't bombed the telecommunications centers. I condemned the hypocrisy of my government for starving the Iraqi people while claiming to punish Saddam Hussein. But the hypocrisy I despised was within me. I continued my life, business as usual, graduating in 1993, and moving on to medical school, with a sadness I could not explain.

Between 1991 and 1997, I finished my Bachelor's degree at Swarthmore and earned my medical degree from the University of Pennsylvania. During the same time-period, economic sanctions achieved the chronic malnourishment of nearly 1,000,000 children in central and southern Iraq.[4] According to Philippe Heffinck, then UNICEF Representative in Baghdad, "It is clear that children are bearing the brunt of the current economic hardship."[5] By the following year, the mortality rate of Iraqi children under five years old was a shocking 500,000 deaths higher than predicted since 1991.[6]

I knew these figures, but I didn't have time to think about them. I had begun a residency in general surgery, first at the University of Maryland, and then back at Penn for a year of research. I was constantly working, ever more sleep-deprived, and miserable, yet I remained unconscious of the internal contradiction fueling my unhappiness. After three grueling years, I convinced myself that changing fields would bring me contentment. I switched to a training program in anesthesiology at Georgetown University Hospital, where I began working in June, 2000. My experiences there would prove to be the final straw.

Most residencies are abusive, and this one was no different. But the environment became even more hostile following the events of September 11, 2001.

"I don't want to operate on any Middle Eastern people," one attending physician muttered.

"We should blow up the countries of each of the hijackers," another said vengefully.

These were my supervisors—medical professionals who had taken the Hippocratic Oath. One of the foundations of medical ethics is supposed to be *primum non nocere* ("First, do no harm"). I wasn't feeling that sentiment in what these doctors were saying. And based on the hostility they were directing towards "Middle Eastern people," I worried about potential backlash against me, if they learned what my background was. I swallowed the lump in the back of my throat, along with my voice, and continued to work under them, business as usual. Protecting myself within my workplace took priority for me that day, over speaking against injustice. I condemned these physicians for their hypocrisy, but my silence was dishonest as well.

By early 2002, the US had invaded Afghanistan, and the American government was telling lies to build support for invading Iraq. My relatives, from whom I still was separated, had been starving under sanctions for more than twelve years. Now, we were going to shock and awe them. My tax dollars would help foot the bill.

"We should just nuke 'em," my attending physician proclaimed.

In September of 2002, overwhelmed by the hypocrisy without and the painful conflict within, I couldn't continue business as usual. I burned out. I was hospitalized.

I was sure that my stay at the Psychiatric Institute of Washington marked the end of my medical career. With my identity inextricably tied to my work, I reasoned that this crisis was likely the end to my life as well. That finality was what I wanted, confirmed by my new diagnosis of Major Depressive Disorder with Suicidal Ideation (*i.e.*, I was depressed and wanted to die). As such, the months afterwards were precarious and delicate times. The tough professional exterior I had developed as a student and resident had shattered, revealing itself as the façade it was. What remained was a lost, frightened, and very fragile soul who had to start life over again—exposed and unprotected. While the drumbeats for another U.S. war on Iraq were growing louder, I was drifting aimlessly through my days, like a tumbleweed in a ghost town at the mercy of the elements. Then, on March 16, 2003, three days before the launch of Shock and Awe, a single news headline would stop my downward spiral: *"Israeli Bulldozer Kills American Woman."*[7] This woman, Rachel Corrie, would show me that goodness still exists on this earth. She would give new purpose to my existence.

After reading that headline, for the first time in a while, I thought about someone other than myself. Also for the first time in a while, I felt an emotion other than depression. I felt anger. Having been completely immersed in news of the imminent attack on Iraq, I felt blindsided by this report that seemed to come out of nowhere. What the hell is going on here? What happened? From the article:

In a matter of months, Rachel Corrie went from the orderly peace movement of this small liberal city [Olympia, Washington] *to a deadly world of gunfire, violent political conflict and the bulldozer that crushed her to death.*

Crushed to death by a bulldozer? I felt my stomach turn and I tasted nausea. What kind of horrific torture did she endure? My God. What the hell is going on in this miserable, Godforsaken world? Who was she?

Corrie, 23, a student at The Evergreen State College in Olympia, died Sunday in Gaza while trying to stop the bulldozer from tearing down a Palestinian physician's home.

I sat staring at the monitor, the words of the *USA Today* article blurring as I tried to make sense of the news. She was so much younger than me. I thought to myself that she had no apparent ties to the Arab World. Why was she there? Why was she halfway around the world in Palestine, while I sat in the comforts of the U.S.A.? Then the crux of the mystery hit me like a slap in the face: why was SHE dead when I—who wanted to die— was alive and reading about her passing? The horror was unjust; it was nonsensical; it was illogical. The loss of her, someone I'd never known of until that morning, was just stupid. I became indignant.

I searched the internet for everything that I could find out about Rachel Corrie—who she was, where she came from, what brought her to challenge bulldozers in Gaza. (And I wondered, my God, what kind of courage does that take? I couldn't even muster the strength to stand up to bigoted doctors in my workplace.) I found a picture of her. She was so beautiful: all-American-looking, blonde-haired, blue-eyed young woman. She was thin and beautiful, like a dancer. She even looked natural and confident in the standard over-the-shoulder shot which every high school portrait photographer makes you pose. Most of us look awkward. Rachel's picture looked elegant.

The outlines of most human beings are dwarfed by the hulking form of a D-9 Caterpillar bulldozer, armored and used by the Israeli Army for the destruction of land and homes.[8] Rachel's frame, in particular, appeared so delicate in the pictures I could find. She was someone who would never experience racial discrimination based on her looks, the way I felt that I had. What was she doing in Palestine? Like everything I else I looked at, none of this made any sense whatsoever. This tragedy must be some horrible, horrible mistake.

In the midst of my indignation, I suddenly was struck with self-loathing at what I then perceived to be more internal hypocrisy. Why was I so moved by Rachel's death? I knew that Palestinians—and many other indigenous peoples for that matter—were dying every day in their struggles for justice. I didn't want to be racist and mark Rachel's death because she was American, while ignoring others who died because they were the "wrong" nationality. There was actually another young man shot and killed by the Israeli Army that day in Gaza, within hours of Rachel's murder. No news of the loss of his life had broken in the papers of *USA Today*.

But there was something about Rachel and her story that mystified me and captured my attention the way no one else had before. The journey of the next few years would help me decipher why her courage, her life, and her death were so powerful to me. It would take a while for me to understand enough about myself to be able to comprehend why she touched my heart so.

In the short term, however, I considered the bizarre contrast of that day in my mind. The headline could have read, *"23-year-old, all-American woman visited—and was murdered in—Rafah in Gaza, Palestine, while 31-year-old failed physician surfs the internet at home."* The incongruity made me wonder: if Rachel could travel thousands of miles to learn about people she didn't even know, then maybe I should go see my family whom I haven't seen in almost twenty-seven years.

* * *

In February and March of 2004, I made a 19-day journey to Iraq. The first memories of my life were from those early years in Iraq. My life would start over again there, too. With Baghdad International Airport controlled by American occupation forces (as it still is today), I flew to Jordan and made the 10-hour car ride to Baghdad. In Iraq's capital, a year after the invasion, damage from bombing raids was omnipresent. Iraq had been liberated, all right—from sovereignty, security, electricity, and potable water. The new "democratic" Iraq modeled sewage in the streets, rolling blackouts, shootings, and explosions. After several days spent visiting my Baghdadi relatives, I needed to reach my father's immediate family in the south. Ahmed [name changed], one of my cousins from Basra, drove twelve hours round trip with a friend, to pick me up and bring me to visit the rest of the family. With numerous checkpoints and no security, their efforts were Herculean.

To my naïve foreign eyes, Basra's condition appeared to be much the same as Baghdad's, except that the damage seemed more extensive. This city had been destroyed during the Iran-Iraq War of the 1980's, the 1991 Gulf War, bombings during the 1990s, and the 2003 Shock and Awe invasion. Throughout that time, sanctions and neglect had thwarted the city's—and her people's—recovery. I expected to receive resentment during my visit. After all, my immediate family had left Iraq for America during the good days of the 1970s. So much destruction had been wrought against the Iraqi people by my government since then. Every destroyed building we passed, every sewage-flooded street, every child suffering in poverty, I despairingly thought to myself, "You're welcome, Iraq. I helped do this to you." I held resentment towards myself and deep shame as an American in this occupied land.

But I did not feel resentment from anyone else during my brief stay. When we arrived at my uncle's (Ahmed's father's) house, I was welcomed with kisses and hugs, overwhelming love and affection. Though I was meeting my cousins for the very first time, they already knew me, far better than I knew them. My father was a legend in the family and in the neighborhoods of Basra where he had grown up and been both a teacher and a professor. My cousins had tracked his life—and the lives of his children, in turn— with fond attentiveness. They welcomed me as if they had known me their whole lives.

Despite the desperation, the novelty of a visit from a long-lost cousin brought everyone joy, myself included. Getting to know each other for the first time, my cousins and I were like little kids, giggling and joking, whether the electricity was working or not. I was so struck by how thin they all were. "You have no idea what it was like [during the sanctions]," my cousins told me. "We are only alive today because your father helped us." Even with his support during those years of starvation, my Iraqi family had sold furniture and other belongings to get money for food.

My cousins' features were familiar to me, because they were similar to mine: olive skin; thick, curly hair (some of them); and a strong Semitic nose (also described as "large.") But their cheeks were hollowed out, especially on Ahmed's face. His clothes hung on him limply, like they did on their hanger. His physique was paper-thin and his face gaunt, revealing the faint outline of his skull. His appearance reflected years of starvation and war. To me, his emaciated body was a microcosm for the whole of Iraqi society. The people appeared as if they had been newly released from a strangling chokehold. They were laid out, exhausted, gasping to catch their collective breath. Ahmed's weary, sunken, dark brown eyes held the fear, worry, and pain of all of that suffering, all of those years.

My father was one of ten children, so we have a lot of family in Iraq. Seemingly everywhere I was escorted during those six days in Basra, I met blood relatives or my father's former students. Most Basrawis (pronounced "*bas-RAO-weez*," meaning people of Basra) live their whole lives in their hometown. My father had traveled to the U.S. and become successful. During my short stay, I heard so many wonderful accolades about him and his teaching. (When I returned home, I joked with my father about how all the images of Saddam Hussein, destroyed after the invasion, would soon be replaced with his picture, to honor his courage and success.)

I was experiencing joy with my cousins that I had not felt in as long as I could remember. My spirits were up, so much so that I stopped my anti-depressive medications. I felt cured. However, because of the unpredictability of a country without law and order, my stay was cut short. I had to return to Amman via Baghdad to make my flight home. But I promised my family that I would return for a longer stay—very soon, we hoped— when conditions in the new Iraq had improved. I left in early March, 2004. Though we looked toward the horizon for better days, conditions in Iraq went from bad to worse.

17

Electricity and water became scarcer, as did jobs and security. But Iraqis' pain and suffering did not stop there.

The lack of these basic necessities was quickly overshadowed by the monstrous obscenities of the American-led occupation. By April, 2004, the atrocities committed against Iraqis by occupation forces at Abu Ghraib prison (and many other prisons throughout the country) had come to light. In addition, the indiscriminate slaughter of Iraqis continued unabated and even accelerated, as exemplified by the April, 2004 siege of the city of Fallujah, followed by the October, 2004 bombings and November, 2004 massacre of the people of that city. (That November, I had wanted to make my return visit to Iraq, but U.S. Marines had blocked the route of the final leg of my trip, the road from Amman to Baghdad.) Anti-American sentiment in Iraq was skyrocketing to new highs, and with good reason.

In the final months of 2004, and through the start of 2005, kidnappings of Westerners became prominent news stories. Fearing for my safety, amidst ever-escalating anti-American sentiment, my family advised me to stay safely at home. Thinking only of myself, I was undeterred from making another trip to see them. I selfishly gave little thought to the danger into which I was putting my family by asking them to "harbor" an American. The facts that my father was Iraqi and I was on vacation probably wouldn't mean much to those desperate souls who might abduct me, whether seeking expensive ransoms to feed their families or sending a message to foreigners to get out of Iraq.

But I was mostly oblivious to the risks. I figured if I were kidnapped, I could use the few words of Arabic I'd learned growing up (from when my father was angry), in reference to the U.S. government. Surely, I thought, with such skills of wit and a photo of my father, I could get myself out of any sticky situation. By the end of 2005, with no end to the chaos in sight, my family had agreed to host me once again, before the situation deteriorated further.

Because the road from Amman to Baghdad was now exceedingly dangerous, my trip was planned to visit only Basra this time. Hostility still governed relations between Iraq and Kuwait, not only from the era of Gulf War I, but from the decades of territorial disputes, dating back to the early twentieth century. Even with an American passport, I knew my Iraqi background might be sufficient cause for Kuwaiti border officials to make my trip more difficult. But I didn't see any other option. I bought tickets to fly via London to Kuwait International Airport in Kuwait City. This capital city sits about 82 miles (132 kilometers) from Basra, with the Iraq-Kuwait border about halfway in between.

I had a planned layover in London of two days, so that I could attend an anti-war conference on December 10, 2005, organized by a UK-based group, the Stop the War Coalition. My scheduled flight to Kuwait was for the following evening, December 11th. If Kuwait had been my final destination, I could have made the trip without a problem. However, four days before the scheduled December 15 elections, Iraq's borders were sealed for "security" reasons (the few sections of the country's boundaries that were secured, anyway). I had to postpone my trip out of London until the borders were reopened. With bitter sarcasm, I joked with my family that the new Iraq had so much freedom in it that occupation forces had to close the borders to contain it all.

Finally, on Christmas Eve, I got a seat on a redeye flight out of London, and landed in Kuwait City on Christmas morning. Though I was tired, my excitement prevented me from getting any sleep. Exhausted and jet-lagged, I struggled through airport customs and the Kuwait border-emigration process to get to Kuwait's northern border and into Iraq. It was raining, and my kind taxi driver waited so I could have shelter, until the bus arrived to carry passengers across the several kilometers of no-man's-land between the borders of Iraq and Kuwait. I peered out my rain-streaked window to see a soldier (whom I remember as being British), standing over what looked like an oil barrel and brushing his teeth using a small hand-held mirror. It was a bizarre sight, and I started to ask myself where the hell I was and what was I doing.

After what felt like a long wait, finally, the shuttle bus creaked into the makeshift parking area. Upon its arrival, numerous travelers emerged from the cars parked nearby, moving hurriedly with their boxes and bags to climb aboard and escape the desert rain. The bus was old and weather-battered, and in my sleep-deprived fog, I wondered if it was the same bus my parents had ridden when they made the commute in the early 1970s. There I was that day, alone, isolated, physically and emotionally drained, and unsure of what was coming next. Somewhere along that anonymous road, in the sands of a nameless desert, I burst into tears. I thought, "This was the stupidest plan I have ever come up with... why didn't anyone try to stop me?!" Of course, many friends and family had tried to alert me to the dangers and difficulties of this trip. I had ignored them. Now there was no turning back.

I stepped off the rickety bus at the Iraqi border, along with my fellow passengers making the difficult journey into occupied land. I was so tired, from both the long trip and my recent crying. My eyes alternated between staring vaguely into the distance in a sleep-deprived daze, and darting toward all angles of my belongings, making sure nothing got stolen. I was trying to put my thoughts together, to decide what to do next, when I believe I witnessed a divine intervention. My gaze moved up from my cart of belongings to find Ahmed standing right before me. I felt an unbelievable rush of relief and joy. The harrowing part of the journey was over. I believed then that everything would be all right.

Ahmed did all the paperwork for me; he had to since it was in Arabic. We meandered over to a car where another cousin, and their friend who had brought them to pick me up, were waiting. All that I'd brought was loaded into the trunk, and I relaxed into the back seat, feeling safe for the first time in what felt like days. When we arrived at my uncle's house, I got the same, beautifully warm welcome from my family as I had before. It was early afternoon, which was early morning for me back home, and I was utterly exhausted. Though it was rude of me, while the family sat down to the big midday meal made in my honor, I curled up in my cousin's bed and slipped into a deep, serene sleep.

On the following day, my first full day back in Basra, we lost electricity completely. On the second day, we ran out of water. On the third day, we lost telephone service. When we realized the phone lines were dead, Ahmed jokingly predicted, "I think tomorrow, we lose air!" We all laughed. Despite suffering the hardships of war, sanctions, and occupation for their entire lives, my cousins showed amazing resilience and tenacity. I was amazed by their intact sense of humor in unpredictable and dangerous conditions. But this spoiled American accustomed to the luxuries of electricity and running water thought worriedly, "What the hell did I get myself into for the next three months...?"

* * *

Iraqis are still suffering today under the brutal grip of American-led occupation. Life goes on in the hope that one day, circumstances will improve. For now, however, as it has been for decades, they struggle. Electricity, water, and jobs remain scarce. The destruction of Iraq's healthcare system has contributed to the deaths of one aunt, one uncle, and one cousin since my 2006 trip. In August 2007, another cousin was killed in the violence we brought to his country. He left behind a wife; a two-year-old son who keeps asking, "Where's Daddy?"; a heartbroken mother and brother; and an entire family devastated by grief, for whom life will never be the same. These precious souls are only four of the more than 1,000,000 lives (and counting) taken by the illegal invasion and occupation of Iraq.[9]

Every country around the world is made up of families. It is those families who either reap the benefits of their government's actions, or pay the price. Our victims in Iraq (and elsewhere around the world) are dehumanized; through media stereotypes, we have been programmed to dismiss the "other's" humanity.[10] That disconnection from humankind is why my college classmates could celebrate the 1991 Gulf War. That disconnection from humankind is why I had focused on my personal gain, even while my taxes brought suffering to millions. It was Rachel Corrie's generous spirit—and the shocking loss of her life—which reconnected me to what is truly important.

If there are political differences between states, then whatever they may be, no resolution comes from targeting the innocent families of their respective societies. We should respect the humanity of women and children, who are the majority of any population. And if we respect their humanity in Iraq, can we respect their grief as they lose their brothers, fathers, husbands and sons, the same way we mourn with and share the pain of American military families? From Rachel, I learned that the answer is yes. Our human connection is all that we need to reach one another.

Before the Israeli military came to Rafah in armored bulldozers, to level homes on March 16, 2003, Rachel Corrie literally stood up for what she believed. With her courageous stand, she equated her Western life with the lives of the Palestinian families behind her. Perhaps, her actions were an affront to the occupation soldiers staring down from their sixty-ton vehicle, inspiring them to crush her to death. To me, her courage showed hope and strength. She inspired me to follow my heart and find my voice.

With Rachel's example before me, my life has directed me to know my family. I've traveled thousands of miles to go see them and know them. But my work as an activist has also taught me that I don't only have family in Iraq. My relatives are everywhere: in Afghanistan; in Pakistan; in Kashmir; in Vietnam; in Walter Reed Army Medical Center; in Arlington Cemetery; in every village and city around the globe. You have relatives there, too.

My medical career is on hold so that I can call for the immediate, unconditional end of war and occupation on behalf of all of my family.

What would you do for your family?

What will you do?

---

[1] http://www.swarthmore.edu/x18.xml.

[2] http://www.icrc.org/ihl.nsf/INTRO/380, Convention (IV) relative to the Protection of Civilian Persons in Time of War. Geneva, 12 August 1949.

[3] Herring, Eric. "Between Iraq and a Hard Place: A Critique of the Case for UN Economic Sanctions" in Falk, Richard, Irene Gendzier, and Robert Jay Lifton, eds. *Crimes of War: Iraq*. Avalon Publishing Group, Inc. New York, NY. 2006. p .223.

[4] http://www.unicef.org/newsline/97pr60.htm

[5] *ibid.*

[6] http://www.unicef.org/newsline/99pr29.htm

[7] http://www.usatoday.com/news/world/2003-03-16-american-woman-killed_x.htm

[8] http://en.wikipedia.org/wiki/IDF_Caterpillar_D9 ; http://www.israeli-weapons.com/weapons/vehicles/engineer_vehicles/bulldozers/D9_D10.html

[9](a)http://www.alternet.org/world/123818/iraq%27s_shocking_human_toll:_about_1_million_killed,_4.5_million_displaced,_1-2_million_widows,_5_million_orphans/;
(b) http://www.zcommunications.org/more-than-1-000-000-iraqis-murdered-since-2003-invasion-by-orb

[10] Shaheen, Jack G. Reel *Bad Arabs: How Hollywood Vilifies a People*. Olive Branch Press. New York, 2001.

The "Terrorist" Journalist

Abebe Gellaw

Abebe Gellaw was born in Addis Ababa, Ethiopia. He earned his bachelor's degree from Addis Ababa University and a post-graduate diploma in law from London Metropolitan University. He began his career in journalism in 1993, as a freelance writer focusing on human rights and political issues. In 1995, he was one of the founders and editors of an independent, biweekly newspaper, Addis Express, *which by early 1996 had been forced to close down by the government. From 1996-1998, he was a senior reporter and columnist for the* Ethiopian Herald, *the only English daily in the country. In late 1998, he was exiled to London. He started his work in London as a radio producer and broadcaster for* Health Africa. *Then, from 2000-2004, he was the managing editor of* New Vision, *a U.K.-based refugee e-journal. Since 2005, he has been a regular contributor and columnist for such major Ethiopian cyber media outlets as* Ethiomedia.com *and* Abugida.com. *In 2006,* Addis Voice, *a popular Ethiopian online current affairs journal in Amharic and English, was launched, and he became its founding editor. He has received many awards, including a Champions of Change Millennium Award in 2002 for his contributions to refugee media development in the UK. He received a British Telecom Community Connections Award that same year, for his work in creating a cyber network for the refugee community in the UK. In 2010, he was chosen as a Young Global Leader by the World Economic Forum; in 2011, he received Human Rights Watch's Hellman/Hammett award for his commitment to freedom of expression. In November 2011, he became one of the 10 journalists charged by the Ethiopian government with terrorism offenses, for expressing critical views on government policies and rampant human rights violations. Currently residing in Virginia, USA, Abebe replied to the charges by writing an open letter to Prime Minister Meles Zenawi, thanking him for including him in the honor list among Ethiopia's high-profile journalists and activists. Abebe says the charge was rather an acknowledgement of the important work he is doing.*

In May of 1991, before I had even finished my freshman year, the civil war between the military junta of Marxist-nationalist Mengistu Haile Mariam, President of the People's Democratic Republic of Ethiopia, and the northern rebels fighting to topple the regime escalated. The military junta was defeated by rebels spearheaded by the Tigray Peoples Liberation Front. However, the liberators immediately began to waste the great opportunities and political capital they had created, to transform the nation and take it out of the quagmire of famine and abject poverty. Instead of adopting an accommodating system, that would allow every voice to be heard and every citizen to be counted, the new rulers failed the nation again, and began shooting peaceful protesters and jailing critics. In early 1993, ordinary people and university communities, trying to demand accountability and a fair non-discriminatory ethnic policy, faced crackdowns. Some students were killed and many thrown into jails.

My troubles with the current Ethiopian government started in 1993, while I was studying at the Addis Ababa University. When the government introduced a highly divisive ethnic policy, which appeared to be a blueprint for divide and rule, students started peaceful protests across campuses throughout Addis Ababa. As a student activist and freelance journalist, I joined the rallies, and published articles critical of the government's ethnic policy devised to pit one ethnic group against the other.

When the then-U.N. Secretary General, Boutros Boutros-Ghali, came to Addis on a working visit in early 1993, we marched out of the three main campuses, demanding that the U.N. press the new rulers that toppled the military junta, to desist from stoking ethnic hostilities and fragmenting the nation along ethnic lines. The students also demanded the current Ethiopian government to desist from facilitating the secession of Eritrea with its 1000 km of coastline, which would make Ethiopia become completely landlocked. Security forces opened fire on the defenseless peaceful protesters. A number of students were killed and injured; I escaped, sustaining only minor injuries.

The next day, the government closed down all the campuses. When the university was re-opened in the middle of the year, the government took another shocking measure that practically crippled the university: It fired 42 respected professors and lecturers, without even making an effort to replace them, and suspended the student union. Out of the 11 full professors at AAU, six were fired, including Professor Mesfin Woldemariam, the father of the Ethiopian human rights movement, and Professor Asrat Woldeyes, the first qualified surgeon and founder of Ethiopia's first medical school.

Like all conscientious students who stood up for justice, I was outraged. We started gathering again, to condemn the dictatorial measures and demand academic freedom. I was elected as one of the interim student union leaders, mandated to press for the reversal of the unfair dismissal of our professors. Instead of considering our demands and letters of appeal, they rounded up over 200 students, detaining them in a harsh military camp outside the capital. A few of my friends and I escaped the arrest, and began to live in hiding. After the turmoil in the university had subsided, I moved to a different part of the city and came out of hiding, confident that they wouldn't identify my face out of the crowd.

In September of 1993, a friend of mine prepared to start a weekly newspaper. I agreed to be part of it, and even became the editor, but it proved to be an act of foolishness. One morning, just a week after the maiden issue of *Addis Raey* [New Vision] hit the newsstands, I left home, to go to our unmarked office on a nameless street. While I was waiting for a taxi, a Toyota Land Cruiser stopped in front of me. Three heavily armed soldiers jumped out of the car and began kicking and punching me, without telling me the reasons. All of them spoke Tigrigna, a language spoken by most members of the ruling party. They didn't understand my cry to stop the illegal attack. After kicking and bloodying me as much as they wanted, they bundled me into their car and took me to a freezing underground detention center. They handcuffed and chained me with the iron pegs on the freezing floor. They kept me there for three days, without food and drink. I slept on the cold bare cement floor, without a single blanket or a bed sheet.

On the third day, I was almost starving to death and fell sick. They gave me a piece of bread and a cup of water. In the evening, they transferred me to the notorious Addis Ababa district prison, where I endured beatings and other abuses in solitary confinement. I was held *incommunicado* in a dark small cell, where there were a lot of rats, lice and fleas. That was the most horrible part.

Due to the efforts of human rights organizations, including Amnesty International, I was released after two months of hell on bail, on condition that I would not engage in any human rights, journalistic or political activities.

Adding insult to injury, I, along with a number of other students, was suspended from Addis Ababa University for one academic year, from November, 1993 to September, 1994. After the suspension was lifted, I resumed my studies. My academic and individual freedom curtailed, I finished them while being monitored by security as well as by a dorm mate, who turned out to be an undercover agent for the ruling party.

In August, 1995, two of my friends and I launched another newspaper, *The Addis Express*. This was clearly in breach of the terms of my release from jail, but I had always wanted to show them my defiance, despite the consequences. While I was working as the newspaper's editor, someone from the Ethiopian Human Rights Council drew my attention to a book written in English, *Federal Ethiopia at Crossroads*, which was sponsored by the Ministry of Foreign Affairs. The aim of the book, as it clearly stated from start to end, was to discredit human rights organizations, especially Amnesty International, by "exposing their lies."

In its comprehensive report, "Ethiopia: Human Rights in Transition," AI had reported that I had disappeared and was being held *incommunicado*, which was accurate. However, in "Federal Ethiopia at Crossroads," the government alleged that I had never been arrested, and was rather studying at Simon Fraser University in Vancouver, Canada. The trouble was, it was only one of the many fabricated cases compiled in a book to tarnish the image of international human rights organizations. Despite the advice of friends and loved ones, I published an article, in both Amharic and English, refuting the government's lies: "I have never been to Vancouver," I wrote. "I didn't even know that there was a university called Simon Fraser."The story was picked up by other media outlets, causing embarrassment to the regime. That spawned outrage among the officials; I received death threats, and was advised to stop my publication. As a result of the intense threats, we decided to close down the newspaper in January of 1996.

In March, 1996, my friends and I decided to promote human rights and democratic values through civic education. We formed an NGO, Center for the Advancement for Peace and Democracy in Ethiopia [CAPDE]. I was elected to lead CAPDE as its executive director. But CAPDE also faced another difficulty. In 1997, The NGO licensing office declared that it would not allow us to operate legally, unless I resign from my position. The reason given was that I had a record of tarnishing the image of the government. I felt so frustrated and angry, but I chose to resign, since I wanted CAPDE to succeed. However, as soon as I had resigned, they assigned a representative of the ruling party to serve as deputy director, with the co-operation of one of my best friends. They practically hijacked CAPDE, to make it operate according to their whims. To this day, CAPDE has never been effective, except as a fundraising milk cow for the ruling party and its cronies.

While I was working unpaid to set up CAPDE, I also freelanced for various newspapers, including the *Ethiopian Herald*. Nonetheless, I decided to leave Ethiopia, rather than live in fear without being treated as a human being. I began looking for opportunities abroad. I applied for a place at the Fletcher School at Tufts University, in their Masters of Law and Diplomacy program. Fortunately, I was selected among 160 applicants out of 1200. Happy with the outcome of my application to a prestigious graduate school, I was eager to study International Conflict Resolution. Armed with my admission letter, I went to the Ministry of Education to apply for a World Bank

Scholarship, which should have been approved by the ministry. My name became a problem again. I was refused, on the grounds that I had been blacklisted as someone who tried to tarnish the image of the government.

My life became more and more meaningless, as the government, which was supposed to protect my rights, became the biggest obstacle and threat to me. In August of 1998, I received a surprise letter from Reuters. It said I had been accepted for a training fellowship in London. That changed my mood, from despair to hope. In September, I quietly slipped out of Ethiopia, with the help of some people. I arrived in London, and as soon as I arrived at Heathrow International Airport, I sought political asylum in the U.K., as the immigration rule required any asylum-seeker to apply at a port of entry, in order to make a valid case.

In exile

"I feel too bad being an asylum-seeker. When will I have my dignity back?" asked a Somali doctor I met over a decade ago. The tall man in his fifties, who had fled his country leaving behind his wife and three children, had been a director of a Mogadishu-based hospital, destroyed by the senseless infighting among the mindless warlords who have ravaged and shaken Somalia upside-down. Both of us were homeless asylum-seekers, among a group of nervous people from the most turbulent parts of the world, huddled in the cold waiting until a Salvation Army day center near London's Victoria train station opened.

All of us shared a simple dream, to live in peace, free from fear and persecution—or, at very least, to be treated humanely. Unfortunately, escaping from fear in a world full of uncertainties and harsh realities, in failed states as well as stable developed nations enjoying relative peace and tranquility, has been only a pipe dream for too many people.

It was brutally freezing on that typical winter morning in November, 1998, so cold that starting a conversation seemed a bad idea. Most of us were wearing tropical clothes, not exactly prepared for the cold reality. Without much success, the Somali doctor tried to provoke some animated replies. A few of us gave some abrupt answers, not knowing what to say exactly, but the majority kept quiet, due to either lack of energy or the "Tower of Babel syndrome" (fear of miscommunication). Some just stared blankly at the ground. The question wasn't too easy to answer anyway, especially at a time of desperation and despair. It required deep thought and soul-searching.

Hopes, expectations, fears, confusions and anxiety were visibly mixed on everyone's face. We were all in the same boat... destined to an uncertain future. *"When will I have my dignity back?"* I repeated the question in my mind, without thinking about the answer. Fleeing troubles and persecution from Ethiopia, but facing another bout of trouble where I sought peace and refuge, I failed to answer this same question as it lingered on my mind for too long.

At around seven o'clock, the day center flung open its doors, and we flocked in as if we were fleeing the harsh cold outside. We sat down on red and yellow plastic chairs. Three smiling Salvation Army women officers in crisp uniforms offered us their kind hospitality and served us cookies and tea. One of them, a short and slim woman in her early forties, came to us to take down our details.

First, she counted our heads. We were thirteen to be exact; perhaps this was indicative of the bad luck awaiting most of us. Nonetheless, I had never been superstitious. *"What luck do children of troubled nations have?"* I wondered with a sense of pessimism.

"I am Captain Collins. Where are you from?" asked the enthusiastic woman staring at the expectant crowd with her inquisitive blue eyes. The baker's dozen of asylum-seekers shouted our names, followed by the broken countries we had fled: "Afghanistan, Somalia, Ethiopia, Congo, Kurdistan, Rwanda, Kosovo…," we declared our dysfunctional-state origins in turn.

"During the winter, it is really hard to find a room in a hostel," she informed us with a sad voice. "Especially when you are asylum-seekers…," she added after a little pause, as her smile faded slowly.

It took me almost six weeks to find a room, in a hostel for the homeless and ex-criminal offenders. After weeks on the waiting list and sleeping roughly in night shelters and train stations, I was finally given a map, with my new home highlighted in yellow, along with a thick red sweater.

"Keep yourself warm. There isn't tropical weather here," the duty Salvation Officer advised me. She had probably guessed how much I hated the hostile weather and the harsh challenge. I bowed down to thank her. "Good luck!" she said, looking at me with wholehearted sympathy.

I was quite happy to get a roof over my head, after all the gloom, the small victory was worth recording. *"23rd Dec. 1998: I found a hostel finally!"* I wrote in black ink on the wrinkling white paper in my diary, and read the simple Amharic sentence over again, to check if it made sense. The exclamation mark was even bigger than the broken letters written with a shivering hand.

I took the bus to my hostel in Mare Street, inner-city Hackney, one of the toughest neighborhoods in London. After a brief interview with the duty officer at the hostel, I was given a key to room number 129 and a bar of soap. The hostel was a strange, stuffy place filled with smoke. The smell was very bad. Most of the residents were unemployed, and some were ex-offenders. It seemed as if almost all of them smoked all day. I saw some of them nervously passing around strange powders and leaves in the lounges and the corridors. In the toilets and the shower rooms, it was quite common to see needles and syringes littering the floor. Apparently, drugs were rampant, and police raids were quite common.

"Hey, mate! You look confused!" said Mike to me in a baritone voice. It was just a quarter of an hour ago that I had walked into the noisy lounge, where residents were congregated in small groups, talking and smoking. Some surrounded the pool table. Mike, a stocky bald Irishman, was wondering why I just stood there, in the middle of the lounge, clutching my clothes in a grocery-bag. I stood still, like a statue gazing down on passers-by.

"I'm Michael," he said and stretched his big hands to greet me, slowly revealing his rusty teeth. "Fag?" he offered me a cigarette-stub, stuck in the middle of his fingers; maybe he suspected my state of stupor might be caused by a lack of nicotine in my bloodstream.

"No, thank you. I don't smoke," I said quietly, acknowledging his kind gesture.

"You want grass?" he inquired.

"What is that?" I asked.

"Are you clean?" I nodded, without understanding what he meant. I pulled myself to an old stool and sat by the only window, probably too small for the big smoke-filled hall.

Suddenly a tall, familiar figure emerged from the heavy cigarette-fog. I frantically waved my hands to get his attention. "Hey, Mohamed!"

"Hello Abe! Did they send you here, too?" he asked, showing his white, orderly front teeth. It was the inquisitive Somali doctor whom I had met a few weeks ago at the Salvation Army day center. He said he had arrived a few days ago. He sat down next to me, and we talked for a while, about our troubled pasts and nostalgia.

"I didn't know you were a journalist. Why were you jailed?" he asked.

I told him the reasons, as well as the risks of being a journalist under a tyrannical regime with a problem with the truth. "According to Orwell, in times of universal deceit, telling the truth is a revolutionary act," I said, looking down at the floor. It was one of my favorite quotes.

"What do you aspire to do?" he asked me.

Thinking for a few seconds, I replied, "That is a difficult question. I don't really know!"

He told me how difficult it was to work as a professional in the U.K. "I want to work as a doctor and support my three kids," he said gasping anxiously. "But that is impossible."

I fled to the U.K. in 1998, perhaps a bad time for asylum-seekers, but it hasn't become any better since I arrived. So many laws, rules and regulations have been made, and unmade. Well-dressed and graying wise men in parliament are still debating, and devising ways to keep asylum-seekers at bay. The debate continues on the radio, TV and newspaper pages, yet the troubles around the world are still unabated, causing many to flee in search of "safe haven." Some even drown in turbulent seas and some others die in the desert, without reaching that distant mirage of "safe haven."

I had fled my wretched country due to the persistent persecution I faced, as a journalist and a vocal critic of the tyrannical regime messing up Ethiopia. That was a well-known and well-publicized fact. I had fled from fear but still lived anxiously, nervously and fearfully for so long, in a place where I had hoped to find a safe haven.

The debate about asylum was raging on TVs and radio stations as usual. "Asylum-seekers invade Britain… Asylum-seekers ruin the health service… Asylum-seekers rob taxpayers… Asylum-seekers enjoy free ride…" The screaming tabloid headlines declared it all, with a view to stocking fear and hatred toward the strangers. It is typical of lazy journalism to be driven by sensationalizing stories, rather than a mission of telling the truth accurately. They never mention the fact that the majority of displaced people live in harsh refugee camps around the world, or that many die trying to cross the oceans, mountains, and deserts to reach somewhere safer.

None of the scribblers churning out such sensational stories seem to be bothered about the basic principles they learned at journalism schools. None of the stories the tabloids churn out and populist radio talk show hosts air, day-in and day-out, about the outsiders ever appear to be about the heartbreaking stories of those they love to vilify. No human angle, no balance, no objectivity, no impartiality… no fairness. *The Sun*, the *Daily Mail*, the *Daily Express*, the *Daily Star*… they lead the anti-refugee chorus, one after another competitively trying as hard as they can to shore up flagging rating with sensational headlines about asylum-seekers; in the process, they misinform and confuse many, while victimizing the desperate strangers who have dispersed around the world in search of peace and dignity, as a result of untold brutalities and atrocities they suffer. The story continues, and the predicament of those vulnerable strangers will go on.

The asylum law changes all the time, making it much too unpredictable. The strangers are not even allowed to work, earn their living and reclaim their dignity, while they are condemned for surviving in poverty, on welfare benefits against their choice. Unfortunately, the world is at times full of contradictions. As a result, so many people suffer in silence, unable to fulfill a life of dignity and liberty.

Asylum-seekers are guilty until proven innocent in the U.K. Yes, there are many individuals who find safe haven there, but there are a lot more who suffer in silence until they are proven innocent, until they can prove they are not "bogus." No matter how long it takes, without the right to work, they are condemned to live in limbo with too many limitations, barriers and uncertainties; even worse, thousands face detention and deportation back to countries like Ethiopia, Iraq and Zimbabwe.

In the course of the harsh asylum process, so many innocent people lose their self-confidence and self-esteem, and struggle to find meaning out of their predicament. Some even prefer to take their own lives. There are many in detention centers, and many more in invisible jails, never properly counted and with no legal rights.

So many asylum-seekers have neither passports nor a place to call a home, but they are all members of the human race, from different parts of a single planet in turmoil. Nonetheless, the undocumented strangers—in refugee camps, immigration detention centers and 'safe havens'; fleeing persecution, upheavals, grinding poverty and suffering—carry genes in their bloodstreams that are more powerful evidence of their identity than a gold-plated passport. They are just *homo sapiens* in trouble, who need sympathy and understanding.

Though my experience as an asylum-seeker was depressing, I managed to qualify as a teacher of English as a Second Language. When I got a job as a college lecturer, I found it another little leap forward toward having a stable life and a semblance of dignity. The north London college I joined as a staff member was a good place to work, as the majority of students I taught were asylum-seekers, refugees and Eastern European immigrants who shared similar dreams of a better tomorrow and stability in their lives. And yet, waiting for my residence permit, in limbo for so many years, was a very difficult experience as the constant anxiety, uncertainty and insecurity was stressful.

A voice from afar

Following the May, 2005 national elections in Ethiopia, the first contested multiparty elections ever held in the country's long history, the hope for democracy, liberty and justice suffered a serious setback: Allegations of government-sponsored vote-rigging caused spontaneous protest marches, which quickly degenerated into widespread heavy-handed government crackdowns, resulting in the deaths of 193 civilians and serious injuries to nearly 800 others. Over 40,000 civilians were detained in makeshift concentration camps for months without trial.

Free-press journalists and any dissident voices have been the official targets of the government, which believes them responsible for igniting the popular demand for democratic changes. Over 20 prominent journalists were arrested and their newspapers and websites were closed down. All of the most respected independent newspapers that were critical of government policies and conduct (including *Menilek, Ethiop, Asqual,*

Abay, Satenaw, and *Netsanet*) are still closed down, as they have been since November of 2005, although their publishers and editors were released, after spending nearly 22 months in harsh jails.

This was the background that necessitated the creation of such news and current affairs cyber-media as Addisvoice.com, with a view to reversing the media blackout the Ethiopian government deliberately created, in an effort to stifle the popular demand for democratic changes. As an exiled journalist, far from the tentacles of repressions, I decided to put both my web development and journalistic skills to the benefit of Ethiopians, within and outside of Ethiopia. With some assistance from fellow exiled journalists and a budget of $300, Addisvoice.com went online in May, 2006, with a mission to provide up-to-date news, analysis and commentaries on Ethiopia to the rest of the world.

Within a short span of time, I have tried to make Addis Voice (which is totally self-funded and has no budget for operating costs) a strong voice in alternative media, in the absence of a free press in Ethiopia and with the hope of making a small difference. As credible news sources have been jammed by the regime in Ethiopia, Addis Voice has tried to help my fellow Ethiopians (at least those who have access to the Internet) to bypass that regime's firewalls. It is evidently a small effort with a big dream.

This being the case, the government was taken by surprise to see that all their repressive measures failed to completely deny access to reports about the day-to-day realities facing the nation. News stories on the appalling atrocities being committed by government forces and agents started appearing on Web sites and blogs, causing worries and concerns among government officials. Unable to catch up with the speed, sophistication and creativity of cyber-media warriors, it sought the expertise of the Chinese, in filtering and blocking the most popular independent Internet sources. And yet, the regime has failed to silence those of us who have made every effort to be irrepressible voices serving a silenced nation.

My life as an exiled journalist in the U.K. has been very challenging, but I have persevered, and I continue to speak out against the corruption, human rights violations, repressions, injustice and crimes against humanity being committed with impunity by the Meles Zenawi regime. One of the difficult parts of being an exiled journalist is that there is little support to help you continue your profession. Despite all that, I have managed to contribute whatever I can: to write stories, expose the crimes of a repressive regime and articulate my views, focused mainly on issues affecting Ethiopians, both within and outside of their country.

I am currently running and editing Addisvoice.com, one of the most popular Ethiopian cyber-media outlets. Besides this, I have been doing a lot of volunteer work. I am on the Steering Committee of Solidarity Movement for a New Ethiopia, the board of the Global Arts Initiative at the World Economic Forum and also sit on the international board of the Ethiopian Satellite Television Service. Meanwhile, back in Ethiopia, I have been charged with terrorism (along with 10 other journalists, including two Swedes, the reporter Schibbye and the photographer Johan Persson, who all went to Ethiopia, to report the truth).

In a country like Ethiopia, choosing to be a journalist is a suicidal venture, as one must be prepared to face the unpleasant consequences of speaking out, with the truth. But I have come to realize that, unless the truth is told—with passion, vigor and honesty—

tyranny and evil will prevail over the great values that have given life deeper meanings. I believe that freedom is worth sacrificing for, as so many people throughout the world have courageously laid down their lives to safeguard it. I have been convinced since I was a teenager that even dying for a cause, in an effort to make the world a better place for all to live, gives life deeper meaning and purpose.

My passion for journalism has seriously destabilized my life, but I will always believe that security and stability without freedom is meaningless. If the truth we report as journalists terrorizes tyrants and dictators, then being labeled as a terrorist is a badge of honor. Yes, I am a "terrorist" journalist, proud of believing in freedom, justice and dignity.

Prospects for Humanity

Francis Boyle

Francis Boyle is a professor and scholar in the areas of international law and human rights. He is the author of Tackling America's Toughest Questions: Alternative Media Interviews, *as well as* Breaking All the Rules: Palestine, Iraq, Iran, and the Case for Impeachment. *He has written and lectured extensively in the United States and abroad on the relationship between international law and politics. His* Protesting Power: War, Resistance and Law *has been used successfully in anti-war protest trials. As an internationally recognized expert, Professor Boyle serves as counsel to Bosnia and Herzegovina, and to the Provisional Government of the State of Palestine. He also represents two associations of citizens within Bosnia and had been instrumental in developing the indictment against Slobodan Milosevic for committing genocide, crimes against humanity, and war crimes in Bosnia and Herzegovina. Professor Boyle is Attorney of Record for the Chechen Republic of Ichkeria, conducting its legal affairs on a worldwide basis. Over his career, he has represented national and international bodies including the Blackfoot Nation (Canada), the Nation of Hawaii, and the Lakota Nation, as well as numerous individual death penalty and human rights cases. He has advised numerous international bodies in the areas of human rights, war crimes and genocide, nuclear policy, and bio-warfare. From 1991-92, Professor Boyle served as Legal Advisor to the Palestinian Delegation to the Middle East Peace Negotiations. He has also served on the Board of Directors of Amnesty International, as well as being a consultant to the American Friends Services Committee. Currently, Professor Boyle lectures on international law at the University of Illinois College of Law.*

During the 1950s I grew up in a family who rooted for the success of African Americans in their just struggle for civil rights and full legal equality. Then in 1962 it was the terror of my own personal imminent nuclear annihilation during the Cuban Missile Crisis that first sparked my interest in studying international relations and U.S. foreign policy as a young boy of twelve: "I can do a better job than this!"

After the Japanese attack on Pearl Harbor on 7 December 1941, my father, Francis Anthony Boyle, (after whom I am named as the oldest of my parents' eight children) applied for admission to Officer Candidate School for the United States Marine Corps. After an extended period of investigation, he was eventually rejected—telling me it was the most disappointing day of his entire life. He was not given the reason for this rejection, but as a child he had had rheumatic fever, meningitis, and polio. As a boy, he had had to walk around with crutches, and had only gradually managed to wean himself from them. This rejection by the Marine Corps Officer Candidate School undoubtedly saved my father's life, and thus made mine possible. The chances of survival for a young Marine Corps Officer during the Pacific Campaign were infinitesimal. They were expected to lead their troops into battle, literally, in front of their men.

Despite his deep disappointment and his physical limitations, at the age of 22, my father then enlisted in the U.S. Marine Corps on 14 July 1943, and agreed to serve for the "Duration" of the war. By contrast, I entered the Harvard Law School on about 7

September 1971, at the age of 21. I thought of my father a lot during that first year of law school. At about my age, he had been fighting for his life in the jungles of the Pacific. But he would have wanted it this way for me.

According to his Honorable Discharge papers (A108534, Series A, NAVMC70-PD) and war stories, my father invaded Saipan, Tinian and Okinawa. According to him, after the battle for Okinawa, all but two of the Marines from his original Company were either killed or seriously wounded. The Marine Corps then ordered my father and his friend to begin training for the invasion of mainland Japan, where they were scheduled to be among the first Marines ashore because of their combat experience. My father told me that at the time he believed it was a miracle that he was still alive. He knew he would never survive the planned invasion of the Japanese mainland, but had proceeded to train for this invasion anyway, because he had enlisted for the "Duration." *Semper Fidelis.* (My father was a very aggressive, relentless, fearless, and ferocious warrior.)

After his Honorable Discharge from the Marine Corps on 16 January 1946, as a Corporal with "Character of Service" rated as "excellent," my father attended Loyola University in Chicago, Illinois and graduated from their Law School in the Class of 1950, shortly after I was born. He went to work as a plaintiff's litigator for a law firm in downtown Chicago where, his hiring partner told me, he was very aggressive in court and otherwise. Eventually, he opened his own law firm as a plaintiff's litigator in downtown Chicago in 1959. On the night he was transferring his files from the old office to his new firm, my father put me into our 1955 Chevy, the first car he had ever bought, and brought me along for the ride and the opening of the new law firm.

Soon thereafter, he designated me as the Clerk for the firm, and promptly put me to work (at the age of nine) running messages, filing documents in court, taking money to and from the LaSalle National Bank, etc.—all over downtown Chicago, on school holidays and during summer vacations. At the end of a hard day's work around 5:30 p.m., I would walk over to the corner of State and Madison, in order to take the bus home by myself while my father continued to work away at his law practice late into the night. Now, if I did that to my nine-year-old son today, the Illinois Department of Children and Family Services would step in and take him away from me (the "home alone" phenomenon). But that was a different era, and my father was of the old school: spare the rod, and spoil the child. It was not easy being the oldest child, and the namesake of a World War II U.S. Marine Corps combat veteran of invasions of Saipan, Tinian, and Okinawa.

I continued to serve as his Clerk, until he died of a heart attack on 10 January 1968 at the age of 46. Because I worked for him at his law firm for all those years, I was fortunate to have spent an enormous amount of time with my father. I learned a lot about life from him. Two of his favorites were "Son, there is nothing fair about life." and "Just remember, Son, no one owes you anything." (Of course, he proved right on both counts—and many others as well.)

In particular, since I was his oldest child and namesake, at a very young age he began to tell me these astounding, chilling, hair-raising stories about what hand-to-hand combat in the Pacific had really been like, tales that literally left an otherwise talkative boy dumbfounded. My father supplemented these stories, by taking me to see almost every war film ever made about combat in the Pacific, where he punctuated these war movies *in medias res,* telling me whether or not the incidents portrayed therein were authentic, and then comparing them with his own war experiences afterward on the way home. It dawned upon me at a very young age that it literally *was* a miracle that he had survived the war.

My father was very proud of his combat service in the Marine Corps, and for the rest of his life continued to consider himself to be a Marine. He never bragged about his combat experiences in the war, to me or to anyone else that I was aware of. His record in combat spoke for itself. Indeed, when I was a young boy, his fellow warriors elected him to be the Commander of the local American Legion Post, a distinct honor as he saw it. He brought my mother, my next younger sister, and me along for the installation ceremony and dinner that night.

My father had nothing good and nothing bad to say about the Japanese Imperial Army and its soldiers. But it was obvious from his tone of voice that he considered them to be dangerous warriors prepared to fight to the death, as large numbers of them did at his hands. However, my parents never raised any of their eight children to be biased or prejudiced against the Japanese, or any other people for that matter.

According to my father, immediately prior to the invasions of Saipan, Tinian, and Okinawa, his Captain had issued direct orders to his Company not to take Japanese prisoners of war, on the grounds of reciprocity: "The Japs don't take prisoners of our men, so I don't want to see any Nip soldiers cluttering up our rear lines!" Notwithstanding, my father took surrendering Japanese soldiers as prisoners of war, escorted them to the rear of the line, and then returned to battle. When the odds are overwhelming that you will meet your Maker in any instant, you want to do so with a clear conscience. (I tell this story to my law students, when they object that it is unrealistic to expect soldiers to obey the laws of war during the heat of combat. That is the difference between a warrior and a war-criminal.)

At first glance, it appeared that my father had survived the war relatively unscathed. He had picked up a fungus on his leg that stayed with him for the rest of his life, which he called his "jungle rot." Also, his hearing had been impaired by the big naval guns bombarding the coasts while he and his comrades waited on ship to board the landing transports in order to storm the beaches, as well as by artillery, grenades, bombs, machine guns, flame throwers, and other ordnance that he endured, while advancing under withering enemy fire during the day, repulsing *bonzai* charges at night, and repeatedly volunteering for what looked like suicide missions behind enemy lines, etc. It had been Hell on Earth.

Only years later, long after he had died, and as a result of medical research on veterans of the Vietnam War, did I realize that my father had come back with a severe case of Post Traumatic Stress Syndrome (PTSS), something that was undiagnosed at the time. Combat veterans of World War II were simply expected to go home and resume their civilian lives without further adieu. As my father's Marine Corps Honorable Discharge papers state: "Requires neither treatment nor hospitalization." In retrospect, my father should have had medical treatment for Post Traumatic Stress Syndrome, had it been available then.

Despite his untreated PTSS, my father built a very successful law practice as a plaintiff's litigator. Shortly before he died, he told me that he had become almost economically secure enough from his law practice to run for a Judgeship in Cook County, which he had intended to do. Given that he was born Irish on the south side of Chicago, along with his Marine Corps combat record, he would have had no problem being nominated, run and elected by the storied Dick Daley Machine—he had grown with them all. But my father's further ascent in the legal profession had been cut short by the physical condition of his heart. Nevertheless, he always demonstrated heartfelt compassion to those less fortunate than he, and taught all of his children to do the same. My mother still does the same today.

★ While it was likely not my father's intention, his stories told over many years, about the terrors and horrors of combat in the Pacific, turned me against war and violence as a solution to human problems.

With the escalation of the Vietnam War in 1964 and the military draft staring me right in the face, I undertook a detailed examination of it. Eventually, I concluded that this war was illegal, immoral, unethical, and the United States was bound to lose it. America was just picking up where France had left off at Dien Bien Phu. So I resolved to do what little I could to oppose the Vietnam War.

In 1965 President Lyndon Johnson gratuitously invaded the Dominican Republic, which prompted me to commence a detailed examination of U.S. military interventions into Latin America, from the Spanish-American War of 1898 up to President Franklin Roosevelt's so-called "good neighbor" policy. At the end of this study, I concluded that the Vietnam War was not episodic, but rather systemic: aggression, warfare, bloodshed, and violence were just the way the United States power elite had historically conducted their business around the world. Hence, as I saw it as a young man of 17, there would be more Vietnams in the future, and perhaps someday I could do something about it, as well as about promoting civil rights for African Americans. These twins concerns of my youth would gradually ripen into a career devoted to international law and human rights.

I commenced my formal study of International Relations with the late, great Hans Morgenthau in the first week of January 1970 as a 19-year-old college sophomore at the University of Chicago, taking his basic introductory course on that subject. At the time, Morgenthau was leading the academic forces of opposition to the detested Vietnam War, which was precisely why I chose to study with him. During my ten years of higher education at the University of Chicago and Harvard, I refused to study with openly pro-Vietnam-War professors as a matter of principle, as well as on the quite pragmatic ground that they had nothing to teach me.

In the summer of 1975, it was Morgenthau who emphatically encouraged me to become a professor, instead of doing some other promising things with my life: "*If Morgenthau thinks I should become a professor, then I will become a professor!*" I thought. After almost a decade of working personally with him, Morgenthau had provided me with enough inspiration, guidance, and knowledge to last now almost half a lifetime.

Historically, this latest eruption of American militarism at the start of the 21st Century is akin to that of America opening the 20th Century with the U.S.-instigated Spanish-American War in 1898. The Republican administration of President William McKinley stole Spain's colonial empire (in Cuba, Puerto Rico, Guam, and the Philippines); inflicted a near genocidal war against the Filipino people; and illegally annexed the Kingdom of Hawaii, while subjecting the Native Hawaiian people (who call themselves the Kanaka Maoli) to near genocidal conditions. Additionally, McKinley's military and colonial expansion into the Pacific was also designed to secure America's economic exploitation of China, pursuant to the euphemistic rubric of the "open door" policy. Over the next four decades, America's aggressive presence, policies, and practices in the "Pacific" would ineluctably pave the way for Japan's attack at Pearl Harbor on 7 Dec. 1941, and thus America's precipitation into the ongoing Second World War. Today, a century later, the serial imperial aggressions launched and menaced by the Republican Bush Jr. administration, and now continued and expanded by the Democratic Obama administration, are threatening to set off World War III.

By shamelessly exploiting the terrible tragedy of 11 September 2001, the Bush Jr. administration set forth to steal a hydrocarbon empire, from the Muslim states and peoples living in Central Asia and the Persian Gulf, under the bogus pretexts of: (1) fighting a war against international terrorism; and/or (2) eliminating weapons of mass destruction; and/or (3) the promotion of democracy; and/or (4) self-styled "humanitarian intervention." Only this time, the geopolitical stakes are infinitely greater than they were a century ago: control and domination of two-thirds of the world's hydrocarbon resources, and thus the very fundament and energizer of the global economic system: oil and gas. The Bush Jr./Obama administrations have already targeted the remaining hydrocarbon reserves of Africa, Latin America, and Southeast Asia for further conquest or domination, together with the strategic choke-points at sea and on land required for their transportation. In this regard, the Bush Jr. administration announced the establishment of the U.S. Pentagon's Africa Command (AFRICOM), in order to better control, dominate, and exploit both the natural resources and the variegated peoples of the continent of Africa, the very cradle of our human species.

This current bout of U.S. imperialism is what Hans Morgenthau denominated "unlimited imperialism" in his seminal work, *Politics among Nations* (4th ed. 1968, at 52-53):

> *The outstanding historic examples of unlimited imperialism are the expansionist policies of Alexander the Great, Rome, the Arabs in the seventh and eighth centuries, Napoleon I, and Hitler. They all have in common an urge toward expansion which knows no rational limits, feeds on its own successes and, if not stopped by a superior force, will go on to the confines of the political world. This urge will not be satisfied so long as there remains anywhere a possible object of domination—a politically organized group of men which by its very independence challenges the conqueror's lust for power. It is, as we shall see, exactly the lack of moderation, the aspiration to conquer all that lends itself to conquest, characteristic of unlimited imperialism, which in the past has been the undoing of the imperialistic policies of this kind....*

On 10 November 1979 I visited with Hans Morgenthau at his home in Manhattan. It proved to be our last conversation before he died on 19 July 1980. Given his weakened physical but not mental condition and his serious heart problem, at the end of our necessarily abbreviated one-hour meeting I purposefully asked him what he thought about the future of international relations. This revered scholar, whom international relations experts generally consider to be the founder of modern international political science in the post World War II era, responded:

Future, what future? I am extremely pessimistic. In my opinion the world is moving ineluctably towards a third world war—a strategic nuclear war. I do not believe that anything can be done to prevent it. The international system is simply too unstable to survive for long. The SALT II Treaty is important for the present, but over the long haul it cannot stop the momentum. Fortunately, I do not believe that I will live to see that day. But I am afraid you might.

The factual circumstances surrounding the outbreaks of both the First World War and the Second World War currently hover like the Sword of Damocles over the heads of all humanity.

My father's life influenced not only my appreciation of the heroism and sacrifices of U.S. Marines, soldiers, sailors, airmen and now airwomen, but also my understanding and apprehension of its dreadful realities, and the aftereffects upon those who must bear its brunt, and carry its memories throughout the rest of their lives.

It's important to understand these ills, which arrogant and rapacious government officials can perpetrate on those who are expected to sacrifice their very lives, as well as the terrible tragedy that is so characteristic of war itself. War is always the ultimate defeat for the human spirit. War is an abomination on the face of God's Creation. There has to be a better way. Law is that better way.

For my part, I drafted the Biological Weapons Anti-terrorism Act of 1989 (the U.S. domestic implementing legislation for the Biological Weapons Convention of 1972) that was passed unanimously by both houses of the United States Congress and signed into law by President Bush Sr.

In the fall of 1990 I served as Counsel for the successful defense of U.S. Marine Corps Corporal Jeff Paterson, the first military resister as a matter of principle and conscience to Bush Sr.'s Gulf War I. Then I represented U.S. M.C. Lance Corporal David Mihaila, in his successful effort to obtain his discharge from the Marine Corps during Bush Sr.'s Gulf War I as a Conscientious Objector. (Corporal Mihaila was the Clerk of the Court for the Paterson court-martial proceeding, and had been motivated to apply for CO status, as a result of my oral argument for Corporal Paterson.)

Then, at the start of 1991, I served as Counsel for the defense of Captain Dr. Yolanda Huet-Vaughn, who had been court-martialed by the U.S. Army in part because of her refusal to administer experimental vaccines to soldiers destined to fight in the Bush Sr. Gulf War I. After a kangaroo-court proceeding, she got eight months—and we got her adopted as a Prisoner of Conscience by Amnesty International. Later on, I served as Counsel for the successful defense of U.S. Army Captain Lawrence Rockwood, who had been court-martialed for his heroic efforts to stop torture in Haiti after the United States government had invaded that country in 1994.

I later served as Counsel for the defense for Army Staff Sergeant Camilo Mejia, the first U.S. military resister to be court-martialed for refusing to participate in President Bush Jr.'s war of aggression against Iraq. After another kangaroo-court proceeding, he got eight months—and we got him adopted as a Prisoner of Conscience by Amnesty International, as well. I then served as Counsel for the successful defense of Army First Lieutenant Ehren Watada, the first U.S. commissioned officer to be court-martialed for his refusal to participate in the War on Iraq.

We Americans cannot keep sending our young men (and now women) off to fight and to die, or to survive with terrible physical and mental injuries, scarred for the rest of their lives by the horrors of warfare, as my father was. America's endemic cycle of warfare, bloodshed, and violence, both internationally and domestically, must stop with us. We need to teach our children that there is a better way. Given the pervasive American culture of glorifying and worshiping violence, warfare, death, and destruction, we must educate our children about the absolute necessity for peace, justice, human rights, and the Rule of Law, both internationally and domestically.

We need to counteract the outright pro-war propaganda, militarization, and military solicitation currently being inflicted upon our children—by the Pentagon, the news media, and university courses in political science, history, and the other social sciences, which have an inherent bias in favor of power, domination, violence, and warfare. The Peace Movement must continue to oppose the Bush Jr. and Obama Administration's attempt to create an American hydrocarbon empire abroad—in Iraq, the Persian Gulf, Afghanistan, Central Asia, Colombia, West Africa, the Horn, Libya, and elsewhere—by exploiting, manipulating, abusing and deceiving the members of U.S. armed forces to serve as pawns in their geopolitical pursuit of oil, natural gas, and corporate profits, while amassing personal family-fortunes in the process. We need as many loyal, patriotic, humanitarian, and principled American citizens as possible to contemplate these ideas, and then act upon them to stop these wars!

Not surprisingly, the January 2007 issue of the *American Journal of Imperial Law* (otherwise known as the self-styled American Journal of International Law, but originally founded a century ago and still operated by U. S. War and State Department legal apparatchiks and their law professorial fellow-travelers) published an article by Harvard Law School's recently retired Bemis Professor of International Law, Detlev Vagts (who only taught me the required course on Legal Accounting), arguing in favor of the Pentagon's Kangaroo Courts System in Guantanamo, despite the fact that they have been soundly condemned, by every human rights organization and human rights official and leader in the entire world, as well as by the United States Supreme Court itself in *Hamdan v. Rumsfeld* (2006).

I am not going to bother to recite here all the grievous deficiencies of the Gitmo Kangaroo Courts under International Law and U.S. Constitutional Law. Suffice it to say, the Gitmo Kangaroo Courts constitute war crimes, under the Laws of War, the Four Geneva Conventions of 1949, and even the U.S. Army's own Field Manual 27-10, *The Law of Land Warfare* (1956). Field Manual 27-10 was drafted for the Pentagon, by my Laws of War teacher Richard R. Baxter, who was generally recognized as the world's leading expert on that subject. (That is precisely why I voluntarily chose to study International Law with him and his long-time collaborator Louis B. Sohn, and not with the bean-counter Vagts. For most of the post-World War II generation of international law students at Harvard Law School, Louis Sohn shall always be our real Bemis Professor of International Law and never the False Pretender to that Throne known as Detlev Vagts.)

Since those student days I have personally appeared *pro bono publico* in five U.S. military courts-martial proceedings involving warfare that were organized in accordance with the Congress's Uniform Code of Military Justice (U.C.M.J.)—which still does not apply to the Gitmo Kangaroo Courts, despite the ruling by the U. S. Supreme Court in

Hamdan that the U.C.M.J. should be applied in Guantanamo—on behalf of the five U. S. military personnel I've mentioned above, who each acted with courage, integrity, principle, conscience and at great risk to their own freedom.

As I can attest from my direct personal involvement, each and every one of these five courts-martial under the U.C.M.J. were Stalinist show-trials, produced and directed by the Pentagon, that predictably and readily degenerated into travesties of justice. These five U.C.M.J. courts-martial involving U.S. warfare each proved correct the old adage, attributed to Groucho Marx, that "military justice is to justice as military music is to music." By comparison, the Gitmo Kangaroo Courts will not even be run in accordance with the U.C.M.J., despite the fact that the U.S. Supreme Court ruled in *Hamdan* that they should be. The Marx Brothers are running the Gitmo Kangaroo Courts. Whenever they are up and fully operating, the Gitmo Courts will constitute Stalinist Show Trials as well as Kangaroo Courts, and their preliminary proceedings have already proven them to be Travesties of Justice. Even worse yet, fully-functioning Stalinist Gitmo Kangaroo Courts will quickly become conveyor-belts of death for alleged and already tortured terrorist suspects along the lines of the Texas execution chamber operated by George Bush Jr. when he was the "governor" of that state and tortured to death 152 victims by means of lethal injection. Gitmo (and/or Gitmo-North in Illinois) will become America's first-ever Nazi-style death camp. There will be no end to it, which is precisely why we have to stop Gitmo dead in its tracks!

Today the "real and present danger" is the kind of unscrupulous Machiavellian power politics so blatantly practiced by the Neoconservative Bush Jr. administration (and now the Neoliberal Obama administration), around the world and at home. The only known antidote is a combination of international law, international organizations, human rights, and the United States Constitution. In our thermonuclear age, humankind's existential choice is that stark, ominous, and compelling. As Americans and citizens of the world, we must not hesitate to apply this imperative regimen immediately, before it becomes too late for the continuation of our human species itself. It is imperative that we undertake a committed and concerted effort to head-off Hans Morgenthau's final prediction on the cataclysmic demise of the human race.

Life Under an Air War

Fred Branfman

Fred Branfman is a writer and longtime activist who directed the Indochina Resource Center during the war in Indochina. He edited Voices from the Plain of Jars: Life under an Air War, *the only book to emerge from the Indochina war written from the perspective of its villagers. It is also the only book to describe life under the largest and most protracted bombing of civilian targets in history, one which left behind more unexploded cluster bomblets in Laos than in the rest of the world combined.*

"Around that village of mine were green and beautiful mountains, and the land and the fields my neighbors had sweated over and labored on since the time of my ancestors. My neighbors were all farmers, honest and hard-working. Our happiness was full and overflowing because we were content with our lives, even though we lived in the wilderness."   - A 26-year-old nurse from the Plain of Jars, on life before the bombs

"There wasn't a night when we thought we'd live until morning, never a morning we thought we'd survive until night. Did our children cry? Oh, yes, and we did also. I just stayed in my cave. I didn't see the sunlight for two years. What did I think about? Oh, I used to repeat, 'please don't let the planes come, please don't let the planes come, please don't let the planes come.'" - Plain of Jars refugee, on life under the bombs

I awoke in Vientiane, Laos on a day in early September, 1969, with no idea that my life was about to change forever.

I had lived in a Lao village for the previous two-and-a-half years, spoke Laotian, and had finished my alternative to military service as an educational advisor with International Voluntary Services three months earlier. I had remained because I really liked Laos and Lao people, and was at loose ends about what to do next.

My years in the village, which lacked running water and electricity though only eleven kilometers outside Vientiane, had led me to deeply appreciate Lao rice farmers. I knew them as real human beings, neither idealized nor romanticized them, and had certainly met some I disliked. But on the whole, I had never met a group of people whom I liked and respected more. I found them kind, friendly, cheerful, decent, fun, honest, sincere and trustworthy. I appreciated how the villagers looked me in the eye, told the truth, and connected on a deep human level. There may be people as fine in this world, I used to tell my friends, but I could not imagine any finer.

I felt particularly close to Paw Thou Douang, the village elder in whose house I lived. He was a deeply devout Buddhist and lay leader of the Buddhist temple ten yards from our home. He was also a medic, farmer and, I discovered after the war ended, the local representative of the Pathet Lao. He was a cheerful, kind, wise, gentle, much loved man whom I deeply respected, and had become a kind of second father to me.

Laos was then divided into the pro-U.S. Royal Lao Government zone of some 2 million people where I lived, and the guerrilla Pathet Lao zone of some one million, which was closed to westerners. I was spending that day downtown with my friend Tim Allman, a *New York Times* journalist, who asked if I would interpret for him as he went to interview refugees from the Plain of Jars. The first residents of guerrilla zones ever to reach Vientiane, they were being housed at the That Louang pagoda in the center of the city.

I eagerly agreed. Although the Plain was only some 230 miles from Vientiane, it might as well have been on the other side of the moon for all we knew of it. I was curious about life in Pathet Lao zones, and the rumors of U.S. bombing, denied by the U.S. government but reported in *Le Monde* the previous spring.

The first visit: early September, 1969

"At that time my life was filled with great happiness, for the mountains and forests were beautiful: land, water, and climate were suitable for us. And there were many homes in our little village."
- Thirteen-year-old boy, on life before the bombing

Tim hopped on the back of my motorcycle. We drove up to That Louang, and entered a large but sparsely furnished prayer shed the size of a football field, filled with hundreds of refugees spread out on the floor.

We picked one man at random, and began to interview him. When I asked him whether he had seen any bombing, his faced clouded over, as he began to describe being bombed frequently for the previous five years. At one point he crouched down and did something that has been engraved in my memory forever. He draw an "L" in the dust, showing the shape of the shelter he had dug into the side of a mountain, where he had hidden by day for months on end, to escape the bombers that came every day and gradually demolished his entire village. *"We lived like animals!"* he said, explaining how he could only come out at night to try and do some farming, and find some food to keep himself and his family alive.

I was thunderstruck. Seeing this subsistence-level innocent Lao farmer, describing how he had hidden like an animal for months on end, from bombers sent from a rich, comfortable distant land to burn and destroy his fellow villagers, family members, livestock and home—without him even knowing who was bombing him or why, and against whom he had committed no offense whatsoever—seemed to me then (and has seemed to me ever since) among the ultimate evils, lack of humanity, and horrors that I could possibly imagine.

In shock, I went on to interview over a dozen refugees. Every one gave the same basic report: The bombing had begun in 1964, and gradually intensified year by year until, starting in late 1968, they were being bombed daily. Villager after villager described seeing relatives and friends burned and buried alive, their livestock killed, their homes and pagodas demolished. They spoke of living in holes for months on end, and of their intense pain at being forcibly removed from the villages of their ancestors, to wind up as penniless refugees in Vientiane. The main victims of the bombing, every refugee explained, were civilians—particularly older people, mothers and children, who had to remain near their villages to survive. The soldiers moved through the deeply carpeted forests of northern Laos, and were relatively unscathed by the bombing.

The refugee camps: September, 1969 – February, 1971

"Travel between villages was easy because there were so many all close together. Boys and girls playing the flute and enjoying themselves in the village was easy. When it came time to work the fields, we went to work together. We shared the labor in a fulfilling way for us young people. When the field work was finished, we joined in the yearly festivities with the sounds of singing, dancing and laughter." - 39-year-old farmer, on life before the bombing

I heard all of this with a slowly mounting and disbelieving horror, unable to take in all I was hearing, from people who were just like those I had come to love in my village. I suppose if I had not been as close to the people of my village, if I had seen the Plain of Jars refugees only as nameless "bombing victims," I might not have had such a strong reaction. But to me, these fine, decent people whom I respected so much did have names and faces, and family members, and dreams—and at least as much right to them as did I, or those who so had cruelly snuffed them out without a thought. Realizing what was happening to these people I so admired felt unbearable.

It was only as I went back frequently to talk with the refugees over the next 15 months that I was able to absorb the full dimensions of who these people were, what they had been through, and its implications for humanity.

The refugees in That Louang were soon moved out to refugee camps around Vientiane, and over the next six months more were brought from the north, as the numbers of refugees from the Plain grew to some 20,000 people.

During the months of interviewing the refugees, my first level of shock came from realizing that these people had been being bombed for five years, without the knowledge of most outsiders elsewhere in the country, myself included. (At that time, the U.S. government still denied that it was doing any bombing in Laos at all.) Unlike in South Vietnam, journalists were not permitted to go out on bombing runs. It seemed eerie and frightening that a handful of U.S. government bureaucrats had the power to bomb so secretly.

I was deeply disturbed to learn how much unilateral power a handful of U.S. Executive Branch officials had, both Democrats and Republicans, and their callousness in using it. I realized that the problem wasn't that my government's leaders hated these Lao. They simply did not care. They conducted this mass murder not out of malice, but sheer indifference to the existence of these innocent Lao rice-farmers.

I experienced even greater horror at seeing the physical effects of the bombing on the refugees. I interviewed 38-year-old Thao Vong, who had been blinded by an antipersonnel bomb attack in July of 1967. Cluster munitions are unexploded bomblets, which remain in the ground and threaten civilians. The term "antipersonnel bombs" refers both to cluster munitions and bombs designed only to kill and wound human beings at the time of use, such as flechette and fiberglass bombs, as well as to cluster munitions that leave behind duds that fail to detonate, and remain a threat beyond their immediate use.

I saw a young boy missing a leg. I spoke with the father of three-year-old Khamphong, one of six of his children hit by cluster bombs on February 28, 1969, and felt the pellets still in her body. I learned from Pha Sii how her daughter-in-law had been killed in August, 1969, shielding her year-old child with her body. I met a 35-year-old man from Ban Na Sou, whose father, mother, wife and three children had all been killed in a July 15, 1967 bombing raid. I talked with Po Sing Som's wife, who described how her husband, in his sixties, was killed by antipersonnel bombs in a September 16, 1968 raid that wounded her and also left pellets still visible in her body.

Two incidents stood out above all. One was receiving the striking wedding photo of Sao Doumma, a sweet-faced woman, who would be killed in a bombing raid seven years later. It symbolized to me the deep humanity of the unseen and unknown victims of the bombing. The second was meeting the mother of a three-year-old girl who had been burned in her breast, stomach and vagina. I was devastated to return a week later and learn that the child had died.

Words cannot convey the pain I felt seeing the wounds of the survivors and hearing their stories of the painful death of their loved ones, due to bombing that continued week after week, month after month, for five and a half long years, longer than U.S. involvement in World War II.

I was especially shocked to learn that many of the people of the Plain of Jars had no idea who was bombing them or why. It was for them like the *War of the Worlds* science-fiction movie, in which unknown giant machines attacked for reasons no one could understand. I had no real answer when refugees asked me, with genuine curiosity, "Why did they bomb us? Do you know?"

I was also particularly struck by discovering something I had never even heard of before: cluster bombs. I first became aware of them when I noticed a yellow pineapple bomb being used as a lamp in one of their huts. The refugees said it was these bombs that had done them the most damage and which they most feared. Exploding over a wide area, they killed those who could not dive into their holes fast enough, particularly older people slower in running, or children confused by the noise and smoke. They said people had also been murdered by stepping on unexploded bomblets, even when the bombing was not occurring.

By far the deepest level of pain I experienced, however, came from the most disturbing realization of all: "*My God! The bombing is still continuing!*" The realization that there were at that very moment Lao people alive today, who would be bombed to death tomorrow, hit me like a hammer.

I am Jewish, and had been deeply moved when meeting Holocaust survivors some years earlier. In this situation, however, it felt as if I had learned what was occurring at Auschwitz while it was still going on. Without any conscious decision, I soon found myself committed to doing whatever I could to stop the bombing, by trying to expose it to the world.

There were only a handful of reporters permanently stationed in Laos; most major journalists came in from elsewhere to report for a week at a time. Over the next 15 months, I wound up working for reporters from all of the major TV networks, as well as many newspapers. From their perspective they were hiring an interpreter and fixer. From mine, I was trying to get the story of the bombing on media back in the U.S. I also took photos and tape-recorded conversations with the refugees and sent them to Senators Kennedy and Fulbright, escorted visiting peace activists like Noam Chomsky out to the camps, and briefed diplomats and Congressional aides.

During this period, I became friendly with a Plain of Jars refugee, my own age, named Ngeun. He stood out for his obvious intelligence, cheerfulness, warm-heartedness, self-confidence, honesty, and steadfastness. He became the closest friend I have ever had, and I learned that he had been a former soldier, cadre and medic for the Pathet Lao. Ngeun agreed to help me collect essays and drawings from refugees. (He did so at some risk, as he had to hide them under his shirt as he passed through police checkpoints.)

The U.S. Air Force: September, 1969 – February, 1971

"I will tell about my past life in Xieng Khouang, an area with high mountains and scattered open plains. It is naturally beautiful because the climate is cool and misty. In the mornings, fog shrouds the mountain. In the evening, the rays of the sun silhouette the mountain in a most charming scene. And turning, you can see the water cascading from the top of a high mountain." - 16-year-old student, on life before the bombing

My other reaction to discovering the bombing, however, was to try and understand how it had occurred. Learning of this mass murder had destroyed my moral universe, throwing into question my deepest assumptions about my government's officials and humanity. It was obvious that the bombing of these people violated international law, and yet the Nuremberg Principles, the Geneva Conventions and the U.N. Charter might as well have not existed.

Many of my deepest beliefs, which I had taken for granted since childhood, had suddenly become null and void. I learned in those camps that crime does pay, truth and justice do not eventually triumph, and goodness and innocence are not rewarded. I soon learned that U.S. Executive Branch had unilaterally bombed Laos without even informing (let alone seeking permission from) Congress. This clearly demonstrated that my country's state was undemocratic at home, and the authorities a force for much evil abroad.

I found myself wondering what it said about humanity: that the richest and most comfortable of the species had spent five years savagely murdering some of the poorest; that they would deploy the world's most sophisticated technology, against villages that lacked even running water and electricity. How could they be so cruel, merciless and pitiless to such kind, sweet, gentle people, who posed no real threat to them? What did it mean that they were so indifferent to human suffering?

I was particularly haunted by this question: If innocent, kind, gentle Lao people could be slaughtered this way, who among us was safe? If the Lao could not be protected from this senseless savagery, who could be?

I can still remember those first few days standing in the prayer shed at That Louang, and feeling overwhelmed by both these and more immediate questions. *Who had ordered this bombing? Who was conducting it? Why were they using these kinds of weapons? Where were the planes coming from? What on earth was going on?* I literally had no idea.

A Peace Corps volunteer friend of mine named Charlie lived in nearby Udorn, Thailand, the site of a major U.S. Air Force base bombing Laos. During a visit to Vientiane, he offered to introduce me to some Air Force personnel who were against the war. I went to Udorn, where I first began to learn about the giant machine of 50,000 airmen involved in bombing Laos from bases in Thailand and South Vietnam and aircraft carriers in the Gulf of Tonkin. The men I talked to, a small minority, were against the bombing, because they knew their leaders were lying when they denied they were bombing Laos. Many had happened to load cluster munitions onto airplanes, and were horrified to learn what they were doing to civilians. A captain in charge of the ordnance dump at Udorn told me that 75-80 percent of the ordnance on hand were anti-personnel bombs. A sergeant explained how just one sortie carried 1,000 clusters, which sent 250,000 steel pellets over an area the size of four football fields. I later learned that more than 580,000 bombing sorties had been flown over Laos.

In the months and years to come, I visited more airbases in Thailand and interviewed pilots at Danang Air Force Base in South Vietnam. I also met Jerry Brown, a former U.S. Air Force captain who had clandestinely selected targets out of the U.S. Embassy in Vientiane. He was then working in advertising in Bangkok, and agreed to a long series of interviews—primarily because he had been upset at how the C.I.A had taken over the selection of targeting, and deliberately targeted villages. He made it clear that the U.S. Embassy, Air Force and C.I.A all knew full-well that civilian targets were being bombed.

One of the most shattering revelations about the bombing was discovering why it had so vastly increased in 1969, as described by the refugees. I learned that after President Lyndon Johnson had declared a bombing halt over North Vietnam in November 1968, he had simply diverted the planes into northern Laos. There was no military reason for doing so. It was simply because, as U.S. Deputy Chief of Mission Monteagle Stearns testified to the U.S. Senate Committee on Foreign Relations in October, 1969, "Well, we had all those planes sitting around, and couldn't just let them stay there with nothing to do."

I shuddered at learning why the people of the Plain of Jars had been subjected to such hideous suffering, at realizing firsthand the meaning of the philosopher Hannah Arendt's famous description of the Nazi Adolf Eichmann. This "banality of evil" was one of the most striking—and frightening—features of the bombing.

Washington, D.C.: February, 1971 – April, 1975

"The village in which I was born, so pleasing to me, had a cool, fresh climate and rich mountains and forests. There was also much land for rice fields and raising livestock. For many years, I raised cows and buffalo, as my parents had taught me to do. I saw this as very beneficial and enjoyable for someone living in the countryside, for a farmer who inhabited the mountains and the forests." - 17-year-old boy, on life before the bombing

In February 1971, I was singled out for expulsion by the Royal Lao Government, and returned to Washington, D.C. to oppose the bombing—ironically at the height of concern about the war in Laos due to the South Vietnamese invasion of southern Laos then under way. Over the next four years, I directed two peace groups (Project Air War and the Indochina Resource Center) which became major sources of information about the war for Congress, the media and peace groups throughout the nation.

I had purchased an antipersonnel bomb/lamp from one of the refugees, and frequently displayed it when speaking or making media appearances back in the U.S. Audiences were uniformly horrified when I explained how these weapons had mainly wound up injuring innocent Lao villagers, and how they had been fiendishly expanded from being mere steel pellets to flechette arrows, designed to do more damage when being extracted then going in, and thence to plastic pellets (invisible to X-rays).

My antipersonnel bomb became both substance and symbol of what the bombing was all about. Nothing did more real-world damage to civilians. And nothing more symbolized the cruelty of the air war for innocent human beings, whatever its stated purpose.

I briefed Congressman Pete McClosky in some detail about the bombing, including information on where the refugee camps were located, in preparation for his April, 1971 visit to Laos. Upon his return, he generated enormous publicity, charging that the U.S. government was lying when it denied it was bombing civilians.

Senator Kennedy's staff then invited me to attend an April 22, 1971 hearing on the Laos bombing, at which U.S. Ambassador William Sullivan would testify, and said the Senator would call on me from the audience. The giant hearing room was packed. I sat in the audience, remembering the hundreds of refugees I had interviewed who had described losing loved ones, hiding in terror from the bombs, seeing their villages destroyed. When I heard Ambassador Sullivan testify that "the policy of the U.S. is deliberately to avoid hitting inhabited villages," a nauseating shock passed through my body.

Kennedy then did call on me. I stood up, described interviewing over 1,000 refugees who all said their villages had been bombed, said that "the evidence is clear that the U.S. is conducting the most protracted bombing of civilian targets in history," and urged Kennedy to take action. Sullivan then again denied the bombing of civilians. Kennedy simply responded to Sullivan "I don't believe you," and the hearing ended. I left with a sick feeling, knowing that the bombing was continuing to kill the innocent hour after hour, day after day, month after month, year after year. In the end, the bombing of Laos continued for nearly two more years after this hearing, totaling nine years of terror from above.

While the exchange with Sullivan made the *NBC Nightly News* and generated other media coverage, the overall—and devastating—lesson was clear. Senator Kennedy's own staff had published a report seven months earlier, stating that "the United States has undertaken a large-scale air war over Laos to destroy the physical and social infrastructure of Pathet Lao areas. The bombing has taken and is taking a heavy toll among civilians." The Senator clearly knew that a U.S. Executive Branch representative had looked him in the face and lied about U.S. responsibility for mass murder, and was lying to Congress and the American people. But he took no action. Nothing brought home to me more that the U.S. Executive Branch was an all-powerful authoritarian institution when it came to automated war, with Congress playing virtually no meaningful role at all. I had learned firsthand that, when it came to Executive war-making in Laos, the U.S. Constitution had as little significance as international law.

When I had returned to Washington, D.C. in February, 1971, I had brought the essays and drawings by the refugees that Ngeun and I had collected with me. I did not read Lao, however, and had no idea of their significance. They sat in my closet for six months, until I contacted a Lao student studying in Montreal named Hiem Phommachanh, who agreed to help me translate them into English. Hiem, now Deputy Foreign Minister of the Lao PDR, worked side-by-side with me for several weeks. He would translate the essays aloud from Lao into French, and I would write them down in English.

It was one of the most touching and deeply spiritual experiences of my life. We were both moved beyond words by what were reading. And we—a Lao and an American, working in a small room while countless more Lao continued to be killed by countless more American bombing raids—experienced our common humanity on the deepest possible level.

The surreal contrast I had experienced in Laos, while shuttling between Lao refugee camps and U.S. airbases, was intensified during my years in Washington. Each morning, while shaving, I would look at my eyes in the mirror and remember the sad, soulful, gentle eyes of the people from the Plain of Jars, and what the war had looked like from the "bottom up." Each day I would then spend my time discussing the bombing from the "top down," most often fruitlessly trying to convince lawmakers to act to stop it, or journalists to write about it, or audiences to work against it.

The fact that innocent villagers were dying every hour of every day was never out of my consciousness during that period. And it was the surreal disconnect between those ongoing deaths in Indochina and the indifference to them in America that I most remember from those years:

- villagers dying as I debated a U.S. Air Force officer in Senator Clifford Case's office who, shocked at my saying that civilians were being bombed, responded by assuring the Senator with clearly earnest sincerity that "the United States Air Force never bombs people. We only strike enemy combatants." (When I explained this simply wasn't true, he looked at me not with anger but unfeigned amazement that I would make such a statement, as if I had come from another planet. Which I suppose I had.)

- villagers dying as I read the following statement by Major General Robert Ginsburg, the U.S. Air Force chief of public affairs: "I don't understand why people are so upset about anti-personnel bombs because they can't destroy a truck or bridge and only kill people. They are anti-personnel bombs. They are not designed to destroy structures or vehicles."

- villagers dying as I was screamed at by the Speaker of the House to "keep those things in your briefcase!" as I began to pull out some drawings, because he feared I would show him "atrocity photos" of children whose deaths he had earlier funded;

- villagers dying as my Congressman pulled his chair close to mine as I was lobbying him to stop the bombing, and whispered in my ear that I shouldn't go too far, because otherwise the Pentagon would stage a military coup;

- villagers dying as a *CBS Evening News* producer interrupted me, when I began to describe the bombing, to proudly show me the anti-personnel flechettes he was using as thumbtacks on his bulletin board;

- villagers dying as a Los Angeles TV station accompanied the display of the drawings with the instrumental version of the 1940s big-band song "Sentimental Journey," rather than allowing me to read the captions as I normally did.

- villagers dying as I showed a photo on TV of a teenager, blinded by Richard Nixon's Christmas 1972 bombing raids, whom I had recently interviewed in a Hanoi hospital, and was told by Nixon biographer Victor Lasky that "I was just talking with the president this morning, and can assure you that he is just as concerned about the bombing victims as are you";

- villagers dying as the head of the Air Force Pacific Command, drunk out of his mind, slurredly informed me that he too wanted to end the war: "I've always been one of those get in and get out kind of guys, know what I mean?";

- villagers dying as a TV network State Department reporter, who I had taken to the camps and knew firsthand of Secretary of State Henry Kissinger's mass murder of civilians on the Plain of Jars, angrily told me, "I'll have you know that Dr. Kissinger is a close personal friend of mine!" in response to my complaining about the media's disinterest in the bombing and Kissinger's role in it. (When phone logs of him flattering Kissinger were recently revealed, he explained to the *New York Times*: "Am I shocked by the notion that people were sucking up to a very powerful official they relied on for information? ... Frankly, no.")

- villagers dying as I saw my antipersonnel bomb held up by a decent U.S. Senator then running for president at a giant campaign rally, and then saw him suffer a massive defeat by Richard Nixon a week later;

- villagers dying as I saw the architect of the mass murder of the people of the Plain of Jars not only go unpunished, but win a Nobel Peace Prize and become the toast of American high society.

Nonhumanity Above, Humanity Below

"In my family there were 13 people — each one happy and content because the area was so bountiful and beautiful. In the evening, one could see the animals returning to their pens in a great unbroken herd after a day of searching for grass. When I would see that, I would feel content because these animals were my heart. If I needed money, I could sell them or some of my other property." — 51-year-old farmer, on life before the bombing

As the years have passed, it is this contrast between what I have come to regard as the "nonhumanity" of those conducting the bombing, and the profound, rich and moving humanity of those below, that I have found most significant—not only for what happened on the Plain of Jars 40 years ago, but for a 21st century that will be increasingly marked by automated war. Much of war-making has of course historically been intensely "inhuman" conflict between enemies who hate each other, whether Nazis and Russians, Hindus and Muslims, Serbs and Bosnians, or Palestinians and Israelis.

American leaders, however, had nothing against the one million Lao upon whom they dropped two million tons of bombs, as much as were dropped on hundreds of millions through Europe and the entire Pacific Theater in World War II. They simply ignored their existence. The bombing of the Plain of Jars marked the fulfillment of a prediction previously only imagined in fiction, as when Orwell in *1984* described how "war involves very small numbers of people, mostly highly trained specialists. The fighting takes place on the vague frontiers whose whereabouts the average man can only guess at."

The contrast:

Above: For years on end, the most sophisticated killing machines ever invented hovered over subsistence-level villages, looking for any sign of human life so as to eliminate it. There were O1E, 02, and OV10 spotter planes at 2,000 feet; AlE, A26, and T28 prop bombers, AC47, AC54, AC119, and AC130 gunships, rescue helicopters at 5,000 feet; F4, F100, F105, F47, and B57 jet bombers, jet reconnaissance, C47 and EC119 electronic aircraft at 10,000 feet; KC135 supertankers at 20,000; B52s at 30,000; EC130 command and control aircraft at 35,000; and SR71 photo recon aircraft at 70,000 feet.

Below: As a 30-year-old Lao woman described it, "I saw my cousin die in the field of death. My heart was most disturbed and my voice called out loudly as I ran to the houses. Thus, I saw life and death for the people on account of the war of many airplanes in the region of Xieng Khouang. Until there were no houses at all. And the cows and buffalo were dead. Until everything was leveled and you could see only the red, red ground. I think of this time and still I am afraid."

Above: Pilots dropped the most exotic weapons ever invented on these villages: napalm, white phosphorous, fragmentation bombs, standard and delayed-action 250-, 500-, 1,000-, 2,000- and 7,500-pound high-explosive bombs, horizontally exploding ball bearing "pineapple" cluster bombs, diagonally exploding ball bearing "guava" cluster bombs, steel-arrowed flechette antipersonnel bombs meant to prevent doctors from operating because they did more damage coming out than going in, antipersonnel bombs bearing fiberglass pellets which could not be X-rayed, laser and teleguided missiles.

Below: A 28-year-old Lao farmer wrote, "because these airplanes dropped bombs on the village without stopping, the people had no place to go to escape. They had never before experienced anything like this. It caused parents to be taken in death from their children, and children to be taken in death from their parents, in great numbers, causing the people's tears to flow.""

Above: Pilots robotically reported their coordinates and payloads to the command and control ships, waiting for instructions to unload.

Below: A 30-year-old Lao woman: "At that time, our lives became like those of animals desperately trying to escape their hunters. Our lives were confided to the Lord Buddha. No matter when, all we did was to pray to the Lord to save our lives. We didn't know how long we would stay alive. When looking at the faces of my children who were losing the so very precious happiness of childhood, as each and every day we would seek escape somewhere in the forest, I would grow increasingly miserable because of the war and hate it more and more."

Above: Pilots returning to Thailand with unexploded bombs from North Vietnam casually chose to dump them on Lao villages rather than in the forest.

Below: A 26-year-old Lao nurse wrote, "We who were young took our sweat and our strength, which should have been spent raising food in the rice fields and forests to sustain our lives, and squandered it digging holes to protect ourselves. For many days and nights, having enough food to survive on became a gigantic problem which pressed upon our hearts. The fields, paddy and seedbeds all became bomb craters. All that remained for our people were sad faces, and tired and weak hearts, disgusted with hating the war, which was like a large stone weighing upon us. We could not understand or imagine why something like this could happen."

Above: The split-second push of a button, and pilots then returning to their bases for a cold one, nap and night carousing with prostitutes in the giant bars surrounding the airbases.

Below: A lifetime of pain, as described by a 39-year-old farmer: "They dropped eight napalm bombs, the fire from which burned all my things, 16 buildings along with all our possessions inside, as well as maiming our animals. Some people who didn't reach the jungle in time were struck and fell, dying most pitifully. By the time the fire died down it was dark. Everyone came out of hiding to look at the ashes of their houses. Even the rice was all burnt. Everyone cried at once—loudly and agitatedly. Some families had been wounded."

The Aftermath

"The mountains and forests are filled with so many useful kinds of birds and animals. Neither paddy farming nor building homes was difficult, for all the villagers would help one another with the work, and it was extremely gay and happy for us young people. That place, though it was very rural, and composed only of forests and fields, was perfect for me."

- 13-year-old boy, on life before the bombing

When the war ended, I entered domestic politics. I wanted to work to elect a new generation of decent leaders, rather than spend the rest of my life simply opposing the latest crimes by the architects of mass murder we call "President" or "Secretary of State."Although I never forgot the refugees from the Plain of Jars, I assumed that their suffering from the bombing had ended.

I was thus shocked to learn from reports by Jacqui Chagnon and Roger Rumpf of the Quakers, and Titus Peachey of the Mennonite Central Committee, who worked in Laos after 1975, that there were still tens of millions of unexploded cluster bombs that were still murdering and maiming countless civilians.

I observed this directly in 1993, when I visited the Plain of Jars for the first time, with my old friend Ngeun. As people described to me losing friends and relatives from postwar cluster bomb explosions, I saw with my own eyes the monstrous hellscape, in which children thought it normal to grow up amidst hidden bombs that could destroy their lives in an instant.

And I discovered a new dimension of "non-humanity": U.S. leaders had spent over $10 billion on bombing Laos, but had contributed virtually nothing to clean up the unexploded cluster bomblets they had left there.

I also talked with a 50-year-old farmer who had survived the bombing, been evacuated, and returned after the war ended. I knew the importance of water buffalo for plowing their fields, and asked him how many he had. "Eight," he said. "Great!" I said.

"Not so great," he responded, "We had 100 head before the bombing!" I realized with a shock what this meant: if he was lucky, he might some decades from now be back to where he had been, 50 years earlier.

Over the next decade, I gradually became increasingly depressed about the bombing and, by 2003, had reached one of my lowest points since discovering it. I despaired to realize that those who had destroyed the plain had gotten away with it, thus freeing them to continue inflicting similar suffering elsewhere. But what somehow disturbed me most was realizing that this suffering had been almost entirely ignored, that it was as if it had never happened.

It really was possible for a small group of government officials to wipe an entire foreign civilization off the face of the earth, and to then walk away, leaving tens of millions of unexploded bombs to torment their descendants for decades to come, with the world outside neither knowing nor caring. I shuddered at the implications of this for the future of the species.

But then something remarkable happened. I received an email from a young Lao-American woman named Channapha Khamvongsa, who had come across, by accident, some of the original drawings. Astounded that as a Lao she had known nothing of the bombing, and deeply moved by the suffering depicted in the drawings, she had decided to form an organization called Legacies of War, to seek to educate the public and Congress about the need to clean up the unexploded ordinance and to promote, in her words, "history, healing and hope."

Channapha used her first grant to digitize the drawings, both to preserve them and to assist in their wider use. She created a traveling exhibit featuring the drawings, set up an impressive public education effort out of Washington, and became a leader in pushing for more U.S. funding for UXO cleanup. It seemed almost a miracle that Channapha, and her group, existed.

The Convention on Cluster Munitions

*"A life whose only value was death, as every day and every night the planes came to drop bombs on us. We lived in holes to protect our lives. **This kind of bomb would explode in the air and was much more dangerous than other ones.**"* [Emphasis added] - 33-year-old Lao woman, Plain of Jars bombing survivor, describing a cluster bomb

I was further encouraged when I learned of the work to create a Convention on Cluster Munitions. From the perspective of what had occurred on the Plain of Jars, it was clearly both of enormous immediate importance and a symbol of something even more significant.

If the Convention had been in force in the 1960s, many thousands of Lao people who died from cluster bomb explosions, and their descendants, would be alive today. The implementation of the treaty will save tens of thousands of innocent lives in the years to come.

And the Convention also brought hope that additional funding might become available to decontaminate the land of Laos, clearly the world's top priority for cluster munitions cleanup. Well over 50 percent of all worldwide unexploded cluster sub-munitions lie on Lao territory. According to official figures, upward of 270 million bomblets were dropped, more than twice as many as the 113 million dropped on Vietnam and Cambodia combined, and more than five times those dropped on Iraq by U.S.-led coalition forces in 1991 and 2003. Laos today has some 80 million unexploded bomblets, more than the rest of the world combined.

(Please see also the "Timeline of Cluster Munitions Use," on the Cluster Bomb Coalition Web site: http://www.stopclustermunitions.org/wp/wp-content/uploads/2008/10/timeline-of-use.pdf. *Please see also, "The Unexploded Ordnance (UXO) Problem and Operational Progress in the Lao PDR," a fact sheet published by the National Regulatory Authority for UXO/Mine Action in the Lao PDR.)*

Lao officials estimate it could take hundreds of years to clean up existing cluster munitions at the current rate, which has seen only 0.28 percent of the total contaminated area cleared in the past 14 years. If the Convention is to have any real meaning in the real world it will clearly see its signers encourage the U.S. to vastly increase its effort to clean up Laos, and to contribute to doing so themselves. The U.S. spent just $5 million on UXO cleanup in Laos for all of fiscal year 2010—equivalent to what it spent on just eight hours of bombing during the Indochina war.

The U.S. bombing and its deadly legacy of cluster bombs have tormented and tortured the innocent people of Laos for nearly 50 years now. During the war it murdered and maimed them, destroyed their livestock and homes, forced them to live like animals in caves and holes, and turned many into homeless refugees. Since the war, unexploded cluster bombs have killed and wounded tens of thousands more, denied them access to farmland they need to survive, and deprived their children of normal lives. Many are still poorer today than they were in 1964 before the bombing began. If there is any justice in this world, the international community will at least now find a way to clean up the unexploded ordnance still destroying the lives of the innocent, and offer assistance to the victims.

But the Convention is also a creative approach to a broader issue: the urgent need to protect all civilians in a time of war, especially from automated war. International humanitarian law—the law of war—largely focuses on two key issues: (1) preventing "aggressive war"; and (2) protecting civilians once armed conflict has begun.

However one feels about the first in regard to Laos, what happened on the Plain of Jars clearly proves that international law does not protect civilians during armed conflicts involving automated war-making.

From this perspective, the Convention on Cluster Munitions marks a tremendously important and visionary first step toward devising ways to protect civilians in what is certain to be a 21st century increasingly marked by automated war. In a nonhuman age, the Convention thus represents far more than a treaty banning a specific weapon, however significant. It is, above all, a statement that civilian lives matter and that eliminating them is unacceptable to anyone who values human life.

The Convention is, in short, a cry for humanity.

Conclusion

And so too are these voices from the Plain of Jars.

"Why then don't we people love one another? Why don't we live together in equality? Why don't we build happiness and progress together? In reality,

51

whatever happens, it is only the innocent who suffer. And as for the others, do they know all the unimaginable things happening in this war? Do they?"
 - 30-year-old Lao woman, a survivor of five years of U.S. bombing of the Plain of Jars, 1964-69

"In all our years, we had known no more than the word 'airplane.' We were all heavy hearted and mournful almost to the point of losing our minds. The other villagers and I got together to consider this thing. We hadn't done anything, nor harmed anyone. We had raised our crops, celebrated the festivals and maintained our homes for many years. Why did the planes drop bombs on us, impoverishing us this way?"   - 39-year-old farmer

I have never been able to read these essays without feeling like weeping. But, today I hear their cry for humanity, far more urgently than at any time since I saw the first refugee draw that "L" on the floor of the That Louang prayer shed.

These voices provide the clearest possible warning about the new challenges posed by a new age of "non-humanity." It was possible to mobilize against such "inhuman" leaders of the past as a clearly mad and violent Hitler. It is far more difficult, however, to organize against personally relatively decent and sane leaders who today commit mass murder through automated war of which the outside world is largely unaware.

If we listen to these voices, in other words, they can confirm our own humanity. We cannot right past wrongs, as a 26-year-old nurse wrote four decades ago: "the past has melted away. Our lives have passed like a dream. There is nothing which can make up for the sorrow."

But though we cannot make right this nonhuman past, hearing—and heeding—these voices today can inspire us to create a more human future. In a century marked by nuclear proliferation and automated war, we have no higher calling—or need—than to do so.

Seeing the Truth

Ross Caputi

Ross Caputi was a US Marine from 2003 until 2006. He was deployed to Iraq from June 2004 until January 2005. Ross founded and is the director of the Justice for Fallujah Project.

After the resistance movement in Fallujah successfully repelled the first U.S.-led siege of their city in April of 2004, Fallujah became a symbol of heroism and resistance to Iraqis. To Americans, Fallujah was made into a symbol of terrorism. The mainstream media within the U.S. described Fallujah as a "hotbed of anti-Americanism" and an "insurgent stronghold." It gave little mention of the 300,000 civilians who lived there. In November of 2004, the U.S. launched a massive siege on Fallujah that killed somewhere between 800 and 6,000 civilians, forced hundreds of thousands to flee their homes, and left much of the city in ruins. From that point on, Fallujah became a symbol to much of the world of cruelty and occupation.

The suffering inflicted on Fallujah did not end in 2004. Life for the people who chose to return to their city never improved. The U.S. imposed security measures and curfews that made living a normal life in Fallujah impossible. Residents already had to struggle to make ends meet in their dilapidated city, but the constant security checkpoints, ID-card scans, and arrests only made life harder. There has also been a constant lack of necessary medicines and medical equipment. Worst of all, since 2004 there has been a dramatic increase in birth defects, infant mortality, mental retardation, and cancers of all sorts in Fallujah. The birth defects are truly horrifying. Babies have been born with six fingers, scaly skin, missing limbs, two heads, and there has been one case of a child born with a single eye in the center of his forehead.

The few studies that have investigated this health crisis in Fallujah argue that there is "genetic damage" within the population, and that ionizing radiation-exposure is the most likely cause. The authors of these studies believe the U.S. may have used uranium weapons in Fallujah in 2004, and that the people of Fallujah continue to be exposed to radiation from these weapons today. This has led some to say that the health crisis in Fallujah is worse than in Hiroshima and Nagasaki after the atomic bombs. So many children are now being born horribly deformed or with severe cognitive deficits that many women are afraid to have families.

The U.S. occupation has had horrible effects on the Iraqi population, but Fallujah may have suffered more than any other Iraqi city. Fallujah is to the Occupation of Iraq what My Lai was to the Vietnam War, and what Hiroshima and Nagasaki were to World War II.

My name is Ross Caputi, and I was a witness to and an accomplice in the atrocities that were committed during the second assault on Fallujah, Iraq in November of 2004, also known as Operation Phantom Fury. My unit was called the 1st Battalion 8th Marines Alpha Company, and at that time I found myself in Headquarters Platoon, acting as the Company Commander's radio operator. It is difficult for me to admit what we did to the people of Fallujah, but the hardest part is explaining to you how we just could not see the harm that we were doing. Although blessed with the gift of sight, we just could not see things as they really were. Only now, six years too late, can I see the truth.

I want to set the record straight about what really happened in Fallujah, but the truth will not be easy for everyone to accept. Please, if only for a moment, put aside all ideologies, philosophical commitments, and nationalist allegiances and try to look at what I am about to tell you with the objectivity that God would have, taking one life to be equal to another and taking the nationality of the victims and aggressors to be irrelevant.

My unit got called into Camp Fallujah a couple of weeks before the second assault. I was a buck private at the time and had recently been demoted for a number of charges from underage drinking to theft to general conduct unbecoming of a Marine. I was even moved out of my old infantry platoon, because I just was not listening to anyone in charge of me; instead, they made me the Company Commander's radio operator.

Most of the guys in my unit were, like me, just out of high school, and we knew practically nothing about Fallujah. We had heard a lot of rumors that Fallujah was the most dangerous city in Iraq, but besides its reputation we knew nothing about it, or the people who lived there. About a week before the siege began, our command told us we were going to liberate Fallujah from the terrorists who had taken control of the city. They also told us all of the civilians had left, even though they knew that thousands of people remained. They told us our mission was to sweep the city, and kill all the terrorists who chose to stay behind and fight. They also told us we should expect 50 percent casualties, and that this would be the biggest battle since Hue City, Vietnam. They told us this operation would break the back of the Iraqi insurgency, and bring freedom and democracy to Iraq. They told us that we were doing this for Iraqis, and for the people of Fallujah.

Personally, I never believed any of these lies. I did not believe the stories about weapons of mass destruction in Iraq, nor did I believe that America's freedom was at stake, and I stopped believing long before I got to Fallujah that we were helping Iraqis. In fact, everything I had seen in Iraq up until that point told me that we were actually hurting Iraqis, and deep down inside I felt that the Iraqis had a right to defend themselves against us. However, I think everyone else in my unit really believed what my command told them, despite the fact that everything that they were seeing with their own eyes suggested the opposite.

I think they believed those lies, because believing them was easier, psychologically, than it was to ask ourselves the hard questions, and because those lies validated everything we were doing. It must have been much easier for them to dismiss the Iraqi resistance as "terrorists" than to ask themselves what they would have done if a foreign army was occupying their country and was assaulting their city. It must have been much easier to see things as they wanted to see them, and to see themselves as liberators, the good-guys. I did not want to be part of Operation Phantom Fury, but I was not willing to stick my neck out and say that I thought it was wrong. I was not willing to risk my benefits, or my paycheck, and (to be perfectly honest) I wanted a combat-action ribbon, so I could go home and brag about it.

Maybe everyone else in my unit believed that we were fighting against pure evil, and maybe they really believed we were liberating Fallujah. Maybe there is a psychological explanation for why they just could not see how badly we were hurting the Iraqis, and maybe they went into Fallujah with good intentions. All that I can say with certainty is, my participation in Fallujah was for me and for me only.

I believe it was November 8th when my unit loaded up into trucks and drove from our base to the outskirts of Fallujah. We drove a few kilometers along a road that cut through the desert towards the city. I remember riding past groups of women and children who I could see were fleeing for their safety, and I remember wondering how they would survive in the desert. Where would they go? How would they get water? I saw them and I saw their suffering, as everyone could, but we could not see that we were the cause of their suffering. Perhaps it was just too painful a realization for many of us to make, because we saw ourselves as the liberators, the good guys, and to admit that we were hurting innocent people would have contradicted everything we claimed to stand for.

I can only speculate about what the motives were for the people who dreamed up that mission, and decided to make the people of Fallujah flee into the desert. Was it also too painful for the decision-makers, to admit to themselves that we were hurting innocent people? Or were they so evil that they just did not care who we were hurting? Whatever their reasons for doing it were, the fact of the matter is that our entire command was aware that we had forced the majority of the city's population, about 200,000 people, into refugee status, but nobody took responsibility for their well-being, as international law required of us.[1]

We drove to the outskirts of the city and positioned ourselves on a hilltop where we watched the bombing campaign come to a climax. At that point it was nighttime and all that could be seen of Fallujah was the flashes of our bombs and a thick cloud of smoke pouring out of the city. At a certain point I saw us drop white phosphorous from the sky. The white phosphorous drifted slowly downward in glowing white balls that eventually disappeared into the smoke that was billowing out of the city. I could not see if the white phosphorous actually landed on the city or in the desert at the city's periphery. However, with the lack of visibility there was no way to know that we were not dropping it on civilians. It was impossible for us to discriminate targets, as international law, again, required of us.[2]

One day later, my unit was inserted into the center of the city. We quickly seized a building that we called "the mayor's complex," and the captain and I went to the roof along with a few others, so that we could get a good radio signal. We started to take sniper fire and had to take cover behind a retaining wall on the edge of the roof. Suddenly a group of civilians appeared in the street below us with white flags. We lifted our heads over the wall to shout at them to go hide, and as soon as we did sniper fire started to crack over our heads. Everyone around me immediately jumped to the conclusion that this group of civilians had played a trick on us, that they were working with the insurgents to draw us out from behind our cover. There was absolutely no reason to think that they were working with the sniper, who was hundreds of meters away. I am telling you this to illustrate that we did not view the civilians in Fallujah with compassion. We viewed them only with suspicion. We saw no clear distinction between a civilian and what we considered to be a terrorist.[3]

A day later we began sweeping through the city, one house at a time. In the houses that I entered I saw family photos hanging up on the walls. I saw dressers full of clothes, refrigerators full of food… and Marines looting everything that appeared valuable out of their homes. I could see that families had been living in those homes just a short while ago, and I knew that they were the same families I'd seen walking in the desert, but that did not stop me from joining in the looting,[4] too. We stole from their homes, and we convinced ourselves that it did not matter. We were perfectly aware that we had told them to leave, because we were coming through their city guns blazing, but we could not see that we had in fact ruined their lives. Of course not, we were the good guys; we were doing this for them.

Most of the time I was perfectly safe with the officers, and there was no fighting within my immediate vicinity. I was in this weird pocket of safety, but everything around me was destroyed, and just a block away I could hear gunfire and rockets and people shouting and screaming. At a certain point it came over the radio that a civilian had been killed. It was just one transmission and that was it. There was no follow-up, and I do not know of any effort made to identify him or contact his family. I found out later from the guys who were there that an old man had been standing on the side of the road with prayer beads in his hands. Someone shouted "He's got something in his hands!" and then someone shot him. I know the person who shot him, and I am told that right after he did it he shouted "One shot, one kill!", which was a Marine Corps marksmanship slogan. I know this person well, and he is not out to hurt people for the sake of hurting people. He actually thought that he was doing his job. He celebrated it because he thought that he had done his job as a Marine. He could not see what he did as murder.

At another point in the city, one of my friends from my unit came running up to me with a huge smile on his face, saying "Caputi, Caputi, I finally shot someone!" He was so happy and so proud of himself, but you need to know this kid like I knew him to know that there is more to this story. He is the sweetest kid you could ever meet. There is not a mean or cruel bone in his body. He really thought that he had done a good thing.

The looting continued for several days, and my command was perfectly aware of what was happening. At this point we knew there were still civilians in the city, but we began using a tactic called "reconnaissance by fire" anyway (this is when you fire into an area or building, to see if people are there). If you hear silence after your firing, then everything is clear. If you hear otherwise, if you hear screaming or moaning, then there are either combatants or civilians there. This tactic is always indiscriminate (which would of course make it illegal), and our command was very aware that we were using it.[5]

We continued to sweep further into the city and met very impressive resistance, but we always responded with superior firepower. If we suspected that there was a resistance fighter in a house, we would fire tank rounds into it, or radio in for bulldozers to flatten the house on top of him.[6]

I watched as the carnage changed the people around me, and a violent hysteria developed in my unit. At a certain point during the assault I had to carry the radio up to a rooftop, where there were two guys I knew sitting up there with their rifles aimed out into the street. They turned and looked at me, and one of them said "Hey, Caputi, did you kill anyone yet? I only got one kill, but this guy next to me got nine."

Later, a friend of mine came up to me and told me about how his team leader had been cutting up the dead body of a resistance fighter, looking for the adrenal gland[7] and how he tried to drag another dead body in front of an AAV for it to be run over. People were bragging about posing for pictures with the dead bodies of resistance fighters, and about the things they had stolen out of houses, or found in the pockets of the dead.

One day I was up on a rooftop with the radio, and I saw a unit to our right flank bulldozing an entire neighborhood. They were moving fast, and I know they were not checking inside the houses to see if civilians were still inside. On one of the last days of the assault, we came across a house with two resistance fighters and a young boy bunkered inside. The boy was about ten years old. I do not know if any attempts were made to negotiate, or to try to get that boy out of that house in some way and save his life. All I know is that we fired grenades into that house until it collapsed, killing all three of them inside.[8]

Everything happening around me was complete madness, and I do not think that anyone else could see it but me. I was in a really unique position: I was far enough away from all the violence so that it did not get in my head like it did to everyone else's, yet I was close enough to see what was actually happening. However, there was still much that I could not see. I saw the people we had forced out into the desert, I saw their destroyed homes, and their dead bodies, but I did not see what any of that had to do with me. I still could not see myself as being complicit in this. I kept telling myself that I did not want to be here, that I was obligated by contract to do this, that I was just doing what I had to do to get back to my family, but none of that was true. Every day that I decided to follow orders, I made a choice, and I chose to follow orders because it was in my own best interest.

I do not know how to explain the absurdity of our mission in Fallujah, or in all of Iraq for that matter. We occupied a country in order to free it, we assaulted a city in order to save it, and we justified it all by claiming that we were doing this for a people who we considered to be the enemy. We told ourselves that we were liberating the civilians of Fallujah, even though we knew that civilians were being hurt, displaced, and even killed. We justified all of this to ourselves by asserting that collateral damage was a fact of war, and that we were doing this for them, for their freedom and democracy. We justified our actions to ourselves so well, we could not understand why the people of Fallujah were not thanking us. After all, we were risking our lives for them. It seemed like with every civilian that we killed we asserted more strongly and believed with more conviction than before that we were doing this for them.

When we went back home, we were welcomed back as heroes. Our friends and families threw big parties for us, and one guy's hometown threw a parade in his honor. Some guy started interviewing us for a book he was writing called "Fallujah with Honor," and a documentary filmmaker started following us around to make a documentary about us. Most of the guys involved have not been able to think about Fallujah outside of that context ever since. They cannot see our actions as being anything other than heroic, and they cannot think of our friends who died, as having died for anything but a noble cause. What really blows my mind about all of this is how easily decent and normal people can be driven to commit atrocities, and how they can even see their actions as being virtuous.

Thank God I got caught stealing and drinking and doing all the things that I was doing when they kicked me out of my old platoon. If they had not, then I would have been the guy kicking in doors in Fallujah, and I might even have been the guy mutilating dead bodies. I really think you could take any group of people in the world, and if you told them all the same lies we were told, and you told them that half of them were not going to make it back in one piece, nine out of ten would commit all the same atrocities that we committed in Fallujah. It could very easily have been me, I am no better than any of the people I just mentioned; in fact, I am probably worse. The guys that did all those awful things I just told you about might have believed the lies they were told, and they might have gone into Fallujah with noble intentions. But I never believed the lies. I knew better. I knew we were in Fallujah for all the wrong reasons. I knew we were hurting people, but

I followed orders, anyway. I did it because I wanted free college and a combat-action ribbon.

The customary international law rules I am citing here are handily summarized in the International Committee of the Red Cross Summary of International Law. These are the most important rules incorporated in key treaties such as the Geneva Conventions of 1949, the Hague Conventions and Regulations, and the UN Charter. I am listing them here, though, as they are listed in the ICRC Summary for ease of reference.

---

[1] This point refers to Rule 1; "The parties to the conflict must at all times distinguish between civilians and combatants. Attacks may only be directed against combatants. Attacks must not be directed against civilians."
Rule 2: "Acts or threats of violence the primary purpose of which is to spread terror among the civilian population are prohibited."
Rule 129 A: "Parties to an international armed conflict may not deport or forcibly transfer the civilian population of an occupied territory, in whole or in part, unless the security of the civilians involved or imperative military reasons so demand."
Rule 131: "In case of displacement, all possible measures must be taken in order that the civilians concerned are received under satisfactory conditions of shelter, hygiene, health, safety and nutrition and that members of the same family are not separated."
Rule 133: "The property rights of displaced persons must be respected. "
[2] The use of white phosphorus against civilians was banned in the 1980 'Convention on Prohibitions or Restrictions on the Use of Certain Conventional Weapons Which May Be Deemed to Be Excessively Injurious or to Have Indiscriminate Effects' (entered into force in December, 1983 and annexed to the Geneva Conventions, 1949).
[3] Rule 5: "Civilians are persons who are not members of the armed forces. The civilian population comprises all persons who are civilians."
Rule 6: "Civilians are protected against attack, unless and for such time as they take a direct part in hostilities."
Rule 15: "In the conduct of military operations, constant care must be taken to spare the civilian population, civilians and civilian objects. All feasible precautions must be taken to avoid, and in any event to minimize, incidental loss of civilian life, injury to civilians and damage to civilian objects."
Rule 16: "Each party to the conflict must do everything feasible to verify that targets are military objectives."
[4] Rule 50: "The destruction or seizure of the property of an adversary is prohibited unless required by imperative military necessity."
Rule 519(c): "Private property must be respected an may not be confiscated except where destruction or seizure of such property is required by imperative military necessity."
Rule 52: "Pillage is prohibited."
[5] Rule 70: "The use of means and methods of warfare which are of a nature to cause superfluous injury or unnecessary suffering is prohibited;" see also Rules 15 and 16, above.

Rule 17: "Each party to the conflict must take all feasible precautions in the choice of means and methods of warfare with a view to avoiding, and in any event to minimizing incidental loss of civilian life, injury to civilians and damage to civilian objects."

Rule 19: "Each party to the conflict must do everything feasible to cancel or suspend an attack if it becomes apparent that the target is not a military objective or that the attack may be expected to cause incidental loss of civilian life, injury to civilians, damage to civilian objects, or a combination thereof, which would be excessive in relation to the concrete and direct military advantage anticipated."

[6] Rule 7: "The parties to the conflict must at all times distinguish between civilian objectives and military objectives. Attacks may only be directed against military objectives. Attacks must not be directed against civilian objects."

[7] Rule 113: "Each party to the conflict must take all possible measures to prevent the dead from being despoiled. Mutilation of dead bodies is prohibited."

Rule 115: "The dead must be disposed of in a respectful manner and their graves respected and properly maintained."

Rule 116: "With a view to the identification of the dead, each party to the conflict must record all available information prior to disposal and mark the location of the graves."

[8] Rule 135: "Children affected by armed conflict are entitled to special respect and protection."

State Violence
for Corporate Interests
in the Peruvian Amazon

Séverine Neveu

Séverine Neveu was amidst her wandering of the planet for the last 17 years, when I had the pleasure of meeting and travelling with her in the Nepali Himalayas in 2000. When not travelling the world, she journeyed between European cities and occupations, from fruit harvesting or cleaner to chain factory worker, from language teacher or personal assistant to quality management consultant, hence touring schools, consulate, small businesses or multinational corporations in a wide range of activity fields. She currently lives in south France, where she is aiming to settle endeavoring to live in harmony with her ethics and to share a vivacious passion for Life, Earth and Arts.

World Environment Day (WED) was established by the UN General Assembly in 1972 to mark the opening of the Stockholm Conference on the Human Environment. Commemorated yearly on the 5th of June, WED is one of the principal vehicles through which the United Nations stimulates worldwide awareness of the environment and enhances political attention and action. The day's agenda is to give a human face to environmental issues, empower people to become active agents of sustainable and equitable development, promote an understanding that communities are pivotal to changing attitudes toward environmental issues, advocate partnership which will ensure all nations and people enjoy a safer and more prosperous future.[1]

The Amazon rainforest is emblematically concerned by these aims. The rainforest is one of the most biologically diverse places of earth; it is often described as the "Lungs of our Planet," as it simultaneously produces some 20 percent of the world's oxygen and removes a large part of carbon dioxide from the atmosphere. The Amazon rainforest is a critical and threatened natural resource that needs worldwide consideration, and its indigenous inhabitants are every bit as threatened as the forest itself. These people and their cultures are the natural guardians of the forest, and their fate is therefore bound to that of this vital biome. As human beings, they and their ways of life have the right to acknowledgement, respect and justice.

June 5, 2009, the Amazon was sullied with human tears and blood.

In the locality of Bagua Grande, at the foot of the Peruvian Amazon, dozens of people were killed and hundreds injured, after police forces dispersed a road blockade organized by indigenous people, who had been peacefully protesting legislation regarding the exploitation of land and resources that poses a threat to their rights to ancestral lands and livelihoods.

In defense of their land and habitat, the indigenous people were demanding the derogation of a set of legislative decrees. These laws were not only voted in under both abusive and grotesque circumstances, but were also anti-constitutional and violated the

Convention 169 of the International Labour Organization (ILO)[2], which protects native communities and stipulates that governments must allow consultation with the indigenous population, prior to the implementation of any law on their ancestral lands. Seventy-two percent of Peruvian Amazon territory is already under concession for the exploitation of oil and gas, and problems of contamination and health are already a reality.

I was a tourist on a night bus journey, traveling from the Amazonian town of Moyobamba to the coastal town of Chiclayo; because of protesting indigenous roadblocks we had to walk part of the way. We happened to walk through the Bagua Grande road blockade in the early morning of June 5th, when a confrontation between police and native protesters took place. Burdened with our luggage, we walked for about two-and-a-half hours between 5 and 7:30 am, from beginning to end of the area—first, through the zone occupied by the protesters, and then through a makeshift staging ground of heavily armed police. The road went through four barricades, the first consisting of unguarded trucks pushed across the road, then three others made of thorny brushwood, guarded by indigenous protesters.

The indigenous people I saw were mostly young men, clad in worn T-shirts and sandals and armed with rusty spears; their faces, sometimes painted in black, reflected calm determination as they watched us walk past, or helped carry across the few young children among us. By sunrise, we had made it by what seemed the protesters' precarious encampment, and some movement was starting to take place on the hill on our left; there was word of a police operation. Suddenly, there was some commotion. In front of me I saw a small group of protesters running toward the hill with their spears, while the man guarding the narrow pedestrian aperture through the last thorny brushwood blockade urged us to hurry up. Shortly, as our scattered exodus of burdened and exhausted walkers kept going fast-forward alongside the hill, we heard detonations (teargas bombs), and then rifle fire.

Further on, out of the protesters' position, walking past dozens of trucks lined on the side of the road, we met two tanks rushing past, followed by three large troops of police heftily outfitted with anti-riot gear (boots, helmets, shields…) and equipped with heavy firearms (AKM). One helicopter, then two more, hovered above us.

It is there and then that for the first time in my life I literally felt *death drawing near*. It wasn't fear, neither was it fear for my personal safety: I was well away from the action by then, and I wasn't a target. It was a strange feeling, a sort of intoxicating "smell of death" that coursed through my veins, as if a dreadful liquefied intuition had replaced my blood for a moment.

In the evening, only hours after the incident, local media were boisterously headlining the "shocking" police deaths, committed by "barbaric natives." Baffled, distressed and overwhelmed, I spent the following nights and days trying to get to the truth and to understand what had happened. The process of gathering as much (and as objective) information as I could in local and national press revealed a gross lack of transparency, blatant inconsistencies, fierce aggressiveness and contradictions in the government's poses.

Five days later, there were still no official or credible reports on the numbers of victims on the protesters' side. The wide majority of newspapers fixated on the tragedy of police officers' deaths, while virtually denying indigenous loss. From what I had seen of their thorny-bush blockades defended at spear point, compared to the heavily armed and equipped police, I found it hard to believe media or government numbers, even if it was claimed that the dissenters had outnumbered police forces—not really what I had seen, from my passing station...

While chilling rumors ran about, regarding indigenous cadavers having been burned or thrown into the river to curtail losses on the protestor's side, a state of emergency had been ordered in the zone, implementing martial law and a media blackout, imposing a curfew on the inhabitants and preventing indigenous families from searching for their relatives.

No independent observer entered the area until over a month after the event; Amnesty International investigated the incident only in July, 2009. Furthermore, there are allegations that not all the ethnic groups involved have been probed. Moreover, not all indigenous officially "exist." Indeed, I had noticed a campaign for birth declarations and IDs registration on civic boards in the area during an earlier sightseer exploration—a fact also mentioned by some NGOs.

To this day, over a year and a half later, accurate number of dead, arrested or disappeared native people remains unclear. The death of 23 police officers is avowed, but on the protestor's side an equivocal range of "at least ten" (the official assertion) to up to 140 "to be confirmed," the shifting numbers of indigenous people are ambiguously stated.

The information presented through the biased media (written press, as well as radio and TV), at the hands of an overly proud government (who never admitted any responsibility whatsoever over the escalation of violence), widely accused the indigenous of "savagery," in a propaganda campaign which bluntly appealed to fear and distrust toward the indigenous population, while thoroughly discarding its voice; the indigenous Amazonian community of Peru was plainly being cast off.

Despised and treated as "second-class citizens," they were being rebuked for standing in the way of political and ruthless economic purposes of the government, in a background of internal and external political tensions haunted and pressurized by the Free Trade Agreement with the United States, the lure of profit and pressure from multinationals over Amazonian resources (gas, petrol and logging activities).

In this scheme, native communities had been utterly disregarded. No plan to tackle the widespread poverty, so pervasive among the indigenous population, had ever been brought forward. In the imposed decrees, not a single thought was given for collateral prosperity to benefit the local people, even less so on guarantees to limit health, social and environmental impacts.

The plan was basically about net exportation of raw material, for the exclusive gain of the two parties in positions of disproportionate power: investors and a corrupt government unscrupulous about dispossessing and destroying the life of its own people. It was, once again, the timeless sad story of the clay pot against the ironware pot...

I'm not a journalist, I'm not a human rights lawyer, I'm not an environmentalist, I'm only an average person, and here I was a simple solo tourist, who felt something terribly wrong on that June morning: something much bigger than a deplorable and deadly police/protesters clash; something nagging, like injustice. (This initial insight was instantaneously confirmed, by the immediate and frenzied anti-indigenous propaganda, constituting an additional violence done to the Amazon people.) The unanswered question remains: why was such big artillery sent to disperse a peaceful civilian's road blockade? What could explain such a wanton set-up? Isn't uncalled-for brutality typically used as recourse for despotic deliberate prejudice...?

I couldn't, as I still cannot, fail to read between the lines, and see—in capital letters— a scenario that is recurrently plaguing so many places on the planet, always with the same settings and characters: a highly lucrative resource, located in a land inhabited by vulnerable populations (indigenous communities, ethnic minorities or poor/uneducated population-classes), governed by a corrupt and repressive regime and desired by unscrupulous powerful corporations, with the manipulative complicity of the media misinforming and confusing public opinion. The plot is about making a fast buck, regardless of human rights, regardless of any social or environmental consequences, and without concern for international treaties or reasonable laws.

To add to my grief and anger, it is that very day that I found out that the 5th of June had been set as an activist World Environment Day. What a sad irony! All around the world, events and conferences were concerned about how to "save the planet." Maybe some of these assemblies were even about conserving the lungs of the planet...

Meanwhile, on that symbolic date, rifle fire had echoed through a distant Amazonian valley, and never reached the oblivious ears of the world.

To me, this international indifference constitutes a third violence done to the indigenous' cause—and subsequently, to the fate of the Amazon. It highlights the powerlessness (if not the hypocrisy) of well-meaning, expectant, politically correct discourse. So long as there is no real accountability in government and business, with respect to essential ethical issues, stealthy abuses will continue to silence legitimate (if tenuous) voices of dissent. It is as fundamental as it is urgent that truly neutral international social movements, promoting universal principles, attain a tangible cohesion. Good intentions and well-wishing don't replace real and efficient mobilization toward factual achievement of the proclaimed, and worthy intents. Quite to the contrary, on the part of these hypothetically influential and rhetorically disinterested international officialdoms, the endless parade of hackneyed good intentions, every so often tailed by inaction and failure, can only cast additional disenchantment...

It shattered me to realize that these people truly have been abandoned, by a world that claims to be progressing in matters of human rights and fairness. This case is so much more than a Peruvian crisis; it involves questions of human rights and justice, and the current dissonance between profit and peace that crony capitalism has wrought!

About ten days after the Bagua Grande incident, I left Peru. My visa was running out, but what really decided me was sheer exhaustion from an ongoing fiery indignation, and a deep discouraging sense of helplessness. I had participated in a few small pro-indigenous demonstrations; I had tried clumsily and vainly to alert international media; I had signed petitions—but it felt all so insufficient.

Nonetheless, against the ubiquitous and powerful adversary of prejudiced media overshadowed by a coercive government, and the impassiveness of a majority of the Peruvian themselves more preoccupied with their own surviving, I was left crushed with a bitter taste of despondent powerlessness. My faith in idealistic political orientations and their associated organizations had just gotten a little bit more sapped. I thought that if they are not corrupt, they are too weak, and in the face of the hard reality of the worse of human greed and indifference the beautiful ideas too often transmute into naïve utopias.

I couldn't help this poisonous and encompassing sentiment of incensed defeat, while local people, who probably knew better, were quicker to resign themselves to passive fatalism, discarding the topic from their lives.

And this is precisely one of the worse adverse effects of recurrent abusive violence and of the impunity of injustice. Against state violence—whether in arms, invasive rulings or contempt—the individual of a divided and careworn society has only indifference or remoteness as protection, the shaky retreat to withdrawal, back to the individual sphere. It is a vicious circle, a fertile soil for growing impunity, which in turn supports tyranny.

Authoritarian powers are well aware of this power of fear, discouragement and self-censure, and they make full use of it via manipulative propaganda, continuously instilling suspicion and debilitating fear within the population. This is why, along with police or army abuses and interventionism, media is another prevalent and powerful instrument, and an accomplice to violence. What else but brainwashing, in addition to a nurtured deficiency of critical thinking, can explain the immobility of enormous masses of people, in the face of direct or indirect injustices carried out openly and publicly?

Hopelessness and fatalism shrink ideals and courage; enforced submissiveness undermines essential values: dignity, justice and respect. In a setting of unequal forces, where people are made small, insignificant and worthless, overriding violence corrupts and further divides, it's the strategy of everyone to save one's own skin. If the model presented by politics and their institutions is based on unlawful self-indulgence and domination by any means, then accordingly, in a number of people's lives, the means of theft and violence will take over at the level of daily life, instead of creativity and solidarity. In such a nation of permanent threat and emergency, where justice is widely disregarded or crushed by force, people are in survival mode, focused on their frail individual peace and security—rather than on the unconvincing, seemingly unattainable collective and fair aspirations for a peaceful and just society for everyone.

Survival mode is a form of resilience, but resilience is not resistance, though resilience can last and benefit its perpetrator for years, until, in due course, exasperation exceeds fear in a perceptible majority of the population, enabling the people to take the risk of rallying into legitimate and active resistance.

Meantime, the paradox of the bully is that in using violence to deny, to abuse or to set limits to its victims, it ultimately advocates a no-limits opposition. Violence displays the shallowness (either by deficient intelligence and closed-mindedness, or by blind greed) of the entity that makes use of it. The power of threat is the false authority of fools. In the method of his ambition, the oppressor confesses his blatant political inability, his ineffectual leadership and his unsophisticated selfishness, which ultimately validates, or will validate, the instability of his deceptively dominant reign. Such a society can't persist; as it alienates its subjects, it simultaneously corroborates its defiance, and the apparent submission, however long-lasting, can only be provisional.

State violence against nonviolent civilians is self-evident injustice; in spite of the uniforms, the decrees, the gain or the ideology, and perhaps even the necessity behind it, it can never acquire true legitimacy—even less so in a democracy, however bogus it might be. In theory, a democracy's government is the people's employee, with the job of protecting and caring for their general well-being. Exploitation of a population's ignorance or vulnerability for the profit of the political and business elite is therefore wholly illegitimate.

The perception of injustice can vary according to cultural backgrounds, yet there are a few universally implicit fundamentals, ownership rights and freedom included, with freedom of speech (the freedom to disagree) being among the first essential human liberties. To repress this inalienable right is to commit an injustice, and injustice is itself violence.

As in the journalistic maxim, "if it bleeds, it leads," violence is a vicious circle, somehow fascinating for some and easily fueled. It draws from deep instincts such as protection, and from raw powerful emotions like fear. That's why it is possible to create and to maintain a climate of violence: everyone has a response that nourishes it. Even the victim, even the subdued, plays an active role in the sequence.

A despotic power makes sure that people know their place, between those who have the power and those who don't. This discourages challenges, and divides the nation into those who collaborate, those who submit and those who resist, while giving way to a gangrenous corruption, as the strangled mass becomes spectator of its own demise. The indigenous Amazon in Peru had the courage to refuse this common option, but they were too small a presence to overcome the governmental pride in front of them. (Too small, because their comrades, natives making up 50 percent of the Peruvian population—the poorest 50 percent—played the part of spectators, to a wrongdoing that may strike them tomorrow)

On the other hand, justice is closely associated with peace; justice doesn't require oppression, violence or any type of coercion. People go along with justice instinctively; justice and peace are unanimously understood, sought-after and approved. This is a profoundly human inclination. All over the world everyone is seeking happiness. Peace and the concomitant justice and freedom are inherent essential constituents of the universal idea of happiness.

The majority of humans are endowed with fraternal, generous and friendly minds; sensitive, they are intuitively open and respectful of others and they all aspire to live in harmony and peace.

Why peace? Because humankind is attached to progress. In a world of peace, as the collective embraces the individual, the individual will also embrace and participate in the collective—instead of violence's vicious circle, this now becomes a virtuous circle.

Peace and freedom fulfill and empower people, because whereas fear is obsessive, serenity is creative; while anxiety is a narrow standstill, well-being is a progressive movement. I believe that a refined model of peace and justice would reach a compromise with the natural passions and impulses of egos, which are great energies and which, combined with freedom in which to express themselves, would become potent motors of progress, for the self as well as for the society. The seemingly indispensable and unavoidable excitement of violence and wars, obvious outlets of frustration, persistently and to this day dominating the history of humanity, may be substituted for as such.

However peace functions like anything else does, it is not to be taken for granted; like friendship, like love, it is an everyone/everyday attention.

And we've got what it takes. Empathy is the ability of the human being to recognize another member of the species as akin to themselves: to put oneself in another's shoes, and be capable of limiting one's superfluous desires, so as not to ruin the essential needs of others. Everybody has empathy, even if limited and undeveloped—maybe not for the whole world, but at least for our loved ones. As everyone's blood is red, as smiling is an irrefutable and spontaneous universal language, consideration and sympathy are also at hand, within us and in our dreams, to give ground to an alternative style of human interactions.

A world where its two pillars, man and woman, would be together without violence or discrimination, A world where tolerance and cooperation would unite people for the best, so that they would live and work with dignity, with a sense of self-esteem and confidence in the future. A world where sense would prevail over the form and even the substance. A world where the ability to be at peace within ourselves would be encouraged and taught as seriously as mathematics!

Who obliges us to credit the antique model of ash and blood, death and battles, the acceptance of dissolute, unfair competition, licentious rivalry, domination and war?[4] Can't we make peace before *resting in peace*? Can't we get out of the spiral of violence, and the historical mold; can't we install peace, without discrediting it by making a war for it? *We—the* great majority of humans—can't we stop the minority in arms? Together, if we disobey together, we can!

In the incident I witnessed in Bagua Grande, however strong in arms the oppressor, legitimacy was without a doubt in the hands of the indigenous. By their desperate fortitude against the iniquity of both the method and the purpose of the government, they eventually succeeded, at least momentarily, in sapping the unscrupulous aggressions on their lands and livelihoods and having the ominous legislative decrees suspended. But for how long?

Peruvian President Alan Garcia has since rescinded two of the most controversial decrees. Peru has kept moving forward on oil and gas development, despite the controversy conveniently well out of the interest of international mass media or administrations. Oil firms already operating in the area include Repsol (Spain), Perenco (France), Pluspetrol (Argentina), Petrobras (Brazil), Maple Energy (United States) and Petroperu (Peru), while most South American explorations are working on behalf of the U.S.-based Hunt Oil, which includes among others SK Energy of South Korea and Marubeni of Japan.[4]With the complicity of the Peruvian government, hefty and far-reaching interests worth millions of dollars are the main players of an abysmally unbalanced situation, at the expense of both the forest and its indigenous communities. Only a few human rights and environmentalist NGOs seem unanimously concerned about the ongoing human tragedy and the ongoing ecological disaster.[5]

In the realm of the xenophobic and stubborn myopic gluttony of the current Peruvian regime, the spiral of hostilities is still going on by way of intimidation and harassment against the few still fighting for truth, justice, and their property rights.

It seems it's not tomorrow that the Amazon indigenous will be empowered into becoming the active human face of sustainable and equitable development of their ancestral land (the sensible setup promoted by WED[6] that, especially regarding the Amazon, is also crucial to all of earth's inhabitants). Peace to the native communities of the Amazon is important not only for them, but for all of us.

In the course of my two-and-a-half years of solo traveling, between Asia and Latin America, this terrible Peruvian incident remains one of the most tragic and "spectacular" manifestations of authoritarian abuse of power I witnessed. However, throughout my journey, I've come across other abuses of power—no less-shocking, no less-surreptitiously violent and no less-outrageous—damaging people's everyday lives, freedom and dignity.

It's not happening tomorrow, but who knows when the awareness of an urgent need to change will materialize into global drastic acts? Who knows what will trigger the cry of millions of people scorned every day by a minority in arms? It could be in a long time, after many wars and much pain, after humankind has finally achieved to destroy the wonderful planet we live on and in doing so sentenced itself to death.

But since we are capable of feeling and dreaming; since John Lennon's "Imagine" is as popular all around the world as Michael Jackson's "Thriller"; since Revolution, including pacific revolution, is also part of human history; since what defines the human race is its aptitude to change; since we have invented the concept of utopia and the entertainment of science-fiction… why, it could be tomorrow!

On June 5th, 2009, a somewhat-large chunk of my faith in humanity was wounded; at the same time, a somewhat crazy and passionate hope survives in me. I must pay tribute to the courage and fortitude of the "small" people, determined to never give up, against all odds and sometimes facing great perils, toward making a better life for themselves and others—dignified people all around the world, who resist with their small means and grand will against repression.

For them, for me, I keep hoping. Much more than that, I resist! Every day I am vigilant about any abusive and undeserved humiliation of my own human dignity, ready to jam the slightest abuse of power, and not give it any ground on which to grow. Whether it is an unfair law in my country, France, or whether it is harassment on the part of an administration or an employer, I stand up, not making it easy for them.

For now and for tomorrow, for me and for others: I am attentive about not being manipulated, confused, disheartened, or worn down into indifference or helplessness; I check my inner conflicts and work at the peace within myself; I recognize when I come across the better side of humanity—and I celebrate it! I fight along, contribute along, every day, within my reach and with my small means, for the sake of peace, and with the sentinel of the deep conviction that Peace belongs to Justice and Freedom.

Our Deepest Fear

"Our deepest fear is not that we are inadequate. Our deepest fear is that we are powerful beyond measure. It is our light, not our darkness that most frightens us. We ask ourselves, Who am I to be brilliant, gorgeous, talented, fabulous? Actually, who are you not to be? You are a child of God. Your playing small does not serve the world. There is nothing enlightened about shrinking so that other people won't feel insecure around you. We are all meant to shine, as children do. We were born to make manifest the glory of God that is within us. It's not just in some of us; it's in everyone. And as we let our own light shine, we unconsciously give other people permission to do the same. As we are liberated from our own fear, our presence automatically liberates others."

- Marianne Williamson, from *A Return To Love: Reflections on the Principles of A Course in Miracles,* and quoted in Nelson Mandela's address on the occasion of his investiture, 1994.

[1] Source : UNEP (United Nations Environment Programme)

[2] See the explicit convention : http://www.ilo.org/ilolex/cgi-lex/convde.pl?C169

[3] Inspired by beautifully eloquent short story « Ensemble » by French author Christiane Singer – 2000

[4] http://www.huntoil.com

[5] See for instance a series of articles on : http://news.mongabay.com

[6] UN World Environment Day

When Will We Learn?

Harry Browne

Harry Browne was a free-market libertarian writer, and the Libertarian Party's 1996 & 2000 candidate for President of the United States. He was also a well-known investment advisor for over thirty years, author of "Harry Browne's Special Report." a financial newsletter published from 1974 to 1997, author of 19 books and thousands of articles, Co-founder and Director of Public Policy of the Downsize DC Foundation, host of two weekly network radio shows (one political, the other financial), and host of an ETV (internet-based television) show called "This Week in Liberty with Harry Browne" on the internet-based Free Market News Network. *Harry died of Lou Gehrig's Disease on March 1, 2006 at his home in Franklin, Tennessee with his wife, Pamela, beside him. He was eulogized in the U.S. Congress by Representative Ron Paul.*

Part 1 – published September 12, 2001 on WND.com

The terrorist attacks against America comprise a horrible tragedy. But they shouldn't be a surprise. It is well known that in war, the first casualty is truth—that during any war truth is forsaken for propaganda. But sanity was a prior casualty: it was the loss of sanity that led to war in the first place.

Our foreign policy has been insane for decades. It was only a matter of time until Americans would have to suffer personally for it. It is a terrible tragedy of life that the innocent so often have to suffer for the sins of the guilty. When will we learn that we can't allow our politicians to bully the world without someone bullying back eventually?

President Bush has authorized continued bombing of innocent people in Iraq. President Clinton bombed innocent people in the Sudan, Afghanistan, Iraq, and Serbia. President Bush, senior, invaded Iraq and Panama. President Reagan bombed innocent people in Libya and invaded Grenada. And on and on it goes.

Did we think the people who lost their families and friends and property in all that destruction would love America for what happened? When will we learn that violence always begets violence?

Teaching lessons

Supposedly, Reagan bombed Libya to teach Muammar al-Gadhafi a lesson about terrorism. But shortly thereafter a TWA plane was destroyed over Scotland, and our government is convinced it was Libyans who did it.

When will we learn that "teaching someone a lesson" never teaches anything but resentment—that it only inspires the recipient to greater acts of defiance.

How many times on Tuesday did we hear someone describe the terrorist attacks as "cowardly acts"? But as misguided and despicable as they were, they were anything but cowardly. The people who committed them knowingly gave their lives for whatever stupid beliefs they held. But what about the American presidents who order bombings of innocent people—while the presidents remain

69

completely insulated from any danger? What would you call their acts?

When will we learn that forsaking truth and reason in the heat of battle almost always assures that we will lose the battle?

Losing our last freedoms

And now, as sure as night follows day, we will be told we must give up more of our freedoms to avenge what never should have happened in the first place. When will we learn that it makes no sense to give up our freedoms in the name of freedom?

What to do?

What *should* be done?

First of all, stop the hysteria. Stand back and ask how this could have happened. Ask how a prosperous country isolated by two oceans could have so embroiled itself in other people's business that someone would want to do us harm. Even sitting in the middle of Europe, Switzerland isn't beset by terrorist attacks, because the Swiss mind their own business.

Second, resolve that we won't let our leaders use this occasion to commit their own terrorist acts upon more innocent people, foreign and domestic, that will inspire more terrorist attacks in the future.

Third, find a way, with *enforceable* constitutional limits, to prevent our leaders from ever again provoking this kind of anger against America.

Patriotism?

There are those who will say this article is unpatriotic and un-American – that this is not a time to question our country or our leaders. When will we learn that without freedom and sanity, there is no reason to be patriotic?

Part 2 – published September 14, 2001 on WND.com

My article last Tuesday "When Will We Learn?" provoked more controversy than anything I've ever written. In case there was any misunderstanding, here is what I believe:

The terrorist attack was a horrible tragedy and I feel enormous sympathy for those who were personally affected by it. I wrote my article hoping that, however unlikely, it might be possible to prevent such a thing from ever happening again.

1. I hope anyone responsible for the attack who didn't die in it will be found, tried, and punished appropriately.

2. Terrorism by definition is the killing of innocent people in order to bring about some political or social change.

3. Terrorism may cause some changes in the short term, but it never leads to a conclusive victory, because it provokes a never-ending cycle of escalating violence on both sides.

4. The U.S. government has engaged in acts of terrorism over the past few decades—bombing and starving innocent people in foreign countries, supposedly to force their leaders to make changes the U.S. government desires. Terrorism doesn't become "policing" or "justice" merely because it is our government doing it.

5. All Iraqis are not Saddam Hussein; all Serbs aren't Slobodan Milosevic; all Afghanis (or Saudis) are not Osama Bin Laden.

6. Killing innocent people in retaliation for the sins of other people isn't justice—it is terrorism. The terrorists were wrong to kill Americans to satisfy their grievances against American foreign policy. And to react to them by killing innocent foreigners would also be terrorism.

7. You can't make productive decisions at a time when your mind is clouded by anger resentment, or thoughts of revenge.

The reactions I've received have been roughly 50-50 regarding my position. Here are some of the objections people have made against my position.

Timing

"This was a bad time for you to say, 'I told you so' in such a poor fashion."

I'm not saying, "I told you so." I'm trying to stop future madness—against Americans and against foreigners. Should I wait until after our military invades Afghanistan before speaking out?

"Now, of all times, is the time when we must support one another for the best."

That doesn't mean supporting the ill-conceived policies that led to this event.

"It is time for our people to pull together against these sick terrorists. We could use your help too."

To do what? Encourage our politicians to continue doing the very things that led to this? You're demonstrating why I had to write the article. If we stand behind our leaders now, letting them speak for us "as one voice," nothing will change. We will continue to see more acts by our government that will lead to more terrorist attacks on the U.S.

"Don't tell me to 'stop the hysteria.' This event merits hysteria, anger, sadness, and fear. I will be hysterical because it is the only thing I can do to show my countrymen that I mourn them."

Hysteria creates lynch mobs and more killing of innocent people. Grief, anger, and resentment are all natural reactions to what happened. But letting your emotions make bad decisions is not a productive reaction.

"What's done is done and now we're in the middle of this terrible mess. Maybe you're right, maybe we should not be surprised that something was

bound to happen. But, now what? We don't need people criticizing our past mistakes at this moment. Save that for later. Right now we need immediate action."

If we don't understand the past mistakes, the "immediate action" taken will simply repeat those mistakes. Is that what you want?

My Motives

"You have lost my support by your political posturing in a time of crisis."

Political posturing? Do you really think I expected to receive adulation for writing an article that goes so sharply against current public opinion?

"It sickens me that you would use this tragedy this way."

In what way? To try to stop it from happening again? To try to stop our politicians from running off and bombing more innocent people? As a normally public voice, should I sit quietly by and not point out that our politicians are continually putting innocent Americans in harm's way by terrorizing innocent foreigners?

I understand your outrage and emotional reaction, but we must hold our own politicians accountable for the anger they are causing around the world with their careless, dangerous, show-off tactics.

"Please leave the United States. You do not deserve to remain here with this type of un-American diatribe which only serves to support the voices of moderation."

I thought this is supposed to be a free country in which everyone was allowed to speak his mind. I guess I misunderstood. I didn't realize it was a crime to try to stop a lynching.

The Libertarian Party

"Using this event as a means to bolster the Libertarian Party is despicable and it is disgusting."

It appears that standing up for what one believes isn't a way to bolster the popularity of the Libertarian Party. But that's what Libertarians often do— especially when no one else will.

"You have forever ended any chance of my supporting the Libertarian Party, unless you resign from any and all leadership positions immediately."

You'll be pleased to know I don't hold any leadership position in the Libertarian Party. I am a private citizen who grieves for what the politicians have done to my country and to the innocents who die in America and abroad. Many Libertarians disagree with my position, so you shouldn't judge the Libertarian Party by me.

Retaliation

"We must deter the next attack with the fiery sword of vengeance, not some limp, liberal, why-can't-we-be-let-alone weak response."

We have done that already: bombing Libya, invading Panama, bombing a perfume factory in the Sudan, bombing Afghanistan. Did those "fiery sword(s) of vengeance" deter the next attack?

"Bomb Kabul into oblivion."

As I recall, Kabul is the capital of Afghanistan, which is run by the same "Freedom Fighters" our own government gave so much money and military hardware to in the 1980s. Before we run off bombing innocent people (or is every Afghani guilty of the World Trade Center bombing?), shouldn't we question the American foreign policy that put those people in power in Afghanistan? Or is it bad timing to bring that up now?

"Once you know the face of your enemy destroy him completely and you will never need fight him again. America is at war. To win a war it must be fought in totality."

A war against whom? Against people like the one million Iraqis who have died of starvation or disease because of the American blockade? Against people like the innocents who died in the bombings of the Sudan and Afghanistan? Every time our leaders say, "We must make sure this will never happen again," they do something to assure that it *will* happen again. I wrote my article in the vain hope it might help people to think twice before demanding the wrong action.

"Do you think these terrorists can really be reasoned with?"

I didn't say they could. I said we shouldn't give them legitimate reasons to direct their misguided zeal at the U.S.

"Don't you think a soft response would just encourage more terrorism?"

I hope the people who were involved are found, tried, and punished. I don't consider that a soft response. But I don't want any more innocent people hurt— Americans or foreigners.

"This is not the time to run and bury our heads in the sand. Someone has to stand up to bullies wherever they are! Like the Nazis; the only good Religious Fundamentalist is one that is in heaven! Not only is it a time for the U.S. to take action but to OCCUPY ALL ARAB LANDS, since their Religious leaders 'preach' the Jihad."

Did I mention that there was a lot of hysteria and a lynch-mob sentiment right now?

"You totally lost your credibility with me when you suggest that any military response will basically serve no purpose."

The U.S. went to Vietnam to stop the Communist dominos from falling, and the entire region fell to the communists. The U.S. invaded Panama, supposedly to end drug-dealing there, and today Panama is more overrun with the drug trade than ever. After years of arming Saddam Hussein, the U.S. invaded Iraq to get rid of him, but he is still held up as a terrible threat to the world. The U.S. bombed Libya to teach terrorists a lesson; so the terrorists hijacked the Pan American plane over Scotland.

Perhaps you could give me an example of where U.S. military response in the past several decades has achieved any purpose.

Obviously, the individuals involved in the attacks should be found, prosecuted, and punished. But going to war against another country or some vague conspiracy will solve no more than the examples I just gave.

"At this time, past wrongful deeds committed by Americans should not play a role in our reaction to this horrible event. We have to retaliate once we confirm who is responsible. Otherwise, even more horrific events are sure to occur in the future."

We *have* retaliated in the past, and still horrific events followed. What I'm hoping for is a different kind of reaction this time—one that will actually change American policy so that we never again suffer what happened this week.

Corrections & Caution

"I would like to point out that the airliner destroyed over Scotland was a PanAm plane, not TWA."

You are right. In my haste to get the article finished, I was careless in relying on my imperfect memory and not looking it up.

"I put my Harry Browne for President stickers back up in my dorm room yesterday."

Please, take them down before you get lynched.

Part 3 – published September 17, 2001 on WND.com

In my last commentary, I pointed out that killing innocent people is terrorism, no matter who does it—freelance terrorists, an international conspiracy, a foreign government, or our government.

It would be wrong for our government to respond to last week's tragedy by committing further acts of terrorism against innocent foreign people.

Find the terrorist conspirators and punish them—yes. Bomb innocent people—no.

Friday I commented on some of the common themes we're hearing now to justify rash action by our government against foreign countries. Here are some more of what I've received in my mail:

Civil liberties

"I don't mind giving up some more of my liberty in order to put a stop to these despicable acts."

I understand your sentiments, but I respectfully disagree with them—for two reasons:

First, you have no idea what liberties are going to be taken from you. And whatever they are, you can have no expectation of ever getting them back—even if the underlying problem goes away completely. (For just one obvious example, income tax withholding was instituted as a war measure in 1942, and it is still with us today.)

Second, taking away our liberties rarely achieves the goals used to justify the new oppression. Because of the drug war, our government now rummages through your bank's records, looking for suspicious transactions you may have entered into; you and your property can be searched and seized without a warrant, without being convicted of anything, without even being accused of anything. And yet drugs are as widespread today as when these intrusions were put in place.

It's easy to say you support intrusions that you believe aren't likely to affect you personally. But I can assure you that any invasion of civil liberties will affect *you* more than they do the truly guilty (who will quickly learn about the invasions and how to circumvent them).

World War II

"What about the situation in the 1930s, where the British under Chamberlain tried to appease rather than oppose Hitler, with horrible results?"

Many historians believe that if Chamberlain hadn't signed the Munich pact in 1938, but had instead gone to war immediately with Germany, an unprepared England would have been defeated easily. Instead, the delay gave England time to get ready to resist Hitler—and even then, a better-prepared England just barely survived.

But "Munich" has become an all-purpose cliché to justify striking out violently against any foreign power that displeases our politicians: "If only Hitler had been stopped at Munich!" (as though at the time anyone had the resources to stop him). We need something more substantial than clichés to prevent future terrorist attacks.

"There are people like Adolf Hitler who are pure evil. You can't hide your head in the sand and pretend they don't exist. Our government must intervene overseas to root them out—just as we did in World War II."

There are people with diseased minds in every part of the world—from your neighborhood right on up to heads of state. Once you accept the idea that a preemptive strike is justified, where do you stop?

It is easy to cite World War II as an example of our government's proper intervention in world affairs—but only if you start the story in the 1930s, just as people are starting the terrorist story at last Tuesday. In 1917, World War I was winding down to a close. Germany was suing for peace. A negotiated settlement was close, and the world could have returned to its pre-war borders and peace. But it was not to be.

At that point, Woodrow Wilson took America into the conflict. That intervention changed history irrevocably for the worse. Millions of fresh American soldiers streamed into Europe—tipping the balance of power, and overwhelming an enemy exhausted from three years of war. Germany and Austria surrendered, the German emperor fled to the Netherlands, and the Allies imposed devastating conditions upon a defeated Germany.

America's action transformed a functioning Germany with Kaiser Wilhelm on the throne into a prostrate Germany eager for revenge. And so a nation of great artistry that had produced the likes of Goethe and Wagner was willing to accept a dictator who promised to help them get even. The humanitarian spirit that propelled America into a war to "end all wars" laid the groundwork for two of history's worst murderers—Josef Stalin and Adolf Hitler.

Although no one can say for sure, it seems very likely that if America had stayed out of World War I there would have been no World War II. And without that war and without a Soviet Union, there would have been no Cold War, no Korean War, no Vietnam War. The 20th century wouldn't have been an era of perfect peace, but it would have avoided being history's bloodiest 100 years.

Could Woodrow Wilson—or anyone else—have foreseen all this in advance? No, and that's the point. Once you embark on the use of force—for any purpose—you have no idea what will fly up out of Pandora's box. If you don't look for the causes that precede the events, you have no hope of ever preventing a repetition of the events.

What the terrorists did last Tuesday was wrong. But if we don't inquire into the background, and instead go off around the world on a holy *jihad* of our own, we will unleash consequences none of us can predict. But we can be almost positive that they won't be to our liking.

> *"Don't you think that if we were to withdraw from the Mideast, that eventually some Arab dictator would unite the Arab-Islamic world (violently) and pose a real threat to us?"*

Arab dictators aren't going to give up their fiefdoms to a single ruler. Nasser tried it with the United Arab Republic, but it lasted only a year or two. Bureaucrats in Europe love a central authority because it gives them *more* dictatorial power. But that isn't likely to happen in the Middle East. And what you suggest could be possible anywhere in the world. Does that justify the U.S. running the entire world? (Speaking of a single dictator!)

> *"Isn't it occasionally right to intervene on the behalf of people that are being massacred, such as in Serbia?"*

In a free country, you should be free to send money—or even yourself—to any country in the world to aid any cause you believe in (which, incidentally, isn't completely legal under federal law today). But the American government shouldn't use your money to intervene or stir up resentments for causes you may not believe in.

"The world is our business, we all live here. Should people be suffering in East Timor or Iraq or Ethiopia/Eritrea and we just stand by and let it happen if we can do something? I don't think so. Taking more responsibility for all the people of this planet and all the nations of the world would be a better stance."

That should be your choice. You should be free to help anyone anywhere in the world. But our politicians should not have the power to inflict violence on people in other countries in your name—making you a target of retribution.

"We are a world power and we must act like one. This means being unpopular. This means intervening in the world because we have a responsibility to the world."

And it means having people attack us violently—no matter how many security measures are taken and no matter how many liberties you give up. Is that what you want?

"You speak of our government meddling in other people's affairs. Give some specific examples."

Our government has been giving money and military hardware to prop up dictators for over 50 years—including people like Manuel Noriega of Panama, whom our government then kidnapped and put in prison in America, and supporting the very Afghanistan government that supposedly today is harboring Osama bin Laden. Although a lot of the support for dictators was explained as a way of fighting communism, it continues today.

Yes, I know that often the people who eventually replace the dictators are just as bad, but that doesn't justify our government giving your money to either the dictators or their replacements. Did you know that our government *still* gives foreign aid to Afghanistan? Yes, the same country Bill Clinton attacked with Cruise missiles. And we have troops stationed in almost a hundred countries even today.

If dictators took over America, how would you feel about foreign countries that helped keep those dictators in power? How would you feel if foreign troops were stationed in your city? Do you really think there's anything strange about foreigners who love McDonald's but hate our government?

Good words

I'm thankful to everyone who took the time to write me to voice a personal opinion—for or against what I've said. I'm sorry that the volume of mail is so great that I couldn't possibly respond and thank you personally. Although I've focused here on a sampling of the many complaints I've received, I've also received many supportive comments. Here is one from Katie Sweeney that makes an additional point:

"Thank you for asking the question that none of the 'experts' or politicians or news media will ask, which is: Just what have we done to make these people hate us so much?

"The politicians say it is just because we're a free country. That is the propaganda needed to get everyone riled up to join the military and give their lives in 'a battle of good vs. evil.' But the truth is what you said, 'We can't allow our politicians to bully the world without someone bullying back eventually.'

"Today, I am filled with tremendous sadness. I am sad for the people who lost their lives and for their families and loved ones. But I am also sad because I know that nothing is going to be solved, and it will only get worse. The leaders will not speak the truth, and I don't even think the people want to hear it. The only talk is of revenge, not of following your three wise suggestions of what we should do. I feel very powerless to change the course that history is taking and very vulnerable to its consequences."

Part 4 – published September 19, 2001 on WND.com

I now have received over a thousand emails in response to my articles on the terrorist attacks. I regret that I can't reply individually to them. Nor is it possible even to reply in print to many of the thoughtful suggestions, complaints, or proposals that readers have offered.

But there is one common theme I can deal with here—one that runs through all the proposals for retaliation—the assumption that the retaliation can be done in a way that achieves many good purposes with no bad consequences. It can be summarized in the statement, "believe we can retaliate with few innocent people killed, and Afghanistan may be a better place when we leave."

But something very important is overlooked in almost every proposal I've received: When you believe the U.S. government can eradicate the terrorist threat, you're assuming it will design, create, and carry out the plan the way *you* imagine it.

When you endorse the idea that our government should invade Afghanistan, or occupy the Middle East, or conduct "surgical strikes" against terrorist sanctuaries, or round up a particular class of people within the U.S., you automatically assume it will be done as you imagine—with no bad side effects.

(This is a problem common to all government programs. You see suffering or danger, and in your imagination you see a government program eliminating it. But in the real world the program could operate as you expect only if you were a dictator—having at your disposal all of government's power to compel everyone involved to do things your way.)

Never happen

But in fact it won't be done your way. This isn't Burger King.

The program you support will be carried out by the same kind of people who bombed a pharmaceutical factory in the Sudan, who fired cruise missiles into the terrorist camp that wasn't there in Afghanistan, who saw American troops humiliated in Lebanon and Somalia, who went to war with Iraq to keep oil plentiful but then forcibly prohibited the buying of most Iraqi oil afterward, who were going to stop Panama from being a drug conduit and instead left Panama completely defenseless against the drug trade.

That doesn't mean the same kind of failures will happen again, but it does mean almost certainly that what you propose is not what you'll get. What's overlooked in the support for unleashing the military, the FBI, the CIA, and other crime-fighting or war-making agencies is simply this: The government that's supposed to win the War on Terrorism is the same one that's been waging the War on Drugs, the War on Poverty, the War on Crime, and the War on Illiteracy. Perhaps we should pay more attention to its track record.

President Bush said, "We will rid the world of the evil-doers." Perhaps he could start with Washington, D.C.—and if he gets rid of the evil-doers there, he could move on to some other part of America—and if he succeeds there, he could extend the program to the rest of America—and if he succeeds there, he could ask the Canadians if they want our help—and if he succeeds there, he could go on to the Mexicans, the Haitians, the rest of Latin America, and then the Europeans, and so on.

But start with the whole world? Doesn't that seem a little pretentious for a government with such a sorry record of failures? If that sounds flippant, I'm sorry, but I get pretty tired of hearing all these promises made to justify taking more of my life away from me—when none of the thousands of promises made already has come even close to being fulfilled.

Why government fails

Why does government fail to keep its promises?

Whenever you ask the government to do anything, you transform what had been a financial, scientific, military, moral, or social matter into *a political issue*. The program you propose will turn into one more Christmas tree on which every politician can hang his favorite pork-barrel boondoggle—and can use to sneak through his favorite scheme for controlling your life and money.

Government programs too often wind up doing the opposite of what their original supporters had expected. Look how programs to end racial discrimination have produced racial quotas, how federal programs to improve education have turned schools into laboratories for crackpot social theories, how "welfare reform" has greatly increased the cost of welfare, how "good works" to foreign countries have produced such ill will.

Political programs produce such strange results because the "public servants" who design and execute the programs have a wholly different agenda from the public who support them.

You aren't a dictator

You don't control the government. And your dreams of what government can achieve are just that—dreams. They bear no resemblance to what government will really do if your program is enacted.

If government is going to do someone's bidding, is it likely to be *your* bidding—or that of people far more determined, far wealthier, and far more influential than you are—people who see the operation as a chance to further their own self-interest?

That's why libertarians are so all-fired determined to reduce government to as small an entity as we can—where it can do as little damage as possible and be used as little as possible for someone's gain at someone else's expense.

That's why it makes no sense to entrust government with the job of bringing peace to the world. It can no more do that than Caesar could. And it can no more rid the world of evil-doers or make it "safe for democracy" than it can stamp out drugs or poverty.

So long as government is supposed to be the instrument of our protection, we can ask it to seek out, capture, try, and punish the specific people involved in the specific attacks—and hope that it doesn't kill too many innocent bystanders in the process. But think twice—no, think a hundred times—before sending it on a mission to cleanse the world of evil.

For our long-term safety, we must quit entrusting our government with world police powers.

When will we learn that government is not our salvation?

The following are excerpts from *A Foreign Policy for America* by Harry Browne (adapted from "Freedom from War," in *The Great Libertarian Offer*, Liamworks, July, 2000)

A Dangerous World

Because America has taken sides in so many conflicts, because America has armed so many countries' enemies, because America has imposed so many "solutions" on so many people, because American troops occupy so many countries, the world has become dangerous for America...

Politicians & Death

War is justified by blurring the distinction between foreign rulers and their subjects. Our politicians cite the sins of foreign rulers, and then ask us to join in killing their downtrodden subjects.

The politicians want us to forget that wars and "police actions" kill innocent people. They talk about teaching a foreign dictator a lesson, but the dictator never gets hurt. Instead, American bombs kill thousands of innocent civilians who may hate the dictator even more than our politicians claim to.

For example, since the Gulf War in 1991, our government has brow-beaten other governments to ban trade with Iraq—in order to force Saddam Hussein from power. In the eight years of trade sanctions through 1999, it is estimated that at least 1,700,000 Iraqi civilians have died for lack of imported foreign food and medicine.

And, although it doesn't seem to make the newspapers very often, from time to time American planes continue to drop bombs on innocent Iraqi civilians.

Politicians call the deaths of the innocent "collateral damage." And President Clinton and the Republican Congress have steadfastly supported the policy of starving and bombing, even though it has achieved nothing but death and disease...

...Isn't there a better way?

Solutions

War is the first resort of political scoundrels, but the last resort of a free people... Government's role isn't to police the world—or even to win wars. Government's role is to keep us out of wars—and to protect us from foreign enemies, not create them.... Our foreign policy would be simple: *We are always ready to defend ourselves, but we threaten no one.*

America's foreign policy should rest on four principles:

1. Non-Interference: Our government should express good will and a desire for peace toward all—threatening no foreign country, interfering in no other countries' disputes, arming or aiding no foreign governments, and giving terrorists no motivation to influence our government.

Any American who wants to volunteer to a foreign government to fight in its war, to negotiate its peace, or to send money to help defend it should be free to do so with no interference from the U.S. government.

But no American should be forced to participate in or pay for such activities. And our politicians should quit committing Americans to these futile attempts to settle other people's problems.

When the politicians drag us off to someone else's war, they always offer plenty of reasons—too many, in fact, to be taken seriously. The typical menu of justifications for a single intervention might be: We must interfere to keep the conflict from spreading, to head off the emergence of a new Hitler, to protect our allies, to do the moral thing, and to end violations of human rights.

But how can our politicians protect human rights in other countries? They don't even respect *our* rights. They try to disarm you, they allow the police to invade your life and property, they use the insane War on Drugs to impose police-state surveillance on all of us, and they try to censor the Internet. So how can they claim to care about human rights in other nations?

2. No Foreign Aid or Military Assistance: The Constitution grants our government no authority to take your money to support foreign governments.

Not only is it unconstitutional, it is unfair by almost any standard. Little of the money reaches the average citizen in the target country. Most of it enriches the rulers—and it helps them stay in power and continue the policies that keep their countries poor.

As Fred L. Smith pointed out, foreign aid taxes poor people in rich countries for the benefit of rich people in poor countries.

Foreign aid originally was justified as a way of arming countries against Communist encroachment. But Cuba, China, and Vietnam all fell to the Communists *after* receiving massive amounts of American money and weapons. In fact, much of the military equipment given to fight the Communists eventually fell into their hands.

So the politicians no longer bother trying to justify giving your money to foreign governments. They just do it. And, not surprisingly, most of the money has strings attached—requiring that it be spent with politically connected industries in the U.S.

Much foreign aid is spent to fix problems that might not exist but for our government. For example, many Americans understandably worry about Israel's security, fearing that without American aid Israel will be overrun by its neighbors. But the most effective thing our government could do to help Israel would be to *stop arming Israel's enemies*.

Our government's eagerness to take sides in Middle East disputes has put billions of dollars of weapons in the hands of Saudi Arabia, Syria, Iraq, and Iran. Small wonder that it seems necessary to rush to Israel's defense when hostile governments can use American weapons to intimidate Israel.

Every American should be free to send money or weapons to Israel or any other government in the world. But our government has no business taxing you for the benefit of any foreign government.

3. Security against Attack
… [text removed]]

4. Target the Aggressors, Not the Innocent
… [text removed]]

Do We Trust Government To Make Us Safe?

Those who tell us America can bring peace and democracy to the world don't seem to recognize that they're talking about the same American government that can't keep the streets safe in Washington, D.C. It's the same government that bleeds us with taxes, pits group against group in battles over quotas and privileges, and has devastated our cities with a futile War on Drugs.

If it fails to achieve any of its domestic goals, if it imposes alien values on its own people, why should you expect it to attain lofty goals overseas?

Politics Is Usual

And don't forget: we're talking about the government, after all.

Military decisions are made politically—just as new pork-barrel projects are chosen politically. The government's foreign policy is determined with reference to polls, voting blocs, rewards, and punishment. For example, Bill Clinton sent troops to Haiti in 1994, killing people along the way, just to gain the support of the Congressional Black Caucus for his domestic political agenda.

It's easy to imagine how our government could intervene to bring peace to some foreign region or to support "American interests" overseas. But the actual policy will never be the one you imagine, implemented in the way you envision. Instead, the politicians will define those interests by relying for "counsel" on those who have the most political influence.

To expect foreign policy decisions somehow to be separated from politics is as unrealistic as to expect politicians to refrain from buying votes with your tax money.

In short, foreign policy is as much a political boondoggle as any other government project. So be careful what you urge the politicians to do.

Enforcing Peace

The U.S. Constitution was the best attempt ever made to limit the power of government. But because it wasn't self-enforcing, the politicians eventually found that they could ignore it with impunity. I believe we need a new Constitutional amendment to restrain the politicians' ability to draw us into war. Here is my proposal:

Section 1. The United States shall be at war only after a declaration of war, naming the specific enemy nations, is approved by the President and by a two-thirds vote of the eligible members in both houses of Congress.

Section 2. The members of the House of Representatives and the Senate eligible to vote on a declaration of war are those who are between the ages of 18 and 35, or who have children, grandchildren, or great-grandchildren between those ages.

Section 3. In the absence of a Congressional declaration of war, the President may deploy the military to repel an armed invasion of the United States, but may not deploy troops or engage in hostilities outside the United States.

Section 4. The United States shall enter into no treaty with any nation or organization if such treaty could oblige the United States to be at war without a declaration of war by Congress, and the United States shall not be bound to engage in war by any action taken by any organization of which they are a member.

Section 5. Except in time of war, as specified in Section 1, the United States will provide no weapons or other resources to foreign governments, will engage in no military action outside the borders of the United States, and shall deploy no military personnel or weapons outside the boundaries of the United States except that at any one time up to one thousand members of the military may be outside the United States for no longer than thirty days.

Section 6. Upon any violation of this article by the President, Congress shall institute impeachment proceedings within 14 days.

Section 4 doesn't preclude a missile defense or any other kind of defense of this nation. It only requires the President to wait before attacking a foreign nation until a declaration of war has been issued. Even if some incapacity prevents Congress from making a declaration quickly, America could still defend itself. It just couldn't attack anyone else.

This amendment is, I believe, an important first step in finding a way to keep politicians away from loaded weapons forever. That's the one kind of gun control that really will save lives.

"[And] you will know that your children will never fight and die in a foreign war — and terrorists will never target your city."

Sudan: Genocide
in the Nuba Mountains

Eric Reeves

Eric Reeves has published extensively on Sudan, nationally and internationally, for more than a decade. He is the author of A Long Day's Dying: Critical Moments in the Darfur Genocide.

The Kauda valley in the very center of the Nuba Mountains of South Kordofan, Sudan is a beautiful place, one of the most beautiful I've ever encountered. The hillsides are alive with *tukuls* (traditional thatched huts) and terraced landscapes that give the impression of always having been there—of belonging there. During my days there I took long walks into the more remote regions of the valley, taking many pictures and communicating awkwardly with folks I met. My camera seemed the perfect translation tool, as most of the people I photographed had never had the experience before, especially the children. And when they saw themselves—typically for the first time in their lives—in my flip-out monitor, the inevitable reaction (once recognition took place—not always an immediate process) was unconstrained laughter. I'm not sure I understood the laughter, or that there was much to understand, beyond the fact that seeing themselves was hugely entertaining and out of the ordinary.

I attended a local church service in Kauda town, where I was welcomed graciously, and every word not sung was laboriously (and in places bewilderingly) translated for me. This made the service rather long, but it was a sign of real appreciation. Afterward there was a beautiful interweaving of communicants, walking in opposite directions around the church. All the women and children were in colorful finery, and the men were dressed in their best attire.

But I also attended a much grimmer gathering, in the rocky hillside well above Kauda: a meeting of Nuba military and civil society leaders, led by the deputy governor of the region (the governor was in Nairobi), in a large tent set up for this occasion. They were determined that I should hear their story, and they were deadly serious. Again and again I felt the force of decades of anger and disappointment pushing me back in my seat. I learned firsthand how bitter the people of the Nuba were, having been left out of consideration at the time of independence (1956), and in the Addis Ababa peace agreement (1972) that ended Sudan's first civil war. They would not be left out of the next peace agreement, they insisted with a vehemence that was almost shocking, and clearly meant to be conveyed to those in whose hands their fate rested.

This was in January 2003—shortly after the cessation-of-hostilities agreement (October 2002), but well before the Comprehensive Peace Agreement (January 2005) was signed by Khartoum and the southern Sudan People's Liberation Movement (SPLM). The Nuba knew that key decisions were going to be made about their future, and they wanted a voice. Most of all, they wanted self-determination, even as they knew that the Nuba Mountains were not only in the North but nowhere contiguous with what was to become the Republic of South Sudan on July 9. Their fear was that they would be left alone in a North Sudan dominated by Khartoum's ideological Islam and Arabism (the ethnically diverse African people of the Nuba follow a number of religions, including Islam). Their worst fears have been realized.

Historical memory in this part of Sudan is defined by the terrible experiences of the 1990s, when the Khartoum regime mounted a full-scale genocidal assault on the people of the Nuba, killing and displacing hundreds of thousands. This was *jihad*, and it was based on a *fatwah* issued in Khartoum in January 1992. With this justification, a total humanitarian blockade was imposed on the region, and many starving people were driven into "peace camps," where receiving food was conditional upon conversion to Islam; those refusing were often tortured or mutilated. It is hardly surprising that Deputy Governor Ismael Khamis would tell me bluntly, "Khartoum doesn't regard us as human beings."

Judging by the nature of the genocide that is rapidly developing in South Kordofan, there can be little quarreling with Khamis' assessment. Clear patterns have emerged from the many scores of reports that have continued to come to me from the region. Human Rights Watch has confirmed that Khartoum's regular military and militia are undertaking a campaign of house-to-house roundups of Nuba in their capital city of Kadugli. Many of these people are hauled away in cattle trucks or summarily executed; dead bodies reportedly litter the streets of Kadugli. The Nuba are also stopped at checkpoints grimly similar to those in Rwanda; those suspected of SPLM ("southern") political sympathies are arrested or shot. The real issue, however, is not political identity but Nuba ethnicity; one aid worker who recently escaped from South Kordofan reports militia forces patrolling further from Kadugli: "Those [Nuba] coming in are saying, 'Whenever they see you are a black person, they kill you.'" Another Nuba aid worker reports that an Arab militia leader made clear that their orders were simple: "to just clear."

Yet another Nuba resident of Kadugli ("Yusef") told Agence France-Presse that he had been informed by a member of the notorious Popular Defense Forces (PDF) that they had been provided with plenty of weapons and ammunition, and a standing order: "'He said that they had clear instructions: just sweep away the rubbish. If you see a Nuba, just clean it up. He told me he saw two trucks of people with their hands tied and blindfolded, driving out to where diggers were making holes for graves on the edge of town.'" There have been repeated reports, so far unconfirmed, of mass graves in and around Kadugli. We should hardly be surprised that the charges of "ethnic cleansing" and "genocide" are coming ever more insistently from the Nuba people, observers on the ground and in the region, and church groups with strong ties to the region.

Just as shocking is Khartoum's renewed blockade of humanitarian assistance to the people of the Nuba, hundreds of thousands of whom have already fled into the hills or mountainsides. The Kauda airstrip, critical for humanitarian transport, has been relentlessly bombed, and the UN now reports that it is no longer serviceable for fixed-wing aircraft. The airstrip has no military value, as the Sudan People's Liberation Army (SPLA) forces have no aircraft. The concerted bombing, with high-explosives producing enormous craters, is simply to deny the Nuba food, medicine, and shelter.

The same assault on humanitarian efforts is under way in Kadugli and other towns under Khartoum's military control. The UN World Health Organization warehouse and offices in Kadugli have been completely looted, as have those of other UN humanitarian agencies. The Kadugli airport has been commandeered by Khartoum's military forces, and all humanitarian flights into South Kordofan have been halted. The World Food Program has announced that it has no way to feed some 400,000 beneficiaries in South Kordofan. As in Darfur, Khartoum intends to wage a genocide by attrition—defeating the Nuba by starving them.

What Khartoum seems not to have fully understood is how determined the Nuba SPLA are. These are not southerners, but true sons of the Nuba; they cannot "return to the South," because they are from the north. And they are well-armed and well-led by Abdel Aziz el-Hilu, a former governor of the region and a fearsome military commander. They believe they are defending their homeland and their way of life. They have no alternative: as Khamis said to me during our 2003 meeting, "we have no way out." Given the geography of South Kordofan, there can be little quarreling with this assessment. These people will fight to the death.

Princeton Lyman, the U.S. special envoy, declared on June 16—eleven days after the killing began in Kadugli—that the United States "doesn't have enough information on the ground to call the campaign 'ethnic cleansing.'" This is an astonishing claim, given what the UN is saying in its confidential reports on the situation in Kadugli, what Human Rights Watch has reported, what is revealed by satellite photography, what escaping aid workers have told journalists, and what is revealed by photographs of the bombing of the airstrip at Kauda. Again, the airstrip has no military purpose: it is being attacked solely to deny humanitarian access to the Nuba people. And it is working: the World Council of Churches, an organization with close ties to the Nuba, reported on June 10 that as many as 300,000 people were besieged and cut off from humanitarian relief.

There can be no reasonable doubt about the reality of widespread, systematic, ethnically targeted destruction of the Nuba people. The Khartoum regime is attacking innocent individuals. I think back to my time at Kauda, and the beauty of the people and the hillsides—now much of it in flames, and all of it under the most intense and unjust assault.

The Unwilling Laboratory

Nebojsa Malic

Nebojsa Malic was raised in Sarajevo, Bosnia (then Yugoslavia). He holds a Bachelor of Arts in History and International Relations. Nebojsa emigrated from Bosnia in 1995 and currently lives in the United States. He has been a columnist for Antiwar.com *since 2000.*

Winston Churchill is alleged to have said that the Balkans produce more history than they can consume. Whatever its origin, the quote is accurate enough. Yet it is difficult to discuss the notions of war, peace and liberty without at least some historical context.

There twice was a country called Yugoslavia. It was first set up at the end of the Great War, in what its founders believed was the fulfillment of a century-long dream of freedom. It is difficult to say whether the great experiment in social engineering might have succeeded eventually, given enough time. Probably not. Either way, Yugoslavia ran out of time in April 1941, when it offended Adolf Hitler by reneging on his offer of "friendship." What followed was four years of chaos and carnage. After the Nazi occupiers put down the insurrection with mass reprisals, the rival Royalist and Communist resistance movements turned against each other. Meanwhile, in the state of Croatia established under Nazi sponsorship, a genocidal pogrom against the Serbs, Jews, and Roma appalled even Hitler's envoys.

As Soviet armies arrived in late 1944, the Communists took control of the country. They re-established Yugoslavia, yet echoed the wartime partition by creating six "socialist republics" (Slovenia, Croatia, Bosnia-Herzegovina, Serbia, Montenegro, and Macedonia) and two autonomous provinces (Vojvodina and Kosovo, within Serbia). The system was designed to produce controllable tensions between the various ethno-religious communities, both historical and newly engineered, thus making the country more governable for J.B. Tito, president-for-life. Politically incorrect history, including the fresh horrors of Croatia's genocide, was suppressed under the slogan of "brotherhood and unity."

Fresh revolutionary zeal fueled the rebuilding of the country—at least until a "New Class" of Communist apparatchiks arose to enjoy the life of power and privilege they once preached against. Royalists and nationalists were executed or exiled at the end of the war, and anyone suspected of "nationalism" was dealt with harshly thereafter. Communists who fell afoul of the ever-changing party line (e.g., following the split with Moscow in 1948) ended up in labor camps.

Tito's regime systematically dismantled traditional institutions of society. Small farms were forced into collectives. Religion was prohibited to Party members, yet without Party membership it was difficult to advance in public service. Private property was nationalized, though eventually some small businesses were permitted to exist. Social engineers came up with ambitious projects such as "directed secondary education" and "workers' self-management." All avenues of economic, personal and social advancement led through the Party. And then Communism ended.

The system was set up to fail: under the 1974 Constitution, the republics became virtual states, and Yugoslavia a confederacy thereof. When Tito died, six years later, the system that depended on his authority began to collapse. By 1990, feuds between Party leaderships of the republics became intractable. One by one, the republics organized multi-party elections. As Communist regimes toppled all over Europe, in Yugoslavia the old apparatchiks reinvented themselves as ethnic and religious nationalists. The emerging European Union, eager to establish itself as a meaningful entity in the flux following the end of the Cold War, sent envoys to mediate the conflict. They did so by declaring Yugoslavia nonexistent, and recognizing the republics and independent states.

The problem with this approach is that it ignored the very same history that the Communists had suppressed for decades. With Communist controls gone, the social reactor suffered a catastrophic meltdown. All the memories, identities, religions and grievances—real or imagined—rushed into the ideological vacuum. The result was an explosion of violence.

First came a skirmish in Slovenia. It was a half-hearted effort by the collapsing central government to keep Yugoslavia together, a slaughter of raw conscripts the Slovenian propaganda turned into a "glorious victory against Serbian aggression." That's when it became obvious the succession wars would be ethnic, not ideological.

In Croatia, a Catholic nationalist government sought to disenfranchise the sizeable Serb Orthodox population, which had historically inhabited the old border with the Ottoman province (and later Yugoslav republic) of Bosnia. Following the WW2 genocide perpetrated by Nazi-allied Croatians, Tito had declared Croatia a state of Croats and Serbs alike. The new government removed the Serbs from the Constitution and welcomed the return of pro-Nazi exiles. When the Serbs revolted, Croatia claimed "Serbian aggression." From there, the war quickly spilled over into Bosnia-Herzegovina.

I turned fifteen the day Alija Izetbegovic, chairman of Bosnia's collective presidency and leader of the Bosnian Muslims, met with the last American Ambassador to Yugoslavia. Subsequent reports claim that Warren Zimmerman told Izetbegovic that he didn't have to sign the power-sharing agreement between the republic's Serb, Croat and Muslim communities. Zimmerman himself denies it, but the fact remains that Izetbegovic did renege on the agreement, choosing instead to unilaterally declare independence. Croatian Army units were already in Bosnia at that time. With all political avenues of resolution thus closed, the Serbs took up arms.

There is a curse in the Balkans, origin unknown, that goes "May you have, then have not." It perfectly describes the horrors of medieval warfare using 20th-century technology. Inflamed by hatred, driven by grievances real or imagined, people went at each other using everything from rockets to knives. The Other was accused of the most heinous atrocities, while one's own were considered fully justified, in righteous self-defense. Delusions and distortions were a major weapon of the war, which was fought with cameras more so than cannons.

Izetbegovic's strategy was simple: have his people bleed on camera as much as it takes, until the outside world intervenes. Bosnia's capital, Sarajevo, was the ideal stage. Host to the 1984 Olympics, site of the 1914 assassination that set off WW1, it was a city the Serbs and Muslims shared—and quickly became a battlefield. Foreign press and UN observers and peacekeepers were there already, covering the events in Croatia. Heavy battles between Serb and Muslim militias in March and April of 1992 ended up dividing the city, with the Serbs controlling the access roads and the airport. Then it became a siege.

"War is hell," U.S. general William T. Sherman said as he torched Atlanta in 1864. In Sarajevo, it most certainly was. Civilization vanished within days. Power lines went down. Water pumps failed. Stores had been looted. With power out, even those who stockpiled food soon found themselves starving, between spoilage and inability to cook anything. Scrounging up ancient wood and coal stoves took weeks, learning to use them even longer. By then, food was running out; in July 1992, the first UN food aid began to arrive. Military rations were considered a delicacy—in any case, preferable to weeds and roots. Pigeons, once common in the city, vanished. They probably replaced chicken in many improvised recipes; I don't think I've ever eaten one (that I know of, anyway). The food situation was especially dire in the winter of 1992-93 and remained erratic until 1994. Eventually people began to tend their own vegetable gardens on balconies and windowsills and whatever small plots of land they could safely till. Displaced people from the countryside taught urban dwellers how.

In those early days of the war, everyone was on a crash course to learn 19th century skills such as chopping wood and bathing in a bucket. With no steady water supply, drinking water required trips to wells, often under fire. Rainwater was collected for flushing. Baths were reserved for the rare days there was a slight surplus of reasonably clean water. Even that was recycled for flushing. That's the worst thing about a water outage: waste disposal. Toilet paper ran out very quickly, and we had to improvise. Disease became a major concern, with epidemics of dysentery sweeping the city from time to time.

Then there was the light—or rather, the lack thereof. Candles ran out quickly, so people made do with lamps made from jar lids, with old shoelaces as wicks, dipped in gasoline, stale oil or rancid lard. Eventually, the government set up its own power grid, serving the military and the occasional government building. People ran cables to those wires and stole power, mostly just enough to run a single light and a TV. The pirate cables were cut every so often, but would soon reappear. Having a source of light meant one could read in the short winter days and TV was a somewhat effective cure for boredom. As in the old description of the trenches, war was long stretches of boredom punctuated by moments of sheer terror; except it was right there on our doorstep, and not in some distant land.

Meanwhile, a low-intensity trench war was waged in the suburbs, with sniping and small-arms exchanges occasionally escalating to a storm of artillery. Early on, everyone hid in the cellar at the slightest sound of an explosion. We quickly learned, however, to tell apart the incoming and outgoing fire and the type of weaponry used. Most people stayed in their homes, avoiding the rooms facing the frontline (when possible) and avoiding the windows. Just about all glass in the city had shattered by the end of 1992, and everyone's windows were covered with UN-supplied plastic foil.

Sometimes survival needs trumped common sense. As most trees were chopped up for firewood, there was less cover from sharpshooters. Improvised pipes and garden hoses tapped into the natural gas supply, which was unreliable at best. Gas explosions, while infrequent, were uniformly fatal.

What war does is strip away all of the outer layers of humanity, every trapping of civilization, manners and breeding, until only the raw human nature remains. The good, the bad, the ugly—all show their true faces. War burns away all illusions, those about the government in particular.

Governments exist because they promise protection. They cannot provide it. We all groused about the incompetence of the government to fight the war, distribute the food aid, or secure the utilities. But few knew how much calculated malice was behind it.

Most of the food that arrived in UN convoys was stolen. Some of it ended up on the black market. The bulk went to feed the military and select government officials. The first to take up arms were the criminals, who were more concerned with "liberating" everything of value than fighting. Although most everyone was issued "work orders" (commanding them to show up for work no matter what), press gangs roamed the city hauling people off to dig fortifications, often under fire. Sometimes people would disappear even when there had been no fighting.

In 1995, intervention came. Though for over three years Sarajevo was center stage for the bloodthirsty media audience—with its inhabitants willing or unwilling actors—it was events elsewhere that tipped the scales. In August, NATO launched an air campaign against the Serbs in Bosnia and Croatia. The peace treaty ending the hostilities in Bosnia was negotiated in November, at a U.S. Air Force base in Ohio. It closely resembled the original power-sharing agreement. Meanwhile, almost 100,000 lives had been lost and the country was in ruins.

Where once there was Yugoslavia, there are now six (or seven, if one counts Kosovo) successor states. Slovenia, Croatia, Bosnia and the Albanian-run Kosovo draw legitimacy from the 1990s wars. More than just the "health of the State" (per Randolph Bourne), war for them is the *source* of the State.

In Bosnia, the three communities have three different narratives of the war. For the Muslims, it was a heroic, holy and just war of defense against "Serbian aggression and genocide." Serbs consider it an imposed war of self-defense, against Muslim and Croat bid to wipe them out. They point to Croatia's "Homeland War," where the expulsion of the Serbs is celebrated as a national holiday.

Governments are so fond of conflict because it allows them to increase their power and silence opposition. Faced with danger, people become a herd, and the instinct of the herd is to "fall in line." Everyday politics is a low-intensity conflict, a smoldering fission reaction politicians believe they can control and exploit. War, on the other hand, is akin to a full nuclear blast, uncontrollably obliterating everything it its path. And yet the belief persists that it can be controlled, harnessed, and used for "creative destruction."

Without a war, the Slovenian government would not have been able to claim a large chunk of Yugoslavia's foreign currency reserve. By the admission of its founding President, Franjo Tudjman, the Croatian government needed a war in order to disenfranchise and eliminate its substantial Serb population. War enabled Alija Izetbegovic to rally the Bosnian Muslims around his agenda of Islamic revolution, and become their unquestioned leader.

Serbia's Slobodan Milosevic, accused by both the separatists and the West of being the aggressive despot and an evil mastermind behind the wars, claimed he was only fighting to protect Yugoslavia. Yet he didn't, and even as Serbia itself was being blockaded and strangled for its alleged "aggression," Milosevic maintained he was not actually at war. He kept trying to negotiate with the West, not realizing that the treaties weren't worth the paper they were printed on. In 1999, NATO bombers backed the ethnic Albanian separatist movement and occupied Serbia's Kosovo province. Milosevic was overthrown in October 2000, in what was presented as a popular revolution—but was, in fact, a coup sponsored by the U.S.

If outside intervention in the Balkans wars was bad, intervention in the Balkans peace turned out much worse. For all its flaws, Yugoslavia of 1990 was a far better place than the sum of its shards twenty-one years later. Economic, social, financial statistics all point to that. So does the nostalgia among the people who still remember the time before the wars.

In Bosnia, the wounds of war not only never healed, but have been exacerbated by 15 years of essentially colonial rule. The original compromise state, entrusted only with essential functions by the mistrustful communities, has been transformed into a modern managerial state in the Brussels mold. A stream of imposed "reforms" over the years has been aimed at expanding, strengthening and making all-pervasive the power of the State—all in the name of "the people." But *which* people? By attempting to coerce a fantasy Bosnia into being, foreign viceroys have only made reconciliation in actual Bosnia that much less likely.

A similar protectorate was established in Kosovo, but it did absolutely nothing to prevent the pogroms, arson and abuse directed against the non-Albanian population, which has practically disappeared. Despite the extensive presence of NATO and UN troops and police in the province, not a single case of murder, rape or property destruction whose victims were Serbs has been punished. In February 2008, the Albanian provisional government in Kosovo declared independence, which remains disputed.

The "Democratic Opposition" that came to power in Serbia in 2000 deserves its own entry in political science textbooks as an example of democracy utterly perverted in form and function. Having accused Milosevic of communism, they never bothered to dismantle the system of government they seized, choosing instead to use its absolute power for personal gain. By blaming everything on Milosevic, his successors have been able to commit a veritable train of abuses against their citizens with impunity.

Widespread corruption, organized crime, school violence, nepotism, party patronage and spoils system, massive foreign debt, infrastructure embezzlements—those are just the tip of the proverbial iceberg. The "democratic" government is busy accepting blame for the Succession Wars, extraditing its entire police and military leadership to be tried for war crimes and recognizing the secession of Kosovo—while the country's industry and agriculture lie in ruins, and the people are starving.

Though Serbia was once a parliamentary democracy with a commitment to liberty, today the self-proclaimed liberal-democrats are the most outspoken opponents of free speech, while "legalist" has become an insult. The country is run by foreign ambassadors and foreign-funded "civil society" groups.

Adding insult to injury is the issue of war crimes. An ad-hoc tribunal (ICTY) set up by the U.S. under UN pretense has accused every high-ranking Serb official from Croatia, Bosnia and Serbia of a grand conspiracy to attack, occupy, ethnically cleanse and even commit genocide against everyone else. Most Serbs protest that these charges are trumped up, but recognize that atrocities happened and deserve to be prosecuted. On the other hand, just about every other group argues that anything they'd done during the wars was by definition legitimate, since they were "only acting in self-defense." Their atrocities were therefore right, proper, even heroic—not atrocities at all. The ICTY has more or less supported this "logic" so far.

Yugoslavia's succession wars were not only an illustration of the failure of the state, but also of the failure of supra-national institutions. The UN has been thoroughly compromised, having effectively taken sides in local conflicts while pretending to be neutral, and turning over most of its authority to the U.S. and NATO. Organizations like the Organization for Security and Co-operation in Europe (OSCE), which were supposed to be neutral and law-abiding, helped create ways of circumventing international law and justify brute force in Bosnia and Kosovo. In 2010, the International Court of Justice tortured language, law and logic by redefining the ethnic Albanian provisional government in Kosovo in such a way that its declaration of independence, though clearly against UN Resolution 1244, was not necessarily illegal.

From the initial decision by the newborn EU that Yugoslavia was "in dissolution" and recognition of its republics as independent states, through the insistence on sanctity of republic borders (except in the case of Serbia), to the demands for centralization in Croatia and Bosnia and *decentralization* in Serbia and Macedonia, it ought to be apparent that foreign approaches to the Yugoslav question had very little to do with any sort of principle or coherent logic, save one: that might made right. It wasn't an issue of double standards, on top of the savageries of war, but of no standards at all.

Having thus compounded the self-inflicted Balkans misery, the self-appointed white knights went on to proclaim their interventions a great success and a model for the future. Kosovo 1999 made possible Iraq in 2003 and Libya in 2011.

Worse yet, the Balkans conflicts helped interventionists create another form of interference: the "democratic revolution." Cynically exploiting non-violence and popular protests, they've used the model first employed in 2000 in Serbia to overthrow governments throughout the former Soviet Union (Ukraine, Georgia and central Asia) and more recently, manipulate the events in North Africa (Tunisia, Egypt). Between the "bombs for peace" and the "revolution business," the fruits of misery grown in the unwilling Balkans laboratory are now going global.

Missing Justice in Afghanistan

Daphne Eviatar

Daphne Eviatar is a New York-based lawyer and journalist, and a Senior Associate for Human Rights First.

It was a cold February morning when I arrived at the sprawling prison complex on the outskirts of Kabul known as Pul-e-charki. A notorious site of torture and brutality during the Soviet occupation of Afghanistan, Block D of the complex was more recently supported by the United States, which transferred national security prisoners there from its own detention center at the U.S.-run Bagram airbase.

An affable prison director greeted our small group—my colleague Gabor Rona, an interpreter, and me—and gave us a tour of the Block D facilities. Though not exactly attractive, the conditions of the cement-block prison seemed decent. So did the Afghan food, which our guide insisted we sample. But as we talked over tea with Major Yaar Rahme Abibzai, the prison's legal director, a darker picture emerged.

The U.S. helped support this prison for years during the Bush administration, even planting roses outside the front gate. But it has since shifted its attention elsewhere, to a newly-built U.S.-run prison at Bagram. Since then, say Block D's directors, although the prison's physical structure has been reasonably maintained, its basic services have not. For example, there are no longer any medical supplies or even basic equipment available for sick prisoners. Although there's a rudimentary clinic in the prison, it doesn't even have the means to test a blood sample, or the resources to send one to a lab, according to the young doctor who was visiting the day I was there. And Block D prisoners cannot be taken to a hospital, for security reasons. As a result, Abibzai said, one prisoner had been lying paralyzed on side of his body for two weeks without treatment. There was nothing they could do for him. The Ministry of Defense had simply failed to put a line item in the budget for medical care for Pul-e-charki prisoners.

The problem of Block D at Pul-e-charki doesn't bode well for the future of Afghanistan. It also raises serious questions about whether the United States is committed to following through on the civilian goal of its military project here: creating a stable society that can resist future takeover by the Taliban.

Indeed, what struck me repeatedly when I visited over the winter was the apparent disconnect between the United State's stated intentions in Afghanistan and the reality on the ground.

Take the condition of Kabul. The capitol city is a mess of congested traffic crowding mostly dirt roads and dust-covered buildings hidden behind concrete security walls and barbed wire. It takes over an hour to cross town, since the roads are in such bad shape and there are almost no traffic lights. The ones there are don't work. And the city, built for 700,000, is now home to some four million people.

Any place you're likely to visit in Kabul is guarded by men with AK-47s. The compounds used by the United States and the United Nations are, not surprisingly, the most heavily fortified. They're set far back from the road behind multiple blast-proof walls topped with concertina wire, shielded by guard stations and automatic weapons. U.S. Embassy staff are not allowed to leave the embassy compound except on official business and in secured vehicles. U.N. staff operate under similar restrictions.

On the one hand, these restrictions make a lot of sense. Suicide bombings are still fairly frequent in Kabul and often target foreigners. But if after ten years of U.S. and NATO involvement here the place is still in such bad shape, is it likely to change much by the time the U.S. withdraws its troops in 2014? And if U.S. and U.N. personnel are too afraid to leave their compounds without armed guards, what will they really be able accomplish for the country?

The disconnect between foreign forces and ordinary Afghans is fueling a growing anger among locals that's palpable in Kabul. In addition to their annoyance that the foreigners tend to have the most money and best living conditions, and live separate and apart from any Afghans, locals complain about the horrible traffic, caused mostly by the influx of foreign forces and their contractors.

The U.S. military makes matters worse by rolling its huge armored tanks down the only paved roads in the area, stalling traffic behind them and scrambling local cell phone connections. (U.S. military vehicles are equipped with devices that automatically block cell phone connections in their vicinity, since cell phones can be used to trigger Improvised Explosive Devices, or IEDs.) And if you're unlucky enough to be stuck in a vehicle behind one of these painfully slow U.S. military convoys, you feel like a sitting duck: you're now situated right behind a major target for insurgent fire. Even worse, if you try to pass it, you become a target of the convoy—even if it's only traveling five miles per hour.

Not surprisingly, since the surge of U.S. forces in 2009, support for the Americans among local Afghans has declined. A December 2010 ABC News/Washington Post poll found that only 32 percent of Afghans rated U.S. actions in their country positively.

My purpose in going to Afghanistan wasn't to gauge public opinion. I was there on behalf of Human Rights First, a U.S.-based NGO, to see whether the U.S. is providing fair hearings to the 1700 or more prisoners it now detains as part of its war in Afghanistan. Human Rights First has been monitoring the treatment and conditions of U.S. prisoners in the "war on terror" since 2002.

When I first saw the description of the new hearing procedures, back in New York, I was mildly impressed. It looked as if the Obama administration had significantly improved past practices. The previous administration didn't give the detainees a hearing at all. But as is often the case, the facts on the ground didn't quite match the plan on paper.

When I arrived at the Bagram Air Base early on a Monday morning, I was escorted by affable young soldiers to a waiting room in the Parwan Justice Center, part of the new $60 million prison complex completed last year. The waiting room is the same place the military brings local Afghans who come to observe or testify at the prisoners' hearings—usually family members or people from the detainee's village. Although a simple pre-fabricated room inside the detention center complex, the floors were covered in Afghan rugs, and cushions for seating lined the walls, all in an effort to mimic a customary Afghan home. And because Afghans in their homes always offer guests tea and snacks of nuts and dried fruit, the U.S. military has its version of this tradition: a folding table stocked with Lay's potato chips and packaged blueberry muffins.

"The Afghans love the muffins," the colonel in charge of handling visitors to the hearings assured us with a smile.

It was clear from talking to her and others that U.S. soldiers at Bagram are trying hard to improve the bad situation they were handed when they arrived. But muffins aren't enough.

Being at war, the military has so far refused to give detainees real trials. Instead of a trial, the U.S. military provides what it calls "Detainee Review Board" hearings every six months for its prisoners. The board consists of three military officers who hear the detainee's case. The case is presented by another officer, called a "Recorder," who acts essentially as a prosecutor. And each detainee is assigned another U.S. officer called a "personal representative" to represent him at the hearing.

All of this is certainly far better than the practice under the Bush administration, when prisoners never had a chance to tell their side of the story. But prisoners still don't get lawyers to represent them ("personal representatives" have no legal training), and the detainees often aren't allowed to see much of the evidence against them, since the military has deemed it classified. Usually that means it comes from a secret informant whose identity the U.S. military does not want to reveal. While that's understandable, it places the detainee in the unfortunate situation of being unable to challenge the evidence. And the military's informants are not always reliable—particularly in Afghanistan.

I don't know how much of the evidence was secret in the hearings I saw, because like the detainee, I was excluded from the classified portion. But I was able to see enough to understand that what passes for justice at the Bagram Air Base would not meet any ordinary understandings of the concept.

Take the case of Gul Alai, whose hearing I saw at Bagram when I visited. The U.S. military holds up to a dozen such hearings a day. I was permitted to sit in on four.

The prisoner wore a white *shalwar kamiz,* (a tunic length shirt and loose-fitting pants, the traditional Afghan dress) and was wrapped in a gray blanket. He sat facing a board of three military officers. His hands and feet were shackled. He'd been imprisoned since last spring.

The Recorder summarized the case, saying Gul Alai owned a compound that was raided by Afghan and U.S. troops, who discovered explosives there. Gul Alai's clothes did not test positive for explosive residue, but he was assessed to be a facilitator for improvised explosive devices.

Eventually Gul Alai was allowed to make a statement. He stood in his shackles. "Yes, that's my house, where I was detained," he said, through a Pashto interpreter, explaining that he lives there with his father, mother, uncles and his wife. "The other house I don't know," he said, referring to another house inside the compound where the explosives were found. "It doesn't belong to me."

One of the judges interrupted: "You own the house or the compound?"

Gul Alai: "I own only the house, not the compound. I do not own the other house where those things were found. That is owned by an old man who lives in Kandahar city." Apparently there had been an error in translation somewhere, or a secret informant who had provided misinformation to U.S. forces. It wasn't clear.

That's because neither the prosecutor nor anyone else introduced any evidence about who owned the house or the compound, or why the military thought Gul Alai was somehow connected to the explosives. In fact, no one produced any witnesses or any evidence at all.

Instead, the judge changed the subject. "What do you think of the Taliban? Do you like the Taliban, or do you hate the Taliban? Do you have friends who have engaged in anti-coalition activity?"

"I am busy with my family," Gul Alai replied, looking bewildered. "I don't understand this business of Taliban. I am a farmer; this is the first time I am detained." Asked about his neighbors, Gul Alai said he doesn't really know them. He can't even see over the wall surrounding their house.

Then his "personal representative" stood up. "How have you been treated here?" the soldier asked.

"I've been treated very well," Gul Alai answered.

His personal representative had no further questions. He sat down.

This is what passes for justice at the U.S. prison at Bagram. The detainee can make a statement, but there is little or no actual evidence presented in open court. The prisoner is not represented by a lawyer, and if there is evidence against him, he often can't see it. After the open portion of the hearing, he must leave while the board holds a classified session.

During my time in Afghanistan, I met with many defense lawyers and former detainees. They all worried that the classified "evidence" against a detainee consists of accusations made to U.S. forces by an enemy of the detainee or a member of a rival tribe. Unfortunately, across the country, longstanding tribal, family and land disputes provide fertile ground for false accusations.

It's a common problem that even U.S. military officials acknowledge. In Paktika province, near the border of Pakistan, for example, villagers told U.S. forces that the Taliban had built a road near their village. Actually, a rival tribe had built the road to harvest timber. "The other villagers blamed the Taliban to get the coalition to target those guys," Lt. Col. David Womack, a U.S. battalion commander, told a New York Times reporter.

If U.S. prisoners in Afghanistan were entitled to a normal trial, then information about the informants and their possible motives would all come out in court. But because these hearings are nothing like trials, the identity and credibility of the informants is never tested.

The U.S. military will say that this is a war, so it can't possibly provide everyone lawyers and a real trial. Soldiers' lives depend on keeping the identity of their informants and their means of collecting information secret, says the military.

Interestingly, Israel, which also has a big problem with terrorism and insurgent warfare, does provide lawyers and trials to the alleged enemies it captures. And it sometimes deals with a much larger volume of prisoners than does the United States in Afghanistan. In May 2002, for example, Israel Defense Forces on the West Bank seized nearly 7000 suspected enemy combatants. They quickly processed and released over 5000, and gave the remaining 1600 suspects access to defense counsel and to independent courts within a matter of weeks. It's not clear why the U.S. can't do something similar.

To some extent, the United States is trying to kick the problem down the road. Over the next few years it hopes to turn over most of its prisoners to the Afghan government, and let them become the Afghans' responsibility. (The U.S. won't relinquish its right to detain people in Afghanistan, though, so it could continue to detain hundreds of Afghans into the future.)

To that end, the U.S. military is trying to train Afghan judges and lawyers to handle national security-related criminal cases. But it's not at all clear that the United States has the ability to transform the Afghan justice system, which is notorious for incompetence and corruption, into a legitimate and functioning set of tribunals capable of meting out real justice. Even if the United States can help improve the system, can the Afghan government sustain those improvements when the United States withdraws its military?

While I was in Afghanistan, I observed an Afghan trial, visited an Afghan prison, met with recently-released prisoners and interviewed Afghan lawyers and U.S. officials. It was evident that the United States faces a steep challenge in its effort to establish some modicum of a justice system in Afghanistan. Even the concept of a defense lawyer to represent an individual accused of a crime is a novelty in many provinces there. And most Afghans believe that whether you're convicted in court and how long you spend in prison depends on what you pay Afghan officials, not the facts of your case.

Still, a legitimate, functioning justice system is critical to the United States' goal in Afghanistan: developing a stable democracy that Afghans will support over Taliban militants.

The U.S. military is taking some steps in that direction. At the Bagram prison, a military task force directs a new Justice Center, which not only sponsors Afghan trials but provides training for prosecutors and defense lawyers and mentoring for judges. The hope is to train them to do basic things, like introducing forensic evidence in criminal cases—for example, fingerprints or

DNA evidence—instead of merely reciting the charges against a defendant and relying on secret intelligence to convict him.

Unfortunately, the Afghan trial I watched at the Parwan Justice Center, part of the U.S. mentoring effort, was not encouraging. The defendant was a 24-year-old farmer named Kamal. Wearing a coffee-colored shalwar kamiz and beat-up sneakers with the backs folded down, he stood and explained that yes, he had been at the mosque with his uncle, but that he did not participate in any fighting. At the age of 15, he had been diagnosed with a heart condition, he explained, which prevented him from walking very much, let alone fighting.

While he was in the mosque, it was raided by U.S. forces, and a shoot-out ensued, which left his uncle dead. Kamal insisted that had not shot at anyone, though. He said that when he heard shots, he ran and hid in a stairwell.

The entire trial lasted less than a half hour. The panel of judges left the room to deliberate. Ten minutes later, they returned and announced that they had acquitted Kamal of the charges of armed assault, due to the lack of evidence. He was convicted of being a member of the Taliban, however, although no evidence was presented to support that charge, either. The prosecutor had merely stated that the Afghan intelligence agency claimed that the prisoner had "participated in destructive activities." The agency's statement was presumed to be true.

The state of the Afghan justice system, even as sponsored by the Americans, doesn't bode well for the U.S. project. Still, eager to withdraw, U.S. officials are adamant that it can succeed. While they seem sincere, those currently most invested in the project are senior commanders in the U.S. military. What happens when the military withdraws from Afghanistan, as it's promised to do over the next three years? What will happen to the United States' commitment to justice reform? Will the training of lawyers and judges and the introduction of actual evidence at trials go the way of the medical supplies at Pul-e-charki?

Former prisoners I interviewed in Afghanistan, although insistent that they were detained by the Americans without cause, were still more afraid of being sent to an Afghan prison and forced to stand trial in an Afghan court. "There, I would have to pay the judge to get out of prison, and my family doesn't have any money," said one man in his mid-40s from Khost province.

The United States wants to withdraw from Afghanistan as soon as it can. The American public is rapidly turning against this war, and it's not clear what the trillions of dollars we're spending on it is getting us. Violence was up sharply last year in Afghanistan, and Gen. David Petraeus has said he expects the situation to be even worse this year.

It's tempting to throw our hands up, pull our forces out and walk away. But in the end, that won't help anyone. If Afghanistan is left to descend into lawlessness, it will be that much more vulnerable to being re-taken by the Taliban—which will just spark U.S. national security fears all over again.

The United States needs to work out a way to quickly and responsibly withdraw its military forces from Afghanistan. But it cannot turn its back on the place altogether. The U.S. needs to commit to long-term civilian support for transforming the Afghan justice system. It must transition from waging war to supporting the conditions necessary for a sustainable peace.

That will require serious commitment and coordination among the many different NATO nations now providing so-called "rule of law" support. And it could take a decade or more. But it's a far less costly way to build Afghans' confidence in their government and bolster security in Afghanistan and at home than maintaining 100,000 U.S. troops in the country—or detaining thousands of potentially innocent Afghans.

We know it's time to end this war. The question now is whether the American public and its leaders are willing to invest in a long-term strategy for peace.

War Would
End the Recession?

It Just Ain't So

Steven Horwitz

Steven Horwitz is the Charles A. Dana Professor of Economics at St. Lawrence University and the author of Microfoundations and Macroeconomics: An Austrian Perspective.

[*This essay was originally published in* **The Freeman** *- January/February 2011* • *Volume: 61* • *Issue: 1:* http://www.thefreemanonline.org/departments/it-just-aint-so/war-would-end-the-recession/]

In his September 28, 2010 *New York Times* blog post [tinyurl.com/363mza3], Paul Krugman announced that "economics is not a morality play." That turn of phrase is his way of defending the idea that in unusual times, such as the sort of deep recession we are in, we can get strange relationships between economic cause and effect. The result is that actions which we might find highly distasteful can have positive effects. Thus we cannot afford to be overly concerned with morality if the goal is to get out of the recession.

Specifically, Krugman defends the claim that World War II got us out of the Great Depression, because "this is a situation in which virtue becomes vice and prudence is folly; what we need above all is for someone to spend more, even if the spending isn't particularly wise." Even spending on something destructive like war, he argues, is what is needed to solve the problem, especially when the "political consensus for [domestic] spending on a sufficient scale" is not available. In Krugman's version of Orwell's Newspeak, destruction creates wealth, and war, though not ideal, is morally acceptable because it produces economic growth.

Thankfully, we can get behind his Newspeak to see the fallacy of his economics. To believe that spending—any kind of spending—is the cure for what ails us is to ignore the subjective nature of wealth and the microeconomic basis of economic growth in favor of an absolute reification of economic aggregates such as GDP and unemployment. Spending trillions of dollars fighting a war can certainly bring idle capital and labor into employment, driving up GDP and lowering unemployment. But this does not mean we are any wealthier than before.

Wealth increases when people are able to engage in exchanges they believe will be mutually beneficial. The production of new goods that consumers wish to purchase is the beginning of this process. When instead we borrow from future generations to spend on goods and services connected not to the desires of consumers, but rather to the desire of the politically powerful to rain death and destruction on other parts of the world, we are not allowing individuals the freedom to do the things they think will make themselves better off. And we are certainly not extending that freedom to those killed in the name of our economy-enhancing war. At a very basic level, the idea that any kind of spending is desirable overlooks the fact that spending on war (and, I would argue, public works as well) actively prevents people from enhancing their wealth through production and exchange linked to consumer demand.

Employing people to dig holes and fill them up again, or to build bombs that will blow up Iraqis, will certainly reduce unemployment and increase GDP, but it won't increase wealth. The problem of economics is the problem of coordinating producers and consumers. This coordination happens when we produce what consumers want using the least valuable resources possible. That is why it is wealth-enhancing to dig a canal using earth-movers with a few drivers rather than millions of people using spoons, even though the latter would generate more jobs.

Sending soldiers off to war is a waste of human and material resources, and is almost by definition wealth-destroying, no matter what it does to GDP or unemployment rates. The only way one can view economics amorally, as Krugman wishes to, is if one is only concerned with total GDP and not its composition. However, it is the composition of GDP, in the sense of how well what we've produced matches consumer wants, that ultimately matters for human well-being. It's easy to create jobs and generate spending, but those do not constitute economic growth, and they are not necessarily indicators of human betterment.

So yes, Professor Krugman, it does matter how we try to get ourselves out of depressions. The world is not upside down and vices aren't virtues. War isn't peace and destruction isn't creation. The real solution to digging out of a recession is to remove the barriers to the free exchange and production that actually comprise wealth creation. Borrowing trillions more from our grandchildren to spend on building the equivalent of pyramids or on blowing up innocents abroad only digs the hole deeper. And when one is reduced, as Krugman is, to saying we "needed Hitler and Hirohito" to get us out of that hole in the 1930s, one has abandoned morality to worship at the altar of economic aggregates.

No critic of free-market economics can ever again accuse us of being irrational and immoral when it is Paul Krugman who says destruction creates wealth, and war is an acceptable second-best path to economic growth. Don't let Krugman's Newspeak fool you: War and destruction are exactly what they appear to be. To argue as Krugman does is to abandon both economics and morality. Big Brother would be proud.

*   *   *

Free-Market Money:

A Key to Peace

[This essay was originally published in **The Freeman** *– January 2008 • Volume: 58 • Issue: 1 -* http://www.thefreemanonline.org/featured/free-market-money-a-key-to-peace/ *]*

When I teach money and banking, I begin the section on the history of the American monetary system by asking my students what the following dates in U.S. history have in common: 1812–1816, 1863, 1913, and 1971. The obvious answer is, "times of war or close to it." (If you count the Great Depression as a metaphorical war in the eyes of politicians, you could add 1934–35 to the list.)

The answer I am looking for, however, is, "times of increased federal government involvement in the monetary system." That both answers are correct is no coincidence. For hundreds of years governments have intervened in monetary institutions in order to use them to raise revenue through the manipulation of money and credit, and most often that revenue has been used to make war.

War finance has long been the overt and covert rationale for an expansion of government's role in the banking system. For classical liberals, exploring this historical relationship sheds light on the sources of both government control over money and the duplicity with which the state often heads to war. The connection illustrates that government intervention in money has no justification in the failures of free-market monetary systems, but rather grew out of the need for revenue. However, it also illustrates the ways in which government can mislead with respect to war by subverting the democratic process and using less-than-transparent means to finance wars, especially unpopular ones.

That classical liberals believe both that government should get out of the money-regulation business and stick to defending the territory of the United States from attack, rather than intervening in the domestic affairs of other nations, often strikes proponents of the "conventional wisdom" as odd. This sort of reaction has greeted Ron Paul's presidential candidacy, which has argued for an immediate withdrawal from Iraq and for the gold standard. Most conservatives, of course, deride the former position, while the left (and some on the right) do the same to the latter. What few if any seem to realize is that these two positions have a deep and important historical connection: If you want to make it harder for the U.S. government to act like an imperial power, you need to find ways to reduce the resources available for it to do so. Preventing the state from creating money would eliminate its ability to manipulate the monetary system to raise funds surreptitiously for foreign adventurism.

Fighting wars requires resources. Governments have only four ways to raise revenue: sell off assets, borrow, tax, or inflate/manipulate the currency. If we assume that states interested in making war are also ones interested in accruing power, selling off assets is unlikely, at least as anything but a last resort.

Both borrowing and taxing have their limits. The most common strategy for financing wars is to sell war bonds. If governments go in this direction, they better have buyers, which assumes that the populace is in general agreement with the conduct of that war. War bonds are a hard sell for unpopular wars. For example, World War II bonds sold well as the public was convinced it was proper to respond to the direct attack by the Japanese and to attempt to stop the Nazis. However, you will look in vain for any Vietnam War bonds, nor have any Iraq War bonds been available since the 2003 invasion. When governments wish to conduct unpopular and often unjustifiable wars, engaging in borrowing tied directly to that purpose is unlikely to succeed.

Raising taxes to fight a war also requires at least some public agreement with the policy because tax-raising politicians may well be voted out if the war is unpopular. For politicians the downside of raising taxes (like the downside of using conscription to obtain soldiers rather than paying them market wages) is that it is an obvious and painful grab for resources by the state. Taxes make the costs of war very visible and spread them across the whole population. (Conscription is very visible, but more concentrated on the draftees.) From the standpoint of political actors, it would be preferable to raise the necessary resources in a way that is much less obvious and therefore has less potential for political conflict. Whenever politicians can disguise and/or delay the true costs of their programs, they will do so. This is where the monetary system enters the picture.

Governments that can either create money directly or use regulation to force banks to provide the resources will be able to conduct war more often and with less political resistance than those that cannot.

From 1791 to 1811, the federal government had partial ownership of the First Bank of the United States, which did not charter or regulate banks, but instead produced a limited amount of currency and served as the government's bank. With the completion of the War of 1812, it became convenient for the federal government to have such a bank in operation again, and so the Second Bank of the United States was created in 1816 (lasting until 1836).

In 1863 the federal (Union) government for the first time offered charters for individual banks. With charters came regulations, one of which was the requirement that bank-issued currency be backed with U.S. government bonds. Whenever a federally chartered bank wanted to give its customers paper currency, it had to purchase such bonds, whose face value slightly exceeded the value of the currency, and then present them to the Comptroller of the Currency in Washington, who then printed the bank's notes. Aside from the effect on war finance discussed below, this cumbersome process was the root of the periodic currency panics that struck the post-Civil War banking system and ultimately led to the Federal Reserve System as the "solution" in 1913.

Guaranteed Bond Market

The stated rationale for the bond-collateral requirement was that it provided safety in case the bank failed and could not redeem its notes in gold. However, Congress also knew that the requirement would, in theory, create a guaranteed market for U.S. government bonds, which in turn would enable the Union government to have revenue to pay for the Civil War. Interestingly, when the federal government first offered the charters, almost no banks signed up; they kept their state charters because the federal charters offered no advantages and some minor disadvantages. Not content to lose that way of financing the war, Congress quickly passed a 10 percent tax on the banknotes of state-chartered banks. This now made federal charters notably more advantageous, leading a significant number of banks to apply. By the end of the 1860s federally chartered banks were proliferating and the large market for the bonds had come to pass. Between the original bond-collateral requirements and punitive tax on the state-chartered banks, the federal government used its power over the monetary system to ensure a market for bonds to pay for the Civil War.

Although the Great Depression was itself not a war, it certainly took on many of the characteristics of one, as the Roosevelt administration attempted to pass legislation and programs that were of questionable constitutionality and popularity. Like many wartime activities, it is plausible to argue that the New Deal programs benefited business constituencies more than the public at large. (Halliburton's role in the Iraq War provides a contemporary example of this sort of damaging corporate capitalism.) The administration's outlawing of private gold holdings in 1934 and the Banking Act of 1935, which created a variety of new federal interventions—the most notable giving the Federal Reserve new powers to create money through bond purchases—were both examples of using the monetary system to provide resources for a growing state. These powers were certainly useful when the government took the country into World War II a few years later.

Vietnam Inflation

The Vietnam era provides an example of a direct connection between inflation of the money supply and war finance. The Johnson administration made a conscious decision to finance the Vietnam War through inflation rather than higher taxes. The increase in money was accomplished by buying up government bonds from financial institutions; as payment, the government simply credited the institutions' accounts. This saved interest payments on those bonds and therefore also allowed the government to issue additional Treasury securities at the same total interest cost they had before the new money was created. The bottom line was that the Fed created additional money and allowed Congress to run more debt at no greater cost in the process.

At the time Federal Reserve Notes held by foreign central banks were still redeemable in gold at the Fed. As a result of the inflation (depreciating dollar) of the late 1960s, the Fed saw a massive flow back of Federal Reserve Notes from foreign governments, which began to reduce U.S. gold holdings. This drain of gold reserves led President Nixon to close the "gold window" in 1971, breaking the last remaining link between the dollar and gold. With excess supplies of money no longer generating any direct negative economic consequences for the Fed, the even-greater inflation and macroeconomic disorder that characterized the rest of the 1970s and '80s were no surprise.

Thus the need to finance the Vietnam War led to increased government control over money, which led to macroeconomic disorder (much as we saw in the late nineteenth-century banking panics), which in turn led to calls for more government intervention. Aside from the direct problems of financing the warfare state, increased control of money by the state often sets off what Ludwig von Mises called the "interventionist dynamic," in which one state intervention has negative unintended consequences that create the perceived need for more intervention. The business cycle is one example of this process.

One can tell similar histories about the creation of central banks and other forms of government monetary intervention in other countries across the globe. The need to fund war and empire has been behind the creation of many a central bank. It's easier to pay for bombs and bullets if you have the equivalent of a printing press at your fingertips.

Because inflation's costs are normally dispersed, subtle, and longer term, politicians find it a politically more palatable way to raise revenues, especially for unpopular causes. This point is even more important because politicians play up the very short-term benefits of inflation as if they were a panacea for a stalled economy. Persuading the public to accept those ephemeral and small short-term gains without an understanding of the long-term costs is part of the general deception often used to promote empire-building wars.

Why COIN is
Doomed to Failure

Shaukat Qadir

Shaukat Qadir is a retired Pakistani Army brigadier and university instructor; he is also former founder and Vice President (and, briefly, former President) of the Islamabad Policy Research Institute.

How Peace

Counter Insurgency Operations, or COIN, are destined to fail—particularly when carried out by militaries in terrains of countries other than their own, or against ethnic/racial groups which are unequal citizens of their own country; the only question is: why?

Forgive me for starting with the very basics: if there is a *counter*insurgency operation, this means there is an insurgency. If there is an insurgency, it could only begin if the people have a complaint, which they cannot convey to those who are in the corridors of power. Therefore, they have taken recourse in the use of force, to make their complaint(s) audible to the blind and deaf individuals manning the corridors of power.

Once this premise is clearly stated, it becomes obvious that retaliatory use of force is not, and cannot, be the solution. This is not to deny that, more often than not, retaliatory use of force is essential to COIN, but the use of force cannot even win battles, let alone the war; all it can do is to buy time. The solution lies solely in removing the complaint(s) that gave rise to the insurgency. All other aspects of COIN revolve around this; it is the essential ingredient.

That is why COIN, based on retaliatory use of force, is doomed before it begins!

My first exposure: the former East Pakistan, now Bangladesh

In early 1971, as a newly promoted captain of the Frontier Force Regiment (Infantry), I volunteered for "Combat Adventure Training" in what was then East Pakistan. I landed in Dacca on April 15th for a two-month stint. I was fortunate, inasmuch as I was involved in very few inland operations and spent the bulk of my stay on the Indian border; beating off attacks by *Mukti Bahini* (Freedom Fighters), who were trained and occasionally assisted by Indian troops. Although we were under strict orders not to cross the border into India, I would periodically do so.

Each raid I carried out gained us a few days of peace, until I finally got fed up. We raided one of the training camps, destroyed it and returned with an Indian Army prisoner of war. Pleased with me, my superiors kept getting my stay extended. Fortunately, I was finally ordered back on October 16th and returned to fight the real war in West Pakistan, before the surrender.

I was well shy of my 24th birthday when I arrived in Dacca, and still a month short of it when I left. I had arrived a cocky youngster, over-confident, sure that we were in the right in quelling these "rebels." Even though I had been involved in only five operations inland, they sufficed to introduce me to the horrors of the kind of war we were engaged in. I wish I could plead innocence, but in all honesty I cannot. I would like to believe that my "excesses" were less stark than most of my colleagues, but I cannot even swear to that!

I left Dacca, a disillusioned war veteran, gloomily convinced that we had lost East Pakistan. Even at that stage of life, I realized that peoples cannot be governed by force. However, it was not until my Uncle discussed my experiences with me that the bulb finally lit. Finding myself cornered, and on the defensive to his questions, I replied in some heat, "But Uncle, *they* started it, what else could *we* do?" Very calmly, with half a smile, he responded, "You have spoken the words of a Sage and decided the outcome. When you club them all to say 'They started' and 'We ended'; 'They' are no longer part of 'Us'!"

I was shocked then; the words remain seared in my mind to this date.

Balochistan

Zulfiqar Ali Bhutto, the then-prime minister of Pakistan, was a feudal autocrat who could not brook competition. Nawab Akbar Bugti of Balochistan was Bhutto's mirror image. Bhutto sought to restrict him by doing away with the traditional tribal hierarchical system in Balochistan. Though politico-economic deprivation of the Baloch was the real cause, in 1973 Bhutto's attempt to change the tribal system triggered an insurgency in Balochistan.

After the war, I had been posted to a brigade HQ on a staff assignment. However, when my unit was ordered to move to Balochistan on COIN operations, I opted to accompany it.

A few years older now, and a veteran of COIN in East Pakistan, a war in West Pakistan, and numerous small actions thereafter, I was considerably more sober and had lost most of my cockiness.

Balochistan was very different; East Pakistan had been green, marshy, interspersed with rivers, dense jungles; Balochistan was a vast expanse of hilly desert, very sparsely populated. The people were harsh, bred to a harsh life in an inhospitable terrain. Water was so scarce that there were places where humans and animals shared the water of the same pond.

However, this COIN was being conducted differently. Then-Prime Minister Zulfiqar Ali Bhutto was a devious, cunning individual, but he had witnessed the loss of East Pakistan and had no desire to lose more of his territory.

Nonetheless, there were still instances of excessive use of force and few, if any, were punished. Despite this, the insurgency ran its brief course and was finally resolved peacefully in 1976. Troops returned to established cantonments, and the Baloch tribal system was restored. There was nothing to indicate that there had been an insurgency, except that the army had constructed some new cantonments deep inside Balochistan.

But the most significant aspect here is that the use of force was restricted to "creating conditions for a negotiated settlement," which is why it succeeded.

Complaints from the insurgent tribes were addressed and resolved through politico-administrative means, and NOT by the use of force.

Indian Kashmir

Ironically, after the partition of India in 1948, Indian Kashmir had its own prime minister for some years. Relations with India had remained troubled from 1948 onwards; but it was the blatant ballot-rigging during the 1987 elections that triggered an unrest in Indian Kashmir. Indian state forces in Kashmir were reinforced, peaceful demonstrations were met with force by Indian state troops, and the violence began to increase, cyclically and incrementally.Kashmiri protestors began to disappear, only to be found dead in some ditch. Women and children were maltreated. Rumors of rape of women in isolated areas grew in numbers, until finally, in 1989, Indian Kashmir rose up in arms against the state repression.

I had served in Azad Kashmir (Free Kashmir, as the portion of Kashmir under Pakistani control is titled by Pakistan) as a youngster, and had participated in the usual border skirmishes that ran through entire summers, since winters were snowed in. However, in 1992, when I took command of the brigade in Kel, the remotest corner of Azad Kashmir, on the banks of the breathtakingly beautiful Neelum River, Indian Kashmir was in the throes of the uprising. And Pakistan, officially promising only moral and political assistance, was in reality helping train and arm the insurgents. I was now to witness COIN as one helping the insurgent!

What a different perspective: state forces were clearly the oppressor; the insurgents were clearly fighting for self-determination and their rights to life, liberty, and pursuits of happiness.However, I could also hark back to my earlier experiences for ironic comparison!

In many ways, it was a humbling experience. People from all walks of life— university professors, their students, physicians, laborers—all crossed over from Indian Kashmir for a couple of months of training, to return and fight for their freedom. The experience was both humbling and inspiring.

Depending on the perspective, I had arrived at just the right or just the wrong moment in time. Either way, I was destined to witness this idealistic effort being corrupted.

When the Indian Kashmiri's struggle for freedom had begun in 1989, it was indigenous and, although led by the majority, the Kashmiri Muslims, the movement ran across that ethno-religious divide, also enjoying the tacit, passive (and occasionally active) support of the Kashmiri Sikhs and Hindus. Being inquisitive by nature, I accompanied the Kashmiri freedom fighters on a few of their forays inside Indian Kashmir. Like I said, there was a sense of *déjà vu,* coupled with the feeling that Alice must have had, when she went through the looking glass!

I could see myself through the eyes of the East Pakistanis and the Baloch, and what I saw was an ugly sight.

And so I had arrived, at the cusp of the Indian Kashmiri freedom struggle. I witnessed it while it was pure and uncorrupted, and then saw it being converted from a legitimate movement for the freedom of the peoples of Kashmir into a *Jihad* (crusade), a purely Muslim movement, one motivated by hatred, revenge and tyranny. I witnessed the arrival of increasing numbers of non-Kashmiri Pakistanis, as well as Muslims from foreign lands, including veterans of the Afghan freedom movement against Soviet occupation.

The latter were people used to violence and its indiscriminate use. They would terrorize the Kashmiri Muslim, who was not an active freedom fighter. They would terrorize the Hindu Kashmiri Pandits, who were an integral part of the Kashmiri culture, forcing them to migrate to mainland India. They were not above rape or torture. In other words, they were no better than the Indian state forces. The Kashmiri was damned either way.

This cooptation caused the greatest damage to the Indian Kashmiri freedom struggle. Apart from *Jihad* in Kashmir being unacceptable to the international community (for fear that it could become contagious in other Muslim majority countries!), the conduct of the non-Kashmiris in Indian Kashmir served to legitimize Indian state forces' use of force and, once again, Pakistan was the "bad guy."

It became obvious to me that, by corrupting the pure freedom struggle in Indian Kashmir, the Pakistani Government had sentenced its own death. Recent developments leading to the Indian Kashmiri *Intifada* might change things; time will tell.

Afghanistan

Chronologically, I witnessed the Afghan freedom struggle more than a decade earlier than the struggle in Indian Kashmir. In 1979, when Soviet forces moved in to occupy Afghanistan, my unit officers were among the many tasked to carry out a reconnaissance of the Durand Line (the de-facto border between Afghanistan and Pakistan). Sitting on top of the Nawa Pass on the Durand Line, I witnessed a Soviet attack on an Afghan village and the ferocity with which Afghans fought back. I was struck by the placidity and calm of the women, the elderly, and children crossing over to Pakistan. They were fearless and tearless. This was not a people who would accept defeat.

However, it was years later that I was to see things firsthand.

In 1993, I was posted from Kel to command the brigade in Thal, in the Kurram Agency in our tribal area. This was the pre-Taliban era of chaos in Afghanistan. During my stay there, I saw the arrival of the Taliban and their initial period of just and representative rule. I was posted out in 1995 and I saw them change, from a distance, and then again as I kept returning after I retired in 1998.

In 1996, Osama bin Laden arrived in Afghanistan. Shortly thereafter, things began to change. From a strictly representative rule, the Taliban turned autocratic and later despotic. A very strict version of the extremist *Wahabiist* Islam was imposed. Women again ceased working in public places, even schools. The hitherto well-mannered "Religious Police" suddenly found itself all-powerful. They could, and very frequently, did stop people in the streets, measuring the male for the size of his beard and inspecting the female for her dress. The slightest violation, real or imagined, of the policeman's interpretation of Islamic edicts could result in the individual (male or female) receiving public lashing on the buttocks. The proud Afghan stood publicly humiliated.

I witnessed some of these acts of Taliban oppression, and the disillusionment of the Afghan and our Pashtun. The Taliban's downfall was greeted with jubilation on both sides of the Durand Line in 2001. However, the jubilation did not last long. The Americans had entered at a moment in time when everything was in their favor. Afghans and Pakistani Pashtun were ready to fight alongside them, and garland them for relieving them of Taliban oppression. The Afghans would have pointed out Taliban and Taliban supporters, and would have led US forces to the cave in Tora Bora, where Osama bin Laden and the Al-Qaida hierarchy were to be found.

Regrettably, US forces did not believe this. They treated all Afghans as "probable Taliban," with suspicion and contempt. In their desire to search for Taliban, they would enter houses where only females and children were present—an unacceptable violation of local culture. They arrested anybody who they thought looked suspicious, often laying their hands on females in the presence of their men. The Afghan was again humiliated and, what was worse, this was humiliation suffered not at the hands of fellow Afghans, but at the hands of a *Kafir* (non-believer) *Farangi* (fair-skinned). This was as bad as the period of Soviet occupation! What was different?

Soon, disillusionment with the occupying American army resulted in the beginning of another Afghan Freedom Movement—this time against the American forces of occupation. I witnessed the revolt in our tribal areas, by tribes that wanted to fight the American Army of Occupation, as they had done against the Soviets, but were being prevented by Gen Musharaf's government; so they revolted against Pakistan, "The American Lackey."

Yes, Pakistanis are suffering due to the extent of our government's support to the U.S. government. Now, of course, we are back in the dock on both sides: the U.S. government calls the Pakistan government a fickle ally, and our extremists target us to avenge themselves against the U.S.—they believe that, not only the Pakistan government, but also the Pakistani people—anybody not actively engaged in combat with the U.S.—are, in effect, an extension of the U.S.!

Even before joining the army, I was familiar with our tribal areas; however, having spent much of my service in and around them, I made lots of friends. With many of these, I am in contact to date. So permit me to conclude my experiences with the American venture in Afghanistan.

Why doesn't the US learn?

Of all governments in the world, the U.S. has more experience of COIN than any other: Korea, Vietnam, Nicaragua (by stoking and assisting the insurgency), and now Afghanistan and Iraq. And yet it doesn't learn. Why?

Actually, this question was answered in the opening three paragraphs of this chapter. The U.S. experience of COIN is confined to countries other than its own. What is more, as a state, there is an unbearable degree of arrogance in the U.S.'s conduct, and an indifference to the loss of non-American lives. Militarily, it has begun to rely overwhelmingly on its firepower.

By 2001, Afghans were fed up with the Taliban oppression and the constant humiliation at the hands of their representatives. As news of the imminent U.S. invasion grew to a certainty, not only Afghans, also Pakistani Pashtuns, were jubilant and celebrating their forthcoming "liberation" from the Taliban.

Everything was favorable for the U.S. invasion. If they had understood the mood of the people, they could have just walked in, smiling, and Afghans would have taken them to the Taliban, Taliban supporters, and Al-Qaida. But the U.S. troops didn't trust any Afghan, least of all Pashtuns. They only trusted their allies, The Northern Alliance.

Let us take an overview of the U.S. invasion of Afghanistan from a purely military perspective, starting with the famous Clausewitzian dictum that "war is an extension of policy" (meaning that all wars are intended to achieve a political purpose, one unattainable without going to war). Therefore, a war must have a clearly defined political objective. From this political objective, the military spells out its "military aim," through which the political aim is intended to be achieved. Clearly, therefore, if the political aim is not sufficiently lucid, the military is bound to err in defining the "how"—the military aim!

The U.S. invaded Afghanistan with the announced political aim of destroying/dismantling Al-Qaida and its leadership, and bringing about a regime-change to oust the Taliban oppressive regime, which was harboring Osama bin Laden and Al-Qaida; it was a moral and laudable aim. (There may have also been undisclosed ulterior imperial motives of acquiring strategic bases to encircle the Russian Bear and the emerging threat of China, as well as accessing the untapped resources of Central Asia.)

But if the professed objectives were the political aims, it could not have meant waging a war on the Afghan people or enslaving them—obviously not! What is more, a regime change could only work if it was people-friendly and, if the ulterior motives were to be realized, it would be possible only if the people were happy with the Americans.

So everything was just right: the environment was favorable, the Afghans wanted to be relieved of Taliban, even Pakistan and Saudi Arabia, staunch Taliban supporters, backed the U.S. invasion; for whatever reasons. What could possibly go wrong? But something obviously did!

In fairness to the American forces, it needs to be pointed out that there is a difficulty to fighting forces indistinguishable from the local population; in this case, though, the local population would willingly have identified the Taliban supporters to the invading U.S. troops in 2001, if the invading forces had only trusted them. Unfortunately they didn't, and are paying the price of that error to date!

What's more, if the U.S. state is arrogant, its military is even more so. Military plans, therefore, end up being made with the following mindsets: 1) we are superior in all respects; 2) we are indifferent to the loss of lives of the local population; 3) American loss of life is to be minimized at all costs, and any hint of threat is to be treated as real, to be responded to with excessive use of force;

4) our military machine has the deadliest weapons and can and will be employed at the discretion of all levels of command; and 5) since we are all powerful, we should be able to destroy the enemy in the shortest span of time.

The last of the above is frequently compounded by political expediency. In the case of Afghanistan, Bush (touting his image of a "war-time President") was pushing the military to get it over with ASAP.

Had cooler heads prevailed, the invading forces would have delayed the invasion by a couple of months, to obtain accurate intelligence of who-was-who and who-was-where. Intelligence, that most invaluable ingredient of all military operations, was missing. Had they bided their time to find out who-was-where, a number of precise strikes could easily have "taken out" the Al-Qaida and Taliban leadership. Then, with the active support of the locals, Taliban supporters could have been identified and dealt with. Afghans would have been embracing U.S. forces!

But the U.S. went in like the proverbial bull in the china-shop, and turned loose their allies, the Northern Alliance, which butchered Afghans indiscriminately, as did the invading U.S.-led forces. Those who weren't butchered were humiliated. (American forces were even unaware that in December, 2001 they had Mulla Omer surrounded in a village close to Kandahar. The intrepid Mulla Abdul Ghani Baradar rescued him on a motorbike, dressing Omer in a woman's veil!)

Because of their conduct, by mid-2002, Afghans had become disillusioned with the U.S., which began in late 2002 what should have been called "Another Afghan Freedom Movement against Foreign Occupation." But that title was as unacceptable to the Pentagon, CIA, and U.S. administration, as it was to the 'free' U.S. media. Instead it was intentionally and falsely referred to as "the resurgence of Al-Qaida and the Taliban."

While the occasional scandal relating to the conduct of U.S. troops would surface, only to be played down, it was Wikileaks that finally broke the bubble.

Some Examples

In August, 2008, the *New York Times* carried a report in which a UN investigation established that American troops had killed 90 civilians, including 60 children during an attack on one single village!!

In "The Kill Team," published in *Rolling Stone Magazine* on March 27, 2011, Mark Boal revealed the exploits of 'Bravo Company,'\ in which Staff Sergeant David Bram and Corporal Jeremy Morlock on one fine morning in early 2010 decided to chalk up kills of innocent Afghans. They picked them at random during their patrols or 'cordon and search' operations, took them to a ditch and shot them, collecting tips of little fingers as souvenirs and taking hundreds of photographs. Everyone was in on the kills, many others joined in. The whole company was jubilant, taking photographs of each other with the dead bodies; one smiling, the other rakishly smoking a cigarette!

No effort was made to stop or discipline these men; in fact, all officers of Bravo Company helped cover for them, even as they continued their killing spree. Finally, when one of their colleagues 'ratted' on them, they threatened to kill him on their next outing. Even that was covered up, but fortunately for the rat, the story broke before his elimination.

According to Boal, Gen McChrystal and Hamid Karzai learned of this scandal in May, 2010. Both joined in the cover up, destroying whatever documents, disks, hardware, software, photographs, and any other incriminatory evidence that could be found; meanwhile, the killing continued.

In early April, 2011, Morlock was finally sentenced to twenty-four years, although no action is being initiated against any officer at any level! Boal concludes his exposé with this:

"Toward the end of Morlock's interview, the conversation turned to the mindset that had allowed the killings to occur. 'None of us in the platoon—the platoon leader, the platoon sergeant—no one gives a fuck about these people,' Morlock said.

"Then he leaned back in his chair and yawned, summing up the way his superiors viewed the people of Afghanistan. 'Some shit goes down,' he said, 'you're gonna get a pat on the back from your platoon sergeant: Good job. Fuck 'em.'"

In another incident in 2010, American helicopter-borne snipers killed nine children gathering wood outside a village close to Kandahar. An ex-Marine immediately described the act as deliberate murder. According to him, with the technology available, there was no possible way for trained snipers to mistake 9-to-13-yearolds gathering wood, for armed militants!

Herat is a non-Pashtun, predominantly Darri speaking province. It has always been considered among the most peaceful areas in Afghanistan; no turbulence of any kind. Gul Khan has a small land holding, not in a far flung village, but only a dozen miles out of town. He has a harrowing tale to tell. He had heard of atrocities committed by U.S. troops, but always thought these were exaggerated. In early 2009, he saw a convoy headed towards Herat, and some five vehicles broke away to approach him while he was tilling his lands. He is not certain, but thinks that the troops were American.

He greeted them warily and was addressed by a soldier with stripes on his shoulders, in Pushto. He responded in rather broken Pushto, since he spoke Darri. Immediately, he was thrown to the ground, handcuffed and the soldiers began to beat him up, shouting 'Pakistani xxxx'! His wife and sons, aged eight and six at that time, all ran out screaming. They too were greeted with expletives and slapped; when he tried to help his family, someone broke both his arms. Fortunately, a neighbor who was fluent in Pushto came up and begged that Gul and his family be released.

A large crowd of local neighbors, hearing the hue and cry, began to approach when one of the soldiers let loose a full magazine from his automatic weapon; after this, the soldiers hurriedly left. Gul was still in handcuffs and in agony. When the handcuffs were taken off and he finally got to see a doctor, he remained in splints for over four months. Today, his right arm is almost fully functional but the left one is withering, below the elbow.

Gul has now become a Taliban supporter. He explains, "We now grow poppy; when government troops approach, Taliban fight them and defend us. Taliban buy the poppy from us at the same price that I could get (in Pakistan), without any deduction. I have requested them that each time they kill an American, I will pay whatever they want, for his balls, but they laughed and told me that they kill the *Kafir* (infidel) in battle, and we will force him to leave our country. But they promised me that if they capture an American alive, they will give him to me as a gift; I live only for that day. May Allah bless them!"

Asked why he had not gone to the Afghan government, he spits before commenting in contempt, "Karzai? He is not Pashtun. He lends his ass not only to any American, but also to any Tajik or Uzbek who wants it! I will let the Americans rape each member of my family before going to him. Even [Burhannuddin] Rabbani [a Tajik] is better."

Such references to Karzai can be heard through the length and breadth of Afghanistan; across the ethnic divide. Even non-Pashtuns holding office under him speak of him derogatively!

In a mid-sized town in the Pashtun region, a middle-aged, middle-class, bald, short, clean-shaven, rotund, unctuous shopkeeper, who himself has a modest landholding as well, looks nothing like an Afghan warrior, and speaks fluent English. He has a son studying in the States and a daughter in a Pakistani university. He had this to say last year, "When the Taliban came, we welcomed them as liberators, then they began to show their true colors and we had no choice but to suffer in silence. When Americans came, we welcomed them, expecting that we would be freed from oppression; but they are far worse, and they are infidels. They treat us like animals. I can speak their language but they deliberately abuse me in my hearing. They killed my father last year (2008) in a 'chance' encounter, because he opposed them vocally and abused them in Pushto in retaliation. Karzai is worse than the Americans. He is. If I have to choose between the US and Karzai on one hand and the Taliban; I will choose our home-grown evil; the lesser of the two. Long live Taliban."

My last narration is the crowning one. Zoe Gul is a Hazarvi, now living in Quetta. He belongs to a village near Kandahar. Anyone who knows about the Hazarvis is aware that, throughout history, they have suffered at the hands of the Pashtun, Afghan and Pakistani. In the early winter of 2009, some American troops surrounded Zoe's house when it was approaching dusk. Zoe's brother and newly married wife were visiting.

The soldiers searched the house and, finding nothing incriminating, spoke to each other smilingly, eyeing Zoe's attractive sister-in-law. They asked Zoe's brother and his wife to accompany them. On inquiry, the soldiers politely told him that since his brother was a visitor, they were taking him and his wife for some routine questions.

Zoe's brother was never found but his wife returned the next morning, disheveled and in torn clothes, witnessed by many villagers. Zoe knew what had happened, but he never asked her. With generations of suffering, they dared not even initiate an inquiry, and suffered in silence with the villager's sympathy. When Zoe saw his sister-in-law getting big with child, he decided to migrate to Quetta, where he had relatives. His sister-in-law gave birth to a dark-complexioned, curly-haired child in July of 2010. She committed suicide the same night.

You just have to wander through the remote villages. The stories are endless. If a genuine poll were conducted in Afghanistan today, you would get a 99 percent result to the question, "What, in your opinion, is the problem in Afghanistan?" The response: "U.S. and Karzai."

So please, U.S. government, go. Stop messing your COIN in Afghanistan. All you continue to breed is regional insecurity and increasing hatred for all Americans. We don't deserve the insecurity; and the average American certainly doesn't deserve to be hated for what the U.S. government does around the world.

Mere Anarchy
Loosed Upon the World

Bretigne Shaffer

Bretigne Shaffer was a journalist in Asia for many years. She is the author of
Memoirs of a Gaijin *and* Why Mommy Loves the State. *She blogs at*
www.bretigne.com.

As I write this, my son is running around the house naked, even though I've
asked him twice to put his clothes on. I can hear the bathroom sink swooshing
on and off as he makes a swimming pool for his zoo animals. I weigh getting up
and possibly waking his baby sister, who is sleeping on my chest, against the
lesser likelihood that he will catch a cold from running around the house naked
and wet. I decide to stay put. The swooshing continues.

I wonder how a man named Scott Oglesby would deal with my son's
exuberance, his lack of "respect for authority," his occasional noisiness. Last
December, 2010, Oglesby, a police officer, was at Stevenson Elementary School
in Bloomington, Illinois, when he heard a seven-year-old special-needs boy
having a seizure. Oglesby ran into the room where the boy was being restrained
by a school psychologist, shouted "you're giving me a headache!" and grabbed
the boy by the throat, holding him up in the air until he turned red, before
throwing him down in a chair. Oglesby is now on "restricted duty," but no
criminal charges will be filed against him.

I'd like to think that cases like Oglesby's are rare exceptions. But every
week there seems to be another story about someone being shot with a taser over
a traffic violation, or for not responding the way the officer wanted them to.
There was the paralyzed man thrown from his wheelchair by an officer in a
Florida jail; the New York City cop who stopped a woman from driving her
dying daughter to the hospital; the mentally handicapped teenager who was
tasered to death after waving a stick around; and, in May of 2010, in another
increasingly common militarized raid on a family's home, the shooting death of
seven-year-old Aiyana Jones as she lay sleeping next to her grandmother. (There
is little doubt as to what happened: the 20 officers who burst into the girl's home
had brought with them a camera crew for a reality-TV show.)

> *"Turning and turning in the widening gyre*
> *The falcon cannot hear the falconer;*
> *Things fall apart; the center cannot hold;*
> *Mere anarchy is loosed upon the world..."*

When I first read Yeats' "The Second Coming," years ago, I saw in the first
stanza a lament about the loss of a central authority, of political authority. Now I
think he meant something else.

I have to believe that there was a time when people would have responded to the likes of Officer Oglesby by unceremoniously dipping him in tar, tossing a bucket of feathers over his head and casting him out from civilized society. Today he and his ilk are given "administrative leave" at best, and are soon back on the streets to endanger the rest of us. At the same time, more than half a million Americans sit in prison for the crime of using or selling substances the government disapproves of. Our nation has the highest per-capita prison population in the world by a very wide margin. Yet people like Officer Oglesby and the officers who killed Aiyana Jones do not count among the incarcerated. We are told that it is a punishable crime to ingest certain prohibited substances, a bigger crime to sell them. But, it is not a crime to shoot a seven-year-old girl in the head while she lies sleeping next to her grandmother. We have become deeply confused as to who the criminals are.

*   *   *

The question "why peace?" seems a silly one. Doesn't everyone want peace? Isn't that one thing we can all agree on? Everyone says they want peace, but very few are truly opposed to war or other forms of aggression. When she was US ambassador to the UN, Madeleine Albright famously told the world that whatever was gained from the economic embargo of Iraq was "worth" the deaths of half a million children. But I bet she says she wants peace. The assertion—almost always conditional—has become meaningless.

As the United States government prepared to invade Iraq in late 2002 and early 2003, I did everything I knew to do to prevent it from happening. I engaged in debate, I signed petitions, I handed out pamphlets in sub-zero temperatures, and on February 15th, 2003, I marched in New York City, along with hundreds of thousands of others who were opposed to the war. On my way to the demonstration, I wondered how many would show up. I had the sense that I was in a minority, that most people didn't care that much, or were too busy living their lives to do something like march for peace.

When I stepped out of the subway station, I was taken aback. Pouring into the street from every direction were people of all ages carrying signs and waving banners. As far as I could see, the streets were filled with people who shared my desire to prevent this war. I started to believe that maybe the sheer force of our humanity, our collective "no!" to more bloodshed, could prevent it. Barely a month later, the U.S. government began its invasion and occupation of Iraq.

I learned from that experience that demonstrations do not prevent wars. I was heartened by the outpouring of public opposition to war, but realized that we would need to come up with something much better than an appeal to those who are committed to waging war if we were to change anything. I also realized that most who said they were "anti-war" were really "anti-some-wars"—and not only out of political partisanship, but out of a desire to be taken seriously.

Nobody wants to come out and say that ALL war is wrong, that it is never justified. That would be unreasonable. Everyone knows that war is sometimes necessary. Everyone knows that sometimes there are just evil governments that invade other countries or commit atrocities against the people living under them.

It is awful, it may even be unthinkable, but even if war is never good, there are times when it is necessary, and the practical and right thing to do is not to shy away from this reality but to be an adult and make the tough decision. Everyone knows that.

The problem with what everyone knows, though, is that it is quite often laced with omission and untruth.

Most children in American schools are taught very carefully about war, and why it is sometimes necessary. This lesson has to be very carefully planned and executed, because much earlier, those same children have been taught that "two wrongs don't make a right." Adults might rightly fear that such children would not find it easy to reconcile the two positions. So we are taught about the American Revolution. We are taught about the Civil War. And then, at some point (for me it was in seventh grade) we are taught about World War II, the Holocaust, and the horrors of the concentration camps. I had nightmares about stormtroopers and gas chambers after those lessons, and I'm sure other children did too. I don't remember precisely what those seventh-grade history books told me, but I came out of that class believing that the U.S. government went to war to save the Jewish people from the gas chambers, that it was right and just and that every once in a while, government does the right thing and this was one of those times. I'm sure other children did too.

Only later did I learn that saving the Jews was not the reason for the U.S. entering the war; that the government that supposedly cared so much for Jewish victims of the Nazi regime would not allow those same people to land in America—an act that might have saved many hundreds of thousands or even millions of lives without any military action at all; that the justification for US entry into the war, the Japanese attack on Pearl Harbor, was not an unprovoked act, as we had been taught; that the nuclear bombs were not dropped on that country in order to end the war; that the Japanese government had been trying to surrender but balked at doing so unconditionally, a demand the US later easily revoked after the real purpose of the bombings of Hiroshima and Nagasaki—a show of force to the USSR—had been achieved.

It was only much, much later that I even thought to ask the question, relevant only to the version of history that had been presented to me: Why does saving innocent people in Germany justify killing innocent people in Japan? I still have yet to hear a satisfying answer to my question.

Far from proving the need for military intervention to deal with murderous madmen, the example of WWII shows precisely how the institution of war and the special rules that sustain it protect such sociopathic killers—as long as they are on the winning side. Former Secretary of Defense Robert McNamara has admitted as much, saying that the firebombing of Japanese cities and the nuclear attacks on Hiroshima and Nagasaki would have been considered war crimes had the U.S. lost the war. They still should be. "What makes it immoral if you lose and not immoral if you win?" asked McNamara, who by all accounts spent his later years haunted by his roles both in World War II and in the Vietnam War. Of course there is no answer to this question that makes any sense. So why are the rest of us not haunted? Why do so many of us refuse to apply consistent standards of morality to those who make war?

* * *

My son is now making a jam sandwich in the kitchen. Every once in a while he comes back to show me what he's done, blueberry jam smeared across his face and hands, and I tell him to go wash his hands so he doesn't get it all over everything. He ignores my request and runs back into the kitchen, squealing with delight. He is "defying authority," and I am relieved. Too many of the problems I see in the world are the direct result of obedience and respect for authority.

We have lost our center. The little boy who was choked by Officer Oglesby understood that what that man was doing to him was wrong. "Mommy, didn't that police officer's mommy say he shouldn't do that to people?" he asked later. That little boy has more clarity than the adults whose comments defending such abuse litter the blogosphere. He still knows the difference between right and wrong. It has yet to be wrenched from him by the system meant to "educate" him.

When I was in high school, someone once pointed to a bunch of kids who were teasing a mentally handicapped boy. "See? That's what happens in anarchy!" He announced proudly, apparently demolishing my arguments against the state. Incredibly, it didn't occur to me to point out that this wasn't happening in "anarchy" but in the very controlled and authoritarian setting of a government school. It didn't occur to me to tell him about my experiences in a Montessori school, where such behavior was unheard of.

Maria Montessori believed that children have a natural instinct for learning and a natural instinct for civilized co-existence. When teachers do not interfere, children learn; when children are treated with respect, they naturally become respectful; when they are encouraged to resolve their conflicts peacefully, they do so. I went to school with a little boy who had Down Syndrome, and I never saw any child treat him with anything other than compassion and decency. In the years I spent there, I witnessed some conflicts, and even a few rare instances of someone being hit. But the stereotype of abusive, bullying playground behavior was an alien thing that I never even heard of until I entered public school.

There, the lessons were just the opposite: That children are savages and must have learning and respect forced upon them. Oddly, this is to be accomplished not by showing them respect, but by treating them as lesser beings, while demanding that they respect those more powerful than them. Is it any wonder they soon start bullying those smaller than themselves? The lesson here—the lesson that goes on to inform adult decisions, institutions and problem solving out in the world—is that might makes right. Children are told to respect authority simply because it is authority. Simply because grown-ups are bigger and can punish them if they don't obey. Nothing more.

An old Cherokee tale tells us that there are two "wolves" fighting inside each of us, two opposing sides of human nature: Good vs. evil; peace vs. aggression; compassion vs. hatred. The battle between the two sides rages in each one of us, and the side that wins is the side that we feed. Most of what we call "education" feeds the bad wolves. It works against our better nature and feeds what is worst in us, allowing it to grow at the expense of what is best. It may be true that violence, hatred, and even cruelty each come from a place within our nature. But a healthy society does not exalt them. It does not try to magnify and expand the very worst of our nature, making it dominant. A healthy society discourages these attributes of human nature. We are not a healthy society and what we have become is unnatural.

It is hard to explain to people who have only known the culture of this kind of schooling that there is another way, not only of educating children, but of living in the world. It is hard to get them to see that things don't have to be the way they think they are, that it is within the nature of each of us to live peacefully. That the "law of the playground" is a lie and "Lord of the Flies" is a work of fiction. That there is always another way.

* * *

It was a long time before I really questioned the underlying premises of war: Primarily, that killing innocent people can ever be a legitimate form of self-defense or retaliation against a violent aggressor. At some point, I was presented with the absurd hypothetical thought experiments to which the apologists for war must always resort when asked to defend its morality. I was asked to believe that a bizarre set of circumstances, combined with a certainty of outcomes possible only in a purely academic construction, offer a passable analogy to the real-world situation faced by the war-makers. I was asked to accept the premise that killing is always the only possible solution and I was further asked to accept the assumption that the war-makers are concerned with preserving innocent life. Confronted with the question, I realized that yes, I would be willing to kill an innocent person in order to save myself or someone I loved. But I also realized that the act would still be a crime, though perhaps one mitigated by my necessity. In war, such crimes—all but the very few exceptions that prove the rule—are dismissed. In war, an act that ought only even be contemplated under a set of bizarre, highly unlikely, and strictly controlled circumstances is institutionalized and made routine.

Wars of aggression must always masquerade as defensive wars. From the Spanish-American war to Vietnam and now Iraq, we have all become familiar with the lies and propaganda used to justify what many call the "illegitimate" wars. That time after time these claims turn out to be false is no accident of history. This is the nature of the institution of war itself, which grants nearly unlimited powers to do violence to a single entity within a geographic sphere. To expect that the war machine thus spawned will act on behalf of anyone's interests other than those at its helm; to expect it to use its powers to promote freedom or to protect the lives of the innocent is to believe in fairy tales. Even support for the best of all possible "good wars" must necessarily have these fairy tales at its foundation.

To believe that war can ever be "good" is to believe not only that the academic hypotheticals are accurate representations of the real-world conflict and that violence is always the only solution, we must also believe in lies that are deeply ingrained in most of our psyches. One of the most pernicious of these, one that persists in the face of centuries of evidence to the contrary, is that governments act in the interests of the people they govern.

Americans seem particularly susceptible to this line of reasoning. We vote for the people who rule our lives, the logic goes, and therefore we control them and are responsible for what they do. Most of us cling to this line of thinking and no amount of crony bailouts, "Constitution-Free Zones," indefinite detentions without charge, SWAT-style raids on unarmed Americans in their homes, sexual molestation as a condition for air travel, or executive orders allowing for the murder of any American citizen at the whim of the president will convince us otherwise.

It's funny to me that so many in the anti-war movement fail to recognize this, insisting instead that the problem is one of undue corporate influence on government. Many of these people distrust corporate monopoly, yet have no problem with the monopoly powers granted to the far more deadly state. They seem to believe that, in the absence of corporate pressure, the state would suddenly begin to act in the interests of those it governs. Until anti-war activists begin to comprehend the danger inherent in granting a monopoly to a single entity to "protect" and "defend"—until they learn not to expect anything other than abuse of such a position—they will remain impotent in the face of the war machine.

This first big lie spawns another one: The lie of collective identification with the nations we live in and the governments that rule us. Believing in this allows us to absolve our own government of its crimes against innocent civilians who live under evil or repressive governments. For if we are responsible for the actions of our government, those civilians must likewise be responsible for the actions of theirs, and "we" are therefore justified in using violence against them. This bloodthirsty collectivist thinking prevents us from recognizing the enemy we have in common with those civilians: Not "their" government and not "our" government, but the very institution of the war-making state itself, and the privileged position it occupies in our societies.

Even Christian just-war theory carves out a unique moral code for the war-makers, laying out conditions under which it is acceptable to kill innocent people. Why? There are no such conditions allowed for the rest of us. No matter how threatened we may believe ourselves to be, we are never permitted by the laws of society to kill an innocent human being without serious consequences. This is the biggest lie of all. It is the lie that says in some situations murder is no longer a crime; it is the lie that tells us the lives of some people are worth less than the objectives of others. Made concrete, it is the lie that in the most real and final way possible allows some people to pass judgment on the value of the lives of others.

* * *

You wouldn't necessarily know it to see him tear around the house yelling at the top of his lungs, but my son is actually very civilized. He is reasonable and can be reasoned with. But he asks lots of questions and he wants to be treated with respect. I worry about how he will fare in a world that demands obsequious obedience to arbitrary authority. My daughter suffers from seizures. They are under control now, but what happens if she has a seizure when she is older and encounters an Officer Oglesby? Or is simply surrounded by people who are increasingly conditioned to see anything unusual as a threat? And whose first impulse is often violence?

Earlier this week, there was a story about some young American soldiers in Afghanistan who decided it would be "fun" to kill some civilians. After shooting a 15-year-old boy, they posed for pictures with his body. After the boy's grief-stricken father had identified his body, the platoon's leader, Staff Sgt. Calvin Gibbs, "started 'messing around with the kid,'" wrote *Rolling Stone* Magazine, "moving his arms and mouth and 'acting like the kid was talking.' Then, using a pair of razor-sharp medic's shears, he reportedly sliced off the dead boy's pinky finger and gave it to (pfc Andrew) Holmes, as a trophy for killing his first Afghan."

I find myself looking at people differently than I used to. I see young children in military fatigues and camouflage and I wonder what their parents can possibly be thinking. I wonder about the young men I see around me. How many of them are war veterans? The guy in front of me in line at the grocery store has a crew cut. Has he ever cut the finger off the corpse of someone's child that he killed? Does he still have it somewhere? What does he do now? Is he in law enforcement? Would he fire on unarmed Americans if ordered to? Or if he just felt like it? Grab my son by the throat and hold him up in the air if he annoyed him? I don't know who the people around me are anymore.

* * *

My own answer to the question "why peace?" is an easy one: *Because I unconditionally oppose the killing of children, and because I do not believe the lie that it is "sometimes necessary," or that it can ever be "justified."* I suppose I could add to this "...or innocent adults," since there is certainly nothing more moral or just about killing them. But for me it is the systematized and sanctioned killing of children that makes war intolerable.

"Serious people" aren't supposed to bring this up when talking of war. In the days and weeks leading up to a war, we don't hear the talking heads pontificating about the deaths of children. Instead, they ask how much the war will cost, how long it will last, what the goals are and whether "we" will accomplish them.

Nobody ever asks, "*How many children will we kill? How many will we maim? Mutilate? And how will we kill them? Will we blow them into little pieces with 'smart bombs'? Will we poison them with toxic sprays? Will our soldiers shoot them in the head? How many will they rape first? And how many children will die simply because they no longer have access to clean drinking water, or because the hospitals have been destroyed?*"

To ask these kinds of questions is to reveal oneself as a "kook," "naïve," a "bleeding heart" and "unrealistic," and to lose any hope of being taken seriously in the debate. Yet what could possibly be more serious?

Among the footage from the US war on Iraq, there is a scene in an Iraqi hospital. In it, a man carries the body of a baby that is either dying or already dead. Not because the baby has been shot or because his or her home was bombed, but because as a result of the UN-imposed economic embargo, there is no medicine available to treat the baby's condition. The look on the man's face as he carries the bundled up child helplessly should haunt anyone who so much as missed one opportunity to speak out against that murderous policy.

The scene is one of hundreds of thousands of such personal tragedies from that one act of war alone, some of which have been captured on camera, most of which have not. Each time I see one, I am jolted into an awareness that the images could well be of myself or my child. Thankfully it is not me, not my family, and it is purely by accident of where I was born that it is not. Knowing this, I feel some kind of responsibility to those who, purely by accident of where *they* were born, have these horrors inflicted upon them.

I am not a pacifist. I do believe that violence is sometimes justified. But war is not simply "violence," and one need not be a pacifist to oppose war. One need not renounce all violence in order to oppose the establishment of a class of people who are above the law; a special situation under which it is acceptable to kill innocents. If the moral codes upon which our societies are built are to mean anything at all, then we must oppose war. If we believe that people have a right to their own lives, a right not to be killed or assaulted by others; and if we believe that that each person has as much right to be here as anyone else, that no-one is above the law, whether by virtue of political, social, economic or any other status, then we cannot believe in war.

Of all the lies that support war, one runs deeper than the others. It is a lie that was given to most of us at a very young age. It is a lie about who we are, what we are capable of and what is the true source of the violence in our world. It tries to make us believe that the way we live now—with our Officer Oglesbys and fire-bombings and economic embargoes and the cutting off of fingers of other people's children—represents the natural order of things. That because we are such flawed beings, we can expect no better.

"As long as humans have a proclivity for violence," this lie tells us, "there will always be war." This is utter nonsense. War does not persist because human beings are flawed or unenlightened, or even because we are violent or hate each other. Even if all of this is true about us, it does not explain war. War is not just another form of violence. It is the institutionalization of unrestrained violence with no meaningful accountability for those who inflict it.

Our problems are not caused by our flawed nature, but by flawed institutions. There will always be Officer Oglesbys in our world. There will always be some people who don't mind using violence to get what they want. There will always be criminals. The question is whether we have systems that protect the rest of us from the criminals, or systems that enable and even encourage the real criminals, while criminalizing those who are peaceful.

We would do well to disabuse ourselves of the notion that institutionalized violence creates order. It does not. It creates a safe place for people like Officer Oglesby, the men who killed Aiyana Jones, the Robert McNamaras and Curtis LeMays and the countless thousands of others who murder with impunity under cover of the state. It creates anarchy—the anarchy of Yeats' poem, spinning us out of control and taking us further and further away from anything that can legitimately be called order.

But these institutions also eat away at our center. They eat away at who we are, conditioning us to accept force, violation and disrespect as part of our daily lives; to accept the doctrine that might makes right, and to believe that nothing else is possible. They tear us from our own centers, our own moral centers, our knowledge of who we are.

"Why peace?" The reasons to abhor war are numerous, from an unyielding belief in the sanctity of human life, to fears for our own children's future. But the simplest answer, the most obvious answer, is the one that seems to elude most of us, either because we have forgotten it or had it "educated" out of us: *Because it's what we're made for.*

American Dominion:
Global Interventionism
Jeopardizing U.S. Security

Charles V. Peña

Charles V. Peña is a senior fellow at the Independent Institute in Oakland, CA and author of Winning the Un-War: A New Strategy for the War on Terrorism. *This essay was written when he was the director of defense policy studies at the Cato Institute in Washington, D.C. and originally published in* Global Dialogue *(a quarterly journal published by the Center for World Dialogue in Cyprus), Volume 7, Number 1–2, Winter/Spring 2005, pp. 86-96, which was an issue dedicated to the topic of humanitarian intervention.*

Preface:

This essay was written and published during the Bush administration at the height of the Iraq War. *Why Peace* is being published during the Obama administration but, unfortunately—despite his campaigning on the need for change—much of the critique and analysis about Bush is just as relevant to Obama. Indeed, the Obama administration's National Security Strategy is, for all intents and purposes, "Clinton *redux*" or "Bush lite." It's still about advancing democracy, universal values, and spreading democracy and freedom abroad. To be sure, Obama may disagree with his predecessor about how to accomplish these goals ("...*will not seek to impose these values through force...*"), but it's a difference of style, not substance.

Like the neoconservatives in the Bush administration before them, the liberal internationalists don't understand that U.S. national security isn't dependent on whether a particular country is a democracy (however "good" that might be in some general sense), but whether it represents a direct military threat to America and our way of life. Moreover, the terrorist threat represented by radical Islamic ideology is not due to a lack of democracy in the Muslim world. Indeed, it is not necessarily true that all future democracies will be friendly to the United States, especially democracies in Muslim countries. Indeed, if completely free and popular elections were held in most of the Muslim world, the resulting governments would likely be anti-American.

Finally, the fact that the global default has not changed (even though administrations have changed) is best illustrated on three counts:

- First, the U.S. defense budget remains enormous: over $500 billion, nearly what the rest of the world spends and more than the GDP of all but about the 20 richest countries in the world.

- Second, U.S. military forces maintain a sprawling footprint around the globe; even though U.S. troops have withdrawn from Iraq, they remain in Afghanistan well over 100,000 active duty military are deployed in over 150 countries.
- Third, President Obama's decision to take military action against Libya is no different than President Bush's decision to invade Iraq; both were unnecessary military interventions rationalized on humanitarian grounds and neither represented a direct threat to U.S. national security.

* * *

In the past, the primary threats to the United States and U.S. interests were posed by nation-states. Since the end of the Cold War, however, the United States has been in a unique geostrategic position. The military threat posed by the Soviet Union is gone. Two great oceans act as vast moats, protecting America's western and eastern flanks. America is also blessed with two friendly and stable neighbors to the north and south. Thus, the American homeland is relatively safe from a conventional military invasion. Meanwhile, the U.S. strategic nuclear arsenal acts as an effective and credible deterrent against possible nuclear attack by state actors—even so-called rogue states that might eventually acquire nuclear weapons. As Jeffrey Record points out:

> [T]here is no evidence to suggest that Saddam Hussein was anything other than successfully deterred and contained during the 12 years separating the end of the Gulf War and the launching of Operation Iraqi Freedom. Unlike fanatical, shadowy terrorist organizations, which are relatively undeterrable if not undefeatable, Saddam Hussein—who always loved himself more than he hated the United States (even to the point, in contrast to his two sons, of meekly submitting to his own capture by U.S. forces)—ruled a state, and states contain such assets as territory, population, armed forces, and governmental and economic infrastructure that can be held hostage to unacceptable U.S. retaliation.[1]

One would think that this favorable strategic situation could have allowed the United States to scale back its global military presence, and cash in the peace dividend yielded by the end of the Cold War. Yet the last two presidents have done just the opposite.

Beyond Containment

In September 1993, acknowledging the fact that the United States was no longer threatened by the Soviet Union, President Clinton's national security adviser Anthony Lake outlined a post-Cold War strategy of "enlargement" in which the United States moved beyond mere "containment" of communism and autocracy and sought instead to enlarge the community of free and democratic nations. Lake based this new strategy on four components:

First, we should strengthen the community of major market democracies—including our own—which constitutes the core from which enlargement is proceeding.

Second, we should help foster and consolidate new democracies and market economies, where possible, especially in states of special significance and opportunity.

Third, we must counter the aggression—and support the liberalization—of states hostile to democracy and markets.

Fourth, we need to pursue our humanitarian agenda not only by providing aid, but also by working to help democracy and market economies take root in regions of greatest humanitarian concern.[2]

And in a speech at the United Nations that same month, President Clinton declared: "Our overriding purpose must be to expand and strengthen the world's community of market-based democracies. During the Cold War, we fought to contain a threat to the survival of free institutions. Now we seek to enlarge the circle of nations that live under those free institutions."[3]

The administration of George W. Bush came to the White House intending to change radically the focus of U.S. foreign policy, promising "humility" in the conduct of foreign affairs. In practice, however, Bush's foreign policy has proved to be rather Clintonesque. For example, some of the goals outlined in the Bush administration's *National Security Strategy*, released in September 2002, include to:

- *champion aspirations for human dignity ...*
- *ignite a new era of global economic growth through free markets and free trade; [and]*
- *expand the circle of development by opening societies and building the infrastructure of democracy.*[4]

In September 1993, Anthony Lake had stated that "the idea of freedom has universal appeal." The *National Security Strategy of 2002* promises that the United States will "defend liberty and justice because these principles are right and true for all people everywhere" (p. 3). According to Lake, "to the extent democracy and market economics hold sway in other nations, our own nation will be more secure." Likewise, President Bush spoke of spreading democracy as a rationale for invading Iraq: "The world has a clear interest in the spread of democratic values, because stable and free nations do not breed the ideologies of murder. They encourage the peaceful pursuit of a better life."[5] Indeed, the Bush administration's National Security Strategy seeks "to help make the world not just safer but better" (p. 1).

The Clinton administration generally conducted its foreign policy under the auspices of the United Nations and/or NATO, whereas the Bush administration is comfortable acting outside those institutions. But when it comes to the issue of spreading democracy worldwide, the strategies of both administrations considerably overlap. Both presuppose the false belief that the best and only way to achieve US security is by forcibly creating a better world.

This argument underpinned both the Clinton administration's intervention in Serbia and the Bush administration's intervention in Iraq. Both were military actions against sovereign states conducted without the formal approval of the U.N. Security Council. Neither country represented an imminent threat to U.S. national security. And both actions ultimately were rationalized on humanitarian grounds—punishment respectively for Slobodan Milosevic's atrocities in Serbia and Saddam Hussein's brutal rule in Iraq.

Ultimately, both Clinton and Bush national security strategies are based on the belief that preventive U.S. military intervention overseas is necessary to safeguard American security. However benevolent the intent, U.S. humanitarian intervention is seen by many abroad as an expression of American empire.

Rather than pursue interventionism, U.S. policymakers—guided by America's relatively secure position in the world—should shift the focus of U.S. security strategy, and concentrate on those individuals and groups which present the gravest threat to the United States. Anti-American terrorist groups cannot be deterred by our nuclear arsenal or military contingents deployed around the globe. They use unconventional means of attack and cannot be stopped in a traditional military way, because they do not occupy a specific geographic area and they hide among civilian populations in numerous countries.

Terrorism feeds on anti-American resentment worldwide. Americans can simply no longer afford to ignore the linkage between an interventionist foreign policy and terrorism against the United States. As a 1998 study for the U.S. Department of Defense reported, much of the anti-American resentment around the world stems from an interventionist U.S. foreign policy.[6]

Therefore, rather than trying to do more everywhere in the world (including creating democracies at gunpoint), the United States needs to stop meddling in the internal affairs of other countries, except when they directly threaten US national security interests (*i.e.*, when the territorial integrity, national sovereignty, or liberty of the United States is at risk). By this standard, military action in Afghanistan was legitimate, insofar as it was retaliation against the Taliban regime that was sheltering the al-Qaeda terrorist network. On the other hand, the invasion of Iraq cannot be justified in terms of protecting the homeland because Saddam Hussein's regime, however despotic and disrespectful of human life, did not constitute an imminent threat to U.S. security.

Empire Reduces Security

A reorientation of America's global military posture, combined with a new national security strategy that avoids unnecessary military interventions, is essential in reversing the virulent anti-Americanism that enables al-Qaeda leader Osama bin Laden and others to recruit would-be suicide terrorists. This change in direction can occur only if policymakers reject calls for the embrace of an American empire, such as those from:

- *Washington Post* columnist Sebastian Mallaby, who finds "the logic of neo-imperialism too compelling ... to resist." He advocates an "imperialist revival" led by the United States, in which orderly societies "impose their own institutions on disorderly ones."[7]
- *Atlantic Monthly's* Robert Kaplan, who urges policymakers to look to the Greek, Roman, and British empires for guidance in the conduct of foreign affairs. "Our future leaders could do worse than be praised for their ... ability to bring prosperity to distant parts of the world under America's soft imperial influence."[8]
- The author of the best-selling book *Empire*, Niall Ferguson, who asserts that "the United States is an empire ... in fact, one of the most powerful empires in all history, and the only remarkable thing about it is that so many Americans are unaware of the fact."[9]

Although many reject the term "empire," the conduct of U.S. foreign policy is clearly guided by a presumption that the United States is, and shall remain, the world's only superpower. The Bush administration's *National Security Strategy* declared that the United States shall maintain its predominant position in the world at all costs, acting even before would-be rivals emerge; the document embraces a sweeping doctrine of preventive war should potential rivals "appear likely to emerge." This language echoed earlier claims, for example, when Clinton administration officials spoke of "conditional sovereignty"[10] and asserted for the United States—the so-called indispensable nation—the right to overthrow odious regimes, even if such regimes posed no threat to the people of the United States.[11]

It is the professed selflessness of our foreign policies that is said to distinguish the United States from empires of the past. Americans are not imperialists, and the sprawling U.S. military presence abroad is not a manifestation of empire, defenders of the new strategy assert, because the United States has good intentions. But the defenders of the French, Spanish, and British empires all made precisely the same arguments. And those whom they colonized inevitably sought to overthrow foreign rule. One by one, nationalist movements expelled their imperial occupiers from foreign lands, at grievous cost to their former colonial masters, and typically at even greater cost to those whose lands were being liberated.

Such nationalist sentiments are a constant threat to empires, and no less so in the twenty-first century. Drawing on the lessons of history, the objections to an imperial foreign policy can be summed up in a single sentence: empire is counterproductive abroad and threatens liberty and security at home. In a modern context, empire is a flawed model for protecting Americans from foreign threats because it is far more costly, and far less effective, than alternative strategies.

The high costs of empire derive, in part, from the fact that the practice of building and maintaining an empire is likely to encourage, rather than discourage, the very attacks against Americans that we wish to prevent. The mere presence of US military forces abroad incites others to commit acts of violence. A better approach to national security policy would be for the United States to adopt a less interventionist policy and to pull back from its Cold War-era extended security perimeter (with its attendant military commitments overseas). Such an approach recognizes that local foreign conflicts do not automatically jeopardize U.S. national security. It also recognizes that many of the problems plaguing the world, such as civil wars and ethnic strife, are largely impervious to external solutions (even from a country as powerful as the United States), as seen in central Africa and the Balkans.

Rather than maintaining a major military presence in disparate parts of the globe, the United States should allow countries to establish regional balances of power. As the world's dominant military power, the United States could always step in as a balancer of last resort if a serious imbalance jeopardizing vital U.S. national security interests were to develop. And instead of viewing all foreign crises and conflicts as vitally important, the United States would be able to distinguish between those demanding its attention and those best left to regional actors.

Attempts to maintain American global dominance, even if such efforts are couched in benign terms, could "alarm other nations and peoples and thus provoke" new coalitions to counterbalance the United States. US assertiveness abroad also creates "incentives for other nations to acquire weapons of mass destruction as an insurance policy against American military might."[12] Indeed, in order to protect themselves from an American intervention, dictatorial regimes look to nuclear weapons as the guarantor of last resort and, accordingly, have stepped up their nuclear research.

Interventionism and Terrorism

The essential problem of empire is that a sprawling U.S. global military presence (no longer needed to check the advances of a superpower enemy) exacerbates, rather than reducing, the terrorist threat to America. The Bush administration holds that other countries and people hate the United States simply for "who we are." This ignores the facts, such as public statements and public opinion polls in foreign countries. Throughout the world—including the Islamic world—there is admiration and appreciation for American accomplishments, culture, and values (including democracy and capitalism). But many of those same people hate U.S. policies. That is, anti-Americanism is fuelled more by our actions than by our cultural values.

A Zogby International poll conducted in the spring of 2002 among the residents of five Arab nations (Saudi Arabia, Kuwait, Egypt, Jordan, and Lebanon), three non-Arab Islamic countries (Iran, Pakistan, and Indonesia), and two others (France and Venezuela), revealed that Muslims are favorably inclined towards America's democracy and freedom, with the numbers especially high in Kuwait (58 percent).[13] Residents of Muslim countries also think highly of U.S. technology, science, and even films and television programs. However, when asked whether they approve of U.S. foreign policy in the Middle East, only a small fraction (9 percent of Pakistanis and just 1 percent of Kuwaitis) said yes.

"In essence, they don't hate us; they don't hate what we are about," pollster John Zogby remarked. "When the president said they hate our way of life, they hate our democratic values, at least in this first poll in the region, we did not find that was the case."[14]

Another poll by the Pew Global Attitudes Project has found widespread acceptance in Muslim countries of the basic ideas and principles of democracy and free markets, but that negative views of the U.S. have spread beyond the Middle East to Muslim populations in countries such as Indonesia and Nigeria.[15]

Even the Bush administration admits to the relationship between an interventionist U.S. policy and retaliatory acts of terrorism. According to Deputy Defense Secretary Paul Wolfowitz (whom many consider to be the strongest proponent and architect of the Iraq War), U.S. forces stationed in Saudi Arabia after the first Gulf War were "part of the containment [of Iraq] policy that has been Osama bin Laden's principal recruiting device, even more than the other grievances he cites."[16]

Yet U.S. policymakers continue to ignore the obvious conclusion: interventionist policies abroad—however noble and well-intentioned—breed anti-Americanism and, subsequently, terrorism. The United States must do everything in its power to dismantle the al-Qaeda international terrorist network, but it cannot afford needlessly to make new terrorist enemies or fuel the flames of virulent anti-American hatred in the Islamic world.

Imperial Burdens

America's imperial foreign policy and the military infrastructure necessary to sustain an imperial presence also pose a financial burden that threatens America's economic security for generations. The United States boasts the world's largest military budget. In 2002, U.S. military spending constituted almost 40 per cent of all such expenditures worldwide. If U.S. and global defense spending follow their current trends, the United States will probably outspend the rest of the world combined before the end of this decade.

Instead of admitting that the costs of empire are indeed great and growing, many advocates of American empire dismiss them with a shrug. The most common refrain, that the cost of whatever we are doing is far less than the costs of another terrorist attack, is deceptively simple because one cannot prove a negative. In the highly unlikely event that there is never another attack, we will never know how much such an attack might have cost. In the more likely event that another terrorist attack does occur, the defenders of the strategy of empire will undoubtedly declare that the attack would certainly have had far graver effects, or that there would have been far more attacks, if the money hadn't been spent. And we can then expect them to turn around and call for yet more money to solve the problem.

Some are already arguing that our military expenditures are not nearly large enough. The mission statement of the Project for a New American Century, a Washington-based institution that has been promoting a *pax Americana* since 1997, calls for significant additional increases in U.S. military spending.

According to the Council for a Livable World, "many military experts, including former Reagan Defense Department official Frank Gaffney, Marine Corps Commandant Gen. James Jones and former Army Chief of Staff Gen. Gordon Sullivan, have suggested military spending should be between 4 and 4.5 percent of GDP."[17]

But the United States cannot sustain an empire indefinitely. Even casual observers can do the arithmetic in their heads: the United States has military facilities in over one hundred countries, already spends more on its military than the next fifteen wealthiest countries combined, and aims to "rescue" the fully one-half of the world that currently does not live within free political systems under democratically elected governments. The true costs of empire may never be known with precision, but if creating a decent, democratic regime in Iraq, for example, is expected to cost hundreds of billions of dollars, then the cost of doing this in dozens of countries is certainly very large.

Although the United States already spends more than any other country on defense, its armed forces—in terms of the number of men and women in uniform—are relatively small, and they are already being stretched to breaking point policing the far corners of the sprawling American empire: from Tuzla to Tikrit and from Kabul to Kosovo. The active-duty force has been augmented by thousands of reservists since 11 September 2001, and the effect on the U.S. economy from the loss of workers in the civilian sector is felt all over America, in large cities and small towns.

Further, although the purpose of reserves is to supplement active-duty forces in conflicts—which should be engaged in only to protect and defend America in the face of serious threats to U.S. security—many reservists today are serving in places that have nothing to do with the war on terrorism. At one point in 2004, approximately 40 per cent of the troops serving in Iraq were drawn from the ranks of the National Guard and Reserve. In fact, the practice of using reservists for routine military missions was established long before the war on Iraq or even before the 9/11 attacks.

Faced with the prospect of extended deployments in the pursuit of dubious missions that have little to do with defending American security, young men and women may choose not to join. Those already in the service may choose not to re-enlist—when they are allowed to quit.

The key question for modern-day imperialists, therefore, is whether Americans have the stomach for empire. If the ranks of the all-volunteer force can no longer be filled, if enough young men and women cannot be induced to volunteer for military service, will the United States have to return to conscription? Some in Congress have already called for a return to the draft. The pressure for draconian new measures to staff the military will certainly increase if recruitment and retention falter.

A far better solution would be to reduce the number of missions the U.S. military is asked to perform, and then to follow this sensible change with reductions in the size and structure of the military itself. This would save American taxpayers hundreds of billions of dollars over the next decade, while at the same time reducing U.S. vulnerabilities abroad and enhancing our ability to combat anti-American terrorism.

Empire Threatens Liberty

If one can envision the government being given the power to subvert an individual's most basic liberty—the right to control one's own life—in the service of some higher collective end, then the subversion of other rights and liberties could follow. And, in practice, empires traditionally have stifled dissent and trampled individual liberties.

There are already ominous signs that the strategy of empire has begun to erode our fundamental rights and liberties in the United States. Beginning immediately after 9/11, the Bush administration asserted sweeping theories of executive authority, including the exclusive right to declare individuals, even U.S. citizens, "enemy combatants," and to deny these same individuals the ancient writ of habeas corpus and the related right to legal counsel. There were secret arrests, secret subpoenas, secret deportations, and even talk of secret trials.

Although some of these assertions of executive authority were struck down by the Supreme Court in June 2004 in the *Hamdi vs. Rumsfeld* case, and the related case of the Guantanamo Bay detainees, the very fact that the White House claimed the right to loosen long-standing constitutional protections is extremely worrisome. These incidents, combined with the relaxation of *posse comitatus* restrictions, and the erosion of privacy inherent within the Pentagon's abortive "Total Information Awareness" project,[18] constitute a series of challenges to well-established civil liberties, and they collectively point to the many ways in which imperial power is and can be used to threaten individual rights.

Many Americans say they are willing to forego some measure of freedom in exchange for security, and so far the costs for most U.S. citizens have been fairly modest. Removing one's shoes at airport metal detectors, or showing picture identification before boarding an airplane, hardly constitute great intrusions on personal privacy. It is true that people are less likely to pay attention to small infringements of their civil liberties, but the impetus of such a policy and the increasing bias in favor of the government are indeed troubling.

Ignoring the Founders

Americans have traditionally resisted the imperial impulse. They were guided by the Founders' oft-stated warnings that a republican form of government was incompatible with an imperial foreign policy. The Founders feared empire because it subverts the freedoms and liberties of citizens at home while simultaneously imposing its will on sovereign peoples abroad.

The eighteenth century still holds important lessons for the twenty-first. In an era when much of the globe was dominated by a few imperial powers—especially Great Britain, Spain and France—both Washington and Jefferson admonished their countrymen to avoid entangling themselves in the affairs of foreign powers. James Monroe declared in the famous doctrine that bears his name that the United States would concern itself only with events in the western hemisphere. In his Independence Day speech to the House of Representatives in 1821, John Quincy Adams summarized the core beliefs of the Founding Fathers in conducting foreign policy when he declared, "[America] goes not abroad in search of monsters to destroy. She is the well-wisher to the freedom and independence of all. She is the champion and vindicator only of her own."

Since the nation's founding, Americans have generally heeded these warnings. In the few instances where policymakers strayed—such as in the Philippines and in Vietnam—the costs proved too onerous to bear, and the public forced political leaders either to recant their imperial ambitions or pay a political price.

Today, the costs are potentially far greater, and they will be paid by politicians and citizens alike. Americans living in Teddy Roosevelt's time never feared Filipino insurrectionists conducting suicide attacks in New York. In the 1960s and 1970s, the Viet Cong posed little threat to Americans in San Francisco or St Louis. But Osama bin Laden and others like him have demonstrated their capacity, and their willingness, to communicate their rage at U.S. policies in ways that threaten the safety and security of all Americans, even those who had nothing to do with the implementation of these policies.

Therefore, elected officials must refocus their attention on addressing the real and tangible threat to their constituents and eradicating those responsible for the horrific events of 11 September. They must also recognize that interventionist foreign policies, and the attendant military presence abroad, do nothing to enhance American security, but instead serve as the vehicle for recruiting a whole new class of terrorists for years to come.

Killing to Save Lives

The use of military force to advance humanitarian goals is ultimately counterproductive because it ignores one unalterable fact: wars kill people. This is true even when the military achieves its mission with remarkable skill. For example, despite America's use of precision-guided munitions intended to minimize collateral damage, many thousands of civilians have been killed in Iraq (both by U.S. military action and by insurgent and terrorist violence). Beyond the casualties of war is a host of unforeseen consequences, many of them dangerous as well as tragic. Although direct damage to civilian infrastructure by U.S. munitions was limited, the American invaders found virtually all aspects of the Iraqi state to be near total collapse. The frustration of Iraqis never enamored with Hussein's brutal rule is now directed at the men and women of the U.S. military pressed into service as armed social workers.

And even if the U.S. military had been truly perfect—if not a single innocent civilian had been hit by a stray bomb, a ricocheting bullet, or a misplaced artillery round—the achievement of military victory would still have been dependent upon the killing and wounding of soldiers in the Iraqi military.

This is a point that the proponents of humanitarian military intervention seem to ignore completely. The schools can be rebuilt. Electrical power can be restored. The water can flow. All of the physical reminders of war's brutal reality can be erased. But even in a "perfect" war against a tyrannical regime, a war in which all military firepower is focused exclusively on the sources of that regime's authority, people will die. Those killed may all be soldiers, and under traditional norms of armed conflict "legitimate" military targets, but these men are fathers, brothers, and sons. The supposedly clear picture of the legitimacy of targeting them in the pursuit of humanitarian ends is further clouded by the realization that many of these individuals served against their will, drafted into the military under penalty of prison or death.

Some believe that the United States performs a great and moral mission when it uses its military might to overthrow undemocratic regimes. We should not be surprised, however, if those who lose fathers, brothers, and sons don't see it that way.

Changing the Global Default

Whenever there is a humanitarian crisis somewhere in the world, advocates of humanitarian intervention claim that the United States has an obligation and responsibility to respond because it is the world's most powerful country, both militarily and economically. It's time to change this global mindset.

To begin with, the limited powers granted to the federal government in a constitutional republic call for providing for the common defense of the citizens of that republic. In other words, the U.S. military does not exist to play "globocop" or armed social worker, but rather to confront direct threats to US security. On the campaign trail in 2000, then-presidential candidate George W. Bush endorsed this principle. Unfortunately, the Bush administration did not stick to it and instead turned its fight against anti-American terrorist groups into a global crusade against other misbehavers in the international arena.

Because the United States has an enormous military capacity, many mistakenly assume it has unlimited ability to intervene anywhere in the world. Indeed, this was the sentiment expressed in 1993 by then-U.S. ambassador to the United Nations Madeleine Albright when she complained to then-chairman of the Joint Chiefs of Staff Colin Powell: "What's the point of having this superb military you're always talking about if we can't use it?"[19]

Yet the strain that the occupation of Iraq is placing on the US military certainly calls into question the ability of the United States to intervene anywhere and everywhere. It is precisely because the military is over-committed around the world that the Pentagon has resorted to the use of so-called stop-loss orders to prevent individuals from leaving active duty when their terms of enlistment expire, a tactic that some have called a back-door draft. Others have been summoned back to active duty from civilian life.

Even if the Iraq War had not compelled the U.S. government to resort to such draconian measures for maintaining the strength of its military, there is no good reason why other countries cannot assume the mantle of defending their own interests in their own regions, independent of the United States. For example, in 2003 the combined economic output of the European Union countries was $11.6 trillion, compared to $10.9 trillion for the United States. Yet U.S. taxpayers spend more than twice as much on defense than their European counterparts. The Europeans have the economic wherewithal to maintain a military capability that is nominally comparable to that of the United States. If they were to do so, they would enhance their ability both to defend themselves and to intervene elsewhere—if they were willing to make that choice.

Indeed, because the European nations are often the first to demand international action in response to a humanitarian crisis, they should be the first to develop such a capability. Yet their default response is to expect that the United States will act for them. American power, the theory goes, carries with it global responsibilities.

The only way to alter the global default setting is for the United States just to say "no." Instead of being the first responder to crises that do not threaten U.S. security, it must encourage states in the crisis region to take action. If these states require additional assistance, the European Union should be encouraged to play a role, assuming the situation is of concern to the Europeans. Such an approach would re-establish a prudent model for dealing with humanitarian crises. By encouraging countries to safeguard their own security and attend to crises in their own neighborhoods, the United States can change the default settings for solving regional problems and simultaneously start to devolve its imperial status.

1. Jeffrey Record, "Nuclear Deterrence, Preventive War, and Counterproliferation," Cato Institute Policy Analysis no. 519, Cato Institute, Washington, D.C., July 8, 2004, p. 20.

2. Anthony Lake, "From Containment to Enlargement" (remarks at School of Advanced International Studies, Johns Hopkins University, Washington, D.C., September 21, 1993).

3. William J. Clinton, "Confronting the Challenges of a Broader World" (address to the UN General Assembly, New York, September 27, 1993).

4. White House, "The National Security Strategy of the United States of America," Washington, D.C., September 2002, pp. 1–2.

5. "President Discusses the Future of Iraq," White House press release, February 26, 2003.

6. Defense Science Board, *The Defense Science Board 1997 Summer Study Task Force on DoD Responses to Transnational Threats*, vol. 1, Final Report (Washington, D.C.: U.S. Department of Defense, October 1997), p. 15.

7. Sebastian Mallaby, "The Reluctant Imperialist: Terrorism, Failed States, and the Case for American Empire," *Foreign Affairs* 81, no. 2 (March/April 2002), p. 6.

8. Robert D. Kaplan, *Warrior Politics: Why Leadership Demands a Pagan Ethos* (New York: Random House, 2002), p. 153.

9. Niall Ferguson, quoted in "The United States Is, and Should Be, an Empire: A

New Atlantic Initiative Debate" (transcript of discussion at the American Enterprise Institute, Washington, D.C., July 17, 2003).

10. Richard N. Haass, "Sovereignty: Existing Rights, Evolving Responsibilities" (remarks to the School of Foreign Service and the Mortara Center for International Studies, Georgetown University, Washington, D.C., January 14, 2003).

11. Madeleine Albright, quoted in Michael Dobbs and John M. Goshko, "Albright's Personal Odyssey Shaped Foreign Policy Beliefs," *Washington Post*, December 6, 1996.

12. Ivan Eland, "The Empire Strikes Out: The 'New Imperialism' and Its Fatal Flaws," Cato Institute Policy Analysis no. 459, Cato Institute, Washington, D.C., November 26, 2002, p. 1.

13. See James Zogby, "It's the Policy, Stupid!" Media Monitors Network, April 15, 2002 [http://www.mediamonitors.net/zogby49.html].

14. Quoted in David T. Cook, "Monitor Breakfast: John and James Zogby," *Christian Science Monitor*, April 12, 2002.

15. Pew Global Attitudes Project, "Views of a Changing World: War with Iraq Further Divides Global Publics," Pew Research Center for the People and the Press, Washington, D.C., June 3, 2003.

16. Quoted in Karen DeYoung and Walter Pincus, "Despite Obstacles to War, White House Forges Ahead," *Washington Post*, 2 March 2003.

17. Dan Koslofsky and Jeremy Bratt, "Indefensible Spending: The Rhetoric behind a Rising Military Budget," Council for a Livable World Education Fund, Washington, D.C., September 2001, p. 11.

18. "Total Information Awareness," first publicly reported in 2002, was a proposal by Admiral John Poindexter to create a "grand database" to discern terrorist activity by tracking American citizens via credit card purchases, phone records, medical prescriptions, educational history, Internet use, e-mail correspondence, foreign and domestic travel, and other transactions and communications. No search warrant would have been required for the collection of these records. To date, Congress has denied the project any funding.

19. Quoted in Colin Powell, *My American Journey* (New York: Random House, 1995), p. 576.

Lockheed Stock and
Two Smoking Barrels

Richard Cummings

Richard Cummings worked as a lawyer for the United States Agency for International Development, Near East South Asia region, as the lawyer for the aid program in Israel and Jordan. His articles on foreign policy, terrorism and intelligence have appeared in Playboy, Tikkun, The American Conservative, the International Journal of Intelligence and CounterIntelligence, The New York Times, Evergreen Review *and others. He is the author of* The Pied Piper-Allard K. Lowenstein and the Liberal Dream. *An international lawyer, Richard is a graduate of Princeton and Columbia Law School and holds the Ph.D. in Social and Political Sciences from Cambridge. He has lectured on the Middle East at Princeton, the United States Naval Academy and the Center for International Relations of Boston University and taught international law at the Haile Sellassie I University in Addis Ababa, Ethiopia. He resides in Sag Harbor, NY.*

Introduction

When I wrote "Lockheed Stock and Two Smoking Barrels" for *Playboy*, which commissioned me to write the article, I had already done a considerable amount of research on military contractors and their role in making policy for a possible book. As I narrowed down my research for the *Playboy* piece, I concluded that Lockheed Martin was, by far, the biggest player, and that its CEO actually met with the top Pentagon officials, not only to inform them of weapon development but to assist them in making decisions about military policy. In other words, Lockheed had the ability to tell the Pentagon, based on available weaponry, where, when and how it could make war. I also began to see a pattern of Lockheed's actions and the value of its stock, which began a startling increase in value as the country moved closer to war with Iraq.

At the same time, the Lockheed lobbyists were working full time, making contributions to members of Congress, increasing the amount of money Lockheed made to Democrats who might otherwise have opposed the war. I also discovered that Dick Cheney owned a considerable amount of Lockheed stock and that his wife, Lynn Cheney, served on the board of Lockheed, for which they paid her hundreds of thousands of dollars to do virtually nothing but attend four meetings a year. Instead of a "military industrial complex," America had something called "the iron triangle," consisting of the contractors, the lobbyists and Congress, an unbreakable alliance that benefited all three at the expense of the tax payers. Lockheed's biggest project in its history, the F-35 Joint Strike Fighter, was worth several hundred billion dollars, even though the plane was plagued with problems.

How much has changed? The British military contractors, BAE Systems, which partners with Lockheed in the construction of the F-35 along with Northrop, is now the world's biggest, replacing Lockheed as number one. This is because BAE, with a history of corruption that outstrips even Lockheed's, has expanded its American subsidiary considerably. It took on top rung retired military and intelligence officials, putting them on BAE Systems America's branch's board. They soon began to pick up an ever increasing amount of Pentagon business, cutting into Lockheed's.

But don't worry about Lockheed. Its profits are still right up there and its CEO, Bob Stevens, has seen his multimillion-dollar salary increase. Robert Gates had called for cuts in military programs, like the competing engine for the F-35, but Congress is seeking to restore it even as it cuts domestic programs, calling for a balanced budget. There have been increasing fears that the F-35 itself is not viable and Gates has forced Lockheed to pay part of the costs of the delays and run-overs. But with America now involved in five wars, (Afghanistan, Pakistan, Iraq, Yemen and Libya), the military contractors are a sound investment. The revolving-door continues, with Pentagon officials leaving to work for the industry and industry executives leaving to take high rankings posts at the Pentagon. This remains a growth industry, and will be so for the indefinite future in the age of perpetual war.

Lockheed Stock and Two Smoking Barrels
(Originally published in *Playboy* Magazine, January, 2007)

In November of 2002, Stephen J. Hadley, deputy national security advisor, asked Bruce Jackson to meet with him in the White House. They met in Hadley's office on the ground floor of the West Wing, not far from the offices of Vice President Dick Cheney and then-National Security Advisor Condoleezza Rice. Hadley had an exterior office with windows, an overt indicator of his importance within the West Wing hierarchy.

This was months before Secretary of State Colin Powell would go to the United Nations to make the administration's case for the invasion of Iraq, touting the subsequently discredited evidence of weapons of mass destruction. But according to Jackson, Hadley told him that "they were going to war and were struggling with a rationale" to justify it. Jackson, recalling the meeting, reports that Hadley said they were "still working out" a cause, too, but asked that he, Jackson, "set up something like the Committee on NATO" to come up with a rationale.

Jackson had launched the U.S. Committee on NATO, a nongovernmental pressure group, in 1996 with Hadley on board. The objective of the committee, originally called the U.S. Committee to Expand NATO, was to push for membership in the NATO military alliance for former Soviet bloc countries including Poland, Hungary and the Czech Republic.

What Bruce Jackson came up with for Hadley this time, in 2002, was the *Committee for the Liberation of Iraq*. The mission statement of the committee says it was "formed to promote regional peace, political freedom and international security by replacing the Saddam Hussein regime with a democratic government that respects the rights of the Iraqi people and ceases to threaten the community of nations." The pressure group began pushing for regime change—that is, military action to remove Hussein—in the usual Washington ways, lobbying members of congress, working the media and throwing money around. The committee's pitch, or rationale as Hadley would call it, was that Saddam was a monster—routinely violating human rights—and a general menace in the Middle East.

"I didn't see the point about WMDs or an Al Queda connection," Jackson says. In his mind the human rights issue was sufficient to justify a war.

Jackson had long been a proponent of unseating Hussein, and the committee dovetailed with his quite real sense of mission. In addition to his role in the Committee for the Liberation of Iraq and the U.S. Committee on NATO, he had also been president of the Project for Transitional Democracies, organized to "accelerate democratic reform" in Eastern Europe.

Still, there is another way to view Jackson's activities. As *The New York Times* put it in a 1997 article, "at night Bruce Jackson is president of the U.S. Committee to Expand NATO, giving intimate dinners for senators and foreign officials. By day, he is director of strategic planning for Lockheed Martin Corporation, the world's biggest weapons maker."

That's how D.C. works. Many of the people making decisions have been in and out of the same set of revolving doors connecting government, conservative think tanks, lobbying firms, law firms and the defense industry. So strong is the bond between lobbyists, defense contractors and the Pentagon that it is known in Washington as "the iron triangle." And this triangle inevitably gets what it wants. Why? Because in the revolving door system, a defense contractor executive can surface as an official in the Department of Defense, from which position he can give lucrative contracts to his former employer, and his prospects for an even better paying job in the private sector brighten. Former aides to members of congress become handsomely paid lobbyists for the companies they were able to help in their position on Capitol Hill. Such lobbyists can spread their corporate-funded largesse to the friendliest members and their aides on the Hill. And so on.

These "blow-dried Republican lobbyists," as one Washington district court judge calls them, wield far more power than most of the elected officials in town. Forget dime-a-dozen congressmen. It's these operatives who get the best tables at the *Capitol Grille*, where the power brokers lunch and sup. The lobbyists have their own lockers there, with personalized nameplates, where they store their vintage wines, ports and whiskies. They dine on the fine aged beef you can see through a window that allows guests to gaze into the refrigerated meat storage area. These people make up the K Street oligarchy that, despite all the vituperative rhetoric in recent years about campaign finance reform and insidious special interests, run Washington.

Bruce Jackson is a perfect example of this. While vice president for strategy and planning for Lockheed from 1999 to 2002, Jackson, by his own account, was also "responsible for the foreign policy platform at the 2000 Republican National Convention," to which he was a delegate. (The platform involved a dramatic increase in defense spending.) His title at the convention was chair of the platform subcommittee on foreign policy. He also served as co-chairman of the finance commission of Bob Dole's 1996 campaign. Prior to joining Lockheed, Jackson had served as executive director of the Project for the New American Century (PNAC), the think tank whose principles included Dick Cheney. PNAC served as the Bush administration's blueprint for preemptive war and authored a 1998 open letter to President Bill Clinton calling for military force to oust Saddam Hussein.

But forget Jackson. In 2002, he was on the outside. Stephen Hadley, looking out of the windows from his West Wing office, was on the inside. Sure, Hadley had the requisite government experience for a deputy national security advisor. He had been an assistant secretary of defense under Bush's dad. But he had been through the revolving door, too: Stephen Hadley, the point man for justifying the invasion of Iraq, had also lawyered at Shea & Gardner, whose clients included Lockheed.

Of course, all the frothing at the mouth about lobbyists, money and special interests can seem from outside the Beltway as much ado about nothing. The government hands out contracts. The beneficiaries or those who want to be beneficiaries buy steak dinners for the officials who hold the purse strings. Big deal. The problem, though, is that, upon closer scrutiny, this is not how the system works. It's actually much more sinister than that, allowing the interests of America to be subverted by the interests of corporate America. As you'll see here, your elected officials did not deliberate on how best to protect their constituents, decide bombing Iraq was the best way and then order some provisions and weapons. On the contrary, this is the story of how Lockheed's interests, as opposed to those of the American citizenry, set the course of U.S. policy after 9/11.

For the war companies, things have worked out perfectly. Whatever the rationale for the invasion of Iraq, business is booming. Not long after Bush took office, Lockheed Martin's revenues soared by more than 30 percent, as it was awarded $17 billion in contracts from the Department of Defense, a far cry from the lean years of the Clinton administration. (Under Clinton, it did win $2 billion in contracts with the Department of Energy for nuclear weapons activity; recently Bush called for 125 new nukes a year, opening up new contract horizons in that area, as well.) Its stock went from 16.375 in October of 1999 to 71.52 in June of 2002. As professor of finance at the State University at Buffalo Michael Rozeff observes, "the stock market anticipates many events."

Lockheed Martin reported 2002 sales of $26.6 billion, a backlog of more than $70 billion and free cash of $1.7 billion. And that was before the war in Iraq.

When it came to organizing the Committee for the Liberation of Iraq, Jackson, by his own admission, "knew nothing about Iraq." So while he agreed to serve as its chairman, he turned day-to-day operations over to Republican operative Randy Scheunemann, who took the position of executive director. Scheunemann was a member of the board of directors of PNAC, served as treasurer of Jackson's Project on Transitional Democracies, and had been a consultant on Iraq to Donald Rumsfeld. He had also been a staffer for Mississippi Senator Trent Lott when Lott was the senate majority leader— Scheunemann had in fact authored the Iraq Liberation Act. The act authorized the $97 million in Pentagon aid that would fund the Iraq National Congress, led by Ahmed Chalabi, who subsequently got close to *New York Times* reporter Judith Miller, explaining to her where Saddam Hussein's WMDs were supposedly located.

Jackson then turned to his old friend Julie Finley, whom he refers to as the "grande dame" of Washington Republican politics and fundraising, to serve as treasurer of the Committee for the Liberation of Iraq. She had held dozens of positions in Republican affiliated groups, and had served as chairman of the board of directors of Jackson's Project on Transitional Democracies. She also knew how to leverage her connections: Among those signing on as board members of the Committee for the Liberation of Iraq in 2002 were Richard Perle, then the chairman of the Defense Advisory Board, former U.N. Ambassador Jeanne Kirkpatrick and former CIA Director James Woolsey. Former Secretary of State George Schultz signed on to the advisory board.

A key member of the Committee for the Liberation of Iraq was Rend Al-Rahim Francke, the founder of the Iraq Foundation, which, according to its tax return, was 99 percent funded by U.S. government grants. The Iraq Foundation, in turn, provided logistical support for the anti-Saddam Hussein propaganda documentary *Voices of Iraq* and facilitated its distribution. The objective was the manipulation of public opinion to support regime change to oust Saddam Hussein, all in support of the goals of the Committee for the Liberation of Iraq.

If the names and organizations connected to the Committee for the Liberation of Iraq seem to blur together, it's no coincidence. Many of the people involved had been in and out of that set of revolving doors connecting government, conservative think tanks, lobbying firms and the defense industry. And many shared another common bond, as well: a link to Lockheed Martin.

By the time the committee had assembled, they had a number of contacts in the Bush administration—many of whom also had Lockheed connections. Bush had appointed Powell A. Moore assistant secretary of defense for legislative affairs serving directly under Secretary of Defense Donald Rumsfeld. From 1983 until 1998, when he had become chief of staff to Republican Senator Fred Thompson of Tennessee, Moore was a consultant and vice president for legislative affairs for Lockheed.

Albert Smith, Lockheed's executive vice president for integrated systems and solutions, was appointed to the Defense Science Board. Bush had appointed former Lockheed chief operating officer Peter B. Teets as undersecretary of the Air Force and director of the National Reconnaissance Office, where he made decisions on the acquisition of reconnaissance satellites and space-based elements of missile defense. Former Secretary of Transportation Norman Mineta, the only Democrat appointed by Bush to his cabinet, worked for Lockheed, as did Bush's Secretary of the Navy, Gordon England. Haley Barbour, chairman of the Republican National Committee before becoming the governor of Mississippi, worked for a Lockheed lobbying firm. Joe Allbaugh, national campaign manager of the Bush-Cheney ticket and director of FEMA during the first two years of the Bush administration (he appointed his college friend Michael Brown as FEMA's general counsel), was a Lockheed lobbyist for its rapidly growing intelligence division.

Dick Cheney's son-in-law, Philip J. Perry, a registered Lockheed lobbyist who had, while working for a law firm, represented Lockheed with the Department of Homeland Security, had been nominated by Bush to serve as general counsel to the Department of Homeland Security. His wife, Elizabeth Cheney, serves as deputy assistant secretary of state for Middle Eastern affairs.

Vice President Cheney's wife, Lynne, had, until her husband took office, served on the board of Lockheed, receiving deferred compensation in the form of half a million dollars in stock and fees. Even President Bush himself has a Lockheed Martin connection. As governor of Texas, he had attempted to give Lockheed a multimillion-dollar contract to reform the state's welfare system.

Soon after taking office in 2001, Bush had also appointed Lockheed president and CEO Robert J. Stevens to his Commission on the Future of the United States Aerospace Industry. The future of that industry was, of course, in an expanding defense budget, and a war in Iraq wouldn't hurt Lockheed's bottom line.

Jackson has the perfect pedigree for this insular, incestuous world of interconnections. His father, William Jackson, was the first person to hold the position of national security advisor, under Dwight Eisenhower. Growing up, his neighbors had included the historian and diplomat George Kennan, author of the doctrine of containment during the Cold War, and William Bundy, a Johnson administration hawk. Jackson graduated from the elite St. Mark's boarding school in Massachusetts and then attended Princeton. In the 1980s Jackson worked for presidents Reagan and Bush under Secretary of Defense Caspar Weinberger, as well as Richard Perle and Paul Wolfowitz.

Next Jackson worked in proprietary trading at Lehman Brothers, an investment bank, before leaving for Martin Marietta, then one of the top defense corporations. Jackson's role was director of strategic planning and corporate development projects, which involved the merger of Martin Marietta with the 800-pound gorilla of the industry, Lockheed. Jackson remained with the new entity, Lockheed Martin.

Today Jackson's Washington apartment is discreetly elegant. Aside from shelves of books, there is another item on the wall in Jackson's apartment worthy of note: It is a signed photograph of George W. Bush together with Jackson and Julie Finley, the fund-raiser who was treasurer of the Committee for the Liberation of Iraq. Sitting in his apartment, which also serves as his office, Jackson describes his role at Lockheed Martin as "non-technical." He worked at developing strategies to improve sales and find new markets, moving the company in directions that were profitable.

Meanwhile, in his "spare time," Jackson worked to promote the expansion of NATO and Iraq liberation, worked to get Bush elected and helped establish the administration's foreign policy. While Jackson sees his role as head of the United States Committee on NATO as an idealistic one, separate from his job,

NATO expansion proved a valuable marketing tool for Lockheed Martin, as Eastern European and Central Asian counties upgraded their obsolete militaries, and, as we'll see, also provided a way to gain support among former Soviet bloc countries for Bush's coming war in Iraq.

The collateral benefits of Jackson's activities to Lockheed Martin were unambiguous, leading one to conclude that while he might have thought he was using them, in reality they were using him. Jackson argues that only "literary types" would see a connection between Lockheed Martin and the Iraq war as "seamless." He insists that his own activities were "not part of my day job. What I did at other times was my own business. There are lesbians who work for Lockheed Martin. One of them might be a belly dancer at night."

As for the same names—many of them people with Lockheed Martin connections—appearing on the letterhead of groups pressing for military action in Iraq and for NATO expansion, Jackson quips: "How many intellectuals are there in Washington? Twenty? We all share the same concerns."

Jackson acknowledges that he "gave William Kristol money" to help start the *Weekly Standard*, which advocated military action to remove Saddam Hussein, just as he had earlier joined with Kristol at the PNAC—all by virtue of their shared ideology, as he explains it. But if the connection between Lockheed Martin and the Iraq war was not seamless, neither was it serendipitous. For example, Lockheed also supported the pro-war *Weekly Standard* as a paying advertiser.

"It used to be just an airplane company," John Pike, a military analyst and director of GlobalSecurity.org says about Lockheed Martin. "Now it's a warfare company. It's an integrated solution provider. It's a one-stop shop. Anything you need to kill the enemy, they will sell you."

They also will tell you who the enemy is. And whether it was seamless or serendipitous, Stephen Hadley, referred to by *The New York Times* as one of the more significant Lockheed operatives in the Bush White House, was there to tie it all together.

Still, while Lockheed Martin may look invincible now, it was not always so. Its rise has been fraught with disaster and catastrophe, even near-extinction, from which it ultimately became determined to insulate itself, free from the vicissitudes of the free market.

During Lockheed's dark days, its failures were so notorious they inspired *Captain Lockheed and the Starfighters*, a 1974 concept album by Robert Calvert, the lead singer of the British prog rock band Hawkwind. Ian "Lemmy" Kilmister, Hawkwind's bassist prior to founding Motörhead, also contributed to the LP, a send-up of the true story of West Germany's experiences with Lockheed's Starfighter jet, the F-104G.

Rejected by the American Air Force, Lockheed sold the Starfighters to the West German air force. Of the 916 jets sold to West Germany, 292 crashed, killing 116 pilots.

The opening track on *Captain Lockheed and the Starfighters* is cumbersomely titled, "Franz Joseph Strauss, Defence Minister, Reviews the Luftwaffe in 1958, Finding It Somewhat Lacking in Image Potential," done by

Calvert in a crazed German accent, impersonating, in Monty Python-manic style, the "Uber-Teutonic Defence Minister." But German officials were not laughing, and government investigations of the purchase ensued. Meanwhile, Lockheed also sold the Starfighter to the Japanese, with 54 of their F-104Gs also falling from the sky.

As a manufacturer of civilian airliners, Lockheed had foundered from the time its propeller-driven Constellation was grounded in 1946 by the Civilian Aeronautics Board after a series of crashes that year. It also discontinued its Electra turboprop commercial airliner two years after it was introduced in 1959 when three crashed in one year.

Its legendary Super Constellation—a mainstay of American transatlantic commercial aviation from 1951 to 1955—faced competition in 1956 from the DC-7, the first aircraft capable of regularly flying non-stop in both directions across the North Atlantic. To keep up, Lockheed created the 1649 Starliner, but it was overtaken by the faster Bristol Britannia and then rendered obsolete by the jet-powered Boeing 707 and the Havilland Comet 4. Lockheed built only 44 Starliners and failed to recoup its investment on what proved to be its last propeller commercial aircraft.

To add insult to injury, the Navy, by now moving into jets, canceled a contract for the W2V-1, a military version of the Model 1649 designed to serve as an airborne early-warning craft. Not only were the 1649s unable to compete with new jets, their engines were temperamental" by Lockheed's own admission. And while Lockheed was able to offset some of these losses by going into the missile business with the founding of Lockheed Missile Systems Division (later Lockheed Missiles and Space Company) and promoting its Polaris and Trident series—which served as the company's cash cows during hard times—its bad business decisions and overruns continued to threaten its profitability.

Finally shifting to jet aircraft, Lockheed still foundered. The company designed and built the JetStar, thinking it had a guaranteed market with the Air Force, which led Lockheed to believe that as many as three hundred of the aircraft would be ordered if Lockheed won the competition for the UCX, or "utility transport, experimental." In the event, the Air Force bought only 16 of the advanced aircraft, leaving a residual sense of "betrayal" in the company, as executives interviewed by Walter J. Boyne expressed in his corporate history of Lockheed, *Beyond The Horizons.*

As Boyne details, Lockheed fared no better in the commercial jet sweepstakes, precipitating a crisis that almost destroyed the company. By failing to acquire Douglas when it had an opportunity to do so, Lockheed allowed McDonnell to beat them to the punch in 1967, a lesson Lockheed management would not forget. Lockheed had hoped to allow Douglas to go under because of late deliveries of both its DC-8 and DC-9, and then pick it up at a cheap price, transforming Lockheed into a much larger and more powerful company than Boeing. Instead, Lockheed found itself in competition with McDonnell Douglas to fill the commercial jet niche between the Boeing 707 (and its counterpart, the DC-8) and the new 747. Its answer was the L-1011 TriStar.

Designed with three engines for non-stop transcontinental flights, Lockheed opted to go with Rolls-Royce for the engines because of Rolls' willingness to provide needed funding for development. Also, American Airlines appeared to favor the Rolls-Royce engine, and Lockheed assumed it would therefore be able to sell American the TriStar. But Franklin Kolk, American's chief engineer and father of the wide-body jet, favored a twin engine aircraft and, disappointed in Lockheed for not following his advice, pushed American to purchase DC-10s instead.

Dan Haughton, Lockheed's CEO, who had previously headed its nuclear missile division, frantically offered the L-1011 TriStar to Eastern and TWA at a drastically reduced price. But since there were Congressional rumblings about Lockheed using a foreign engine—with dollars leaving America for Britain—Haughton concocted a scheme to announce a sale of 50 L-1011s to Air Holdings in Britain to show that money would be coming into the United States to more than offset what was going out to Rolls-Royce. GE offered its engine to United Airlines at a favorable rate, assuming that Lockheed would switch from Rolls-Royce to win a United contract. But Lockheed refused to redesign the TriStar to accept the GE CF6 engine because of the $100 million cost of such a conversion. Haughton, believing he still had the American deal, was convinced United would fall in line and accept the RB 211 engine from Rolls-Royce. But United used its leverage to drive down the price of the competing engines and planes. Then it stabbed Lockheed in the back by going with the Douglas DC-10, announcing its intention to buy 60 with an option to buy 30 more.

With the deck stacked against it, Lockheed proceeded with the Rolls-Royce engine that, unexpectedly, then failed the standard test for "susceptibility to bird-strike damage." When three dead chickens were fired into one of the engines while it was in operation, it blew apart. Rolls was obliged to redesign the engine, producing one that was heavier and more costly and increasing the cost of the TriStar.

Competition from GE drove down the price of engines, causing Rolls-Royce to hemorrhage money. On February 4, 1971, it declared bankruptcy. Lockheed was thrown into turmoil. Having created a $50 million state-of-the-art facility to produce the L-1011s, it suspended production and laid off 4,000 employees. But Richard Nixon and Ted Heath, Britain's prime minister, joined forces to attempt to salvage Rolls-Royce and Lockheed.

Heath arranged for Britain to take over Rolls-Royce as "Rolls-Royce 1971," as it was registered on the London Stock Exchange—a bit of socialism for the privileged. Nixon's Secretary of the Treasury, John Connally, negotiated a deal between Britain and the United States to continue production of the RB 211 and the L-1011 TriStar, with Britain agreeing to make the engine as long as America would guarantee the L-1011 would continue to production. As part of the deal, Lockheed agreed to pay $120 million more for the engines. It was all in vain, however, as Lockheed was eventually obliged to discontinue the L-1011 in the wake of a bribery scandal during their attempts to get Japan to buy the aircraft. *Beyond the Horizons* offers an excellent look at this entire episode.

Lockheed learned a number of things from the L-1101 experience. First and foremost, it didn't pay to compete in the private sector. Instead, the company shifted gears; these days 80 percent of its business comes from federal government contracts. Moreover, Lockheed would load the government with its own people and then hire former defense department employees, creating a revolving door that would guarantee friends in the right places. That goal, of course, has been achieved and sustained.

Also in the wake of the L-1011 debacle, Lockheed's business practices became aggressive in the extreme. It charged the Pentagon $646 for a toilet seat and delivered C-5A transport planes—that cost millions of dollars—without installing thousands of essential parts. It paid bribes to foreign officials to help unload planes no one wanted, including giant long-distance transports to Indonesia, the Philippines, Brazil and Italy, until the passage of the Foreign Corrupt Practices Act of 1977 made such actions illegal. Undeterred, in 1995 Lockheed paid an Egyptian official $1.2 million to secure a contract for three C-130 cargo planes. A Lockheed executive promised a federal judge that the company would henceforth make a "commitment to the highest ethical standards of conduct," but this was not until it was obliged to pay $145.3 million in penalties. Also, in 1994, Lockheed received a $13 million fine under the Arms Export Control Act when it supplied information that could have been used to improve the accuracy of Chinese ballistic missiles. The U.S. government charged Lockheed with 30 violations of arms export laws in connection with having aided Chinese satellite technology.

Lockheed also learned never again to miss out on the chance to gobble up other defense contractors or merge with them on favorable terms. After developing the F-22 (later known as the F/A 22) with General Dynamics and Boeing, Lockheed took over General Dynamics' Forth Worth aircraft division. And in 1995, it made the decision that would change the face of the industry. Lockheed would merge with Martin Marietta, which itself had gobbled up the aerospace division of General Electric. President Clinton wanted the merger so a new, more technologically advanced company could emerge, capable of building a new Joint Strike Fighter supersonic warplane.

Lockheed met secretly with its financial advisor, Morgan Stanley, which considered the deal beneficial, at least to the stock market. Dick Cheney served on the Board of Morgan Stanley. His 2004 financial disclosure statement lists Lockheed stock options and $50,000 in Lockheed stock, but also investments in a number of Morgan Stanley funds. In 2000, *The New York Times* reported that "Mr. Cheney has a much larger brokerage account at Morgan Stanley Dean Witter, on whose board he serves, but he did not report any trades in that account on his and his wife's tax returns.... Mr. Cheney and his wife Lynne had previously disclosed only the first two pages of their tax returns for 1990 through 1999, holding back the supporting documentation that show details of investment income."

Overall, the new Lockheed Martin received about $1 billion from U.S. government coffers for costs related to the merger which, as Geov Parrish noted in *Mother Jones*, included "approximately $31 million" paid in executive bonuses.

But all did not go well with the merger. Lockheed Martin incurred further debt when it acquired the defense electronics and system integration business of Loral Space & Communications. Joint ventures with Russia to launch satellites also cost Lockheed Martin a considerable amount of money. Lockheed poured almost a billion dollars into the ventures as of 1999 before security issues limited the number of Russian launches of U.S. built satellites to 20.

Then, in 1999, with profits tumbling, Vance Coffman, the chairman and now CEO, shook up the company, reorganizing its management structure to create what it described as a "new customer focused organizational realignment." In short, it was a strategy designed to respond to another lesson learned in the course of doing business: By becoming part of the decision-making process, Lockheed Martin could ensure that defense budgets would expand and not contract.

The shakeup got into high gear as the price of its shares tumbled to its all-time low of $16.375. Executives left in droves. Lockheed Martin announced the retirement of Peter Teets, the company's president and chief operating officer. (Two years later Teets was appointed as undersecretary of the Air Force in the Bush administration.) Coffman chaired a search committee for new blood, eventually appointing as CFO (and in 2001, CEO) Robert J. Stevens, formerly a vice president of Lockheed Martin's strategic development organization. Stevens, says Jackson, is "as straight arrow as you get, an all-American guy," who "polishes his own shoes."

While working as head of strategic planning, Stevens had devised a strategy he could implement as CEO to turn Lockheed Martin around and make it the master of its fate. And as he served on Bush's Commission to Examine the Future of the United States Aerospace Industry from 2001 to 2002, he had the president's ear.

In 1999, when Stevens left strategic planning to become chief financial officer, Jackson became vice president for strategy and planning, their careers intersecting at a crucial time. Stevens developed the strategy for Lockheed to outpace Boeing, General Dynamics, Raytheon and Northrop Grumman as the top Pentagon contractor through aggressively pursuing federal contracts while eschewing the risks of the marketplace in the private sector. He started pouring large sums of PAC money to members of Congress to garner their cooperation and hired the armies of lobbyists for which Lockheed Martin became famous. According to Jackson, Lockheed Martin has hired "200 lobbyists," who in turn "hire other lobbyists" to work on Lockheed accounts. (One of them is Katherine Armstrong, daughter of a policy aide to Ronald Reagan. It was Katherine Armstrong who hosted the infamous Dick Cheney hunting party at Armstrong Ranch where Cheney accidentally shot a leading Republican lawyer.) Fees to lobbyists in a given year likely exceed $10 million.

When the United States gives military aid to its allies, the benefits accrue to Lockheed Martin, too. Israel, for example, spends much of the $1.8 billion a year it receives in military aid from the U.S. on planes and missile systems from

Lockheed—and that's in years when it is not actively at war with Hezbollah. Lockheed's market is worldwide, selling F-16 fighters, surveillance software and other equipment to more than 40 countries. The United Arab Emirates, forced to give up its deal to run American ports through its state-run Dubai entity, has been a major customer, spending more than $6 billion on F-16 fighters in 2000 as it looked forward to the Bush presidency. No wonder Bush threatened to veto legislation barring the ports deal.

Stevens has boasted that Lockheed Martin not only creates the technology, it makes military policy as well. He told *The New York Times* in November of 2004 that Lockheed stands at "the intersection of policy and technology," which, he observed, "is really a very interesting place to be. We are deployed, entirely in developing daunting technology" that "requires thinking through the policy dimensions of national security as well as technology." He acknowledges "this is not a business where in the purest economical sense there's a broad market of supply and demand."

And although he may shine his own shoes, Stevens is paid $7 million a year, not counting bonuses and stock options. In 2002, Stevens left Bush's aerospace commission, becoming a member of the influential Council on Foreign Relations, and Jackson left Lockheed Martin to work on the Project on Transitional Democracies and the Committee for the Liberation of Iraq. Stevens and Jackson were tag team wrestlers, Mr. Inside and Mr. Outside, of Team Lockheed. And, increasingly, the distinction between Lockheed Martin and the government began to blur as the war in Iraq became inevitable.

With the 2002 election over and Democrats increasingly hawkish on Iraq, Bush made his State of the Union address on January 29, 2003, uttering this now famous line: "The British government has learned that Saddam Hussein recently sought significant quantities of uranium from Africa." The threat of Saddam Hussein was established and the American people bought it. And the person claiming responsibility for leaving that line in was Hadley.

In February of 2003, Jackson helped draft a declaration for the 10 Eastern European foreign ministers—all countries up for NATO membership and associated with Jackson's expansion efforts—that became known as the "Vilnius Ten," rebuking French President Jacques Chirac's opposition to attacking Iraq. The declaration stated: "The newest members of the European community agree that we must confront the tyranny of Saddam Hussein and that the United Nations must act now." Jackson achieved this success when he attended a dinner party at the Slovak embassy in Washington and told assembled diplomats from the countries, according to *The American Prospect*'s John B. Judis, that signing the declaration would help win U.S. approval of their membership.

On March 20, 2003, America attacked Iraq. "Shock and Awe" began at night, with Lockheed Martin Stealth F-117 Nighthawks leading the assault. Looking like gigantic, venomous black bats, the V-shaped killers with their sharply spiked tail wings swept over Baghdad in search of the concrete shelters and reinforced bunkers where it was believed Saddam Hussein and his inner circle were concealed. Light ground forces moved swiftly toward Baghdad. An American blitzkrieg had been launched.

The F-117 had been reconfigured to carry a 2,000-pound bunker buster bomb, accurately guided by new technology to hit its target at a vertical impact angle with a warhead called the BLU-109. The Lockheed Missiles and Space Company manufactured it. Lockheed's Keyhole and Lacrosse satellites beamed images from the war back to the military, employing its Theater Battle Management Core Systems, specialized software used to coordinate communications between intelligence systems and ground forces to assist the air campaign. Lockheed U-2 and the SR-71 Blackbird spy planes joined with its F-16 and the F/A 22 jet fighters in support of the F-117s. Army and Marine ground troops unleashed Lockheed Hellfire laser-guided anti-armor missiles to demolish helicopters and land attack vehicles, and PAC-3 missiles, a highly agile, "hit-to-kill" interceptor, to provide air defense for ground combat forces. Lockheed Javelin portable missiles were used to considerable effect, particularly later in the invasion of Fallujah. Lockheed's "arsenal of democracy" was in full display.

Five days later, Bush asked Congress for $74.7 billion to pay for six months of combat, separate from the regular defense budget. But by June, it had become obvious that the "uranium from Africa" intelligence had been deeply flawed and erroneous. Acknowledging the CIA had warned him in two separate memos that the Agency would not stand by the information suggesting Iraq was trying to buy yellowcake uranium in Niger to reconstitute a nuclear weapons program, Stephen Hadley had this to say about it: "When the language in the drafts of the State of the Union referred to efforts to acquire natural uranium, I should have either asked that they—the 16 words given to that subject—be stricken, or I should have alerted DCI Tenet. And had I done so, this would have avoided the whole current controversy. And in my current position, I am the senior-most official within the NSC staff, directly responsible for the substantive review and clearance of presidential speeches. The president and the national security advisor look to me to ensure that the substantive statements in those speeches are the ones in which the president can have confidence. And it is now clear to me that I failed in that responsibility in connection with the inclusion of these 16 words in the speech that he gave on the 28th of January."

Yet when Colin Powell resigned as secretary of state and National Security Advisor Condoleezza Rice took his place, Stephen Hadley was promoted to take her position as national security advisor. Hadley's "error" had enabled Bush to go to war, the big payoff for Lockheed Martin.

But how had the British government gotten the intelligence on the African uranium so wrong? How had MI6, the most fabled intelligence service in the world, allowed itself to be misled by dubious sources? While Tony Blair and his government deny any pressure was put on its intelligence services, the stakes were high for Britain to join America in the war. And here again Lockheed loomed large.

In October of 2001, the Pentagon announced it was awarding Lockheed Martin a nearly $20 billion contract for the next phase of the development of the Joint Strike Fighter, called the F-35. To the industry, it was "the deal of the century," despite the fact that the century had only just begun. In beating out Boeing, Lockheed asserted itself as the undisputed leader of military contractors for decades to come, if not forever. But it did not go it alone. It brought in on the deal not only Northrop Grumman, but also the beleaguered BAE Systems, Britain's, and Europe's, largest defense contractor. Under the terms of the contract, BAE was responsible for building the aft fuselage and the tails; Lockheed the forward fuselage and wings; and Northrop the middle fuselage.

On September 30, 2005, following Britain's participation in the invasion of Iraq and with its ground troops still on the ground as other coalition partners, such as Spain, pulled out their troops, according to John A. Smith of Lockheed's Fort Worth operation: "Lockheed Martin and the U.S. Department of Defense formalized a $25.7 billion Joint Strike Fighter system development and demonstration contract that effectively replaces the $19.7 billion SDD contract under which the JSF was operating previously." As this was all covered by the fiscal year 2005 Congressional budget, it "requires no additional Congressional funding."

Smith explains that nine countries will use the F-35—the United States, the U.K., Italy, the Netherlands, Turkey, Canada, Australia, Denmark and Norway—with all nine negotiating for what they will buy in the future, with sales worth $257 billion. (Israel has recently indicated its intention of converting its air force to F-35s in a deal worth $5 billion.) He explains that this is the fifth year of 12 in the systems development stage. Smith further explains that there is "no fixed percentage" as to how the three participating companies receive money, which is paid out on an "as needed" basis.

Bush couldn't go into Iraq without a major ally and Lockheed knew it. To sweeten the pot for Blair, Lockheed dragged BAE Systems into the F-35 deal. When BAE still struggled prior to the war (Goldman Sachs reported that BAE would have to cut its dividend), Lockheed began renegotiating the contract—with the new version unveiled in 2005, giving BAE billions more to be paid "as needed." This put BAE back on its feet, able to build the Typhoon jet fighter for sale to Saudi Arabia in a $70 billion deal, saving 10,000 BAE jobs and 4,000 Rolls-Royce jet engine building jobs.

Meanwhile, a government accountability office report for Congress says the Defense Department is investing too heavily in the F-35 without knowing whether the aircraft will work properly. The report criticizes the Pentagon plan to spend $49 billion on 424 fighters before full testing on the stealth plane is completed in 2013. "Starting production before ensuring the design is mature through flight testing significantly increases the risk of costly design change that will push the program over budget and behind schedule," the report concludes. But that is all light years away, as far as Lockheed and BAE are concerned. As Bob Elrod, a senior executive at Lockheed's fighter plane division boasted, "We're looking at world domination of the market."

To make things even better for Blair, Lockheed brought the British in on the new presidential helicopter deal, notwithstanding the loud protests of then-Democratic Senator Joseph Lieberman from Connecticut, where Sikorsky—America's leading helicopter manufacturer and the losing bidder—is located.

Meanwhile Jackson closed down the Committee for the Liberation of Iraq in June 2003 because its human rights rationale for the war had been abandoned.

"We were cut out," Jackson explains, "after the whole thing went to Rumsfeld. The Department of Defense didn't want anyone looking over their shoulder. Rumsfeld took it all away from State." Jackson had lined up people like Vaclav Havel of the Czech Republic, Natan Sharansky of Israel and Carl Bildt, the prime minister of Sweden, to support the Committee for the Liberation of Iraq, but Bush and Rumsfeld took off in another direction. Stephen Hadley explained to Jackson that "terrorism and WMDs" were now the rationale for the war, not human rights.

News of torture at Abu Ghraib prison undermined all of Jackson's efforts and, to his credit, he called for Rumsfeld's resignation. He acknowledges that things are not going well in Iraq, but still sees the removal of Saddam Hussein as morally justified. He declines to predict how it will all end.

Poland, one of the countries Bruce Jackson helped gain membership in NATO, also joined the "coalition of the willing," sending troops to Iraq as a desperate Bush scrambled to find allies in the war. Poland also spent 976 million Euros (more than $1.6 billion) in 2006 upgrading its military, almost all of it going to Lockheed Martin for the first eight F-16 warplanes to be delivered this year, part of a total of the 48 F-16s it has ordered. Mounted on a wall in Jackson's apartment is a glass case containing an ornate antique Polish sword and scabbard, a gift in appreciation of his efforts. Lockheed Martin must have been appreciative, as well: Jackson can tell you the exact price of Lockheed Martin shares.

But Jackson and Hadley—promoted to national security advisor despite his "error" on the uranium—weren't the only beneficiaries among the core group of war advocates. In Washington, the revolving door is already working to the benefit of many involved. Randy Scheunemann, for instance, the president of the Committee for the Liberation of Iraq, became president of the Mercury Group, which lobbied for Lockheed Martin and other corporate clients, before setting up his own firm, Scheunemann and Associates, and then Orion Strategies, which, among other things, consults with companies and countries seeking to do business in Iraq. Rend Al-Rahim Francke, a member of the Committee for the Liberation of Iraq and founder of the Iraq Foundation that facilitated the film *Voices of Iraq*, was appointed Iraqi ambassador to the United States in November of 2003.

When Assistant Secretary of Defense Powell Moore left the government in 2005, though not an attorney, he joined the powerful international law firm McKenna Long & Aldridge, which specializes in aerospace and defense, as managing director of federal government relations. According to the firm's description of its activities, it provides "legal services to some of the largest and fastest growing companies in the aerospace, electronics and information technology field, names such as Lockheed Martin, Boeing, Northrop Grumman, SAIC and TRW."

Edward C. Aldridge, who was the undersecretary of defense for acquisitions, technology and logistics responsible for the November 2001 approval of the Lockheed contract to build F-35, left government in 2003 and now serves on Lockheed's board of directors. That's Washington in an era when the war companies run things.

What, if anything, can be done about the oligarchy of the war companies and the K Street lobbyists pulling the strings in our capital? Is there no way to break the iron triangle? Jackson agrees that contractors doing business with the government should be prohibited by law from making political contributions. He says the contractors would favor this because the situation is not as most people think it is. He insists it's the elected officials who "shake down" the contractors for contributions and not the other way around. Of course, this may be the best indicator, in a roundabout way, of just how powerful the war companies are—in the name of special interest reform the legislators would be cut out of the action from the flow of defense money they can apparently no longer control.

Former Long Island Democratic Representative Otis Pike, who served in the Marines and was a hawk on Vietnam, once said privately, while still in office, that the only solution was to "nationalize" the defense industry. Pike's attitude regarding national security evolved as a result of experiences chairing the Pike Committee investigating abuses by the CIA in the 1970s. Since half of Lockheed Martin's business now comes from its IT division, there is no reason why it should not be broken up under the anti-trust laws into two separate companies, without any damage to its ability to innovate. Also, a war-profits tax of the type imposed by Britain on its military contractors during World War I to help pay for the cost of the war—since they were profiting from it—might be in order.

But none of this is the concern of the beautiful and the brilliant young techies, black, white, brown and yellow, male and female, gay and straight, who throng to Washington to work for the subcontracting firms locating there in droves. In March of 2005, Lockheed Martin acquired Sytex, which provides "personnel and technological solutions to the Pentagon's Northern Command, the Army Intelligence and Strategic Command and the Department of Homeland Security," making Lockheed one of the biggest recruiters of private interrogators, "unaccountable to any legal authority or disciplining procedure," as Corpwatch puts it.

In March of 2006, Lockheed Martin won the lion's share of a $20 billion contract by the U.S. Army to develop cutting-edge technology to support the Army's "reconnaissance, communications, surveillance and intelligence gathering in combat situations." According to Lockheed spokeswoman Wendy Owen this was a "major victory" for Lockheed Martin, which has been aggressively promoting its systems and information technology divisions, which account for half of its business. It already provides surveillance services for United States ports.

That night, March 16, when the local press announced the $20 billion contract, Cafe Citron, off Dupont Circle, was packed with revelers. Latin music throbbed as they laughed and shouted, partying with abandon, knocking down the drinks. For those in the war business, life is good.

Why Peace

The Ties That Bind
(Lockheed Is the Biggest Operator, But Not the Only One)

Here's a quick look at some of the iron triangle interconnections at other defense firms also making a killing in the current war climate:

The Boeing Company: **Defense Revenue (2004):** $17.1 Billion

Defense Products: P-8 Poseidon anti-submarine aircraft, KC 767 air-to-air tanker.

Bedfellows: Richard Perle's venture capital firm, Trireme Partners, received $20 million from the Boeing Company. He's also a member of the Pentagon's Defense Policy Board. James Roche's resignation from the post of secretary of the Air Force was prompted by the investigation Senator John McCain launched into a shady non-competitive Boeing tanker deal Roche encouraged. The investigation eventually landed two of the defense contractor's officials in jail.

Northrop Grumman: **Defense Revenue (2004):** $11.9 Billion

Defense Products: B-2 Bomber, RQ-4 Global Hawk unmanned aerial drone, "Star Wars" laser systems.

Bedfellows: Former undersecretary for defense and current president of the World Bank Paul Wolfowitz is a former Northrop Grumman consultant. Former Pentagon official Douglas Feith has been investigated several times for distorting prewar intelligence on Iraq. In addition to holding the number three position at the pentagon, Feith founded the Feith & Zell law firm, whose clients included Northrop Grumman. He can be credited for creating the now disbanded Office of Strategic Intelligence, which, among other things, provided fake news items to the foreign media in order to gain support for the war in Iraq.

General Dynamics Corp.:   **Defense Revenue (2004):** $9.6 Billion

Defense Products: M1 Abrams Main Tank, Trident subs, EFV Amphibious Assault Vehicle.

Bedfellows: Gordon England, former secretary of the Navy, began his career with no prior military or government experience. Rather, he was plucked by the Bush administration from the position of executive vice president of General Dynamics. Former Secretary of State Colin Powell served on the board of Gulfstream Aerospace—a company whose clientele included Kuwait and Saudi Arabia, and which was taken over by General Dynamics.

Halliburton: **Defense Revenue (2004):** $8 Billion

Defense Services: Provides the military with services such as construction, clean-up and troop support.

Bedfellow: Vice President Dick Cheney was CEO of Halliburton from 1995 until his resignation in 2000, and has been accused by Democrats in Congress of having an influence on no-bid contracts awarded to the company he once ran.

The Berlin Wall:
An African Perspective

Temba A. Nolutshungu

Temba A. Nolutshungu is the Director of the Free Market Foundation, Cape Town. He is a trustee of several boards. He travels widely and publishes regular papers on a variety of issues.

This essay is adapted from an article published by www.AfricanLiberty.org on November 8, 2009.

> *Those that can give up essential liberty to obtain a little temporary safety deserve neither liberty nor safety* - Benjamin Franklin, 1759

Having lived in Apartheid South Africa, I feel my experience qualifies me to comment on tyranny, be it in South Africa, Korea, Germany, or wherever throughout Africa. The history of the Berlin Wall demonstrates the truth that a free society, based on private ownership of the means of production, best delivers what people want; liberty and prosperity.

I had some bitter experiences as a black South African on the receiving end of apartheid laws. I was first thrown into a police holding cell at the age of sixteen, languishing there for days with my family not knowing where I was. This was an experience to be repeated as had happened to so many other blacks. As a black consciousness political activist, I was detained twice in solitary confinement under the Terrorism and General Law Amendment Acts, draconian laws that forbade freedoms of expression and association.

My paternal grandfather, whose name I carry, built a house for his family on land provided by his employer, the mining company Crown Mines. He also built a tennis court, the envy of everyone including whites, which he allowed others to use. When he died, the property was expropriated without compensation, by virtue of the fact that he was black. Blacks had no legal title to land. His family was dispersed throughout what was then the Transvaal province. His youngest child, my uncle Graham Tainton Nolutshungu, left South Africa on a one-way passport (exit passport as it was then known) and established himself in Sweden. He still recalls vividly and with profound sadness the melodrama surrounding the expulsion of the family from Crown Mines.

My maternal grandmother ran a small subsistence retail grocery outlet in Cape Town, and instilled in us a work ethic. She nursed my grandfather for many years during his illness. He was unable to come to terms with the consequences of losing his land because of the Natives Land Act of 1913. The Act expropriated black-owned land at the stroke of a pen, ensuring that blacks would be forever hewers of wood and drawers of water. My grandfather's grief brought home to me the cruelties of the apartheid system. Tragically, he kept

157

reading the agricultural journal, *Farmer's Weekly*, when he no longer had any land and was denied any right to own land. He could not let go. I seldom saw him smile. And that is how he was when he died.

My grandmother always said that if the government would leave us alone and not interfere with and dictate to us black people, we would take care of our own. While this did not sound politically sophisticated, I believe my grandmother was talking about freedom in the classical liberal sense. I know my ancestors must be proud that I have dug a trench and hoisted a flag in the cause of individual liberty for all people, wherever they might be in the world.

As I ponder the significance of the fall of the Berlin Wall and the implosion of the socialist and communist systems, I am inspired by the courageous and noble struggle of our people to overcome the suffocating stranglehold of the repressive system of apartheid. I understand why all over the world people migrate from repressive systems to freer countries. It is not surprising that the freer the country, the greater the proportion of refugees attracted to it.

I became aware of the existence of the Berlin Wall, without appreciating its political significance, soon after its construction in 1961. This was the time when I was cutting my political teeth and discovering the forces that rule the world. The all-pervasive apartheid system that was in force in South Africa inevitably politicized many of us, and socialism seemed to offer an appealing solution to the prevailing state of affairs. The SA government displayed a systematic and deep-seated hatred of communism, which was manifest on an almost daily basis in the propaganda generated by the communications network at the disposal of the various state organs. This anti-communist sentiment was echoed in the relatively free press, which was owned and run by whites. So, for us blacks, the equation was simple. The oppressors, who had inflicted so much suffering on our people, hated communism. So what the enemy hated had to be good for the oppressed people. After all, communism was about a classless society and how the people shared everything.

As I matured politically, I immersed myself in a thorough study of the philosophy of communism. I began asking myself how communism worked in practice, and found it hard to come up with credible answers. This further stimulated my curiosity. I wondered about the Berlin Wall, built by the Russian and the East German governments to keep the people living inside the workers' paradise, communist East Germany, from fleeing to the capitalist West, which typified man's exploitation of his fellow man.

Before its construction, East Germany had experienced a dramatic exodus of people to the West consisting of thousands of educated young people—a brain drain of major proportions. After the Wall was built, with its guard towers, trenches and checkpoints, thousands of individuals risked death attempting to cross into West Berlin. It disturbed me that the refugees included people from all walks of life: artists, scientists, students, and professionals among others. They seemed not to be deterred by the threat of death, as they sought to cross the Wall in defiance of East German law.

I began to perceive the Berlin Wall as symptomatic of the merits or demerits of the two contrasting systems, capitalist democracy and communist dictatorship ('the dictatorship of the proletariat'). After World War II, capitalist West Germany had gradually grown into the second biggest economy in the world, while East Germany remained stuck in the economic doldrums. West Germany was a free democratic country, while East Germany was clearly a police state.

I cast my precocious mind on South and North Korea. The same scenario was patently obvious. As with Germany, it concerned the same people, same culture, same language, with relatives on both sides of the divide. But there were such glaring incompatibilities. The desperate attempts of individuals to flee from the communist grip of the North to the capitalist democracy of the South needed closer study.

In Africa, most liberation movements, which sought to overthrow repressive European colonialism by force, had embraced variations of communism or socialism. Once in power and transformed into political parties, these movements implemented economic policies informed by a socialist perspective.

Gradually, it became clear that these policies were very much to the detriment of the welfare of their people. For quite a while, though, the vision of the nirvana that socialism would bring, along with an awareness of the manifest injustices of the colonial past (which were blamed largely upon capitalist interests), bought the new parties time and caused people to put up with the consequent suffering. The seductive vision of popular ownership of the means of production through the medium of the state appealed to many and still does in some circles within South Africa.

Only with experience has it become clear to me that the nationalization of productive assets doesn't actually mean that they are owned and controlled by either the proletariat or the people and operated for their collective benefit. Rather, they are owned, controlled, and managed by the state, which in reality means the elites or elite factions which wield power and control the state. It gradually became apparent that, as with East Germany and North Korea and other communist countries, the leadership of these African socialist states was the only class to derive any real benefits from their collectivist policies. As in the case of East Germany, it eventually transpired that attempts to impose communist systems in Africa were economically unsustainable, politically tyrannical and morally bankrupt.

As I scrutinized the apartheid system more closely, it became clear that it had more in common with a communist state than with a free capitalist society. Under apartheid, the government controlled every facet of black peoples' lives, from the cradle to the grave. Consistent with the policy of racial segregation, it decreed where black people could be born, where they could live, and where they could carry out limited subsistence trade in accordance with all sorts of restrictive conditions.

My grandmother's shop and the few other businesses allowed to operate in black areas were subject to a myriad of regulations, including restricted trading hours and a description of the nature and quantity of the goods that could be stocked and sold. Blacks were also prohibited from operating any type of business outside designated black areas.

Apartheid denied blacks property rights, mandated where they could get the legislatively prescribed form of education, where they could work and what form of work they could do, which hospitals and amenities they could use, how and when they could move from place to place, and even where they could be buried. Blacks had to carry identity documents, generally known as "passes," which had to be produced on demand to policemen. Forgetting the pass at home meant being thrown in prison for the night. The pass I carried stipulated where I was allowed to live, and, if I was employed, the name and address of my registered employer.

Getting a job was a real struggle. As I lived in a province designated a "colored" preferential area, employers would typically be denied the work permits they needed to employ me. Curfews prohibited blacks from being outside my stipulated residential area after the curfew time, which generally meant after dark. To blacks passes were a symbol of oppression, and, not surprisingly, the public burning of passes was to become an important act of defiance. With apartheid, blacks were effectively nationalized by the South African government.

Apartheid, a ubiquitous and omnipotent system, was, like its communist cousins, economically unsustainable, politically tyrannical and morally reprehensible. And, as with communism, the few who benefited vehemently rejected this characterization of the system.

For me, the fall of the Berlin Wall proved some very important truths. People value freedom above ideologies. The system that fails to acknowledge this definitive attribute of human nature will eventually succumb to pressure, however long that might take. The system that does not obstruct this natural human state will unleash the spirit of enterprise that runs through all cultures and all nations. This is encapsulated in the words of Joseph Stalin's daughter, Svetlana Alliluyeva, "It is human nature that rules the world, not governments and regimes."

Communism corrodes human freedom. In its zeal to redistribute resources, abolish private ownership of the means of production, and re-engineer the structure of society, it necessarily resorts to the use of force. It subsequently denies individuals the freedom to act in their own best interests, and it denies them the fruits of their own labor and initiative. It is not surprising, therefore, that communist leaders such as Joseph Stalin, Mao Ze Dong, Pol Pot, Eric Honecker, Nikolai Ceauşescu and many others were obliged to rely so much on coercion, violence and a body of spies to maintain their regimes, and in the process slaughtered hundreds of millions of their own people. (Vladimir Lenin used a now infamous metaphor, to remind his followers that an omelet cannot be made without breaking eggs.)

My understanding of the history of the Berlin Wall, the circumstances surrounding its historic breach on November 9, 1989, and its subsequent destruction by popular demand has fundamentally contributed to my own ideological metamorphosis. For me, the history of the Wall proves the truth that a free society best delivers what people want for themselves and their loved ones: liberty, peace, and prosperity.

The deconstruction of the Berlin Wall signifies the triumph of the human instinct for freedom over imposed ideology, but for Africans faced with a plethora of trade barriers and protectionist measures, which impede the free flow of their products to Europe, it seems that the fortress mentality lives on in Europe in another guise. There is a Berlin Wall of tariff protection which hamper free trade of African agricultural products to European markets and consumers. This is also an immoral and tyrannical wall. In the interest of human rights, justice, and peace it too should be brought down.

Peace is also a necessary condition for the free flow of goods within and between nations. Political instability and war are generally detrimental to trade. The reasons are quite understandable. Where there is strife and violence, trade becomes uncertain and unsafe. Furthermore, under conditions of political instability or outright war, the institutions which support democracy and the rule of law are often compromised.

But peace requires liberty in order to thrive. Liberty and peace are so intertwined that the former can rightly be said to be a precondition for the latter. Enduring peace cannot be realized until people, as individuals, feel truly free to interact with one another without the coercive intrusion of government or vested interests which enjoy the favors of government. The quest for peace presupposes that everyone accepts that, in general, all interactions among individuals are permissible provided that they involve neither force nor fraud. The quest for personal freedom is so ingrained in humans that it is almost instinctive. This truth, while obvious to most, is inexplicably elusive to those with autocratic designs. Even in primitive societies this was the governing wisdom which acted like a glue to ensure that socio-economic transactions would ultimately serve the interests of the community at large. It is precisely the adherence to this principle which explains the social cohesion in communities and nations, long before the advent of the modern-day state.

Apartheid, as with all variations of socialism or other totalitarian systems, was antithetical to freedom. Apartheid relentlessly sought to control human conduct through its legislative prescriptions. But ultimately, as is the case with the former socialist systems and the present unraveling of autocratic regimes in the Arab world, the instinct for freedom prevails over even the most autocratic and totalitarian regimes, no matter what their ideological or religious basis.

It can thus be clearly seen how any political system or ideology that is based on the subjugation of the individual will to collectivist or statist dictates has embedded within itself the seeds of its own demise. The desire for individual freedom has driven revolutions throughout history. Human beings wish to pursue their individual aspirations unimpeded so long as this pursuit does not hurt one's fellow humans. Sadly, as has sometimes happened, vested interests take over and start to interpret or articulate these aspirations from narrow sectional perspectives which rely on the hijacking of state institutions for the implementation of their goals. In this regard, the wise words of Thomas Paine (*The American Crisis*, No 4, 1777) are particularly poignant especially in these times: "Those who expect to reap the blessings of freedom must, like men, undergo the fatigue of supporting it."

Encountering Humanity

Luke Hansen

Luke Hansen, a scholastic in the Wisconsin Province of the Society of Jesus (Jesuits), coordinates the Red Cloud Volunteer Program on the Pine Ridge Indian Reservation in South Dakota. In 2010, he earned a Masters degree in Social Philosophy from Loyola University, Chicago; his thesis is titled, "Countering Terrorism with Justice: a Catholic response to U.S. policies of indefinite detention in the fight against terrorism." Luke is also active with the Witness Against Torture community (www.witnesstorture.org).

A shorter version of this essay appeared in the Winter 2011 issue of *Jesuit Journeys*, a publication of the Wisconsin Province of the Society of Jesus (www.jesuitswisprov.org). Used with permission.

Our pilgrimage to Bermuda to meet with former Guantánamo detainees

Khalil Mamut speaks fluent English, loves to play soccer, and deeply misses his mother in East Turkestan. Abdulla Abdulqudir has difficulty speaking to his father on the phone; his father cries uncontrollably, longing to reunite with his son after almost a decade. Ablikim Turahun had a wife and son, but since there was little hope to ever reunite with them, he told them to move on, not wanting them to lose their own lives during his long imprisonment. His wife has since remarried.

Visiting with these three Uyghur men (along with a fourth, Salahidin Abdulahad) in Bermuda, I learned that they love their families, enjoy playing soccer, work hard to earn money, offer generous hospitality to strangers, desire justice and fairness for others, live a devoutly religious life of prayer, and experience the usual joys and struggles of life. Simply put: in many ways, these men are quite ordinary, and a lot like us.

Yet their story is also unique and has involved untold suffering at the hands of both China and the United States: persecuted by the Chinese government as an ethnic and religious minority; forced to leave their livelihood in Afghanistan as U.S. bombs devastated the country in late 2001; doubled-crossed and arrested in Pakistan; handed over to the U.S. military in exchange for bounties; interrogated and imprisoned in Guantánamo for seven years; and finally, resettled on a small island—thousands of miles from family—with few Muslims and no fellow Uyghurs.

In July 2010, I had the privileged opportunity to personally visit with these men and listen to their stories. I traveled with two friends, Jeremy Kirk and John Bambrick, from *Witness Against Torture*—a faith-based movement to close Guantánamo, end torture, and forge human ties with the prisoners and their families. In Bermuda, we visited the Uyghurs' apartment, shared meals, cruised the island on their motorbikes, played soccer on the beach, and swam in the ocean. Our various conversations during the weekend, which ranged from light-hearted to emotional and serious, helped us to begin building relationships with the men we had long advocated for, but had never met.

I became involved with *Witness Against Torture* through my friendship with members of the Catholic Worker movement (www.catholicworker.org), several of whom had traveled to Cuba in 2005 to bring light to the injustices of torture and indefinite detention, and to personally visit with the detainees, fulfilling the Christian mandate to "visit the imprisoned." Even though the twenty-five pilgrims were ultimately not permitted to enter the U.S. Naval Base, they were able to hold a 24-hour fast and vigil outside its gate. This prophetic action strongly resonated with me and inspired me. For my Catholic Worker friends, Guantánamo was not only a "political issue," but a reality and an injustice that affected hundreds of our fellow human beings and their families.

The detainees are human beings became a mantra of our movement. The detainees are not "bottom of the barrel dregs" and "genuine human debris," as Rush Limbaugh claimed. They are fathers and sons, uncles and brothers. Whatever the detainees are accused of, they remain human beings—and recognizing this truth changes everything. It's never moral to torture a human being. And it's never moral to imprison a human being without due process. Essentially, this is why I am involved in this work, and why I visited with the Uyghur men in Bermuda. I wanted to cut through the rhetoric, characterizations, and condemnations in order to meet the *human beings.*

Arrest and imprisonment

All four men—Khalil, Abdulla, Ablikim, and Salahidin—are ethnic Uyghurs from East Turkestan, also known as the Xinjiang Uyghur Autonomous Region in China. The estimated twenty-five million Uyghurs who live in the vast region (four times the size of California) do not identify as Chinese; they consider themselves Turks from Central Asia. The land, resource, and cultural disputes between the Chinese government and the Uyghur people are well-documented. So is Chinese persecution of Uyghurs, though the situation of the Tibetans receives much more international attention.

In a Guantánamo tribunal hearing in November 2004, Ablikim described how the Chinese government systematically persecutes the Uyghur people. Uyghurs are constantly threatened by unjust incarceration, torture, social and cultural marginalization, stolen resources, unemployment, and inhumane abortion laws, he said.[1]

"The Uyghur people only have the privilege of having two children," Ablikim testified. "If a female gets pregnant with a third child, the government will forcibly take the kid through abortion." He then asked the tribunal members, "If they torture us every day and pressure us too much, then what are we going to do? How are we going to live? In the future, what will our next generation do? How will they survive?"

In this desperate situation, the four Uyghur men left their native land and traveled to Afghanistan, the only country in the region where Uyghurs can work without documentation, and without fear of being returned to China. In Afghanistan, the men had found jobs in exchange for housing and meals in a

Uyghur settlement, but they were forced to find refuge in Pakistan after the U.S. began its bombing campaign in late 2001.

"We crossed into Pakistan and there were tribal people there and they took us to their houses and they killed a sheep and cooked the meat, and we ate," Ablikim explained to a military tribunal. Later, the men were taken to a mosque, served bread and tea, betrayed into the hands of Pakistan authorities, and later transferred to U.S. custody in exchange for $5,000 bounties. When the men realized that they were in U.S. custody, they actually felt relieved. They recognized the United States as a strong supporter of Uyghur causes, and thus expected to be quickly processed and released. This was the "war on terror," however, and not even favorable Uyghur politics would save these men from ultimately being transferred to Guantánamo and falsely labeled as terrorists.

Resettlement efforts

After early interrogations revealed that the Uyghur men had no connection with the Taliban or al Qaeda, the U.S. government faced a difficult predicament: They could not return the men to China, because of the possibility of torture and unjust imprisonment in that country. At the same time, more than one hundred countries rejected U.S. pleas to resettle the Uyghur men, because of Chinese political and economic pressure. And the last remaining option—resettlement on U.S. soil in an established Uyghur-American community in Fairfax, Virginia— never gained any traction within the Bush administration.

For nearly eight years, the Uyghur men received news of favorable tribunal decisions (recommending transfer to a third country), along with several U.S. Supreme Court victories, including the *Boumediene v. Bush* (2008) decision, which extended the constitutional right of *habeas corpus* to Guantánamo detainees. In October 2008, a federal judge ruled the continued detention of the Uyghurs to be unlawful, and he ordered their immediate release into the United States. While the Bush administration conceded that the Uyghur men were not "enemy combatants," their legal team successfully blocked the transfer of the Uyghur men onto U.S. soil.

The U.S. courts failed to deliver their promise of justice for the Uyghur men, but U.S. politics brought new hope in the election of Barack Obama. In April 2009, the White House's top lawyer, Greg Craig, developed a plan to resettle two of the Uyghur men in Fairfax, Virginia. According to a *Time* magazine report,[2] Secretary of Defense Robert Gates and Secretary of State Hillary Clinton approved the plan, and "it was a matter of days, not weeks," until the transfer would take place.

The hope: if two Uyghurs were successfully resettled on U.S. soil, more would follow. And with the U.S. taking the lead on Guantánamo-detainee resettlement, the State Department would enjoy more credibility in asking other countries to do the same, ultimately helping to shutter the infamous Guantánamo prison.

On April 24, however, news of the Uyghur resettlement plan hit the media, and politicians and pundits quickly and relentlessly criticized the President for planning to release "hardcore terrorists" into American neighborhoods. In a May

14 opinion piece in *The Washington Examiner*,[3] Newt Gingrich shamelessly and falsely accused the Uyghur men of being "trained mass killers instructed by the same terrorists responsible" for the September 11 terrorist attacks, even though the Bush administration conceded that this wasn't the case, and the courts unanimously agreed.

The persistent attacks paid off, however, and the damage was done. With public opinion strongly against the resettlement plan, President Obama acquiesced, and the Uyghurs' long imprisonment became even longer. "It was a political decision, to put it bluntly," acknowledged a White House aide (*Time* magazine report). President Obama decided to reserve his political capital for domestic initiatives, such as health care legislation. The cost: the continued unjust imprisonment of seventeen Uyghur men.

One month later, something finally broke on the resettlement front: Bermuda, an overseas territory of the British government, agreed to resettle four of the imprisoned Uyghur men. After seven grueling years in Guantánamo, these four men finally had an opportunity to begin new lives on a tiny island in the North Atlantic Ocean.

Abdulla's perspective

I loved being with Abdulla, who demonstrated a full range of emotions as we shared stories, told jokes, and engaged in serious conversation about religion, politics, and his experience of imprisonment in Guantánamo. When we laughed together, Abdulla grinned widely, nodding his head to the side, eyes sparkling. At other times, however, his facial expression revealed a very different story. He could become stoic, serious, and (justifiably) angry.

When telling us about his long imprisonment, Abdulla's eyes would widen, his speech would become hurried, and he would repeat, "Am I a terrorist? I am not a terrorist!" He explained the difficulty of being told—early on—that they were innocent and would soon be released, only to wait for years and years while hundreds of other detainees were being repatriated or resettled in third countries. (More than five hundred detainees were released from Guantánamo during the Bush administration.) "If we are innocent, why must we continue to wait?" he asked.

This kind of waiting—never charged with a crime, never brought to trial, never knowing when the imprisonment might end—tested their faith and resolve more than anything else at Guantánamo.

"George Bush should spend one day in Guantánamo," Abdulla suggested. "Give him one day behind the cage, taking orders from the MPs [military police], having to 'step back' behind the line to receive his meals. If he asks to leave, they can tell him to be patient. See if he lasts two hours before he tries to hang himself." (In imagining this scenario, Abdulla was not motivated by hate or revenge. He simply wanted others to empathize with the suffering they endured. Only then, Abdulla seemed to suggest, would the absurdity and injustice of Guantánamo be revealed.)

Sometimes Abdulla shared very freely. At other times, especially when talking about the conditions of confinement or the difficulty of being separated from family, Abdulla (in mid-thought) would politely ask to change topics. "I can't say anymore," he would say. "It's too tough to talk about it." We respected his wishes and gladly redirected the conversation. In these moments, I gained a better sense for the gravity of the harm inflicted upon these men. I, too, felt anger and frustration… and remorse.

Faith and family

We asked the Uyghur men what gave them hope during seven years of imprisonment in Guantánamo. "Faith in Allah and asking Allah for patience. Also the knowledge that if released, we could possibly see our families again," Khalil explained.

In Bermuda, I felt inspired by their genuine faith in God and accompanying religious commitment. Their innate sense for the divine touches every aspect of their lives; it affects what they eat, when they pray, their perspective on suffering and hope, and their plans for marriage and children.

For these men, faith and family are intricately tied together. They acknowledged a religious obligation to marry and have children, and they explained that being in Bermuda (with few Muslims and no Uyghurs) made this difficult to fulfill. The Uyghur men constantly spoke about how much they love and miss their families who are thousands of miles away. "I miss my mom," Khalil simply and poignantly expressed. It broke our hearts to hear and feel Khalil's sadness, and we realized how much freedom we enjoy (and take for granted) to see our families.

The Uyghurs' primary concern, however, did not rest with their own hardship, but that of their imprisoned brothers. While seventeen Uyghurs have been transferred from Guantánamo to third countries, five Uyghur men remain in Guantánamo to this day. From our perspective, the solution is simple: Congress needs to rescind the ban on detainee transfers to U.S. soil, and the Obama administration needs to make this resettlement a reality. We understand that welcoming former Guantánamo prisoners into our neighborhoods would require a major shift in public opinion, but we believe that it is possible. Having encountered the humanity of these men in Bermuda, we feel renewed in our commitment to the freedom of their unjustly imprisoned brothers.

"Our happiness will come when the brothers are out," Khalil explained. "Whenever I eat, whenever I pray, I think of them intensely." We unite with Khalil in these prayers, and we invite others to join this struggle for justice.

1. Combatant Status Review Tribunal Transcripts: Ablikim Turahun, "The Guantánamo Docket," *The New York Times*. Available online at http://projects.nytimes.com/guantanamo/detainees/320-ablikim-turahun/documents/4.

2. Massimo Calabresi and Michael Weisskopf, "The Fall of Greg Craig, Obama's Top Lawyer," *Time* magazine (Nov. 19, 2009).

3. Newt Gingrich, "Let's NOT meet the Uighurs," *Washington Examiner* (May 15, 2009). Available online at http://washingtonexaminer.com/newt-gingrich/2009/05/lets-not-meet-uighurs. For a direct response to Gingrich's article, see Nury A. Turkel, "Meet the real Uyghurs," *Foreign Policy* (May 20, 2009). Available online at http://experts.foreignpolicy.com/posts/2009/05/20/meet_the_real_uyghurs.

From Utopia to Dystopia

My Disillusion with the U.S. Government

Jamshid Marvasti

Jamshid A. Marvasti, MD, is a child and adult psychiatrist who has practiced for more than 30 years in the U.S. He is a specialist on psychological trauma, terrorism, and child maltreatment on which he has published articles and edited books, including Psycho-Political Aspects of Suicide Warriors, Terrorism, and Martyrdom (2008), *and* War Trauma in Veterans and Their Families (2012). *Dr. Marvasti is an Instructor in Psychiatry at the University of Connecticut School of Medicine.*

If I wanted to live in a country where the government cheats, deceives, tortures, brainwashes, and violates human rights, I would have stayed in the Middle East. —The author

Introduction

I am an American by choice, rather than by birth. In this writing, when I refer to "the U.S." or "America," I use these to refer to the United States government, and *not* the citizens of the United States. Likewise, terms such as "we" do not refer to you and me personally, but rather to the administration. I have respect and admiration for American citizens (in fact, I married one), and I presently consider most Americans to be victims: exploited, deceived, and brainwashed by major news media and the government, which, in my opinion, are both greatly controlled by the same elite group.

Before Entering the U.S.: The Dream of "Camelot"

We are to be that shining city upon a hill. —Pres. Ronald Reagan

I was born into a military family in Iran, and grew up in an educated middle class home. My mother, a midwife, worked day and night, but more so at night because, as she used to say, "Babies come at midnight." My father was a major in the Iranian Army when I was born, and eventually he became a general.

I remember the summer of 1953 (28th of Mordad), when the CIA carried out their coup in Iran (I nicknamed this "the Iranian Nakba"). The coup resulted in the overthrow of democratically-elected nationalist Dr. Mohammad Mossadegh and the installation of Mohammad Reza Shah Pahlavi's dictatorship. I was only a child, but I remember watching my father, then a colonel, as he stayed up all night listening to the radio and smoking cigarettes. Once in a while I would hear the name of my father's friend on the broadcast. I did not understand as a child on that night how significantly the destiny of my country had changed. (*See notes at bottom of this chapter*).

This coup became a thorn in the sides of many Iranian nationalists. They felt resentment toward the U.S. Government, whose leaders seemed to think they were in a position to know what was best for Iranians; as if Iranians did not know how to take care of themselves (2). I, however, was able to rationalize this incident and felt that maybe the American CIA agents knew something that we Iranians did not. Perhaps they had information that ordinary people were not privy to concerning the plans of the Soviet Union. The Soviets were pushing for a regime change in Iran through their communist party, Toudeh. At that time we received constant propaganda from the Soviet Union. They were critical of America and thought of Americans as victims and slaves of capitalism. (I did not believe this, until I began to practice medicine in the United States and found that the political system here and its interventions were forcing some of my elderly patients to choose between their medication and their food. In fact, according to the government's own data, their policies are making the rich richer and the poor poorer).

Eventually, I passed the medical exam necessary for entering residency training in the United States. My father encouraged me to "Go to the West" for my education, and my mother would always add, "Learn science, and bring it back." In some ways the U.S. did look like Camelot: a center of art, science, and freedom.

At that time, Iran was a police state, with corrupt government officials and a notorious security service, SAVAK, which brutally tortured many opponents of the government. SAVAK had been created under the guidance of the CIA and the Israeli intelligence agency, the Mossad, in the 1950s. According to Jesse J. Leaf, a former CIA analyst in Iran, SAVAK was instructed in torture techniques by CIA agents. In fact, after the 1979 revolution, Iranians found a CIA film made for SAVAK on "how to torture women" (Blum, 1995).

The country was run by a pseudo-political party under the Shah, and all of the news was censored and controlled by the Shah's government. There was no arbiter of justice to whom anyone could complain about SAVAK and the police.

Any demonstration at my university, no matter how peaceful, would end with police invading the area, beating up students, and arresting them. Several of my classmates were arrested and tortured. As a medical student in Iran, I worked with one hospital physician who had graduated from a school in the U.S. After returning to Iran he was arrested, tortured, and sentenced to years in jail for his opposition to the Shah. This was a time when people were executed because of their leftist/communist ideologies.

At that time, Iran was a country in which a Shakespearean play could not be shown because of its content. The regime believed that if an emperor such as Julius Caesar could be assassinated, it might give Iranians the idea that their king could also be killed (as if Iranians could not figure this out on their own).

The Beginning of my Disappointment/Disillusion

If I sit silently, I have sinned. —Dr. Mohammad Mossadegh

In 1973, I came to the U.S., leaving behind the dictatorship of the Shah of Iran. Even though the Shah's dictatorship was fully supported by the U.S., I still had positive feelings toward the U.S. system of government. By comparison, the neighboring citizens of the U.S.S.R. had less freedom to speak or travel, and less certainty that their leaders would respect their human rights. While in Iran I also learned that, even in anti-communist America, members of the communist party had the freedom to believe in their own ideals, and even to vote for their own presidential candidates. In school I had learned Lincoln's famous quotation about a government, "of the people, by the people, for the people." I found this deeply moving, and wanted to learn more about the U.S. system of government.

I was always fascinated with the idea of freedom, especially freedom of speech and news media. Gradually, I started to adjust to American life in the 1970s, and continued to have positive feelings toward the U.S. government. Here, there were Iranian students who openly opposed the Shah, and were even able to write about it. In political terms, they ranged from left-communist Marxist Maoists to right-wing religious believers. I began to meet them and to read their anti-Shah literature, published by the Iranian opposition in the United States. This writing also criticized the U.S. government as the greatest supporter of the Shah, and it was exciting for me to see that the government here did not censor these newspapers or prevent their publication. How different from the way things were in Iran at that time, where every newspaper, every bit of written material, had to first be cleared for publication by SAVAK.

During the '70s I did not have any major complaints about the U.S. system, although by then I had started to read material by Howard Zinn and Noam Chomsky. While I felt that they might be right some of the time, I generally didn't fully believe in their analysis of and allegations against the U.S. government.

I was in denial. Looking back, I see that this denial was necessary for me at the time. In the field of psychiatry, we call this "denial in service of ego." I compare myself to one of my patients from long ago, a woman whose husband had been carrying on multiple affairs. There was ample indication of his infidelity, but because it was too painful for her to believe or accept it, she remained in denial. This was similar to my relationship with the U.S. government.

It happened gradually, but over time my denial decreased and bitter reality began to take a more prominent place. Eye-opening experiences began to bring forth undeniable truths about the U.S. government. For example, it was only after the 1979 revolution in Iran that we learned some of the secrets of the Shah's dictatorship. Revelations of wrong-doing came from the Iranian people, not the government of the revolution. During a visit to Iran after the revolution I spoke with people who filled me in on what had happened with regard to human right violation by Shah. (For further information, see Rejali, 2007 and Blum, 1995).

The most shocking allegations involved American CIA agents who had taught various torture techniques to members of SAVAK, and had even sold them high tech torture machines. It seemed the Iranians were in the habit of torturing the opposition to the point that they became unconscious or died. The U.S. agents set out to teach them the nuances of torture, explaining that the goal is to inflict maximum pain, but cause only a minimum amount of loss of consciousness, permanent bodily injury, or death. They explained that the purpose of torture is to break the detainee's will, to control them, get a confession, and gain the names of their friends and collaborators (Rejali, 2007 and Blum, 1995; 2000). This baffled me. I could not understand how the same government that was supposed to protect individual rights to due process could teach torture.

Conversation with Clergyman

I recall a conversation with a clergyman from the Middle East, years ago, when I was still idealistic about the U.S. I criticized the number of political arrests in his country, where members of the opposition were being detained without legal justification. I remember asking him why his government was keeping these people in detention for months without any charges, and subjecting them to isolation and torture. He defended his country by telling me that they were surrounded by enemies: the CIA, Mossad, the KGB, and Iraq's Saddam Hussein. And not only that, he said, they had terrorists inside the country as well, all plotting against them.

He pressed me to explain why I stayed in the U.S., and I told him that it was because these types of human rights violations would never happen here. He emphasized that the U.S. was not in any kind of jeopardy nor facing threats to national security, and he insisted that the U.S. would act the same way if faced with any real danger. I challenged him by reminding him that President Reagan had been shot by a would-be assassin, yet still, law enforcement officials had to go through all of the proper channels before they could even obtain a search warrant to collect evidence from the suspect's home. He countered that this event was not a true threat, and that if Reagan had been shot, another one just like him would take his place.

Sadly, if I were to meet this man again, I would have to confess that the Bush/Cheney and Obama/Biden administrations have proved just how wrong I was, and how right he was. Our modern government should remember the words of Benjamin Franklin, who said, "Those who sacrifice liberty for security deserve neither."

Elements of my Disillusion

When I go to fight the darkness, I carry a torch, not a sword
. —Zarathustra (Iranian prophet)

My disillusion did not develop overnight. I was full of disdain when I heard that Chomsky believed the U.S. was a "leading terrorist state." He referred to the U.S. Army's guidelines on "low-intensity warfare," comparing these practices with terrorism. Slowly, and over time, I began to recognize that he may be, at least partially, right. Terrorism has generally been referred to as a technique of the weak. However, Chomsky explained that Western regimes also commit terrorism, but they refer to it as "counterterrorism."

Looking back, it is possible for me to pinpoint some of the precise elements of my disillusion:

1) The Similarity between Terrorism and Counterterrorism

You will never end terrorism by terrorizing others. - Martin Luther King, Jr.

Terrorism is the war of the poor, and war is the terrorism of the rich.
—Sir Peter Ustinov

One of my first disappointments was over the Reagan administration's monetary and military support for the armed Contras, who engaged in terrorism against the legitimately elected Sandinista government of Nicaragua (Parry, 1997, Parts 1 & 2). Next was the U.S. support for the apartheid government of South Africa, which was also operating as a terrorist government and providing support for white rule in South Africa through military, intelligence, nuclear, and economic cooperation (Davis, 1997). The Apartheid regime was terrorizing blacks and those who supported them. Such policies bothered me, and I began to wonder how "terrorism" was actually different from "counterterrorism."

Both Reagan and George W. Bush have claimed that other countries hate us because we represent freedom and democracy. This assertion was, by then, no longer believable for me. I had come to realize that the United States had long supported, and continues to support, some of the world's most brutal dictators. It is only logical that the citizens of the corrupt foreign governments that we support will resent us.

Former U.S. Air Force lieutenant colonel, Robert Bowman, made a keen observation about the U.S. role in other countries. He had flown many bombing missions in Vietnam before becoming a Catholic priest, then an Archbishop. He said, "We are not hated because we practice democracy, value freedom, or uphold human rights. We are hated because our government denies these things to people in Third World countries whose resources are coveted by our multinational corporations."

I was dismayed to realize that Western governments ignored or downplayed their own behavior in contributing to the creation of opposition and terrorism in other countries. This was especially true after 9/11. I thought of the proverb made popular by Hillary Clinton, "It takes a village to raise a child." We could also say "It takes *two* villages to raise a terrorist." The American government had become one of those villages. Our "village" contributes to the development of terrorism by invading, occupying, and colonizing the other village's land and resources, and humiliating its citizens.

Western counterterrorism operations tend to rely solely on killing the suspected terrorist, while disregarding the fact that many innocent civilians are also killed in the process. One example was an incident in which coalition forces bombed a house in a Pakistani village, based on information that a suspected terrorist might be inside. In this case, they also knew that the house contained women, children, and other civilians. That, however, did not deter them from bombing. The local villagers later denied that the home had been harboring a terrorist, and were left to mourn for the loss of the dozen civilians inside the home, who had effectively been sentenced to death despite their innocence. No Western authority questions the morality of such massacres; not the major corporate media, nor the legislators who fund these killings with taxpayers' wealth. The perpetrators, from the President to the drone operators in Nevada, will not have to face a war crimes tribunal.

There are two sets of rules at work here. On our own soil, police and law enforcement officials are instructed that, whenever possible, they are not to shoot at an offender if he or she is holding a hostage, because the hostage may get hurt. In fact, law enforcement officials are trained not to shoot at any time when civilians are present, due to risk of civilian injury. Yet, overseas, we knowingly bomb innocent civilian areas with impunity.

2) Double Standard

When fascism comes to America, it will be wrapped in the flag, carrying a cross. | —Sinclair Lewis

I have also been increasingly bothered by the double standard that is such an obvious part of U.S. policy. For example, when President Reagan was asked why the Nicaraguan Contras were not being called terrorists, despite the fact that they employed all of the tactics associated with terrorism, he replied that the Contras were "freedom fighters." This justified his willingness to support them as they went on destroying farms, killing civilians, and engaging in illegal arms and cocaine trafficking (Blum 2006).

More recently, Libya has been criticized by U.S. leaders and the media for using cluster bombs in civilian areas, which is a violation of international legal conventions against the use of such weapons. These munitions explode into hundreds of "bomblets," which, if left unexploded, can remain in the landscape where they can harm civilians for decades. The International Criminal Court (ICC) brought a case against embattled Libyan leader, Col. Muammar Qaddafi. ICC prosecutor, Luis Moreno-Ocampo, said, "Those responsible for attacks on civilians must be held to account" (Gilligan, 2011). Yet, the U.S. considered it okay to use cluster bombs in Iraq and Afghanistan.

In March of 2011, U.S. forces began using B2 stealth bombers to target sites in Libya. They carry 2,000 pound bombs, including the massive "bunker buster"(Hartley-Parkinson, 2011). Members of the Libyan opposition (anti-Qaddafi rebels) complained bitterly about the impact of these air strikes on civilians and members of the resistance. Yet in France, Foreign Minister Alain Juppe defended the U.S. and NATO, by saying that Qaddafi's forces were the problem since they were located in heavily populated civilian areas (*Associated*

Press, 2011). On May 16th, Britain's top military commander proposed that NATO begin widening the air campaign to include electrical power grids and fuel dumps in government held regions (Burns, 2011). In late 2011, the International Criminal Court started to investigate the allegation of war crimes which committed by NATO in Libya (McElroy, 2011 Nov).

To the average person our leaders may seem preoccupied with exporting "democratic" elections and government to other countries. However, this concept of "democracy" is very much distorted. The U.S. Government encourages democratic elections in Third World countries; as long as the citizens of those countries choose the candidate that the U.S. likes. If they do not, they may be punished through economic sanctions, or even a plot of regime change.

3) News Media, Lies, Distortion and Dis-information

A half-truth is a whole damned lie.   —Yiddish proverb

Many of us remember the infamous video footage of the Kuwaiti "nurse" that was released immediately prior to the first Gulf War. The sobbing woman recounted how Iraqi soldiers had stormed a hospital in Kuwait. They reportedly removed babies from their incubators, throwing them to the floor, so they could steal the incubators and send them to Iraq. The video was circulated as part of a plea to save the Kuwaiti people from the evil atrocities of Saddam Hussein. After several months, human rights organizations learned that the woman had been an actress, and the video was allegedly the product of a Washington D.C. public relations firm (MacArthur, 1992). For me, this kind of propaganda was an unforgivable sin.

Later, after 9/11, I found it unsettling when Vice President Dick Cheney adamantly claimed that there was a connection between Saddam Hussein and Osama Bin Laden. From a historical point of view, of course, the two men were enemies. The President and the CIA, under pressure from reporters, denied that there was any connection. Even so, the major corporate news media failed to demand that Cheney disclose the source of his information. This was a deceptive exploitation of 9/11 used to justify the U.S. invasion and occupation of Iraq. I can't help but recall Susan Sarandon's question, "Before our kids start coming home from Iraq in body bags, and women and children start dying in Baghdad, I need to know, what did Iraq do to us?"

My faith in the government/military's portrayal of events continued to diminish. Another example was during the second Iraq war, when Private First Class Jessica Lynch was reportedly "captured" by Iraqis during an ambush. Army Rangers and Navy Seals stormed the hospital where she was being held and "rescued" her, while a military cameraman filmed the event. It was later discovered that this incident had been staged, and that the Iraqi hospital had, in fact, offered to return Private Lynch by ambulance days earlier. When confronted, the commander in charge was reported to respond by saying that we needed a hero, and by rescuing her we made her into one.

In reality, there is no shortage of actual heroes in America; indeed, you will find memorials and monuments to them in every town. Jessica Lynch herself denied being a hero, and admitted that the entire incident had been greatly overblown.

Unfortunately, the news media does not seem to be getting better at reporting the truth. In early 2011, *The Hartford Courant* (February 12, 2011) ran the headline, "Egypt Is Free," on the day Mubarak resigned. (Ironically, during the more than thirty years that Egypt was *not* free, *The Courant* never ran a story about their lack of freedom. Mubarak visited the U.S. multiple times, and was even welcome in the White House without criticism).

Another discrepancy in U.S. policy was evident in our backing of protesters in Libya. We supported these citizens in praise of democracy, and yet somehow ignored their contemporaries in Bahrain, Yemen, Jordan and Saudi Arabia. The governments of these four countries, although dictatorial and brutal, remain our allies.

4) War, Occupation, and Deception

I just want you to know that, when we talk about war, we're really talking about peace. —George W. Bush

This business of burning human beings with napalm, of filling our nation's homes with orphans and widows, of injecting poisonous drugs of hate into veins of peoples normally humane, of sending men home from dark and bloody battlefields physically handicapped and psychologically deranged, cannot be reconciled with wisdom, justice and love.

—Rev. Martin Luther King, Jr.

After more than 30 years of life in America, I find it disheartening that war is so often the first choice for the U.S. government, and not the last. We forget the Bible, which teaches us that "*He, who lives by the sword, dies by the sword.*" Recall President George W. Bush's phrase, "pre-emptive strike" as he sought military action in Iraq. Over time, I have come to realize that the hasty invasion of Iraq indicates the extent of just how influential the war industry is. Is this what Eisenhower feared when he expressed concern that the U.S. would become a military industrial complex?

I remember finding it odd when President Clinton chose Senator William Cohen, a Republican from Maine, to become his Secretary of Defense. Years later, President Obama made a similar move by picking Robert Gates, a well-known Republican, to be his Secretary of Defense. It seems to me that their choices had little to do with the actual platforms of either the Republican or Democratic parties. What message are these two presidents giving us with their selections? That war is our business, and business should be as usual, regardless of who is in the White House. Also, by choosing Republicans for their Secretaries of Defense, these two Democrats were effectively absolving their own party from criticism. They were telling the other party that in no way should they criticize the war, because to do so would be to criticize one of their own men.

5) Our Best Friends are Among the Worst Brutal Dictators/Torturers

You can't do wrong things in a right way. —Proverb

It saddens me to know that the U.S. Government has supported some of the most brutal authoritarian regimes, such as that of General Augustus Pinochet, and those of South Africa during Apartheid, Haiti, Egypt, Saudi Arabia (where Christians are not allowed to have churches, and women cannot have drivers licenses), and at times Saddam Hussein.

To give an example, I will discuss the case of General Dostum, a top commander who is "on our side" in the Afghani government. American television news spent considerable resources focusing on his activities, which reportedly included such brutalities as skinning his enemies alive (Williams, 2001). Later, it was announced that the American-backed government had chosen him to be deputy defense minister for Karzai (Shiberghan, 2009). Thus, a torturer became a U.S. favorite (Global Security, 2005; 2009). The major U.S. news media abruptly stopped reporting on any negative aspects of this brutal general.

We must remember that the entire fiasco in Afghanistan began with the U.S. support for Mujahedeen in that country, which became the Taliban. (*Mujahedeen* means 'persons who struggles against oppression'; *Taliban* is plural for 'students of the clergy'). These were the root organizations for Osama Bin Laden's militants who were fighting a progressive secular Afghani government. The only problem with this government, as far as the U.S. was concerned, was their affiliation with the Soviet Union.

The July, 2010, cover of *Time Magazine* featured a photo of an Afghani woman whose nose and lips had been cut off by order of a Taliban commander. The directive was carried out by her husband and brother-in-law, after she reportedly fled from abusive in-laws.

There is no doubt that this story is a tragedy, and represents the fates of many women who are forced to live under the Taliban's law. What we are quick to forget, however, is the U.S. involvement in bringing the Taliban to power, by offering them money, arms, and political support from American taxpayers. It seems that the U.S. Government has no problem with brutality when it suits its own interests. The message that the foreign policy of the U.S. gives us is, "If you side with us, you can get away with murder."

Could we request our democratic government to disclose the name of the U.S. politicians or agents who supported the Taliban and Bin Laden? Are they still in decision-making positions?

6) Torture

The U.S. is committed to the worldwide elimination of torture and we are leading this fight by example. I call on all governments to join with the U.S.

and the community of law abiding nations in prohibiting, investigating and prosecuting all acts of torture.

— George W. Bush

Only the winners decide what were war crimes. — Gary Wills

For me, Abu Ghraib was the straw that broke the camel's back. In this case, the camel's back was the reputation of the United States as that "shining city upon a hill." Seeing the now infamous image of a man with a hood over his face and his arms extended, who could help but think of Jesus on the cross? Even more troubling to me was the lying, cheating, and distortion by government officials who told us that this was the work of a few "low-ranking bad apples." One of these pictures showed a sophisticated type of torture used by the Brazilian Army. I asked myself how "a few low-ranking bad apples" could know such techniques. Months later it was discovered that the authorization for torture had come from Washington.

Before the invasion of Iraq, President Bush and Vice President Cheney had promised that, once Saddam Hussein was overthrown, there would be "no more torture chambers in Iraq." However, Abu Ghraib is evidence of the futility of this promise. Doctor Hamid Dabashi, an Iranian scholar and professor at Columbia University, reported that there was an attempt to justify the human rights violations of Abu Ghraib due to the demands of counter-terrorism policies.

Yet, he explains, "the eventual revelations about the United States torture chambers at Bagram Air Force Base in Afghanistan, in Abu Ghraib in Iraq, in Guantanamo Bay in Cuba, and throughout an entire network of interrogation dungeons in Europe," plus discoveries of sporadic war crimes (rape, murder and massacre) of civilians in Fallujah, Haditha, and Mahmoudiya in Iraq) have entirely "discredited the Unites States as an arbitrator of human rights abuses." Doctor Dabashi also referred to western writers and politicians who "theorized the legal and moral necessity of torturing people" to support these policies (Dabashi, 2007).

I remember when the *Hartford Courant* published a front-page story about a factory in the nearby town of Bloomfield, CT. This company, operating with the permission of U.S. authorities, was making torture devices and selling them to foreign governments (3). According to Amnesty International, there are no fewer than six U.S. companies selling equipment used for torture. China, in comparison, lists half that many (Amnesty International, 2003). There is a saying that, to the man who has only a hammer, every problem looks like a nail. Likewise, those who develop machines and technology for torture seek out human targets and soon see them everywhere.

Other reliable journals have reported about the School of the Americas (renamed the Western Hemisphere Institute for Security Cooperation), in Fort Benning, Georgia, a military school that has been teaching torture to foreign students for years according to author Stephen Lendman (2011). This practice of "rendition," or kidnapping a foreign citizen and secretly transporting him or her to another country for torture, is extremely disturbing to me. An example is the twenty-six CIA agents, who allegedly kidnapped an Italian clergyman and took him to Egypt to be tortured and interrogated, before ultimately establishing his innocence. In an interview after his release, he said they had kidnapped him, not because he was connected to terrorists, but because he was deeply trusted by many of his followers and the CIA wanted him to spy on them—a task which he refused. In essence, this man was tortured because he was too good and too well-trusted.

My great disappointment in President Obama is that, contrary to his pre-election promise, he has decided against prosecuting American agents involved in torture, explaining that they should not be prosecuted because they were under orders. This excuse did not work in the Nuremberg Court that America helped set up, and it should not work now. He also defended and continued the practice of rendition, whereby we allow other governments to torture prisoners on our behalf. When the security of a country is based on the practice of torture of prisoners, that country creates more enemies than friends. A government that trains its young men and women to torture detainees for the sake of "national security" is also securing sadism and savagery in its nation. This is one thing that the enemy cannot do to us; we can only do it to ourselves.

Karl Menninger stated that "Love not only cures the one who receives it, but also the one who gives it." I say, "Torture not only destroys the one who receives it, but also the one who gives it."

The Last Hope: American Citizens

One never loses his desire for Camelot.   — King Arthur

I'm tired of being labeled anti-American because I ask questions.
    —Susan Sarandon

Do I miss my dream of Camelot? Yes, I do, and I still pursue it, even despite negative events that continue to surround us. In 2011, a Florida clergyman publicly burned the Koran (here, in a country established on the basis of religious freedom), with no legal repercussion for his message of hate. This reminded me of another lesson in history. On May 10, 1933, the Nazi regime burned thousands of books (from Freud, to Hemingway, to Helen Keller). Years before that, the German poet Heinrich Heine had written, in his play *Almansor*, "Where they burn books, they will end in burning human beings." How sadly true his prediction was in the case of the Nazis. I am proud of the thousands of American people who denounced that Florida clergyman, and it is my deep hope that American citizens will continue to advocate for mercy, kindness, and care for humanity. We must work together to ensure that the words of Heine will never again materialize.

When not fed misinformation by the mainstream news media, Americans draw important conclusions from the information to which they gain access. Once the truth becomes clear, we can make distinctions between American citizens as a society and the U.S. government. For example, it eventually came to light that Khaled El-Masri, a German citizen, was kidnapped by the U.S. government from Germany and taken to a secret prison in Afghanistan where he was tortured. He was held without counsel for five months until they determined he was innocent and had no ties with terrorism. He then traveled to the U.S. and Germany and brought a suit against the CIA over their involvement in his abduction. While on a visit to the U.S. he said, "I will never forget an elderly couple in Richmond, Virginia, who came to support my case against the government, holding signs that read 'Stop the Torture Flights.' That is the real face of the United States. The people who kidnapped me represent the hidden and false face of America" (Abadi, 2007).

Sometimes an American, usually right-wing and very "patriotic," will criticize me and ask me why I choose to remain in this country when I don't like what our government is doing here. I answer by paraphrasing a former president who said, "There is nothing wrong with America that can't be corrected by what is right with America." And so, I am here to correct and to support what is right in America.

Notes

1. My father and several other colonels were pro-Mossadegh, and together they were devoted to supporting him against the Shah. After the coup, some of his friends were arrested, while he was still working in the justice system of the army. His boss was suspicious of him and wanted to test his loyalty, so he planned to make him prosecute his friends. My father went to his brother, who was a physician, and asked him what he should do. My uncle called his doctor friends and arranged for my father to be hospitalized for one month in a military hospital to avoid prosecuting his friends. It was not unusual to make a false medical diagnosis for officers.

2. My father rarely talked about the coup, but he was obviously devastated and traumatized. He mentioned a few times that on the day of the coup he had been on the roof of the military building with his commander. He saw many sergeants and lower-level military personnel holding Korans over their heads and supporting the Shah, with the intention to go to the street to overthrow Mossadegh's regime. He told his commander, "Let us shoot them and prevent the coup." His commander answered that the order should come from a higher level and not from him.

When Kennedy became president, he was concerned about the Shah's dictatorship and corruption, which he felt would advocate communism rather than prevent it. Under his pressure, the Iranian regime did some correction. As a result, my father became a general and prosecuted some of the corrupt generals and officers, including the first Iranian four-star general. Later on, it began to look like my father was siding with the Shah; however, he was abruptly retired by the army. SAVAK had taped his phone conversations with one of the members of the government opposition (Mr. Haerizadeh Yazdy) and used this information against him.

3. One Iranian political prisoner reported that he had been tortured with a high-tech machine that could not have been built in Iran. Apparently, whenever he screamed, his screams would be amplified in his ear and the pain would somehow increase. He had to learn to suppress his screams.

References

Abadi, C. (2007, Spring). Disappeared but not silenced. *Amnesty International, 23*, p. 12-15.

Amnesty International, (2003). *The Pain Merchants, Security equipment and its use in torture and other ill-treatment.* www.amnesty.org/en/library/info/ACT40/008/2003

Associated Press, (2011), "Libyan rebels complain about NATO airstrikes" www.wsvn.com/news/articles/world/21003978486393/

Blum, W. (1995). *Killing Hope*, Chapter on Iran, 1953, Common Courage Press, at Third World Traveler, http://www.thirdworldtraveler.com/Blum/Iran_KH.html

Blum, W. (2000), *Rogue State; A Guide to the World's Only Superpower*, Common Courage Press, reproduced in Third World Traveler, online http://www.thirdworldtraveler.com/Blum/Torture_RS.html

Blum, W. (2006*),* "The CIA, Contras, Gangs, and Crack," *Information Clearinghouse* www.informationclearinghouse.info/, November 2006

Burns, J. F. (2011, May 16), "Broader Campaign Needed to Drive Qaddafi Out, British Commander Says,*" New York Times,* http://mobile.nytimes.com/article?a=789763&f=20

Dabashi, H. (2007). *Iran: A People Interrupted*, New York: The New Press, p. 239

Davis, J. (1997). "*Foreign Policy in Focus*, South Africa," FPIF, A project of the Institute for Policy Studies, www.fpif.org/reports/south_africa.

Gilligan, A. (2011). Arrest warrants sought for Col Gaddafi, son and intelligence chief, *The Telegraph*, www.telegraph.co.uk/news/worldnews/africaandindianocean/libya/8516915/Libya-arrest-warrants-sought-for-Col-Gaddafi-son-and-intelligence-chief.html

Global Security, (2005), profile, Abdul Rashid Dostum, Deputy Defense Minister of Afghanistan www.globalsecurity.org/military/world/afghanistan/dostum.htm

Global Security, (2009) Report, Abdul Rashid Dostum,
http://www.globalsecurity.org/military/world/afghanistan/dostum.htm

The Hartford Courant (February 12, 2011) "Egypt Is Free", p.1.

Hartley-Parkinson, R. (2011), "Touchdown: B-2 stealth jets return after epic 11,500 mile journey to bomb Libyan aircraft shelters," *Daily Mail News.* www.dailymail.co.uk/news/article-1368337/Libya-crisis-B2-stealth-bombers-25-hour-flight-Missouri-Tripoli.html#ixzz1MYY3O3vm

Lendman, S., (2011, April 11). "Police Brutality in Honduras," *RENSE.* http://www.rense.com/general93/hond.htm

MacArthur, J.R. (1992, Jan. 6), "Remember Nayirah, witness for Kuwait?" *The New York Times* Op-Ed.

McElroy, D. (2011, Nov 02).Libya: NATO to be investigated by ICC for war crimes. The Telegraph. http://www.telegraph.co.uk/news/worldnews/africaandindianocean/libya/8866007/Libya-Nato-to-be-investigated-by-ICC-for-war-crimes.html

Parry, R. (1997, Part 1). Lost History: Contras, Dirty Money & CIA. *Consortium News*, http://www.consortiumnews.com/archive/lost17.html

Parry, R. (1997, Part 2). Lost History: Contras, Dirty $ & CIA, *Consortium News*, www.consortiumnews.com/archive/lost18.html

Rejali, D. (2007). *Torture and Democracy,* Princeton, NJ: *Princeton University Press,* http://press.princeton.edu/titles/8490.html

Shiberghan, (2009). Returned Afghan general throws weight behind Karzai, Tehran Times, http://www.tehrantimes.com/index_view.asp?code=201204

Williams, A., (2001). W*ar on Terror: Freedom Fight:* Prisoners skinned alive, women raped, victims tortured, should we call these killers our friends? *The Free Library,* http://www.thefreelibrary.com/WAR+ON+TERROR%3A+FREEDOM+FIGHT%3A+Prisoners+skinned+alive,+women+raped,...-a079947043

Beyond Interfaith Dialogue

Confessions of a Post-Zionist American Jew

Mark Braverman

Mark Braverman's roots are in the Holy Land: his grandfather, a fifth generation Palestinian Jew, was born in Jerusalem, then emigrated to the U.S. as a young man. Growing up in the United States, Mark was reared in the Jewish tradition, studying Bible, Hebrew literature, and Jewish history. Trained in clinical psychology and crisis management, Mark devoted his professional career to working with groups and individuals undergoing traumatic stress. Returning to the Holy Land in 2006, he was transformed by witnessing the occupation of Palestine and by encounters with peace activists and civil society leaders from the Muslim, Christian and Jewish communities. Since then, Mark has devoted himself full-time to the Israel/Palestine conflict. Mark is a co-founder and Executive Director of Friends of Tent of Nations North America, a nonprofit organization dedicated to supporting Palestinian land rights and peaceful coexistence in historic Palestine. He serves on the Board of Directors of the Israeli Committee Against House Demolitions-USA, and the advisory committee of Friends of Sabeel North America. He is a charter member of American Jews for a Just Peace and has recently been appointed Consultant for Evangelicals for Middle East Understanding. Mark is the author of Fatal Embrace: Christians, Jews, and the Search for Peace in the Holy Land. *His website is* www.markbraverman.org.

It wasn't going well. The people entering and leaving the building were not happy about our presence on the street outside the Washington, DC Conference Center. No one would accept the printed information we offered, and all efforts to engage anyone in conversation or even a brief verbal exchange failed—unless you count the occasional accusation of "shame on you!" It was March, 2007. I was standing outside the annual conference of the American Israel Public Affairs Committee, more commonly known as AIPAC, or the "Israel Lobby." We were protesting our country's massive, unconditional U.S. military aid to Israel, and the U.S.'s blanket diplomatic protection of the Jewish state in the international arena.

We were arguing that, although we supported Israel's right to live in peace and security, the U.S. should call Israel to account for its human rights violations and its flouting of international law in its treatment of the Palestinians. In a handout we pointed out that changing our policy was not only the right thing to do, it was in our self-interest: our support of Israel's oppression of the Palestinians was further isolating us globally. A YouTube clip shows me being interviewed outside the Convention Center that day, explaining why I felt that, using the words of progressive rabbi Michael Lerner, AIPAC, is "bad for the United States, bad for Israel, and bad for the Jews!" [1]

I was protesting that day as a Jew who was heartbroken about and, frankly, horrified by the actions of a state that purportedly existed to keep me safe in a world that for millennia had persecuted my people. But I was also standing there as an American objecting to my own country's failed policy in the Middle East. It had failed because rather than addressing the root cause of the Israel-Palestine conflict, which was the dispossession of the indigenous Arab population to make way for the Jewish state, the United States had supported and perpetuated the injustice. Since the founding of Israel in 1948, the U.S. has backed Israel diplomatically and financially, ignoring the plight of millions of refugees, abetting the continued taking of land, and sanctioning these abridgements of human rights by blocking UN resolutions and appeals to the Geneva Conventions by the international community.

I had a deep attachment to Israel: I had lived there as a young man, spoke the language and had deep family roots in Jerusalem. But I could not be silent or passive in the face of behavior that I knew was wrong and that was tearing at the fabric of Israeli society. I knew that the path to peace would be found not through military might or in walling out the Palestinians, but in finding a way to share the land with the people who were already living there when the Jews from Europe, seeking a haven from persecution, had begun to arrive in the late 19th century. I had been taught from an early age that the conflict that had plagued the Jewish state for its entire history arose out of the eternal hatred of the "Arabs" for the Jewish people. But I had just come from there, and I had met the Palestinians, and I knew that they didn't hate me.

In my hands that day was a stack of copies of a recent *Los Angeles Times* opinion-piece, in which a Palestinian American professor made an eloquent, balanced appeal for Palestinian rights. My goal was to get people to accept the handout, and, even better, to engage in conversation. After hours of having no luck on either score, I was considering giving up and going home. Just then a well-dressed man on his way into the conference walked up to me, looked me in the eye and said, "I'll take one." "Great!" I said, and handed it to him. Taking it, he tore it into shreds, threw it in my face, and walked away without another word.

How, I have often asked myself in recalling this incident, *did I get here?*

My journey

I was born into the safe, prosperous context of the post-World War II Jewish community in the United States. I swam in the deep, protecting waters of an old and majestic tradition. My early life was enriched by beautiful rituals, splendid holidays, a monumental literature—and, perhaps most of all, the claiming of an illustrious history. As Jews, we feel well-deserved pride for having survived and, over the course of 3000 years, having made extraordinary contributions to civilization. But this upbringing had another side, one with which, as I began to venture out of my insular Jewish world, I grew increasingly uncomfortable. It was a paradox: I grew up in the open, if somewhat bland and racially segregated culture of metropolitan East Coast America in the 1950s. I never experienced anti-Semitism—but then I never ventured very far into what I had learned to call the "non-Jewish world." The dark side of growing up Jewish was that I was taught to avoid and to fear the "goyim"—as my grandmother, born in Europe, and even my own American-born parents would call the society surrounding the Jewish bubble in which we lived. "*Goyim*," from the Old Testament Hebrew, means simply "the nations." But throughout the centuries, and right into mid-twentieth century America, the word had become freighted with darker meaning. Although it was not always made explicit, one fact about the *goyim* was very clear to me: They were dangerous.

That's why we had Israel.

I was raised in a potent combination of Rabbinic Judaism and political Zionism. I was taught that a miracle—born of heroism and bravery—had blessed my generation. The State of Israel was not a mere historical event; it was redemption from millennia of marginalization, demonization, and murderous violence. The legacy of this history was a collective identity of brittle superiority for having survived, despite the effort, "in every generation"—so reads the prayer we recite every Passover—to eradicate us. In order to survive in this hostile, murderous world of the goyim, we had to remain ever vigilant, mistrustful, and—in a not always obvious but nevertheless profound way—apart. Whether justified on a biblical basis by religious Jews, or simply by virtue of our history of suffering (as the non-religious Zionist founders claimed), the State of Israel existed to ensure our safety and to underscore our unique identity in a world that could never be trusted. The story of the birth and survival of the young state partook of this legacy of separateness, vulnerability, and specialness. I embraced this legacy. I treasured the reality of Israel, "the first flowering of our redemption."

Until I saw the Israeli occupation of Palestine.

Traveling in Israel and the Occupied Territories during the summer of 2006, I experienced first-hand the damage inflicted by the occupation, on the Palestinian people and on Israeli society. I witnessed Israel's separation wall, snaking through the West Bank on stolen land (any Palestinian will tell you that the wall has no defensive efficacy, and a look at the map clearly shows that the wall functions as a land grab, following the boundaries of huge illegal settlement blocs), the humiliating checkpoints restricting Palestinian movement, the network of Jewish-only highways, the massive, continuing construction of illegal settlements and towns, the vicious acts of ideological Jewish settlers, and the destructive impact of militarization and ongoing conflict on Israeli society.

I realized that a humanitarian crime was being committed, and that the role of occupier was leading Israel toward political disaster and the Jewish people down a road of spiritual peril. Standing before that huge barrier of concrete and steel, the grim consequences of our national homeland project became agonizingly clear to me. Not that I did not understand—I felt it in my cells—"the hope of 2000 years, to be a free people in our own land" as expressed in the Israeli national anthem, *Hatikvah*. But my confrontation with the occupation of Palestine was pushing me to question the very concept of the Jewish state. I was beginning to understand that we had to move on, into a new world and toward a renewed Jewish identity, where freedom from fear meant walls being dismantled, not being built higher. On that day, the wall inside me began to come down.

The wall, however, was very real for me that summer in Israeli occupied Jerusalem. For centuries, Jews, Muslims and Christians had lived together peacefully in an undivided Jerusalem. The troubles started in the early 20th century with the accelerating pace of Jewish immigration. Palestinians began to understand that the bands of plucky, idealistic settlers who had begun to arrive from Eastern Europe in the 1880s, followed in the 1930s by waves of desperate escapees from Hitler's Reich, added up to a colonial project aimed at displacing the indigenous population.

Conflicting British promises to both Arabs and Jews beginning in the post WWI period further fed the growing conflict and set the stage for the 1947-1949 Arab-Israeli war. In 1948, Jerusalem was divided when Jewish forces retreated from the walled Old City and the eastern half of Jerusalem in the face of the Arab Legion. A Berlin-type wall was erected, dividing the Israeli western side from Jordanian-controlled East Jerusalem. In 1967, when the Israeli Army recaptured the eastern side in the Six-Day War, the wall of wood and mortar that had bisected the city came down—but the ethnographic barrier remained, and persists to this day.

That was the Jerusalem that I encountered in 2006. That summer, I lived in two worlds. I woke up every morning in the home of my uncle and aunt in the German Colony section of West Jerusalem, a neighborhood of stately homes that, until 1948, housed well-to-do Palestinian families now displaced and living in the West Bank or abroad. The neighborhood is now one of the most fashionable in West Jerusalem, and it is peopled entirely by Jews. None of them ever venture into Arab East Jerusalem except for the occasional shopping excursion to the Arab marketplace in the Old City or for a religious pilgrimage to the Western Wall, near the site of the Jewish Temple destroyed in 70 CE.

Every morning, I left Jewish West Jerusalem and walked to the east side, to rejoin my delegation for a day of meetings with Israeli and Palestinian organizations devoted to activism and education. I crossed the street that once marked the boundary wall, and in one step—like a cinematic special effect—I left the Jewish west side and entered Arab East Jerusalem. In contrast to sedate, devout, manicured, and ordered West Jerusalem, East Jerusalem was riotous in color and tempestuous in emotion. Daily, I experienced the vivid contrast between the two cultures. On the one hand, there was the indigenous Palestinian culture: passionate, industrious, wise, connected deeply to the land. On the other was the new Israeli civilization: transplanted from Europe, carved into the ancient landscape, marvelously creative, hardworking, and hungry for life... and ignorant of the people it was displacing. I stopped a distinguished-looking man in traditional Arab dress to ask for directions, and almost began to address him in Hebrew. I had forgotten that I had crossed the invisible barrier that separated Jew from Palestinian.

For my first fifty-eight years, "Jerusalem" had been the Jewish city. I had now discovered the whole city, and it was split in half. In this divided capital, I would have to choose which side I would prefer to live in, which language I would speak. As I made this daily crossing, eastward in the morning and back west at night, I realized that it was in the east side that I was feeling at home, on the east side that I wanted to be. I felt increasingly alienated in West Jerusalem, among my people, where I spoke the language and understood the culture. In contrast, I felt increasingly comfortable in Arab East Jerusalem, among Muslims and Christians, in the midst of a culture that was new to me and where I didn't even speak the language. I was profoundly disturbed by this. What was happening to me?

The Wall comes down

One day, not long after my first confrontation with the wall, I sat in the offices of Sabeel in East Jerusalem. Sabeel is an organization of Christian Palestinians. The people of Sabeel—the Arabic word means "the way," and also "source of life-giving water"—confront the challenges of life in Palestine today by emulating the mission and life of Jesus. Sabeel does this by embracing nonviolence. This includes supporting and collaborating with nonviolent activist groups of the three Abrahamic faiths in Israel/Palestine, creating and disseminating educational materials, organizing local and international conferences, and working with youth.

A woman named Nora Carmi spoke to us. Nora is a Jerusalemite, a refugee in her own land—her family lost their West Jerusalem home in 1948. The conflict has brought Nora—a mother and a grandmother—pain, loss, and fear. Yet these troubles have only strengthened her faith. I asked Nora how she deals with being dispossessed and occupied. I will never forget her answer: "We follow Jesus." She went on to explain: Who was Jesus? He was a Palestinian Jew living under Roman occupation. Faced with an Empire that sought to destroy not only the physical but the ethical basis of Jewish society in Palestine, he did not turn to hatred of his oppressors, nor to fomenting rebellion; in contrast, he taught love of humankind, commitment to God's requirement to pursue social justice, and persistent, stubborn nonviolent resistance to oppression. "Love your enemies," Jesus instructed his people: do not allow them to take away your dignity, or to come between you and your devotion to the commandments to love your neighbor and to be responsible stewards of the earth. "We follow Jesus," she said. "Empires come and empires go. We are here." A stone had dislodged itself from the wall inside me. Here was a woman whose family was driven from the neighborhood, perhaps the very street, where I was staying with my aunt and uncle in West Jerusalem, a woman whose faith and courage were inspiring me in ways I had not felt in a very long time. Leaving Sabeel that day, I took with me a copy of *Justice Only Justice: A Palestinian Theology of Liberation,* by Reverend Naim Ateek, the Palestinian Anglican priest who founded Sabeel. Ateek was eight years old in 1948, the year of my birth, the year that Jewish forces expelled his family from their home, their church, and their village.

He spoke to me from the pages of his book, a book that recounts how his experience of dispossession and occupation had led him directly to his belief in the centrality of justice in his faith. Ateek traces a direct line from the Old Testament prophets to Jesus of Nazareth. The questions and answers came quickly. Did I believe in the prophets' call for justice? Had I not been taught that the core of my Jewishness was a commitment to compassion for humankind? I realized that the outrage I was experiencing about the violations of human rights I was seeing was the most Jewish thing I had ever felt, and that working for justice in Palestine was the most Jewish thing I could do.

The Mount of Memory

Jerusalem is full of memorials. Not long after my confrontation with the Attali memorial, our delegation visited one of the most famous in Israel, if not the world. On a hilltop in the hills west of Jerusalem sits Yad Vashem, Israel's national memorial to the Jewish victims of the Nazi genocide and its museum of the Nazi Holocaust. Approaching the museum, I passed under a huge archway inscribed with the words of the prophet Ezekiel from the famous vision of the Dry Bones: "I will put my breath into you and you shall live again and I will set you upon your own soil" (*Ezekiel 37:14*). Contemplating this inscription, I was rooted to the spot. I had been in Jerusalem and the West Bank for four days. I was bursting with outrage at what I had seen. I was not feeling close to the redemptive Zionist dream. Since my last visit to Yad Vashem six years before, the museum had been rebuilt; this was the new and improved version, taking much from the original museum and housing it in a new architectural format and adding new exhibits, the first of which confronts you as soon as you enter.

I stood before a huge wall, on which was projected a movie depicting the lost world of the Jews of Eastern Europe. Moving before me, across a map of Russia, Poland, and Germany, was a heartbreaking photographic record of the world that had been lost: artisans, musicians, laborers, teachers, villages, houses of study, children. All gone. The movie ended with a photograph of a choir of Jewish children, somewhere in Europe, and on the soundtrack they are singing *Hatikvah* ("The Hope"), the Zionist poem and the national anthem of the State of Israel.

I was shattered. A hand had reached into me, grabbed hold of my heart, and drawn me back into my past, into the collective memory of my people. How could I turn my back on this? How could I walk away from my history, from this incalculable, unfathomable loss, and, more so, from Israel, my deliverance? It had worked. I was hooked. What was I to do now? I had no choice. Emptied, numb, and confused, I turned and walked down the hall into the museum.

It's a brilliant exhibition. One walks down into it. It is subterranean—no windows, no light, no escape. You are led through corridors and tunnels, with no control and no way out but through. One traverses the whole, familiar story: from the laws enacted in the thirties, the walls of isolation, privation, and degradation closing in, to the Final Solution: the ovens, the stacked bodies, the faces of the children. Darkness closes your heart—you feel you will never escape from this horror, this black hole of evil and despair. Then, as you turn a corner into the final gallery, on display are the blown-up photos of the ships bringing the refugees to the shores of Israel, faces shining with hope and gratitude. There is David Ben-Gurion reading from the Israeli Declaration of Independence. And then, suddenly, you emerge. Ascending a wide flight of stairs, you are outside, in the light and the open air, standing on a wide patio that looks out on the Jerusalem Hills. *It's the final exhibit.* And then it hit me—this was no mere museum. This was a lesson, this was indoctrination: from the biblical quote at the entrance, into the depths, and to this sight—*The Land. The reward. Our destiny.*

As we left the museum, my fellow delegate Diane turned to me and asked if I had taken note of how the Nazis acted to marginalize, dispossess, and banish the Jews, the part before the extermination camps and the ovens. She asked if I had seen that this was what we had witnessed over the last few days. Yes, I had seen. And something let go.

Another stone fell from the wall. Treading, as I had so many times, the sacred ground of the Holocaust, I had, for the first time, broken The Rule: our Holocaust, *The* Holocaust, must not be compared to any other disaster, genocide, or crime. It has to stand as the ultimate humanitarian crime. I had also broken a rule not often articulated but nevertheless fundamental: one may never compare Israeli policy to Nazi crimes. The comparison has been called "obscene." I now know that what is obscene is to deny the comparison—to say, "this is them; this cannot be us." Seeing what I had seen, I realized how dangerous this rule is to the Jewish psyche, as it would be to any group or individual claiming an exceptional right to victimhood. I saw this as I stood before the separation wall. I saw this as I walked the streets of a Jerusalem being taken, stone by stone, neighborhood by neighborhood, by my own people seeking to establish their spiritual redemption and physical security at the expense of the Palestinians. To close one's eyes to this evil was the obscenity.

Leaving the museum, I now knew how to understand the calamity of the Nazi Holocaust in the context of contemporary Jewish history. For one thing had not changed: even though I had been born three years after the fall of the Third Reich, the murder of six million of my people would continue to be the formative historical event of my life. But now, finding the meaning of the Holocaust meant working for justice for Palestine. There were too many parallels, too many ways in which Israel was doing to the Palestinians what the Nazis did to us. No, we had not built death camps. But we were turning into beasts, and we were killing a civilization.

Outside the museum, I sat with our Palestinian guide, Said. We had grown close over a few short weeks. I told him the story, explaining to him how intense it had been to look in the mirror in this way, and I talked about my horror about what my people were doing to his people, and my realization at my own country's complicity in this crime. He was silent, taking this in calmly.

"This is my community," I said. "This is who I am returning to."

Said answered, "Then you know what you have to do."

I accepted the charge. But carrying it out would prove difficult. Returning to the U.S., I found that the mainstream Jewish community was closed to my message—what I was saying about Israel was unacceptable and was not to be countenanced. The most charitable characterization of my position was that I was "naïve," manipulated by people and forces who wished us ill. The arguments varied, but they were all based on a single assumption: defense of the Jewish state was paramount. Yes, it was unfair that innocent Palestinians had to suffer, but concern for the security of Israel trumped all other considerations. The wall was regrettable, but it kept Israel safe from terrorism.

No, Israel was not perfect, but allowing criticism of Israel to surface would give aid and support to those who sought our destruction. Didn't I realize that anti-Semitism was everywhere, that we had to defend ourselves against the implacable hatred of our enemies? And besides, even if we were to acknowledge that the Palestinians had been dispossessed, how could we consider remedying that without destroying the Jewish character (i.e. the Jewish majority) of Israel?

These arguments came not only from Jews who were politically conservative, or from organizations who saw anti-Semitism everywhere and who were prepared to mount well organized attacks on anyone challenging the status quo. They came just as readily from Jews who were otherwise politically progressive, but who, because of their ignorance of the facts, were uncritically pro-Israel by default. Yes, there were Jews who shared my feelings—a small number of Rabbis who were beginning to speak out, and organizations of Jewish activists devoted to challenging Israel's human rights abuses and our government's policy of supporting this behavior. But the established Jewish community—the religious denominations, the philanthropic and social service agencies, the advocacy and watchdog groups, the political action committees—were arrayed to silence any word of dissent or questioning of the basic assumptions of political Zionism. [xi] They would fight to protect the huge, no-strings-attached financial and diplomatic support that Israel has enjoyed. Anyone, especially a fellow Jew, who challenged the dominant narrative of a vulnerable Israel beset by powerful enemies faced a juggernaut of opposition and accusations of anti-Semitism.

The call

As is often true, when one door closes, another opens. The Jewish establishment was dug in—stubbornly, blindly, and in my view tragically—refusing to acknowledge the trouble Israel was in and the tragic wrongness of its course. I mourned this and frankly it scared me. But I was not given the time to brood about it. At the same time that I was confronting the resistance of the Jewish community, I made a discovery that was to change my life. The group I had travelled with in Israel and the West Bank was mostly Christian. We had made a covenant to speak about our experience once returning to the U.S. My new friends, therefore, began to arrange for me to speak in churches.

And an extraordinary thing happened: *the doors flung open.* I found that Christians, like most Americans, were ignorant of what had happened to the Palestinians in 1948, and were equally unaware of the oppressive conditions under which they currently lived. When my audiences heard about the historic and present injustices visited upon the Palestinians, they responded as they would to the story of any oppressed people. As I spoke in church after church, I sensed a deep passion for justice and a largely untapped store of commitment for this cause.

I began to realize how important the church could be in breaking the political deadlock that was so disastrous, not only for the Palestinians, but for the Jewish people. At the same time, I saw that a huge barrier stood in the way. Everywhere I went I encountered Christians who gratefully received my message that something had to be done about Israel's mistreatment of the Palestinians, but who felt that because the church bore such a heavy responsibility for Jewish suffering, they could not say or do anything that might hurt the Jewish state, or that might even be perceived as critical of Israel.

I had left Palestine with the question: "Why are my people doing this?" This was now joined by a second question, a question that I was asking, not of my own people, but of the Christian world: *Why are you helping us to do it?* My agony about the American Jewish community's blind support for Israel was now accompanied by the realization that the Christian world had been enabling Israel's illegal and self-destructive behavior. This was happening both because of the active support of Israel and the Zionist vision at congregational, denominational and ecumenical levels, as well as passively, through Christians' silence.

People I met in the churches and denominational conferences, who were appalled as I was by Israel's behavior but as Christians felt caught on the horns of their dilemma, appealed to me to continue my work with the churches: "You need to keep on doing this," I have heard so many times I have stopped counting. "As a Jew you can say these things—we can't." I disagreed with the premise, but I accepted the assignment. New to the culture of the American church, I was discovering something surprising and inspiring about the Christian world, and it was this: for many Christians—and for some congregations in particular –being "churched" was not about attending worship on Sunday and returning to their lives for the balance of the week. Rather, it meant committing themselves to relieving suffering in their own communities and around the world. Driving this commitment was not just an impulse toward charity or humanitarian acts—it was a felt imperative for social justice, deeply rooted in their faith. Taking an active stance against racism, poverty, and injustice was what it meant to follow Jesus and, further, to leave behind what some saw as the doctrinal sterility and exclusivism that characterized much of the institutional church.

Welcome to our synagogue

After a life where my exposure to religion was limited to the inside of my Jewish bubble, it was good to connect so powerfully with another faith tradition. I did not regard this as a rejection of Judaism or of my Jewish identity. It is just the opposite; responding to this call, I have embraced the deepest part of me, the Jewishness I have always felt at my core, the Jew I have been in the process of becoming. One evening, I found myself speaking to a group in a church sanctuary in New England. I was asked by someone, as Christians tend to do—everyone wants to know where you worship—what synagogue did I belong to? The question was unexpected, and so was my immediate, spontaneous answer. I said, "You're sitting in it. This work, this witness, is my place of worship. It is how I express my devotion to the values of my faith tradition."

We were in a Catholic church. A crucifix—and it was a large one, almost life-size—was suspended over the altar behind me. I continued: "And I know that the Galilean rabbi and visionary whose image hangs over my right shoulder would fully endorse that statement. So (and with this I opened wide my arms)— welcome to our synagogue!" I saw the jaws drop—and then they broke into applause. And I knew that the approbation was not for me. It was an acknowledgement of the significance of this moment—of a Jew, standing in a church, speaking out for justice for Palestinians and claiming in that witness the legacy of another Jew who spoke out for his own oppressed people 2000 years ago.

Here is what was happening. A faith community was celebrating its devotion to social justice—a core value that, although often out of sync with the prevailing political system or national culture, was finding its expression in the embrace of a just cause. I was learning that a fierce, focused commitment to justice and compassion was precisely the genesis and spirit of the early church, grassroots outposts of nonviolent resistance to tyranny in the midst of the Roman Empire, a civilization and power structure that was attempting to undermine those essential values. That evening in that New England church, and in other gatherings of this kind that were growing in number and gaining in momentum, the distinction of Jew, Christian, Muslim was fading before the imperative to work for justice in the Holy Land. What I was discovering as I met people from all faiths, in religious as well as in secular contexts, is that a commitment to a just peace in Israel/Palestine cuts across the faith communities.

I have found this justice imperative operating on multiple levels in the American church. I have discovered small but determined pockets of activism in congregational mission committees, in denominational human rights taskforces, and in local peace groups, who, if they had not yet taken up the plight of the Palestinians, were ready to place Israel/Palestine at the top of their agenda. This is unfolding across a truly ecumenical landscape. It can be seen in progressive Catholic organizations and orders, hosting speakers and sending nuns and priests to Palestine to defend Palestinian human rights; in the persistent and courageous actions of mainstream American Protestant denominations, introducing resolutions to divest from companies involved in the occupation of Palestine; and in ecumenical conferences on the relationship of land theology to the struggle for human rights in Palestine and other areas of conflict around the globe.

I have met evangelicals who, breaking the stereotype of religious extremists calling for Jewish domination of Jerusalem in order to hasten the end-times, are expressing solidarity with the Palestinian call for justice and sending delegations of support to occupied Bethlehem. I realized that I was looking at a huge force: deep, wide, and passionate, poised to take on this cause on a global level. I recognized it as a nascent movement that would change the politics of the conflict, a force equal in power and commitment to the pastors and church bodies that led the American Civil Rights movement and the worldwide campaign to bring down South African Apartheid. I was inspired, encouraged, and deeply moved by the people I met, and struck by their hunger—there is no better word for it—to become educated about the situation and to find ways to become involved.

One State or Two States?

As we contemplate the disaster of stalemate and blindness that characterizes Israeli politics today (and the equally destructive, bankrupt and politically pusillanimous U.S. policy that enables Israel to carry them out), and as the occupied territories continue to sink into a morass of violence and repression, denial begins to yield to the realization of the need for a radically new look at the fundamentals of the state. One way that this push for a new direction is manifesting itself is in the reemergence of the movement toward a "one-state solution." It is not a new idea, but it has resurfaced in an alliance of Palestinians who have had enough of the endless and fruitless "peace process" and Israelis—many in exile in the United Kingdom and the United States—who, with an increasing sense of urgency, have devoted their academic and political careers to saving their country.

These Israelis have joined the ranks of Palestinians and others in declaring that the emperor has no clothes: that successive Israeli governments have been committed, not to progress toward a negotiated settlement, but to a policy of endless delay. Meron Benvenisti, the former deputy mayor of Jerusalem, stated the obvious in a recent article in Haaretz, "The Binationalism Vogue," appearing on April 30, 2009. In it, Benvenisti pointed out that the new Netanyahu government has no intention of moving toward the establishment of an autonomous Palestinian state. The government's use of the term "two states" can only be described as a "smokescreen of imagined progress toward a dead end" ((Benvenisti, 2009).

The idea of a single state for Jews and Arabs emerged in the early twentieth century. It was championed by such Jewish luminaries as Martin Buber and Judah Magnes, who were joined in the 1920s by Albert Einstein and a number of Zionist organizations. The notion of one state for both peoples, always a minority position, suffered significant setbacks in the wake of Arab-Jewish violence in the late 1920s and the Arab revolt of 1936 to 1939. In 1937, the Peel Commission, appointed by the British Crown to recommend a political solution to the conflict between Jewish and Arab interests, concluded that the best solution lay in the separation of the two peoples through the partition of Palestine. Any further discussion about sharing the land was smothered in the ashes of Auschwitz-Birkenau and drowned out by the cheers of most of the Jewish and Western world that greeted the declaration of the State of Israel in 1948.

Arab nationalist sentiment, faced with the reality of the Jewish state, similarly rejected the idea of bi-nationality in the framework of a state so designated and so constructed. The concept only resurfaced in the aftermath of the 1967 war, in which Israel gained control of the West Bank and Gaza. It remained, however, the province of a small handful of Palestinian and non-

Jewish Western analysts until recently. Critics of the one-state solution say it's a dream, the obstacles too daunting. Those committed to keeping the idea in play counter that, with the colonization and fragmentation of the West Bank all but complete, the two-state option has already passed us by. For over half a century a discounted or frankly ignored concept, the idea of a single state for Jews and Arabs in Palestine is now receiving attention in the public forum.

Stephen Walt, professor of International Relations at Harvard's Kennedy School of Government and coauthor of *The Israel Lobby,* weighed in on this issue in an article in the April 2009 issue of *Foreign Policy.* "So what are Israel's options?" he asks. "One alternative would be to make the West Bank and Gaza part of Israel, but allow the Palestinians who live there to have full political rights, thereby creating a bi-national liberal democracy. This idea has been promoted by a handful of Israeli Jews and a growing number of Palestinians, but the objections to it are compelling. It would mean abandoning the Zionist vision of a Jewish state, which makes it anathema to almost all Israeli Jews, who want to live in a Jewish state." (Walt 2009).

But what is it that is "compelling" about these objections to the idea of a liberal, pluralistic democracy in the territory of historic Palestine? Does the simple fact that some Jews do not want to accept the idea of a shared state render it somehow unacceptable or outside the bounds of allowable discourse? The question must be asked: do Jews want to live in a Jewish state, or a secure and prosperous one? Can the vibrant Jewish society that has been created in Israel retain its Jewish character and also be part of something else, something more diverse, something that encompasses a vision bigger than the cherished right, granted by the Jews to themselves over one hundred years ago, to a national homeland in historic Palestine?

Is it possible that those who insist on seeing the state as a prize awarded to a privileged, exclusive group might become a minority in Israel, much like the marginalized ultra-nationalists and ethnic supremacists that exist in the midst of other pluralistic, democratic societies the world over? Could it be that the Jews of Israel, and indeed the Jews of the world, find themselves on the cusp of accepting for consideration the concept of historic Palestine as "a country for all its citizens" as the subtitle of a recent conference on one state for Palestine reads? Could we begin to understand that a solution fulfilling this simple description, whatever political form it may assume, is the one that might save Israel, whatever it becomes and whatever it is called?

Of one thing we can be certain, and Walt makes this very clear in his piece: time is running out for the two-state solution. It is increasingly clear that Israel's current government is not committed to the establishment of a viable, autonomous Palestinian state in the West Bank and Gaza. Walt appeals to Israel's supporters here in the U.S. to use every possible means to support the Obama administration in taking a firm stance with the Netanyahu government. "If they don't," he warns, they may someday have to explain to their grandchildren why they watched Israel drive itself off a cliff and did nothing to stop it."

What are the alternatives to the non-democratic, apartheid reality which is rapidly coming to pass? There are two: In the first, Israel withdraws to the 1949 armistice lines, the *de facto* recognized border and the one that has now been accepted by the Arab League and several Arab governments, including Palestinian governments. It must dismantle the settlements; relinquish control of the roads, borders, and water resources of the West Bank; allow for the return or resettlement of Palestinian refugees; and cease and reverse the project to Judaize "greater Jerusalem," an expanded metropolis that effectively cuts the West Bank in half. The second alternative is to contemplate a unitary, multinational state, perhaps through a federated structure. Which scenario is more plausible?

The Treason of the Hawks

In the 2009 piece, Stephen Walt named Netanyahu's approach to power "the treason of the hawks," using the term coined by Fred Iklé, Ronald Reagan's Undersecretary of Defense, describing "those tragic situations where hardliners stubbornly refuse to make peace and thereby lead their countries to disaster" (Walt 2009). As we contemplate the actions of successive Israeli governments, and now the rhetoric of Israel's present leadership, Walt's historic analogy is chillingly apt. As Americans we must reject the "treason of the hawks," those who would lead Israel into one disastrous war after another, and consider not the end, but the future of the Jewish people. As American Jews we must ask, can we not be Jewish in the United States and the other countries of our so-called Diaspora?

Could we not be Jewish in a new Israel, an Israel—whatever it is called and however it is politically fashioned—in which we live alongside and as equals with the other peoples of the land? Of course we can, if—to borrow Herzl's famous statement at the inauguration of the Zionist project over one hundred years ago—we really want it. Jews are facing a threat to their continuation that is as critical as that faced in the inhospitable Europe of Herzl's time. But, unlike the situation in Europe, the present threat is not external. It is, rather, our own inability to shift from the defensive position learned during centuries of persecution. What is required is not easy: we must recognize that the greatest threat to our survival today is not the existence of an external enemy. The threat, rather, is our unwillingness to embrace the other people in whose midst we live and with whom we are called to reconcile.

I often think back to the day I stood protesting against AIPAC in Washington, DC. What had brought me there? Yes, it was my outrage and horror at the violations of human rights that I had witnessed, but what had turned me was meeting the "Other"—whom I was supposed to fear—and realizing the destructive power of that fear. What had changed me was looking into the eyes of my supposed enemies and knowing, clearly, that they didn't hate me. And what had set my life on a new course was meeting the "Others" in my own backyard, and seeing them as my partners, as my now expanded and deepened community of faith. It is this emerging community that represents the best hope for a future of peace for Israelis, Palestinians, and the whole community of humankind.

---

[1] **Rabbi Michael** Lerner's definition is worth quoting: "When I talk about the Israel Lobby I mean to refer not only to AIPAC or The Conference of Presidents, but to a range of organizations, including the American Jewish Congress, the American Jewish Committee, the World Jewish Congress, B'nai Brith, the Anti-Defamation League (ADL), Hadassah, the Wiesenthal Center, the Federation, and the United Jewish Appeal (UJA), the various Jewish Community Relations Councils, most of the local Hillel Foundations on college campuses, most of the Hebrew schools and day schools introducing their students to Judaism or Jewish culture, the array of Federation sponsored newspapers that are distributed in almost every Jewish community in America" (2007).

Intervention in Cambodia:
A Double-Edged Sword

Sophal Ear

Sophal Ear is an Assistant Professor of National Security Affairs at the US Naval Postgraduate School in Monterey, CA. He was a TED Fellow in 2009, a Fulbright Specialist in 2010, and was honored as a Young Global Leader in 2011 by the World Economic Forum. A graduate of UC Berkeley and Princeton University, Sophal moved to the United States from France as a Cambodian refugee at the age of 10.

Introduction and Background

Cambodia, known as an "Island of Peace" in the 1960s, is like any other typical post-colonial country—groping its way through development—except for one inconvenient truth: it suffered one of the worst abuses of humanity in the 20th Century, thanks to a fanatical Maoist group known as the Khmer Rouge, when 1.7 million people or a quarter of the population died.

During the 1960s, the economy was strong—Cambodia exported more rice than it imported—and it was such an example of development that even Lee Kuan Yew came to Cambodia to learn about nation-building after he led Singapore as a self-governing state. Paradoxically, it was during this time that a war raged on next-door in Vietnam and the secret bombing of Cambodia by American B-52s would start. More bombs fell on Cambodia in subsequent years than all of World War II Europe. Little did anyone know what future decades would hold for this "Island of Peace."

Coming from Cambodia, I'd like to frame this in a more personal context and share a bit about my family. My late mother was born in 1936 and had a typical Cambodian childhood. She had seven years' schooling but learned several languages throughout her life, one of which was Vietnamese. It would prove to be extremely useful and important to her later in her life, the lives of my four surviving siblings, and my own.

I was born in late 1974. Within months, the Khmer Rouge came to power. Their rule resulted in a complete reordering of society, a literal reboot to "Year Zero" when money was banned and all one could own was a spoon. Describing the Khmer Rouge, Michael Paterniti has written:

> *Once upon a time—1975, actually, in Cambodia—there was a regime so evil that it created an antisociety where torture was currency and music, books, and love were abolished. This regime ruled for four years and murdered nearly 2 million of its citizens, a quarter of the population* [1]

Paterniti could not have formulated a better description.

My parents lived in Phnom Penh, the capital of Cambodia, and when the

Khmer Rouge entered (sullen but resolute in their quest to cull from the country all bourgeoisie), Mom and Dad, along with over two million other residents were forcibly relocated to the countryside. There, they were made to work in rice fields like water buffalos and to contribute their labor and energy for the "greater good" of this anti-society. As a Western academic apologist of the Khmer Rouge lamented,

> *What the urban dwellers consider 'hard' labor may not be punishment or community service beyond human endurance ... Such associations [with memories it invokes of Russian history] take what is happening in Cambodia out of its historical and cultural context.*[2]

What other Solzhenitsyn Gulag-like context could there be? One can only think of the Cultural Revolution in China. The end-result of this revolution was that one in four Cambodians died (possibly even three, depending on the actual population of Cambodia at the time, a number that remains disputed), including my own father of malnutrition and dysentery and my oldest brother, who has been missing since 1975.

The death of what is now generally agreed to be 1.7 million people was due to direct state violence resulting in genocide and crimes against humanity. The policy to empty cities, which the Khmer Rouge ruthlessly implemented on 17 April 1975, led to famine as a result of botched agrarian policy and massive deaths from treatable diseases. My wife's own father was picked-up by the commune chief one day and told that he would be going to a nearby village. In fact, he was taken away and beaten to death. A boy who spied for the Khmer Rouge reported this to other commune members, who then sent word to my mother-in-law. My wife's father had been targeted from the get-go, made to clean human and animal waste because he had been skilled at injecting prescribed medicine during the *ancien regime*.

It is estimated that of the 400 to 600 legal professionals in existence before Democratic Kampuchea, only six to twelve survived.[3] (In Cambodia, they really did "kill all the lawyers.") Examples of state aggression, oppression, and personal and economic rights infringements in Cambodia include, for example, the banning of private property (except for one's spoon) and the destruction of families by systematically breaking-up children from parents and teaching them to respect the "Angka" (the Khmer Rouge organization) above all. Individual and societal effects of this state aggression include post-traumatic stress and a total disinclination towards confrontation with the state even decades later, lest one disappear. Ignorance, or feigning ignorance, meant survival. Questioning authority (or even wearing spectacles) meant death.

Support for the Khmer Rouge

Despite the death toll, the Western academic quoted earlier was not alone and not the exception in her support. Another was Malcolm Caldwell, a lecturer at the School of Oriental and African Studies at the University of London. He was an ardent supporter of Pol Pot, the Khmer Rouge's top leader, and visited Democratic Kampuchea, as Cambodia had been rechristened during the Khmer

Rouge's reign. Ironically, he was murdered on Christmas day, 1978, the very night after he personally interviewed Pol Pot.

In a conference that took place in Stockholm, Sweden, from 17-18 November 1979, following the invasion of Cambodia and ouster of the Khmer Rouge by the Vietnamese government, participants met to discuss how the Khmer Rouge could return to power and be rid of Vietnam. A speaker at the conference named George Hildebrand had collaborated with Gareth Porter on one of the first books on the Khmer Rouge Revolution, entitled *Cambodia: Starvation and Revolution* (New York: Monthly Review Press). This 1976 book presented the Khmer Rouge in a positive light. Replete with propaganda pictures from the Khmer Rouge, it even justified the forced evacuation of hospital patients from Phnom Penh. Noam Chomsky cited the Porter and Hildebrand book favorably, describing it as:

> *...a carefully documented study of the destructive American impact on Cambodia and the success of the Cambodian revolutionaries in overcoming it, giving a very favorable picture of their programs and policies, based on a wide range of sources.*[4] (Later, Porter agreed that the Khmer Rouge regime was guilty of mass killings and mass starvation.)

The conference included a Khmer Rouge delegation headed by Ieng Thirith, the Minister of Social Affairs for Democratic Kampuchea. Her husband, Ieng Sary, was Foreign Minister for Democratic Kampuchea. After three decades of freedom and wealth, both now await trial at the Khmer Rouge Tribunal taking place near Phnom Penh.

Passport to Freedom

Returning to the personal, the only reason that my four siblings and I are alive today is because my mother spoke Vietnamese, and was able to use that language as a passport to freedom. At the time, my mother received word that she would be able to leave Cambodia if she could prove that she was a Vietnamese national. She decided to pretend being Vietnamese. Her Vietnamese was so bad that she had originally given all the boys girls' names and all the girls boys' names. If it were not for a Vietnamese lady whom she had befriended, who told her of this mistake, we would all have been sent to the gallows. With this Good Samaritan's assistance, my mother was tutored for three days in the repatriation camps at Koh Thom and Koh Tiev before each of her language interviews. In retrospect, this woman was an intervener. Because of her kindness, my mother was able to pass two exams, one by the Khmer Rouge and one by the Vietnamese cadres, to prove herself as Vietnamese.

But the intervening did not end there. After Vietnam, we planned on traveling to France, but to get to France was another incredible experience involving the kindness of others, in particular, a Frenchman named Bernard Guyader. A distant cousin, who was a starving Parisian student, had the difficult task of getting us to France, even though he had no means of doing so. He had to find someone to run the paperwork and also locate another person who had the same last name as my mother, to prove some kind of familial relationship in order for us to be sponsored to go to France. One day, despondent, he bumped into Bernard who in turn cared enough to intervene. He helped my family with the paperwork and found the needed individual with the same last name as my mother. Bernard persuaded her to sign the paperwork and mail it, but they got lost in the mail. He simply forged the signature the second time around. (When the French Ministry of Foreign Affairs had already locked its gate at the close of business, Bernard simply hopped over it to gain access to the counter, whereupon he declared that by his watch it wasn't yet closing time.)

Human Rights and Intervention for Peace

But how does this personal history and experience particularly relate to the human condition, human rights, and intervention for peace? Forming the base of my experience is the idea that without human rights defenders, or interveners, I and countless millions would not be here today.

For those who have not shared similar experiences to my own, I have another angle to relate to: natural rights. Natural rights are essentially rights that you are born with, that are "natural" to you, and not necessarily given by a government. These rights are, for example, captured in the ideas of "life, liberty, and the pursuit of happiness" and "all men are created equal,"[5] enshrined in America's Declaration of Independence.

Tip O'Neill's adage that "All politics is local" is also useful. If we look back to the 1950s and 1960s and the great Civil Rights Movement that sprouted then, we can see that it was certainly a period that highlighted the injustices of Jim Crow laws that kept races "separate but equal." Equality under the law cannot be separated.

Human rights can seem like something foreign, but in fact, human rights as explained in the Universal Declaration of Human Rights, sound strikingly familiar: "All human beings are born free and equal in dignity and rights."[6] Natural rights are civil rights which in turn are human rights. As citizens of the world, the global becomes the local and vice-versa. Events that happen thousands of miles away from us still have an impact on us. As much as we may think "out of sight, out of mind," we now live in a global village, and what happens in Darfur does not stay in Darfur. It happens to all of us. And, when individuals are aggressed against there, it is equally unjust and harmful.

George McGovern, who was the Democratic Party's candidate for the 1972 presidential election, had opposed the Vietnam War. He had a firm anti-war stance. However, he strongly advocated humanitarian intervention in Cambodia when he realized what the Communists had wrought to the country. He firmly believed that "the rise of the Khmer Rouge was one of the greatest single costs of U.S. involvement in Indochina."[7] As sovereign rulers, the murderous Khmer Rouge regime killed Cambodians under the lawful backing of the international system, which turned a blind eye to abuses happening inside Cambodia. What is now happening in North Korea is no different.

Conclusion

Cambodia's story is a cautionary tale of antagonists and protagonists when it comes to intervention. While some academics have checkered pasts with respect to Cambodia, encouraging intervention by the Khmer Rouge to reorder society into an agrarian utopia, they have long been forgotten. Some, like Ben Kiernan, have apologized and have gone on to become celebrated leaders in genocide studies. Other paid with their lives. The Good Samaritan story that is really my life story shows that were it not for strangers along the way, and their personal interventions, it would be impossible for me to write these words today.

Acknowledgements: Jim Chhor and Richard Chhuon provided excellent research assistance. The views expressed are Sophal Ear's alone, and do not reflect the views of the Department of the Navy or the Department of Defense.

---

[1] Michael Paterniti. "Never Forget", GQ, July 2009. Available: http://www.gq.com/news-politics/big-issues/200907/cambodia-khmer-rouge-michael-paterniti

[2] Laura Summers, "Defining the Revolutionary State in Cambodia," *Current History*, December 1976 p. 216.

[3] Neilson, Kathryn E. "They Killed All the Lawyers: Rebuilding the Judicial System in Cambodia." CAPI Occasional Paper #13. Victoria: Centre for Asia-Pacific Initiatives, 1996.

[4] Chomsky did this with Edward Herman repeatedly. First in an article in *The Nation* entitled "Distortion at Fourth Hand" on 25 June 1977 and then in 1979 in their book *After the Cataclysm: Postwar Indochina & the Reconstruction of Imperial Ideology* (South End Press) on page 161.

[5] Preamble to the Declaration of Independence. Available: http://www.archives.gov/exhibits/charters/declaration_transcript.html

[6] Article 1 of the Universal Declaration of Human Rights. Available: http://www.un.org/en/documents/udhr/index.shtml

[7] Samantha Power, *A Problem from Hell: America and the Age of Genocide*, Harper Perennial Edition, 2007, p. 133.

If War is the
Health of the State,
What is Peace?

Karen Kwiatkowski

Karen Kwiatkowski retired from the USAF in 2003 as a Lieutenant Colonel. She has an MA in Government from Harvard University, an MS in Science Management from the University of Alaska, and has completed both Air Command and Staff College and the Naval War College seminar programs. She earned her Ph.D. in World Politics from the Catholic University of America in 2005, with a dissertation on Overt/Covert War in Angola: A Case Study of the Implementation of the Reagan Doctrine. *While in the USAF, Karen has authored two books on African security issues,* African Crisis Response Initiative: Past Present and Future *and* Expeditionary Air Operations in Africa: Challenges and Solutions. *Her final military assignment was as a political-military affairs officer in the Office of the Secretary of Defense, Under Secretary for Policy, in the Near East South Asia (NESA) Policy directorate. Karen left the military to write and publicly speak out against government excess and fraud in national security politics, and has contributed to several books, including* Ron Paul: A Life of Ideas, Why Liberty: Personal Journeys Toward Peace and Freedom *and* Neo-Conned, Again.

When I contributed to the recently published *Why Liberty*, the assignment was easy. After all, liberty is a condition that men and women everywhere instinctively love and need, even if it isn't always well-articulated. Liberty speaks to a way of self-government that is human-centered and fundamentally humane. Liberty defines human rights in a way that is supremely just, and liberty, by its very nature, is antithetical to force. Liberty is the natural condition of man, and most individuals share this ideal. Peace, on the other hand, for Americans born in the past 70 years, and for the millions of foreign subjects of the modern American empire, has not been part of their ideals, their ethics or their collective experience.

When we think of the Renaissance philosopher Jean-Jacques Rousseau and his work on individualism, libertarians and logicians alike chuckle at his claim that, "Men must be forced to be free." Rousseau likely meant that we tend to be voluntarily enslaved by our governments and kings, and by our cultures and traditions. He was right on one aspect of human nature. We are often reluctant to give up our fantasies of the justness of our rulers and the righteousness of our traditions.

Americans, in particular, embrace the language of liberty, even as the American state itself has become ominously and voraciously antithetical to liberty. The state pursues its wars in the name of liberty, and the government constantly reminds us that it maintains a large standing army, a massive military establishment, and a heavily integrated domestic police apparatus—all in the name of freedom. We cannot go far in the United States without being reminded that "if we like our freedom, thank a soldier."

To talk about peace in the 21st century, as fresh as we are from the deadly outcomes of the 20th, is a challenge. While it is natural to love liberty, it seems that peace is often argued to be unnatural, uncommon, and unlikely in the human condition. While the claim to liberty is granted by the Creator, claims to peace are not. But practiced liberty, with its prohibition on the use of force to take a man's time, his children, his property and labor, his movement, is the fundamental precursor to peace. A truly free society celebrates individuality, trusts its citizens, respects their private property and industry, and is fundamentally averse to the use of force. A free society is comfortable with the art of trading and deal-making based on marketplace choices, not government edicts. A truly free society is a peaceful society.

In the United States, we once had a vocal combination of thinkers who advocated nonviolence, and opposed the use of force, by individuals and by states. For many decades in our history, the primary opinion in the country was that government was to be limited in size and scope. Statesmen referenced the Constitution as a guide for this limited government, and limiting government (and by extension, war) was considered both valuable and normal. In these previous eras, serious public debate on war and peace was tolerated, and one could read about both war and peace in the newspapers.

But gradually, the state as a source of both assistance to and identity for individuals (increasingly thought of as "citizens") emerged in part with the emigration of the German and other national populists after the failures of the various 1848 revolutions in Europe. These immigrants, unlike previous waves of Europeans seeking freedom of religion and opportunity to farm and produce, embraced ideas of the importance of national unity, and the supremacy of democracy, political ideas that elevate the importance of the state. They were urban-oriented and industrial-minded immigrants, who valued the state as a legitimizer of individuals, and desired a powerful and egalitarian welfare state. They became important political blocs in the country, supporting a strong central rule, workers rights over property rights, majority rule over rule by the more staid and limited Constitution.

Meanwhile, the role of religionists and philosophers in the United States also increasingly saw the state as the mechanism of virtue. The era of Christian progressivism looked to the state to aid sinners in their fight to resist sin, and this very powerful and popular abdication of individual and community responsibility for diktats of state on the individual culminated in the 18th Amendment in 1919, banning sales and consumption of alcohol across the land. From political, economic, and religious perspectives, America as a great state was increasingly valued over America, land of liberty. These Europeans in general opposed Southern slavery. They generally did so as a means to higher paychecks and full employment rather than because they believed in equality of African Americans, or substantially embraced the fundamental concepts of human liberty. Slavery was enforced more effectively in the non-slave North than it had ever been in the South, in part due to racism, and in part due to the widely held view of slaves as economic units of competition.

The state centralized as a result of the war to prevent secession of a number of southern states between 1861 and 1865, and the state militarized as a result of Reconstruction and the post-war "professionalization" of federal civil servants. After 1865, the newly united and powerful federal army enforced both military rule on the South, and invigorated its ongoing efforts to dispossess and relocate remaining Native Americans in the western territories. Dehumanization, destruction of property, unlimited post-war takings by the state, shamefully supported, demanded and cheered on by both business and progressive religious sectors, all challenged constitutional ideas of liberty. Without liberty, and the innate justice that comes from respecting property of others, peace is impossible. As when the Christian churches actually condemned their more peaceful advocates in the abolition movement and came to see the state as an ally in pursuit of common goals of social order, the hypocrisy of some of those who worshipped the Prince of Peace became more and more obvious. The rise of the *Yankee Leviathan*, as phrased by historian Richard Bensel,[1] and the statist church-celebrated *Battle Hymn of the Republic*, written at about the same time, both illustrate the nature of the perversion.

Mark Twain's famous "The War Prayer" was first published in 1923, although it was actually composed in 1904 or 1905. In it, Twain refers to some Christian calls to reconvert the failing Spanish Empire from Catholicism to Protestantism, just as the burgeoning public school movement in America was attempting with the new waves of impoverished Catholic Irish and Italian immigrants. "The War Prayer" indeed captures the hypocrisy of Christians who longed to harness the state for a religious aim, effecting war, death and destruction, often overseas or in another's backyard. This lust for war, equating support of the state with love of country, and confusing government-led collective hate with patriotism, was not something the founders envisioned for the new and free Republic. They certainly understood both the nature of mob thinking, as well as the nature of ruling elites, the latter of which were in a clear position to profit from war. To prevent the nation from adventuring into wars abroad, without the full awareness and support of the people and without a deep public debate on the justness of the war, the founders specified that Congress, representing the people and the several states, was designated the only branch of government that could declare and authorize war.

This seemed to work with few exceptions until the late 1800s. Was it a desire for war, or a desire for global relevance, or just the evolving nature of the American state that caused this shift? Had Americans thrilled to the idea of peace, it seems we would have heard more in the public sphere about how we could achieve it. Instead, we got a 20th century of state-engineered wars on the indigenous, state wars on other states, cold war militarism and fear-mongering, and the militaristic positioning of global alliances against other global alliances. On this foundation evolved domestic and global wars on drugs, wars on illiteracy, wars against poverty, wars on terror, and wars for "humanitarianism," democracy, and human rights.

War is organized in vertical authoritarian structures, and entails force against one's own people through regulation, drafts, and economic mandates from the state. War requires great collective fear of an enemy, as well as great personal fear of one's own state. When Randolph Bourne wrote "War Is the Health of the State" he explained how the state is fully realized only in war:

> The more terrifying the occasion for defense, the closer will become the organization and the more coercive the influence upon each member of the herd. War sends the current of purpose and activity flowing down to the lowest level of the herd, and to its most remote branches. All the activities of society are linked together as fast as possible to this central purpose of making a military offensive or a military defense, and the State becomes what in peacetimes it has vainly struggled to become—the inexorable arbiter and determinant of men's business and attitudes and opinions. The slack is taken up, the cross-currents fade out, and the nation moves lumberingly and slowly, but with ever accelerated speed and integration, toward the great end, toward the "peacefulness of being at war," of which L.P. Jacks has so unforgettably spoken.[2]

And what is that "peacefulness of being at war?" Jacks observed that in the early years of the First World War:

> ...the individual is not more gloomy. He is brighter, more cheerful. He worries less about himself. He is a trifle more unselfish and correspondingly more agreeable as a companion or neighbor. ... This feeling of being banded together, which comes over a great population in its hour of trial, is a wonderful thing. It produces a kind of exhilaration which goes far to offset the severity of the trial. The spirit of fellowship, with its attendant cheerfulness, is in the air. It is comparatively easy to love one's neighbor when we realize that he and we are common servants and common sufferers in the same cause. A deep breath of that spirit has passed into the life of England.[3]

In a sense, there is no way to speak about peace to a 21st century American, except as the absence of war. There is no way to collectively think about the absence of war, because the language of modern America is filled to the gills with talk of war, and a reactionary embrace of the centralized state. War is what we do. War sustains a significant portion of our government, gives our presidents manliness and makes our men and women aggressive and longsuffering patriots. War and munitions makes up over half of our global exports and employs over three million people, not counting men and women in uniform, which is all an enormous drain on our prosperity. The US government is obsessed with war, and in war, both seeks and finds its political and economic identity. This war-obsessed government employs today over 22 million Americans, twice the number of people employed in manufacturing, all a net loss for our wealth.[4]

I have directly been part of this "net loss." I attended college with the help of an ROTC scholarship, and was commissioned into the United States Air Force in December 1982. For nearly a decade, my work was directly justified as part of the global war against communism, specifically the Soviet Union's version rather than the Chinese variant, and this was known as the Cold War. It was supported and funded energetically and competitively by both Republicans and Democrats, and cheered vociferously by neoconservatives within both parties. By 1990, in the immediate aftermath of our "winning" the Cold War, and witnessing the collapse of the Soviet Union and the liberation of its satellite states, I expected a major contraction and reduction in military planning, budgets and activities, and an end of the American empire. I was optimistic for the new opportunities for peace and prosperity for Americans and worldwide. Instead, I observed what could only be described as continual and even accelerated military and governmental growth. In the 1990s, I spent a four-year stint working in military acquisition and within government "quality improvement" circles. This increased my understanding of how government economics really works. I watched the U.S. invoke the world's first "humanitarian war" in the Balkans, and I cringed at new U.S. base-building in Bosnia and Kosovo by the Clinton administration, all with the collective blessing of both liberal and conservative sectors. I began to understand that libertarian non-interventionism made sense, and also that government, including ours, was largely incapable of making moral or economic sense. I had not yet heard of the Leviathan, nor read "The War Prayer," nor understood that "war is the health of the state." However, these concepts, poems, and essays would soon inform my understanding of what my military career really meant.

By the time I was assigned to the Pentagon, in the last several years of my military career, I had read most of Ayn Rand, and had re-read Orwell's *1984*. I had rediscovered my native libertarianism, and had read, in amazement, General Smedley Butler's famous essay, "War is a Racket," detailing the corporate and political collusion in justifying the war on and occupation of the Philippines one hundred years earlier. I learned that our war and empire-seeking national policies had deep roots, and that long before I was born, conservatives actually opposed empire and war. Even so, in May 2002, when I was assigned into the Office of the Secretary of Defense for Policy, covering Middle East activities, I was truly shocked to find that the invasion of Iraq had already been tactically and operationally planned and approved, and that the government propaganda campaign to get the American people on board with this planned invasion had just gotten underway.

I was shocked to see for myself that this propaganda campaign was actively promoting information known by the intelligence community to be false, unsubstantiated, or misleading, or all three. As the next nine months unfolded, I became increasingly disgusted and enraged that my service to defense had come down to this: a cog in the wheel of an extremely powerful and well-funded imperial army, loyal only to its bureaucratic expansion and import, and the politicians who promised that expansion and paid homage to ever-increasing defense budgets and programs. My previous acquisition experience had made me wise to the nature of the military-industrial complex, and the frightening consequences of revolving door, contractor-written and created requests for proposals, cost-plus contracts and the successful imperial strategy of having military production facilities, bases and contracts located in every congressional district.

I wrote informally and anonymously while still at the Pentagon and, after retiring, wrote more extensively in opposition to war and empire, and tried to help others understand what had happened, in effect, to peace and our stated goals of peace. The immediate response by the war-loving right-wing and neoconservatives of both parties was to vilify me and denigrate my assertions and my military experience. These attacks did not last long, however, as Americans increasingly tired of war in the Middle East.

The anti-war voices grew louder and more coherent throughout the 2008 presidential elections, where a purported anti-war Democrat promised to bring troops home, end torture of detainees in the war on terror, and revoke a variety of executive orders that had so enraged so many constitutionalists, conservatives, libertarians, and the opposition Democratic Party.

However, upon assuming the office of the president, Mr. Obama quickly backed away from all promises to reduce the military industrial agenda, its funding, and its ongoing global projects. In fact, in the spring of 2011, he added another illegal and lie-based military intervention, again seeking to unseat a leader of an oil-rich (this time North African) country. The antiwar voices, once unified, remained in disarray after Obama's election, and the true nature of the Democratic Party's love for empire, mirroring that of the Republican Party, was painfully revealed. The business of the United States, as both General Smedley Butler then and the *Wall Street Journal*'s Stephen Moore today would agree, is war.

Yet, for all of this, Americans themselves do value peace, and are increasingly tired of war, and the endless lies and prevarications about the wars that seem to constantly engage us. Happily, the latest flurry of news from the White House about the final end of al Qaeda leader Osama bin Ladin is not producing the presidential political "bump" in the polls that past similar announcements have done, and instead of loud celebrations, Americans seem newly interested in what bin Ladin's death can tell us about our own country's prospects for real peace, and a contraction of our global military empire.

Peace takes on a more concrete meaning when people are struggling to feed families, buy gas, get and keep a job, and make their mortgage payments. As the productive capacity and civil liberties of Americans are shrinking, as they have done radically since September 11, 2001, the idea of living in a constitutional republic rather than an empire or global military enforcer becomes more compelling to the average American. Increasingly Americans are expatriating, and if not fully disengaging from the American state, are seeking second homes in places that truly seem to embody peaceful living.

We are reminded today, almost three generations later, of the emerging prosperity-oriented ideas of the late 1950s. Barry Goldwater called for smaller more accountable government, in the face of a growing and ever more confiscatory state. President Dwight Eisenhower questioned the burgeoning growth of the military-industrial complex and warned all Americans that unless checked, we as a nation would sacrifice both peace and liberty. In 1957, Ayn Rand published *Atlas Shrugged*, posing a last-ditch solution to the monster war-loving state, a "shrugging" off of individual productivity by simply disappearing from the purview of the state. Increasingly, we can find even mainstream media discussing the growing number of ways Americans are seeking some form of escape to Galt's Gulch: through alternative currencies, such as gold, silver, and electronic bitcoins; through lifestyle changes to include emigration, family and community self-sufficiency; and through the withdrawal of individual consent to government edicts, agendas, and policies.

These ideas—all related to peace, all related to prosperity, founded on Renaissance revelations of the intrinsic value of the individual and resting on the Founders' ideas of a Creator-granted organic right of liberty—have persisted, even as the government of the United States has morphed into a war-addicted, liberty-offending, debt-ridden global empire.

Why peace? And why now? We have become a country that cannot afford the luxury of killing human beings and destroying economies around the world. Americans are slowly waking to the ongoing destruction of our own economy, due largely to government spending abroad and government malinvestment in a military sector that dwarfs anything existing anywhere else on the planet. Americans are beginning to separate in their own minds their government's unending interest in military force and intimidation around the world, and their own interest in living a profitable and peaceful life, and seeing their children prosper in their own great land, not die miserably or be damaged irreversibly in some barren mountaintop or scorching desert inhabited by people our government simply does not care about.

Americans are slowly recognizing that the rule of law in this country has been usurped by a new imperial model, where presidential assassinations of enemies of the state around the world are standard, and where American citizens in general are viewed as threats to the state, not as free and valuable individuals, for whom the state must necessarily be submissive and subordinate. Peace is the only way we can resolve and reduce the state's grip on the lives and economies of Americans, even as peace will resolve and reduce our government's grip on much of the rest of the world.

Many Americans increasingly sense that economic hardship and limited freedom is the new 21st century reality for them and their children. They correctly associate hardship and a kind of citizen servitude with the United States global military empire, even as this empire has been slowly evolving, in some ways surreptitiously, for nearly 100 years. We require peace, because we can no longer afford war. More importantly, Americans are beginning, thanks in part to vastly and immediately available access to a wide variety of information, both historical and real-time, to recognize and even laugh at our prevaricating and parasitic political masters in both parties. When major public polling entities begin to regularly pose questions for the "political class" as opposed to "the people" as Rasmussen did in 2010, it is a major sign of impending revolution—

or, if we are fortunate, a peaceful evolution towards a value set that will publically and commonly criminalize war and war-mongering, and celebrate peace, liberty and prosperity at home, and everywhere.

In the dystopian future imagined by George Orwell in *1984*, Winston Smith is advised,

> *There will be no curiosity, no enjoyment of the process of life. All competing pleasures will be destroyed. But always—do not forget this, Winston—always there will be the intoxication of power, constantly increasing and constantly growing subtler. Always, at every moment, there will be the thrill of victory, the sensation of trampling on an enemy who is helpless. If you want a picture of the future, imagine a boot stamping on a human face—forever.*[5]

In this simple description, we see the answer to the question, "Why Peace?" War is intoxication, addiction, and destruction. It is sensation, compulsion, and sin—the enemy not of peace, but of humanity itself. Randolph Bourne correctly observed, "War is the health of the state," and we can clearly see that the converse is also true. Peace is the health of the individual, the family, the community and the land.

We don't have to accept the boot of the state and its wars stamping on a human face forever, even as it is served up daily by the ever-ravenous political class, sitting atop a sand-based pyramid of state paranoia. Peace trumps the zero-sum game of war, and peace is additive, creative, infinitely inventive, and just. Only in peace can a true "spirit of fellowship" be experienced. To use the language of war with which Americans have become so comfortable, peace always wins, even as states inevitably collapse under the weight of their hubris and criminality.

---

[1] Richard Franklin Bensel, *Yankee Leviathan: The Origins of Central State Authority in America, 1859-1877* (Cambridge University Press, 1991).

[2] Randolph Bourne, "War is the Health of the State" 1918. Excerpted from "The State," published posthumously, in *Untimely Papers* (1919). http://fair-use.org/randolph-bourne/the-state/

[3] L.P.Jacks, "The Peacefulness of Being at War," *The New Republic*, September 11, 1915. pp. 152–154, http://fair-use.org/the-new-republic/1915/09/11/the-peacefulness-of-being-at-war.

[4] Stephen Moore, "We've Become a Nation of Takers, Not Makers," *Wall Street Journal Online*, April 1, 2011. http://online.wsj.com/article/SB100014240527487040502045762190738671821 08.html

[5] George Orwell, <u>1984</u> (Signet Classic Paperback, Penguin, New York: 1961): p. 267.

Waging Peace

Fr. Roy Bourgeois, MM

Roy Bourgeois spent four years in the military: two years aboard ship, one year in Greece, and one year on shore duty in Vietnam as a Navy lieutenant. He is a recipient of the Purple Heart. After leaving the military he became a Catholic priest and worked in Latin America for six years. He is the founder of School of the Americas Watch (SOAW), a grassroots organization dedicated to closing the School of the Americas. In 2010, Roy and SOAW were nominated for a Nobel Peace Prize.

[*This essay first appeared in* From Warriors to Resisters: U.S. Veterans on Terrorism, *and has been revised and updated.*]

Growing up in a small town in the bayous of Louisiana, I was taught to be patriotic. When I left college with a degree in geology, and our country's leaders told us we had to go off to Vietnam and stop the spread of communism, I did not question them. I became a naval officer, spent a couple of years aboard ship, and then volunteered for shore duty in Vietnam.

Vietnam became a turning point in my life. We soldiers were young and in a country far from home, knowing so little about its people, culture, and history. We were warriors, believing our cause was noble. Then something happened. The suffering and death and the body bags returning home began to change us. We started questioning our country's violence and began to consider it a dead-end street. At the time I could not articulate it, but I was beginning to feel what Dr. Martin Luther King was saying: "The ultimate weakness of violence is that it is a descending spiral, begetting the very thing it seeks to destroy." Hope, which was always very alive in my life, began to disintegrate in Vietnam.

But grace was at work. I met a missionary at a nearby orphanage who was caring for hundreds of children, many of them wounded by our bullets and napalm. In the midst of all the madness and violence, he was a peacemaker, a healer. Spending time with the children helped get me through my year in Vietnam, helped me hold on to hope.

I returned home to my family and friends, very grateful to be alive. But I came back, as so many of us did, different. I entered a seminary of the Maryknoll Order, a group serving the poor in 28 countries. After being ordained a Catholic priest in 1972, I went to Bolivia, where a slum on the outskirts of La Paz became my home for the next five years.

Bolivia was struggling under a brutal dictator, General Hugo Banzer, who came to power through a violent coup that was supported by the United States government. During this time, the United States government was also supporting the repressive military regimes of Chile, Argentina, Peru, Ecuador, El Salvador, Guatemala, Honduras, and Nicaragua—arming and training the men with the guns, in the interest of protecting private US corporate interests.

Bolivia's poor became my teachers and taught me about oppressive interventionist policies. The majority of the people were struggling for survival. They lived in shacks without running water. They had no schools for their children, and when they got sick there were no medicines to heal them. In short, the poor of Bolivia died before their time. They were hungry for food and they were hungry for justice.

In their struggle for survival, the oppressed became educated. They knew that there were more than enough resources for everyone to live comfortably. But what was there to be shared instead ended up in the hands of small, powerful elites.

Now, as then, those suffering in Latin America are doing what we would do if we lived in such dehumanizing oppression, day after day. They are saying, "*Basta!*" (Enough!) They are organizing and calling for wealth and resources not to be stolen and destroyed and power to be returned to the people. However, as so often when individuals organize and speak out, the men with the guns are there to silence them; the soldiers defend the crony-political system that exploits most everyone.

In Bolivia, it angered me to see my country giving guns and training to the bullies doing the killing. It was all about providing the muscle to protect U.S. economic interests in Latin America, at any cost to the Latin Americans.

The prisons of Bolivia began to overflow with tin miners, factory workers, and university students. With the help of the local bishop, I was able to get a pass and visit political prisoners. Many were being tortured, which I reported to members of the U.S. Congress. I was later arrested and forced to leave Bolivia.

After returning to the United States, I became very involved in activities regarding El Salvador, especially after Archbishop Oscar Romero was assassinated and four U.S. church women were raped and killed by the Salvadoran military. (Two of those women were friends of mine.) The Archbishop and the four women were killed, because they had dared to be outspoken critics of the Salvadoran military's brutality against innocent individuals. I went to El Salvador and, as in Bolivia, I found my own country giving guns and training to those doing the killing.

When hundreds of Salvadoran soldiers started combat training at Fort Benning, Georgia, I rented an apartment near the post. I called it "*Casa Romero*" and started organizing. After I gave talks at local colleges and churches about the U.S.-sponsored repression in El Salvador, it was time to take the message to those soldiers at Fort Benning. The messengers were Linda Ventimiglia, who was in the Army Reserves and had trained at Fort Benning; Fr. Larry Rosebaugh, an Oblate priest who had worked in Brazil; and me.

We dressed as high-ranking military officers and entered Fort Benning at night. We carried a powerful boom box that contained the last sermon of Archbishop Romero, given at the cathedral the day before he was assassinated. His sermon had called for the military to stop the killing. Linda, Larry, and I climbed a pine tree near the barracks of the Salvadoran soldiers and waited. When the lights went out, we boomed Romero's message to the soldiers, and it was like poking a bee hive. We were arrested, brought to trial, and sent to prison for 18 months. But the truth could not be silenced, and we spoke out from prison.

The bloodshed continued in El Salvador. On November 16, 1989, six Jesuit priests, their co-worker, and her 15-year-old daughter were massacred. Like the four churchwomen, the Jesuits had opposed the aggression that the Salvadoran military directed toward their people. A U.S. Congressional task force investigated and reported that those responsible had been trained at the U.S. Army School of the Americas (SOA) at Fort Benning.

The SOA is a military school that trains Latin American soldiers in commando tactics, psychological warfare, and counterinsurgency. Their targets have been religious leaders, landless farmers calling for land reform, human-rights activists, health-care workers, students, and anyone inclined to call out for justice.

I returned to Fort Benning, rented a small apartment just outside the main gate, and began the SOA Watch. Joined by Kathy Kelly, Charlie Liteky, Jim Barnett, and others, we camped at the main gate and went on a water-only fast for 35 days. Our mission was to call attention to this combat school that was hiding behind a wall of secrecy, and to call for its closure. After the fast we started our research. Through the Freedom of Information Act and human-rights reports, we documented hundreds of SOA graduates involved in massacres, torture, and rape.

As word about this school of assassins (all paid for by U.S. taxpayers) began to spread around the country, a grassroots movement was born, rooted in nonviolence and connected in solidarity with those suffering in Latin America. It grew rapidly and became very diverse, made up of thousands of college students, parents, grandparents, veterans, members of religious communities, and others. We worked hard at educating and lobbying our senators and representatives.

A growing number of members of Congress called for the school's closure when it was learned that SOA manuals advocated torture. The Pentagon, realizing the days of their school were numbered, came up with a plan for changing its name. By a close vote in Congress, SOA became the Western Hemisphere Institute for Security Cooperation (WHINSEC) on January 17, 2001.

No one was fooled. It was a new name, but the same shame. The late Rep. Joe Moakley of Massachusetts was right when he said that renaming the school was like pouring a bottle of perfume on a toxic waste dump. Indeed, ten years later, the school is still deadly. It's still about men with guns, still about keeping the militaries of Latin America in power to protect U.S. corporations and U.S. government interests, and still about allowing the privileged to live very well off the backs of the poor.

After the September 11 attacks, the commanding officer of Fort Benning and the mayor of adjacent Columbus said that the U.S. was at war with terrorists, and they requested that the SOA Watch call off its annual protest in front of Fort Benning. But the tens of thousands in the movement said that it was more important than ever to protest. After all, President Bush had repeatedly said that we were at war with terrorism, and should go after those training camps for terrorists wherever they might be. We thought that a good place to start would be on our own soil, at the SOA/WHINSEC... nonviolently, of course.

So on November 17-18, 2001, over 10,000 individuals from all over the country gathered at Fort Benning's main gate and said, "Not in our name!" We remembered those killed in the September 11 attacks, the 75,000 killed in El Salvador, the 200,000 killed in Guatemala, and the thousands dying in Colombia at the hands of a military armed and trained by the United States government.

Thousands continue to gather every November at the main gate of Ft. Benning, to keep alive the memories of the thousands killed by SOA/WHINSEC graduates, and to call for the closing of SOA/WHINSEC. Over the years, more than 245 people from the SOA Watch movement have gone to federal prison for nonviolent protests at Ft. Benning, most serving six-month sentences. Prison is difficult, but whenever the government incarcerates us, the movement is energized and grows.

The United States government produces and sells more weapons than any other nation, and the United States possesses more weapons than ever before. Yet we have never felt less secure than we do today.

I returned to Vietnam some ten years ago. I felt it was important to go back to the place that had had such an impact on my life. I brought with me a letter that said, "As a Vietnam veteran I have returned to your country to apologize for all the suffering and death we caused you. Over these years I have asked God's forgiveness for what we did in Vietnam. I now ask for yours."

One of the many Vietnamese to whom I gave my letter was a Buddhist monk. In our long conversation he said, "Our greatest enemy is ignorance. Our sword must be wisdom."

In light of ongoing training at SOA/WHINSEC and ongoing U.S. government militarism in so many parts of the world, I think about the monk's words a lot today.

The Revolutionary Spirit
in Iraq's Insurgency

Alex Peterson

Alex Peterson is a U.S. Army veteran of the Iraq War living in New Hampshire. Today, he is twenty five years old and a student at the University of New Hampshire. He is currently in his final year of an undergrad degree in History and Political Science and beginning a Masters program in Medieval Archaeology at the University of York in 2012 (In the United Kingdom). Alex is both the founder and an active member of the UNH Young Americans for Liberty chapter, and is involved in organizing college youth activist events. Additionally, he is a member of the Free State Project and volunteers with an Iraqi refugee resettlement program in New Hampshire. Alex aims to share his experiences of the Iraq War in order to promote non-intervention and advocate for peace.

During the years of 2006 and 2007, at the age of nineteen, I was deployed to Western Baghdad in Iraq. Serving in the U.S. Army Infantry, I was eager to finally have an opportunity to use my skills and discover if I could do the job for which I was trained. Coming from a strong neo-conservative family, I fell in step with the belief that the war was justified and serving in the military was a patriotic duty required to maintain "our" freedoms; however, my experience in the war caused a transformation in how I conceived the world around me. In short, I found myself unable to justify the war or foreign intervention any longer.

Looking back, it feels like I was a completely different person during my time in the military. Today, I live in New Hampshire as a member of the Free State Project, am a strong advocate for non-intervention, and involved in both anti-war and liberty activism. Along with this, I participate as an organizer for college youth liberty events at the University of New Hampshire, where I am currently enrolled in classes. The change in my understanding of both the war and politics was substantial when put in contrast to my neo-conservative background. This dramatic shift in perspectives was a direct result of my experience in the war. I came to realize the necessity of peace and the immoral nature of U.S. intervention overseas.

The process I went through in reaching my new understanding of the war took time, as it did for other soldiers who reached similar conclusions. Due to the significant time and effort that a soldier invests in the war, it becomes easy to justify it. For soldiers in the infantry, as I was, the degree to which one becomes invested in the conflict is great. For this reason, despite gut instincts that questioned the morality and justification of the war I was involved in, I tried to defend the conflict as long as I could; however, I could not ignore my conscience forever. It was not until a year after returning home that I accepted the immorality and erroneous nature of intervening in Iraq. I witnessed the destructive nature of U.S. intervention and the numerous lives and families that

213

were destroyed by it. It was several experiences like this that led me to the conclusions I maintain today. Upon forming my new conclusions, I knew I had an obligation to share with others why peace is necessary.

Before I share some of my experiences in the war, it is useful to mention a book that impacted me greatly and guided me to my new convictions. About a year after returning to the states, I read a Russian soldier's memoirs about Afghanistan. A particular quote affected me strongly, due to its relevance to the war in Iraq. Reading this soldier's memoirs caused me to reconsider the awful war I had participated in, as it spoke to me in a voice that represented what I felt but could not yet admit.

The author of this memoir was the Russian soldier Vladislav Tamarov. In one passage, he writes about a monument erected on a Soviet base in 1985 that was created as a symbol for Afghan-Soviet friendship and dedicated to 'soldiers fulfilling their international duty.' Commenting on this monument, Vladislav writes:

> *"We felt differently about it. For us it was a giant gravestone. For us it was a symbol of revenge. We took revenge on them for our friends who remained here forever. They took revenge on us for their brothers who fell after our friends. And the longer we were here, the more vicious this circle became. And that was the true symbolism of this monument."*[1]

Collateral damage always happens in war; every person that is killed is someone's brother, father, son, daughter, mother, spouse, friend, etc… Clearly, this breeds hatred and a desire to resist a foreign-armed force. Although an individual may have no previous quarrel with a foreigner, when they lose family or their home is destroyed, it should be no surprise that an insurgency or resistance would fight back. I found myself accepting the fact that we were often fighting those who were merely defending their homes or getting revenge, creating an endless cycle of violence similar to what Tamarov describes.

If the current administration continues on the current course of action, what occurred during Russia's intervention in Afghanistan will continue to characterize U.S. intervention in both Iraq and Afghanistan. The U.S. is only creating more enemies as foreign intervention continues. How high will the cost become, before American leadership accepts that a non-interventionist policy is morally, and economically, necessary? By the unexpected and simple act of reading this memoir, I finally began to seriously consider my experiences in the war and the adverse and harmful effects the war had on many individuals. Perhaps this volume will help achieve the same for others.

As an example of how intervention in Iraq destroys individual lives, while failing to actually make the United States any safer, one memory comes to mind immediately. In Iraq, I had several encounters with Iraqi citizens who had been detained. Some of the detainees spoke English well, and I was able to talk with them. One such conversation significantly challenged my preconceptions about why they fought. In Baghdad, I discovered one detainee who spoke English surprisingly well had actually been educated in England. Responding to a question I posed asking why he fought, he replied "What would you do if men with guns and tanks drove down your neighborhood street and built bases on your land?" Initially, I was surprised by his response, as I was expecting a religious justification preaching his hatred of America and the necessity of Islamic jihad across the world.

Along with this, he explained how he had been an engineer, who worked a nine-to-five job like many Americans. In fact, his life was not so different from most Americans I knew, and I found myself relating to his situation. He explained that after his home had been destroyed by coalition bombings, killing his wife, he was obviously upset. This tragic loss motivated him to join a militia, not any religious motivation. He was proud of his efforts fighting the U.S. as a member of a Sunni nationalist militia.

With conviction, he asserted that Iraq would be sovereign one day and the U.S. would be forced to withdraw once the costs become too high. The reason his response challenged my preconceptions of the war was not simply because he gave me an answer I had not expected, but that I found myself agreeing with him. With my 'mind's eye' I put myself in his shoes and realized I would do the same in his place. If a foreign military bombed my home and drove tanks down my neighborhood street, I would defend my family and my home, without a second thought. Due to the fact that his answer made sense and reflected an obvious reaction that would be true for most rational people, seeds of doubt were planted which would grow as I began to question the war further.

The Iraqi resistance fighter I had spoken with was a member of a militia that had been giving troops in my area trouble for some time, gaining much support from the local Sunni population. This militia was called the 1920 Revolutionary Brigade. It consisted of Sunnis who had nationalist aims to create a sovereign Iraqi nation free of foreign intervention. Most of my military experience in Iraq during 2006 and 2007 involved the 1920 Revolutionary Brigade. For this reason, I feel this essay will speak with more validity if I limit my discussion to them alone.

By examining the brigade further, the complexity of the war in Iraq is illustrated. The 1920 Revolutionary Brigade was not the only nationalist militant group. Multiple nationalist and anti-occupation militias existed throughout the country. This was an aim of the majority of insurgent or resistance militia's I encountered in Iraq. Religious Islamists were a minority, and organizations like Al-Qaeda were new phenomena in Iraq that can be understood as a reactionary movement to foreign intervention. The longer foreign intervention continued, religious extremists could appeal to a broader audience as a convincing alternative to overcoming occupation. Prior to the war, many of the members of the 1920 Revolutionary brigade had lived peacefully side by side with Shi'ites. Members of this militia were always quick to point out that individuals of different religious sects and communities in the Near East have been able to live together peacefully for some time now, and the recent rise in religious extremism has been due to Western intervention.

Religion is surely an important aspect of Middle Eastern culture, but the Revolutionary Brigade had secular aims, despite its members being Muslim. An example of this can be depicted by describing a routine operation in which I was involved. In one case, Iraqis we captured needed to be prepared to travel into one of the permanent internment facilities. I can remember lining several prisoners up along a wall, as we asked them to identify if they were Sunni or Shiite. The purpose of this was to separate them into different holding areas, so as to avoid sectarian conflict by placing Sunni and Shiite Muslims together. Several of these detainees were members of the 1920 Revolutionary Brigade. When asked which sect they followed, all members of the brigade replied "I am Iraqi." They were proud as they said this, and refused to be distinguished from other Iraqis by religious labels. Their aim was to liberate Iraq, and they had very secular political goals.

Oftentimes, most Americans view the Middle East by what is shown to them on television. The media often shows videos of religious extremists, beheadings, and other Islamist material. What most Americans do not see are the writings and videos produced by the nationalist and liberty insurgent organizations. I came across a plethora of such material in Iraq, without knowing what any of it said at first. It was a surprise to hear this material translated by the interpreter assigned to my unit, as it never seemed to fit the stereotypes we all expected. Occasionally we would get the typical Islamic extremist propaganda you hear about on the media; however, we seized much more material from nationalist organizations like the 1920 Revolutionary Brigade. No matter how much of this we found, military intelligence officers would often ignore it and pass it off as not important, as it did not fit the description of the type of intelligence the government was wanting them to focus on. On the other hand, if any Islamic extremist writing were discovered, military intelligence would jump all over it in a hurry.

It is important for Americans to view material produced by the nationalist militias if they are to have a better understanding of the war. Fortunately, some of the 1920 Revolutionary Brigade messages were written in English and posted on the net. In 2007, we were aware they were doing this but never gave much attention to it. However, it always bothered me when I read what they wrote, I found myself becoming empathetic to some of their grievances. It is not religious in nature and is often very eloquent. The media never shares this side of the insurgency, so I will. Some of this can still be found on forums across the internet or on Arabic news pages.

One statement issued in 2007 read:

"The Resistance has proved to the world that it is through morality and determination that you can achieve and gain your rights and that ideological pretext that is marketed by the US media as being the cause of this war, is nothing but another lie. Religions have coexisted for thousands of years in peace, why is it now a problem. Ideologic and religious fanaticism on all sides is only the excuse and not the reason which is economic gain and influence. The Resistance has also proved that the highly consumable capital based economies cannot fight long wars, and their greed for energy to sustain a specific lifestyle will eventually grind humanity into a global

market of exploitation and slavery only to be followed by total collapse."[2]

Along with this, the revolutionary brigade always had a message for the peace movement and those at home in the U.S. in their statements. For example, in the 2007 address they wrote, "*We also extend our appreciation and respect to all the honorable people around the world, the heroes of dignity and freedom, the brave men and women of the anti-globalization and Peace movements. We in Iraq are thankful and grateful for all what you have done and your continued efforts to end this conflict.*" Many people are unaware of this side of the war in Iraq, I know I was. After interacting with the revolutionary brigade in Iraq, I learned there was more than meets the eye to the war in Iraq.

As I mentioned above, it was nationalist militias that made up the majority of insurgent forces I encountered. This was unexpected, and a key reason I started questioning the war. I still feel as if most Americans view Iraq insurgents as Islamic "terrorists"; this is a common fallacy that has been indoctrinated into our culture by the media, the state, and other institutions. If I were to count the number of insurgent groups I encountered who could actually be defined as Islamic extremists, I could do it with one hand. Because of the misunderstanding of who the Iraqi insurgents are, which many Americans continue to have, it is vital to reveal the reality of the situation if the peace movement is to succeed in convincing others to demand non-intervention. This fear of "Islamic Fascism" is all too familiar, I am sure, to individuals in the peace movement who debate with supporters of the current wars. By educating others on the true nature of the conflict, this obstacle can be overcome.

I tried to justify the war as long as I could. Eventually I accepted that it was impossible to continue defending it. I could find no reason why Iraq was any threat to U.S. security. As soon as my military contract was complete, I left the military in 2009, and was determined to advocate peace and attempt to reverse the damage I had seen done while in the service. The war continues to damage the lives of thousands of Iraqis. I have worked with refugees from the war who have been resettled in the U.S. and the stories they have shared with me are moving.

It is not just Iraq that is harmful; all wars and cases of intervention must be rebuked. The state commits mass murder and calls it war, claiming it has a right to do so by posing as a champion for human rights, democracy, and freedom. In truth, they only bring disorder, death, and poverty. The state has become the greatest legalized mass murderer in history. Peace will always be resisted by the state, as it thrives and expands itself during military conflict.

One of the most important goals of liberty and peace activists everywhere should be aimed at ceasing to support the warfare state. The continuation of the war directly links to problems we face today. Due to both the war and defense spending, the U.S. economy is weak. The war has also been used as an assault on personal liberty through legislation such as the USA PATRIOT Act. Worst of all, it has caused the deaths of Americans, coalition members, and Iraqis. It is a simple concept; the wars in the Middle East violate the basic laws of nature. No individual, group, or officials supposedly representing a collective have any right to aggress against another or rule over them.

War is merely a means of the state to achieve its political ends through coercion. The only moral action is a voluntary action. If something is truly moral, one would not need to compel others with violence to accept it. For this reason, as peace activists everywhere continue to persuade others why peace is needed, the means must reflect the ends. Non-aggressive means is the only way to reach a peaceful end: non-violent civil disobedience, opposition to all intervention and initiation of force, and educational outreach efforts to spread the message of peace and liberty to others.

As a soldier in Iraq, I was always told by my officers that our purpose was to create peace and stability. Our means were coercive and violent, causing an endless circle of violence, much like Tamarov expressed in his memoirs. The above is a clear example of how aggressive means has created violent ends. It is not war which achieves peace, rather peace is achieved through non-aggression. Peace is the only way to create a climate which promotes freedom, open markets, and voluntary exchange.

Sadly, it is viewed as extremist to advocate peace and non-aggression. Many challenges face the peace movement that will have to be overcome. Even if success never comes, at least those who advocate peace refuse to legitimize the warfare state or take part in its immoral wars and numerous harmful interventions at home and abroad. I regret that I was once part of the aggressive military arm of the state, but I am not alone. Many soldiers with whom I served feel the same and are speaking out, some of whom I had never expected would change their perspective. This is encouraging and gives me hope for the peace movement as it moves forward into the future, only increasing in number every day.

Not one more person needs to die for the state; the state needs to die for peace.

---

[1] Vladislav Tamarov, *Afghanistan: A Soviet Soldier's Story.* (Berkeley: Ten Speed Press, 2001), 110.

[2] 1920s Revolutionary Brigades Message To The World. "The Hidden Facts": http://www.uruknet.de/?s1=1&p=36689&s2=27

For a Free North Korea

Park Sang Hak

Park Sang Hak is the founder of Fighters for a Free North Korea. He is a North Korean defector who graduated from Kim Chaek College of Engineering in North Korea. He was from an elite family in North Korea (His father, Park Kun Hee, was decorated several times by Kim Il-sung for his inventions in spy communication technology), but was disenchanted with the regime when millions of people died of starvation in the late 1990's. Park Sang Hak and his family defected to South Korea in 2000 and founded the North Korean Gulag in 2003, a North Korean defectors organization intent to dismantle the North Korean concentration camps, along with Kang Cheol Hwan and Ahn Hyuck, two of the concentration camp survivors. Park Sang Hak was one of the leaders working very closely with the late Mr. Hwang Jang Yop, the top ranking North Korean defector in South Korea. Park Sang Hak founded Fighters for a Free North Korea with the purpose of sending balloons with informative leaflets into North Korea.

Fighters for a Free North Korea is composed of North Korean defectors who escaped to freedom in South Korea. We began to send balloons with informative leaflets, regarding current events and informative propaganda, to North Korea in 2004.

We knew all too well how important the balloon/leaflet project was in our efforts to free our people in North Korea. The South Korean government did not support us, but rather harassed us whenever we tried to send the balloons. We had very limited money. We did not have the technical knowhow to fly the balloons. In short, we had little, but we were determined to carry out this project. (During the Roh Moo-hyun government in South Korea, we had to send the balloons/leaflets to North Korea in secret, since even they suppressed and harassed our activities.)

Kim Dae-jung's administration of South Korea had agreed to the "June 15th Joint Declaration" with the Kim Jong-il regime of North Korea in June 2000. They had declared that the South and the North would work together for peace and reconciliation. Subsequently, the South Korean government decided unilaterally to stop the propaganda campaign against the North Korean government. Since the South Korean government ceased such campaigns, we, the defectors, started the balloon-leaflets project, to let our brothers and sisters in North Korea know the truth outside.

In 2002, Kim Dae-jung's administration had completely stopped the radio broadcasting program, the electric billboards at the Demilitarized Zone (DMZ), and the balloon project. The North Korean people and the soldiers near the DMZ were again entirely cut off from the outside world. (Before I had defected to South Korea, I had on occasion listened to the radio broadcasts from the South, and heard about the leaflets. The Kim Jong-il regime has always been most sensitive to these projects in the South, because the truth and facts from the South could be fatal to the regime.)

One reason I felt I had to do this was the fact that, after my father and our family had defected to South Korea, many of my relatives in North Korea had been taken to the infamous political prisoner's camp and executed. He had been a high-ranking party official in North Korea, working in Room #35 of the NK Labor Party, the intelligence headquarters against South Korea. When a high-ranking party official defected to the South, his relatives were certain to be rounded up and persecuted. I felt I had to do something for all those relatives who had been executed because of our defection.

Not many individuals supported us in South Korea. Defectors pitched in $5, maybe $10 each. It was very difficult all around. Sometimes the balloons fell in Seoul, and not in North Korea. When they fell onto the Blue House, the executive office and official residence of the South Korean head-of-state in Seoul, President Roh Moo-hyun became very angry and publicly denounced our balloon project.

In spite of all the difficulties we encountered, there came an opportunity when the people and the South Korean media heard of and reported on our balloon project. On September 23, 2008, U.S. President George W. Bush and the First Lady had invited dissidents from all around the world to Governor's Island in New York. I was among the dissidents invited to this meeting. In attendance, along with the President and First Lady, were Secretary of State Condoleeza Rice and many other high-ranking government officials. The dissidents came from Myanmar, Tibet, Cuba, and other countries under dictatorship. During this lunch meeting, we talked for more than two hours. I could not believe that I had been invited to this meeting, representing all the North Korean defectors in South Korea. President Bush asked me many questions about North Korean human rights, and the dictatorship of Kim Jong-il in North Korea.

I gave copies of the leaflets to President Bush as a present, and repeated the importance of our work. President Bush said, "You are doing a great service for the North Korean people who do not have eyes or ears under the brutal dictatorship of Kim Jong-il. The dawn is not too far away, however. Dictatorship cannot last forever. Your fight against Kim Jong-il's dictatorship will succeed in the end. I am sure you will be able to go back to Pyong Yang sooner than later." These were words of encouragement from the U.S. President.

CNN reported this event worldwide. The South Korean press picked it up, and people in South Korea heard about the meeting. The North Korean government quickly called for a military conference with the South Korean government. At that conference, the North Korean delegation brought with them hundreds of our leaflets, and demanded an immediate end to the balloon project. They threw the leaflets at the South Korean delegation, screaming, "The People's Army will never tolerate this kind of treacherous propaganda that lies about the heroic revolution in North Korea."

On December 2, 2008, Fighters for a Free North Korea planned to send 100,000 leaflets to North Korea, from the Peace Bridge in Pajoo City at the DMZ. Some fifty members of pro-North Korea organizations like the

Progressive Institute, the Association for the June 15th Declaration, and the South Korean Labor Party came to the Peace Bridge, and tried to stop us physically. They tore the leaflets into pieces and physically assaulted our members.

Five of us from Fighters for a Free North Korea fought back. I fired my gas gun in the air to warn the leftist thugs. One of them suffered head injuries, and sued one of the FFNK members for physical assault. These aggressors were suing the innocent individuals who were defending themselves.

The police and the prosecutor's office sided with the attackers, and charged our member, Park Young Hak (my younger brother) with aggravated assault. The judges convicted him, and sentenced him to a one-and-a-half-year prison term. (This happened, mind you, in Seoul, South Korea, not Pyong Yang, North Korea.)

On December 5, 2008, National Assemblyman, Park Hee-tae, Party Chairman of the majority Grand National Party, asked me and a representative of the Abductees Family Association to come to their headquarters. Park Hee-tae asked us to stop the balloon project, for fear of further provoking the North Korean government. He said that the North had threatened to stop all ongoing talks and projects with the South if we kept sending those balloons into North Korea.

I protested that we could not and would not stop the balloon project, despite Kim Jong-il's threats. We know that the people in North Korea anxiously await news from the outside, and that they benefit from receiving it. How could we stop? I asked him if GNP had ever supported us financially, even 10 cents? We were not sending the balloons to disrupt the governmental projects, or to start a war with the North. The North Korean government had never specifically mentioned our organization, either.

What we were doing with the balloons against Kim Jong-il was entirely in accordance with our Constitution. We were letting our people in North Korea know what we had found in South Korea: that the Republic of Korea is free and democratic, and that the people in South Korea are not starving like those in North Korea. In fact, South Koreans are prospering and live better than most of the world. Read this truth! Kim Jong-il's Military First Policy is a farce!

I continued to explain that the balloon project had not begun the day before. It had taken five years since 2004 to build. Other than defectors, who else had ever showed their interest in our project? Why were they trying to stop us now? How could we ignore and forget our brothers and sisters in North Korea?!

I broke down and cried.

Suzanne Scholte, president of the <u>Defense Forum Foundation</u> (a non-profit educational foundation that sponsors programs on national security, foreign affairs and human rights issues), has helped us greatly. Suzanne has always been out at the front, promoting North Korean human rights, aiding North Korean refugees, and talking about human rights atrocities to the international community. Since 2003, she and I had become big sister and younger brother.

In May, 2007, Suzanne and I went to the DMZ where civilians are allowed, and sent balloons into North Korea. The military police tried to stop us; Suzanne was worried they would take me to prison. I told her that the prisons in South Korea were better than the hotels in North Korea. We both laughed.

We have demonstrated together at the U.S. Capitol, at the European Parliament, and in Seoul, promoting freedom and human rights in North Korea. We have sent balloons together more than ten times, from the land and the sea.

Suzanne is the guardian angel of North Korean human rights. Kim Jong-il must be most afraid of her. She is our champion. I wish there were one angel among South Koreans like Suzanne. Mr. Hwang Jang-yop, our leader, said before he passed away that we should build a statue of Suzanne Scholte in Pyong Yang when we go back to North Korea.

On February 16, 2009, Kim Jong-il's birthday, we put North Korean 5,000-won bills in our leaflets and sent them to North Korea for the first time. The North Korean 5,000-won bill had the portrait of Kim Il-sung, the Great Leader, printed on the money. North Korea threatened to cut off all dialogues between the two Koreas. Lee Myung-bak of South Korea publicly asked us to stop the balloon project. We did not listen to him.

Along with Suzanne Scholte, we sent more balloons with the money-picture on the leaflets. CNN, NKH, and other media reported the event worldwide. Hyun In-tak, Minister of Unification in South Korea, charged me with illegal use of North Korean money, a violation of the South-North Trade Act, or something. My case is still pending.

The balloons were sent from Paek Ryung Island. On May 20, 2010, Fighters for a Free North Korea and the Abductees Family Association sent half a million leaflets and CDs, denouncing the unprovoked sinking of the Chon Ahn Navy warship by the North Korean government.

On December 18, 2010, we sent 200,000 leaflets, 1,000 U.S. $1 bills, and 500 DVD's in balloons, from Yon Pyong Elementary School in Yon Pyong Island to North Korea.

On November 30, 2010, some 300 members of the Fighters for a Free North Korea and the Korean Parents Association sent leaflets from Imjin Pavilion in Pajoo City, denouncing the North Korean attack on Yon Pyong Island a week earlier. The leaflets contained messages like "Let us bomb Kim Jong-il!" and "Father and Son Kims are butchers!"

Why does North Korea protest so viciously against the leaflets? Because they contain messages of truth: *"More than half a million people died in the concentration camps in North Korea... North Korean people should rise up against the dictatorial regime of Kim Jong-il."* The leaflets contain broadcast hours of the Free North Korea Radio, as well as the family tree of Kim's Dynasty: *"Kim Jong-il spent almost $1 billion on his father's memorial in Pyong Yang, while more than 3 million of his own people starved to death. He could have fed his people with that money..."*

Anyone who had been through "the March of Suffering" famine in North Korea (1994-1997) and lost family members would feel betrayed by the regime when they read the messages of our leaflets.

We wrote the truth about the Korean War, the prosperity of South Korea, and the secret funds for Kim Jong-il in North Korea. We published the list of Korean prisoners of war who had never been returned—all 487 of them.

Recently, we have included USB flash drives, carrying videos of the recent wave of popular uprisings against authoritarian rulers in Egypt, Libya and other Middle Eastern countries. These are in vinyl plastic bag leaflets, so they cannot get wet or be destroyed easily. We put $1 U.S. bills in the bag as often as we can afford. It costs from $3,000 to $4,000 to send 100,000 leaflets, including the printing costs, the balloons, gas for the balloons, and the timer. That's three or four cents per leaflet.

Truth is more deadly to the enemy than the guns and swords. Over the past 60 years, Kim Il-sung and Kim Jong-il have brainwashed the population in North Korea. The government blocks all news and media from the outside world. From birth to death, North Korean people are indoctrinated into a one-man personal cult. North Koreans die shouting, "Long live the General!" They are completely conditioned, and they worship the person who impoverishes and restricts them with his government's force.

Kim Jong-il stole the soul of North Koreans; deprived of freedom and human rights, they behave like slaves. They starve to death, but never complain about their Great Leader or Dear Leader. Why? They are completely cut off from worldwide ideas on liberty. They don't have ears or eyes. In this way, the government can continue to rule over them.

This is why the balloons are so important. They contain truth and ideas for North Koreans. Balloons are the only guiding light in the darkness for North Koreans. That is why Kim Jong-il is so afraid of the balloons. And, balloons and leaflets are not guns and cannons. Force is no match for truth and ideas.

It was reported that Kim Jong-il ordered his troops to collect our leaflets, lest the people should learn the truth, and disobey authority and agitate for liberty. At every military conference between the South and the North, the North has demanded that the South stop our balloon project.

Furthermore, the leftist sympathizers in South Korea have tried every means to harass and obstruct our project. The South Korean government and police, instead of enforcing the law on these aggressors, has not protected us, but rather charges us with possessing illegal foreign currency and violating the South-North Trading Act.

The government of South Korea spends billions of dollars on military expenditures to counter the provocations from North Korea. Why do they harass us? We are doing their work by exposing Kim Jong-il for what he is.

For more than 10 years in the name of Sunshine Policy and Engagement Policy under Kim Dae-jung and Roh Moo-hyun, the South Korean government has suppressed the balloon project on Kim Jong-il's demand.

The Sunshine is over. The Engagement is over. We must send in the truth about the third-generation hereditary dictatorship of the Kim Dynasty. It is our responsibility as free people.

The Economics
of Foreign Military
Intervention

Christopher J. Coyne

Christopher J. Coyne is the F.A. Harper Professor of Economics at the Mercatus Center and a member of the Department of Economics at George Mason University. He is the author of After War: The Political Economy of Exporting Democracy.

1. Introduction

I first became familiar with the moral and economic arguments against war and militarism during my undergraduate studies at Manhattan College, where I first read Ludwig von Mises's *Human Action* and *Liberalism*, as well as Murray Rothbard's *For a New Liberty*. However, my interest in formally studying the economics of military intervention began in 2004. At the time, I was pursuing my Ph.D. in economics at George Mason University and was assigned as Tyler Cowen's research assistant. During a conversation, Tyler handed me an article on the U.S. occupation of Iraq; I cannot remember the specifics content of the article, but I do remember it discussed some of the problems the U.S. military was having in reconstructing the country.

Tyler suggested that we co-author a paper on the economics of post-war reconstruction. As I looked through the existing work on the topic, I was surprised that there was little to no research that applied economic concepts to military interventions aimed at transforming foreign societies. There is a large literature on the causes of conflict, mediation in conflict, state building, and various studies on specific cases of intervention. However, there was little applying the core tools of economics—incentives, knowledge problems, and other constraints—to military interventions.

Based on our initial conversation, Tyler and I wrote an article titled, "Postwar Reconstruction: Some Insights from Public Choice and Institutional Economics," and the economic analysis of military intervention became the topic of my dissertation. I feel fortunate to have had an excellent dissertation committee consisting of Peter Boettke (chairman), Tyler Cowen, Richard Wagner, and Jack Goldstone. Each committee member was not only helpful during the dissertation process, but has been extremely supportive of me throughout my career. After graduating from George Mason University, my article with Tyler became the core of my first book, *After War: The Political Economy of Exporting Democracy*. Since that time, my research has continued to focus on the economic analysis of foreign military intervention.

I believe that there are strong moral arguments against most instances of military intervention and that these arguments are very important. However, I have chosen to focus my efforts on the positive analysis of military intervention. In other words, I take the ends stated by policymakers as given and focus on analyzing the means invoked to achieve those ends. While positive analysis does not allow us to make ethical judgments about the ends themselves, such analysis can be used to inform whether ethical positions are feasible in reality.

For example, it might be determined that people have a moral responsibility to help others during a humanitarian crisis. Economics, by itself, cannot judge the moral content of these ends, but it can assist in analyzing whether some means are more or less appropriate for achieving those ends. I have chosen to focus on positive aspects of the issues because discussions of foreign intervention often devolve into ideological debates with no clear resolution.

For instance, Republicans contend that the Democrats are 'soft' on the war on terror and can't stomach the sacrifices that are required to spread democracy and freedom around the world. Democrats often respond that the Republicans botched the current efforts in Iraq and Afghanistan with poor planning and a general lack of 'effort.' If only better planning had taken place prior to occupations, the argument goes, the U.S. would not be mired in these situations.

These debates tend to miss a crucial issue. It is rarely considered whether the U.S. government has the means available to accomplish the desired ends when it intervenes abroad. Economics can shed important insight into government's capabilities, or lack thereof, in this regard. Employing the tools of economics affords the opportunity to put aside ideological issues and focus instead on the ability of the U.S. government to achieve its stated ends of spreading Western-style institutions abroad. The historical record shows more failures than successes. I have argued that there are a few core reasons why this is the case.

2. The Political Economy of Military Intervention

Economists emphasize that people face constraints (*e.g.*, knowledge, information, income, etc.) and respond to incentives. Incentives refer to factors influencing human behavior by changing the relative costs and benefits. When the benefits associated with a certain behavior increase, people engage in more of it. Likewise, when the costs associated with a certain behavior increase, people engage in less of it.

From an economic standpoint, military occupation is all about constraints and incentives. All of the various individuals (members of the military, bureaucrats, policymakers, politicians, citizens and policymakers in the occupied country, politicians in neighboring countries, etc.) involved in foreign interventions face certain constraints and incentives which contribute to ultimate success or failure. The application of the economic way of thinking to foreign intervention goes a long way in explaining why a majority of U.S. efforts to export democracy abroad through military occupation have failed dismally.

2.1 The Knowledge Problem: Creating Incentives for a Free Society

The most significant constraint facing policymakers and occupiers is the fundamental knowledge problem of establishing the foundations of a free society where they do not already exist. Many agree on the general characteristics of a free society (protection of individual and property rights, freedom of speech, rule of law, etc.), but the knowledge of how to effectively design and impose these characteristics is lacking.

The lack of knowledge regarding the factors leading to democracy is captured in the following list of propositions put forth by political scientist Doh C. Shin (1994: 151):

1. There are few preconditions for the emergence of democracy;

2. No single factor is sufficient or necessary to the emergence of democracy;

3. The emergence of democracy in a country is the result of a combination of causes;

4. The causes responsible for the emergence of democracy are not the same as those promoting its consolidation;

5. The combination of causes promoting democratic transition and consolidation varies from country to country; and

6. The combination of causes generally responsible for one wave of democratization differs from those responsible for other waves.

Success in military occupation is not simply a matter of taking the rules that work in one society and imposing them on another one. This point is illustrated not only by the many failed U.S. foreign interventions, but also by the failure of several Latin American countries to effectively mimic the U.S. Constitution.

The ability to transport rules between societies is constrained by the fact that underlying belief systems, values and ideals often differ across societies. What works in the United States will not work in the Middle East, just like what worked in Japan and West Germany following World War II is a very poor guide for current and future foreign interventions.

Given the lack of knowledge regarding the foundations of liberal democracy, why should we expect foreign occupiers to be successful in attempts to establish these institutions at gunpoint? The knowledge problem facing policymakers and occupiers prevents them from designing and implementing the incentives necessary for a free society. This realization alone should lead us to be extremely skeptical of the ability of the U.S. government to 'export' liberal democratic institutions abroad through military intervention.

Unfortunately, the knowledge problem has not stopped U.S. policymakers from using foreign military interventions to foster political, social and economic change. Instead of recognizing the fundamental limitations of these efforts, focus is typically placed on the amount of 'effort' in the form of time spent planning, monetary and humanitarian aid, troop levels, the timing of elections and exit strategy. Unfortunately, this overlooks the deeper issue—policymakers do not have the relevant knowledge to achieve their desired end.

A stark example of the knowledge problem is playing out as I write this. The

U.S. has spent over eight years in Afghanistan and Iraq. Some successes have been achieved, but the governments of both countries are fragile as are their economies. Parallel to these efforts, a series of revolutions have emerged in Tunisia, Egypt, and Libya. These spontaneous revolutions demonstrate that social change cannot be planned or predicted by outsiders. Of course no one knows what the outcome of these revolutions will ultimately be, but that is the very point. Radical societal change toward liberal ends cannot be planned and imposed by outsiders.

2.2 The Economics of Politics

Politics is central to any foreign occupation. Therefore, it is important to consider the incentives facing those involved in the political system and the subsequent impact on military interventions and occupations. To illustrate this, consider a few of the key players in reconstruction efforts:

2.2.1 Elected officials

Economics suggests that the decisions of elected politicians are often shortsighted in nature. For elected officials that are constrained by a term limit, the main focus is on obtaining benefits during their time in office, even if these shorter-term benefits entail great costs that will be incurred in future periods. This is because current politicians will not incur "bills" that come due in the future since they will be out of office. This logic applies to military intervention just like any other policy. For example, in 2002 Larry Lindsey, a Bush economic advisor, announced that the Iraq war could cost in the range of $100-$200 billion. In order to maintain public support for the war efforts, the Bush administration rejected these numbers as a significant overestimation. To date, the war has cost over $500 billion with no end in sight. Further, Joseph Stiglitz and Linda Bilmes (2008) estimate that, when all is said and done and all direct *and* indirect costs are taken into account, the war and reconstruction in Iraq could cost closer to $3 trillion.

2.2.2 Bureaucrats

The occupation and reconstruction of Iraq has been characterized by infighting between various government agencies and bureaus. Many blame this on poor planning and management on the part of the Bush administration. However, the economics of bureaucracy predicts that this is the outcome we should expect no matter which party is in charge. Consider the incentives that bureaucrats face. Absent profit and loss to judge their effectiveness, the success of a bureau is judged by the size of its budget and the number of bureaucrats employed. Foreign occupations provide an excellent opportunity to increase both. The result is that while bureaus are supposed to be working together for a common goal, they end up fighting with each other in the hopes of establishing a dominant position and securing a bigger share of the resources associated with the intervention.

2.2.3 Special-interest groups

In addition to bureaucrats, private firms also seek to influence foreign interventions and secure a share of the associated monetary budget. Central to the process of securing contracts and significant roles in the intervention are the relationships between these firms and elected officials and bureaucrats. One example of this is the role played by Halliburton in the ongoing reconstruction of Iraq. The popular media has highlighted that Dick Cheney was the CEO of Halliburton from 1995 to 2000 as evidence of the connection between Halliburton and the Bush administration. While important, this neglects the more important fact that Halliburton has had a close relationship with the U.S. government for decades. This includes close connections with both Republican and Democratic administrations. While Republicans are often stereotyped as being in bed with 'big business,' in reality both Democrats *and* Republicans foster crony capitalism, through the exchange of political favors for financial support.

The resulting military-industrial complex is a dynamic set of political, bureaucratic, and economic interests seeking to influence foreign policy regardless of the need or viability of this policy. It includes bureaucracies and special-interest groups which view foreign interventions as a lucrative profit opportunity. It also includes politicians from both sides who rely on the fear of foreign threats to maximize their votes. The main takeaway is that the perverse incentives created by political institutions affect foreign interventions by influencing policies and outcomes. The result will often be dysfunction or failure.

3. The Failure of Central Planning (Again) and the Free Trade Alternative

3.1 Foreign Intervention as Large-Scale Central Planning

The main insights from the economic way of thinking regarding foreign intervention and military occupation can be summarized as follows:

1) Policymakers and occupiers face an array of constraints, both internal and external to the country being occupied, which make reconstruction efforts more likely to fail than to succeed.

2) The failure of foreign interventions and reconstruction efforts is *not* a matter of political ideology or the political party in charge. Nor is it an issue of "trying harder" with more troops, money, the timing of elections, or better planning.

3) The failure of foreign intervention and reconstruction efforts is due to the fundamental inability of government to centrally plan the complex array of formal and informal institutions of a free and prosperous society.

Military occupation and reconstruction is an exercise in large-scale, comprehensive central planning. For the same reasons efforts to centrally plan the economy under socialism failed, so too do efforts to centrally plan the complex array of institutions underpinning a free society. Given the abysmal failures of government attempts to centrally plan economies, why should we expect foreign interventions which utilize the same means to be any different?

3.2 Unilateral Free Trade

In the conclusion to *After War*, I proposed a shift in U.S. foreign policy toward a default strategy of non-intervention, coupled with unilateral free trade with all countries. This strategy calls for a withdrawal from current engagements and an immediate unilateral reduction of trade barriers to U.S. markets, granting full access to all countries around the world. The logic behind withdrawal is grounded in the constraints discussed above. The logic underpinning unilateral free trade is that in addition to the economic benefits from trade, free trade also generates cultural benefits through the exchange of ideas, beliefs, and alternative ways of life. What better way to expose people throughout the world to the values of freedom, liberty and tolerance than to practice them ourselves? In other words, I make the argument that this strategy is a more appropriate means to achieve the desired ends as defined by the interveners.

Of course my proposed strategy does not guarantee that societies around the world will adopt western-style institutions. But neither does military intervention, as indicated by the historical record showing more failures than successes.

With the collapse of socialism, there is widespread consensus regarding the futility of economic central planning. This same logic has not been extended to foreign interventions that attempt to centrally plan economic, legal, social and political institutions. Like socialism, these more recent efforts at central planning are likely to fail to achieve the desired end.

3.3 Is Military Intervention Necessary to Spread Markets?

Some who agree with me regarding the importance of trade have pointed out that military intervention abroad is necessary to establish freedom and markets, so that citizens in these countries can engage in trade with the U.S. and other developed countries. I reject this line of argumentation for two reasons. First, the institutions that underpin a free society cannot be planned. This is the equivalent of saying that we must plan and implement markets where they do not exist, precisely because markets allow us to take advantage of dispersed knowledge of time and place. There is no blueprint that instructs people, step by step, how to implement a free society. This must be discovered through a process of experimentation that is often messy and chaotic from the view of those outside the process. Second, the idea of engaging in war in the name of peace runs the risk of "perpetual war for perpetual peace." There will always be some societies that are relatively unfree, meaning there will always be a justification for war in the name of spreading freedom and peace. Militarization, occupation, and imposition under any name are the very antithesis of liberalism.

3.4 Protectionism

Calls for free trade of any kind, unilateral or otherwise, are typically met with calls for some form of protectionism. Protectionism refers to the restriction of trade through government imposed barriers. Examples of protectionist measures would include tariffs—a tax applied to imports and exports—and quotas—limits on the quantity of a good that can be imported. There are several typical justifications for protectionist measures, which I summarize below, followed by a brief response.

The key point to remember in each case is that voluntary trade makes both parties better off, at the time of trade, no matter what their geographic location. We know this because of demonstrated preference—if one of the parties did not expect the trade to make them better off they would simply refrain from interaction and exchange. When one realizes the gains from trade approach, they quickly realize that protectionist measures, by reducing voluntary trade, make people worse off.

One justification for protectionist measures is that a 'free' country can use protectionist measures to force other countries to reduce their trade barriers. This is a form of "benevolent protectionism," whereby a 'free' country imposes protectionist measures until the 'unfree' country reduces or removes its trade barriers. If effective, this policy would ultimately benefit both countries. This justification is peculiar for several reasons. First, the 'free' country harms its citizens by making itself 'unfree,' in order to benefit another country whose government is choosing to harm its citizens. Second, this justification assumes that the trade barriers will eventually be removed. However, the logic of special interest groups indicates that once in place, trade barriers are hard to remove precisely because they benefit vested interests who benefit from their persistence.

A second justification for protectionist measures is that domestic markets need to be protected against 'dumping' and other 'predatory' practices. Dumping typically refers to selling items below the cost of production. The logic goes that foreign firms can take unfair advantage of high domestic production costs by selling their items below cost in the domestic market. For example, Chinese firms can 'dump' their products in U.S. markets by selling below cost, which is viewed as unfair to U.S. firms. The response to the dumping charge is straightforward.

Consider what happens after a major holiday. The price of holiday-specific merchandise is drastically cut due to a fall in demand. Simply put, the demand for Christmas trees falls on December 26. Producers may indeed charge a price that is below the cost of production, but if this is dumping many sales and dollar bins would be unfair. The key point is that prices are not determined by costs, but instead by consumer's subjective valuation of the good in question. A related response to the fear of dumping is the realization that consumers prefer lower prices, all else being constant.

When consumers shop they rarely look to pay more for a given good or services. This implies that even if dumping is occurring it doesn't harm consumers. Of course producers who cannot lower their prices to compete do not like competitors who charge a lower price. But this is a result of those producers being relatively inefficient and not because of the competitors engaging in predatory behaviors.

A third justification for protectionist measures is that they are needed to 'protect' the local economy. But we must ask a fundamental question: why do we want to protect the local economy? Most of us feel fortunate that we do not have to sew our own clothes, grow our own food, build our own housing, etc. Instead, we rely on markets and exchange because this allows us to take advantage of comparative advantage and specialization.

As the extent of the market increases, so too does the range of trading partners. Note that trade openness does preclude one from 'buying local.' You can still grow your own food or buy from a local farm. Protectionist measures, in contrast, force people to 'buy local' by restricting the extent of the market. In other words protectionism imposes the preferences of the 'buy local' supporters on *all* consumers who no longer have a choice.

A related argument, associated with protectionist measures to protect local markets, is that cheap labor undermines more expensive labor in wealthy countries. This, however, misconstrues wages. Wages are based on productivity implying that higher wages in the U.S., relative to other countries, are due to the fact that U.S. workers are more productive. For example, if U.S. wages are three times the wages in Taiwan, this implies that U.S. workers are, on average, three times as productive.

Per dollar spent, the productivity is the same in both places because employers are getting three times as much output in the U.S., relative to Taiwan. This is important because, as Rothbard (1986) notes, "the problem faced by American employers is not really with the 'cheap labor' in Taiwan, because 'expensive labor' in the U.S. is precisely the result of the bidding for scarce labor by U.S. employers. The problem faced by less efficient U.S. textile or auto firms is not so much cheap labor in Taiwan or Japan, but the fact that other U.S. industries are efficient enough to afford it, because they bid wages that high in the first place."

A final justification for protectionist measures is cultural protectionism. The underlying idea is that increased trade erodes local cultures leading to cultural homogeneity. Simply put, there is a fear of a McDonald's on every corner. It is argued that protectionist measures can insulate local cultures from this homogenizing process. One response is that culture is not a static concept. Indeed, culture is constantly emerging and evolving as traditions, beliefs, and conventions change. Further, while trade can indeed have a homogenizing effect on some margins, it can also increase heterogeneity as people specialize in certain niche areas due to increases in the extent of the market (see Cowen, 2002).

Finally, those who are supposedly protected from trade are the ones who incur most of the costs of protectionist measures. It is these people whose range of choices is constrained in the name of cultural protection. Perhaps they want to eat at McDonald's but are prevented from doing so by some outside party who requires them to refrain from certain desirable activities in the name of cultural protectionism. One of the benefits of markets is that they allow for choice. All that is required to stop the spread of specific goods and services is the decision not to patronize the producer of the good or service. Protectionism removes this choice and forces consumers to abide by the preferences of policymakers.

4. Concluding Remarks

With the collapse of socialism, there is widespread consensus regarding the futility of economic central planning. This same logic has not been extended to foreign interventions that attempt to centrally plan economic, legal, social, and political institutions. Like socialism, these more recent efforts at central planning are likely to fail to achieve the desired end.

There have been several responses to my work on foreign military intervention that I find peculiar. My focus on positive analysis—*i.e.*, taking ends as given—has come under attack on two fronts. First, some have accused me of agreeing with the ends of military intervention since I take those ends as the starting point of my analysis. Second, I have been accused of being naïve because I assume that policymakers actually want to achieve the ends that they say they want to achieve. To put it bluntly, policymakers lie, and while they say they want to spread liberal institutions, in reality they have ulterior motives.

I have always been confused by both lines of argument. As economists we try, to the best of our ability, to be value free. Part of this is not judging the ends that people seek to achieve. Instead, we focus on the means to achieve given ends. A perfect example of this is the 'socialist calculation debate.' In that debate Ludwig von Mises and F.A. Hayek did not attack the ends of the stated ends of the socialists—advanced material production. Instead, they focused on the means, arguing that socialism was an ineffective means for achieving this end.

Further, Mises and Hayek assumed benevolence on the part of planners. In doing so, they were not being naïve, but instead establishing the best-case scenario for socialism. They then showed that even under the best case socialism would fail to be an effective means to achieve the desired ends of advanced material production. In taking policymakers at their word regarding foreign intervention, I have attempted to begin from the best case scenario. If military intervention fails under the best case scenario, then we have even more reason to be skeptical as we deviate further and further from that ideal. One benefit of this approach is that it shifts the debate from ideological grounds—e.g., Republican vs. Democrat, etc.—to actual analysis of the problem situation.

Another response to my work is that in a complex world—domestically and internationally—my call for skepticism regarding foreign intervention and my call for free trade is unrealistic and simplistic. Again, this strikes me as an odd line of reasoning. It is precisely because the world is complex that I am so skeptical of the ability of outsiders to centrally plan the extended order of institutions in foreign societies. Which is more simplistic: calls for humility in intervening abroad coupled with recognition of the benefits of trade, or calls for policymakers and the military to attempt to design entire societies according to a grandiose blueprint? In this regard, I have taken my cue from Hayek, who noted that, "The curious task of economics is to demonstrate to men how little they really know about what they imagine they can design" (1988: 76).

In the immediate future, I plan to continue to focus my efforts on the positive aspects of foreign military intervention. I am currently working on a book manuscript entitled *The Ability to Protect: The Limits of Humanitarian Intervention*. State-led humanitarian interventions have become increasingly militarized, as evidenced by the '3D approach' which has come to dominate U.S. foreign policy. This holistic approach attempts to synchronize U.S. defense, development, and diplomacy efforts.

I am applying the tools of economics to international efforts aimed at improving the human condition, because these efforts suffer from many of the same problems noted above. Critiquing humanitarian interventions is often considered off limits, even by those who are staunch opponents of other interventions, such as foreign aid aimed at development. In my view, precisely because so much is at stake in these interventions, it is even more important to engage in critical analysis in order to understand exactly what can, and cannot, be achieved in practice. It is not enough to say that we *must* 'do something' without critically considering what we *can* do.

References

Cowen, Tyler and Christopher J. Coyne. 2005. "Postwar Reconstruction: Some Insights from Public Choice and Institutional Economics," *Constitutional Political Economy* 16: 31-48.

Cowen, Tyler. 2002. *Creative Destruction: How Globalization is Changing the World's Cultures*. New Jersey: Princeton University Press.

Coyne, Christopher J. 2008. *After War: The Political Economy of Exporting Democracy*. California: Stanford University Press.

Hayek, F.A. 1988. *The Fatal Conceit: The Errors of Socialism*. Chicago: The University of Chicago Press.

Rothbard, Murray N. 1986. *Protectionism and the Destruction of Prosperity*. Auburn, AL: Mises Institute.

Shin, Doh Chull. 1994. "On the Third Wave of Democratization: A Synthesis and Evaluation of Recent Theory and Research." *World Politics* 47: 135-170.

Stiglitz, Joseph and Linda Bilmes 2008. *The Three Trillion Dollar War: The True Cost of the Iraq Conflict*, New York: W.W. Norton.

Fights for Peace

Yuri Pérez

Yuri Pérez Vázquez was born in Camaguey, Cuba. His uncle Amado Perez was a political prisoner in Cuba (Causa 32/1971 "Contra los Poderes del Estado") and his father Eliseo Perez has been a political oppositional activist since 1999. Yuri began Law Studies in the University of Camaguey (UC) in September, 2002 and was a student leader of a small-scale strike. His political activism included movements for academic freedom. As a result, he was expelled from University of Ciego de Avila in May, 2006. Yuri worked with a coalition of Cuban youth for freedom, promoting democracy and human rights, until October, 2009, when he left Cuba as a political refugee.

Peace is usually understood as the absence of war. (*"The former, predominant position, which considers war as built into the architectonics of the system of states, defines peace as the absence of war."* (Polant, p. 317)). There are low-level, but intense conflicts where people live without peace. Eventually, these conflicts lead to unrest and even war, as we have witnessed in the Middle East. These conflicts are consequences of state oppression and injustice, conditions with which I grew up and then fought to overcome.

These conditions are especially present under authoritarian regimes, which may be imposed on religious, ideological or nationalistic grounds. Particularly horrible regimes are the ones built by communists. Communists systematically destroy freedoms and violate human rights. In order to do so, as a mean to keep control over all citizens, they establish a state of fear with confiscations, massive incarcerations, killings, and the use of watch organizations that spy on every aspect of individuals' lives.

In the case of the tyrannical, communist government of Cuba, Fidel Castro gained absolute control, including over the economy. He additionally looked for foreign enemies, to justify the system's failures and keep attentions directed overseas. Castro declared an endless war against so-called imperialism and its head, the United States of America. Based on the Bay of Pigs failed invasion, democracy efforts supported by the USA, and US government embargo, Castro has militarized Cuban society, including its children. From elementary school through every single institution, children, women, even the elderly are required (along with the men) to get military training and be prepared for a hypothetical (though impossible) American attack.

Furthermore, Castro's counter-peace efforts have gone from provoking the Caribbean Missile Crisis, when he asked the Soviet Union to install nuclear weapons in Cuba and use them against the United States of America, to the creation and promotion of global violent, revolutionary and terrorist movements that cost bloodshed in both Latin America and Africa. Hostility against the USA, and anti-American activism worldwide, has been the main pillar of Castro's foreign policy. The true war, however, is waged against Cuban citizens. The initial years of Castro's revolution were characterized by thousands of political

234

murders, prisoners and exiles. Systematic purges have been developed since, and against different targets, including the wealthy, farmers, churches, homosexuals, entrepreneurs, prostitutes, the unemployed, dissidents and so on. Such a militarized state has guaranteed Castro's power over half a century. Citizens live in a state of fear, even sometimes terror, and consequently are poorly organized in a very weak civil society, unable to dismiss the tyranny.

The police state is also enhanced by the totally outlawed society, where any non-government authorized activity is illegal. Due to the general impoverishment of Cuban people, as a consequence of more than five decades of communism, every small economic activity is strongly taxed or otherwise persecuted by the government. Thus, every citizen must violate the current legal order, just to to survive. As incredible as it may seem to those living in freer societies, Cuban consumers have only one place to buy milk, beef, or a car, and that is on the black market network.

Most economic activities are developed underground on the Island. Therefore, the secret police's oppressive surveillance machine decides whether or not individuals are allowed to satisfy their needs and those of their families. That way, everybody is afraid of being caught while trading goods and services. In addition, if the secret police believe a citizen is not a Castro follower, then the common police might arrest him or her during a survival exercise. Therefore, the entire society has been criminalized by its tyrannical government. The lack of peace is evident in every aspect of life, too. The mass media is under the absolute monopoly of government and serves as its mouthpiece. The inflammatory language against concord is a daily topic of television, radio and newspapers. The propagandist organization portrays Castro's followers as friends, and those who dislike him as enemies that must be destroyed.

I was born and raised in such a mad environment, living in the lack of peace until coming to the United States of America, when I was granted a political-refugee visa. I had had to participate, since I was a child, in all kinds of warfare activities, as ordered and directed by the government. I still remember how, while in elementary school, all children were supposed to worship Che Guevara, the murderer of many Cubans, every single day.

There, according to Guevara's teachings, I was taught to hate different ideas, looks and behaviors. The Cuban educational system is essentially a tool of indoctrination, designed for the creation of the "New Man," one who is far apart from Western civilization's values, who is intolerant, and who is ready to kill in order to impose the revolutionary ideology.

The construction of the so-called socialist or communist society is a process of anthropological destruction. The individuals face a process intended to destroy previous societal values and replace them with a new revolutionary code. This code is based on absolute loyalty to the revolution, which mandates to discharge individual interests for pursuing the collective goals of the revolution. Therefore, human nature is violated by the new order that sets society and its personification, Fidel Castro, at the highest rank, in disregard of individuals, family and every other value.

At some point, while facing all the human misery generated by communism,

I started to analyze my society. Then those feelings of regret, hate, and victimization took body in articulated thinking. Particularly helpful was the information I was able to get through the Catholic Church and some independent libraries, since books from classical thinkers are both rare and censored. Once at the university, the discussion of controversial issues became stronger, and I had the opportunity to argue in a relatively leveled debate with more open minded-people.

Information exchange, writing, and church-sponsored debates, among other activities, went on there for a while, until the secret police took radical actions. Some students were expelled from university, while the Catholic priests were sent out of Cuba. I was harassed by the Communist Party officials, and decided to move to another province, in hopes of continuing my studies. However, I was expelled from the university because of my pursuit of freedom of speech and academic freedom. A student strike I had organized to fight against unjust administrative decisions, and my refusal to participate in a secret police pogrom against a dissident also played a role in their decision.

Indeed, the pogroms, which have long been a preferred repressive technique used by the Castro tyranny against Cuban people, deserve special remarks. They consist of crowds of low-life people, organized by the secret police, yelling at, harassing and even lynching their victims. The victims are usually members of whatever social group is being targeted at the time. It is one of their most nasty and horrific tools, and has been used periodically throughout the years. Moreover, the pogroms express the nature of Castro's followers and his regime, conformed by people of the worst human condition, able to do the most awful things, as was noted by Hayek while analyzing "why the worst (persons) get on top" in a totalitarian regime (Hayek, 157-170).

After those events I was even more devoted to work against the Castro regime as a political activist, and I have not stopped. To be a freedom fighter against communism is not only a search for liberty, but also a search for justice, the true basis for peace.

There is no peace when a family is destroyed. There is no peace when brothers and sisters are supposed to spy and fight each other in the name of class struggles. There cannot be peace under oppression, when human rights are violated and human dignity is disrespected. Nevertheless, there is hope. Castro's nomenclature is very old and the biological factor will help in obtaining Cuba's freedom. Meanwhile, I have not been alone in my journey toward peace; there is a growing civil society that is pushing for individual rights, liberty and a free market economy.

References:

Coste, Brutus, "Freedom, the Key to Peace," American Journal of Economics & Sociology 25.3(1966): 227-228. Biomedical Reference Collection: Comprehensive. EBSCO. Web. 24, Apr. 2011.

Hayek, F.A, The Road to Serfdom, Definite Edition II, p. 283. Chicago: University of Chicago Press, 2007. Print.

War and Peace
as States of Mind

Butler Shaffer

*Butler Shaffer received his JD degree from The University of Chicago Law
School and teaches at the Southwestern University School of Law. He is the
author of* In Restraint of Trade: The Business Campaign Against Competition,
1918-1938; Calculated Chaos: Institutional Threats to Peace and Human
Survival; *and* Boundaries of Order: Private Property As a Social System.

My own childhood experiences are instructive in understanding the means
by which human energies are so easily mobilized on behalf of the war system. I
was ten years old when World War II ended, and my earlier years were
dominated by wartime events. I lived in a Midwestern city in which a major
bomber base was located, and I was accustomed to seeing formations of B-17s
flying over my home. An uncle (of whom I had been quite fond) was a bomber
pilot whose plane had been shot down by so-called "friendly-fire" during a
training exercise two years earlier. I still vividly recall the pain I felt over his
death.

Through it all, I was constantly—and consistently—told by teachers,
newspapers, radio programs, motion pictures, my parents and other relatives,
that the war was "necessary" and "justified." Countries such as Germany, Japan,
and Italy were (by some process of which I was then unfamiliar) my hated
"enemies," while the Soviet Union and China were my "friends." These same
authorities upon whom I had been relying for my understanding of this war
informed me that America was on the "good" side, while my enemies were on
the "bad" side. I was further told how fortunate I was to live in America, rather
than in the European countries that were being devastated by the war; and that
"God favored America" and would see to it that "we" won the war. No one in
my young life told me anything to the contrary; nor did I have any reason to
doubt that "patriotism" was among the highest of virtues. Accordingly, I eagerly
participated in scrap-paper and scrap-metal drives, and sat on the roof outside
my bedroom scanning the skies for the German bombers that my youthful
innocence told me were on their way.

And America did win the war; and I saw photos of European and Japanese
cities that had been thoroughly destroyed in the process. Newsreels showed me
pictures of thousands of dead and physically emaciated European casualties of
the war, whose fates were readily distinguishable from my own. Why *wouldn't* I
be inclined to believe in the superiority of my "side" in the war, and the
inferiority of the other side? Still, despite the sharp differences I had been
propagandized to see in this conflict, I was able to play with children from two
separate families on my block, whose parents had emigrated from Germany. If
the German people were "evil," as I had been told, why were these families so
decent? That I was able to enjoy their company, without feeling a sense of hatred

I had been trained to have for their nationality, may have planted some doubts in my unconscious mind.

No sooner was World War II over than I discovered something rather remarkable: that war had been replaced by something called a "Cold War" which, interestingly, reversed the "good" guy and "bad" guy roles of the prior combatants. Germany, Italy, and Japan had magically been recast as my "friends," while China and the Soviet Union were just as inexplicably presented as my new "enemies." I recall being puzzled not only by the transformation itself, but by the thoroughness with which it all took place within a matter of two to three years. Upon later reflection, I wonder if the nature of the change might have provided a catalyst for my thinking—and, perhaps, the thinking of others—about the war system?

A fundamental shift seems to have taken place among many Americans in the half-decade between the close of World War II and the Korean War. There was an heroic sense with which young men and women went off to war, following what was then generally regarded as a "sneak attack" upon Pearl Harbor. While subsequent historic research has shown the deceitful and politically-motivated role the Roosevelt administration played in bringing about this attack,[1] such an awareness was not generally present in December, 1941. While there was nothing "heroic" about the government's decision to declare war on Japan (and, in the process, Germany), the men and women who enlisted in the war effort were, I believe, motivated by heroic sentiments. There was an attitude—shared by most Americans—that when *this* war was over, *peace* would prevail in the world.

But the speed with which the Korean War was conjured up by the political system began to raise doubts about the purposes served by the war system. The notion that "America" was under attack from some ill-defined "enemy" forces halfway around the world, triggered the kind of skepticism that ought always attend the exercise of political power. By the early 1950s, Harry Truman had become a very unpopular president because of his promotion of this war, and Democrats and Republicans alike turned to General Eisenhower—who had helped end the war in Europe—as the prospective presidential candidate in 1952.

From the Korean War, to the Vietnam War, to a myriad of other American military exercises, and down to the Iraqi and Afghan wars (that have lasted longer than World War II), the widespread gullibility of Americans, to see wars presented as means to noble ends, has greatly dissipated. While the political and media voices that have always cheered the state's war system will characterize American troops as "heroes," it has become difficult for increasing numbers of men and women to see them as anything other than innocent youths being exploited in the furtherance of corporate-state political purposes. At a time when more American troops die from *suicide* than from *battlefield combat,* we require deeper explanations for war than the simplistic ones offered to children.

Contrary to our politically directed thinking, *peace* is not just the absence of *war,* a condition to be turned on or off as suits the needs of nation-states in manipulating their respective populations. When promoters and conductors of the war system are Nobel Peace Prize-recipients, it becomes evident that the popular meaning of the concept has become little more than a confused and contradictory strategy to be employed in fleeting service to the interests of coercive power structures.

The ease with which we learn to accept such paradoxical thinking can be attributed to the conditioning to which our minds were subjected in our youth. Every institutionally-centered society has inculcated its children in the belief that its organizational arrangements are the only sensible means of social behavior. In the words of Ivan Illich, "[s]chool is the advertising agency which makes you believe that you need the society as it is."[2] "Once young people have allowed their imaginations to be formed by curricular instruction," Illich adds, "they are conditioned to institutional planning of every sort."[3] Institutions are organizations that have become ends in themselves. Their desired permanency is premised *not* upon adapting themselves to satisfy the demands of people, but in conforming people to serve their ends. The institutional order is at war with the changefulness of life itself; coercive power forces life to become what it does not choose to be. It seeks to preserve its rigid, ossified forms through whatever means it considers most effective, whether through propaganda or outright violence.

I dealt in depth with this institutionalization process in my book, *Calculated Chaos*.[4] In order to create and sustain support for the prevailing culture, people have been trained to seek "identities" for themselves in various abstractions. These may include such groupings as nationality, race, religion, ideology, geography, gender, economic interests, or other categories. Such identities are not necessarily confined to a single classification: "African-American," "White-Anglo-Saxon-Protestant," "Christian-socialist," "gay-Republican," are just a few examples of combined identities. However constituted, such practices amount to what has been called "ego-boundary"[5] or "ego-barrier"[6] identity-seeking. We learn to define ourselves less by intrinsic, personal characteristics, and more in terms of our association with abstract categories external to ourselves. In an existential sense, we literally *become* the abstraction. In the process, our lives become a playing out of the implications of what David Riesman distinguished as "*inner*-directed" or "*other*-directed" persons.[7]

Regardless of the specifics of a person's ego-identity, the practice is always premised upon separating one's sense of self from other collective groupings. Ego-boundaries *divide* us from one another, and make it easy for nation-states to generate their self-serving conflicts whose foundations we have already set within our minds. Without such divisive thinking, political systems could not exist. Governments of every nation thrive by promising one or more groups benefits that will be denied to others. Political parties mobilize the energies and expectations of discrete groups bent on using lawful coercion to advance private ends. The professional practitioners of *realpolitik* are then able to play their "musical-chairs" games, freely substituting one group for another as they reinforce the "us" versus "them" mindset that keeps political systems in power. The hated "them" may consist of "communists," "landlords," "labor unions," "terrorists," "illegal immigrants," or any other fungible group capable of being used to evoke a sufficient hostility.

The war system feeds on and nurtures such conflicts, a fact that led the late Randolph Bourne to declare that "[w]ar is the health of the state,"[8] because of its capacity for further concentrating and reinforcing political authority. War provides a respite from *domestic* inter-group contests for special privileges, by shifting attention to *foreign* enemies around which to solidify and increase the power of the state. How wars enhance state power was made evident following the 9/11 World Trade Center attacks. In reaction, the United States government invaded and bombed a nation that had nothing whatever to do with these attacks. The American state was further able to exponentially expand its police, surveillance, and other regulatory powers against its own citizens, thus confirming Bourne's observation.

The symbiotic relationship between the war system and the growth of state power is seen in such practices as military conscription, censorship, the regulation of prices, and the governmental control of resources, to name but a few. More recently, we have witnessed the hurried enactment of the USA PATRIOT Act; TSA groping and fondling of airline passengers; the increased employment of tasers against harmless persons; torture; people being held without trial, or even the right to legal counsel; and the ever-widening search for bogeyman "terrorists" in public transportation, amusement parks, parades, and sporting events, as well as at other major public celebrations overseen by police "snipers" with high-powered rifles.

To regard peace as but the absence of war is to miss the essential dynamics of political behavior in which history pulsates in periods of warfare and non-warfare; but without experiencing the deeper meaning of "peace" that would be fatal to all political systems. Many years ago, while perusing an etymological dictionary, I discovered that the words "peace," "freedom," "love," and "friend" shared some common origins.[9] Might our ancestors have understood something of the holistic nature of our social interconnectedness, an awareness unfamiliar to most of us who play out the destructive implications of our conditioned, divisive thinking? Relating this inquiry to the theme of the earlier book in this series, *Why Liberty*,[10] perhaps we need to explore the concepts of "freedom" and "liberty" (terms we tend to treat as synonyms) to see if we might locate the foundations for social systems that consistently integrate *peace* and *liberty.*

I regard "freedom" as a state of mind; an inner sense of wholeness that arises from living without conflict, contradictions, and moral confusion. To be *free* in this sense is to live what some have called the psychologically and philosophically "centered" life. Those who associate themselves with, and take direction from, collective identities, would seem to be lacking in such an integrated personality. The competing demands of different institutions, groups, and one's self-interested ends, militate against such wholeness. Thus do many political conservatives regard themselves as "pro-life" when considering the question of abortions while, at the same time, defending wars and capital punishment. Likewise, men and women of so-called "liberal" persuasions will defend a "pro-choice" position on the abortion issue, while denying to opponents of their other political programs the "choice" not to be taxed to support them. George Orwell introduced us to the institutionalized expressions of contrary thinking in such "Newspeak" propositions as "war is peace," "freedom is slavery," and "ignorance is strength." The Strategic Air Command's slogan "peace is our profession" demonstrates that such contradictory thinking is not confined to literary works. The image of the soldier "fighting for freedom" raises the question: of what is one *free* when he is *fighting*? How can one who is in such deadly conflict as war be said to be in a state of freedom while killing others? Do not the escalating suicides among soldiers reflect a confused and conflict-ridden personality?

If *freedom* is regarded as a state of mind, then *liberty* would represent the condition in which free men and women live together in society. Herein do we begin to see our ancestral understanding of the connection between "peace" and "freedom." There is one form of division among people which, if recognized, does not engender conflict: respect for the inviolability of property boundaries. (I have explored this topic more fully in my *Boundaries of Order*.[11])

Contrary to the *collective* identities by which the state manipulates us to fight its endless wars against endless enemies, the private-property principle is an expression of the means by which both personal *liberty* and social *peace* coexist, without any limitation upon either. With boundary lines defining the limits of our actions as well as the basis for our claims to immunity from coercion, we are able to see through the state's ersatz forms of shared interests that put us at war with one another, and to discover what we genuinely have in common: our mutual need to respect one another's inviolability. As the Marxist, Max Eastman, so well expressed the point:

> *It seems obvious to me now—though I was slow coming to the conclusion—that the institution of private property, the dispersion of power and importance that goes with it, has been a main factor in producing that limited amount of free-and-equalness which Marx hoped to render infinite by abolishing this institution.*[12]

Perhaps this socially-harmonious insight was shared by our predecessors who found commonality in the concepts "peace," "freedom," "love," and "friend." Perhaps they understood what our political conditioning has trained us to forget: namely, that such qualities can exist only when we do not separate ourselves from one another in conflict-ridden ways.

The interdependency between our divisive thinking and the destructiveness of the war system can be ended only by a fundamental transformation in how we see ourselves. Only in transcending the conditioning by which we have defined ourselves as members of abstract groups with conflicting interests, can we discover how to live peacefully with one another.

"*Why* peace?" is a fairly easy question to answer. Much more difficult is the inquiry into "*how* peace?"

---

[1]   See, e.g., Robert B. Stinnett, *Day of Deceit: The Truth About FDR and Pearl Harbor* (New York: The Free Press, 2000).

[2]   Ivan Illich, *Deschooling Society* (New York: Harper & Row, 1972), p. 163.

[3]   *Ibid*, p. 56.

[4]   Butler Shaffer, *Calculated Chaos: Institutional Threats to Peace and Human Survival* (San Francisco:

      Alchemy Books, 1985); republished (Coral Springs, FL : Llumina Press, 2004).

[5]   Frederick Perls, *Gestalt Therapy Verbatim* (New York: Bantam Press, 1971).

[6]   Ludwig von Bertalanffy, *Robots, Men and Minds* (New York: George Braziller, 1967).

[7]   David Riesman, with Nathan Glazer and Reuel Denney, *The Lonely Crowd* (New Haven: Yale University Press, 1950).

[8]   Randolph Bourne, *War and the Intellectuals* (New York: Harper & Row, 1964), p. 71.

[9]   Eric Partridge, *Origins: A Short Etymological Dictionary of Modern English* (New York: Greenwich House, 1983), p. 235.

[10] Marc Guttman, *Why Liberty: Personal Journeys Toward Peace and Freedom* (Apple Valley, CA: Cobden Press, 2010).

[11] Butler Shaffer, *Boundaries of Order: Private Property As a Social System* (Auburn, AL: Ludwig von Mises Institute, 2009).

[12] Max Eastman, *Reflections on the Failure of Socialism* (New York: The Universal Library), p. 107.

Peace Has
Yet to Come
to Northeast Asia

Noguchi Takayuki

Noguchi Takayuki works as an editor and writer. He is the author of Escaping with North Korean Defectors. *Takayuki was born in Saitama, Japan. He studied political science at Arkansas State University. Meanwhile, he spent 2 years traveling in Asia. After graduation, he moved to New York City and worked for Kawaski Rail Car, Inc. When he returned to Japan, Takayuki began working with Life Funds for North Korean Refugees. He spent eight months imprisoned in China for aiding North Korean defectors escape North Korea through China. Takayuki currently is a board member of Life Funds for North Korean Refugees. I miss our times in New York City and backpacking on trails in the Hudson River Valley.*

"The police are here."

The guide's voice trembled, her face pressed up against the peephole in the door. She turned toward us, all the blood drained from her face. I looked at her frozen face and felt my knees turn to water. We should have escaped detection in Nanning, a small Chinese city near the Vietnamese border. And, yet, out of nowhere there was this knocking at the door.

We ignored the knocking. They started pounding on the door. If we continued to ignore them and they were police, they would just open the door using the hotel master-key. I motioned to the guide to open the door.

"We are Chinese police!" As the door flew open, the room was filled with the sound of heavily-accented English, and plainclothes officers burst into the room.

This is how I was arrested by Chinese security officers in December, 2003. I was charged with one count of illegally transporting people with the intent of crossing the border, and an additional count of attempting to assist in illegally crossing the border. In court, I was sentenced to eight months in prison and fined 20,000 RMB (about US$3,050). All my personal goods, including 340,000 yen in cash (about US$4,100), a video camera, and a cellular phone were also confiscated.

At the time of my arrest, I was involved in a clandestine operation to help two North Korean refugees escape from China. I was working with a Japanese NGO called Life Funds for North Korean Refugees. The plan was to head from Dalian, Liaoning Province, in northeastern China, via Beijing and then south to Vietnam. Instead, I was arrested, along with the two North Koreans, in this hotel room in Nanning, about 200 km from the Vietnamese border.

One of the North Korean refugees was *K*, a 47-year-old woman, whose parents were sent to Japan after the end of the Korean War. Although she was born in Japan, when she was six years old she had moved to North Korea with her mother. The other North Korean refugee was a 60-year-old man, *P*, who had gone to North Korea at the age of 18 after finishing school in Japan. Both had left Japan in the early 1960s.

Why did they go to North Korea? Japan was still a poor country in the 1960s, only 20 years after losing the war. Ethnic Koreans, a minority in Japan, were even poorer than the Japanese. They also suffered from deep-rooted discrimination. Kim Il Sung had already established his dictatorship in North Korea and started a propaganda campaign, urging ethnic Koreans in Japan to return to the "Paradise on Earth" that was North Korea. But it was not only Korean residents in Japan who swallowed Kim's lies: in total, about 100,000 Korean residents and their Japanese spouses had boarded ferries bound for North Korea. The two North Korean refugees with me were among those who had gone to the North in this way.

But North Korea was anything but a paradise on earth. It goes without saying that people had no freedom, but the food situation was also worse than it was in Japan. And starting in the 1990s, the lack of food became a matter of life and death for many. According to some reports, more than 3 million North Koreans have starved to death since the start of the 1990s. Many North Koreans started fleeing into China in search of food, and the number of North Koreans fleeing to South Korea in search of freedom increased drastically. *K* and *P* had both decided that leaving North Korea was a matter of survival, and had turned to their relatives still in Japan for help. Their relatives had in turn contacted Life Funds for North Korean Refugees, and we had begun our rescue operation.

But what was supposed to be a rescue operation ended in arrest and failure. People often ask me why I decided to help North Korean refugees, at the risk of my own safety. This question is always a tough one for me to answer, and I have yet to find a satisfactory answer. But I have no doubt that my travels in Asia in my twenties have had a huge influence. It was through this that I began to realize that the world was full of injustice, and that by a mere accident of birth— by being born Japanese—I had had so many advantages that others hadn't. And I started to feel very uncomfortable with this. The North Korean problem made me ask myself what I could do. And the answer was to use my background to help others.

After my arrest, the two North Koreans with me were forcibly repatriated by the Chinese authorities. *K* was sentenced to six months in a hard-labor camp and *P* was tortured by North Korean security forces; during this time, I heard that *P* had died.

People around the world believe the Cold War ended decades ago. But in fact the Cold War only ended in Europe. If we consider northeast Asia, it is hard to avoid the reality that the Cold War has not ended. The Chinese continue to be ruled by the tyrannical Communist Party, and Kim Jong Il, the supreme leader of North Korea, maintains his rule of terror. Meanwhile, in nearby Russia, journalists criticizing the regime run the risk of dying under suspicious circumstances. Authoritarianism is alive and well in this part of the world. Here, even thinking about freedom is a deadly mistake. Humanitarian activists and groups have also become targets. My arrest and trial, at which I was given an eight-month sentence, was like a throwback to the Cold War.

People who escape to China from North Korea are protected by the 1951 Convention related to the status of Refugees and its 1967 Protocol. Despite being a signatory to the 1951 Convention and the 1967 Protocol, the Chinese government breaches both by refusing to recognize them as refugees, instead cracking down on them as illegal migrants and repatriating them.

Once North Koreans are repatriated to their own country, they are certain to face severe punishment, including the possibility of the death penalty, as stipulated by Article 47 of North Korean Criminal Law. (The North Korean Penal Code criminalizes defection. Article 47 of the Penal Code states that "one who escapes to another country or to the enemy betrays his motherland and people.") Still, many North Koreans attempt defection every year because of food shortages, oppression, and the collapse of their family.

The international community has repeatedly asked China not to repatriate the refugees and to protect them, but the Chinese government continues to ignore such requests.

At present, China is making its presence felt through its economic strength. The economies of numerous countries, including Japan, are dependent on trade with China, making it difficult for them to criticize the Chinese government. The Chinese government is well aware of this and has been throwing its weight around as a result. However, in the background are people like the refugees from North Korea who are suffering as a result of China's inhumane treatment.

Beginning with Tunisia this year, liberty movements have been springing up all over North Africa and the Middle East. There has been a certain amount of wishful thinking that such movements might spread to North Korea, but this seems unlikely. The internet and social networking sites played a large role in the North African and Middle Eastern democracy movements, but there is no such mechanism to allow grassroots communication in North Korea, since the North Korean government has criminalized the internet. There have been reports of sporadic protests, but these seem unlikely to spread throughout the country.

The Berlin Wall came down in 1989, bringing the Soviet Union with it and ending the Cold War in Europe. The fall of the Berlin Wall became the symbol of the democratization of Eastern Europe. It began with East Germans who sought to start a new life in West Germany, passing through Hungary and the former Czechoslovakia. But for North Koreans, there are no such neighboring countries—only China and Russia. Of course, the root of the problem is the Kim Jong Il regime, and we can hardly expect change to come from there. A change in the Chinese government's stance is needed in order to resolve the North Korean refugee problem.

But this is easier said than done. Those of us who help refugees are constantly anguishing over how to resolve the situation. But we should not let the difficulties sideline us. In 2008, China's per capita GDP hit the US$ 3,000 mark, and China hosted the Olympic Games. That per capita GDP is expected to reach US$5,000 in 2012. The Olympics had never before been hosted by an overtly despotic regime. Along with China's economic growth has come a growing middle class, clamoring for their individual rights. In other words, freedom and self-governance.

With this background, we are seeing something new happening in China: cooperation among human-rights activists, including lawyers and writers. Liu Xiabo, last year's Nobel Peace Prize laureate, was one of these. Most of them are fighting a lonely battle, being clamped down on by the Chinese government as they are. Currently, Liu Xiabo is being incarcerated in China as a political prisoner because of his human rights activism and calls for political reform. When the Nobel Committee announced that Xiabo had won the Nobel Peace Prize, the news was at first heavily censored in China. Later, China denounced the Prize being awarded to a "criminal." Celebrations in China were banned; prominent dissidents were detained, harassed and put under surveillance; and Liu's wife, Liu Xia, was placed under house arrest and not allowed to talk to reporters.

The Chinese look to foreign activists and organizations for support and work together to bring about change to make their own country an easier one in which to live. On principle, I oppose interfering with the internal affairs of other countries, but if the individuals in that country are asking for help, I want to do whatever I can to help defend them.

Making the biggest power in northeast Asia more humane would benefit the entire region. And if China were to change, North Korea would change too. I can only hope that changes will happen in China that will also bring freedom and peace to North Korea, and until then I will continue to do whatever I can.

How

Top Secret America

Misfires

Coleen Rowley

Coleen Rowley, a FBI special agent for almost 24 years, was legal counsel to the FBI Field Office in Minneapolis from 1990 to 2003. She wrote a "whistleblower" memo in May, 2002 and testified to the Senate Judiciary on some of the FBI's pre 9-11 failures. Coleen retired at the end of 2004 and now writes and speaks on ethical decision-making and balancing civil liberties with the need for effective investigation.

Governmental obfuscation and cover-up after 9-11, combined with reckless, wrongheaded, and outright illegal responses, served to launch the U.S. "war on terror"; this has motivated me to speak out, and keep speaking out. It's hard for me to fathom the Orwellian belief system that took hold and caused so much violence and destruction in the Mideast; two examples are getting 70 percent of US citizens to believe in early 2003 that Saddam was behind 9-11, and the more recent public belief that the US is bombing Libya as "humanitarian intervention." I attribute much of this insanity to mass-media propaganda, which has effectively manipulated public opinion by pushing people's emotional buttons: fear, hate, greed, false pride and blind loyalty.

I enjoyed a fairly normal career in the FBI, falling as it did for the most part in the lull between the Vietnam War and the post 9-11 wars. I became an FBI agent in January of 1980, just a couple years after the Church Committee concluded its work investigating the COINTELPRO abuses, culminating in the 1978 enactment of the "Foreign Intelligence Surveillance Act"—at the very same time that strict Attorney General Guidelines were promulgated, regulating FBI investigations (and infiltrations of domestic groups). The FISA law was a legal compromise that provided for judicial oversight, and thus put an end to Hoover's "black bag jobs." (However, these Church Committee restrictions upon executive power were greatly resented by some Nixon/Ford-era political officials like Dick Cheney, who eventually made it their mission to undo these restrictions, under the guise of national security and the need they argued for an all-powerful war presidency.) I later helped process files pursuant to Freedom of Information Act (FOIA) releases that documented the abuses of Hoover's FBI during the Cold War and Vietnam Wars.

Criminal justice for me has always been a calling. I have always viewed it as a subset of wider justice, fairness and human ethics. I was transferred to Minneapolis in 1990, after working on various crime programs, including Italian organized crime in New York City. I became the Minneapolis Division's legal counsel, responsible for legal training of agents in that division, which later also encompassed ethics training.

I could not believe the cover-up that ensued after 9-11 about the various mistakes and governmental failures to "connect the dots." And when I got a chance, in connection with the Joint Intelligence Committee's Inquiry (JICI), I wrote and delivered a memo to the FBI Director, the FBI's internal affairs and Senators on the JICI about what I knew involving Minnesota agents being thwarted in their investigation of suspected terrorist Zacarias Moussaoui. I was only hoping the memo would be read and provide better insights, so that the mistakes would not be repeated.

Long story short, that was not to be. Although the memo got some attention when it got leaked to the press, and also resulted in my being asked to testify to the Senate Judiciary Committee in early June 2002 (the same day as the FBI Director and the same day Bush made his "emergency announcement" creating the Department of Homeland Security), it was already too late. My memo led to a two-year-long, comprehensive Inspector General report that ferreted out much (but not all) of the truth behind the FBI's failures, and whose findings figured into the official 9-11 Commission Report. However, by the time those reports came out (summer of 2004), the Bush Administration had long before launched its misguided response, bearing no connection to the pre 9-11 mistakes. The wars on Afghanistan and Iraq; massive "total information awareness" type data collections; the use of "dark side" illegal kidnappings, torture and black sites; warrantless monitoring of Americans; and the creation of the huge "Top Secret America" security-surveillance complex.... All were well underway by the time these official findings were made public.

Having become known as an FBI "whistleblower," I didn't see any option but to try speaking out a second time, in March 2003, warning that the launching of the US invasion of Iraq was unjustified and would prove counter-productive. I began to see history repeating as the FBI and other agencies went along with the "green light" turned on by the Bush Administration, leading to a series of unethical, illegal and counterproductive actions in their "global war on terror." So, I have continued to speak out and, since retirement, organize and engage in anti-war and anti-torture protests.

It doesn't take a Jeremiah to predict that we now stand to reap what we have sown. Whereas almost all religious and philosophical systems are rooted in fundamental notions of karma, yin-yang balancing, divine justice or what the CIA simply terms "blowback," our politicians have really opened the proverbial Pandora's Box, unleashing something they can't control in using these base forms of manipulating people. Large majorities of Americans are now duped to believe in fictional utilitarian propositions, where wrongful and illegal means yield good ends (*e.g.,* that torture saves lives). In fact, just as liberty and security cannot be disconnected, neither can ethics and pragmatism.

There are three insightful books I've read that explain how and why no good can come of the current U.S. reliance on military force and war in seeking its desired "Pax Americana": *War Is A Racket* by General Smedley Butler; *War Is A Force That Gives Us Meaning* by Chris Hedges; and *War Is A Lie* by David Swanson. While most experts believe our country's foreign wars are designed to be permanent, as both hot wars and long-term military occupations, the massive national surveillance and security apparatus in the U.S. has also now turned inward on its own citizens. So, just as Cassandra was doomed to continue her unsuccessful warnings, I don't know what else to do but continue to speak out.

Why has Congress not yet awakened to the fact that since 9-11 we have been sailing into a perfect storm? Here are just some of the turbulent winds blowing and pushing officials in the wrong direction:

- Politicians who stoke the fear of terrorism, while forcing underling officials to promise they can protect the public by "pre-empting" all threats, hyped and un-hyped;

- The erosion of prior legal safeguards, even the firmly entrenched ethical and legal (jus cogens) principles prohibiting torture;

- The broad legal authority given to the Executive by Congress in such laws as the USA PATRIOT Act and Military Commissions Act, as well as the abuse of "presidential war powers" through warrantless monitoring and authorization of offshore, indefinite detention;

- Perverse, counterproductive job and profit incentives for the 854,000 agents, analysts, operatives and private contractors/consultants who staff the "Top Secret America" surveillance-security complex;

- The lack of any effective, independent oversight (despite the 9-11 Commission's prescient and serious concerns, enumerated years ago), as exemplified by the hobbled Privacy and Civil Liberties Oversight Board; and

- The basic need for war presidencies to maintain momentum in the face of popular disapproval of the ongoing conflicts and occupations in the Mideast.

Such systemic forces will always produce a similar bad result—for our rights and our safety.

Even the rather conservative *Washington Post* is quite worried about what's likely to come of this clearly out-of-control pressure cooker called "Top Secret America." If it cannot be quickly reined in, we are almost certain to witness and suffer a revisiting of the worst of Cold War McCarthyism and Vietnam COINTELPRO abuses. That prediction is based on what has happened before, whenever militarist forces turned inward on U.S. citizens. Even if government officials are well-intentioned, these forces increase the chances for error and opportunism. (Some would say we've entered a perfect storm already, given the numerous examples of improper targeting of domestic advocacy groups, most recently the FBI raids on various anti-war activists' offices and homes in Minneapolis and Chicago.)

Let's not forget how the "war on terror" was originally sold to the American public: as "Let's fight them *over there* so we don't have to fight them here." But Homeland Security now admits that the "war on terror" is increasingly being fought at home.

FBI agents are motivated, for instance, to check off "statistical achievements," by sending well-paid, manipulative confidential informants into mosques (and apparently also into various advocacy and anti-war groups). In the Iowa heartland, for instance, FBI surveillance, trash searches, terrorism database paperwork, and "statistical accomplishments" regarding a few student protesters in Iowa City before the 2008 Republican National Convention fill hundreds of file pages, without providing any plausible justification for the operation.

Leaving aside the issue of those the U.S. captured abroad and brought to Guantanamo (half of whom are now believed to have been innocent and 172 of whom still remain locked up indefinitely, without any factual adjudication process commensurate with American notions of due process), the examples of innocents originally inside the United States who have been unjustly detained, brutalized, tortured and who otherwise had their civil rights interfered with are too myriad to list comprehensively. But they range from that first post 9-11 "round-up" of immigrants, who just happened to be in the wrong place (mostly in NYC) at the wrong time, and who were locked up on a "no-bond" policy for several months. (Many ended up also being brutalized by jailers motivated by the FBI's and Department of Justice's daily press releases implying that the mounting number of arrests—with the last press release claiming over 1000 were in custody—corresponded to progress in the "war on terrorism.") Ultimately, though it took almost two years for the Inspector General's critical findings to issue, none of these 762 people with immigration issues were charged with acts of terrorism.

Although the Center on Law and Security at New York University School of Law documents some improvement in terrorism prosecutions after those early incidents in post 9-11 years, other groups like "Project Salam" note that the government's theory of "pre-emptive prosecution" relies on paid informants, who target mostly Muslims. Profiling based on race, religion or ethnicity was prohibited by the Bush Administration's Department of Justice for all criminal matters except national security (where it flourishes). The combined use of profiling and government informants can easily incite and entrap people to do things they would not otherwise do.

Finally come reports, including those by the highly credible Department of Justice's own watchdog Inspector General, who recently confirmed that from 2001 through at least 2006, the FBI spied on the First Amendment-protected activity of nonviolent anti-war, environmental and animal rights groups. "In so doing, the FBI exceeded its investigative authority, intruding on the privacy, free expression and right to assemble of innocent Americans."

Several anti-war activists in Chicago and Minneapolis (including a 71-year-old great grandmother who is a friend of mine) were infiltrated for 2-½ years by undercover police, and were raided and subpoenaed in the fall of 2010 under the USA PATRIOT Act's expanded definition of "material aid to terrorism," which now includes "expert advice and assistance".

These abuses attack our basic constitutional right to dissent, without making us safer. Relatively simple ways to address and reduce each of these counterproductive forces do exist, however—ways that preserve our liberties while actually enhancing our collective security. The list below outlines the most serious current civil liberties problems and the potential fixes. It is based on my years of teaching constitutional criminal procedure to FBI agents and police officers, and also on my firsthand exposure to and understanding of some of the pre- and post-9-11 failures:

1) In the course of arguing the Holder v Humanitarian Law Project case in the Supreme Court (decided in late June of 2011), Georgetown Law Professor David Cole warned explicitly that this law could be used to improperly target and prosecute a wide range of humanitarian, human rights and peace advocacy groups, and prevent them from exercising freedom of speech and other First Amendment rights. However, Cole failed in his arguments to overturn a few words in the USA PATRIOT Act that broadened "Material Support of Terrorism" to encompass "expert advice and assistance" to designated "foreign terrorist organizations." (For more information, see "How Easy Is It for Peaceful People to Violate the Patriot Act?" by Joshua Holland, July 2010.) This problematic Supreme Court decision, which essentially makes advocacy of peace and humanitarian issues illegal with respect to 40-some groups designated by the State Department, is surely something that Congress never intended in hastily passing the hundreds of pages of USA PATRIOT Act provisions in October, 2001. As a result, missionaries, fair election proponents and humanitarian workers could be placed in legal jeopardy. People like Three Cups of Tea author Greg Mortenson, who had to meet with a variety of foreign nationals in war zones in order to forge a consensus to build schools for girls in Pakistan and Afghanistan, could be in trouble, as could former president Jimmy Carter, who engages in pro-democracy efforts to monitor election fraud in many places in the world. The paradox is that true non-government-affiliated efforts aimed at furthering education, humanitarian assistance, free elections and non-violent conflict resolution in other parts of the world are widely recognized as more effective and beneficial than U.S. military or U.S. State Department-controlled efforts.

The **simple fix** would be to revise the phrase "expert advice and assistance" in the USA PATRIOT Act, clarifying that Congress never intended to define "material aid or comfort" to designated organizations so that it would chill or hamper the free speech rights of members of non-governmental humanitarian, peace and pro-democracy groups.

2) "Pre-emptive" security—with its false promise of preventing all future acts of terrorism, and its accompanying pressures—should be understood as a real Mission Impossible (not to say Mission Stupid). It led to the immediate erosion of the post-Church Committee Attorney General (AG) Guidelines that required varying levels of factual justification before targeting any domestic group. Shortly after 9-11, AG Ashcroft began by loosening the old guidelines and

allowing FBI agents to go into churches, mosques and other public places. The final nail in the coffin was the decision by the Bush Administration, in one of its last official acts, to reverse the need to demonstrate some level of factual justification and promulgate a new and very low legal standard for all types of cases. This new standard means, in effect, that the FBI has only to deny that a group has been targeted based *solely* on its exercise of First Amendment rights. Civil libertarians were initially aghast at the prospect of this total erasure of any real investigative guidelines. But knowing of Obama's background as a constitutional lawyer, they thought it better to bring the issue to Bush's successor. It should be noted that the demise of the old AG Guidelines came after the Inspector General (IG) discovered that the FBI had served hundreds of thousands of mistake-ridden and unjustified National Security Letters, and also found many compliance problems in the FBI's opening of cases and handling of informants.

Simple fix: It's fine to create one set of guidelines for all crime programs. However, some reasonable level of factual justification should be required before the FBI or other federal law enforcement agency can target a group or individual. The Department of Justice (DOJ) IG should immediately undertake a review of all "terrorism enterprise investigations" begun by the FBI after 2006, when the IG's prior investigation ended.

3) The blurring of protest activities and dissent with terrorism dovetailed with the launching of U.S. wars after 9-11. For example, in October 2003, the FBI put out "Intelligence Bulletin 89," which focused on protesters' plans for the Free Trade Area of the Americas meetings in Miami and anti-war marches in Washington, D.C. I personally made an IG complaint to the DOJ IG about this blurring, but it was punted back to the FBI and then swept under the rug. *New York Times* reporter Eric Lichtblau exposed the problematic Bulletin; the DOJ retaliated by yanking Lichtblau's press pass, and the FBI ordered its 56 field divisions to cease contact with the reporter. (The sorry episode is described, beginning on page 122 of Lichtblau's book, *Bush's Law: The Remaking of American Justice.*) Perhaps if that overly defensive posture had not been taken, problems would not have reached the proportions later found in the September 2010 report, "A Review of the FBI's Investigations of Certain Domestic Advocacy Groups." The wrongheaded mindset that dominated law enforcement almost immediately after the launching of the Iraq War (and the larger "war on terror") is most clearly seen in what a spokesman for the California Anti-Terrorism Information Center (CATIC) said, when forced in 2003 to defend his agency's unjustified targeting of anti-war protesters without any factual evidence. CATIC Spokesman Van Winkle, apparently without thinking too hard, reasoned that evidence wasn't needed to issue warnings on war protesters: "You can make an easy kind of a link that, if you have a protest group protesting a war where the cause that's being fought against is international terrorism, you might have terrorism at that [protest]. You can almost argue that a protest against [the 'war on terror'] is a terrorist act." (In a similar vein, the Department of Defense (DOD) for years administered an annual mandatory anti-terrorism test that

equated protest with terrorism. The test asked, "What is an example of low-level terrorism activity?" The correct answer was "protest.") Similarly, listen to the compelling testimony of anti-drilling activist Virginia Cody, after she discovered she had been spied on by the Pennsylvania Department of Homeland Security, by authorities who actively worked with industry officials to quash dissent. Also noteworthy is the fact that Joint Terrorism Task Forces (JTTFs) and Fusion Centers combine local and state police jurisdiction with federal jurisdiction. So crowd control, something not usually within federal jurisdiction, becomes a "joint" activity. The CIA has members on these joint task forces and fusion centers, even though the CIA charter bars the organization from operating domestically.

The fix would be to stop equating protest, including acts of civil disobedience, with terrorism. The USA PATRIOT Act's definition of domestic terrorism begins with these words: "Acts dangerous to human life...." Protest and dissent—and even acts of civil disobedience involving trespass and minor property damage— do not constitute acts of terrorism. Issues of crowd control, even during large marches and rallies, do not normally threaten national security and should not involve federal authorities.

4) Front-loaded "statistical achievements" are the main way of evaluating job performance inside the FBI and probably the other 3,000 or so agencies and contractors thought to be operating in "Top Secret America." The 854,000 operatives, agents, analysts, private contractors and consultants (believed to average about $90,000 per year in salary) are under more than a little pressure to prove they are earning their generous paychecks and in competition with each other to move up the ranks. So an elaborate grading system is used that checks the initial projection of work in a quantitative, not qualitative way. An FBI agent, for instance, collects 'stats' for opening files, disseminating information, adding individuals to a terrorist database or a watch list, serving subpoenas and national security letters for records, recruiting and contacting secret sources and informants, executing searches/seizures, making arrests, and getting people charged and/or convicted. Given the change of emphasis from prosecution to intelligence data collection and analysis, more and more 'stats' do not involve any judicial oversight. The danger exists that the pressure on producing 'stats' would encourage FBI agents and personnel of the other 3,000 entities to open fruitless investigations and try to fit garden-variety crimes into the terrorism category. Pressures to "pre-empt," plus lack of oversight in managing "top-echelon informants," lead to repeated examples of opportunistic targeting and entrapment of people not predisposed to commit crimes. Cases that don't pan out or were never justified to begin with, like the "terrorism enterprise investigation" of the students in Iowa City referred to earlier, can fulfill this unending need for 'stats.' Ultimately, if no quality-over-quantity mechanism is found to evaluate work performance, agencies are likely to return to the Cold War-era "post and float" system of "papering files." McCarthyism and COINTELPRO-type abuses are bound to recur, this time with "terrorist" substituted for the old bogey of "communist."

Quick fix: Revise the method of collecting and proving "statistical accomplishments" to favor quality over quantity. At a minimum, ensure that "statistical achievements" are subtracted when actions are found to have unjustifiably targeted advocacy groups or interfered with a person's constitutional rights without proper cause.

5) Because the 9-11 Commission was very concerned about the much greater authority being given to the FBI and other agencies in the "war on terror," three of their 41 recommendations concerned the creation of a Privacy and Civil Liberties Oversight Board (PCLOB). The FBI Director assured the ACLU that civil liberties would be upheld. The PCLOB was statutorily forced on Bush by Congress, but he assured its powerlessness and later dismantled it. Obama has thus far totally ignored the issue by not appointing anyone to the PCLOB.

Fix the situation by immediately appointing five PCLOB commissioners and empower them to interact with and provide mandated training to all national security agencies, contractors and consultants. In addition, allow PCLOB to directly hear and evaluate whistleblower complaints relating to abuses, and to access reports from Civil Liberties/Privacy Officers in each agency, as is done by the Office of Government Ethics.

Intelligence failures as well as abuses are the predictable outcome of massive and irrelevant data collections, which only add hay to the haystack and make it even harder to spot patterns. Abuses and failures result from excessive over-classification (see "WikiLeaks and 9-11: What If?") and improper use of the "State Secrets" privilege, which keeps cases out of the courts and negates government whistleblower protection. The English historian Lord Acton, who observed that power corrupts, also noted that, "Everything secret degenerates, even the administration of justice; nothing is safe that does not show how it can bear discussion and publicity."

A great cartoon drawn by Ben Sargent, where two men are looking at the U.S. Security Intelligence Apparatus diagram, says it all. One man says, "Um...Who actually catches the terrorists?" and the other responds, "Alert T-shirt vendor, usually."

But this only begins to capture the irony of our current situation. While governmental targeting of domestic advocacy, peace and environmental groups are jaw-dropping revelations, the even worse news is that these same agencies have failed to stop real terrorist violence and attempted violence. No government agency connected the dots before Fort Hood shooter Nidal Malik Hasan killed 13 and wounded 30, flight passenger Umar Farouk Abdulmutallab tried to ignite his "underwear bomb" in the air over Detroit or Faisal Shahzad planted his car bomb in Times Square. Yet all of these terrorist events involved individuals in direct communication with the very same Yemeni cleric who was also connected to three of the 9-11 hijackers.

The news gets even worse. We now know that the CIA ignored prior warnings regarding a suicide bomber (one they were hoping to use as a double-agent) who attacked a CIA outpost in eastern Afghanistan, and that the scout who planned the terrorist attacks in Mumbai in 2008 was a former DEA informant who U.S. officials had sent to train in Pakistan—despite the fact that the FBI had been warned years before that the DEA informant worked for Al Qaeda.

Why would joint terrorism task forces go after American students and peace and labor activists, while failing to detect and stop genuine acts of terrorism? This combination of misplaced zeal, incompetence and opportunism has consequences for our freedom and our safety. It is time for Top Secret America to ask itself whether its own flawed and contradictory assumptions and strategies are furnishing "material aid to terrorism."

Editing assistance from Hugh Iglarsh, writer/editor/citizen based in Chicago. A shorter version of this piece originally appeared as an op-ed in the Minneapolis Star Tribune *on January 16, 2011 "Coleen Rowley: We're conflating proper dissent and terrorism."*

Faces of a Drug War

Zack Mellette

Zack Mellette is cofounder of Give Us Names, a 501(c)3 nonprofit organization seeking to improve the lives of displaced Colombians through advocacy and the responsible implementation of strategic development initiatives.

She slaps the haunches of the last mule in the train and allows herself only the briefest glimpse back at her farm and the life she used to share with her husband and four children. Her fifth, only weeks from birth, may never know life in the Colombian countryside. The feel of lush grass under a bare foot, the sweet taste of fresh fruit plucked from the tree, splashing in the gurgling creek to rinse the sweat from an unforgiving afternoon sun... These are some of the simple pleasures that have been enjoyed by traditional Colombian farmers, or campesinos, *for many generations. And this is what Olga and her family are leaving behind. The last of their belongings have been strapped to mules and are now bouncing along the worn, dusty trail leading to the city and their new life.*

According to some international human rights groups, Colombia now has the highest number of internally displaced persons in the world. The country of 45 million also receives the most U.S. military aid outside of the Middle East, and is a strong ally, friend, and trading partner of the United States government. That is why the rapidly growing number of displaced (it is almost 1 in 8 people) is so alarming. How can a country that is receiving so much help from the United States be struggling through such a staggering human rights catastrophe? Why, if we are winning the war on drugs, are more and more Colombians losing their homes, livelihoods, and families?

Colombia has endured a history of violence and its people have lived through generations of conflict and turmoil. Dating back to a period referred to as *La Violencia* in the 1940s, and the resulting Marxist/Communist revolution that would thrust the country into one of the world's longest running civil wars, Colombia has suffered immensely. This strife has held the resource- rich and stunningly beautiful country back from progressing beyond a nation entrenched in political turmoil and economic fragility. Present-day Colombia now faces daily battles among government military, revolutionary militias, and right wing paramilitary groups.

The coca plant is a leafy green shrub that grows natively in Colombia and throughout the surrounding Andean region. For centuries it has been used for medicinal, ceremonial, and a wide array of other purposes, including as an appetite suppressant. It is also the base ingredient for a highly potent chemical concoction that produces a drug popular around the world called cocaine. As demand for cocaine skyrocketed in the U.S. during the 1970s, Colombia quickly became the largest producer and exporter of the drug in the world, and an extremely profitable illegal market exploded.

As U.S. and European demand for cocaine fueled the underground Colombian coca industry, highly lucrative cocaine trafficking funded armed groups, perpetuated violence, and led to an increase in organized crime. This relationship between drug users in the richest nations and drug producers in developing countries has paved the way for many of the current geopolitical dilemmas in Colombia.

In the year 2000, U.S. President Bill Clinton and his Colombian counterpart Andres Pastrana enacted a monumental aid agreement commonly referred to as "Plan Colombia." This package outlined money given to Colombia by the U.S. taxpayers and stipulated how the money was to be spent. The stated intentions of this aid were to decrease the amount of cocaine on the streets of the U.S. and to fortify the Colombian military against the FARC (The Revolutionary Armed Forces of Colombia, the largest guerrilla rebel group) and other armed groups who were funded mainly by narco-trafficking, extortion, and kidnapping.

One of the main mechanisms supported by Plan Colombia, aiming to reduce the cocaine supply, was an extensive aerial fumigation program. In this program, specially armored crop-dusting planes flown by U.S. pilots targeted areas where coca was actively being cultivated and conducted aerial fumigations. These planes would spray a highly potent herbicide from the air, attempting to kill living coca plants and stop the crops from transforming into the later by-product, cocaine. In its simplest theory, if we could kill coca at the source, cocaine production would be dramatically reduced, and less of the harmful drug would make it onto the streets of the United States.

After 10 years of actions sponsored by Plan Colombia, and over $7 billion of U.S. taxpayer money spent, the success of aerial fumigations and the agreement as a whole are still hotly debated. Many in the pro-Plan Colombia camp cite a reduction in coca cultivation in overall hectares as a clear-cut victory in the war on drugs. Opposition voices argue, however, that mere reduction in hectares cultivated is a misleading statistic. Much evidence suggests that aerial fumigations have only pushed coca growing deeper into forested areas, and have caused smaller yet higher-yielding farms to pop up. Reliable statistics for how much coca is actually being harvested and turned into cocaine are hard to find, and vary considerably due to the illegality of the market and lack of any reporting or receipts by buyers and sellers of the illicit products. This has led in many cases to biased reporting and statistical manipulation by those on both sides of the argument to support their respective positions.

What is known, however, is that there is not nearly enough evidence to suggest that cocaine supply reduction tactics such as the aerial fumigation program have successfully curbed the amount of available cocaine in the U.S. market. Since Colombia is the number one exporter of cocaine to the U.S., if supply was drastically reduced, you would expect to see a sharp increase in the street price for cocaine, assuming all other factors remained constant. No drug policy experts or researchers have noted such a phenomenon as a result of this program.

At the end of 2009, I took a trip to Colombia with a few friends, to hear the testimonies of those who have suffered the fate of displacement and to listen to others who are actively trying to fix a broken system. Our six-week trip led us all over the country: from single-room stick-and-trash-bag houses; to universities; NGO offices; and into the capitol. We wanted to learn about the situation from those who are living it.

Our questions were simple: *What is your story? How has displacement affected you and those you know? What can we do about it?* Over and over, from people of varying backgrounds, standings, and beliefs, we were asked to share their stories. "Tell people in your country what you have seen and heard here," they begged. Out of this experience grew an organization called Give Us Names. Our goal is to tell their stories in such a way that those who hear them will not rest until displacement ends, justice is brought to the perpetrators, and the rights of the displaced are recognized and protected.

While I was in Colombia conducting research for the documentary on the relationship between current US drug policy and the displacement that we are producing, I witnessed firsthand many detrimental effects of the aerial fumigation program. Often, in the process of spraying suspected coca fields, winds and inaccuracy causes the chemical used to drift onto undesired areas.

The highly potent herbicide (essentially, "super Roundup") adheres to and destroys whatever it lands on, without discrimination. Though it is designed to kill coca plants, many times native flora and licit agricultural crops are the unwarranted recipients of the deadly concoction. In addition to serious environmental damage related to the practice of spraying an airborne herbicide over one of the most sensitive ecosystems in the world, aerial herbicide spraying can pose health risks to both humans and animals. While in Colombia, we spoke with many farmers who reported skin rashes and lesions as a result of contact with the herbicide. Most shocking of all is the fact that the fumigations have proven to be a direct cause of displacement.

Case in point:

> *Olga and Abelardo had a small farm with chickens, geese, turkeys, yucca, plantains, assorted fruit trees, and cacao (chocolate). They could manage to feed themselves and their children mainly by their various crops, and financed the rest of their needs through the sale of cacao at the local market. The* **criminalized** *coca crop was nowhere on their property. One day, from far out on the horizon, they heard the unmistakable sound of aircraft engines overhead. On its way was a formation of aerial fumigation aircraft coming through to* **spray nearby** *coca fields. Abelardo and Olga's farm lay in the flight path* **of one of** *the aircraft's* **targets** *and was hit by the deadly liquid; this killed their livelihood and left a brown, scarred trail where fertile soil had once yielded the nourishing green plants so critical to their survival. A second round of fumigations a couple of months later finished them off. There was no way to* **produce and sustain** *life from their land any longer, and their* **only choice was to pack** *up and move on.* **Displaced.**

Sadly, the story we witnessed is not a lone tale from an isolated family in Colombia. They are but one of many families who have suffered at the hands of a carelessly executed, government-sponsored program buried deep within our destructive and secretive war on drugs. As you lift the folds around the aerial fumigation program in Colombia, you begin to see just how damaging it is to the *campesino*. He is already living on a paper-thin margin, enduring the same trials as so many subsistence farmers throughout history. Just one lost harvest can put him under, and keep him from providing the needed food to keep his family alive. To a pilot navigating a stressful mission or trying to finish up a long day of work, a poor spraying job is an accident. To the *campesino*, it is his life.

I hugged Olga tightly as she fought back tears before following the mule train carrying pots and pans, blankets, her children's toys, and all their clothes away from her farm. No comforting words came to me as I helplessly watched a family's life being packed up and carried off. Witnessing their displacement was one of the most gut-wrenching sights of my life. Knowing that I helped to pay for it is why I will keep fighting.

A History of Force

James L. Payne

Political scientist James L. Payne has been researching and writing on government for fifty years, writing his first book as an undergraduate at Oberlin College. He received his Ph.D. from the University of California at Berkeley and has written 15 books on many aspects of politics, including foreign policy, Latin American politics, militarism, the history of force, welfare, social science methodology, voluntarism and volunteer groups, taxation, and the U.S. Congress. His articles have appeared in Reader's Digest, *the* Wall Street Journal, Fortune, *and many other publications. For eighteen years, he taught political science at academic institutions, including Yale, Wesleyan, Johns Hopkins, and Texas A&M University. In 1985, he resigned his tenured professorship and moved to Sandpoint, Idaho, where he works as an independent scholar and freelance writer. His latest book,* Six Political Illusions, *distills his half-century of experience into a short, readable primer on government, a volume that explains why people keep seeking more government even when they know it fails to deliver on its promises.*

Introduction

Deploring is one thing; analyzing is another. On the subject of war and other uses of force we tend to expend our energy on indignation. We criticize, we point out how destructive, inefficient, or immoral these practices are. Unfortunately, this normative emphasis tends to shortchange the analytical aspect. In particular, we do not pay much attention to *trends* in the use of force over time. When it comes to the use of force, we are like a primitive people that fears tigers, but do not know how many there are, nor where, or whether, they sleep—or, to bring the analogy closer to the point, whether the number of tigers is diminishing over time.

In *A History of Force,*[1] I undertook to examine the trend in the use of force, and concluded that it was declining. In the excerpts that follow, I explore the underlying explanation for the worldwide decline in the use of force, and suggest how we can put ourselves in harmony with this trend in our own actions and activism.

What History Is Up To

This exploration of historical trends and practices reveals that a broad decline in the use of force has been taking place in the world. Before we examine the specifics of this decline, it would be useful to discuss it in general terms and develop an explanation for it. What accounts for the trend against the use of force?

The best way to answer this question is to trace out the implications of the definition of *force*. In popular speech, we use the word *force* to cover any situation where an action seems strongly motivated. At the bridge table, a player may say, "When George led the queen, I was forced to cover with the king." The meaning given to *force* here is much more restrictive: *deliberate physical action against the person or possessions of another.* Thus, *force* here always refers to physical force. It refers to concrete, physical actions such as cutting, piercing, restraining, and taking, as carried out by physical implements such as hands, clubs, swords, bullets, and bombs. In general, my use of the term *force* refers to those acts that would be called crimes of violence if carried out by a private party, such as murder, robbery, arson, kidnapping, and rape. I use *violence* as a synonym for *force.*

Although there is a distinction between using force and threatening to use it, in most contexts the distinction is an unimportant one. Both can be called a use of force. A robber who physically extracts your wallet from your pocket while holding you down on the ground has used force, but so has a robber who has obtained your wallet by threatening to push a knife into your stomach if you don't give it to him.

It is important to distinguish force—physical force—from the many other ways in which human beings try to control each other's behavior. When George led the queen at the card table, he did not pull a gun on his opponent and say, "Play the king or I will kill you." Therefore, he did not "force" him to play the king in the sense of the term employed here. The opponent played the king motivated by a desire to play successfully within the rules of the card game, not by fear of physical harm.

There are many situations in life where circumstances strongly compel a certain action but do not involve the use of force. We might hear, for example, that an employer "forces" waitresses to wear a particular uniform. Does this usage conform to our definition? Almost certainly not. The employer who requires uniforms is threatening to discharge—that is, not pay—the employee who fails to conform to his wishes. Refusing to buy something from someone is not an act of physical aggression. (Every shopper does it to thousands of merchants every day.) The use of the term *force* would be correct only if the employer drew a gun and threatened the waitresses with bodily injury if they decline to wear the uniform.

What if a waitress could get no other job and might therefore starve if she were discharged? The threat of being fired would certainly strongly compel her to wear the uniform, but she still would not be forced. The definition of *force* does not hinge on the possible consequences of an action. It pertains to the nature of the action itself—namely, deliberate physical injury or threat of injury to the person or his possessions. A woman might drive her lover to take his life by refusing to marry him. People might be tempted to say in this case that "she killed him," but her action is not a use of force, not a crime of violence. All she did was say "no." A person who refuses to give bread to a starving man is not using force, even though his refusal might result in the man's death.

Human beings can harm each other in many ways that do not involve the use of force. Sometimes, in an effort to emphasize their points, writers transplant the language of physical force to these other spheres. They speak of "cultural violence" or "verbal violence" or "economic force" or "psychological force." In each case, the writer may well be pointing to some kind of wrong, some kind of harmful control, but it is not force in the sense of direct physical injury or restraint.

Government Does It, Too

Another aspect of the definition of *force* that needs to be clarified concerns the status of the actors. In our conception, it makes no difference *who* uses physical means against another, whether it be an individual, a group such as a gang or lynch mob, or the agents of a socially approved unit such as a government. It is still force. This may seem an obvious issue, but in practice the confusion between private and governmental uses of force gives rise to many distracting arguments.

The source of this confusion is the fact that all societies have both socially approved uses of force and disapproved uses. This distinction, although perhaps clear enough to the reader of this page, is difficult to maintain in mass communications. Cultures want things in black and white: something is either wrong or right. Because force in the form of violent crime by individuals obviously has to be wrong, modern societies are led to disapprove of force in general. We say killing is wrong, robbery is wrong, and kidnapping is wrong. But this generalized disapproval leaves no room for the socially approved uses of force, specifically the ways that governments kill people or rob them or kidnap them.

The common way to escape this dilemma is to attempt to redefine government's uses of force as not "really" force. We see this confusion clouding the modern interpretation of taxation, for example. Taxation is, simply, government's extracting funds by force or by threat of force. In other words, in physical terms, it is robbery. However, because taxation is a socially approved activity, we don't use the negative-sounding term *robbery* to refer to it. We have an entirely different term—*taxation*—and try to make ourselves believe that it is in no way related to that criminal act. Indeed, many people (especially those Internal Revenue Service officials who are embarrassed about their role) say that taxation does not involve force at all, that it is "voluntary."

This kind of confusion needs to be transcended if we are to have any clarity about historical developments in the use of force. We can debate whether a certain use of force is socially desirable, but this debate should not obscure the fact that it is still force. Governments can and do use force, just as much as private individuals. Indeed, down through the centuries, they have been the greatest users, so to eliminate their actions from the study of force would be to set aside most of the data.

What's Wrong with Force?

Making a distinction between force and the other ways human beings try to influence each other is important not just for semantic clarity. It is essential in order to understand what history has been up to for the past several thousand years. There is no trend, so far as I can discern, against the emotional control of some people by others, or the exercise of economic power or the wielding of cultural influence. The historical trend is against the use of force—physical force. Why has this type of action been singled out?

The broad answer, I believe, is that the use of physical force involves more harm more consistently than other methods of influence—social, economic, psychological, or intellectual. This difference stems from the fact that it is physical, that its user can depend on Isaac Newton's reliable laws about the behavior of mass and energy in causing pain. All other methods of trying to hurt human beings have an indirect and merely probabilistic effect.

Suppose an employer wishes to harm one of his employees. He is so angry with that employee that he wishes him dead. He therefore decides to use his economic power to its fullest extent: he discharges the employee, hoping that this will cause the fired worker to starve to death. This is bad behavior on the employer's part, without a doubt, but the action is not with certainty harmful. The discharged worker can get another job—possibly even a better one—or find income from some other source. Because of all the other alternatives, it is most unlikely that the worker will starve to death. Thus, economic power is limited in its capacity to do harm. Not so with force as defined here. By putting a bullet through the worker's body, the employer can kill him with certainty.

The same point applies to verbal power. Language can be used in many wounding ways, but its harm is both limited and uncertain. An insult, for example, may not wound at all. The hearer may laugh it off. There is no way to laugh off a knife in the ribs. What our fathers told us about schoolmates who taunted us was right: It is, indeed, sticks and stones that break our bones. Perhaps it's too strong to say that "words can never hurt me," but even when they do hurt, their injury is normally much less than that caused by violence. Ask yourself: Would your rather be insulted or shot?

One reason we are poorly equipped to recognize the line between force and other kinds of harm is that religion, which traditionally has been the main source of ethical standards, almost entirely ignores the harm of using force. It dwells, instead, on many lesser wrongs and sins. For example, in the Bible, in both Old and New Testament, one will find only a handful of references to the wrongs of killing, robbing, and raping. Misbehavior like adultery and thinking bad thoughts are mentioned much more frequently. What accounts for the slighting of the wrong of force by religious authorities? One answer is that in earlier times, religious leaders used force to impose their doctrinal views and to punish unbelievers. This made them reluctant to condemn force. After just burning heretics at the stake, a sermon on how wrong it is to kill would be out of place.

Another part of the explanation is that religion sets its sights on perfection. It lumps all the different wrongs together as instances of falling short, or committing sin, that is, transgressing against God or the divine order. Thus, religions do not rank or rate misdeeds according to their degree of injury. For example, the Buddhist preaches the doctrine of "do no harm." It would undermine the transcendental character of this principle to analyze and discuss degrees of harm—by saying, for example, that killing a mouse is four times as bad as killing a fly, or that killing a man is sixty-four times as bad as killing a mouse. Instead, all these acts of transgression against the living universe are viewed as equally wrong. Other religions take a similar absolute view of wrongdoing. They posit an infinite universe of sinful deeds—including sinful thoughts—and religious leaders have been loath to rank these wrongs according to their relative harm. As a result, the simple point that violence is a greater wrong than others is overlooked.

Another reason why religion downplays the evil of force is that the point is considered so obvious that it doesn't need to be dwelt upon. Most parents agree with this point. They spend far more time telling their children to say "please" and "thank you" than reminding them not to kill other children. Of course they consider killing to be a far greater wrong, but it seems obvious that the child already understands this.

For all these reasons, religions fail to emphasize that using force represents a level of wrong greater than other kinds of transgressions. Consider the story of the Good Samaritan. It dwells on the behavior of the Samaritan who gave aid to a traveler who had been beaten and robbed on the road to Damascus. It contrasts his helpful behavior with that of the priest and Levite who passed by the injured traveler without rendering aid. The moral of the story is "render aid to needy strangers." Notice how the real evildoers in the story are not even criticized. They are the robbers who used force, who caused the injury without which there would have been no need for any help. The first moral of the story ought to be "robbing and beating people is wrong," and the account should have severely condemned the vicious robbers. The priest and Levite didn't do as well as they should have done in the situation, but they come off rather well compared to the robbers.

Putting First Things First

If philosophers had sat down at the beginning of history, and decided which evil would be the most important one for the human race to overcome, they surely would have picked the use of physical force. It's not that there aren't other kinds of wrongs and injuries, sins both of commission and omission. But this one stands out as the most important problem to be solved.

It also stands out as being the most *preventable.* It is easy to see and apply the rule that would eliminate the use of force from human affairs: don't initiate physical action against another person or his property. It is much more difficult to arrive at a rule to control the other kinds of harm that humans may do to each other. How would we control verbal abuse, for example? It's not good enough to say, "Don't make insults." People can be offended by words in the form of literary reviews, well-intentioned advice, and the truth. Similarly, how do we prevent economic power from leading to injury? We can't just say, "Don't sell," or "Don't buy," or "Don't fire employees." People may cause some kind of injury with their economic decisions in an infinite variety of circumstances (which is why the effort to define economic crimes is always arbitrary and convoluted).

Or take affairs of the heart. Problems involving love, romance, and sexual relationships certainly cause much woe, but by what rule can they be regulated to prevent this harm? No one should ever fall in love? Boy must never be allowed to meet girl? This is not to say that nothing could ever be done in this field. Dear Abby and Dr. Laura represent a useful beginning. But we are far from even imagining how to arrange matters in this complex and subtle terrain so that no one ever gets hurt.

I think our philosophers at the beginning of history would have grasped this point. They would realize that it makes most sense, in the attempt to improve the lot of human beings, to tackle an obvious, easily preventable harm. Later, when we get really good at righting wrongs and have the genie of force more or less completely in the bottle, we can tackle more obscure and intractable sufferings. Our philosophers would reach the conclusion, then, that from the standpoint of overall human progress, the reduction in the use of force ought to be considered the first priority.

Our philosophers are imaginary, however. Real philosophers almost never think along these lines, nor do moralists, prophets, preachers, or politicians. Worldly thinkers and doers do not make the reduction in the use of force the focus of morality or policy because, as noted previously, like everyone else, they are highly ambivalent about it. Yes, they condemn certain uses of force in certain contexts, but in other contexts they want to use force to accomplish their ends and to uphold their ideals and values. And so this policy—striving to bring about a general reduction in the use of force—remains an orphan in the world of ideas, unendorsed by any significant group, movement, or party.[2]

How then has the human race made progress in reducing the role of force in its affairs? If no party or ruler has consciously pursued this objective, how has it been achieved? One is almost tempted to answer that "History" is the protagonist in this drama. This is not quite fair, of course. Human beings, through their actions and inactions, have brought about the shift. But they have not consciously or directly attempted to reduce the use of force. They simply have tried to make things more sensible or less painful or more efficient, and, time after time, such goals happened to coincide with a reduction of force.

Perhaps an analogy will help clarify this subtle process. Let us suppose that at some point human beings made all their furniture out of straw. Straw was abundant, and they lacked the imagination or ability to make furniture out of any other material. From an analytical, objective point of view, we can see that straw is a poor material for furniture because it has no strength. However, the human beings involved lack this perspective. They believe that furniture has to be made out of straw. That's the way it always has been, they say, and the way it always will be.

Yet in individual instances, the users discover problems with the straw furniture. They discard a straw table because it has collapsed, deciding that it is easier to eat sitting on the floor. Later, someone brings in a plank of wood, which serves as a slightly better table than the floor. Later they support this plank on some logs, which works even better. Eventually they have a wooden table. They refuse to generalize from this experience, however. They still have straw beds, straw chairs, straw bookcases, and so on, and will not listen to the suggestion that straw in general is a bad idea for furniture. Yet one by one, the other straw items of furniture prove dysfunctional and are discarded and replaced, so that in the end little straw furniture remains.

The movement away from coercive institutions has followed this pattern. The human race is unable to take an analytical, objective view of force, unable to apprehend the general principle that force is unhealthy and harmful. But on a case-by-case basis, force-based practices have been discarded because they were seen to be harmful or inappropriate.

As I have mentioned, this evolution has not taken place at an equal pace around the world. It began earlier in some parts of the world than others, and has proceeded faster in some places compared to others. The result is that societies differ considerably on this dimension. In some places, one finds a strongly force-oriented culture where force is widely used, officially and unofficially, to control behavior and punish transgressions, and inhabitants accept, and even approve of, many public and private uses of force. In another region, one might find a less force-oriented culture, where coercive practices found elsewhere have been abandoned, or are applied less frequently. In their attitudes and opinions, the inhabitants of this less force-oriented culture show a degree of hesitation or skepticism about many uses of force.

What accounts for these variations in the orientation toward force? Why do some communities come to reject a certain use of force before others? Why, for example, does a community abandon human sacrifice when it does? Or, why does one country stop arresting writers and printers long before another country? As we shall see as we explore such points, there are no simple answers. However, two broad explanatory variables do emerge: increasing wealth and increasing communication. When people grow richer, so that they are better fed, healthier, and more comfortable, they come to value their own lives, and the lives of others, more highly. I will expand on this theme later; for the moment, I simply note that economic advancement appears to be one broad condition that has fostered a decline in the use of force.

Communication is important in the reduction in the use of force because it enables objective third parties to draw conclusions about the harm of violent practices. The participants in a war, for example, are steeped in subjective hatreds, ambitions, and the desire for revenge. Therefore, to them, war seems a necessary, desirable institution. Far-off observers, untouched by these hatreds and ambitions, are more likely to see the folly and tragedy of the war and thus to begin to learn the lesson that war is unwise. Hence, the development of communication—written language, libraries, universities, printing, and organs of mass communication—plays a significant role in the decline in the use of force. It facilitates the creation of a reflective public opinion that can assess and evaluate the role of force.

These explanatory ideas will take us only so far, however. There is certainly not any one-to-one correspondence between prosperity and communication, on the one hand, and the decline in the use of force, on the other. Many ancient empires were relatively prosperous, yet were strongly force-oriented societies. Furthermore, the movement away from force is not a smooth and consistent one. A culture may go for many centuries with little change in its orientation, and then, in the space of a few decades, it may discard key violent practices. And there are cases of backsliding, when a coercive practice that has been seemingly rejected is momentarily readopted.

The routes whereby uses of force are abandoned are often quite unexpected, even mysterious—so mysterious that one is sometimes tempted to allude to a higher power at work. Time and again one encounters violent practices so rooted and so self-reinforcing that it seems almost magical that they were overcome. One is reduced to pointing to "History" to explain how this immensely beneficial policy—a reduction in the use of force—has been gradually imposed on a human race that has neither consciously sought it nor agreed with it.

Swimming in History's Tide: Lessons for Voluntarists

The study of history is generally thought to be a restful undertaking, one that removes the student from the troubles of the day and immerses him safely in the dead past. Armies march to and fro, but only in the mind's eye, not into our living rooms. A study of the history of force, however, does not afford this degree of detachment. The examination of the violent practices of the past reveals a trend, and a trend is a living, moving thing. It is a finger pointing at historians and their generation, challenging them to declare their loyalties and to announce their intentions.

On this subject, however, our loyalties are divided and our intentions confused. On the one hand, we know that for thousands of years, humankind has been struggling to emancipate itself from the curse of force. And we know that it has been succeeding, with coercive practices being gradually abandoned century by century. Our attitudes and values on the subject are also changing: we are becoming increasingly skeptical about force. Few people today would boldly proclaim, "Force is a sound and proper basis for human institutions." We know that the path of the future and of future achievement lies in moving away from the use of force.

But we also notice many ways that force is still widely used. Judging from some of our practices, we do indeed appear to believe that force is a sound and proper basis for human institutions. The modern welfare state with all its taxation and regulation utterly depends on it.

The upshot is that we are uncertain how to proceed. It is unrealistic, and in some instances counterproductive, to strive to eliminate all use of force. Those who adopt this stance will be viewed as irresponsible cranks. Yet it is also unrealistic to embrace the use of force as a fixed and necessary element of civilization. This stance ignores the real and powerful historical trend against force. The human race is indeed turning away from the use of force, and this movement has accelerated in modern times. Those who say that coercive practices such as war or taxation are an immutable part of the human condition are going to be as wrong as past observers who said the same thing about slavery, dueling, or religious persecution.

We need a middle position, then, one that accommodates force-based institutions in the current stage of social evolution, but also recognizes the historical trend away from them. I have taken to calling this position *voluntarism*. Voluntarism holds that all uses of force, even those that seem most necessary and unavoidable today, are slated for eventual displacement. Therefore, none should be clung to as inevitable or indispensable. Yet the elimination of force-based institutions is an achievement that lies largely over the horizon, beyond our ability to accomplish in our generation. To some degree, it is beyond our ability even to imagine how many of today's coercive practices will be displaced. It will be up to history, subtly altering attitudes and institutions, to take uses of force that today seem essential and turn them into practices that are considered unthinkable. Because this alteration has already happened in many, many instances, we can be rather confident that it will continue to happen.

Voluntarists, then, do not strive to make history or to change the course of history. Theirs is the more modest project of trying to place themselves on history's side, finding ways to support the evolution against force in the context of their time and place. This is by no means an easy assignment because history does not follow a simple linear path. Sometimes the attempt to eliminate a use of force produces a backlash that prolongs that use of force. One thinks, for example, of the 1960s attempt by the U.S. judicial establishment to eliminate capital punishment before the public was ready for the change. In contriving the demise of coercive practices, history has been amazingly subtle and indirect. As we contemplate joining with this evolution, then, we need to appreciate the complexity of the task.

The Limits of Nonviolence

The first issue that reformers need to face is the problem of violent aggressors. Down through the years, many idealists have preached the doctrine of nonviolence, but none of them have come up with a satisfactory answer to the problem of aggressors. A good example of this failing is seen in the case of Leo Tolstoy, the great Russian philosopher and novelist. Tolstoy analyzed the ills of the czarist regime and found, at bottom, that they stemmed from its reliance on physical coercion. In *The Kingdom of God Is Within You,* written in 1899, he condemned the many uses of force prevalent in his day, including wars of conquest, military conscription, taxation, the violent punishment of criminals, the flogging of peasants, the expropriation of lands, persecution to uphold the Russian Orthodox Church, and state censorship of reformist writings (including his own).

He eloquently argued that government's use of force impeded progress: "Violence, which men regard as an instrument for the support of Christian life, on the contrary, prevents the social system from reaching its full and perfect development." He believed that under the influence of a public opinion inspired by Christian teachings, "violence is diminishing and clearly tending to disappear." Tolstoy's solution for hastening the day of nonviolence was to implement the principle of Christian love and follow the commandment to "resist not evil by violence."[3]

Although appealing at first glance, the idea of rejecting all use of force proves to be untenable because it does not address the problem of violent aggressors. Even if the principle of nonviolence were widely accepted, there are bound to be some people disposed to employ force to accomplish their ends. If you refuse to use force to resist them, two bad consequences follow. First, the aggressors accomplish their ends, demonstrating that force is an effective tactic—and thereby making it more appealing. Second, they may well overrun and destroy *you,* the advocate of nonviolence. This is more than a theoretical possibility. A review of the history of war and conquest shows that societies less prone to use force than their neighbors often were overrun, and their more peaceful philosophies obliterated.

What is true among nations also applies to individuals. Advocates of strict nonviolence have never had a solution to the problem of violent crime. Tolstoy, in making the argument that government's use of force wasn't necessary, simply denied the existence of violent aggressors:

Who are these evil men from whose violence and attacks the government and the army saves us? If such men existed three or four centuries ago, when men prided themselves on their military skill and strength of arm, when a man proved his valor by killing his fellow-men, we find none such at the present time. Men of our time neither use nor carry weapons, and, believing in the precepts of humanity and pity for their neighbors, they are desirous for peace and a quiet life as we are ourselves. Hence this extraordinary class of marauders, against whom the State might defend us, no longer exists.[4]

Tolstoy was probably right in thinking that the proportion of violent individuals is gradually declining over time, but it is unrealistic to expect that violent aggressors would ever entirely disappear. The problem of individual violence will always be with us in some degree as long as human beings have free will and the ability to act physically against others.

Most people are fearful about violent aggressors. It seems obvious to them that force has to be used to deter and restrain them, and they will not listen to any philosophy that suggests that they are to submit to being killed in their beds until murderers tire of the sport. This is probably why Tolstoy's views on nonviolence—farsighted and sound in so many ways—have been ignored.

But if we say that the use of force against aggressors is acceptable and necessary, how far should this idea extend? The danger—and history has seen countless examples—is that in response to the threat of aggression, one becomes an aggressor. To meet the dangers of foreign attack, one builds up armaments that threaten opponents. Or a nation may start a preemptive war, attacking another country to upstage a possible attack on itself. The same problem arises domestically. To counter violent criminals, the police are given authority to use force energetically and end up behaving like criminals themselves. In an effort to check crime, draconian punishments are adopted, punishments that brutalize society and provoke retaliation. The policy of matching threat for threat and violence for violence can lead to a continuation, even an escalation, of violence. So it does not reduce the use of force in the world.

There is no simple solution to this difficult dilemma. However, one useful perspective in grappling with it is the *principle of moderated response:* aggression should be met with a response, but with less force than the original provocation. According to this principle, the proper treatment of an aggressor is neither to try to get even following the idea of "an eye for an eye," nor to turn the other cheek, ignoring the aggression altogether. Instead, the rule should be something like "half an eye for an eye." This approach may calm a possible action-reaction cycle and lead the way to a less violent world.

The principle of moderated response is no more than a general perspective. It does not decree any particular policy for responding to the aggressive use of force in specific cases. About the only thing one can say for certain is that, paradoxical as it seems, the goal of reducing the use of force cannot be achieved by applying the principle of never using force!

Who Is to Blame for Force?

When force is used to check violent aggressors, it may be called a *reactive* use of force. The aggressor is the one who initiates the use of force, and agents of society are only reacting to this initiative. This reactive force is not the only socially approved use of force, however. Societies also undertake the *assertive* use of force. That is, they initiate force against peaceful individuals in order to try to solve social or economic problems or as a way of punishing behavior that, though not violent, is considered undesirable.

For example, in bygone days, a person who disagreed with a tenet of the official religion was not being violent in his disbelief. He was not striking anyone or breaking into houses or blowing up buildings. He simply declined to make certain religious declarations—for example, that God consisted of a trinity of Father, Son, and Holy Ghost. But because this refusal to endorse the prevailing doctrine was offensive, government officials would initiate force against him to discourage other people from doing the same thing. Burning people at the stake for their religious beliefs is an example of the assertive use of force.

Today we have moved beyond persecution for religious beliefs, but the general practice of initiating force to address social problems still persists. In thousands of ways, governments initiate force against peaceful individuals to punish them for nonviolent actions that are considered wrong and even to punish them for inactions—that is, for failing to do what the government expected them to do. A person who fails to buckle his automobile safety belt, for example, is not in any sense an aggressor. But he may end up in jail for failing to do it. Taxation is another example of the assertive use of force: government agents initiate force or the threat of force to compel peaceful individuals to give up their money.

Most people endorse this idea of using force assertively in order to improve behavior and accomplish social goals. Many embrace it wholeheartedly, and many others, although not enthusiastic, are resigned to it as an inevitable feature of society. The voluntarist would not be content with the practice, however, and would seek to move society away from it.

One is at first tempted to assume that because government applies the assertive use of force, government is the cause of the problem. All the regulation and other intrusions, one might say, are the doing of arrogant kings and ambitious senators who, throughout history, have sought to impose their wishes on the rest of the world. To check the assertive use of force we just need to reign in government officials. A closer look reveals, however, that the pressure for regulation is much more broadly based.

We see the pattern in religious persecution. Governments did not invent the idea of using force against religious deviants. The practice generally started with ordinary people who were scandalized and frightened by the alien religion. They formed mobs that attacked and killed the deviants and destroyed their places of worship. From the persecution of the Pythagoreans in the sixth century B.C., to French persecution of Huguenots in the seventeenth century, to English persecution of Catholics in the eighteenth century: in each case, intolerant mobs initiated the violence. A government that attempted to practice religious tolerance would have placed itself in peril. To survive, government officials had to go along with popular demands and formalize the policy of persecution.

Another illustration of the same point is the regulation of markets. For thousands of years, governments around the world have attempted to set the prices and control supplies of basic foodstuffs, especially grain and bread. This regulation involves an assertive use of force. When a farmer brings a sack of grain to market and sells it for a certain price, he has not used force against anyone. He is engaging in a voluntary transaction with the buyer. If a government official fines him or puts him in jail because this price is different than the set price, it is the official who is initiating the use of force. The reformer would say, Why not ask government officials to avoid this practice?

But rulers did not take up regulation because they were bored and needed something to do. In most cases, government officials were responding to and attempting to deflect the violence that members of the public were prepared to employ. In earlier times, mass violence in connection with food supplies was common. Crop failures or disruptions in transportation created a shortage of grain. The shortage drove prices up and made it difficult for many people to afford food. Aggrieved consumers formed mobs that attacked stores and warehouses and seized grain. The violence put the government in a difficult situation. If it did nothing, mob action would probably escalate. The rioting might even touch off a destructive civil war—as bread riots did, in fact, spark the French Revolution. Seeing this danger, rulers stepped in to regulate the price of foodstuffs. They sometimes even seized and distributed the stockpiles held by farmers and merchants. In this way, the government defused the riots. In such a situation, it's no good telling rulers that "force is wrong," and it doesn't help to point out that these measures of regulation will aggravate the food shortage. If government fails to act when there are riots in the streets, the violence will escalate. A hands-off policy would be likely to lead to more bloodshed, a result that both rulers and philosophers of peace want to avoid.

The fact is, most people are prepared to use force (or willing to countenance its use) to implement their anger, their intolerance, or their selfishness. Government's force-based systems of subsidy and regulation are for the most part merely a reflection of this human reality. Take the case of tariffs, a policy condemned by so many economic theorists as inimical to prosperity. Policies developed to restrict imports did not begin with theory. They had their roots in the violence of the workers whose products were being displaced by imports. Through riots and attacks on ships and barges, workers imposed *de facto* import prohibitions. To calm the violent scene, government legislated various types of import restrictions. Often, the violence of workers was quite personal. In London in the early eighteenth century, rioting silk weavers roamed the streets attacking women who were wearing Indian calico dresses, stripping the garments off them. A government law limiting the importation of calicoes calmed the disturbances.

Today, all countries have some type of progressive taxation—that is, a system that purports to take from the rich in order to give to the poor. Some academic philosophers may praise these schemes, but the schemes did not begin in academia. They were compelled by street violence. For thousands of years, human societies have been wracked by costly, violent struggles, caused by the have-nots attempting to seize the wealth of the haves. The have-nots never have benefited in any permanent way from all this violence, but that fact has not prevented the upheavals. Therefore, rulers seeking domestic peace have been prompted to engage in some show of redistribution of wealth, as a way of heading off civil war. Even as late as the 1930s, most of the economically advanced countries saw violent mass movements that sought to overthrow the rich in the name of the poor. Policies of progressive taxation and redistribution, such as the New Deal in the United States, were undertaken in part to defuse this threatened explosion. These programs may have been foolish and counterproductive in economic terms, but who can say that, from the standpoint of promoting social peace, they were not needed?

The source of government's use of assertive force, then, lies in the disposition of ordinary people to use force to act out their grievances. They don't like the style of their neighbor's house, or they think it wrong that he pays low wages to his workers or sells a drug they disapprove of or declines to contribute to the local school, and they are willing to resort to violence to make him behave "better." Government's use of force is, in most cases, simply an orderly substitute for the use of force by gangs and mobs.

Attitudes do change, however. As my explorations have shown, people have become less willing to use force themselves and more upset about the prospect of its being used by others. A remarkable reduction has occurred in most kinds of collective, politically oriented violence in the developed world over the past century, which has made possible a decline in government involvement in a number of areas. For example, in most of the economically developed countries, food rioting is a thing of the past—which means that their governments can afford to be less involved in setting food prices. The threat of a violent revolution by the have-nots has also subsided, which, in turn, has made policies of income redistribution less imperative.

Humans haven't become angels, of course. Even in developed countries, workers and farmers on occasion resort to physical blockades to prevent the entrance of lower-priced foreign goods such as lumber (from Canada into the United States) or beef (from Britain into France). The complete abandonment of all tariffs and import restrictions would probably lead to an increase in this type of violence. Government programs are a substitute for citizen violence in many other areas as well. Today there are some "environmentalists" who resort to blockades and the destruction of property to express their anger against what they feel are threats to the natural world.

Drug regulation is another volatile area. If government entirely ceased hounding those who sell drugs such as heroin, it is probable that we would see vigilante mobs using violence of their own against drug dealers. Quite a number of parents feel that drug use will destroy or has destroyed the lives of their children, and they are prepared to attack those who appear to be responsible for an obvious social curse. Government's drug war, misguided as it may be, is a war that many citizens want fought—and would be willing to fight themselves if government declined to do it.

Knowledge and the Use of Force

One factor working to reduce the reliance on the assertive use of force is the growth of knowledge. The use of force always involves harmful side effects. Many times these side effects are so severe that they outweigh the good that was supposed to be accomplished by using force. A war that was supposed to end an international dispute simply leads to another war. An attempt to ban alcoholic beverages leads to a thriving bootleg industry. A program to seize farmland to give to poor peasants leads to mass starvation of those same peasants. Time and again humans have reached for force to solve a problem—only to learn, perhaps generations later, that they only made the problem worse.

In ancient times, when the human race had little ability to analyze social relationships or to recall the effects of past policies, the most absurd policies of taxation and regulation were repeatedly undertaken on nothing more than impulse. Rulers would see a problem and assume that a simple ban or regulation would solve it. One recalls, for example, the Roman emperor Diocletian's sweeping price-control edict that attempted to control inflation (caused by his own debasement of coinage). He killed many people trying to enforce it, but only succeeded in further wrecking the Roman economy. As knowledge about cause and effect in social and economic life has expanded, nations have become better able to avoid those uses of force that are harmful in the long run.

The changing perspective on government regulation of food prices illustrates this kind of development. In olden days, food rioters and government officials may have supposed that they were solving a problem through their use of force, but they were only adding to it. When mobs or the government seized food or forced vendors to sell it at low prices, they discouraged farmers and merchants outside the area from shipping food into the stricken region. Furthermore, the threat of seizures and price control deterred farmers and middlemen from increasing supplies in future years. They were reluctant to plant crops and invest in means of transportation and storage because they feared that the government might seize their supplies or force them to sell below cost. The conclusion is that when force is used, either by mobs or by government acting on behalf of mobs, it aggravates the problem of food shortages.

In ancient times, this problem wasn't recognized. Even if a few people noticed the connection, they didn't have the means of communication to share their insight with others and with future rulers. So mobs and kings would go on with their violent policies of seizure and regulation, wrecking the agricultural economy generation after generation. In modern times, the growth of scholarship and communication has made it possible to bring knowledge to bear on decisions about whether to use force. In England, for example, the development of economic theory by theorists such as Adam Smith in the late eighteenth century began to make rulers somewhat sensitive to the harm caused by attempting to regulate prices. Many came to understand that refraining from using force to regulate commerce was a constructive approach. This policy of laissez-faire was implemented—political conditions permitting—and accounted in no small degree for England's prosperity.

Another example of the role of analysis concerns the treatment of criminals. In olden days, the aim in the treatment of criminals was to cause suffering, to make the wrongdoer feel pain. This was the logic behind punishments of mutilation and painful, degrading incarceration. In more recent times, reformers and scholars began to examine the theory of punishment and to trace out its implications. They began to notice a connection that had been previously ignored: by inflicting physical suffering on a wrongdoer, they degraded and demoralized him, thus making him a burden to society and a menace to his neighbors after the punishment was completed. This analysis is gradually leading societies to reduce the use of physical force in the treatment of criminals.

In broad terms, then, knowledge promotes the evolution away from force. One way to join this historical movement, therefore, is to help develop the understanding of cause and effect in social life.

Voluntary Alternatives

I have said that there is a historical trend *against* force. But a movement away from something can also be described as a movement *toward* something else. One way that reformers can find creative opportunities for assisting history's design is by looking at the positive side of this evolutionary process.

Suppose a community needs a school. Currently, this kind of need is filled through the assertive use of force. A government entity imposes a tax, forcing inhabitants to pay for the school under the threat of being taken to jail or having their property seized. The money collected is then turned over to a bureaucracy to establish and operate a school. This is the prevailing system for funding schools almost everywhere today. It is accepted because even though it involves a use of force, people feel that force is being used for a "good" purpose—and also because many can see no other practical way to accomplish the task.

Voluntarists would like to move away from such coercion-based practices. But how should they proceed? If they think in terms of working *against* force, they will expend their energies in a campaign against the existing force-based school system. This is a negative stance that puts them in the unpopular position of working to destroy schools, dismiss teachers, and deprive children of education.

Tactics and perspectives change entirely if reformers start by focusing on the positive view of history's trend. If history is moving away from force, what is it, necessarily, turning toward? The answer is *voluntary alternatives,* methods of accomplishing social purposes that do not involve threatening friends and neighbors with harm to body or property.

One such alternative is commercial activity—that is, producing, buying, and selling on the basis of economic exchange. We may criticize entrepreneurs' motives, and we may decry the harmful side effects of trade and industry, but neither of these complaints alters the fact that market activities are voluntary: no one uses guns to get people to make things or sell things or buy things. That is the meaning behind the term *free market:* the exchanges are free of force and the threat of force. Sometimes we are so busy criticizing entrepreneurs that we overlook the fact that they do meet human needs. Commercial establishments— restaurants, dental clinics, hardware stores, computer makers—are, literally, community service agencies. They just happen to operate on the principle of economic exchange between suppliers and customers.

Returning to my school example, then, voluntarists do not need to expend their energies in a negative and unpopular campaign against existing force-based schools. They can take the positive route of creating a school that operates on a voluntary basis. They can set up their school as a business that meets its expenses through the fees that parents pay to send children there. Such private schools may be expected to attract growing numbers of students as the frustrations and inefficiencies of the coercion-based school system become increasingly apparent. Thus, the reformers will have promoted a turning-away from the use of force by providing a superior alternative.

Philanthropy

As time goes on, the reformers will probably find that this school, although a useful and constructive institution, does not meet all the educational needs of the community. For example, some poor families may not be able to afford to send their children there. When most people notice this kind of gap, their first impulse is to look to coercion to address the problem. Capitalism, they say, needs to be controlled and supplemented through the action of government. In the case of schools, they say, we have to force people to pay for them, so that poor children can attend.

It is true that systems based on economic exchange cannot address all aspects of all social problems. It does not follow, however, that force is the only way to fill the remaining gaps. Voluntary approaches can meet needs not served by commercial arrangements. One important alternative is philanthropy, the giving of wealth without the expectation of a material personal benefit in return. Generosity is a natural and surprisingly strong human motive, one that often impels people to devote their time and wealth to improving their community. Virtually all of the helpful community institutions we have today—universities, hospitals, libraries, and so on—were originally developed and promoted by philanthropists. Philanthropists built roads and bridges, funded artists and composers, and created endowments for the promotion of every imaginable aim, from medical research to candles for the poor.

Philanthropy takes many forms. There are inventor-philanthropists who develop ideas and products for human benefit—such as Ben Franklin, who gave his famous stove for the benefit of all. There are entrepreneur-philanthropists, individuals who develop a business partly or mainly with the aim of social improvement and are willing to lose money in the process. Such civic-minded entrepreneurs played an important indirect role in winding down the violence of food riots, for example. Applying their interest in scientific agriculture, they established "model farms" to develop and demonstrate agricultural techniques, spurring the English Agricultural Revolution of the eighteenth century.

Education is a community function that philanthropy has widely supported. The United States had, by the early nineteenth century, an extensive educational system rooted in philanthropy, with funds being supplied by wealthy donors, church members, and local merchants. The tradition continues today. Virtually every private school in the country has a scholarship system to support students unable to pay the fees, and philanthropists in dozens of cities have established voucher systems to help inner-city children attend private schools. A reformer who finds a gap in the provision of education by private, fee-paying schools, then, does not need to turn to the coercion of the tax system for a remedy. All he has to do is open his own wallet—and convince his friends to do the same.

Shaping Behavior through Persuasion

Philanthropy may be able to supply funds for community services such as libraries, art museums, hospitals, and schools, but there are many problems that money can't solve. These problems are rooted in the behavior—or rather, the misbehavior—of human beings. For example, the best-funded school system in the world might be a failure if parents don't send their children to it. Traditionally, it has been assumed that government's assertive use of force should be used to correct problems of this kind. To promote school attendance, for example, government threatens parents with fines or even jail for failing to send their children to school, and children found playing hooky are dragged to school or to jail.

But force isn't the only way to get people to do the right thing. Many voluntary methods exist for pursuing the same aim, including advertising, nagging, persuading, offering personal example, shaming, and shunning. To get parents to send their children to school, voluntary reformers might employ billboards and radio ads; they might visit parents and remind them about the importance of sending children to school; they might publish a list of parents who fail to send their children to school. Another voluntary technique to promote good behavior is the use of rewards and payoffs. Parents might be paid to send their children to school, for example, or prizes might be awarded for families with good attendance.

Voluntary methods of social improvement often can be made more effective if reformers band together in a formal organization that enhances their resources and authority. Although one can find examples of voluntary organizations in ancient times, the service-oriented voluntary organization is a rather modern development. Beginning in the eighteenth century, people began to realize that they could address problems by joining with like-minded friends to form a society funded by voluntary donations and sustained with voluntary labor. In the 1830s, the French observer Alexis de Tocqueville noted the "vast number" of private associations in the United States. "Americans," he reported, "make associations to give entertainments, to found seminaries, to build inns, to construct churches, to diffuse books, to send missionaries to the antipodes."[5] Today, the United States has approximately one million voluntary groups. They are numerous in other countries as well. Britain has approximately half a million, Germany 250,000, Spain 110,000. As government comes to be seen as an inappropriate or ineffective method for providing community services, these groups can perform virtually all of the same tasks by relying on voluntary methods of fund-raising and influence.

Limits on the Voluntary Sector

In surveying the voluntary sector today, we should keep in mind that it does not exist in pure form. Voluntary institutions are still tied to and often dominated by the prevailing force-based system. Commercial enterprises are impaired and distorted by government's assertive use of force in the form of taxation, tax subsidies, licensing arrangements, tariffs, regulations, and liability lawsuits. Modern philanthropy is also debilitated by government. The tax system has made philanthropy into something of a tax dodge and fostered the creation of self-serving, self-perpetuating foundations. Furthermore, the looming importance of government has deprived philanthropy of its vision, with the result that many philanthropists and foundations direct their funds to supporting government agencies and government programs.

Government and its readily available systems of coercion also undermine the healthy systems of social persuasion. Those who campaign against bad habits— smoking, drinking, using drugs—do not confine themselves to voluntary methods, but appeal to government to force people to abandon these habits. Those leading efforts to promote tolerance and goodwill toward minority groups have often turned to government to try to force their neighbors to change their prejudiced ways. Not surprisingly, these reformers have generated a backlash of resentment.

Government also weakens and perverts voluntary organizations. Its taxation drains resources from them, its subsidies deflect them into unproductive and self-serving modes of behavior, and its programs of regulation and liability lawsuits block innovation and creativity. Furthermore, government undermines them psychologically. "With its vast resources and powers, government is supposed to handle everything," say prospective donors and volunteers. "Why should we rise from our couches?"

The evolution against force still has a long way to run. In our thinking and practices, we shall continue for many years to look to force-based government to deal with social problems, even as we deplore its institutions and disparage the people who operate them. Beyond the hubbub and cynicism of politics, however, voluntary systems of improvement, systems that do not rely on force to accomplish their ends, are growing.

To be sure, these voluntary approaches lack the flair and drama of government. Coercion always promises sweeping reforms, "comprehensive" measures that purport to solve problems once and for all. Voluntarism, on the other hand, is a humble, piecemeal approach. It does not intoxicate with power, inviting one person or one party to "change the course of history." But at least voluntary methods always work some good. The problem with grand crusades directed at promoting government action is that they often fail, and in failing they waste untold amounts of time, energy, and idealism. Reformers who associate themselves with voluntary efforts are on a more secure path to progress. They directly improve the world through their business enterprises and voluntary organizations, and they have the satisfaction of knowing that, whatever their level of accomplishment, they are working in harmony with history's larger design.

_____

[1] James L. Payne, *A History of Force; Exploring the worldwide movement against habits of coercion, bloodshed, and mayhem* (Sandpoint, Idaho, Lytton, 2004)

[2] Disapproval of the use of force as such appears to be a relatively modern position. Of course, many ancient religions and philosophies stressed the idea of kindness to others, but, as noted earlier, these creeds made no distinction between harmful acts of force and the many other ways humans might be said to harm each other. A focus on force perhaps first appeared with the Anabaptists of the sixteenth century, who disapproved of the use of force by those in authority.

The Anabaptists unfortunately also became embroiled in a disappointingly large amount of violence themselves. The Mennonites, an offshoot of the Anabaptists, were more consistent about avoiding the use of force, as were the English Quakers. In the nineteenth century, anarchists such as Pierre Proudhon and Mikhail Bakunin disapproved of the state's use of force, but they themselves were prepared to use force to destroy the state. Members of William Lloyd Garrison's Christian "nonresistance" movement were consistently opposed to the use of force. Leo Tolstoy echoed their views. In England, Auberon Herbert made an impassioned (and unheeded) plea for "Voluntaryism," a doctrine that focused on avoiding the use of force.

In modern times, skepticism about the use of force has been a central theme for the many libertarian thinkers who emerged around the mid-twentieth century, including Leonard Read, Ayn Rand, and Murray Rothbard, as well as for near-libertarians such as Friedrich Hayek and Ludwig von Mises. In general, libertarians make a clear distinction between the *initiation of force,* which they almost always consider wrong, and the *defensive use of force,* which they generally endorse.

[3] Leo Tolstoy, *The Kingdom of God Is Within You* (New York: Charles Scribner's Sons, 1925), pp. 18, 239. Tolstoy attributes the dictum "Resist not evil by violence" to the nineteenth-century American pacifist Adin Ballou.

[4] *Ibid.*, p. 166.

[5] Alexis de Tocqueville, *Democracy in America,* edited by Phillips Bradley (New York: Vintage, 1945), vol. 2, p. 114.

Battle for the Mind
in the Heart of War

Josh Stieber

Josh Stieber was deployed as part of "The Surge," with the infantry unit depicted in Wikileaks' "Collateral Murder" video, when he was assigned to Baghdad from Feb 2007-Apr 2008. After leaving the army as a conscientious objector in 2009, he and another veteran bicycled across the US to share their experiences and challenge assumptions about war. Josh is currently a student, but continues to speak, write, and organize.

Revolts and revised governments in North Africa and the Middle East have pushed memories of Iraq even further out of the mainstream consciousness than they already were. Despite protests in Iraq, the architects of the Global War on Terror push their new memoirs, hoping we will accept and forget. While promoting his new book, Donald Rumsfeld tried to paint a picture of a reluctant and cautious path to war in Iraq, when Jon Stewart accused the former Secretary of Defense of sounding a loud rally cry for a highly questionable cause.[1]

Looking back on those years, I see my teenage-self, filled with anything but reluctance when I marched through DC with Rumsfeld himself in a "Support the Troops" rally, envisioning the uniform that I would soon don. But now, as the Iraq War fades into history, it is as important as ever—for the veterans, for the Iraqis, for future generations—that those who saw what happened firsthand in Iraq not let the dirty realities get processed into a sanitized and more easily digestible memory.

In the evangelical school that I grew up attending, evaluating calls for war was not a priority. Under the guise of "biblically submitting to the governing authorities," my classmates and I viewed our leaders as the forces of good in a world of darkness. We read a lionizing account of the president called *The Faith of George W. Bush* in my government class. Portraying Bush as a heroic visionary, the book's author quoted him, commenting:

> *"America is good, then, but good nations are not 'spared from suffering.' Instead, we have suffered precisely 'because we are freedom's home and defender.' We are destined for this. It is the price we pay for being good. It is worth the fight... He (Bush) was making language part of the national arsenal, learning the power of a president to impart the moral sense to a nation in crisis."* (136)[2]

Coupled with reports of how evil Saddam Hussein was, I assured myself that Operation Iraqi Freedom was a righteous mission, and one in which I should be on the front lines. With the encouragement and honor of my family and friends, I became an army infantryman upon my high school graduation in 2006.

Good and Evil

Fast forward to one year after I enlisted: The violence in my unit's patrol area in the industrial outskirts of Baghdad had only increased since our arrival in February. My moralistic idealism had collapsed like the crumbled building looming on the other side of the street; when locals had heard that we were moving into a factory in their district, they blew it up. Not getting the message, we moved into another old factory on the other side of the road.

The day we occupied our new outpost further shred my ideals; a swarm of Iraqis had gathered around the building, chanting and waving flags, clearly telling us that we were unwelcome. With our rumbling humvees, we forced our way in, dismounted, and were ordered to wave our rifles in the protestor's faces. A few impassioned young men got too close; they were tackled to the ground and then beaten in a small cell. The images of men, women, and children pleading so earnestly for autonomy made the battle cry, "spreading freedom and giving voice to the oppressed," seem a cruel and ironic joke.

The voice of the people had shouted loudly, and was swiftly ignored. Soon, blast walls surrounded the entire city block that our outpost was in, pushing aside those who lived and worked there. I thought back to my high school history class, where we glorified the American War for Independence, and couldn't help but remember that one of the revolutionaries' chief grievances was the intrusion and occupation of the British Empire's soldiers. Now we were the ones imposing on the populace that we were supposedly fighting to liberate, but that ideal had also gotten turned on its head.

Winning hearts and minds, in my infantry company, had largely become the punch line to the joke, "what do you call two bullets to the chest and one to the head?" Carrying out the desensitization we'd been indoctrinated with in Basic Training, the few of us who would show understanding to the locals were branded as "Hadji-lovers."

The heat of the Baghdad summer brewed together frustration over the gap between the war's rhetoric and reality, with a fear of attacks, leaving most soldiers with only one remaining goal: making it home alive. This dismal recipe had toxic results: as the locals' peaceful demands for us to leave their district had been ignored, they turned to roadside bombs and sniper attacks. With little ambition beyond mere survival, most of my platoon went along with our Battalion Commander's order: to shoot anyone on the street when a bomb went off. The desperate philosophy that claimed to justify this twisted bloodshed argued that if we made the locals more afraid of our barrage of bullets after an explosion than they were of the insurgents laying the bombs, then the people would be vigilant against those planting bombs; in other words, we were trying to out-terrorize the terrorists.[3]

When another soldier and I refused to shoot civilians, we were quickly chastised, and I soon lost my job as a gunner. This taught me a new lesson as my ideals were shattered even further: in the U.S., it's easy to assume the moral high ground, the force of freedom fighting against a depraved enemy, but my experiences were showing that morality had more to do with material conditions than an intrinsic goodness. I'm certainly not excusing the many cruelties of different insurgent groups, but I also think it is unfair to say that without the U.S.'s wealth and technology that Americans wouldn't turn to equally desperate tactics if they had no better alternatives. American rhetoric can and does often turn into debates of absolutes—of good vs. evil—but the difference, I was seeing up close, was more one of degree.

Late one night while I pulled guard duty, one of my platoon's staff sergeants came to visit the watch tower where I sat. Quickly tiring of small talk, I asked this three-combat-tour soldier, "Sergeant, how do you think Americans would respond if another army came in and acted towards them the way we act towards the Iraqis?" At that point, I was too disillusioned to care if this leader got offended at my question. His quick response, however, was anything but offensive. "Are you kidding? Smashing in people's doors in the middle of the night, scaring their kids, abducting their husbands and sons—nobody in the U.S. would stand for that," the sergeant explained animatedly, adding "I don't blame these people for doing whatever it takes. They don't have the same technology as us. If I was in their shoes, I'd consider strapping a bomb to myself, or even my kids!"

I realized that I'd been making excuses for far too long. Even in Basic Training, I'd had qualms: we would watch videos of bombs being dropped on villages and people being killed, and most trainees would chant along to the background music blaring, "Die Terrorist Die." Despite my concern that such training was a betrayal of my prized morality, I—along with church leaders to whom I would write back home, asking for advice about my doubts—would give the excuse that building up callousness was needed to take on the duty of killing to keep one's country safe.

Upon arriving in Iraq in early 2007, several of my leaders took me and the other new soldiers into a room, one by one, asking a series of questions, leading up to the key test: "Stieber, if you were in an open marketplace, full of civilians, and you saw a *Hadji* pull out a weapon, would you open fire on him, even if there were civilians standing beside him?" I began asking a clarification question: wrong answer. "You don't have time to ask questions," my leaders shouted, warning, "if you're not ready to do what it takes, then you'd better *get* ready, or else you or one of your friends is going to get shot up!" Glares from my leaders ushered me out of the room. I didn't want to imagine myself shooting civilians—I'd enlisted with the naïve notion that war would be like a video-game—where the enemy was clearly defined, with no moral ambiguity involved—but I knew my leaders might be right that hesitancy to fire could cost my friends or myself our lives, so I crossed my fingers, hoping their scenario wouldn't become manifest.

But as training had transformed into direct actions with real world consequences, I'd seen these excuses clear the way for the dejected position that I now found myself in. I knew my whole paradigm had to change. Sure, there may have been good intentions, but we weren't righteous heroes who only compromised our ideals in the direst of necessity; we were human beings, acting on our priorities and influences.

After a few months in Iraq, hardly any soldier talked about freedom or democracy; the blunt priority was to make it home alive. The influence, since the early days of training, was of being prepared to meet the goal of survival. Lackluster run-times, failure to scream "blood, blood, blood, makes the green grass grow" during bayonet training, and other shortcomings were met with the threat that "if you don't do what you're told to now, then it'll probably lead to getting killed in Iraq." Morality, on the other hand, was based on convenience, not an inherent American birthright.

Friends and Enemies

Had I spent more time in high school reading books that challenged my preconceived notions, instead of mostly ones that justified my selective worldview, then perhaps I wouldn't have had to learn this lesson the hard way. The president that my family, friends, and I all ardently supported had assured us that Saddam Hussein was evil. That black-and-white diagnosis was far easier to accept than to examine the history of the U.S. government's support of Saddam, the Taliban, or others of our government's allies who became branded in all-encompassing moral terms when political convenience was lost.

Time in Baghdad passed slowly, forcing me to reflect on the ideas I had failed to consider before enlisting. Though the Green Zone, the center of political action and publicity, lay only a few miles to our west, the power struggle around our lonely outpost seemed worlds apart. The days went by in sets: three days of searching homes and going on raids, until the disapproving looks of mothers and the forlornness of our prisoners was relieved by three days of guarding the outpost; the boredom of guard duty would then be lifted with a transfer to an Iraqi police station for even more guard duty at night, and controlling a gas station by day; nine demanding days would then be replaced with a return to the main base for vehicle repairs, laundry, weapon cleaning, and just enough of a taste of comfort and security to make us feel unnatural, before we'd hit the streets again for another cycle.

In the spare hours of this cycle, I tried to learn more about how this war, whose mission was declared "accomplished" years before, had descended to the fury transpiring around me. In talking to our platoon's interpreters, who were Iraqi natives, as well as reading the few news sources that were available, I began to see a much different picture than one of a massive majority pushing for democracy against a few terrorists who hated it. Instead, U.S. leaders like Paul Bremer barged into Iraq with "freedom" as a catchphrase, but with little understanding of the country's history or sociology. The interpreters, as other experts have also reaffirmed, explained that Iraqis did not see themselves primarily as Sunni and Shiite. Bremer, however, oversimplified Saddam's Baathist party as Sunni, though it was mixed; compared them to Hitler and the Nazis; and thus propelled Shiites to fill the power vacuum. Many Sunnis, outraged at American ignorance in this scapegoating, refused to participate in the new government, and sought to grab power from the ground up, instead. In this quickly shifting political atmosphere, Iraqis scurried to their newly imposed ethnic identities, forcing out or slaying the opposing group in the quest of local dominance.

Compounding this factionalism, which soon escalated into a bloody civil war, was another early U.S. imposed policy of disbanding the Iraqi Army, along with Baathist government employees. This massive number of unemployed, now with understandable bitterness towards the occupation that plucked them from their livelihoods, provided prime, disgruntled recruits for the array of factions vying for power.[4]

It was in this context that the broader questions of who is a friend and who is an enemy, and which side is just and which side is depraved, became localized for me. As roadside bombs continued to be planted, the policy of spraying the entire area continued to be enforced; I continued to refuse, losing my job as a gunner. What I learned in my reassigned role, however, gave me an inside view at the moral ambiguity—the dirty politics—that had been so distant from presidential speeches, classrooms lessons, and church prayers.

Taken out of the gunner's turret, I was placed as the radio operator for my infantry platoon; a main part of my job description involved taking notes for the platoon officer as he met with local leaders. Within the first couple of weeks in my new role, I found myself in a meeting with the district mayor, who sat behind a broad, wooden desk, cigarette-smoke dancing in front of his deep, shifting eyes. After a few minutes of awkward small talk, my First Sergeant demanded of the man known as al-Shradr, "We need the names of the people who have been planting the roadside bombs."

Waving his hand like a mafia don, al-Shradr chuckled, and announced that we need not worry about capturing the bomb makers, because he had the situation under control. Though the faces of several U.S. Army leaders around me betrayed dissatisfaction with this answer, none of us could deny that our situation had improved in the last few months—thanks in large part to negotiations with al-Shradr.

It was now October of 2007, and we were over halfway through with our fourteen-month deployment as part of "The Surge" campaign. In the eight months since arriving in this impoverished, industrial outskirt of Baghdad, our relationship with Al-Shradr had changed dramatically. The first time I had seen the man who now sat smugly behind the commanding desk, he was being shoved into a tight seat of an armored Humvee, tied and blindfolded. Arrested for participation in an IED (Improvised Explosive Device) ring, al-Shradr had been destined for the miseries of a military prison... until we discovered that he was the district authority. Following his release, the number of attacks had actually decreased, as we negotiated with educational and medical supplies as bargaining chips.

Al-Shradr also factored into the national scene: he had ties to the Shiite militia group known as the Mahdi Army. Most, if not all, of the attacks we faced were from this brutal group as they desperately sought to fill the power vacuum left in Saddam's removal. Despite the Department of Defense declaring that the Mahdi Army "has replaced Al Qaeda in Iraq as the most dangerous accelerant of potentially self-sustaining sectarian violence in Iraq," our values were elastic enough to negotiate with this group.[5] The greatest reduction in violence during my fourteen months in deployment occurred not from shooting more bullets, but came from the cease fire that the anti-American leader of the Mahdi Army, Muqtada al-Sadr, issued to his followers. When the cease-fire was lifted, our months of patrols, searches, and detentions could not prevent our outpost from being burned to the ground, the day after we turned control over to a new Army unit.

Though "The Surge" was largely heralded a success, due to the superior firepower of more troops on the ground, scenes like this negotiation with a man who had attacked us just months earlier are a key element to understanding how the Iraq War unfolded. Despite all the claims that "you can't negotiate with terrorists" and the black-and-white portrayal of the war, it was clear that partnership with former enemies changed the political scene far more than a greater use of force.

Rebuilding

With all my preconceived notions toppled, I set about trying to rebuild an adjusted outlook from the scattered pieces of idealism. I had joined to free an oppressed people, but many of our actions could not simply be brushed aside with the claim that, "at least we're not as bad as Saddam." The brutality of the groups with whom we partnered, along with the bloody ethnic cleansings that they sparked, made defining "oppression" highly subjective. My other goal—making my nation safer—was also brought into question as I realized that, as vengeful as 9/11 had made Americans, the countless civilians hurt and killed during Operation Iraqi Freedom had given even more people a reason to loath U.S. foreign policy.

When I boiled it down, I knew that I would not have stood for what I had contributed to in the lives of others, had it been done to me. I finally stopped making excuses for why I should go along with what I believed to be wrong, and decided to take action. Presenting several plans to Army friends, all ending in removal from the military system, they insisted that the best option was to not worry about the effects of our actions; just do our time, stop asking questions, and get out. I could no longer accept this option, so I began planning to go AWOL and then turn myself in, to finish my time in prison, where I would no longer harm innocent civilians.

Our deployment ended in April of 2008, and most of May was set aside for visits with our families. The time in between exposed the psychological frailty of fresh veterans, as friends began turning to alcohol and prescription drugs to escape their inner turmoil. False promises of a nation supporting its troops also became exposed, as these same friends were turned away from mental health facilities, cracked down on for their drunken antics, and demeaned through articles about Post Traumatic Stress Disorder, posted on walls with the word "pussy" etched over them.

If those of us, who had seen how far the reality of the War in Iraq was from the rhetoric that supposedly justified it, didn't start speaking out, then I didn't know who else would, and the myths would continue. My Army friends were mentally falling apart as they tried to push the memories from their mind, which made me even more resolute to not suppress my own conscience. I visited home, and informed my friends and family of my plan, that could have landed me in prison. Some told me about conscientious objection—a formal application for release from the military, based on one's beliefs no longer conforming to military expectations—and forcing me to struggle through whether or not I opposed participation in all wars.

Ironically, the reaction of friends and family to the possibility that I would go to prison for my beliefs helped me make my decision. Despite the high levels of morality with which I'd been raised, I was warned instead that my decision could harm a future career and leave me poor. I realized that most of the worst events throughout history had taken place not only through despotic individuals, but through the masses who turned blind eyes, and focused instead on personal comfort and security. For me, the decision became one of passively pursuing my own well-being, while my nation stockpiled weapons waiting for provocation to use them reflexively, versus proactively living out my ideals, and trying to shape events before they descended to violence.

I chose the latter, returned to my stateside military base, and began the conscientious-objection process. Most of my fellow soldiers thought it was an unworthy hassle, but weren't hostile to my action. Then it came time to train to kill again. We would shoot at targets that were enlarged photos of stereotypical-looking Middle Easterners. Like Japs and Gooks of past wars, we were given "Hadjis" to direct our ignorant hatred toward. Many of the disturbing scenes I'd witnessed in Iraq, however, had stemmed from a disrespect of all Iraqis, and I knew that the battle for the mind largely determined the physical battlefield. Building up further hatred by shooting at these targets was the opposite direction of where I wanted to go, so I refused.

When my First Sergeant found out, he had an arsenal of choice words that he unloaded on me. I was tempted to try to yell louder and hurl colder insults than him, but I thought back to all the lessons I had learned in Iraq. Our trying to be more fearsome than our enemies had only provoked more intense attacks and led to more loss of life and deeper hatred. Understanding, on the other hand, even with those who had attacked us, had created far more progress. So I employed these lessons, trying to respect my angry leader, and show him that I wasn't just trying to get out of work. This left me scrubbing toilets and delivering papers most days, but my steadfastness to my convictions slowly changed my leader.

Ten months after I had applied as a conscientious objector, I was finally granted status, and as I prepared to leave the Army, the man who had been as angry as I had ever seen a person gave me a hug and wished me luck on my life after the military.

Amazed by the dramatic transformation of my leader in how he treated me—and noting my own changes as well—I wanted to utilize that largely untapped, proactive force that I saw changing people from the inside-out, rather than through external force. Soon after leaving the military, I embarked on a six-month journey on foot and bicycle, to share the lessons I had learned, to learn more from others, and to visit people all across the country who were working to address problems before they boiled into the spilling of blood.

At the *Central Asia Institute*, I learned of a much different approach to creating change in the Middle East: their 145 schools were alleviating the causes that can drive people to violent extremism, while focusing on local partnerships to accomplish their mission. Volunteering at the *Matthew 25 Ministries*, I saw the potential of the individual in a man whose goal of using items that people typically discard, as a means to serve needy places around the world, had bloomed into a massive warehouse of supplies. In Ashland, OR, I found a community who had prepared themselves for the return of deployed soldiers to a local base by training themselves in compassionate listening and in college application procedures to help comfort and give options to fresh veterans.

I met a former Marine Sergeant who had gone through a similar transformation as I had and joined me for half of the journey. We met our share of people who weren't thrilled with what we had to say, but by patiently hearing out their perspectives (though tempted at times to dismiss certain individuals as racists), we were able build enough mutual respect for others to consider our perspectives as well. In one case, a man who initially tried to convince me that "killing Arabs and Asians isn't the same as killing an American," eventually, after several long conversations, broke down in tears over what he'd seen in his Korean War experience. Often the deepest demonstrations of hatred emerged from those who tried hardest to cover their own suffering.

The long path that had taken me through the brutality and contradictions of war, through military scrutiny and then to many interactions in my travels, had shown me a deeper meaning of the words that had been invoked generously when I was growing up. *Good and Evil* were not monopolized by any one group; *Courage* wasn't just following orders to go into dangerous situations, it required standing up to those giving the orders if they demanded injustice.

These deeper definitions ultimately flow from the belief that *freedom* does not mean bending to whatever standard allows one's will to dominate. A fuller *freedom* is the inward fortitude that allows a person to live out their convictions, even in the face of the harshest threats. My hope is that these words will not be exploited again as catchphrases, to misrepresent some shadowy cause in the future. This will be thanks to the partnership of dedicated activists whose work has continued to inspire me as I've travelled across the country. We're going to do everything we can to keep that from happening.

---

1. http://www.thedailyshow.com/watch/wed-february-23-2011/donald-rumsfeld-pt--1
2. Mansfield, Stephen, *The Faith of George W. Bush*, (Tarcher) 2003.
3. Harvey, Ryan, "Wikileaks in Baghdad." *The Nation.* 29 July 2010. Web.
4. Rosen, Nir. *Aftermath: Following the Bloodshed of Americas Wars in the Muslim World.* New York: Nation Books. 2010. Print.
5. "Al-Mahdi Army / Active Religious Seminary / Al-Sadr's Group." *GlobalSecurity.org.* Web.

War Is Horrible, but . . .

Robert Higgs

Robert Higgs is the Senior Fellow in Political Economy for the Independent Institute. He is the author of nine books, including Crisis and Leviathan *and* Depression, War, and Cold War, *and the editor or co-editor of six other books, including* Arms, Politics, and the Economy *and* Opposing the Crusader State.

Anyone who has done even a little reading about the theory and practice of war, whether in political theory, international relations, theology, history, or common journalistic commentary, has encountered a sentence of the form "*war is horrible, but ...*" In this construction, the phrase that follows the conjunction explains why a certain war was (or now is, or someday will be) an action that ought to have been (or still ought to be) undertaken, notwithstanding its admitted horrors. The frequent, virtually formulaic use of this expression attests that nobody cares to argue, say, that war is a beautiful, humane, uplifting, or altogether splendid course of action, and therefore the more often people fight, the better.

Some time ago—in the late nineteenth and early twentieth century, for example—one might encounter a writer, such as Theodore Roosevelt, who forthrightly affirmed that war is manly and invigorating for the nation and the soldiers who engage in it: war keeps a nation from "getting soft." Although this opinion is no longer expressed openly with great frequency, something akin to it may yet survive, as Chris Hedges argues in *War Is a Force That Gives Us Meaning* (2002). Nowadays, however, even those who find meaning for their lives by involvement in war, perhaps only marginal or symbolic involvement, do not often extol war as such.

They are likely instead to justify a nation's engagement in war by calling attention to alternative, even more horrible outcomes that, retrospectively, would have occurred if the nation had not gone to war or, prospectively, will occur if it does not. This seemingly reasonable "balancing" form of argument often sounds stronger than it really is, especially when it is made more or less in passing. People may easily be swayed by a weak argument, however, if they fail to appreciate the defects of the typically expressed "horrible, but" apology for war.

Rather than plow through various sources on my bookshelves to compile examples, I have availed myself of modern technology. A Google search for the exact term "war is horrible but" on September 11, 2006, identified 1,450 instances; the same search on January 7, 2011, yielded 30,400 instances. Rest assured that this larger, more recent number is still smaller than the entire universe of such usage—some instances have yet to be captured electronically. Among the examples I drew from the World Wide Web are the following fourteen statements. (I identify the person who made the statement only when he is well-known.)

1. *"War is horrible. But no one wants to see a world in which a regime with no regard whatsoever for international law—for the welfare of its own people—or for the will of the United Nations—has weapons of mass destruction."* - U.S. Deputy Secretary of State Richard Armitage

This statement was part of a speech Armitage gave on January 21, 2003, shortly before the U.S. government unleashed its armed forces to inflict "shock and awe" on the nearly defenseless people of Iraq. The speech repeated the Bush administration's standard prewar litany of accusations, including several claims later revealed to be false, so it cannot be viewed as anything but bellicose propaganda. Yet it does not differ much from what many others were saying at the time.

On its own terms, the statement scarcely serves to justify a war. A regime's disregard of international law, its own people's well-being, and the will of the United Nations, combined with possession of weapons of mass destruction—these conditions apply to several nations. They no more justified a military attack on Iraq than they justified an attack on Pakistan, France, India, Russia, China, the United Kingdom, Israel... or the United States itself.

2. *"War is terrible, war is horrible, but war is also at times necessary and the only means of stopping evil."*

The *only* means of stopping evil? How can such singularity exist? Has evil conduct never been stopped except by war? For example, has shunning—exclusion from commerce, financial systems, communications, transportation systems, and other means of international cooperation—never served to discipline an evil nation-state? Might it do so, if seriously tried? (If these questions give the impression that I am suggesting the possibility of a resort to embargo or blockade, that perception is not exactly correct. Although I support various forms of voluntary, peaceful withdrawal of cooperation with evil-doing states, I do not endorse state-enforced—that is, violent or potentially violent—embargoes and blockades.)

Why must we leap to the conclusion that only war will serve, when other measures have scarcely even been considered, much less been seriously attempted? If war is really as horrible as everyone says, then it would seem that we have a moral obligation to try very hard to achieve the desired suppression of evil-doing by means other than resort to warfare, which is itself always a manifest evil, even when it is seemingly the lesser one.

3. *"No news shows [during World War II] were showing German civilians getting fried and saying how sad it was. It was war against butchers and war is horrible, but it's war, and to defend human decency, sometimes war is necessary."* - Ben Stein

Stein is a knowledgeable man. He surely knows that the U.S. government imposed draconian censorship of war news during World War II. Perhaps the censors had their reasons for keeping scenes of incinerated German civilians away from the U.S. public. After all, even if Americans in general had extraordinarily cruel and callous attitudes toward German civilians during the war, many Americans had relatives and friends in Germany.

Stein appears to lump *all* Germans into the class of "butchers" against whom he claims the war was being waged. He certainly must understand, however, that many persons in Germany—children, for example—were not butchers, and bore absolutely no responsibility for the actions of government officials who were. Yet these innocents, too, suffered the dire effects of, among other things, the terror bombing the U.S. and British air forces inflicted on many German cities.

To say, as Stein and many others have said, that "war is war" gets us nowhere; in a moral sense, this tautology warrants nothing. Evidently, however, many people consider all moral questions about the conduct of war to have been settled, simply by their having labeled (or by their having accepted someone else's labeling of) certain actions as a "war." Having chanted this exculpatory incantation over the state's organized violence, they believe that all transgressions associated with that violence are automatically absolved—as the saying goes, "all's fair in love and war." It does not help matters that regimes treat some of the most egregious transgressors as heroes.

Finally, Stein's claim that "to defend human decency, sometimes war is necessary" is, at best, paradoxical, because it says in effect that sometimes human indecency, which war itself surely exemplifies, is necessary to defend human decency. Perhaps he had in mind the backfires that fire fighters sometimes set to help them extinguish fires. This metaphor, however, seems farfetched in connection with war. It is difficult to think of anything that consists of as many different forms of indecency as war does. Not only is its essence the large-scale wreaking of death and destruction, but its side effects and its consequences in the aftermath run a wide range of evils as well. Whatever else war may be, it surely qualifies as the most indecent type of action people can take: it reduces them to the level of the most ferocious beasts and often accomplishes little more than setting the stage for the next, reactive round of such savagery. In any event, considered strictly as a way of sustaining human decency, it gets a failing grade every time, because it invariably magnifies the malignity that it purports to resist.

4.   *"War is horrible, but slavery is worse." - Winston Churchill*

Maybe slavery is worse, but maybe it's not; it depends on the conditions of the war and the conditions of the slavery. Moreover, if one seeks to justify a war on the strength of this statement, he had best be completely certain that, but for war, slavery will be the outcome. In many wars, however, slavery was never a possibility, because neither side sought to enslave its enemy.

Many wars have been fought for limited objectives, if only because more ambitious objectives appeared unattainable or not worth their cost. No war in U.S. history may be accurately described as having been waged to prevent the enslavement of the American people. (Some people talk that way about World War II or, if it be counted as a war, the Cold War, but such talk has no firm foundation in facts.)

Some may object that the War Between the States was fought to prevent the ongoing slavery of the blacks then held in thrall. But however deeply this view may be embedded in American mythology, it is contrary to fact. As Abraham Lincoln made crystal-clear in his letter of August 22, 1862, to *New York Tribune* editor Horace Greeley, he had not mobilized the armed forces to free the slaves, but only to prevent the seceding states from leaving the Union: "My paramount object in this struggle *is* to save the Union, and is *not* either to save or to destroy slavery. If I could save the Union without freeing *any* slave I would do it, and if I could save it by freeing *all* the slaves I would do it; and if I could save it by freeing some and leaving others alone I would also do that."

When Lincoln brought forth the Emancipation Proclamation—a document carefully drawn, so that at the time of its promulgation, it freed not a single slave—he issued it only because at that time it seemed to be a useful means for the attainment of his "paramount object," preserving the Union. The slaves, including those in states that had not seceded, were ultimately freed for good in 1865, by the ratification (at gunpoint in the former Confederate states) of the Thirteenth Amendment, which is to say, as a ramification of the war, which itself had not been undertaken in 1861 in pursuit of this then-unforeseen outcome.

5. *"You may think that the Iraq war is horrible, but there may be some times when you can justify [going to war]."*

Perhaps war *can* be justified at "some times," but this statement itself in no way shows that the Iraq war can be justified, and it seems all too obvious that it cannot be. If it could have been justified, the government that launched it would not have had to resort to a succession of lame excuses for waging it, each such excuse being manifestly inadequate or simply false. The obvious insufficiency of any of the reasons put forward explains why so many of us put so much time and effort into trying to divine exactly what *did* impel the Bush administration's rush to war.

6. *"War is horrible, but sometimes we need to fight."*

Need to fight for what? The objective dictates whether war is a necessary means for its attainment. If the objective was to preserve Americans' freedoms and "way of life," the U.S. government certainly did not need to fight most of the enemies against whom it waged war historically. Oddly enough, the only time the enemy actually posed such a threat, which was during the Cold War, the United States did *not* go to war against that enemy directly, although it did fight (unnecessarily) the enemy's less-menacing allies, North Korea, China, and North Vietnam. In the other wars, the United States might well have remained at peace had U.S. leaders been sincerely interested in peace, rather than committed to warfare.

7. *"Of course war is horrible, but it will always exist, and I'm sick of these pacifist [expletive deleted] ruining any shred of political decency that they can manage."*

Many people have observed that wars have recurred for thousands of years, and therefore will probably continue to occur from time to time. The unstated insinuation seems to be that in view of war's long-running recurrence, nothing can be done about it, so we should all grow up and admit that war is as natural, and hence as unalterable, as the sun's rising in the east each morning. Warfare is an inescapable aspect of "how the world works."

This outlook contains at least two difficulties. First, many other conditions also have had long-running histories: for example, reliance on astrologers as experts in foretelling the future; affliction with cancers; submission to rulers who claim to dominate their subjects by virtue of divine descent or appointment; and many others. Eventually, people overcame each of these long-established conditions. Science revealed that astrology is nothing more than an elaborate body of superstition; scientists and doctors discovered how to control or cure certain forms of cancer; and citizens learned to laugh at the pretensions of rulers who claim divine descent or appointment. Because wars spring in large part from people's stupidity, ignorance, and gullibility, it is conceivable that alleviation of these conditions might have the effect of diminishing the frequency of warfare, if not of eliminating it altogether.

Second, even if nothing *can* be done to stop the periodic outbreak of war, it does not follow that we ought to shut up and accept every war without complaint. No serious person expects, say, that evil can be eliminated from the human condition, yet we condemn it and struggle against its realization in human affairs. We strive to divert potential evildoers from their malevolent course of action. Scientists and doctors continue to seek cures for cancers that have afflicted humanity for millennia. Even conditions that cannot be wholly eliminated can sometimes be mitigated, but only if someone tries to mitigate them. War may belong to this class of events.

Finally, whatever else one might say about the pacifists, one may surely say that if everyone were a pacifist, no wars would occur. Pacifism may be criticized on various grounds, as it always has been and still is, but to say that pacifists "lack any shred of political decency" seems itself to be indecent. Remember: war is horrible, as everybody now concedes, but many immediately put out of mind.

8. *"Every war is horrible, but freedom and justice cannot be allowed to be defeated by tyranny and injustice. As hideous as war is, it is not as hideous as the things it can stop and prevent."*

This statement assumes that war amounts to a contest, between freedom and justice on one side, and tyranny and injustice on the other. One scarcely commits the dreaded sin of moral equivalence, however, by observing that few wars present such a stark contrast, in which only the children of God fight on one side and only the children of Satan fight on the other. One reason why war is so horrible is that it invariably drags into its charnel house many—again, the children are the most undeniable examples—who must be held blameless for any actions or threats that might have incited the war.

Even if we set aside such clear-cut innocents and consider only persons in the upper echelons of the conflicting sides, it is rare to find only angels on one side and only demons on the other. In World War II, for example, the Allied states were led by such angels as Winston Churchill, who relished the horrific terror bombing of German cities; Josef Stalin, one of the greatest mass murderers of all time; Franklin D. Roosevelt, of whose moral uprightness, the less said the better; and Harry S Truman, who took pleasure in annihilating hundreds of thousands of defenseless Japanese noncombatants first with incendiary bombs and ultimately with nuclear weapons. Yes, the other side had Adolf Hitler, whose fiendishness I have no desire to deny or minimize, but the overall character of the leadership on both sides sufficiently attests that there was enough evil to go around. (As for the ordinary soldiers, of course, everyone who knows anything about actual combat appreciates that the men on both sides quickly become brutalized and routinely commit atrocities of every imaginable size and shape.)

It is far from clear that war is always or even typically "not as hideous as the things it can stop and prevent." On many occasions, refusal to resort to war, even in the face of undeniable evils, may still be the better course. When World War II ended, leaving more than 62 million dead, most of them civilians, and hundreds of millions displaced, homeless, wounded, sick, or impoverished, the survivors might well have doubted whether conditions would have been even more terrible if the war had not taken place. (The dead were unavailable for comment.)

To make matters worse, owing to the war, the monster Stalin had gained control of an enormous area, stretching from Czechoslovakia to Korea; and soon, because of the defeat of the Japanese Empire, the monster Mao Zedong would take complete control of China, and impose a murderous reign of terror on the world's most populous country that cost the lives of perhaps another 60 million persons (as many as 77 million, according to one plausible estimate). It is difficult to believe that the situation in China would have been so awful even if the Japanese had succeeded in incorporating China into the Greater East Asia Co-Prosperity Sphere.

9. *"I grant you the war is horrible, but it is a war, after all. You have to compare apples to apples, and when I do that, I see this war is going well."*

This statement about the U.S. war in Iraq exemplifies what some call the not-as-bad-as-Hamburg-Dresden-Tokyo-Hiroshima-Nagasaki defense of brutal warfare. If we make such pinnacles of savagery our standard, then sure enough, everything else pales by comparison. But why should anyone adopt such a grotesque standard? To do so is to concede that anything less horrible than the very worst cases is "not so bad." In truth, warfare's effects are sufficiently hideous at every level. What the Israelis did in Lebanon a few years ago bears no comparison with the February 1945 Allied attack on Dresden, of course; however, the sight of even one little Lebanese child, dead, her bloody body gruesomely mangled by an explosion, ought to be enough to give pause to any proponent of resort to war. Try putting yourself in the place of that child's mother.

10. *"[Certain writers] all agreed that war is horrible, but said the Bible gives government the authority to wage war to save innocent lives."*

Biblical scholars have been disputing what Christians may and may not do in regard to war for two thousand years. The dispute continues today, so the matter is certainly not resolved among devout Christians. Even if Christians may go to war to save innocent lives, however, a big question remains: Is the government going to war for this purpose or for one of the countless other purposes that lead governments to make war? Saving the innocent makes an appealing excuse, but often, if not always, it is only a pretext. "Just war" writers from Augustine to Thomas Aquinas to Grotius to the latest contributors have agonized over the ready availability of such pretexts, and warned against the wickedness of advancing them when the real motives are less justifiable or even plainly immoral.

For centuries, European combatants on all sides invoked God's blessing for their wars against one another. As recently as World War II, the Germans had *"Gott Mit Uns,"* a declaration that adorned the belt buckles of Wehrmacht soldiers in *both* world wars. Strange to say, in 1917 and 1918, Christian ministers of the gospel in pulpits across the United States were assuring their congregations that *their* nation-state was engaged in a "war for righteousness" (the title of Richard M. Gamble's splendid book about this repellent episode). The invocation of Biblical authority really doesn't get us very far: The enemy may be invoking the same authority.

Nowadays, of course, one side invokes the Jewish and Christian God, whereas the other calls upon the blessing of Allah. Whether this bifurcated manner of gaining divine sanction for the commission of mass murder and mayhem represents progress or not, I leave to the learned theologians.

11. *"War is horrible, but thank God we have men and women who are willing and able to protect our people and our freedom."*

These men and women may be willing and able to supply such protection, but do they? Our leaders constantly proclaim that their wars are aimed at protecting us and our freedoms—"we go forward," declared George W. Bush, "to defend freedom and all that is good and just in our world"—but one had to wonder, considering that in the entire history of warfare, each major U.S. war (with the possible exception of the War for Independence) left the general run of the American people with fewer freedoms after the war than they had enjoyed before the war.

In my book, *Crisis and Leviathan* (1987), I documented this ratchet effect in detail for the two world wars. After World War I, the government not only kept taxes far above their prewar levels, but also retained newly court-sanctioned powers to conscript men for foreign wars, to interfere with virtually any private transaction in international trade and finance (Trading with the

Enemy Act of 1917), and to suppress free speech in a draconian manner (Sedition Act of 1918).

After World War II, the government again kept taxes much higher than they had been before the war; retained for the first time a large peacetime military apparatus; created the Central Intelligence Agency as a sort of personal presidential intelligence and quasi-military outfit; continued to draft men for military service even during peacetime; and engaged much more pervasively in central management and manipulation of the private economy. The people, for their part, gained the privilege of living with the very real threat of nuclear holocaust hovering over them for four decades, while the U.S. government kept the Cold War pot boiling.

The so-called War on Terror has struck deeply into Americans' rights to privacy by vastly enhancing the government's surveillance activities and virtually gutting the Fourth Amendment's protection against warrantless searches and seizures. It has also led the government to create an agency now empowered to commit acts in U.S. airports that, if committed by others, would be prosecuted as sexual assault and battery and as criminal molestation of children. This "war" has also served to justify one of the greatest military-spending run-ups in U.S. history, leaving U.S. military-related spending—if correctly measured –greater than the comparable spending of all other nations combined.

Nevertheless, Americans are no safer because of these sweeping infringements of their liberties, many of which have been *de facto* pork-barrel projects, while others have been nothing more than security theater. War, whether real or make-believe, serves to justify huge increases in government spending, taxing, borrowing, and exertion of power over private affairs, and such government surges attract opportunists galore, while doing little or nothing to improve people's real security. Indeed, in the War on Terror, the government has added fuel to the fire of Muslim rage against Americans in the Middle East, while achieving nothing positive to compensate for this heightened threat.

Every time the rulers set out to protect the village, they decide that the best way to do so is to destroy it in the process. Call me a cynic, but I can't help wondering whether protection of the people and their freedoms was really the state's objective, and after fifty years of thinking about the matter, I've come up with some pretty attractive alternative hypotheses. One of them is that, as Marine General Smedley Butler famously expressed it, war is a racket, but I have other alternative hypotheses, too.

12. *"War is horrible, but some economic good came out of World War II. It brought the United States out of one of the greatest slumps in history, the Great Depression."*

This venerable broken-window fallacy refuses to die, no matter how many times a stake is driven through its heart. Most Americans believe it. Worse, because less excusable, nearly all historians and even a large majority of economists do so as well. I've been whacking this nonsense for several decades, but so far as I can tell, I've scarcely made a dent in it. Should anyone care to see a complete counterargument, I recommend the first five chapters of my book *Depression, War, and Cold War* (2006).

In brief, the government did not—indeed, could not—create wealth, simply by spending vast amounts of money (much of it newly created, as a result of cooperative Federal Reserve policies) on soldiers and weapons. The government did wipe out unemployment during the war, but only by putting millions of men in the armed forces. During World War II, these forces absorbed, primarily by conscription, sixteen million persons at one time or another (about three times the number of persons officially counted as unemployed in 1941), while causing a similar number of people to be employed in military-supply industries.

The economy looked prosperous because everybody was working and (except those in the armed forces) earning seemingly good wages and salaries. Yet the supply of civilian goods and services actually shrank, and many ordinary goods were not available at all (e.g., new cars) or were available only in limited, rationed amounts (meats, sugar, canned foods, gasoline and tires). Private investment also dropped sharply, as the government took over the allocation of capital, directing it into arms-related projects. So the apparent "wartime prosperity" was spurious. Only when the war ended and the military machine was largely dismantled did genuine prosperity return, for the first time since 1929.

13. "War is horrible, but whining about it is worse. Either put up or shut up."

Some people always reject the denunciation of any familiar social institution or conduct unless the denouncer offers a "constructive criticism," that is, unless he puts forward a promising plan to eliminate the evil he denounces. I admit at once that I have discovered no cure for the human tendency to resort to war, when much more intelligent and humane alternatives are available. I'm trying to convince people that, on nearly all occasions, they are allowing their rulers to bamboozle them and to turn them into cannon fodder, for purposes that serve the rulers' interests, not the people's. I'm getting nowhere in this effort, but I'm going to keep trying. I'm also going to continue to denounce stupidity, ignorance, ugliness, bullying, bad breath, and rap music, even though I don't expect to succeed on those fronts, either.

14. "Of course, war is horrible, but at present, it's still the only guarantee to maintain peace."

The statement as it stands is self-contradictory, because it affirms that the only way to make sure that we will have peace is by going to war. Perhaps, if we are feeling generous, we may interpret the statement as the time-honored exhortation that to maintain the peace, we should *prepare* for war, hoping that by dissuading any aggressor from moving against us, our preparation will preserve the peace. Although this policy is not self-contradictory, it is dangerous, because the preparation we make for war may itself move us toward actually going to war. For example, preparation for war may entail increasing the number of military officers, and allowing the top brass to exert greater influence in foreign policymaking. Those officers may believe that without war, their careers will go nowhere, and hence they may tilt their advice to civilian authorities toward risking or actually making war, even when peace might easily be preserved.

Likewise, military suppliers may use their political influence to foster international suspicions and fears that otherwise might be allayed. Wars are not good for business in general, but they are good for the munitions contractors. Certain legislators may develop an interest in militarism; perhaps it helps them to attract campaign contributions from arms contractors, veterans' groups, and members of the national guard and military reserve organizations. Pretty soon we may find ourselves dealing, as President Dwight D. Eisenhower did, with a military-industrial-congressional complex, and we may find that it packs a great deal of political punch and acts in a way that, all things considered, diminishes the chance of keeping the country at peace.

From the foregoing commentary, a recurrent theme may be extracted: those who argue that *"war is horrible, but..."* nearly always use this rhetorical construction not to frame a genuinely serious and honest balancing of reasons for and against war, but only to acknowledge what cannot be hidden—that war is horrible—and then to pass on immediately to an affirmation that notwithstanding the horrors, whose actual forms and dimensions they neither specify nor examine in detail, a certain war ought to be fought.

The reasons given to justify its being fought, however, generally amount to claims that cannot support a strong case. Often they are not even *bona fide* reasons, but mere propaganda, especially when they emanate from official sources. Sometimes they rest on historical errors, such as the claim that the armed forces in past wars have somehow kept foreigners from depriving us of our liberties. Often the case for war rests on ill-founded speculation about what will happen if we do not go to war.

People need to recognize, however, that government officials and their running dogs in the media, among others, are not soothsayers. None of us knows the future, but these interested parties lack a disinterested motive for making a careful, well-informed forecast. They have, as the saying goes, an agenda of their own. "The best and the brightest" of our leaders and their kept experts generally amount to little more than what C. Wright Mills called "crackpot realists," and on occasion, such as the one since 9/11, they don't meet even that standard. Hence, lately, these geniuses, equipped with all that secret information they constantly emphasize their critics don't possess, have put forward forecasts of a "cake walk" through Iraq, a "slam dunk" on finding lots of weapons of mass destruction there, and liberal-democratic dominoes falling across the Middle East—forecasts that fit more comfortably in a lunatic asylum than in a discussion among rational, well-informed people.

The government generally relies on marshalling patriotic emotion and reflexive loyalty, rather than on making a sensible case for going to war. Much of the discussion that does take place is a sham, because the government officials who pretend to listen to other opinions, as U.S. leaders did most recently during 2002 and early 2003, have already decided what they are going to do, no matter what other people may say. The rulers know that once the war starts, nearly everybody will fall into line and "support the troops."

If someone demands that the skeptic about war offer constructive criticism, here is my proposal: always insist that the *burden of proof* rest heavily on the warmonger. This protocol, which is now anything but standard operating procedure, is eminently judicious precisely because, as we all recognize, war is horrible. Given its horrors, which in reality are much greater than most people appreciate, it only makes sense that those who propose to enter into those horrors make a very, very strong case for doing so. If they cannot—and I submit that they almost never can—then people will serve their interests best by declining an invitation to war. As a rule, the most rational, humane, and auspicious course of action is indeed to give peace a chance.

Wartime Confessions
of a Talk Radio Heretic

On Going Forth
a Lamb among Wolves

Charles Goyette, a longtime award winning talk show host from Phoenix, has been noted for his outspoken anti-war views, his opposition to the war in Iraq, and his economic commentary. He is the author of the New York Times *bestseller* The Dollar Meltdown: Surviving the Impending Currency Crisis with Gold, Oil, and Other Unconventional Investments. *His latest book is* Red and Blue and Broke All Over: Restoring America's Free Economy.

(A speech given in Phoenix, Arizona, March 19, 2003,
the very night the Iraq War was launched and the bombs started falling)

I left my radio studio this evening to be here just as President Bush's ultimatum to Saddam Hussein expired. The bombing of Iraq, which has been going on more or less continuously since 1991, at this hour assumes a new intensity, joined by helicopter gunship attacks, and a ground invasion. A headline in the foreign press (I have, after all, become accustomed to getting my news from foreign press) blasts: *"EXPECTING IRAQI MOTHERS RUSH TO GIVE BIRTH BEFORE WAR! Baghdad: The sound of screaming filled the maternity ward at the Elwiyah Hospital on Tuesday, as women rushed to give birth ahead of an impending US invasion. Many pregnant women demanded to have caesareans, rather than risk delivering their babies during war, even though they were sometimes well short of their natural due date."*

Under the circumstances, there is little reason for me to marshal yet again the arguments against war, as I have been doing on my daily radio talk show. In any event, the rationale for the war that America wants has shifted so many times, one can hardly know which to refute: Is this war, in defiance of the wishes of the United Nations, a war to uphold the sacred honor of UN Resolutions? But that seems logically inconsistent. Is it a war against Al Qaeda and Osama bin Laden? Or was that last year?

Well, it could hardly be about 9/11, since the architects of this war had the blueprints finished years before the attack on America, even before the election of President Bush. Perhaps we need the war for the good of the stock market as we've been told by the likes of Lawrence Kudlow and William Seidman. So far that hasn't worked out too well and the long-term impact of this policy on the American economy and the dollar may hold some very unpleasant surprises. Any significance that Iraq's oil riches can have for this war has been so vehemently denied, one almost feels foolish believing there actually is oil

299

beneath the ground of Iraq.

(I should say parenthetically that since oil certainly has nothing to do with it, I hardly know what to make of the 1998 letter to President Clinton, urging America to war alone against Iraq because Saddam Hussein is a "hazard" to "a significant portion of the world's supply of oil". Those who signed that letter more than five years ago include: current US Secretary of Defense Donald Rumsfeld; Deputy Secretary of Defense Paul Wolfowitz; Richard Perle, a current Pentagon adviser; Richard Armitage, Deputy Secretary of State; John Bolton and Paula Dobriansky, Under Secretaries of State; Elliott Abrams, the presidential adviser for the Middle East and a member of the National Security Council; and Peter W. Rodman, Assistant Secretary of Defense for International Security Affairs. That's a mighty impressive list of officials to have all been deluded about the presence of oil in Iraq.)

Perhaps the best reason for this war, or if not the best at least the latest reason for this war, is to liberate the Iraqi people. (Yeah, liberation, that's the ticket!) We've been so very busy liberating people in the Middle East these many years—liberating them from the difficulty of finding their own way, by propping up their shahs, sheiks, and sultans. *Liberate Iraq*, the way we liberated them in the Gulf War Part One, when we encouraged them to revolt, incited revolution with broadcasts from our CIA posts in Cyprus. *Liberate Iraq*, and set the people free with Operation Shock and Awe. We wouldn't want anybody getting loose with any weapons of mass destruction, so let us open the heavens and rain down some three thousand cruise missiles and bombs in the first 48 hours. And then there's the new MOAB bomb the Massive Ordnance Air Blast or Mother of All Bombs, 21,000 pounds of explosive—more than ten tons of bomb. It flattens everything around, leaving behind only a mushroom cloud... and a liberated Iraq.

This is how force rules. It has become a tried and true proposition. In Vietnam, we had to destroy the village in order to protect it. In Waco, we had to kill the children in order to save them. And in Iraq, we're sorry, but it will be necessary to slaughter the people in order to liberate them.

Of course hand in hand with liberation of Iraq is democracy for the entire Middle East. *Democracy.* We believe in democracy. There'll be democracy for everybody! Of course, when our representatives voted to pass the Constitutional buck on the war, nobody had told them it was to bring democracy to the Middle East. And you wouldn't want to put it to a vote in the United Nations General Assembly or even a vote of the Security Council. We'll install democracy, just as soon as the Palestinians quit choosing leaders we don't like. *Democracy.* Even if we have to underwrite the Generalissimo in Pakistan who tossed out the elected government. *Democracy.* Even if we have to spend billions to bribe the government of Turkey to betray its people, 90 percent of whom oppose this war. Even if we have to vilify European leaders, for not defying their constituents who want no part of this war.

Well, you can understand how perplexing it is to enter the ring of public debate and wrestle with this shape-shifting rationale for war. You may be convinced that we are in a foreign adventure because Karl Rove discovered after

9/11 that Bush polls 20 points higher dressed in a bomber jacket. But no sooner do you have it pinned down fair and square, it morphs into something new. A new focus group shows three out of five Americans' pupils dilate and palms sweat when Bush says, "My job is to protect the American people." You know they've discovered a new phrase that pays, when you hear it uttered in response to every question asked in White House press conferences. And if they really need a boost, the President will say it while actually wearing a bomber jacket. Aboard an aircraft carrier.

So then, war is a *fait accompli*. Mr. Bush shall have his bump in the polls like his father before him. His presidency, indeed by his own acknowledgment his life, is given meaning. But I am a lonely dissenter because I see this wolf of war walks on three legs: fear, deceit, and collectivism.

A heretic in the propaganda business

1. Fear

Since September 11, 2001, my industry—the news industry—and most particularly cable television news and talk radio, has been in the fear business. With the exception of greed, there is nothing quite so motivating, no sell quite as easy as fear. And we've been selling it by the tankload.

I am in this business because I enjoy the bare knuckles of debate about policy, lively discussion of issues, and a laugh about the foibles of our age. But the continual promotional announcements about mushrooms clouds; the near-hysterical tone in which the most trivial developments are presented as breath-taking breaking news; the frenzied dance of government and news anchors, of official pronouncements and heightened alert levels… create a weird symbiosis, in which the media serves the state in its relentless grab for bigger budgets and greater police powers, while the state feeds the media's need for high drama and the narcotic of fear.

The disproportionality of our continual state of alarm, our addiction to fear, is evident in the air-traveler's submission to utterly pointless and humiliating treatment; in the outbreak of panic at the presence of powdered donuts (whatever did happen to that anthrax investigation by the way, and will we have to bomb Maryland when the truth comes out?); and in the rush to buy plastic sheeting and duct tape—which resulted in more than one death by suffocation. We are witnessing a level of hysteria not seen in a generation, since bomb shelters and school children cowering under their desks.

This is not to say that proportionate measures are not needed in dangerous times, but fear of imminent attack is mesmerizing, as we watch and listen and learn where the threat will erupt next. It brings in new viewers, creates extended time spent listening, and higher ratings.

Fear sells.

2. Deceit

Deceit has ever gone hand-in-glove with war. The Spanish-American War of 1898 and the suspicious circumstances of the sinking of the battleship Maine may be ancient history, but it shouldn't be hard to recall the tale of Frederic Remington's request to return home from Cuba because nothing was going on. He was famously told by William Randolph Hearst to remain. "You furnish the pictures and I'll furnish the war." In no time the Hearst and Pulitzer press frenzy, on no evidence, had the public demanding intervention in Cuba.

Perhaps it is true that the truth comes out eventually, but as Napoleon said, the truth doesn't need to be completely suppressed. It just needs to be delayed until it no longer matters. Does it matter any longer that after 59 years of cover-up, secret documents released under the Freedom of Information Act reveal the extent of the President's foreknowledge of the attack on Pearl Harbor? See Robert B. Stinnett's *Day of Deceit,* if it matters to you.

I had Daniel Ellsberg on the show a few days ago, famed for risking prison to release the Pentagon Papers. He describes the deceit behind the Gulf of Tonkin Resolution, the act that gave Johnson the same unlimited authority to wage the Vietnam War that Bush has been given in the War on Terrorism. The Gulf of Tonkin Incident. The lie that became the pretext for the course of action that had already been designed. Sound familiar? Another gulf, another blueprint for war, drawn up well before the triggering event. If that doesn't sounds familiar, how about this from President Johnson: "We are not about to send American boys 9 or 10,000 miles away from home to do what Asian boys ought to be doing for themselves." Half a million American boys overseas later and 58,000 dead, we have to wonder why anyone believed him. Couldn't anyone at the time remember similar assurances from Wilson and FDR before their World Wars?

Those who do remember the deceit always vow not to get taken in next time. "*We won't get fooled again!*" But a generation later, we're told that this time it's different. It's like the high-tech bubble. This is a whole new paradigm, or so the story goes. But reality, like the market, has a way of crashing in. It's the same old paradigm. "*Meet the new boss, same as the old boss!*"

Surely we should remember Bush the Elder telling a Joint Session of Congress of the threat to Saudi Arabia during the prelude to Gulf War I. The Defense Department—under the same officials pushing Gulf War II—was estimating there were as many as 250,000 Iraqi troops and 1,500 tanks in Kuwait poised in the south to roll into Saudi Arabia. So a reporter at a small Florida newspaper persuaded her bosses to spend $3,200 on satellite photos. No troops, no tanks. No threat.

Meet the new boss, same as the old boss.

3. Collectivism

Wars are built on fear and deceit. And collectivism. It is to be expected that we would link arms, circle the wagons in times of danger. There is nothing destructive in seeking mutual aid and security in the company of one another. It is only natural to have a special affinity for, and obligations to our own countrymen, those with whom we share community, custom, and culture. This wholesome patriotism is quite unlike a national collectivism that deifies the state, a nationalism that demands obedience.

Just as my love for my children cannot detract from your love for your own, the pride I feel for my country should not detract from that which others have for theirs. But a national collectivism that incites contempt and hatred for others is something else entirely. This collectivism, the state raised to divine status, is a prerequisite for aggressive war. If the state is a god, not only can it command all the resources needed for war, but its enemies are nothing but devils and must be destroyed. That this destructive nationalism rules is seen when the talking heads of TV indulge in dehumanizing the opponent. It is heard as the radio hosts encourage a frenzy of hatred for the enemy's culture, institutions, and people. Of course there is no moral accountability for this behavior because each individual is dissolved in the collective.

One last ritual is demanded to make the collectivism complete, one last act of capitulation that I must make along with everyone else who opposes this war. We must make a holy vow that we "support our troops." What this affirmation would mean in reality is almost too silly to contemplate. As if I could refuse to pay the taxes that actually provide for our armies and support our troops. As if I'm somehow empowered to decide what troops and which missions I will support.

Support the troops? I'm risking my livelihood trying to keep them from being sent on these deadly and needless foreign adventures. I've been nothing if not outspoken that I want these young men and women all to come home to their lives and families. (Or in the alternative, in calling for the middle-aged architects of these wars, the armchair chickenhawks of the War Party, to go to the front lines in their place!) How much more supportive can it get?

But the demand for the public declaration is really about something greater than the individual men and women in uniform. It is demanded with a vehemence by those whose doubts are forcibly suppressed, whose own responsibility in this blood affair must never be acknowledged. The sin that the aggressive war represents must be a universal sin. All must be stained by the guilt equally, in the hopes that there are no individual consequences. This confession of "support for our troops" (sometimes "support for our president," which achieves the same effect but can be harder for some die-hards to spit out) is a final act of surrender to collectivism.

My Heresy

This collectivism is also responsible for what could be described as the cowardly behavior of the media, their obsequious deferral to the governing authorities. The party line—or it could even be called the Patriotic Line—is established after a crisis. It is encapsulated in slogans: "*They hate us for our freedom*"; "*They hate us because we are good*"; "*You are either with us or against us*"; and a host of other Big Brotherisms.

Most journalists are willing to toe the Patriotic Line, at least for a while, sometimes because they doubt their own contrary views, sometimes just out of fear. Dan Rather told the BBC last year that it was a form of self-censorship, of patriotism run amok. So how do I account for my own heresy, as a talk show host on an explicitly conservative station surrounded by what have been called "The Windbags of War"?

My view is a Socratic one: that self-knowledge is the basis of all wisdom. One might wish that it would be given us to see not just ourselves, but our country, as others see us. Just as we can be psychologically blind to our own faults, so too do we shut our eyes to the deceit, hypocrisy, criminality and violence of our own government. Jung makes clear that this quest for self-knowledge can be an unpleasant undertaking and is preoccupied with bringing to light the psychological shadow, one's own dark and rejected nature. Oh, yes, terrible things happen, but it is always others who do them. Yes, children are starved and deprived and die by the thousands, but we have no complicity. Yes, we have been bombing them for years, but we have solid legal grounds for doing so. In fact, says Jung, a persistent disregard for our own collective shadow can make us an instrument of evil.

This call to self-knowledge is, I have found, a pretty hard sell in the popular media. We know ourselves to be good, and we mean well, and we have laws, and besides, only left-wing America-haters blame America first. And in regarding ourselves as harmless we add stupidity to our destructiveness.

Pro-war vs. anti-war

One last point that I would like to make, although I feel I should warn you that I may not make it well, because its outlines are just becoming clear to me in the course of the public debate. There is a sense in which being pro-war and being anti-war are very much alike. The stakes are raised, antagonists are spotlighted and vilified, battle-lines are drawn, casualties are created. Emotions run high; anger and hatred fill the psycho-sphere! In their extreme form, the pro-war want their enemy's land nuked into a glass bowl, while the anti-war hope for the kind of widespread calamity that will vindicate their position. War, god I love it! Anti-war, glorious anti-war! Locked together in an eternal embrace of action and reaction! But I am not sure that peace is created in such battles of force and resistance. The *I Ching* says the only effective way to overcome evil is to make continual progress in the good. Jesus spoke of the same spiritual principle.

This group has often invoked the wisdom of the late Leonard Read, who founded the Foundation for Economic Education at the end of the last world war. Read was a wonderful champion of freedom and self-improvement. He understood this philosophy of continual progress in the good. A volume of his essays, which he generously signed for me before his death, begins with an epigram from Emerson:

> *"Great men are they who see that spiritual is stronger than material force, that thoughts rule the world."*

304

Peace Through Justice,
Justice Through Video

David Weingarten

David Weingarten is a videographer from Newmarket, Ontario, Canada. He is the producer of the grassroots documentary Unfair Dealing *and his latest documentary* Fortress Toronto. *A graduate of the Broadcast Journalism course at Seneca College, David has previously worked on-air for University of Toronto Radio and produced for national broadcaster CBC/Radio-Canada. He currently volunteers as a video activist and operates a video production business.*

Peace is a concept that widely lends itself to interpretation. It can represent profoundly a halt to military hostilities or simply the refreshing slumber that comes with a clear conscience. Peace may be found externally among the policies of nation-states or within the accomplishment of an individual who has struggled and achieved their own personal objective.

In order for peace to thrive—in any form—the role that truth and transparency play within that grand ideal must not be forgotten. The pacifying role of truth and transparency is easily illustrated in instances like the Iraq War, where greater transparency would have sustained peace by shattering the West's impetus to invade. More obscure, however, is the peace that can be found in the disclosure of evidence against a criminally accused suspect because, as the Canadian Supreme Court succinctly puts it, *"(Evidence is)... the property of the public to be used to ensure that justice is done."*

With justice comes peace, and whether it regards evidence of a fraudulent war or justification for the infringement of personal liberty, truth and transparency provide the fair context necessary to achieve it.

It's been my personal experience that video documentation serves as a highly effective tool for achieving justice, though my path to that realization was an unlikely one. I was raised in a white, suburban, upper-middle class family. My father, a Princeton-educated physician, had instilled in him a strong work ethic that he passed on to his children. My mother, an equally hard-working administrative professional, fondly supported the Canadian government, having immigrated from communist Poland at a young age. Growing up, my parents rarely discussed politics, and social justice issues were hardly a topic of conversation amongst my friends and classmates. These conditions formed to provide me with a safe, comfortable existence, and as I look back I realize it may have been that insulated life contrasted against the daily realities of the world - and the immense shock of discovering that disparity—which led me to become an activist videographer.

Throughout public school I cultivated my ability with the English language and, despite losing interest in traditional academic pursuits, came to the conclusion as a young man that an education would be the most effective way to do *something* important with my life. I figured my command of the English language would assist me in the field of journalism, as would my affinity for storytelling. I enrolled at Seneca College, gaining acceptance into the Broadcast Journalism course.

Broadcasting seemed like an attractive field to work in, with sociable colleagues and the potential to create unique and individualized work. Meanwhile, I found the craft was less wordy than print journalism, using the power of images and sound rather than text to deliver a story in its entirety. Since then I've often thought, if the pen is mightier than the sword, and a picture is worth a thousand words, video documentation must be worth 30,000 words per second, and makes small foe of the sharpest blade. It was a moment of my life full of great optimism; the impression had been set upon me that with hard work I could attain a high-ranking position in a noble field that provides valuable information to the public. If I was really good I might even become the talking head of a major media outlet, reading the evening news to an audience of millions.

That train of thought eventually changed during a night shift, while working for CIUT-FM at the University of Toronto. I was researching the events of September 11, 2001 and came across troubling information regarding the attacks of that day. Conspiracy theories aside, I will say there is substantial evidence contradicting the official 9/11 story many people believe, publicly regurgitate, and allow to dictate their personal lives. There is information which, if analyzed in a proper and unbiased manner, would force the public to confront a very sobering reality as I did.

At least some of that information came to me in the form of an internet documentary entitled *Loose Change*, produced by New York residents Dylan Avery, Jason Bermas, Matthew Brown and Korey Rowe. These young men transformed years of research into an engaging 80 minute video, raising questions about 9/11 which many of us didn't know existed. *Loose Change* was my first exposure to video footage of World Trade Center Building 7 (WTC 7), a 47-storey building that collapsed mere hours after the Twin Towers did.

WTC 7 was not hit by a plane, yet collapsed in a fashion similar to WTC 1 and 2, by crumbling vertically into its own footprint with a speed and totality previously only accomplished by controlled demolition. What caused this building to disintegrate? Why was its collapse omitted from the 9/11 Commission Report? Having been introduced to this footage so late in 2006, I initially thought the WTC 7 footage was a hoax. But as I came to accept the truth about WTC 7, other questions began to gnaw at me. Specifically, with the glaring enigma presented by WTC 7, why was I forced to learn of its existence from internet documentarians whom most in the mainstream media would call "kooky conspiracy theorists"?

Loose Change was impressive for the fact that, with a budget of less than $10,000, it was such a critical work and reached such a wide audience. More astounding was that the seemingly alchemical combination of passion, information, video-editing software, and the force of the internet could produce something so revolutionary, despite its simplicity. At the root of this revolutionary gesture was one basic element: the truth.

Facts largely ignored by the mainstream media were placed front and center in *Loose Change*, and it seemed that independent journalists and filmmakers were filling the informational void left by our fourth estate. It dawned on me like an epiphany how truly effective independent videography was at making a real difference by sidestepping editorial control and letting the facts take us where they may, as uncomfortable a place it may be.

Had the media seized upon the mystery of Building 7 with the same tenacity it did upon the culpability of Osama Bin Laden, perhaps public opinion would have demanded a full independent inquiry into 9/11 rather than a full-scale war in the Middle East. Where would a true investigation have led us? What would it mean for the lives of millions of Afghans and Iraqis, had the media diligently forced us to confront the questions raised by the collapse of Building 7?

The answers to these questions illustrated for me the true power that video has to compel real transparency and justice, and realizing the neglect of our media to use that power to such effect, I was drawn closer to video activism.

Over the course of a year, disillusionment with the mainstream media shifted my focus to one less geared toward society's paradigm of success. I became less concerned with grooming myself for corporate-media stardom, and more inclined to research the *real* inconvenient truths behind current events. Investigative journalists like Greg Palast and Gary Webb convinced me through credible, methodic research that North America isn't the beacon of righteousness and liberty many of us are raised to believe. In fact, their respective investigations into U.S. election fraud and CIA involvement in cocaine-trafficking reveal a country that could easily resemble a despotic regime. Although Palast's report wasn't broadcast in the U.S., and Webb's career dwindled away before he sadly committed "suicide" with two gunshots to the head, these gentlemen succeeded in bringing powerful information to the light of public scrutiny. How widespread and effective such scrutiny becomes is uncertain, but this is the manner in which transparency brings about justice. Once an ugly truth has made itself apparent, we are forced to remedy it for we can no longer live in ignorance of it.

Further research and a desire to contribute locally led me to investigate Canada's largest post-9/11 anti-terror operation. In 2006, the "Toronto 18" arrests appeared to be Canada's definitive "homegrown terror" sting, arriving on the heels of the London 7/7 subway bombings in 2005, and the Madrid train bombings the year before that. The "Toronto 18" was originally presented as a core group of eighteen individuals, ranging in age from 15 to 43, who were plotting to bomb targets in southern Ontario. We were told they had the intent, they had the resources, and that an attack was imminent, although my cursory research on the matter indicated otherwise. I set out to produce a video that would critique the true threat posed by the "Toronto 18," hoping to emphasize the important, lesser-reported facts of the case. With the help of my college mate Adil Lakhani, I released *Unfair Dealing* via internet in early 2008.

Through this humble video project, we established that the "Toronto 18" was a loosely connected group, rather than the organized "terrorist" cell being depicted by the government. The group was so loose, in fact, that some of the suspects only first met each other after being arrested. Of the eighteen suspects, only five were involved in the bomb plot, which itself had only been realized with the extensive assistance of a paid government informant, described by his handlers as "vindictive," and "motivated by money."

The remaining suspects were, in one way or another, involved in a winter camping trip that was arranged with the help of another government informant. It was during this camping trip that many of the participants displayed their ineptitude—and even outright rejection of extremism—leading the informant to dub the expedition "operation potty-training." Many of the suspects were simply unaware of the "sinister" nature of the camping trip, and their activities were apparently benign enough to elicit a shocked reaction from the informant upon hearing of the arrests. Although our information was easily available to the mainstream media, *Unfair Dealing* was the only source that depicted the warehouse where the bomb-making materials were delivered – and the fact that *it is next door to a detachment for the Royal Canadian Mounted Police.*

In the case of the "Toronto 18"—as in many, many others—the government held a monopoly on information. The Royal Canadian Mounted Police (RCMP) declared the guilt of the suspects during a stately press conference, and security agents solidified the perception of homegrown terrorism through anonymous, often untruthful, leaks to the press. With the myth of the "Toronto 18" firmly established in the Canadian psyche, a publication ban was subsequently enacted, ensuring the myth was all the public had access to.

But what would the public's reaction have been if they were shown imagery of an RCMP detachment next door to the terrorists' "hideout"? Would they have questioned the extent of the informants' involvement? Would they as easily have fallen prey to the RCMP's frightening portrayal of a self-sufficient homegrown terrorist threat? Consider for a moment that amidst all the sensationalism, the "Toronto 18" were used as justification for many things including increased security funding and continued Canadian military involvement in Afghanistan. It's interesting to think how public opinion, and ultimately our collective willingness to go along with a law-and-order agenda, would have been affected had our mainstream media given scrutiny to these details rather than grudgingly mention them in passing, if at all.

In the end, 11 suspects were convicted and 7 released. At least 3 of the convicted suspects "should never have faced charges" according to the RCMP informant, and 7 innocent Canadians spent eighteen unnecessary months detained in prison, much of that time in solitary confinement. I believe *Unfair Dealing* was successful in defending the "Toronto 18" suspects, but to what extent I'll never know for sure. We received nominal media coverage, and I'm told that Crown prosecutors were well aware of the video, but I doubt any of them would reveal what influence we had on them dropping charges against the 7 suspects.

There are countless, more easily quantifiable, examples of video documentation bringing social justice. For example, in 1988 director Errol Morris released his documentary *The Thin Blue Line*. Many are already familiar with this film, which retells the story of a murdered Dallas police officer through interviews and reenactments. Through investigative work, reexamination of the facts, and an entertaining visual presentation, Morris was able to compel the release of a man imprisoned for more than 12 years who, at one point, had come within three days of execution. By revisiting the facts and presenting them in a calculated manner through video, Morris was able to bring justice and closure to a situation that threatened the life of an innocent man.

In another more recent example, video evidence has provided some justice and peace for the family of Robert Dziekański. This Polish immigrant arrived in Canada at the Vancouver International Airport in 2007, where he lost his life after being tasered multiple times by the RCMP. Since the incident, the RCMP have accepted many recommendations of a federal watchdog agency, the Dziekanski family has received financial compensation, and the police have publicly apologized to Dziekanski's mother. Even the Polish government has become vocal, calling for criminal charges against the four RCMP officers involved in Dziekanski's death. The interesting thing is that this reaction came only after video footage of the incident surfaced—video footage the police tried to suppress, and which disproved the RCMP's version of events. The release of the Dziekanski video managed to discredit the police, shift public opinion, and elicit the governmental response it did by simply showing the *truth*. While Dziekanski died at the hands of the RCMP, perhaps his family can be afforded peace in the fact that video documentation has preserved his character.

While not as dramatically as the Dziekanski case, the video camera has also proven for me to be an invaluable source of protection against dubious police behavior.

In the summer of 2010, the city of Toronto became a police state in the weeks leading up to the G20 Summit and I, with my co-producer Shaun Hanley, set out to document the transformation of our city. It was our prerogative to keep the cameras rolling during encounters with the RCMP, Canadian Security Intelligence Service (CSIS) agents, and private security. While private security attempted to detain myself and Shaun, a camera captured the interaction as we asserted our right to retain the footage we had shot. We posted the video online, entitled *Detained at the MTCC Prior to G20 Summit*, to demonstrate that our actions were civil and peaceful. It was probably a wise thing to do, since the encounter prompted CSIS agents to show up at my home, and visit Shaun at his office. Weeks later during the protests, we preserved evidence of Shaun's arrest on video, importantly, because the charges against him—and many hundreds of other activists—later vanished without a trace.

For those unfamiliar with the Toronto G20 Summit, it was venue to the largest mass arrest in Canadian history, and one of the most egregious violations of Canadian civil liberties. It was during this summit that the public was fooled into believing the police had special, temporary powers to search residents without probable cause, and arrest any citizen who dared step within 5 meters of the Metro Toronto Convention Center without identification. In reality no such police powers existed, and the propagation of that lie is one example of how police transparency would have preserved the personal peace of Toronto's citizenry.

Had the public—and the police, for that matter—been fully aware of the true extent of the temporary legislation, hundreds of incidents would have been prevented in which innocent Canadians were, sometimes violently, forced to empty the contents of their knapsacks. Though the Toronto Police Service would like to give the impression that no illegal searches took place that week, it is because of the myriad of videos posted online that we know for a fact they did. Likewise, the police would be happy to bury the notion they made countless illegal arrests at Toronto's G20. The fact that over one thousand arrests were made, yet only a small percentage pursued in court, shows that police *greatly* overstepped their authority. Because there was no documentation for most of the arrests (including Shaun's), the police avoided accountability for their actions in a court of law, and detained protesters were unable to find closure by facing their accusers. The injustice to hundreds of detainees was left a painful, unresolved memory.

For many of the protestors victimized that weekend by state-sanctioned abuse, the complaints system was not an option for reaching justice either. During the protests, many police officers had concealed the names and badge numbers on their uniforms, hiding information required by the public to file a complaint against a specific officer. This problem was exemplified by the case of Adam Nobody, who suffered a broken nose and cheekbone at the hands of the police. Although Toronto Police Chief Bill Blair characterized Nobody as armed and violent, video footage surfaced disproving the allegations. More importantly, one of the police who concealed his name and assaulted Nobody was eventually identified through the video, leading to the first charges against an officer for assault at the Toronto G20.

What a relief it must have been for Nobody, after being assaulted and publicly vilified, to have tangible video evidence that *he's not the bad guy the police want you to think he is.* As in the Dziekanski case, video of the Nobody assault discredited the police by exposing their lies. For the hundreds of other, similarly "violent" detainees, I wouldn't doubt their credibility enjoyed a small personal victory too.

Recently the police have threatened to damage my own credibility, and were it not for video documentation they may have succeeded. Near the end of 2010, I was shaken during an incident in which police cruisers pulled up to my home, shining powerful floodlights into my residence, in what seemed like an obvious attempt to intimidate me. To this day, despite multiple correspondences with my local police department, I have not been able to determine the purpose of that particular visit. Instead, I have been given several, demonstrably false explanations in regards to the incident, as I've documented online in a video entitled *Police Brutality and Harassment in York Region: Police Caught Lying On Hidden Camera.* I posted this video online because since I've complained about this episode of harassment, the York Region Police have tried to convince me it never happened. Additionally, in my pursuit of an explanation for the visit, I have had investigating officers accuse me of having "mental health issues" for my desire to hold them accountable. Knowing, as I do now, the power of video to expose the truth, I have decided to forfeit the approval of a systemically flawed police complaints system. I believe that by letting the camera tell my story, any viewer will be able to reach their own conclusion, and I will reach a far better standard of justice than the police would allow.

One commonality among such varied circumstances as cause for war, the imminent execution of an innocent man, the death of an immigrant, or deception by the police, is that greater transparency can achieve justice in each of them. Citizens must not forget that their right to video-document is as inalienable as their right to free speech and peaceful public assembly. As long as we continue to exercise that right, the greater chance we have for truth, transparency and justice to prevail, and with that the opportunity for peace to remain a constant in our lives.

Pakistan:

Losing Hearts

and Crushing Minds

The Implications of America's Undeclared War

Malou Innocent

Malou Innocent is a Foreign Policy Analyst at the Cato Institute. She is a member of the International Institute for Strategic Studies, and her primary research interests include Middle East and Persian Gulf security issues and U.S. foreign policy toward Pakistan, Afghanistan, and China. She has appeared as a guest analyst on CNN, BBC News, Fox News Channel, Al Jazeera, Voice of America, CNBC Asia, *and* Reuters. *Innocent has published reviews and articles on national security and international affairs in journals such as* Survival, Congressional Quarterly, *and the* Harvard International Review. *She has also written for* Foreign Policy, the Wall Street Journal, Asia, the Christian Science Monitor, Armed Forces Journal, the Guardian, Huffington Post, the Washington Times, *and other outlets, both in the United States and overseas. She earned dual Bachelor of Arts degrees in Mass Communications and Political Science from the University of California at Berkeley, and a Master of Arts degree in International Relations from the University of Chicago.*

> *"The art of economics consists in looking not merely at the immediate but at the longer effects of any act or policy; it consists in tracing the consequences of that policy not merely for one group but for all groups."* — Henry Hazlitt, *Economics in One Lesson*

Introduction

Following the terrorist attacks of September 11, 2011, the United States launched a covert campaign of targeted assassinations against Taliban and al Qaeda suspects in the tribal region of Pakistan. On May 1, 2011, U.S. President Barack Obama, who accelerated and expanded the C.I.A.'s drone program, announced that he authorized a "targeted operation" in Abbottabad, Pakistan, that killed Osama bin Laden, the hunted mastermind behind 9/11.[1] While U.S. officials boast that drone strikes, ground raids, and other covert activities in Pakistan have decimated al Qaeda's senior leadership, these operations have also inadvertently increased the Pakistani public's hatred of the United States, provoked terrorism on American soil and contributed to the dangerous destabilization of the Pakistani state.

U.S. Strategy in Pakistan in the Post-9/11 World

A year before leaving her post in Pakistan, Anne Patterson, former U.S. Ambassador to Islamabad, warned her superiors that while the "unilateral targeting of al-Qaeda operatives and assets" was important to countering terrorism, it also "risks destabilizing the Pakistani state, alienating both the civilian government and the military leadership, and provoking a broader governance crisis without finally achieving the goal."[2] Official unclassified U.S. government reports show that suicide operations, bombings, and other violent incidents—once limited to geographic areas bordering Afghanistan, including Balochistan, the Federally Administered Tribal Areas (FATA), and the North-West Frontier Province (NWFP)—have spread to major urban centers, such as Karachi, Peshawar, Lahore, and Islamabad.[3] War on Terror policies have made it politically unpopular—if not downright suicidal—for them to explicitly support U.S. counterterrorism policies. That predicament was captured in the waning years of General Pervez Musharraf's regime (1999-2008), and is presently on display under the weak, civilian-led leadership of President Asif Ali "Mr. 10%" Zardari (2008-present).[4] As the Ambassador alluded to, unilateral targeting is not a comprehensive policy. It does precious little to bring about a power-sharing arrangement in Afghanistan, or to address the low-intensity proxy war between arch-adversaries Pakistan and India. Whatever the precise number of militant or civilian fatalities, targeted operations produce mixed results across the board.[5]

The U.S. government's undeclared war in Pakistan has been a double-edged sword. On the one hand, targeted operations have been an effective instrument for targeting militants without large numbers of U.S. boots on the ground; on the other, targeted operations have also been fodder for radical worldviews and an inspiration for violent extremism.Indeed, the semi-secrecy of targeted operations alone has been an enduring challenge that has plagued Washington's post-9/11 relations with Islamabad.

The political fallout from the Raymond Davis affair is but one example. On January 27, 2011, Raymond Davis, a former U.S. Army Special Forces soldier, shot and killed two Pakistani citizens he claimed threatened him at gunpoint in that nation's second-largest city, Lahore. A U.S. Consulate vehicle summoned to help Davis then accidentally struck and killed a motorcyclist, speeding away from the scene. The incident quickly triggered a diplomatic crisis.

"With respect to Mr. Davis, our diplomat in Pakistan," U.S. President Barack Obama declared at a press conference on February 15. "We've got a very simple principle here, that every country in the world that is party to the Vienna Convention on Diplomatic Relations has upheld in the past and should uphold in the future, and that is, if our diplomats are in another country, then they are not subject to that country's local prosecution."[6] That same day, U.S. Senator John Kerry, Chairman of the Senate Committee on Foreign Relations, flew to Lahore to help secure Davis' release.[7]

As public anger spread throughout Pakistan, Davis' diplomatic cover became a matter of heated debate.[8] For many in Pakistan, the incident symbolized the impunity with which the U.S. government could operate inside their territory. When the story first broke, the notoriously conspiratorial Pakistani media alleged that Davis was affiliated with U.S. intelligence. These suspicions were stoked by equipment police confiscated from Davis' car, including an unlicensed pistol, a long-range radio, a GPS device, an infrared torch, and a camera with pictures of buildings around Lahore.[9] However, those reports seemed spurious amid coexisting claims in the Pakistani press that Davis was providing al Qaeda terrorists with "nuclear fissile material" and "biological agents" in order to "re-establish the West's hegemony" over South Asia.[10] But on February 20—a full 25 days after the shooting—the *Guardian*, a British publication, confirmed that the 36-year-old former special forces soldier was employed by the C.I.A.[11] On February 22, *ABC News* reported that "Davis first arrived in Pakistan in December, 2008, and was posted at various times in Islamabad, Lahore and Peshawar. Until last August, Davis was stationed in Pakistan, as an employee of the company once known as Blackwater, now called Xe Services, and contracted to the CIA."[12]

The Elephant in the Room is the Foreign Presence Next-Door

In early-August 2008, a colleague and I traveled to Pakistan. Our first night there, we met one of Karachi's high-powered businessmen, part of the country's new rising class of entrepreneurs. On a remote beach in the province of Sindh, we talked about the presence of foreign troops next door in Afghanistan. For millions of Americans, the operation in Afghanistan was a justifiable response to the atrocities of September 11. That perception was shared neither by our hosts nor by many within their government.

Whether in Peshawar, Lahore, or Karachi, almost everyone we spoke to believed that 9/11 was an inside job carried out between the United States and Israel, that the U/S/ government is fomenting instability along the "Af-Pak" border as a pretext to remain in Afghanistan and to sabotage China's influence in the Indian Ocean basin, and that the U.S. military presence in the region threatens their country more than al Qaeda or the Taliban. One widely held conspiracy theory holds that the United States and India want to seize Pakistan's nuclear weapons and dismember the country. Fear of partition is especially pervasive, in light of Pakistan's amputation in 1971 at the hands of India and Bengali separatists, a humiliating experience that came less than a quarter century after its bloody birth in 1947. Many people we met kept referring to 2015 as the year when New Delhi and Washington would succeed in splitting Pakistan's provinces. "America forced the break-up of the Soviet Union," was heard throughout the country, "so why not Pakistan?" Panic over Indian encirclement as a precursor to future conflict has intensified since 9/11. In recent years, deepening ties between India and Afghanistan have heightened this sense of encirclement.

People we spoke with were unanimous in their condemnation of U.S. government policies. One Western-educated federal judge we spoke to believed that Wasshington was trying to create what he called a "crescent of containment" that encircles China, contains Muslim countries, and protects petroleum resources. One prominent media commentator, whose television show is broadcast throughout the country, not only believes that regional militants were U.S. government proxies, but also that India is supporting Chinese-Muslim separatists and using its influence in Afghanistan to subvert Chinese influence. A former ISI official we spoke to (who praises the father of the Taliban, Hamid Gul, as "brilliant") alleges that India has infiltrated the Taliban and is funding insurgents in Pakistan's Balochistan province.

Of course, these fringe and unsubstantiated theories go on and on, and numerous polls in the country conducted by the Pew Research Center's "Global Attitudes Project" confirm the troubling levels of anti-American animosity we gleaned from our dozens of interviews. In fact, even before 9/11, the United States was suffering from a crisis of legitimacy, with favorable opinion of America polling at 23 percent in 1999/2000.[13] In 2002, following the 9/11 attacks, America's favorability rating fell to 10 percent and rose to a mere 13 percent in 2003. America's favorability hit its peak of 27 percent in 2006 when Washington contributed a large amount of aid following a massive earthquake in Pakistan. However, these numbers then dropped into the teens, and have remained there ever since. After the U.S. Navy SEAL operation that killed Osama bin Laden, nearly two-thirds (63 percent) of Pakistanis expressed disapproval of the raid, according to a poll released by the Pew Research Center. More than two-thirds (69 percent) said they think of the United States as more of an enemy.[14] In Washington, such beliefs are deemed absurd, and are therefore subsequently dismissed. But Pakistani viewpoints should be the starting point of the U.S. government's discussion about the future of militancy, as America is fighting both perceptions and reality.

"There is no doubt among intelligence officials," the *New York Times* reported in May 2010, "that the barrage of attacks by C.I.A. drones over the past year has made Pakistan's Taliban (which goes by the name *Tehrik-i-Taliban*) increasingly determined to seek revenge by finding any way possible to strike at the United States."[15] American officials believe that many post-9/11 militants—as compared to their pre-9/11 predecessors—are driven less by religion, and more by a sense of responsibility to the *ummah*, or global Muslim community.[16]

"They're killing Pashtuns," exclaimed an incensed Faisal Shahzad, a Pakistani immigrant who in 2010 pleaded guilty to trying to detonate an S.U.V. packed with explosives in Manhattan's Times Square. Among Shahzad's motives was the killing of Muslims by the U.S.-led drone campaign.[17]

America's Pakistan Policy

At the 2011 Aspen Security Forum, Michael E. Leiter, the former head of the National Counterterrorism Center, challenged assessments that claimed al-Qaeda was on the verge of collapse. The basis for his contention was Shahzad, who had been trained by the *Tehrik-i-Taliban*. But this conclusion, which epitomizes the U.S. government's tendency to overreact to terrorism, is troubling for what it implies. In Pakistan, the long-term success of counter-terrorism depends on the people's repudiation of extremism. Unfortunately, however, at his confirmation hearing before the Senate Intelligence Committee, Matthew Olsen, President Obama's choice to replace Mr. Leiter, said that he would define the strategic defeat of al Qaeda as "ending the threat that al-Qaeda and all of its affiliates pose to the United States and its interests around the world."

If—as senior American intelligence officials and Muslim-world scholars claim—jihadists of the post-9/11 variety are driven to commit acts of terrorism out of a sense of obligation to fellow Muslims, then America's strategy, tactics, and perceived objectives must all be reexamined. Even unwavering proponents of drone operations must stand back and recognize that bombing remote villages in nuclear-armed Pakistan serves to intensify the level of anti-American sentiment in the world's most volatile region. Because the virus of anti-American radicalism ripples beyond a county's borders, other post-9/11 policies—including the aggressive wars of occupation in Iraq and Afghanistan and the expanded drone campaigns in Somalia, Yemen, and Libya—also serve to reinforce the militant narrative that they are fighting for the *ummah* and against a greater injustice.[18]

Conclusion

For far too long, politicians and pundits have danced around the uncomfortable truth that the pervasive fears and anxieties exhibited by the Pakistani public provide, at best, passive acceptance and, at worst, popular backing of militant groups.[19] However, it is well past time for planners in Washington to thoroughly explore the notion that U.S. policies are inadvertently contributing to anti-American radicalization. Reining in the West's interventionist foreign policy will not eliminate the number of people and organizations that seek to commit terrorist attacks against the United States, but it will certainly diminish it.

---

[1] Peter Bergen and Katherine Tiedemann, "Washington's Phantom War: The Effects of the U.S. Drone Program In Pakistan," *Foreign Affairs,* July/August 2011.

[2] "U.S. Embassy Cables: The Documents," *The Guardian,* http://www.guardian.co.uk/world/us-embassy-cables-documents/226531.

[3] North-West Frontier Province (NWFP) was renamed Khyber Pakhtoonkhwa. It is referred to herein as "NWFP" for consistency. For U.S. government findings on violence in Pakistan, see: Office of the Coordinator for Counterterrorism, "Chapter 2. Country Reports: South and Central Asia Overview," *Country Reports on Terrorism 2010*, August 18, 2011, http://www.state.gov/s/ct/rls/crt/2010/170258.htm; Office of the Coordinator for Counterterrorism, "Chapter 2. Country Reports: South and Central Asia Overview," *Country Reports on Terrorism 2009,* August 5, 2010, http://www.state.gov/s/ct/rls/crt/2009/140887.htm; National Counterterrorism Center, *2010 Report on Terrorism,* April 30, 2011,

http://www.nctc.gov/witsbanner/docs/2010_report_on_terrorism.pdf.

[4] Following a November 2011 NATO airstrike that killed two dozen Pakistani soldiers, Pakistani streets and newspaper editorials were brimming with anti-American sentiment. That incident threatened to widen the gulf between Pakistan's senior military leadership and its junior officer corps, and make Islamabad's alliance with Washington even more of a liability. Salman Masood and Eric Schmitt, "Tensions Flare between U.S. and Pakistan After Strike," *New York Times,* November 26, 2011, http://www.nytimes.com/2011/11/27/world/asia/pakistan-says-nato-helicopters-kill-dozens-of-soldiers.htm; "Pakistan Protests Deadly NATO Attack,"*Reuters,* November 28, 2011, "JD Vows to Make Pakistan a Taliban State," *The Express Tribune,* November 30, 2011, http://tribune.com.pk/story/299747/lash-back-jd-vows-to-make-pakistan-a-taliban-state/.

[5] "This is the least indiscriminate, least inhumane tool we have," said C. Christine Fair, an expert on South Asia at Georgetown University. Her research shows that civilian casualties from drones are very low, but she cautions that the secrecy surrounding the program allows propaganda to thrive. See Scott Shane, "C.I.A. Is Disputed on Civilian Toll in Drone Strikes," *New York Times*, August 11, 2011, http://www.nytimes.com/2011/08/12/world/asia/12drones.html; and C. Christine Fair, "Drone Wars," *Foreign Policy,* May 28, 2010, http://www.foreignpolicy.com/articles/2010/05/28/drone_wars

[6] Laura Rozen, "John Kerry Visits Pakistan Amid Uproar Over Official," *Politico,* February 15, 2011, http://www.politico.com/news/stories/0211/49571.html.

[7] Jake Tapper and Lee Ferran, "President Barack Obama: Pakistan Should Honor Immunity for "Our Diplomat," *ABC News,* February 15, 2011, http://abcnews.go.com/Blotter/raymond-davis-case-president-barack-obama-urges-pakistan/story?id=12922282.

[8] Craig Murray, "This CIA Agent is No Diplomat," *the Guardian,* February 28, 2011, http://www.guardian.co.uk/commentisfree/cifamerica/2011/feb/28/cia-agent-diplomat-pakistan-raymond-davis?INTCMP=SRCH

[9] Declan Walsh and Ewan MacAskill, "American Who Sparked Diplomatic Crisis Over Lahore Shooting Was a CIA Spy," *the Guardian,* February 20, 2011, http://www.guardian.co.uk/world/2011/feb/20/us-raymond-davis-lahore-cia.

[10] Quiser Butt, "CIA Agent Davis Had Ties with Local Militants," *International Herald Tribune,* February 22, 2011, http://tribune.com.pk/story/122105/cia-agent-davis-had-ties-with-local-militants/.

[11] Walsh and MacAskill.

[12] Matthew Cole, "U.S. Fears for Life of Outed CIA Contractor in Pakistan Prison," *ABC News,* February 22, 2011, http://abcnews.go.com/Blotter/ray-davis-us-fears-life-outed-cia-contractor/story?id=12968878&nwltr=blotter_featureHed.

[13] Pew Research Center, "America's Image in the World: Findings from the Pew Global Attitudes Project," March 14, 2007, http://pewglobal.org/2007/03/14/americas-image-in-the-world-findings-from-the-pew-global-attitudes-project/.

[14] CNN Wire Staff, "Poll: Most Pakistanis Disapproved of U.S. Killing Bin Laden," June 21, 2011, http://articles.cnn.com/2011-06-21/world/pakistan.bin.laden.poll_1_pakistani-army-taliban-affiliated-pakistani-government?_s=PM:WORLD.

[15] Mark Mazzetti and Scott Shane, "Evidence Mounts for Taliban Role in Bomb Plot," *New York Times,* May 5, 2010, http://www.nytimes.com/2010/05/06/nyregion/06bomb.html?pagewanted=all.

[16] Andrea Elliot, "Militant's Path From Pakistan to Times Square," *New York Times,* June 22, 2010, http://www.nytimes.com/2010/06/23/world/23terror.html?pagewanted=all.

[17] *ibid.*

[18] Julian Barnes and Charles Levinson, "U.S. Drones Hit Targets in Libya," *Wall Street Journal,* April 25, 2011, http://online.wsj.com/article/SB10001424052748704489604576282703009692640.html.

[19] For more, see Daniel Byman, "Confronting Passive Sponsors of Terrorism," *Brookings Analysis Paper,* No. 4, February 2005, http://www.brookings.edu/fp/saban/analysis/byman20050201.pdf; and Jacob N. Shapiro and C. Christine Fair, "Why Support Islamist Militancy? Evidence from Pakistan," *International Security 34*, no. 3 (Winter 2009/10): 79-118, http://belfercenter.ksg.harvard.edu/publication/19922/why_pakistanis_support_islamist_militancy.html.

The War on Terror
Comes Home

Matthew Harwood

Matthew Harwood is a journalist working in Washington, D.C. His work has appeared at Alternet, Common Dreams, Columbia Journalism Review, Freedom Daily, The Guardian, Huffington Post, Reason, Truthout, *and* The Washington Monthly. *He holds an M.Litt in International Security Studies from the University of St. Andrews in Scotland, and is currently working on a book about evangelical Christian rhetoric and aggressive US foreign policy.*

> *And now you do what they told ya / Now you're under control*
> -   Rage Against the Machine

Peace is a concept with a morbid, ironic history.

Those who preach it rarely survive. States and thugs drive nails into their limbs, shoot bullets through their bodies and brains, and hang them like bloody ornaments from posts and trees.

But terror and state aggression isn't the only way to stop peace's procession.

When violence doesn't strike down those who protest in peace's name, the peacemakers are marginalized. The goal is normally achieved through misrepresentation. In the United States, the most oft-used caricature is that of the campus hippie, the unkempt buffoon with the straggly hair who exists in a haze of pot smoke, foolishly waving his two figures in the air, and regurgitating the platitudes of love. This is the image those who preach for peace encounter, not the heroic visage of Jesus or Martin Luther King Jr. or Ken Saro-Wiwa,[1] but that of Cheech & Chong.

The truth is that many people who promote peace have cauldrons of fire searing inside their guts. We are an angry lot. Angry that people can always be marshaled to man the trenches, storm the beaches, drop the bombs, and pilot the drones in a self-destructive program that eviscerates the life, liberty, and property that humans struggle to create during their short, often miserable, time on earth.

To count yourself anti-war, you only need to abide by two precepts:(1) your life is no more valuable than anyone else's; (2) absent a threat to your immediate safety, you mingle with this mass of humanity around you as peaceably as possible.

For the truth of these precepts to register only takes a bit of moral imagination. It's this bit of empathy that most Americans so sorely lack. Americans have been miseducated to ignore their government's bloody trail through Native America, Mexican America, the Caribbean, the Philippines, and—in the aftermath of World War II—Latin America and Eurasia. Most Americans remain loyal to the idea that the United States government is never

319

the aggressor: this city on the hill never starts the fight, its citizens merely finish it. Many scoff indignantly at words like those of MLK at Riverside Church, when he called the United States the "greatest purveyor of violence in the world today." Not much has changed since King uttered those words—indeed, American imperialism may have gotten worse.

Currently somewhere in the ballpark of 750 U.S. military bases[2] take up space across the world, tangible reminders of who's in charge of this small speck of water and terrain within the Milky Way. Imagine a vast military base full of intruders just down the road from your neighborhood WalMart. For even those Americans not obsessed with 2nd Amendment solutions, the mere idea of a foreign power's military presence on American shores would create a bloodlust. It isn't hard to imagine an American teenager's rite of passage becoming a night pegging rocks and lobbing Molotov cocktails at a foreign base, like something out of *Red Dawn*.

But our presence is much worse in places like Iraq and Afghanistan, where the American military actively flexes its muscle and erects massive military bases, setting down American government roots where they don't belong. Sometimes it's necessary to put on someone else's blood-soaked shoes and walk a few last dying steps to understand what American intervention has wrought, and what it would look like if it washed up on our shores. Here is a photo-negative tour of what the War on Terror is, *Twilight Zone*-style:

- Somewhere in Kabul, a drone pilot sees his target. The three-car convoy of militants speeds down I-95. It passes the Philadelphia Eagles' Lincoln Financial Field as a missile vaporizes it. But the convoy isn't full of militants, and the drone operator has just liquidated three cars full of weekend travelers unfortunate to be on the interstate at that time, mistaken for hostiles.[3] Shrapnel from the attack rips through a tailgating party outside the stadium. *Collateral damage.*

- In St. Louis, a car containing a man with his young son quickly approaches the Iraqi soldier manning a checkpoint. The soldier signals the car to stop. The driver ignores it. Fearing an attack, the soldier riddles the vehicle with bullets. The car slows to a stop, just yards away from the soldier. The soldier approaches the car and opens the door. The father, half his face gone, falls out of the driver's seat. What's left of his son decorates the back seat. The soldier, stricken with grief, says to himself, in a language we can't understand: "Why didn't they stop? Why didn't they stop?"[4]

- In New York City, a speeding convoy of Iraqi diplomats, surrounded by private military contractors, careens through the intersection of Broadway and 42nd Street. A private military contractor manning a turret watches, as a white Toyota Camry approaches and opens fire. His comrades join in. As the smoke clears and the casings come to a rest on the asphalt, 14 unarmed American theatre-goers lie dead in pools of blood, as the three people in the car are splattered across its interior.[5]

- A pack of adolescent boys goes down to the banks of the Green River to play. This can be a dangerous proposition with the Af-Pak military patrols in the area, hunting down Seattle guerrillas, who use the woods as a safe haven. Coming through the clearing towards a pool of water, the boys see the bloated corpses of four guerrillas bobbing face down in the water, shot execution-style.[6] Right there, three of the boys decide to take up arms when they get older, to repel the invaders. A new generation of young men has decided to fight and die, and continue the cycle of violence.

It wouldn't take many examples of these imperial indignities—which occur regularly in our wars (all wars)—to create massive pockets of resistance in an effort to once again liberate their territory, no matter their ideology, race, or religion. No doubt the invaders would see these militants as ultraviolent barbarians without the benefit of civilization, much like the American people see Afghans, Iraqis, Pakistanis, and Yemenis.

To understand the carnage of war means to imagine what it would look like on your street, in your town, across your country. It is the ability to look out across our vast oceans, and see people just like us who only want the opportunity to go about their lives in peace, find work that agrees with them, and protect their family.

Right now, this moral imagination is in short supply. And because of this, in many places around the world, the name of the United States is a nightmare. It is the noun that drops bombs and tears flesh and shatters backbones.

We are a country with a tremendous mythology of liberty and decency. It's time to make the soothing whispers we tell ourselves a reality, to exorcise the demons that deny us our principles—and others, their lives.

---

[1] Ed Pilkington, "14 years after Ken Saro-Wiwa's death, family points finger at Shell in court," *The Guardian*, 27 May 2009, Online: http://www.guardian.co.uk/business/2009/may/27/ken-saro-wiwa -shell-oil

[2] Chalmers Johnson, "737 U.S. Military Bases=Global Empire," *Alternet.org*, 19 February 2007, Online: http://www.alternet.org/story/47998

[3] David S. Cloud, "Anatomy of an Afghan war tragedy," *Los Angeles Times*, 10 April 2011, Online: http://www.latimes.com/news/nationworld/world/la-fg-afghanistan-drone-20110410,0,28 181 34, full.story

[4] David Harrison, "Wikileaks: Civilians gunned down," *The Telegraph*, 23 October 2010, Online: http://www.telegraph.co.uk/news/worldnews/middleeast/iraq/8082605/Wikileaks-Civilians-gunned-down-at-checkpoints.html

[5] David Johnston and David M. Broder, "F.B.I. Says Guards Killed 14 Iraqis Without Cause," *New York Times*, November 13, 2007. http://www.nytimes.com/2007/11/14/world/africa/14iht-14blackwater.8327313.html

[6] Abbie Boudreau and Scott Zamost, "Army tapes reveal motive in Iraq prisoner killings," *CNN.com*, 17 November 2009, Online: http://articles.cnn.com/2009-11-17/us/army.tapes. canal.killings _1_soldiers-18th-infantry-regiment-prisoners?_s=PM:US

Free at Last

Steve Kubby

*Steve Kubby is an avid skier and outdoors person. He is especially concerned
with healthcare issues, due to his own personal experience as a cancer survivor.
Thirty-eight years ago he was diagnosed with adrenal cancer and given six
months to live. Crediting medical marijuana, inner determination, and the love
and support of family and friends, Steve has become the first person to ever
survive so long with his form of cancer. Steve earned a B.A. degree from
California State University at Northridge in 1968 and holds a lifetime teaching
credential. He has also written two critically acclaimed books,* The Politics of
Consciousness *and* Why Marijuana Should Be Legal. *In 1970 he founded Earth
Camp One, featured in* National Geographic *and* Newsweek *for its innovative
and successful approach to child development. He also launched* Ski West
Magazine, *which became the top selling ski magazine in seven countries, before
it was sold. In 1996, Steve played a key role in the passage of Prop. 215, and
was subsequently asked to run for Governor on the Libertarian ticket. Although
massively outgunned by his wealthy opponents, the Kubby for Governor
Campaign received far more coverage than any previous third party campaign,
including national coverage on the* Bret Hume Show. *Steve's campaign brought
together many talented people and the campaign's TV commercial won top
awards. Steve currently serves as National Director for the American Medical
Marijuana Association, a national organization dedicated to protecting the
rights of seriously ill patients who use cannabis. He is also now heavily involved
in another California initiative, to* Regulate Marijuana Like Wine, *scheduled for
the 2012 ballot.*

I'm pleased to report that all charges against me have been dismissed and my
record has been expunged. I am a free man with a clean record. Yes, you read
that right, thanks to the incredible support of so many individuals, I not only
survived, I PREVAILED!

Because of those who cared enough to help me and my family, I survived an
indictment for 19 criminal counts, amounting to a minimum of 40-years-to-life
in prison. That indictment was backed by a $10 million grant by the U.S.
government to put me, and the medical marijuana revolution, behind bars.

For the crime of passing and then attempting to utilize a law that police,
prosecutors and judges all hate, I faced the wrath of the DEA, California
Attorney General, IRS, State of Nevada, Child Protective Services, Immigration
Canada, Royal Canadian Mounted Police, and Placer County DA.

You should know that I should be dead. That's what the doctors told me just
before my 28th birthday. I was diagnosed with terminal cancer, and told I had six
months to live. At first, I refused to believe it. I went and saw other doctors at

prestigious medical centers across the U.S. Everywhere it was the same, grim prognosis.

I tried the medications the doctors gave me, but they just made me sicker and took away my will to live. I had lost 60 pounds, I was rapidly losing my hair and I was in constant pain. Then I tried marijuana, and my health began to improve dramatically.

That was twenty years ago. Today I run several companies, publish one of the top magazines on the Internet, have authored two books on drug policy reform, and served a key role in qualifying a medical marijuana initiative for the California ballot. I still have cancer, but I'm living an active and productive life—all because of this extraordinary herb. I can tell you that just about everything you've been told about marijuana… is a lie.

Marijuana prohibition has forced us to pay a terrible price in pain and suffering, especially for those who are critically ill and might otherwise benefit from this unique herbal medicine. The drug warriors assure us that "marijuana has no medical uses." The truth is that as long as marijuana is illegal, all of us are being denied a valuable medicinal choice, which can provide to many non-toxic, long-lasting relief, and can even cure a host of common ailments.

Of all the reasons to legalize marijuana, none are more compelling than medical use. In 1988, the DEA's own Administrative Judge, Francis Young, found marijuana "the safest therapeutic substance known to man," and urged its reclassification and distribution for medical uses. That finding was totally ignored by the DEA and the U.S. Government. Even the U.S. Circuit of Appeals for the Distinct of Columbia has ruled that listing marijuana as a Schedule 1 drug (no medical use) is "illogical."

After years of suppression by governments, the truth about medical marijuana is finally coming out. As Dr. Tod Mikurya, a former director of marijuana research for the U.S. government, explained,

> "Marijuana has been scientifically shown to help patients with AIDS, cancer, glaucoma and chronic pain. There is also evidence that marijuana also functions as an immuno-modulator, helping patients with auto-immune diseases such as arthritis.... I was hired by the government to provide scientific evidence that marijuana was harmful. As I studied the subject, I began to realize that marijuana was once widely used as a safe and effective medicine. But the government had a different agenda and I had to resign."

Just as our health has suffered from marijuana prohibition, so has the health of the planet. In the 1930s, an unholy alliance of forest magnates, ex-Prohibition agents, chemical and industrial pharmaceutical companies used the public's fears (of drugs and for kids' safety) to outlaw not only marijuana, but also industrial hemp. The marijuana laws were used to replace natural hemp products and pharmaceuticals with high profit synthetic substitutes. Ironically, it was the prohibition against marijuana and hemp that created a far more deadly form of addiction—our addiction to petroleum and plastics. As a result our environment has become more toxic.

American farmers are frustrated that at a time when the family farm is vanishing, the U.S. government refuses to allow farmers to grow hemp, despite the fact that industrial hemp is currently grown legally in Europe, Asia, Australia and Canada. In contrast to the U.S. refusal to even consider industrial hemp cultivation, the European Union now offers subsidies to its hemp growers.

For the past 45 years, governments have waged an international war on marijuana. The drug warriors who promote this War on Pot talk about "getting tough on crime," yet studies have shown that getting tough on drugs has had the inevitable consequence of decreased policing of crimes unrelated to drugs. The War on Pot, it turns out, has not only failed to control marijuana consumption and has wasted billions of dollars each year, it has generated more violent crime by creating lucrative black markets, diverting law enforcement, and overwhelming prison resources. Here in the U.S., about half a million citizens are arrested for marijuana each year. This policy is clogging up the criminal justice system and resulting in the early release of thousands of violent criminals each year.

Politicians and law enforcement, corrupted by forfeitures and drug money, are perpetuating this War on Pot, depriving the sick of a valuable medicine, preventing farmers from growing this productive crop, jailing otherwise law-abiding citizens, promoting violent crime, wasting billions of dollars and harming the very freedoms they are sworn to protect. In addition, many innocent people are harmed in the crossfire of the Drug War and in turf battles.

U.S. citizens can lose everything they own if they are just accused of a marijuana crime. Eighty percent of the people whose assets are seized by the U.S. Government under drug laws are never formally charged with any crime. Many states now mandate a six-month driver's license suspension if citizens are convicted of possession of any amount of marijuana, even if it is nowhere near a car. The state can force convicted marijuana consumers to surrender custody of their children.

A number of states revoke professional licenses of convicted marijuana offenders. This affects not only doctors and lawyers, it also includes state-licensed plumbers, beauticians, educators, and so on. In some states, if an otherwise law-abiding citizen is arrested for possession of marijuana and has a loaded rifle in the home, he will be sentenced to a mandatory 5-year prison term just for possession of the rifle. This penalty is in addition to those that apply to the marijuana crime itself. The Internal Revenue Service may audit citizens, solely because they've been convicted of a marijuana offense. Many states have bogus taxes on pot, and assess fines against those convicted of marijuana crimes.

This is not what freedom is about. The time has come to abandon the failed policies of drug prohibition, beginning by repealing the repressive marijuana laws and returning this valuable plant, once again, back into service for all humanity.

In 1996, my friends and I wrote California Proposition 215, the Compassionate Use Act. It was intended to fully exempt medical marijuana patients from criminal prosecution. The Attorney General even said so when he wrote his official Title and Summary to Prop. 215 and told the voters in their

1996 Voter's Handbook: "*…Exempts patients and defined caregivers who possess or cultivate marijuana for medical treatment recommended by a physician from criminal laws which otherwise prohibit possession or cultivation of marijuana.*" Despite the proposition being passed by California voters, sick, disabled and dying patients throughout California are still being raided by SWAT teams, arrested, jailed, humiliated, treated like criminals, bankrupted, having their children abducted by Child Protective Services, and are made to be even sicker.

When a jury voted to convict me on a possession charge, involving a psilocybin mushroom stem and a few peyote buttons (a felony) found in our guest bedroom, I was sentenced to 120 days in jail.

In 2001, exercising my legal right to appeal the conviction for peyote possession, I obtained the court's permission to move to Canada with my wife and two children. My family and my legal advisors were concerned that hostile police and prosecutors were determined to prove their theory that I didn't really need medical marijuana, and would find a way to arrest and incarcerate me. The Kubby family had only been in Canada for a few months, when the terms of my appeal were changed (without my knowledge or consent) by two judges, who were recused from my case for bias, illegally making me a fugitive. Although I made every effort to resolve this legal fraud from Canada, I was asked to leave by the Canadian government and I complied.

Upon my voluntary return to the US, under a 30-day departure order (not deportation, as was widely reported), I was pulled off a plane and roughed up by heavily armed officers from Homeland Security, U.S. Immigration, and U.S. Customs.

Two days later I was in solitary confinement in cell number 420 (cops' humor, I suppose, but that really was my cell number), pissing blood, suffering horrible pain from my damaged kidneys, and cut off from the world. After years of relatively good health, I was now suddenly battling for my life. But people didn't forget me. Many came to the jail and shook the jail walls with their protests and billowing clouds of marijuana smoke. So many media showed up that the local paper complained of the "media circus." Hundreds of people showed up. Even my former wife, Rebecca Maidman, pitched in and raised several thousand dollars to purchase the Marinol (synthetic THC, legal but very expensive) that kept me alive through my ordeal.

Oh, how I wish you could have seen how they came to me and told me their phones were all tied up, "The medical complex can't do a thing because of the constant ringing of phones! The entire jail complex is on HIGH ALERT, because we have no phone communications! Worst of all, there was marijuana smoke in the prison ventilation system!"

Yes, I wish you could have seen their faces when they came and told me that the San Francisco Board of Supervisors had passed a resolution calling for me to be released immediately. Truly, they looked like deer caught in the headlights. (Actually, these were all big deputies, so it was more like hippos!)

Most of all, I wish you could have seen Placer County Sheriff Ed Bonner, coming to visit me in jail and greeting me with a big smile and a warm handshake. Bonner told me straight up that he thought medical marijuana was a fraud, but now he knows it is real, and that law enforcement is going to have to obey the new law.

It's sad that anyone should have to go through something like this, especially when someone has followed the rules and changed the law. However, as Dennis Peron, the true author and driving spirit behind Prop. 215, recently told me, "It is our suffering that changes the world."

To which I can only add, "It is individuals, supporting those of us on the front lines, who make real change possible!"

Bhutan: A Struggle for Human Rights and Democratic Reforms

Tek Nath Rizal

Tek Nath Rizal is the Chairman of the Bhutanese Movement steering committee and a political and human rights activist in Bhutan. He was imprisoned by the government of Bhutan from 1989 to 1999 at the Chamgang jail after protesting against the Bhutanese government's approach to the Bhutanese refugee problem. According to Amnesty International, he was held by Bhutan "for the peaceful expression of his political beliefs, in particular his campaign against government policies unfairly affecting members of the Nepali-speaking community in southern Bhutan." He was sentenced in 1993 to life imprisonment. Rizal was released from prison during an amnesty granted by the king in December 1999. He attributed his release to the efforts of activists from around the world who pressed for his release. He is the author of Torture - Killing Me Softly *(available as a free download on* www.teknathrizal.com*), as well as* From Palace to Prison *and* Ethnic Cleansing and Political Repression in Bhutan.*

1. Introduction

Bhutan is a small landlocked mountainous kingdom of about 38,400 square kilometers in an area on the southeastern part of the great Himalayan range. It is bordered by the Tibetan Autonomous Region of China to the north and by India on its three sides to the south, east and west, with open borders and free access for the Bhutanese people into the Indian territories. The present population is around 700,000[1] which has suddenly decreased from the official figure of one million when Bhutan joined the United Nations back in 1971. Further decreases in the population have been due to the mass evictions of the Southern Bhutanese and the forced exile of the many Eastern Bhutanese. The country was isolated until 1960, and thus its history is rather vague, caused by both illiteracy in the country and the fact that hardly any historian is writing independently about Bhutan. Most writing has been dependent entirely on the government version of events, in which the ruling elites have been portrayed in greater glory. Thus, the country's early history hardly mentions its southern and eastern regions, and has no substantial record, especially about the first half of the twentieth century.

Bhutan has three main ethnic groups: the *Ngalongs,*[2] the *Sharchhokpas*[3] and the *Lhotsampas.*[4] The Ngalongs form the ruling group with the monarchy, as well as most of the senior government officials who have also dominated the economy since the early seventies; they inhabit the northwest region of the country. They are primarily of Tibetan ancestry, speak *Dzongkha*[5] and follow the *Drukpa Kargyupa*[6] sect of Mahayana Buddhism. The Sharchhokpas in the eastern and central region are mostly of Tibeto-Burman ancestry; they speak *Tshangla*[7] and follow the *Nyingmapa*[8] sect of Mahayana Buddhism. Lhotsampas (literally, "inhabitants of the south") are the Nepali-speaking people restricted by law to live in the foothills and lower-middle Himalayas of southern Bhutan. From the Anglo-Bhutan War of 1864 until the 1950s, the Lhotsampas, mainly Hindus, were responsible for guarding the Indo-Bhutan frontiers..

In addition to these three dominant groups, there are a dozen of other smaller ethnic groups, who are believed to be the indigenous tribes of Bhutan. They include the Khengs, Brokpas, Mangdepas, Kurteopas, Doyas, Totos, Adivasis and Lepchas. The Tibetan refugees who arrived in Bhutan in the fifties and early sixties were naturalized in the late sixties and early seventies, and have commingled mostly with the Ngalongs. Those Tibetans who chose to retain their identity were all evicted by the end of the seventies and early eighties, after the attempted coup by the supporters of the Tibetan mistress of the third king, on behalf of her son during the coronation of the fourth king in June, 1974. All Tibetans living in Bhutan had then become targets of the regime's indignation.

The three main ethnic groups had migrated to Bhutan at different points in time before the turn of the 19th century, with a small trickle from the north and the west even in the first half of the 20th century. For this reason, Bhutan has often been called a country of immigrants. For centuries, the people of these different groups lived in harmony and cooperation. Religious tolerance and compromise have been the hallmarks of the Bhutanese society despite the autocratic feudal rule, which began to sow the seeds of racism among the ethnic groups and discrimination in the late seventies. This resulted in political turmoil in the late eighties and nineties, and culminated in a mass exodus of Lhotsampas. The persecution of Sharchokpas has led to the exile of several of the active leaders and a few thousand people now living in refugee camps or scattered in the Indian states of Meghalaya, Arunachal Pradesh and Assam.

2. Political Entity and Systems

Bhutan (*Druk Yul*[9]) was established as a nation by Ngawang Namgyal, the religious leader of the Drukpa Kagyupa sect of Buddhism. Popularly called the Shardrung, he unified the tribal chieftains who by 1637 ruled each valley as a separate entity, and established the theocratic rule while also teaching them the rudiments of Tantric Mahayana Buddhism. Shabdrung had fled the Druk Ralung Monastery in Tibetalong with his followers in 1616, escaping religious persecution by other sects of Tibetan Buddhism (especially the Gelugpa Sect). He traveled south to Lho-Mon and named it *Druk Yul*. Under his theocratic leadership, Shabdrung ruled Bhutan as the Dharma Raja, and selected the Deb Raja to support the temporal affairs of the state.

This theocracy continued until 1907, when it was replaced by the hereditary monarchy after the Tongsa *Penlop*,[10] Ugyen Wangchuck, established his supremacy over all other chieftains and abolished the theocracy. In place of the Shabdrung, the monarch would select the senior-most monk in the monastery, who had absolute allegiance to the monarchy to head the monk body as the chief abbot (called *Je Khenpo*) responsible for all religious matters. King Ugyen was recognized as the head of the state by the British ruling over South Asia, the King of Nepal and the Chogyal (king) of Sikkim.

For over a hundred years, four hereditary monarchs have ruled Bhutan with an iron fist, crushing any anti-monarchy factions or people's movement for greater freedom. It was only in 2008, after a hundred years of feudal oligarchy, that the fourth king, Jigme Singye Wangchuck, abdicated the dragon throne in favor of his son, to prevent any family feud among his sons and their cousins over succession issues if he were to pass away while in office. Thus he ensured the hereditary throne for his eldest son by his second wife. In addition, the fourth king shrugged off taking responsibility for his role in making refugees of almost one-seventh of the population of the country.

It may be recalled that ever since the monarchy took over the reins of the country with its establishment in 1907, the country has faced several intrigues opposing this autocratic feudal monarchy that chose to treat the citizens as serfs or mere subjects. These feuds include the conspiracies and assassinations of the various incarnations of the religious leader Shabdrung Nagawang Namgyal in the twenties and forties. Shabdrung had been the theocratic leader who unified Bhutan in the seventeenth century, until the established dual rule in Bhutan was usurped to establish the Wangchuck dynasty in 1907. In the early fifties, the Lhotsampas established the Bhutan National Congress to demand equal rights and democratic reforms in Bhutan after India's independence. This led to the establishment of the National Assembly in Bhutan, and opened doors to modern development.

In the sixties, when the plot to assassinate the child-incarnate of Shabdrung was being hatched, the then-representative of India in Bhutan, Nari Rustomji, whisked him out of the country to Shillong in Meghalaya, then to Delhi and finally into Himachal Pradesh. However, he was murdered after the regime's agents poisoned him in Pedong in West Bengal, and he passed away at Velore in 2005 under mysterious circumstances. (All descendants of Shabdrung are more revered by the common people than the kings, and thus have been targeted for assassination, even as children.) The assassination of the first Prime Minister, Jigmie Dorji, by the king's relatives in 1964 threw the country in turmoil, which also saw the exiling of several leaders and supporters of the prime minister. The 1974 episode culminated in the eviction of Tibetan refugees, who had been given asylum in Bhutan after leaving Tibet when the Chinese had annexed Tibet under the communist regime in 1959. Thus, Bhutan has faced intrigues several times and each time any dissention has been ruthlessly trampled and most of the Bhutanese have always been suppressed—except the privileged Ngalongs—the ruling class of the country.

2.1 From Absolute Monarchy toward Democratic Institutions

Bhutan has come a long way from the absolute monarchy established under the powerful chieftainship of Ugyen Wangchuck with the support of British India to the present system of purported democracy. Jigme Thinley, the former king's most trusted man for more than three decades, is the country's first elected Prime Minister. He defeated his rival, the present king's maternal uncle, Sangay Ngedup Dorji, in an uneven political playing field; the two political parties with the blessings of the king are basically the chessboard game of the two families.

The first and second monarchies prior to 1952 witnessed a primitive form of governance: a handful of officers at the helms of what can be called administration; a hierarchical monk-body and officials at each district, under a *Dzong*[11] called *Dzongpon*[12], to administer the country by word of mouth laws; and the southern frontiers, being governed by *dewans*[13] with *muktihars*[14] and *mandals*[15] appointed by the hereditary office of the *Gylakhap Kutshap*[16] in Kalimpong. Kaji Ugyen Dorji, the first Gylakhap Kutshap, was succeeded by his son, Raja ST Dorji, who was married to the Princess Chunni of Sikkim. Raja ST Dorji married his daughter Kesang Choeden Wangmo to Prince Jigme Dorji Wangchuck of Bhutan, who ascended the throne in 1952 as the third dragon king. Together with his well-educated brother-in-law, Jigmie Palden Dorji (who succeeded his father Raja ST Dorji as the Gyalpoi Kutshap), they began to modernize Bhutan, starting with the administrative system and educating of the people. Even before the relationship and ascendancy to the throne, the royal house of Sikkim and the Dorjis influenced the royals of Bhutan, enabling modern education with British tutors and exposure to British India and the outside world for Prince Jigme Dorji Wangchuck, his half-brother Namgyal Wangchuck and their sisters and cousin.

When Jigme Dorji Wangchuck ascended the dragon throne as the third king, Jigmie Palden Dorji with his modern education joined the administration as his advisor and close confidant. In 1952, King Jigme Dorji Wangchuck established the National Assembly of Bhutan, with representatives from all over the country. That was the first time the public from Southern Bhutan had been initiated into the national mainstream of Bhutan to participate in the state's affairs.

The king was a visionary, and has rightly been called the Father of Modern Bhutan. In his early years, he toured some of the southern districts with his trusted aides, interacting with the local people. Through these closer interactions, he realized the potential of the southern subjects, and thus gave final shape to his visions by opening the country from its long era of isolation. In 1958, he abolished serfdom and enacted the first Citizenship Law, whereby all the people who could show ten years of residence in the country and ownership of land were granted Bhutanese citizenship.

This was a remarkable step in bringing all the people within the political boundary of Bhutan into the mainstream of national development, in addition to getting representation from all corners of the country in the National Assembly. The king named Jigmie Palden Dorji the first Prime Minister of the country, and rapidly embarked on modernization of the government and the country as a whole. He established an amicable relationship with the newly Independent Indian—especially Prime Minister Nehru, who took a keen interest in the development of the country by visiting Bhutan in 1957 and helping Bhutan launch its first Five Year Plan in 1961, with most of the funding coming from India.

The door of the isolated dragon kingdom was thrown open with the beginning of the construction of two national highways—one in the east from Samdrup Jongkhar to Tashigangand, the other in the west, as the gateway to the country's capital Thimphu from Phuntsholing. Realizing the importance of education, health and infrastructure, efforts were made to open new schools, recruit teachers, medical workers and professionals (doctors and engineers) from India to convert Bhutan into a vibrant developing country. Recognizing the multi-ethnic characteristic of the country, efforts were made to provide scholarships to all Bhutanese to study in India and abroad for building its human resource base. Thus the visionary King and his Prime Minister were able to sow the seeds of modern Bhutan among its professionals who comprised a large fraction from Southern Bhutan. The proximity to India and the influence of relatives and friends across the border had enabled the Lhotsampas to obtain education across the border mainly in the adjoining district of Darjeeling, which was the main education hub—not only for Bhutan, but Nepal, Sikkim, other parts of West Bengal and northeast India, as well as Thailand and Malaysia. The office of the former Gyalpoi Kutshap, known as Bhutan House, acted as a liaison office for providing scholarships in Indian schools and colleges of West Bengal especially Darjeeling districts. Some were even sent to other parts of India for higher education, after which they were directly recruited as officials in the administration.

Unfortunately, this rapid pace of development of the country threatened the traditionalists, and the main advisor of the King, PM Dorji, was assassinated in an unprecedented turn of events. It is believed that this horrendous act was the conspiracy of the king's brother, Namgyal, who was getting over-shadowed in the affairs of the state by the Prime Minister. In addition, the brothers of the Prime Minister with education from India and exposure to the outside world had taken over the country's commerce and gained prominence. Thus, Namgyal conspired to get rid of the PM Dorji such that he would be able to consolidate the affairs of the state and its commerce more for the Wangchuck family and thus sideline the more popular Dorjis especially in Southern Bhutan. The PM JP Dorji was known as the *Kumar Saheb*[17] and was very popular with the Lhotsampas. It may have been his closeness to the Lhotsampas that caused the jealousy as he was personally responsible for educating many Lhotsampa officials and professionals who were given influential positions in the government.

Despite the setback by the assassination of the PM at the hand of his own close confidants, the visionary king went ahead with his modernization such that the development issue took centre stage and the king established the Cabinet of Ministers, the Royal Advisory Council, and introduced the system of electing village chiefs by the people, in a popular one-family-one vote, to find candidates suitable to carry out the affairs of the state at the grass-roots levels. These activities included collection of taxes, meting out local justice at the village level, conscripting a national laborer force, assisting developmental activities in the village (water-supply, malaria eradication, primary education) and a host of other infrastructure-development activities.

The opening of the country and the building of roads opened the southern district to the north, as well as making the northerners realize the presence of almost half of the population in the south, who could equally contribute to the national building process that had begun with the third monarch. The national infrastructure projects, mainly the seat of government at Thimphu and the two national highways, were made with the national workforce, with technical and financial assistance of the Indian Military Engineering Services. Joining the United Nations in 1971 paved the way for greater development well into the times of the fourth monarch who took over the reins of the government after the sudden and suspicious demise of his father during a hunting safari in Nairobi. As a regent of the young king, Prince Namgyal Wangchuck carried on the work of his brother until he handed over the responsibilities to the king in 1974 while he himself remained as the most influential minister in the cabinet and also had recruited the kings' two elder sisters into the Cabinet as the king's representatives in key ministries of Finance and Development.

Thus the third monarch's reign saw the devolving of the administration, from absolute monarchy toward a more constitutional form, with a written law called the *Trimsung Chenpo* and two elected bodies (the National Assembly and the Royal Advisory Council), although there was demographic non-representation with respect to the Lhotsampas. Other changes included a Cabinet of Ministers, decentralized government with development activities at the district level, and other social amenities to the public with a stress on improving health and education in the country. In becoming a member of the United Nations, Bhutan was enabled to be a part of the international development agenda, and began to receive not only bilateral assistance from India but also multilateral assistance from various other developed countries.

In the national polity, the most remarkable initiative has been the vote of confidence introduced in the National Assembly for the King himself every three years; the first vote was conducted with one vote against the monarch. Due to his opening of country doors to a modern era with various democratic reforms, King Jigme Dorji is regarded as the Father of Modern Bhutan. However, the king passed away mysteriously at a young age, without seeing his dreams fulfilled. Truly, 37 years after his demise the foundation he laid has finally given rise to an elected government, though more as an outward fashion. Perhaps Bhutan would have seen true democracy much earlier without the trauma of evictions, had the country not lost its charismatic king in 1972.

3. Centralization of Power

The Golden Era of modern Bhutan under the third monarch ended with his untimely mysterious demise. The regent and the young king began introducing measures to consolidate power under the monarchy, with the introduction of greater roles for the royal family members, and greater concentration of commerce under the immediate family members of the Wangchucks. The regime under the monarch (and in the shadow of his uncle) enacted one draconian law after another, with the "approval" of the majority in the Cabinet, which basically consisted of the ruling elites.

The power-broker uncle and the fourth king had the triennial Vote of Confidence on the king's leadership removed from the National Assembly's hands. As the new king grew more mature, the first new draconian law was the Marriage Act of 1980, which placed restrictions on Bhutanese who married foreign spouses, and was made effective retroactive to 1977. In 1980, to centralize the country vertically, he abolished the office of the Southern Commissioner at Sarbhang, realigned and renamed the southern districts and converted the country into four zones, each assigned to a Zonal Administrator from among his chosen ones, thus complicating the otherwise decentralized district level administration. In the same year, he passed the Land Act of 1980, placing a ceiling on the size of landholdings to 25 acres of land. which was strictly implemented in the southern districts. This curtailed the agricultural activities of the Lhotsampas subsistence-farmers, as the land =-ceiling included orchards and grasslands for cattle. The land survey that followed made a large part of the already cultivable land illegal for the subsistence farmers. (Meanwhile, in the western districts, the ruling elites and the rich relatives even placed land holdings in the names of their pets, to keep the 25-acre limit in place.)

The Green Belt Policy was adopted in 1984, ostensibly to create a green animal corridor one kilometer wide on both sides along the Indo-Bhutan border. It was in reality a clever but obvious ploy to confiscate prime cultivable land from the farmers, and hand it over to the forest, ultimately to be distributed to those the king favored. This Green Belt would never have been implemented from the Indian side (already lush green with tea gardens), but the regime would have succeeded in displacing a sizeable population of the south. However, this unilateral policy, aimed at displacing the Lhotsampas, proved a fiasco; the final straw was the Citizenship Act of 1985, which disqualified all the provisions in the previous Acts and made it retroactive to 1958, without any basis. Thus, with its implementation as a third-degree strategy for displacing the Lhotsampas, the King selected individuals for census teams, mentoring them through the office of the Deputy Home Minister Dago Tshering, a radically racist individual, while another racist official, Dorji Tenzing, headed the Department of Immigration and Census, to implement his depopulation strategies.

This was coupled with the land survey, which was meant to "correct" the previous survey geodetically, so that all excess land resulting from the (accurate) land survey, as well as the land holdings of anyone with more than 25 acres, was confiscated. In cases when no tax receipts were available for the land tilled, the survey teams confiscated the land, making hundreds of families landless. Thus, the centralization of power, by the king and his close relatives who stood to benefit, finally culminated in his legalizing his relationship to four sisters, who by 1988 had borne him seven children out of wedlock. This legalization and consolidation of his family rule continued until his abdication in 2008. He had proved himself incapable of resolving the crisis he had created by evicting over a hundred thousand Lhotsampas through his Reign of Terror in the late eighties and early nineties, with the implementation of several royal family welfare policies.

4.   In the Service of the Nation

It was during the late sixties that I began my journey into the administrative and developmental corridors of Bhutanese oligarchy, during the reformative years of Bhutan's rapid move toward modern development under the compassionate monarch, King Jigme Dorji Wangchuck. Twenty-seven years later, all my services to the nation in various capacities abruptly ended under the regime of the fourth monarch, who became utterly disillusioned and turned racist in his efforts to protect his large family interests. He danced to the tune of corrupt members of his family in the government service, and of the other inept bureaucrats who also brought him largesse as shares of spoils from their own fraudulent practices. Thus, the man who had once considered me his best public representative, for bringing to light the misuse of state resources by the oligarchy and its sycophants, chose to throw my contribution to the development and well-being of the country and its people out the back door, as he embraced the powerful corrupt oligarchy to save the vast wealth amassed with their help. And I, in my patriotic zeal to the nation, now found myself rendered an unrecognized refugee, one who has not as yet been granted refugee status by the international refugee agency, even after seven years.

My contribution to the developmental activities of my country began with my first summons to the capital city from my home in Lamidara, Chirang in order to supervise the renovation of the Tashichho Dzong, the national secretariat at Thimphu. It was being renovated with the contribution of manpower from all the districts of Bhutan. Volunteers came in turn from various parts of the country, and encamped in the valley of Thimphu to contribute to the country's development, without even receiving the wages and other basic amenities paid to any worker under international conventions.

Upon my arrival, I came to understand the pathetic working conditions of the laborers being engaged, and strove hard to improve their living conditions. Once the work was done, I headed back to the districts, and engaged in various activities leading to the building of the infrastructure of the country. As a Labor Officer, I was instrumental in recruiting a National Work Force (NWF) for Bhutan, for meeting the needs of various infrastructure projects within the country.

4.1 Public Representative and Development Activities

While serving the government of Bhutan, in various capacities and in a large number of developmental activities, I was also engaged in various social/communal and religious activities. This enabled me to get elected as a Member of National Assembly (MNA) from Lamidara in 1977, which I served for two terms. During my tenure as a MNA, I worked with fellow MNAs to bring about several pieces of legislation in Bhutan, all aimed at making the country more self-reliant in the comity of nations. Some of the main ones were:

1. The introduction of citizenship identity cards for all Bhutanese, enabling each individual to have valid proof of nationality. This was widely carried out in a national census; photographs were taken, and later identity cards were issued to all citizens.
2. A cadastral survey of the land, by which each family with ownership of land could have documented evidence of land holdings.
3. The introduction of a national integration program, by which students from northern schools were encouraged to study in southern Bhutan, while the Lhotsampas students were taken to northern or eastern Bhutan, enabling them a better understanding of the culture and traditions of other ethnic groups, and thus moving toward national integration.
4. An increase of trade and commerce with Bangla Desh, for the export of agricultural products fruits and forest produce in exchange for precious hard currency.
5. A decentralization of public works, along with other infrastructure and engineering activities to the district level, with community involvement for greater effectiveness.
6. The establishment of Community Development programs, headed by community leaders at the village level.
7. The initiation of the Department of Civil Aviation and the expansion of the Druk Air services outside India.
8. The establishment of the Royal Civil Service Commission from the erstwhile Manpower Department.
9. The establishment of higher centers of learning within Bhutan (instead of having to depend on outside institutions).
10. The abolition of free labor to the military camps in southwestern Bhutan by the people of Samchi district.

Based on my work as a NMA and contribution to the national mainstream, in 1981 the people of the Chirang and Samchi districts selected me to represent them in the Royal Advisory Council (RAC). As a representative of the people, I brought forth several pieces of legislation, for the benefit of all the Bhutanese. However, some of the legislation passed by the majority in the cabinet were aimed at depopulating the south. Despite my protest against such measures, the issues were not debated in the National Assembly, but were passed and implemented clandestinely by the Cabinet. Among them, as mentioned before, the Marriage Act of 1977, the Citizenship Act 1985, Green Belt Policy and Implementation of the Cadastral Survey (with the aim of reducing land holdings) are worth noting, as they were all aimed mainly against the Lhotsampas.

In 1982, upon becoming the Royal Advisory Councillor for the two districts of Samchi and Chirang, I was assigned duties directly under the cabinet as a member. Also as a member of the Royal Civil Service Commission, I was also assigned the responsibility for heading the newly formulated National Investigation Bureau (NIB). NIB was especially designed to unearth all the cases of embezzlement of developmental funds at the district level, especially by district officers (Dzongdas) and their deputies in collusion with district engineers and central government officials.

4.2 Bridging the Gap between the King and the People

As a member of the National Assembly, it was mandatory for most of the members to work for the government as civil servants, due to the acute shortage of manpower. The work was mainly in coordination with the Dzongdas and other administrative officials in each district and sub-division. The main activities were the development of public amenities (construction of schools, dispensaries, hospitals and agricultural centers in the rural areas), and thus all members were fulfilling an important task of bridging the gap between the King and the people.

In the course of working in rural areas on development projects, I realized that along with the development of infrastructure, human resource development was a key factor in the country's modernization and thus the administrative system needed modernization. Hence the first step was the institutionalization of the Royal Civil Service Commission, to enable the educated and qualified people to play a vital role. As time went by, the country witnessed the beginning of the Druk Air Corporation, formulations of the plan for National Workforce and implementation of family planning and mother-child welfare.

4.3 Community Development and its Impact

In 1982, I was sent by the king to Australia to learn English as well as understand the process of how the country had developed. That was a great opportunity for me to learn the process how a country—a land of immigrants—was managing its affairs while moving toward the development process; this made it one of most advanced countries with a flourishing economy, yet a comparatively small population. It was in Australia during my English courses that I was able to learn about community development systems under a community leader.

Upon my return, I introduced the system in Lamidara, the sub-division I represented as National Assembly Member, as our version of Community Representative System or "*Samaj Pati Pratha.*" This proved to be a success, and was later coined by the name *Gewog Tshogpa* (Block Representative System) for each block now in practice. This system became instrumental in many developmental activities at the village level, although it was misused by the district officials, to implement their own agenda of conscripting forced labor for the government activities.

This was evidenced by the *Gongda Woola* (forced free labor) recruitment and the *Chunidom* system, in which each family was required to contribute one month free labor, with nothing in return. Earlier in the sixties and seventies, people of Samchi district had been required to carry military supplies to the military bases at Pathibhara and Kupuk area on the northwest border between Sikkim and Tibet (China), where a small garrison of Bhutanese military was stationed. The place was accessible on foot or by mules only, although it is a well-known fact that all Bhutanese military supply and transport was paid by the

Indian military budget.

5. (National) Census in Southern Bhutan

Bhutan is a small country, and all senior officials above the level of deputy director or the sub-divisional officer are selected by the King, and thus known to him and all the ministers. Similarly, both a *Dzongda* (district officer) and a *Thrimpon* (district magistrate) know all the village heads and their assistants, as it is just a handful of people. Similarly, a National Assembly Member knows each family in his constituency; hence, each officer assigned for administration at the *Dungkhag* (sub-district) level knows almost all the households under his/her sphere of work. Knowing that all Lhotsampas were genuine citizens under the 1958 Citizenship Act, and that they also fell under the Citizenship Act of 1985 (except for the non-Bhutanese spouses married to Bhutanese men and women), the Census enumeration exercise was implemented in a hush-hush manner. The arrangements were also made in a typically racist manner, with only Northerners involved in the census teams, without involving the village headmen and elders or the Gewog Tshogpas in providing information. It may be recalled that the Citizenship Act of 1985 required people to prove their existence in Bhutan prior to 1958 with tax receipts only, and that any non-national married into the family after 1958 was declared illegal, despite the fact that they had been recognized and issued citizenship identity cards after the 1978 Census exercise and the making of identity cards. Despite this fact, the royal regime began to implement the Census in southern Bhutan, with ulterior motives and in a grossly inhumane manner, as the selected and trained teams proceeded to harass the public. The following sections will portray how the census exercise became the tool for the King, and his coterie's design for uprooting a large fraction of elite Lhotsampas, thereby decreasing the demographic balance to enable the ruler to continue its oppressive rule in the south.

5.1 The King's Designs to Uproot People

Bhutan had never revealed its true population to the world, once it had given the fictitious figure of about one million in 1971, when it joined the United Nations. That figure was based on the advice of India (Foreign policy advisor per the Indo-Bhutan Friendship Treaty of 1949), and was designed to help Bhutan get more assistance based on its more than double-counted population. The other possible aim in the early seventies was to increase its population to that level, if India managed to make it another state after Sikkim. So the actual figure was classified information, never known by the public but remaining within the close confidants of the ruler.

Thus when the king and his coterie led by Namgyal Wangchuck realized that the Lhotsampa population was about to become more than 50 percent of all Bhutan, the conspiracy to decrease the Lhotsampas was hatched. In addition, the literacy level among the Lhotsampas was higher, which was a concern to the royalists; with the winds of change blowing from eastern Europe and the Soviet

Union, it would be only a matter of a few years Bhutan would have to transition to a democracy. When this happened, the nation's rule would surely fall into the hands of the Lhotsampas.

Already, at the technical level, the Lhotsampas had become a dominating force in the country. Those in the fertile lands in the southern foothills were adopting modern farming methods and orchards, making the Lhotsampas economically better off. Greed and envy overwhelmed the regime, which could not digest the idea of southern Bhutan becoming agriculturally self-reliant. Thus, the king and his coterie conspired to thwart this possible democratic threat to their feudal survival from a larger ethnic group.

The king knew very well that the only way to tilt the demographic balance was to depopulate southern Bhutan by uprooting the people, despite their firm roots in terms of citizenship, landholdings and literacy-level. The first attempt was the hypocritically ill-conceived Green Belt Policy, in collusion with India, for an animal corridor. This policy would have evacuated thousands of Lhotsampas from the one-kilometer belt of prime land on the foothills, but it seemed to impact all the literates and even some Northerners who had made home in the south. So the next step of census exercise was designed to hit the Achilles' heel, for which sufficient background checks were done. The teams were instructed to be radical and even racist in executing their duties, and give utmost harassment, especially to the vulnerable and the least capable of defending themselves.

5.2 The Beginning of Oppressions

As envisaged by the regime, the deployed teams began the execution of the census with ruthlessness and extreme impunity. Those people who failed to produce any evidence (in the form of tax receipts from 1958) of their legitimate residency were declared illegal and forced to leave the country. It might be known that in 1958, the literacy level of the people was barely 10 percent, and many families had never kept the tax receipts safely. Some had kept them in bamboo containers, others in glass bottles; many others had been lost to the weathering effects of thatched huts, or destroyed in fire or by insects.

In addition, there were people with edicts of grant of land (from the then-*Gyalpoi Kutshap* in Kalimpong, or by Paro Penlop), which were confiscated and declared invalid documents. Often, marriages had occurred between various districts and settlements. The individuals or families who had resettled in one district from another were ordered to get a Certificate of Origin (CO) from that district's census team or the administrator; these requests were most often delayed or even denied. There was no question of entertaining any spouse married from India or Nepal, who were summarily declared non-national even if they had been granted citizenship identity cards. These documents were confiscated by the teams.

Many families were told to separate from the spouse from outside Bhutan, or forced to leave the country. Under this repression, when forced to leave her family and the country, one woman in Lamidara committed suicide . When these oppressive measures of census enumeration were in full swing, simple village folks and even village headmen began to seek the help of the elites: National Assembly Members (NAM) and Royal Advisory Councillors (RAC). The village folk realized that unless they appealed through the relevant authorities, they would be made stateless by the census team. In such a scenario, many people rushed to the capital, seeking the help of their own village elites and public representatives to voice their grievances. When they complained to the village heads (or *Mandals*) of their plight, they were advised to seek help of the NAM or RAC, or even their own elite relatives in the corridors of the government.

5.3 My Appeals to the King for Basic Rights

There were two of us, Bidhypati Bhandari and me, elected by the Lhotsampas as Royal Advisory Councillors and given position as members of Cabinet. I was engaged in the National Investigation Bureau, under direct orders of the king. The village folks, *Mandals* and NA Members began to stream to Thimphu, bringing their petitions directly to me and my colleague. Some villagers came with their elite relatives or officers to complain of the excesses of the census teams.

More than a thousand petitions came to me, to help redress the distresses and the oppressive measures of the census exercise. We decided to consult with senior Lhotsampa officials like Minister Om Pradhan, Secretary LB Gurung, Directors RB Basnet, Meghraj Gurung and Bhim Subba, Judges DN Katwal, Dawa Sherpa, KB Ghaley and many others. We convened several meetings, and it was decided that I should seek the advice of the king. The king then advised me to write a petition to submit to him, whereupon we councillors and senior colleagues wrote a petition, submitted on 09 April 1988 and highlighting all the issues and concerns. I filed the public petitions from the villagers and the *Mandals* as evidence. There was an emergency meeting of the Cabinet, which excluded us RACs, and was thus dominated by the regime's radical elements.

I understand now that it was what the regime needed: to malign all the work I had done and that of my colleagues. During the NIB audits, I had sincerely worked to unearth widespread corruption cases, and indicted a number of very senior officials, including some members of the royal family (the most important being Namgyal Wangchuck) in huge corruption cases. Similarly, all my associates in the petition-drafting and several rounds of meetings could be ensnared within one fence.

In one single onslaught, the villagers were terrorized by the teams, and their elites ensnared. It was a very clever ploy to implement the first act of their depopulating strategy. The second cabinet meeting declared me guilty of treason against the *Tsa-Wa-Sum,*[18] stripped me of my public post in the most humiliating manner possible, and forced me to leave the capital—after signing an agreement in which I would not speak to more than three people outside my family. That decree made me a virtual prisoner in my own home in Gaylegphug, where I was under the constant surveillance of the security intelligence.

The regime had seen very well the events unfolding as the people rallied around me, as the most vocal representative against injustice to the people; I was also closely networked with senior Lhotsampa officials. By declaring me a traitor, despite my most loyal service to the nation, they sought to instill fear in my colleagues and the people, so that the oppressive measures could be carried out without any opposition. The regime went a step further, by creating a condition totally contravening normal means, to coerce me into exiling myself from the country amid a campaign of great humiliation and negative character assassination carried out against me.

This dramatic episode also indicated that the King was a very highly unpredictable person, who would go to any extremes to keep his close coterie pleased, and could turn into a racist animal at his own whim. When the situation became intolerable for living in my own country, I exiled myself, to give voice to the common masses for the injustices being meted out to the poor rustics and the whole of Bhutanese in general. As soon as I left the portals of my motherland, I was declared a traitor and *persona non grata* in my own country.

5.4 The King's Steps Towards Silencing the Rights

The King was fully aware of the happenings in the south through the network of intelligence reports. He took immediate drastic steps to silence the growing discontent over his actions of suppressing the rights of the Lhotsampas to their rightful citizenship, despite all evidence. The King was fully prepared to use force, if needed, to get his policies implemented. In addition, the plan was reinforced when he informed the Indian PM Rajiv Gandhi (during his holiday visit to Bhutan) that the regime would begin thinning out the Lhotsampas. That tacit agreement (whose support he had gained through the then-Chief Minister of West Bengal, Jyoti Basu, through various means of exotic gifts and largesse in cash and kind) became one of the supporting pillars for his invasion of Southern Bhutan.

Meanwhile, the regime began to gather information on the allegiance of all the officers who provided me support for drafting the petition regarding the excesses in the census exercise. I came to know from reliable sources that most Lhotsampa officials of the middle level who had supported me were threatened if the issue of the census was brought into question. Some senior officials were taken into the coterie's confidence, while others were placed under constant security vigil.

I could find no solace in staying idle, without voicing my concern for human rights in Bhutan. I therefore sought assistance, through activists and intellectuals in the adjoining state of Assam and Sikkim. All my efforts were met half-heartedly by the people concerned, so I finally moved to Nepal. West Bengal was already in the folds of the regime, and the Gorkhaland agitation in Darjeeling had just been crushed. Hence, a person of Nepali origin talking about fundamental rights in north Bengal, for the local citizens or for Bhutan, was as unwelcome as the Naxalites in India. So I decided to move to Nepal, where an underground movement for reinstatement of democracy was in full swing.

In Nepal, after due consideration of the ongoing situation and advice from several human rights activities, I launched the People's Forum for Human Rights in Bhutan (PFHRB) on 07 July 1989, with Adrasha Kafley as its Founding

General Secretary, a large following from within Bhutan and the external support of Indian and Nepali human rights and political activists.

6. Peaceful Movement for Human Rights

The first activity I envisaged after the launching of the forum was an information campaign to highlight the human rights violations and atrocities going on in Bhutan, especially with respect to the southern and eastern Bhutanese. The establishment of the PFHRB had the sole objective to institutionalize basic human rights and fundamental reforms in Bhutan, for the benefit of the whole Bhutanese people suffering under the yoke of the feudal monarchy. Initially, the regime had been happy to know I had exiled myself, and they could do what they pleased with the main voice of opposition in the form of a public representative out of their way.

However, as the oppressed people inside the country became more and more aware of our human rights forum, the media in Nepal and India also highlighted this human rights movement from its cradle. Thousands of Bhutanese visited Nepal, and were eager to know the activities and the course the movement would take. Of course, the overwhelming response to the establishment of PFHRB was viewed as a threat to the Bhutanese regime, even though it had been launched in exile. Hence, the regime began to conspire to thwart it with whatever means it could, even if it meant wasting precious national resources or donor funds.

6.1 Monitoring of the Movement

First of all, the regime began monitoring our activities, with an unlimited budget to spend for those involved in gathering the intelligence reports. One main technique used was to establish a network of informers: hiring people to report on activities; bribing Nepali police officials to keep a watch on me and my colleagues with reports of all related activities; hiring hoodlums in the border areas of southern Bhutan as paid agents who could be used for criminal activities if needed; and posting police officials well-versed in Nepali and Hindi in southern Bhutan, to monitor the travel and activities of mainly the elites working in the south.

These officials also monitored the activities of the Lhotsampa officials on tour to the South. Thus, all activities even remotely related to the fledgling human rights movement were reported to the Home Ministry. In addition, it sent delegations to meet the Chief of Darjeeling Hill Council; Subhash Ghissingh, the Chief Minister of Sikkim; Nar Bahadur Bhandari, the CM of West Bengal; Jyoti Basu; and the CM of Assam, Prafulla Mahanta. All but the CM of Sikkim assured the delegation of their support in monitoring the movement.

Then, to twist the issue dramatically, Bhutan began a disinformation campaign against the CM of Sikkim and the Bhutanese movement, as a design for a Greater Nepal conspiracy which gathered support against the people of Nepali ethnicity in West Bengal and Assam, despite the support of Subash Ghissingh to the regime. In addition, delegations to Nepal (which was still a monarchy) were being sent, to understand the status of the Bhutanese human rights movement and the support it might be receiving from the Nepalese government and the public. Thus, the King's men worked in every possible manner to follow the activities of the human rights forum.

6.2 The Precursors

Among the pre-movement activities on the side of PFHRB had been my efforts to meet with regional leaders in Assam, West Bengal, Sikkim and Nepal. This had been closely watched by the regime. Thus, some of these precursors allowed the regime to know my whereabouts and my activities.

Interestingly, while my efforts to voice the injustices being meted out to the Lhotsampas in general (and the denial of basic rights to the common masses throughout Bhutan) were going on, people within Bhutan had begun to demonstrate their own defiance toward the regime's ill-conceived policies. By now, these went beyond the census enumeration, to include dress codes, language obligations and denial of teaching Nepali language in the southern schools, as well as the imposition of Buddhist culture (albeit slowly) onto the non-Buddhists, who mainly comprised the Hindus.

The young graduate groups and students in southern Bhutan, the National Institute of Education in Samchi, Sherubtse College in Kanglung and the Royal Bhutan Polytechnic in Deothang, had begun to form the Student Union of Bhutan (SUB), which exists to this date although in exile. The students were gaining momentum, while young graduates and senior officials were unhappy with the situation in the southern districts, where the regime had unleashed its Reign of Terror, nicknamed the "Black Census."

The main precursor for the movement was the exposure of the corruption and nepotism right under the nose of the king, and the impact of this shook the very foundation of those considered royal and noble in the country. The shame of potential exposure became the fear that prompted the invasion on the society, who were proving to be greater patriots, with higher ethical values, than those elites of the ruling class acting like blood suckers.

The obliteration of the teaching of the Nepali language in southern schools, with the staunch support of Fr. Mackey (educationist-turned-stool-pigeon for the regime), was successful in promoting the policy of "One Nation, One People," followed by z single national language (and, more slowly, one religion, one culture and one ethnicity) that would follow with the eviction of the Lhotsampas.

6.3 Kidnapping of a Former Public Representative

All the regime's efforts to suppress and agitate the Lhotsampas were working well, as it also used the golden "Divide & Rule" policy. It took into confidence, and even provided largesse to, those who would report any anti-regime activities. The regime was also creating a scenario of repression with its low-key methods of atrocities encouraging more people to join the dissident group; thus, the regime could clamp down and call them "anti-national."

The movement for human rights was growing, and the information campaign on the issue of human rights violations inside Bhutan—not only against the Lhotsampa community, but against all others—was being highlighted. What the king thought to be a sectarian movement limited to the Lhotsampas increased its proportions to the eastern and central part of Bhutan, the regions which had been traditionally suppressed by the regime run by the Ngalongs. Thus, the maligning of Lhotsampas, as well as alienating them from the national mainstream, was intensified, to keep the movement sectarian and make the Ngalongs and Sharchokpas view Lhotsampas as enemies of the nation.

The regime had to prove that it could curb the movement, and it wanted to eliminate the leadership. Hence, it kidnapped me (with the help of King Birendra, who was also trying to suppress the movement for democracy in Nepal). The regime also arrested Ratan Gajmere in Samchi and intimidated Man Bahadur, who was later reported as having committed suicide—a claim still debated.

The regime had by then established a clear link between the people inside and the movement in exile. So after months of monitoring my activities and those of my associates, the regime schemed with the Nepalese police and intelligence (as instructed by the Nepali Palace and the then-Prime Minister Marichman Singh) to extradite me. It succeeded in its covert operation, in which I and two of the most active members of PFHRB, Sushil Pokrel and Jogen Gajmere, were arrested in my residence at Anarmani in the middle of the night. We were taken to Kathmandu, from where the regime had made arrangements to take us directly from the Nepalese policy custody to the Druk Air flight from Delhi waiting at the tarmac for takeoff.

While we were being abducted to Bhutan through the royal channel of Nepal, preparations were being made to arrest others closely linked to PFHRB through the monitoring process. While we were taken to Thimphu to begin our incarceration in inhumane conditions, arrests were being made all over the country. Among them, Mandals, students, government officials, and business people were detained in police headquarters and forced to give statements related to the movement. Seven of us, including Deo Dutta Sharma (abducted from India) and Bhakti Bhandari, Vishwanath Chetri and Rattan Gajmere (arrested in Bhutan), were sent to solitary confinement at the dreaded Military Rabuna prison in Wangi Phodrang. After about 30 months, only I was left in the prison and Deo Dutta was shifted to another one and later released. Then I was moved to the capital, where I continued to be incarcerated without trial, among common criminals, for four more years.

The movement mushroomed even more after my abduction by the regime and the mysterious disappearance of the Founding General Secretary, Adarsha Kafley. DP Kafley carried on the legacy, and many members of the human rights group formed the Bhutan People's party (BPP) in exile. Both organizations peaked in their movement for institution of human rights and democratic reforms in Bhutan with the September, 1990 mass peaceful demonstrations in southern Bhutan, that caused near-paralysis of the regime for a period of about two months.

The regime was taken aback at the popular uprising against its cumulative atrocities and suppression, while I was in solitary confinement under the most inhuman conditions of detention. Strangely enough, the regime blamed me for the uprising, and for inspiring people to rebel against the regime. Truly, the mass peaceful demonstrations exemplified how the people in Bhutan wanted a change from the autocratic regime, and how the rustics had been so unjustly treated by its instruments. This put the traditionalists and vested interest groups in such a position that they would be losing their superiority and privileges if human rights were instituted and democratic reforms brought about at that juncture. So the royal government, in collusion with its beneficiaries within the country and well-wishers outside its borders, began the Reign of Terror by evicting people in pockets of resistance. Encouraged by its success of forcing the people to leave and the mass arrests of the demonstrators, the King himself first went around northern and eastern districts, garnering support and widening the ethnic gap by instilling racist feelings among the officers, common people and members of the security. Then he moved to the south, public asking people to speak their problems during the day, and sending his hoodlums in the security forces to plunder, loot, rape and force people to leave the country, while the government machinery forced them to sign the voluntary migration forms.

During the king's campaign throughout the country, he portrayed me as the country's number-one enemy, who had masterminded the uprising; he asked people how he should punish me. In my solitary dungeon, I was not even aware of anything that was going on in Bhutan. His stooges put words in the mouth of a select few rustics, to ask for "death sentence or life imprisonment" as my punishment. Later the regime faked a trial, based on the National Security Act 1992 (enacted three years after my arrest) and gave me life imprisonment.

My release was achieved after 6 years under pressure from international organizations as a royal clemency, but the regime created such conditions that I was forced to cross the borders of Bhutan to live in exile a second time—first in India for a few months, and now in Nepal, without even refugee status. The UN Refugee Agency still refuses to recognize me as a refugee or evictee from Bhutan. What an irony!

6.4 The Making of Refugees

The regime had planned to thin the population of Lhotsampas with their various policies and forced evictions, and by coercing individuals to sign what they called Voluntary Migration Forms (VMF). The strategy for VMF was simple: the regime targeted the heads of the family (primarily the male members) and arrested them, while forcing the female members of the family to sign the forms. Once signed, these families were evicted, with no chance of appeal. To that effect, even former *gups/mandals*, national assembly members and their families, civil servants' families and family members of security forces were mercilessly evicted. One wonders how the same people who had been helping the administration could suddenly become illegal in the eyes of the regime, and thus one comprehends the conspiracy of the racist king. Almost all demonstrators and their relatives, either recorded or reported by stooges and bribed neighbors, began to be evicted with the coerced signings of VMFs.

Numerous acts of horror were committed by the police and security forces, and then blamed on the dissidents outside Bhutan. The regime charged the movement as a terrorist organization, perpetrating terrorizing raids in villages, and they declaring they had been committed by the activists. Thus, it maligned the movement and garnered support of the northern Bhutanese against the Lhotsampas, instilling into them the seeds of ethnic hatred against not only Lhotsampas but the entire Nepali Diaspora, additionally saddling them with the fictitious "Great Nepal" bogey.

6.5 Evictions and Exodus

The dissidents and the people being forced out of Bhutan began to trickle into India and then into Nepal, where the Nepal Red Cross Society and CARITAS Nepal came to their rescue. UNHCR finally entered the scene when the refugees swelled to a large enough number. While it made propaganda of the 'voluntary migration' with the world media, the regime did not flinch an inch in its bluff to the global stage, which believed that thousands of people would suddenly choose to leave their land, property, jobs and business, to migrate to Nepal as refugees in a country already suffering under its own democratic turbulence and instability, after King Birendra had yielded to the popular uprising of the Nepali masses in 1990.

I often wonder how the world readily believed one lie after another, and chose to keep mum, despite the recognition of the crisis by the UN. It is amazing to know how the trauma of the refugees was weighed against the false propaganda campaign of the regime. The truth would never prevail in the eyes of the Indian and many other governments that continued to pour in financial and technical support to the regime to drive out more people.

6.6 Efforts to Internationalize

The PFHRB, with the support of various NGOs in Nepal and India, the Bhutan People's Party formed in 1990 and the newly established Human Rights Organization of Bhutan (HUROB), campaigned to internationalize the issue of human rights violations and evictions. Amnesty International (AI) and the International Committee of the Red Cross (ICRC) campaigned to penetrate the feudal fortress of the Royal Government of Bhutan to reach the political prisoners. They were able to save many of us prisoners, who could as easily have perished, like so many of the Tibetan prisoners of the early seventies.

It is reported that as the refugee influx swelled, various international agencies were invited to work with UNHCR in refugee relief programs. The Nepalese Government, which had invited the UNHCR to rehabilitate the Bhutanese asylum-seekers, began registering them as refugees, while seeking to internationalize the issue of the influx. To that effect, the then- Prime Minister of Nepal (the late Girija Prasad Koirala) called all the ambassadors, chiefs of diplomatic missions and NGOs in Kathmandu, and informed them of the plight of the refugees; he thus managed to garner considerable attention among the world community. Many European countries, along with Australia, Canada, the U.S. and Japan, took keen interest and visited the refugees' camps, while providing various means of humanitarian support to UNHCR to help assuage the trauma of the refugees. Thus, at the humanitarian level, the issue of ethnic cleansing by the Bhutan government and the resultant influx of Bhutanese refugees was finally acknowledged by international society.

The UN Refugee Agency admitted in various media and to visitors that the Bhutanese refugee camps of eastern Nepal were the most peaceful camps UNHCR had even managed, with well-disciplined people. On the contrary, the royal regime was using its entire means to describe the rustic refugees as terrorists and anti-nationals, or as illegal immigrants (who had voluntarily migrated). The Bhutanese regime had managed to hoodwink the international community, bribing the media and providing red-carpet treatment to local leaders and international visitors, journalists, statesmen, and intellectuals.

6.7 Bilateral Efforts by Nepal

All efforts by Nepal to come to an agreement on the exodus and stop it with its bilateral initiative ended at the wall posed by India (which always claimed the refugee issues as bilateral, despite the fact that the Indian states of West Bengal and Assam had been fully involved in making the evictions a success for the regime). At the Indian corridor, the refugees were often transported free of charge across the border to Nepal, or even dumped at the camp areas. Special transport systems were used to see the evicted citizens cross the border into Nepal, but the Indian government simply washed its hands of the issue. Over more than 20 years, fourteen rounds of bilateral talks between Bhutan and Nepal only wasted precious resources of the international community in hosting the refugees, without a proper solution.

Except for the ongoing resettlement process, initiated with the American leadership when it saw that Bhutan was not budging from its seat by the side of the heavyweight India, the plight of the Bhutanese refugees in the UNHCR camps would have aggravated. Thus, Nepal failed to protect the movement when it was budding, handed over its leaders to the scheming Bhutan and ultimately failed in the bilateral talks. The hope for repatriation of the refugees has dimmed day by day. Only a drastic change in Bhutan, like the Arab Spring with mass democratic changes and institution of human rights, could eventually usher a repatriation process.

6.8 Interventions from the West

Since 2000, the U.S. has led the comity of several western nations aiding the refugees, to finally resettle them in 2008. Now the bulk of them are being resettled in the U.S,, while others are scattered around Canada and Europe. Finally, the refugees have gotten much awaited humanitarian justice, though not political justice.

7. Concluding Remarks

As I conclude this paper, I wish to highlight the contribution of various entities in making Bhutan what it is today. First of all, our immediate and most helpful neighbour India, and our ancestral land Nepal, that provided shelter to all of us in our years of desperation, and the international community that has come to the rescue of Bhutan and the Bhutanese in its own way.

The international community helped save thousands of Bhutanese refugees, after their evictions by the racist regime, from trauma and assimilation in the vast sea of humanity in India and Nepal. It is their efforts that somehow kept the issue of Bhutanese refugees alive in the camps, although those refugees were not allowed to practice their political campaigns freely. We are indeed thankful to the countries that are now giving a new chance to all the refugees to live as others do, study, work and earn a decent living as citizens with fundamental rights.

At this juncture, it is our duty as Bhutanese who have been forced to become refugees to keep the flame alive as Bhutanese, and to hope of a return to the homeland one day, when the country Bhutan will need qualified manpower it is lacking even now. The opportunity given to the refugees to excel, which they are already doing in various fields—especially the younger generation, who will one day make the resident and non-resident Bhutanese society proud of the achievements of its members. Therefore, establishing a Non-Resident Bhutanese (NRB) association would definitely help make the NRBs an intellectual force on the world stage. The lost generation who were evicted by the ruthless racist regime has suffered the maximum, along with their offspring. Yet now, the younger generation, who grew up in the camps or were born outside Bhutan, can live a wholesome life, rather than melt as non-entities into the vast poverty stricken masses in south Asia.

As a human rights activist, and a leader (for the last 22 years, ten of which I spent incarcerated) of the movement to usher in democratic reforms and establish human rights in Bhutan in place of the royal democracy, , I am still hopeful. I am hopeful that one day our country will realize the crime against one-sixth of its population by the regime of the fourth king, and take back all willing NRBs to play significant roles in the development of the country, which is still 30-40 years behind any developed nation in terms of infrastructure and education. However, it is also my fervent hope that, for crimes against his own people, the fourth Dragon King, Jigme Singye Wangchuck, who abdicated when he could not solve the problem he created, shall be brought to justice by the United Nations Administrative Tribunal.

My only question to the people of Bhutan, India and Nepal, and the entire international community with a soft corner of their hearts for Bhutan, and its people is this:

"Was Tek Nath Rizal, a public representative who spoke on behalf of the people he represented in the then Royal Government of Bhutan, justly treated by the fourth King Jigme Singye Wangchuck who incarcerated him for ten years on fabricated charges and denied him a dignified court hearing?[19]*"*

---

[1] One million was the inflated population figure given to the U.N. when joining it in 1971 (possibly to prompt more U.N. assistance).

[2] *Ngalongs* are western Bhutanese of basically six districts of Ha, Paro Thimphu, Punakha and Wangdi. Ngalong is derived from the Tibetan word *Ngalop* used for dissidents of the Tibetan spiritual oligarchy in the 16th and 17th centuries.

[3] *Sharchokpa* means "resident of the east": the eastern Bhutanese.

[4] *Lhotsampa* is a resident of south; thus people of Nepali ethnicity living in southern Bhutan are called Lhotsampas.

[5] *Dzongkha* is derived from Choekey (the language of Lamaism Buddhist text and prayers, used mostly in monasteries in Tibet and Mongolia). The Dzongkha grammar is derived from Choekey grammar (which has roots in Sanskrit) as well as a majority of the words used in it. Only in the late seventies did Bhutanese scholars (Lopon Nado and Lopon Pemala) make changes in Choekey grammar to make it more simpler and adaptable for common use.

[6] This sect of tantric Mahayana Buddhism is an offshoot of the sect under the Druk Ralung monastery in Tibet. The abbots of this sect wear red hats.

[7] *Tsangla* is a dialect significantly different from Dzongkha and spoken in various adapted forms in eastern Bhutan.

[8] Mahayana Buddhist abbots of this sect wear yellow hats and differ in religious practices from the red hatters.

[9] *Druk* means "dragon" and Yul means "land"; thus, Dragon Land.

[10] *Penlop* means "Governor" in Choekey

[11] Dzong is a fort built during the time of Shabdrung as the seat of power as well as a monastery.

[12] Dzongpon is the temporal administrator of a Dzong and the language used in the Dzong is called Dzongkha.

[13] Dewan was like a deputy commissioner for a district.

[14] A *muktihar* was regional chieftain for several villages. One Dewan has around 10-15 Muktihars under him.

[15] A *mandal* is the head of a block. One Muktihar has several mandals to help him.

[16] *Gylakhap Kutshap* means "country representative," the position entrusted to Kaji Ugyen Dorji at Kalimpong in 1898, acting as the representative of Bhutan to the British India as well as administering south Bhutan and settling people in what was once a malaria-infested region.

[17] *Kumar Saheb* is the short form of Raj Kumar (Prince); "Saheb" means officer (a term of respect)

[18] *Tsa-Wa-Sum* means "3 Gems of the country": the King, Country and Government

[19] Those who read either this article or my book, Torture: Killing Me Softly, please email your frank answers to me at tnrizal47@gmail.com.

A Startling Awareness:
Transforming Fear
into Compassion

Richard Forer

Richard Forer was born in Trenton, New Jersey in 1948. His younger brother is an attorney and former president of one of the largest Reform synagogues on the East Coast and his identical twin brother is a prominent member of an Ultra-Orthodox sect of Judaism. A former member of AIPAC (American-Israel Public Affairs Committee), Forer is a practitioner of the Meir Schneider Self-Healing Method, a unique system of healing developed by an Israeli.

[This piece has been adapted from *Breakthrough: Transforming Fear Into Compassion: A New Perspective on the Israel-Palestine Conflict* by Richard Forer. [Insight Press, 2010]]

> *On three things does the world endure: justice, truth and peace....*
> *Mishnah: Pirkei Avot* (Chapters of the Fathers) 1:18a

On Wednesday, July 12, 2006, Hezbollah (party of God), the nationalistic Lebanese political and military organization, abducted two Israeli soldiers and murdered three in a cross-border raid into northern Israel. Within two hours, Israeli tanks and armored personnel carriers entered Lebanon. In the fighting that followed, five more Israeli soldiers died, four when their tank drove over a powerful bomb. An unknown number of Hezbollah soldiers also died in the fighting. Israel's cabinet immediately authorized "severe and harsh" retaliation. The Second Lebanon War had begun.

Upon hearing this news, I was overcome with fear and despair. And coming just three weeks after Hamas's kidnapping of Israeli soldier Gilad Shalit from the Southern Gaza border, I was stunned. Once again, Israel was the object of undeserved scorn and hatred and, in its endless struggle for permanence, was forced to strike back against blatant acts of aggression, which I took to be personal and execrable attacks against myself and all Jews. Like my fellow Jews, I only wanted to live in peace. Although I had no history of discord with anyone of Arab heritage, this latest incitement proved that the adversary I had read about in Sunday school, the enemy of the Old Testament, was determined to wipe Israel and its Jewish inhabitants off the face of the Earth.

As the war raged on, I anxiously watched television and read the newspapers, anticipating a quick and successful end to the conflict. My hopes, however, were dashed by Hezbollah's unexpected strong resistance to the powerful Israeli military. I bristled at the damage to Israel and the loss of Israeli lives, victims of rocket attacks dispatched by Hezbollah.

350

When I read about the devastation to Lebanon, I had no difficulty rationalizing the deaths of hundreds of innocent civilians and the displacement of nearly one million. The deceased were victims of the wanton disregard their countrymen had for the sanctity of human life. There was no mistaking the fact that Islamic terrorists had intentionally embedded themselves within local populations. Hezbollah's premeditated and cynical strategy was to attract enemy bombs, in order to provoke the international denunciation of Israel that would follow. These extremists had cavalierly sacrificed the lives of their own people just to smear the integrity and reputation of the Jewish nation. In the light of that depravity, the proposition that Hezbollah was fighting for the rights of its populace was nothing more than a pathetic excuse to hide its genocidal intentions. Clearly, the Arabs would do anything to achieve their heinous objective. In contrast, Israel's plan of self-defense, which some called excessive, seemed reasonable to me. "We" were fighting a war, while making every effort to avoid harming civilians, even at the cost of increased risk to our own troops.

* * *

As I look back at that difficult period, I can see the unreserved one-sidedness of my disposition. Back then, however, no one could have convinced me that my views were biased. Facts alone dictated my position. And the fact that I was fortunate enough to have been born Jewish and American, rather than Muslim and Arab, did not implicate me in any kind of prejudice.

A different identity, however, was silently waiting to be born, and with a more sweeping perspective than I ever could have imagined. By the time Israel ended its naval blockade of Lebanon on September 8, 2006, my perception of the world had been radically transformed, my lifelong conditioning released, my tendentious beliefs overturned and my inborn compassion manifested. From this new place of freedom the roots of conflict were gracefully revealed to my conscious mind.

* * *

Growing up during the 1950s and 1960s, I attended Sunday school at my reform synagogue from the time I was six until a year after my *bar mitzvah*. Like most people, I naturally identified with my religion and culture. Knowing who I was gave me a sense of pride and participation in something deep and mysterious.

The overwhelming majority of Jews I knew were honest and fair in their dealings with others and, taken as a whole, appeared to be more socially and politically aware than other groups of people. Their respect for different cultures impressed me as kind and considerate, especially when contrasted with the racial slurs and ethnic stereotypes I often heard from Gentiles.

I appreciated the humor, the food, the warmth, the intelligence and the contributions to humanity spawned by my ancestry; but more than anything else, I willingly embraced my Jewish heritage because of my people's history of wandering and persecution. To question my identity would have felt like a betrayal of an ancient tradition and indifference toward the suffering of my people.

After graduating from elementary school, I regularly attended Friday night and Saturday morning religious services. Occasionally, I would overhear some of the men discussing the possibility of a global nuclear catastrophe. They all agreed that the most likely place for war to be triggered was the Middle East. That region was a powder keg just waiting for a spark, and the spark was Arab hatred of Israel.

Faced with that prospect, I would often ask myself what we had done to cause the Arabs to hate us. The answer was simple. We had done nothing. We were Jews; that was enough. That had been the rule since time immemorial. But, as I would finally figure out many years later, the most honest and accurate answers to my question were not so one-dimensional. The anger the Arab nations felt over Israel's existence had more to do with territory than with inborn hatred for the Jewish people.

As I grew older, I rarely dwelled on the enmity between Israel and the Arabs, but I never lost sight of Israel's vulnerability, situated among hostile neighbors, each resenting its very existence and insensitive to the six million unspeakable acts of cruelty that had exterminated a third of world Jewry a generation earlier.

In 1996, I was introduced to Joan Peters' influential work, *From Time Immemorial: the Origins of the Arab-Jewish Conflict over Palestine.* A best-seller, the book claimed that the Palestinian people never existed. They were Arab immigrants who had migrated to Palestine from other areas of the Middle East for the jobs made available by Jewish landholders. Any uncertainty I'd had about the circumstances surrounding Israel's birth was completely erased by this remarkable book. *From Time Immemorial* articulated the justification for a Jewish State and provided detailed evidence that enabled me to infer that any and all accusations by Israel's enemies were not only false but anti-Semitic.

* * *

Anxiety for Israel's well-being and a corresponding disregard for Lebanon led to arguments with close friends who were critical of the Jewish state. Their inability to grasp the obvious logic of my position fanned the flames of fear and despair and compelled me to take action, to disprove them and all of Israel's critics. I decided to research the history of the Jewish state.

When I began my study, I was determined to read Jewish authors only, knowing that if I chose non-Jewish authors I would suspect bias. First, I went on the internet and scanned reviews of books by Israeli and other Jewish writers. Then I noticed a book by an American professor, Norman Finkelstein. The writer's surname met my chief requirement and the title drew my attention: *Beyond Chutzpah: On the Misuse of Anti-Semitism and the Abuse of History.* After compiling a few other possibilities, I drove to my local library.

Browsing through the bookshelves, I found Finkelstein's book. Perusing the inside jacket, I read that Joan Peters' book *From Time Immemorial* had been "exposed as an academic hoax." Given my enthusiasm for Peters' work, the statement was provocative and threatening. As I was beginning to recover my balance, the jacket held another surprise: it said that Finkelstein was highly critical of the Israel-Palestine analysis that Harvard Law professor Alan Dershowitz had communicated in his book *The Case for Israel*. Although I had not read that book, I had always regarded Dershowitz as an independent and fair-minded thinker. I had admired him, along with Peters, for a long time. I had barely begun my investigation, yet I was already faced with the prospect that long-held, nearly sacred beliefs were about to be deflated.

My inner turmoil had pushed me into a corner. Seeing something I almost wished I hadn't, I was simultaneously repelled and attracted. In the face of this unforeseen impasse, I was left with no choice but to borrow Finkelstein's book from the library as the only possible relief from my dilemma.

Back home the awareness that I was about to venture into terrain that did not appear to be as clearly demarcated as I had always supposed became more pronounced. Feeling somewhat anxious, I decided to sleep on my decision and see how I felt after a night's rest.

The following morning I sat alone in my living room. It was very quiet outside. There was nothing to distract me, nothing I really wanted or needed. At ease, I was finally ready to uncover any evidence that might clarify the issues that had caused such consternation. Resigned to the fact that I was about to discover unsavory details about Peters and Dershowitz, I picked up *Beyond Chutzpah*.

Over the ensuing days, I read Finkelstein's words with as much tolerance as I could muster. There was no doubt in my mind that I was studying the work of a brilliant scholar who possessed a great deal of confidence in his arguments. Furthermore, Finkelstein was meticulous about documenting the evidence he was presenting. Because of these qualities I restrained myself from abandoning his book, sensing that my endurance would lead to some kind of resolution, though I had no idea what form it might take. Most of the time my reading was marked by an inner struggle: on the one hand, a desire to get to the truth and alleviate my torment; on the other, a curiosity to ascertain whether Finkelstein was in fact a disturbed academic and anti-Semite (an ironic possibility, given that the book was purportedly about the misuse of anti-Semitism). For me the question became: Who was actually misusing anti-Semitism, him or me?

Part one of *Beyond Chutzpah* was entitled, "The Not-So-New 'New Anti-Semitism." Here Finkelstein tackled the modern Jewish penchant for ascribing "any challenge inimical to Jewish interests" to anti-Semitic tendencies. He criticized a wide variety of Jewish sources for their blind and uninformed support of the Israeli government and their attempts to silence voices that spoke out against its policies, even when those voices were respected human rights organizations like Amnesty International or Human Rights Watch. He especially ridiculed the hypocritical stance of some prominent Jews in defending Christian fundamentalist leaders, like Jerry Falwell of the Moral Majority and Pat Robertson of the Christian Broadcasting Network, because they backed a "militarized Israel," while ignoring the fact that their theology "reeked of anti-Semitism." Although I was impressed with the clarity of Finkelstein's reasoning, I was not fully persuaded. He had not (yet) overcome my sensitivity to the undercurrent of anti-Semitism in my society and the threat it posed to my people.

By the third day, I began to experience a succession of distinct emotions, but was so engrossed in the book that it took awhile before I could articulate them. When I eventually shifted my attention onto my mental-emotional state, I remembered the feelings of shock and disbelief that had come over me upon reading that the Israeli government had bulldozed hundreds of homes in the Palestinian areas, sometimes with the inhabitants still inside; that Israel was siphoning off disproportionate amounts of water from those areas for its own use; that collective punishment was a common practice; and that Israel was the only country in the world that legalized torture. As a Jew, I was acutely bothered that human beings were being mistreated in my name and in the name of my people. Considering that I had never treated anyone with such brutality, it seemed unfair that I should have to carry such a burden of culpability.

Pausing briefly, I put the book down and tried to find some respite from this onslaught of disturbing information. After taking a few deep breaths, I forged ahead, only to discover that Israeli security forces had killed or injured dozens of unarmed Palestinians attempting to pass through checkpoints. I also learned that tens of thousands of Palestinians had been tortured or harshly treated, frequently without any evidence that they had committed acts of defiance toward the Israelis.

After reading these and other allegations, my disbelief and shock turned into anger at my Israeli brethren for their unjustified and inhumane deeds. My anger then turned inward, as I reflected on my past failure to pay attention to this struggle. My face flushed with heat and a righteous fury seethed within me for the suffering of an entire ethnic group that I had continually ignored. The cries of millions had never even touched me. Waves of remorse passed through my body and I shuddered at the thought that I had rejected their claims of persecution as propaganda and lies. I was ashamed that I had demonized an entire culture and judged its people as irredeemable. In acknowledging my heartlessness, I was obliged to silently confess to my history of delusion and denial. Many of the positions I had taken on behalf of Israel and against the Palestinian people were factually incorrect.

These positions, so prevalent within my culture, had appeared reasonable, even unassailable. They had taken shape during the impressionable years of childhood and were suffused with the common accounts of my parents, rabbis, Sunday-school teachers, relatives and friends. Most significantly, they were founded upon two interconnected, governing beliefs, which were the substratum out of which all other judgments arose.

The first was that Israel unfailingly acted with integrity in its dealings with others. There was never any doubt in my mind that when mistakes were made, Israel's overriding rectitude ensured that the mistakes were redressed. The second and more prominent belief was one that had wielded its authority from the deeper recesses of my mind, indifferent to the fact that I had never been a religious Jew: God had promised the land of Israel to the Jewish people and, at last, after thousands of years of persecution, that promise had been fulfilled.

And, just as the patriarchs Abraham, Isaac and Jacob had acted under God's guidance and protection, so too had Israel. Thus, the judgments I had regarding the Israel-Palestine issue—empowered by holy writ—were so unshakable there had never been any thought of deserting them.

Under the influence of these beliefs, I had further rationalized Israel's actions with other, subordinate beliefs that I presumed were equally incontestable. Among these were that the Israeli government, when forced to retaliate against its enemies, did so with great reluctance; that Israeli soldiers did not violate civil rights or kill indiscriminately; that Israel's Supreme Court was a bastion of justice for all citizens, including the Palestinians; and that the reason the Palestinians always subverted Israel's sincere attempts to establish a fair peace was because their true goal was to push the Israelis into the sea.

Since I had always believed the United Nations was the primary arena for resolving conflict around the world, I had been chronically upset with its myopia to the truth of what was happening in the Middle East and its insensitivity to the suffering of the Jewish people. Only anti-Semitism could explain such ignorance. I had also been unable to comprehend why some Jews were convinced the Palestinian cause was just. That reasoning was nonsensical to me, so I had attributed their confused logic to misguidance and misinformation.

But now my mind was in the crosshairs, its conception of reality threatened by powerful reasoning and compelling research.

My shame and embarrassment receded, and a heavy sadness enveloped me for the oppressive treatment that so many Palestinians had suffered.

*   *   *

Although I had always considered myself capable of clarifying most matters on the basis of my own scrutiny, I saw that when it came to Israel I had brushed aside challenging questions, in favor of an irrational but emotionally satisfying appraisal. This realization quickly passed when I noticed that I could no longer detect an exclusive identity, or "me," differentiated from anyone or anything else. Given my customary outrage at the world's non-acceptance of my people, it was hard to believe at first that I was evaluating my experience accurately. Briefly I speculated that such an evocative ending to a core identity should be accompanied by dramatic emotional, mental and physical overtones. But that was not the case. And too, as hard as I tried to reanimate my Jewish identity— not out of fretfulness, but to confirm the validity of my unanticipated observation—it would not return. So I surrendered to the inevitability of the moment, and calmly accepted that I was not separate from members of other religious or ethnic groups. I had lost my individual identity as a Jew, and discovered my common humanity with all people. I was as much Palestinian as Israeli, as much Muslim as Jew.

My Jewishness had never felt like a burden to me. It was "who I am," or so I'd thought. But now that I was no longer bound to one identity and separate from another, I felt a great relief. This new consciousness of non-separation imbued me with the freedom to reflect upon the lifelong dominion my former identity had held over me.

Initially, my reflection took the form of a simple exercise. I relaxed and settled into my body. Then, from that calm space I began to compare the new self-sense with the old. At a certain point I noticed an almost imperceptible sensation in my upper abdomen, around my solar plexus. As the sensation captured my attention, a memory arose from early childhood. The memory took the form of subtle bodily recoil at the communication that who I was could be defined by others, that I was Jewish and an American.

This recoil, which I experienced as doubt, was a natural response to the delimiting of my being—to being informed who I was and, therefore, who I wasn't. It was a warning from my deepest internal perception that, by capitulating to a limited identity, my most basic understanding of myself would be undermined. But the warning disappeared as fast as it had appeared and the communication became a part of how I would come to identify myself. I had made a choice, but the choice was not borne of thought; it was borne of innocence, vulnerability and trust. It was a decision from the heart.

As I matured into adulthood my identity became more entrenched within cultural and social boundaries, beyond which I had no awareness or understanding. These boundaries were analogous to having bridle reins connected to the sides of my head, prescribing how far I could turn in any direction. I could see only that part of the world the restraints permitted, and was so habituated to the restraints that I didn't even know they existed. As a result I took for granted that the world I saw was all there was to see. With such a worldview it was not possible to comprehend the motivation for the behavior of those I perceived as threats to me and my people. What was possible was to label them "terrorists." My irrational fear had reduced them to objects intent on my demise. Only after I was free of irrational fear did I become aware that I had objectified anyone.

Now I could see just how primitive my thinking had been. A reasonable need for safety had been transformed into an irrational fear that could be satisfied only by incapacitating or destroying the objects of my fear. Only then would no harm befall me. Fear persuaded me to deny the humanity of others and more easily condone their destruction. By interpreting the world through the prism of fear, my mind had created enemy images and then superimposed those images onto other people, unconsciously presuming that they actually existed as reality. I had played God by determining the substance of a man or a woman, without even knowing that man or woman. Those whom I defined as enemies, as threats to my being or way of life, were transmuted by fear into monsters, whose potential for violence could never be discounted.

Deceived by a belief system consisting of antagonists and protagonists and aligning myself with the presumption that one part of the world represented sanity and the other insanity, I was supporting indiscriminate and massive destruction; in a word, insanity. This careless choice emanated from a single error in consciousness: my unquestioned devotion to a limited identity. Until I acknowledged the profound influence of this primal error, my participation in the generational reenactment of hatred and retribution, of chronic hostility and mistrust, was destined to continue.

I noticed that I didn't seem to suffer a fear of terrorists. Where once there was fear, now there was emptiness, and this emptiness manifested as the absence of any impulse or desire to judge or define the other. My curiosity was stirred, so I designed an experiment to check the accuracy of my observation. Like someone who pinches himself to see if he is really awake, I visualized a series of horrifying scenarios that were similar to news reports that once stimulated great agitation within me. My objective was to see if I could rekindle my former feelings.

I imagined bloody atrocities against innocent children and meditated on nightmare visions of my brutal death at the hands of Islamist extremists. Surprisingly, the physical and mental stress that normally sprang from such images did not appear. What materialized instead was a feeling of equanimity. There was an immeasurable relief in knowing that the rage extremists felt was not based solely upon irrational hatred. With this understanding they became human, and the irrational fear and anger I once felt for them were translated into compassion, equal to the compassion I felt for Jews. Compassion became the doorway to understanding the suffering of my former enemy.

In classical psychology, projection is defined as "the attribution of one's own ideas, feelings, or attitudes to other people or to objects; *especially*: the externalization of blame, guilt, or responsibility as a defense against anxiety." (*Merriam-Webster's online dictionary: m-w.com/dictionary/projection; 6b.*)

Although I was familiar with this defense mechanism, I had really only understood it with my intellect. Now I understood it with the natural intelligence of my heart, and I found myself able to inquire directly into the grievances that catalyze the anger of others.

I realized that my past appraisal of the motivations of the extremists had more to do with me than it had to do with them. Believing that my fear and hatred were justified, I had been certain that my intentions arose out of fairness, while theirs arose out of hatred. That was pure projection. Their anger simmered and then exploded, because my culture withheld the fairness they longed for. Now I had to consider the possibility that they didn't become our enemies because of *who we were*; they became our enemies because of *what we did*.

Before, I had scoffed at their torment and ridiculed as fiction the reasons they gave for their anger. Now I could feel how callous that attitude had been and I understood why the level of violence in parts of the Muslim world had grown over the years and why my fellow man could act with such murderous intent. After years of frustration, of not having his hopes and needs considered, he was enraged. Demoralized by the deaths of family and friends and anguished over the persistent inequality between his people and their occupier, he was intent on ridding his homeland of an unwelcome and foreign presence. Once I understood how these feelings ignited his passions, I knew that what the Palestinian people truly wanted was not the gratuitous deaths of Israelis but the implementation of the same God-given rights citizens of Israel possess: self-determination and equality.

Notwithstanding my continued abhorrence for premeditated acts of violence, I had to admit that no matter how coldhearted I judged their behavior, the extremists had adopted the only means they knew to pursue the quest for justice that was hidden within the heart of their struggle. They had as much right to self-determination and equality as anyone else. Also, I understood why so many Jews and Americans were emotional, even hysterical, in their condemnation of Islamist extremists and how—as I had once done—they generalized that reaction to include all of Islamic society.

* * *

Our beliefs convince us how the world *should* appear. When we look out at the world, if it does not conform to our beliefs—and especially when we see conflict and violence—we suffer fear, anger and despair. These difficult emotions, especially fear, stimulate confusion. Our natural intelligence then succumbs to cultural prejudices and unconscious thought processes that doom us to conflict. The paradigm of this ancient process is the belief in "us" against "them," good against evil. This belief, and the dualistic thinking that produces it, has held us in its grip for most of our lives. In order to free ourselves from this oppression, we need to question the certainty of our views and begin to understand how easily we can deceive ourselves into supporting policies that favor some at the expense of others, and how our views often induce us to deny the humanity of those whose actions arouse our fear and anger. We will need to continually ask: *Why? What is the history behind their outlook?* Not our particular version of their history, not the selected evidence that supports our beliefs, not the facile language we use to condemn them—but the reality of their history.

The responsibility for uncovering and verifying the facts is ours alone. If we abdicate this duty, there will be no one to blame but ourselves for the turmoil that results—not terrorists, politicians, religious groups, governments, or radical cults. Until we come to a hard-earned understanding of the causes of a particular conflict and the lessons its history contains, peace will remain a distant fantasy.

If we honestly commit ourselves to a real peace, a new understanding will reveal itself. We shall see that in truth we have much in common with our so-called enemy. We are both the product of our history, and we are both often distracted by pain and confusion. We both want to avoid suffering. Most importantly, we both share a common desire for peace within ourselves and within the world. This understanding of our common reality produces compassion.

My experience is that compassion is a profound relief. It is inborn. When it was reawakened, I was instantly freed from irrational fear and my natural intelligence was restored. Then I knew that a real peace can never come about through aggression or as a result of one group's superiority over another. Real peace can only come about through insight and compassion.

How George W. Bush
Changed My Life

David R. Henderson

David R. Henderson is a research fellow with the Hoover Institution and an associate professor of economics in the Graduate School of Business and Public Policy at the Naval Postgraduate School. He is author of The Joy of Freedom: An Economist's Odyssey *and co-author, with Charles L. Hooper, of* Making Great Decisions in Business and Life. *His latest book is* The Concise Encyclopedia of Economics. *David has also testified before the House Ways and Means Committee, the Senate Armed Services Committee, and the Senate Committee on Labor and Human Resources.*

A friend and colleague of mine at the Hoover Institution, Peter Robinson, wrote a book a few years ago titled *How Ronald Reagan Changed My Life*. In this excellent book, Peter tells of how his time as a speechwriter for Reagan changed his life in a good way. Peter, by the way, was the author of the famous line, "Mr. Gorbachev, tear down this wall." It was one of the best lines in Reagan's whole political career: Reagan used his moral and powerful righteousness to appeal to Gorbachev's better nature rather than making threats. And, oh, by the way, it worked. Even though many people, including me, wondered why Reagan bothered, the fact is that although Gorbachev didn't literally tear down the wall, he didn't intervene with force when the East German government allowed it to be torn down. Instead, peaceful, freedom-loving East and West German citizens took care of the wall's demise.

Just as Ronald Reagan changed Peter Robinson's life, George W. Bush changed mine—only not in the same way. Reagan changed Peter's life by demonstrating positive character traits that Peter emulated; George W. Bush changed my life by making war on people in other countries. Whereas I had a fair amount of admiration for Ronald Reagan, who had been my big boss when I was at the President's Council of Economic Advisers, there is nothing about George Bush that I would like to emulate.

Nevertheless, George W. Bush did change my life. Before Bush became a wartime president, my professional work, in both academic and popular articles, was almost entirely in domestic economic policy. I had written academic articles about taxation and supply-side economics, tariffs on oil, the International Energy Agency's oil-sharing agreement, and military manpower. I had written popular articles on free trade, taxation, health care, government subsidies, government regulation, immigration, and the drug war. In all of these articles, I made the case for less taxation, less spending, and less regulation of people's lives.

But before September of 2001, the number of articles I had written on war and foreign policy could be counted on the fingers of one hand. Not that I hadn't thought about it, and not that I wasn't antiwar. It's just that my specialty was domestic economic policy. Only when the first President Bush planned a war on Iraq did I write a piece about the war, and that one made the narrow case that one could not justify the first Iraq war on the basis of Saddam Hussein's threat to the world oil supply. My column, published in the *Wall Street Journal*, made quite a splash, leading *Washington Post* editorial writer Richard Harwood to write an editorial, "War—or Folly—in the Gulf," pushing my argument and leading CNN to have me on live for an interview on Labor Day, 1990. But then I returned to my domestic knitting.

Until 9/11. Like almost everyone else in America and, indeed, most people in the world, I was outraged by the 19 criminals who murdered 3,000 innocent victims. But when George Bush said, on that very same day, "Freedom itself was attacked this morning by a faceless coward … and freedom will be defended," I smelled a rat. In saying that freedom was attacked, Bush was saying something about the motives of the attackers, even though he couldn't have known that soon what their motives were. It seemed clear to me that Bush was trying to set the groundwork for a war, rather than trying to go after the higher-ups behind the perpetrators. I turned out to be right. In response to 9/11, George Bush made war on Afghanistan and, depending on which audience he and Dick Cheney were speaking to, a response to 9/11 was more or less part of their motive in attacking Iraq.

That's when I started to inform myself regularly on foreign policy. My first piece on war after 9/11 was on a topic with which I was quite familiar, even without knowing much about foreign policy: the economics of war. I had thought it was obvious that war hurt the economy, but on Sept. 14, 2001, *New York Times* columnist and economist Paul Krugman committed what economists call "the broken window fallacy." He wrote, "Ghastly as it may seem to say this, the terror attack—like the original day of infamy, which brought an end to the Great Depression—could even do some economic good." His argument was that the destruction of buildings in New York would lead to the construction of more buildings to replace them.

Krugman, apparently, was unaware that over 150 years earlier, French economic journalist Frederic Bastiat had shown the problem with that reasoning. When a window is broken, noted Bastiat, it's true that there is a need to replace the window. That's *what is seen*. What is not seen but should be foreseen, wrote Bastiat, is that the resources used to make that window could have been used to produce something else, something that now won't be produced. The bottom line, concluded Bastiat, is that destruction is not profitable for society.

I *had* to reply. On Nov. 28, 2001, I pointed out his mistake, among other things, in "The Economics of War" published in the *San Francisco Chronicle*.

I decided that I wanted to speak out, in print and orally, on these subjects. But to do so, I would need to inform myself the same way I did when I wrote on domestic policy issues: read articles by the people who disagreed with me, take careful note of their arguments and evidence, and ask questions, by e-mail or phone, of experts in the field. Bit by bit since then, I have become a foreign policy analyst. One of my first chances to speak on this was in June of 2002, when, in a talk to admirals taking a special class at the Naval Postgraduate

School, I made the case against war on Iraq. I argued that although I did not know whether Saddam Hussein had weapons of mass destruction, even if he did, the U.S. government could deter him from using them. Moreover, I said, the worst thing the U.S. government could do was attack him, because then he might use them. There was amazingly little pushback. Virtually all of those who expressed any thoughts on the issue agreed with me. So I felt confident enough to write an article, "A Case for Not Invading Iraq."

In October 2002, Congress rolled over for Bush on Iraq, voting 296-133 in the House of Representatives and 77-23 in the Senate to let him make war. I was sure we were now in deep trouble, so I started paying even closer attention to war and foreign policy.

I realized that, although I had been teaching military officers at the Naval Postgraduate School for almost 20 years, I had thought amazingly little about how to apply the same economic tools to analyzing war and foreign policy that economists have successfully applied to domestic economic policy. When I started reading the academic literature on the economics of war and foreign policy, I found amazingly little had been written about such obvious questions as the incentives of politicians to make war and the unintended consequences of war, to name two. I found that the same pillars of economic wisdom that helped my students and me understand domestic economic policy could help us understand foreign policy. It's just that few economists had studied foreign policy using those tools, so there was a lot of low-hanging fruit.

I wrote an academic article on that issue, titled, "The Economics of War and Foreign Policy: What's Missing?" Among the conclusions I derived is that a government will do more destruction to people in a foreign country than to its own people, because its own people have little information about what the government does to other people, and because those foreigners don't vote in the home country's election. We should expect, therefore, that foreign policy will be more destructive than domestic policy and, sure enough, it is. We don't see the U.S. government bombing certain high-crime areas of Los Angeles, for example, even though the arguments the U.S. government make for bombing neighborhoods in Iraq could just as easily be applied to Orange County's urban areas. This is obvious when you think about it, but I had never found it written anywhere.

In 2005, after hearing me speak on foreign policy, Eric Garris, managing editor of Antiwar.com, asked me to write a regular column for the Web site. With some trepidation (would I have enough to say and would I be able to back up my claims, while still keeping and being productive in my day-job?) I accepted.

None of this would have happened had George Bush not turned into such a war-making president. I don't thank him for this, and neither should you. I would much rather have continued writing about health or energy policy. But the stakes are bigger in foreign policy, and very few of my economist colleagues are writing about war. Someone needs to do it. My biggest disappointment about many of my fellow economists is their unwillingness to write about such momentous issues. But that's another story.

There's another way George W. Bush has changed my life. By focusing on war, he let the U.S. bureaucracy get out of control. For example, the Food and Drug Administration is way more restrictive than it was when he took office; one reason is that Bush and his staff paid it so little attention. That means that drugs that would have been introduced and saved lives will never see the light of day, or will appear years later than otherwise. That could well affect my life— and yours. George W. Bush certainly has changed my life, and I haven't even mentioned all the lives he has ended.

I Don't Have to Fight You

About eleven years ago, I boarded a small United Express airplane in Los Angeles. When I got to my row, a man was sitting in the aisle seat, and I asked him to move, so that I could get to the window seat. He scowled at me, but grudgingly got up to let me in. While getting to my seat, I accidentally stepped on his foot. I apologized immediately, but as soon as I was seated, he turned to me and said, "I'm gonna beat the s**t out of you!" I tried to ignore him, but he persisted. "Let's go out on the tarmac and get it on," he said. You've probably heard the saying "fight or flight." I think it's what we men are supposed to do when threatened. That is, we're supposed to either fight or get out of there. I certainly did think of both alternatives immediately. I sized him up and decided I wasn't at all sure I could take him. (I'm a 5'5", 160-pound man with powerful legs but weak arms. He was at least 10 years younger, taller, and obviously full of some kind of upset that might make him very powerful physically.) More important, even if I could take him, I might not get out of it undamaged; I was also pretty sure that in the noise of the open plane, no one had heard his threat, and so I might have trouble flying in the future if it looked as if I had started a fight. More important than any of those reasons, I hate fighting. The times I've avoided fights have always worked out well for me; the one time as an adult that I didn't, I regretted.

I also thought of running, but I figured he would just chase after me. Neither alternative seemed satisfactory. I thought of pushing the flight-attendant call button, but realized that he might beat me up by the time she got there, and that even once she got there, it was his word versus mine. There was one other alternative; wait him out. So I focused on looking straight ahead, not confronting, not talking to him, and waiting to see if he escalated or calmed down. About half an hour later into the short flight to Monterey, the putative pugilist passenger seemed to have calmed down. We hadn't spoken a word since his threat, so I thought I'd try something.

A week or two earlier I had been at a men's workshop run by two men I admired, Charlie Kreiner and Fred Jealous, who had talked about men's alternatives to violence. One of the exercises had gotten one of the men so worked up he had started swinging his fists at those around him, and various men had held him down. Either Fred or Charlie (I've forgotten who) had then gotten down close to his ear and said something to calm him down. It had worked. Then Charlie used it as a teaching moment for all of us, talking about how men are conditioned to fight, and that we need other ways of getting our rage out and ways to solve problems without fighting. Now I thought to myself, "Wow! Here's a chance to see if this works. This guy has just threatened me. But as long as he doesn't do it again, I'm fine. I don't need to beat him physically or in any other way. Wouldn't it be interesting to see if we can have a civilized conversation?"

I pulled a pack of gum out of my pocket, put a stick in my mouth, and held out the pack to him. He shook his head fiercely. I put the gum away. But that was the opening. A minute later he said, "I'm sorry about what happened back there. I just came in from the East and I've been flying for the last day. I don't mean the East like New York; I mean China. I'm having a bad day." His apology reminded me of how many politicians apologize, by talking about "what happened" as if they bear no responsibility for their actions. Nevertheless, it *was* an apology. I felt powerful for having handled things the way I had.

Does this story apply to foreign policy? *Big-time*, as former Vice President Cheney likes to say. Five years ago, I attended a round-table academic conference in which we spent a fair amount of time discussing war and foreign policy. One participant mentioned that after the Japanese government (he actually said "the Japanese") bombed Pearl Harbor, it was obvious that the U.S. government (he said "we") had to go to war with Japan. I replied that that wasn't obvious to me at all. First of all, as my co-author, Charles Hooper, and I point out in our book, *Making Great Decisions in Business and Life*, and as philosopher David Kelley has so eloquently put it, there's almost nothing we *have* to do. And you don't think clearly by starting from falsehoods. Although one might argue that the U.S. government *should* have made war on Japan, the U.S. government didn't have to: it had a choice.

Second, I said, it wasn't obvious to me that the U.S. government should have made war on Japan. While it's awful that more than 2,000 Americans were killed at Pearl Harbor, it was not a good bargain to lose 407,000-plus additional American lives, not to mention 2.6 million Japanese lives, 700,000 of them civilian. Interestingly, no one argued with me, possibly because they didn't have a good argument, or possibly because they wanted to discuss other things. One might argue that it was worth it because otherwise the Japanese government would have moved on and attacked the U.S. mainland. If that fact could have been established, then I would have favored attacking Japan. But, just as in my airplane story, the U.S. government had had other options.

There were two main differences. One was that the other passenger was angry at me because I had accidentally stepped on his foot, while the Japanese government was angry at the U.S. government because it had purposely tried to cut off Japan's supply of oil (Funny how that upsets people). The other difference was that the guy hadn't laid a finger on me, whereas Japan's government had attacked the United States.

One obvious solution would have been for the U.S. government to back off on trying to strangle Japan's economy—in return for, say, an apology from the Japanese government and, say, $1 billion (a lot of money in those days) in reparations. Of course, this wouldn't have accomplished the U.S. government's main goal, which was to get the Japanese government to withdraw from

Indochina and China. But why should that have been a goal of the U.S. government? And notice that if the U.S. government's concern was to keep the Chinese people from being ruled by a bloodthirsty government, it didn't succeed: Chairman Mao saw to that.

So what did "we" get from going to war with Japan and Germany? Four hundred thousand more deaths and a hostile, mass-murdering government in China. That doesn't sound like a bargain to me. Maybe that's why I didn't get any argument from the attendees, virtually all of whom were well informed about 20th-century history.

But here's the problem. Neither Roosevelt nor the leaders of Congress who pushed for war on Japan actually put themselves at risk by going to war themselves. They also made a quick decision, on Dec. 8, based on something that had happened on Dec. 7. That's one of the problems with government solutions: the decision-makers often make quick, bad decisions because they rarely bear the costs of their decisions. If Roosevelt had been willing to consider alternatives to war, 407,000 American lives and a few million Japanese lives might have been saved. That sounds like something worth thinking about.

After the session ended, various people came up to me and told me that I was the most radical antiwar person there. I think, but I'm not sure, that they meant it as a compliment. They said it made them look like moderates. Now don't get me wrong: I love compliments, I just don't see it their way. I think it's kind of radical to advocate an action that kills a few million people, and kind of moderate to advocate thinking first and coming up with solutions that save those same lives. I guess I'm strange.

Baghdad:
The Questions Pour In

Kathy Kelly

*Kathy Kelly co-coordinates Voices for Creative Nonviolence, (*www.vcnv.org*) a campaign to end U.S. military and economic warfare, which has organized peace-team efforts in several war zones and campaigns within the U.S. to stop all funding for U.S. wars and occupations. Earlier, with Voices in the Wilderness, she and her team members organized 70 delegations to Iraq, defying the economic sanctions, and remained in Baghdad throughout the 2003 "Shock and Awe" bombing.*

U.S. Marines were setting up a checkpoint at the intersection just outside of Baghdad's Al Fanar hotel. Umm Zaineb, the desk clerk's wife and mother of little girls Zaineb and Miladah, was at the window watching them. I did not know she was crying.

Two days earlier, we had watched, wide-eyed, as the Marines approached, traveling slowly in a long line of beige-colored military vehicles on a street that parallels the Tigris River, and then halting in front of our hotel, the Burge Al Fanar. Did this mean the bombardment was ending? Cut off from all communication since the first week of bombing, we'd been without any information about the course of the war. As the Marines arrived, we had held up our banners that said "*War = Terrorism*" and "*Courage for Peace, Not for War*," but seeing that they looked tired and thirsty, we had also gone out to meet them, carrying bottled water and dates. The owner of the Al Fanar had invited them inside to take turns cooling off in the overstuffed lobby chairs and even to take showers. Not the flowers and chocolates of gratitude (gratitude for weeks of bombardment?), but simple compassion and hospitality.

Now they were setting up their checkpoint.

Since 1996, delegations like mine from the Voices in the Wilderness (VitW) campaign had headed for this small, family-owned hotel (or another much like it) whenever we arrived in Iraq, duffel bags generally full of medicines and medical relief supplies we'd been officially forbidden to bring. Our campaign had organized close to 70 such delegations, all in open and public defiance of U.S./U.N.-imposed economic sanctions against Iraq. The sanctions had supposedly been designed to punish Iraq's dictator, Saddam Hussein, for possessing weapons of mass destruction, but U.N. statistics showed that they had directly contributed to the deaths of over 500,000 children under age five. Our campaign sought to nonviolently resist the imposition of such brutal punishment on innocents, delivering our interdicted healthcare equipment directly to Iraqi families and hospitals.

From previous trips, we knew exactly where to find overwhelming evidence of a weapon of mass destruction. Inspectors had only to enter the wards of any hospital in Iraq to see that the sanctions themselves were a lethal weapon, destroying the lives of Iraq's most vulnerable people. In children's wards, tiny victims writhed in pain, on blood-stained mats, bereft of anesthetics and antibiotics. Thousands of children, poisoned by contaminated water, died from dysentery, cholera, and diarrhea. Others succumbed to respiratory infections that become fatal full body infections. Five thousand children, under age five, perished each month. 960,000 children who were severely malnourished bear lifelong consequences of stunted growth, brain deficiencies, disablement. At the hands of UN/US policy makers, childhood in Iraq had, for thousands, become a living hell.

Repeatedly, the US media described Iraq's plight as "hardship." Video footage and still photographs showed professors selling their valuable books. Teenage students hawking jewelry in the market were interviewed about why they weren't in school. These are sad stories, but they distracted from the major crisis in Iraq under sanctions, the story still shrouded in secrecy. This was the story of extreme cruelty, a story of medicines being withheld from dying children. It was a story of child abuse, of child sacrifice, and it merited day-to-day coverage.

A *Reuters* TV crew accompanied our delegation to Al Mansour children's hospital. On the general ward, the day before, I had met a mother crouching over an infant, named Zayna. The child was so emaciated by nutritional marasmus that, at seven months of age, her frail body seemed comparable to that of a seven-month premature fetus. We felt awkward about returning with a TV crew, but the camera person, a kindly man, was clearly moved by all that he'd seen in the previous wards. He made eye-contact with the mother. No words were spoken, yet she gestured to me to sit on a chair next to the bed, then wrapped Zayna in a worn, damp and stained covering. Gently, she raised the dying child and put her in my arms. Was the mother trying to say, as she nodded to me, that if the world could witness what had been done to tiny Zayna, she might not die in vain? Inwardly crumpling, I turned to the camera, stammering, "This child, denied food and denied medicine, is the embargo's victim."

I felt ashamed of my own health and well-being, ashamed to be so comfortably adjusted to the privileged life of a culture that, however unwittingly, practices child sacrifice. "It's a difficult choice to make," said Madeleine Albright, when she was asked about the fact that more children had died in Iraq than in Hiroshima and Nagasaki combined, "but," she continued, "we think the price is worth it." Iraqi oil must be kept off the markets, at all costs, even if sanctions cost the lives of hundreds of thousands of children. The camera man had moved on. "I'm sorry, Zayna," I whispered helplessly to the mother and child. "I'm so sorry."

Camera crews accompanied us to hospitals in Baghdad, Basra and Fallujah. They filmed the horrid conditions inside grim wards. They filmed a cardiac surgeon near tears telling how it feels to decide which of three patients will get the one available ampule of heart medicine. "Yesterday," said Dr. Faisal, a cardiac surgeon at the Fallujah General Hospital, "I shouted at my nurse. I said, 'I told you to give that ampule to this patient. The other two will have to die.'" A camera crew followed us into the general ward of a children's hospital, when a mother began to sob convulsively because her baby had just suffered a cardiac arrest. Dr. Qusay, the chief of staff, rushed to resuscitate the child, then whispered to the mother that they had no oxygen, that the baby was gasping her dying breaths. All of the mothers, cradling their desperately ill infants, began to weep. The ward was a death row for infants.

Associated Press, Reuters and other news companies' footage from hospital visits was broadcast in the Netherlands, in Britain, in Spain and in France. But people in the US never glimpsed those hospital wards.

And yet we were shown magnificent hospitality: hotel staff, hospital personnel, shoeshine boys, several extended families and kind, faithful drivers had housed us and shepherded us through Iraqi cities and towns, many, many times. So as war again seemed imminent, we couldn't imagine separating ourselves from them, seeking safety as they stayed in mortal peril. In August, 2002, Voices activists met in Chicago to plan the Iraq Peace Team, resolving to live alongside ordinary Iraqi people despite threats of looming war, not as "human shields" of any description, but as friends seeking to return many favors of solidarity and service, hoping we could be witnessing eyes for an all-too-blind Western world and convinced that "where you stand determines what you see."

War, of course, came with a heavy aerial bombardment of all parts of the city. Umm Zaineb had moved her children into the hotel where Hassan, her husband worked, both for safety, and for certainty, throughout the bombing, that from moment to moment everyone in the family was still alive. Sometimes Umm Zaineb (the name means "Mother of Zaineb" in the Iraqi fashion in which parents take the names of their children) would bring her children to the lobby so that Hassan could help her hold and comfort them. I began to take turns with them as well.

The little girls, Miladah and Zaineb, seemed always eager to play. I tried my best to think of new games to distract them from the sickening thuds, earsplitting blasts, and deafening concussions of explosions heard at varying distances. Cradling the little girls in my arms helped ease the anguished helplessness I myself felt after daytime visits to some of the city's hospitals, witnessing at the bedsides of children whose bodies had been torn apart by my government's bombs.

But I also felt a spark of simple joy and happiness each time I was with the girls and their mother. The children were simply beautiful, and it was a privilege to befriend them and to have earned the trust and friendship of their mother.

Now I couldn't help but feel some relief as the U.S. Marines built their checkpoint in front of our hotel. We had survived! We had seen an end to the terrifying days and nights of bombing. And, in spite of the menacing force of which they were part, the Marines outside our hotel had been friendly to us.

I now thought I'd like to take Miladah and Zaineb outside and introduce them to several of the Marines with whom we had been conversing, although I had second thoughts when I saw the Marines uncoiling large segments of barbed wire to block off the nearby intersection. Nonetheless, reassured that I could securely hold one in each arm, and somewhat clueless as to how their mother was seeing the new activity around her, I walked over to where Umm Zaineb sat, and cheerily asked her if her girls and I could finally go out and get some (relatively) fresh air (burning oil-filled Iraqi defensive trenches, combined with bomb blast pollutants, had roofed the city in eerily heavy, dark clouds).

Umm Zaineb was staring out the window and crying. I asked her what was wrong. "Kathy," she said, "never before did I think that this could happen to my country. And I feel very sad. And…," she struggled to continue, "I think that this sadness… it will never go away."

I felt overwhelmed with dismay and no little shame at the terrible reality of her words. I was cheerfully imagining my return to Chicago, after only six months in Iraq, but she couldn't imagine any possible return to safety, to normalcy, or indeed to happiness. Her tears flooded out as the questions poured in; among the terrible questions deluging her:

Where were her brothers? They lived in Najaf.

Had they survived the war? No phone service, no way to find out.

What had become of her other relatives? Would her husband have continued work, in the hotel or elsewhere, in these new conditions? He had worked the night shift at a hotel which apparently had the Hussein regime's approval; would he be accused, by the troops, by others, of having collaborated with the government?

If accused, would he be taken from her? Tortured? Who would govern their lives? How could she protect and educate her little girls? What future would they face?

For many of us in the U.S., the war simply meant that Saddam was now out of power; case closed, and no further questions. The U.S. would somehow be safer, and the Iraqis, if not greeting our soldiers with flowers and chocolates, would soon come to thank us. We at least had helped them out by getting rid of Saddam.

Umm Zaineb's tearful questions were sadly and disastrously prophetic for so many families, if not her own. In the summer of 2010, Iraqi scholar Dr. Adil Shamoo reported that "Iraq has between 25 and 50 percent unemployment, a dysfunctional parliament, rampant disease, an epidemic of mental illness, and sprawling slums. The killing of innocent people has become part of daily life."

"Since the US-led coalition invasion of Iraq in March 2003, accurate casualty figures for Iraqi civilians have been almost impossible to confirm," according to a July 28, 2011 article posted on *Al Jazeera*'s website. "One of the highest estimates was published in the UK medical journal *The Lancet*, which said that over 600,000 violent deaths occurred between the invasion and June 2006. Most other estimates of civilian deaths are much lower, with the Iraq Index published by the Brookings Institution in Washington DC reporting nearly 115,000 civilian deaths from March 2003 to April 2011."

[http://english.aljazeera.net/indepth/spotlight/iraqschallenge/2011/06/201162864
91536746.html]

I've tried very hard to find Umm Zaineb, Hassan, Miladah and Zaineb. The Al Fanar owner sold the hotel; one of the workers died of a heart attack and another was shot dead in the street. People are afraid to be in touch with westerners. When we would call on the phone, they would ask us to find someone who could speak Arabic, because it was dangerous to speak with an English-speaking person. Truthfully, over time, our hands were so full trying to help Iraqi families that had fled to Jordan and Syria that we couldn't imagine taking on more families that might be in need. Nevertheless, I've been thinking so much of this family.

Warfare brings so much darkness, and of course it utterly obscures the truth. Our leaders act on detached, impersonal military accounts that try to fit war's consequences into tidy timelines and benchmarks and make it possible to listen to the war without hearing it; a flood of certainty deafening them to Umm Zaineb's questions, the superimposed order of statistics concealing, because incapable of amending, the absolute chaos, violence, and upheaval of war.

In this context, peace activists must try to expose, to illuminate, the fear gripping war's victims. We must help people to imagine the metallic fumes of old bomb-smoke in the mouth and lungs, to see the children in Iraqi hospital wards and hear new amputees not yet turned twelve ask if they will always be this way?

The truth about warfare is told through children; because children are the future and it can be a bleak future, it can be made so. And those of us concerned for the future do not trade in certainties, we don't accept the "mission accomplished"—we don't easily accept the mission— and we are deluged with questions. This truth shows in the eyes of parents who can no longer shelter their children, who know with a terrible understanding that they can no longer hope to keep their children safe. But we all have a future to protect. And wherever we are, we can work—every day we can find a way to work—to make sure the questions ring out a little louder, to make our leaders not only listen but hear, so that never again will we demolish futures like the futures I saw dying that year in Iraq.

War and Inflation

Llewellyn H. Rockwell, Jr.

Llewellyn H. Rockwell, Jr. is founder and president of the Ludwig von Mises Institute in Auburn, Alabama, editor of LewRockwell.com, and author of Speaking of Liberty *and* The Left, The Right and The State.

This talk was delivered at the Future of Freedom Foundation's conference on "Restoring the Republic: Foreign Policy and Civil Liberties," on June 6, 2008, in Reston, Virginia.

The U.S. central bank, called the Federal Reserve, was created in 1913. No one promoted this institution with the slogan that it would make wars more likely and guarantee that nearly half a million Americans would die in battle in foreign lands, along with millions of foreign soldiers and civilians. No one pointed out that this institution would permit Americans to fund, without taxes, the destruction of cities abroad and overthrow governments at will. No one said that the central bank would make it possible for the U.S. to be at large-scale war in one of every four years for a full century. It was never pointed out that this institution would make it possible for the U.S. government to establish a global empire that would make Imperial Rome and Britain look benign by comparison.

You can line up 100 professional war historians and political scientists and talk about the twentieth century, and not one is likely to mention the role of the Fed in funding U.S. militarism. And yet it is true: the Fed is the institution that has created the money to fund the wars. In this role, it has solved a major problem that the state has confronted for all of human history. A state without money or a state that must tax its citizens to raise money for its wars is necessarily limited in its imperial ambitions. Keep in mind that this is only a problem for the state. It is not a problem for the people. The inability of the state to fund its unlimited ambitions is worth more for the people than every kind of legal check and balance. It is more valuable than all the constitutions ever devised.

The state has no wealth that is its own. It is not a profitable enterprise. Everything it possesses it must take from society in a zero-sum game. That usually means taxes, but taxes annoy people. They can destabilize the state and threaten its legitimacy. They inspire anger, revolt, and even revolution. Rather than risk that result, the state from the Middle Ages to the dawn of the central banking age was somewhat cautious in its global ambitions simply because it was cautious in its need to steal openly and directly from the people in order to pay its bills.

To be sure, it doesn't require a central bank for a state to choose inflation over taxes as a means of funding itself. All it really requires is a monopoly on the production of money. Once acquired, the monopoly on money production leads to a systematic process of depreciating the currency, whether by coin

370

clipping or debasement or the introduction of paper money, which can then be printed without limit. The central bank assists in this process in a critical sense: it cartelizes the banking system as the essential conduit by which money is lent to the public and to the government itself. The banking system thereby becomes a primary funding agency to the state, and, in exchange for its services, the banking system is guaranteed against insolvency and business failure as it profits from inflation. If the goal of the state is the complete monopolization of money under an infinitely flexible paper-money system, there is no better path for the state than the creation of a central bank. This is the greatest achievement for the victory of power over liberty.

The connection between war and inflation, then, dates long before the creation of the Federal Reserve. In fact, in America, it dates to the colonial era, and to the founding itself. The fate of the Continental currency, printed massively during and after the Revolutionary war, for example, was a very bad omen for our future, and the whole country paid a very serious price. It was this experience that later led to the gold clause in the U.S. Constitution. Except for the Hamiltonians, that entire generation of political activists saw the unity of freedom and sound money, and regarded paper money as the fuel of tyranny.

Consider Thomas Paine: *"Paper money is like dram-drinking, it relieves for a moment by deceitful sensation, but gradually diminishes the natural heat, and leaves the body worse than it found it. Were not this the case, and could money be made of paper at pleasure, every sovereign in Europe would be as rich as he pleased.... Paper money appears at first sight to be a great saving, or rather that it costs nothing; but it is the dearest money there is. The ease with which it is emitted by an assembly at first serves as a trap to catch people in at last. It operates as an anticipation of the next year's taxes."*

But the wisdom of this generation, subverted by Lincoln, was finally thrown out during the Progressive Era. It was believed that an age of scientific public policy needed scientific money machinery that could be controlled by powerful elites. The dawn of the age of central banking was also the dawn of the age of central planning, for there can be no government control over the nation's commercial life without first controlling the money. And once the state has the money and the banking system, its ambitions can be realized.

Before the creation of the Federal Reserve, the idea of American entry into the conflict that became World War I would have been inconceivable. In fact, it was a highly unpopular idea, and Woodrow Wilson himself campaigned on a platform that promised to keep us out of war. But with a money monopoly, all things seem possible. It was a mere four years after the Fed was invented under the guise of scientific policy planning that the real agenda became obvious. The Fed would fund the U.S. entry into World War I.

It was not only entry alone that was made possible. World War I was the first total war. It involved nearly the whole of the civilized world, and not only their governments but also the civilian populations, both as combatants and as targets. It has been described as the war that ended civilization in the 19th-century sense in which we understand that term. That is to say, it was the war that ended liberty as we knew it. What made it possible was the Federal Reserve. And not only the U.S. central bank; it was also its European counterparts. This was a war funded under the guise of scientific monetary policy.

Reflecting on the calamity of this war, Ludwig von Mises wrote in 1919 that "One can say without exaggeration that inflation is an indispensable means of militarism. Without it, the repercussions of war on welfare become obvious much more quickly and penetratingly; war weariness would set in much earlier."

There is always a price to be paid for funding war through the central bank. The postwar situation in America was a classic case. There was inflation. There were massive dislocations. There was recession or what was then called depression, a direct result of capital dislocation that masked itself as an economic boom, but which was then followed by a bust. The depression hit in 1920, but it is not a famous event in United States economic history. Why is that? Because the Federal Reserve had not yet acquired the tools to manufacture an attempt to save the economy. Instead, neither the Fed nor Congress nor the President did much of anything about it—a wholly praiseworthy response! As a result, the depression was brief and became a footnote to history. The same would have happened in 1930 had Hoover not attempted to use the government as the means of resuscitation.

Sadly, the easy recovery of 1920-1922 tempted the central bank to get back into the business of inflation, with the eventual result of a stock market boom that led to bust, then depression, and finally the destruction of the gold standard itself. FDR found that even fascist-style economic planning and inflation could not restore prosperity, so he turned to the ancient method of looking for a war to enter. Here is where the history of the United States and the Fed intersects with the tragic role of the German central bank.

The German government also funded its Great War through inflation. By war's end, money in circulation has risen fourfold. Prices were up 140 percent. Yet on international exchange, the German mark had not suffered as much as one might expect. The German government looked at this with encouragement and promptly attempted to manufacture a complete economic recovery through inflation. Incredibly, by 1923, the mark had fallen to one-trillionth of its 1914 gold value. The U.S. dollar was then equal to 4.2 trillion marks. It was an example of currency destruction that remains legendary in the history of the world—all made possible by a central bank that obliged the government and monetized its war debt.

But did people blame the printing press? No. The popular explanation dealt directly with the Treaty of Versailles. It was the harsh peace imposed by the allies that had brought Germany to the brink of total destruction—or so it was believed. Mises himself had written a full book that he hoped would explain that Germany owed its suffering to war and socialism, not Versailles as such. He urged the German people to look at the real cause and establish free markets, lest imperial dictatorship be the next stage in political development. But he was ignored.

The result, we all know, was Hitler.

Turning to Russia, the untold truth about the Bolshevik revolution is that Lenin's greatest propaganda tool involved the sufferings by the Russian people during World War I. Men were drafted and killed at a horrific level. Lenin called this capitalist exploitation, based on his view that the war resulted from capitalist motives. In fact, it was a foreshadowing of the world that socialism would bring about, a world in which all people and all property are treated as means to statist ends. And what made the prolongation of the Russian role in World War I possible was an institution called the State Bank of the Russian Empire, the Russian version of the Fed.

The Russian war itself was funded through money creation, which also led to massive price increases and controls and shortages during the war. I'm not of the opinion, unlike the neocons, that the Russian monarchy was a particularly evil regime, but the temptation that the money machine provided the regime proved too inviting. It turned a relatively benign monarchy into a war machine. A country that had long been integrated into the worldwide division of labor and was under a gold standard became a killing machine. And as horrific and catastrophic as the war dead were for Russian morale, the inflation affected every last person and inspired massive unrest that led to the triumph of Communism.

At this juncture in history, we can see what central-banking had brought to us. It was not an end to the business cycle. It was not merely more liquidity for the banking system. It was not an end to bank runs and bank panics. It certainly wasn't scientific public policy. The world's major economies were being lorded over by money monopolies and the front men had become some of the worst despots in the history of the world. Now they were preparing to fight each other with all the resources they had at their disposal. The resources they did *not* have at their disposal they would pay for with their beloved machinery of central banking.

In wartime, the printing presses ran overtime, but with a totalitarian level of rationing, price controls, and all-round socialization of resources in the whole of the Western world, the result of inflation was not merely rising prices. It was vast suffering and shortages in Britain, Russia, Germany, Italy, France, Austria-Hungary, the US, and pretty much the entire planet.

So we can see here the amazing irony of central banking at work. The institution that was promoted by economists working with bankers, in the name of bringing rationality and science to bear on monetary matters, had given birth to the most evil political trends in the history of the world: Communism, socialism, fascism, Nazism, and the despotism of economic planning in the capitalist West. The story of central banking is one step removed from the story of atom bombs and death camps. There is a reason the state has been unrestrained in the last 100 years and that reason is the precise one that many people think of as a purely technical issue that is too complicated for mere mortals.

Fast-forward to the Iraq War, which has all the features of a conflict born of the power to print money. There was a time when the decision to go to war involved real debate in the U.S. House of Representatives. And what was this debate about? It was about resources, and the power to tax. But once the executive state was unhinged from the need to rely on tax dollars, and did not have to worry about finding willing buyers for its unbacked debt instruments, the political debate about war was silenced.

In the entire run-up to war, George Bush just assumed as a matter of policy that it was his decision alone whether to invade Iraq. The objections by Ron Paul and some other members of Congress and vast numbers of the American population, was reduced to little more than white noise in the background. Imagine if he had to raise the money for the war through taxes. It never would have happened. But he didn't have to. He knew the money would be there. So despite a $200 billion deficit, a $9 trillion debt, $5 trillion in outstanding debt instruments held by the public, a federal budget of $3 trillion, and falling tax receipts in 2001, Bush contemplated a war that has cost $525 billion dollars, or $4,681 per household. Imagine if he had gone to the American people to request that. What would have happened? I think we know the answer to that question. And those are government figures; the actual cost of this war will be far higher—perhaps $20,000 per household.

Now, when left-liberals talk about these figures, they like to compare them with what the state might have done with these resources in terms of funding health care, public schools, head-start centers, or food stamps. This is a mistake because it demonstrates that the left isn't really providing an alternative to the right. It merely has a different set of priorities in how it would use the resources raised by the inflation machine. It's true that public schools are less costly in terms of lives and property than war itself. But the inflation-funded welfare state also has a corrosive effect on society. The pipe dream that the inflation monster can be used to promote good instead of evil illustrates a certain naïveté about the nature of the state itself. If the state has the power and is asked to choose between doing good and waging war, what will it choose? Certainly in the American context the choice has always been for war.

It is equally naïve for the right to talk about restraining the government while wishing for global war. So long as the state has unlimited access to the printing press, it can ignore the pleas of ideological groups concerning how the money will be raised. It is also very silly for the right to believe that it can have its wars, its militarism, its nationalism and belligerence, without depending on the power of the Federal Reserve. This institution is the very mechanism by which the dreams of both the fanatical right and the fanatical left come true.

The effect of the money machine goes well beyond funding undesirable government programs. The Fed creates financial bubbles that lead to economic dislocation. Think of the technology bubble of the late 1990s or the housing bubble. Or the boom that preceded the current bust. These are all a result of the monopolization of money.

These days, the American consumer has been hit very hard with rising prices in oil, clothing, food, and much else. For the first time in decades, people are feeling this and feeling it hard. And just as in every other inflation in world history, people are looking for the culprit and finding all the wrong ones. They believe it is the oil companies who are gouging us, or that foreign oil dealers are restricting supply, or that gas station owners are abusing a crisis to profit at our expense.

I wouldn't entirely rule out the possibility that price controls are around the corner. When Nixon imposed them in 1971, neither he nor his advisors believed that they would actually result in controlling inflation. Rather, the purpose was to redirect the target of public anger from the government and its bank over to retailers, who would become scapegoats. In this sense, price controls do work. They make people believe that the government is trying to lower prices while the private sector is attempting to raise them. This is the real political dynamic at work with price controls.

The question is whether you will be taken in by these tactics. It is long past time for us to take note that the cause of the real trouble here is not the manufacturers or even the war as such but the agency that has been granted a legal right to counterfeit at will and lower the value of the currency while fueling every manner of statist scheme, whether welfare or warfare. We need to look at the Fed and say: this is the enemy.

Note that the Federal Reserve is not a political party. It is not a recognized interest group. It is not a famed lobby in Washington. It is not really even a sector of public opinion. It seems completely shielded off from vigorous public debate. If we truly believe in liberty and decry the leviathan state, this situation cannot be tolerated.

I say to the sincere right, if you really want to limit the state, you will have to give up your dreams of remaking the world at the point of a gun. Wars and limited government are impossible. Moreover, you must stop ignoring the role of monetary policy. It is a technical subject, to be sure, but one that we must all look into and understand if we expect to restore something that resembles the American liberty of the founders.

I say to the sincere left, if you really want to stop war and stop the spying state, and put an end to the persecution of political dissidents and the Guantánamo camps for foreign peoples, and put a stop to the culture of nationalism and militarism, you must join us in turning attention to the role of monetary policy. The printing presses must be unplugged. It's true that this will also hit programs that are beloved by the left, such as socialized health care and federalized education programs. But so long as you expect the state to fund your dreams, you cannot expect that the state will not also fund the dreams of people you hate.

And let me say a few words to libertarians, who dream of a world with limited government under the rule of law, a world in which free enterprise reigns and where the state has no power to interfere in our lives so long as we behave peacefully. It is completely absurd to believe that this can be achieved without fundamental monetary reform. And yet, until the most recent Ron Paul campaign, and aside from Murray Rothbard and the 26-year-long work of the Mises Institute, I don't recall that libertarians themselves have cared much about this issue at all.

In 1983, the Mises Institute held a large academic conference on the gold standard, and we held it in Washington, D.C. (There were scholarly papers and Ron Paul debated a Fed governor. Ron won.) Even back then, I recall that D.C. libertarians ridiculed us for holding such a meeting to talk about the Fed and its replacement with sound money. They said that this would make the Mises Institute look ridiculous, that we would be tarred with the brush of gold bugs and crazies. We did it anyway. And all these years later, the book that came out of that conference remains a main source for understanding the role of money in the advance of despotism or resistance to it, and a blueprint for the future.

Of course the Austrian tradition fought paper money and central banking from the beginning. Menger was an advocate of the gold standard. Böhm-Bawerk actually established it as finance minister to the Habsburg monarchy. Mises's book on the topic from 1912 was the first to show the role of money in the business cycle, and he issued dire warnings about central banking. Hayek wrote powerfully against the abandonment of gold in the 1930s. Hazlitt warned of the inevitable breakdown of Bretton Woods, and advocated a real gold standard instead. And Rothbard was a champion of sound money and the greatest enemy the Fed has ever had. But generally, I've long detected a tendency in libertarian circles to ignore this issue, in part for precisely the reasons cited above: it is not respectable.

Well, I will tell you why this issue is not considered respectable: it is the most important priority of the state to keep its money machine hidden behind a curtain. Anyone who dares pull the curtain back is accused of every manner of intellectual crime. This is precisely the reason we must talk about it at every occasion. We must end the conspiracy of silence on this issue.

I was intrigued at how Ron Paul, during his campaign, would constantly bring up the subject. Most politicians are out to play up to their audiences, so they say things that people want to hear. I promise you that early in the campaign, no one wanted to hear him talk about the Federal Reserve. But he did it anyway. He worked to educate his audiences about the need for monetary reform. And it worked. For the first time in my life, there is a large and very public movement in this country to take this topic seriously.

Monetary economist Joseph Salerno was called the other day by C-Span, which wanted to interview him on television on the need to restore gold as the basis of our currency. As I watched this excellent interview, I was struck by what a great triumph it truly is for liberty that this topic is again part of the national debate. In the 19th century, this was a topic on everybody's minds. It can be again today, provided we do not eschew the truth in the formation of our message.

It might be said that advocating privatization is politically unrealistic, and therefore a waste of time. What's more, we might say that by continuing to harp on the issue, we only marginalize ourselves, proving that we are on the fringe. I submit that there is no better way to ensure that an issue will always be off the table than to stop talking about it.

Far from being an arcane and anachronistic issue, then, the gold standard and the issues it raises gets right to the heart of the current debate concerning the future of war and the world economy Why do the government and its partisans dislike the gold standard? It removes the discretionary power of the Fed by placing severe limits on the ability of the central bank to inflate the money supply. Without that discretionary power, the government has far fewer tools of central planning at its disposal. Government can regulate, which is a function of the police power. It can tax, which involves taking people's property. And it can spend, which means redistributing other people's property. But its activities in the financial area are radically curbed.

Think of your local and state governments. They tax and spend. They manipulate and intervene. As with all governments from the beginning of time, they generally retard social progress and muck things up as much as possible. What they do not do, however, is wage massive global wars, run huge deficits, accumulate trillions in debt, reduce the value of money, bail out foreign governments, provide endless credits to failing enterprises, administer hugely expensive and destructive social insurance schemes, or bring about immense swings in business activity.

State and local governments are awful and they must be relentlessly checked, but they are not anything like the threat of the federal government. Neither are they as arrogant and convinced of their own infallibility and indispensability. They lack the aura of invincibility that the central government enjoys.

It is the central bank, and only the central bank, that works as the government's money machine, and this makes all the difference. Now, it is not impossible that a central bank can exist alongside a gold standard, a lender of last resort that avoids the temptation to destroy that which restrains it. In the same way, it is possible for someone with an insatiable appetite for wine to sit at a banquet table of delicious vintages and not take a sip.

Let's just say that the existence of a central bank introduces an occasion of sin for the government. That is why under the best gold standard, there would be no central bank, gold coins would circulate as freely as their substitutes, and rules against fraud and theft would prohibit banks from pyramiding credit on top of demand deposits. So long as we are constructing the perfect system, all coinage would be private. Banks would be treated as businesses, no special privileges, no promises of bailout, no subsidized insurance, and no connection to government at any level.

This is the free-market system of monetary management, which means turning over the institution of money entirely to the market economy. As with any institution in a free society, it is not imposed from above, and dictated by a group of experts, but is the de facto result that comes about in a society that consistently respects private-property rights, encourages enterprise, and promotes peace.

It comes down to this. If you hate war, oppose the Fed. If you hate violations of your liberties, oppose the Fed. If you want to restrain despotism, restrain the Fed. If you want to secure freedom for yourself and your descendants, abolish the Fed.

Americans Have
Lost Their Liberty

Paul Craig Roberts

Dr. Roberts is formerly an Assistant Secretary of the U.S. Treasury, associate editor of the Wall Street Journal, *a member of the Congressional staff, and has held academic appointments at Stanford University, Georgetown University, Virginia Tech, Tulane University, George Mason University, and the University of New Mexico. He is the author or co-author of nine books, has had numerous articles in scholarly journals, and been a contributor to many books and to economic dictionaries and encyclopedias. He was awarded the U.S. Treasury's Silver Medal and the French Legion of Honor, and has testified before committees of Congress on 30 occasions. He was* Business Week's *first outside columnist and was a columnist for the Scripps Howard News Service and Creators Syndicate in Los Angeles. Dr. Roberts was educated at Georgia Tech, the University of Virginia, the University of California at Berkeley, and Oxford University, where he was a member of Merton College. His latest book,* How The Economy Was Lost, *was published by Counterpunch/AK press in 2010.*

> *A state of war only serves as an excuse for domestic tyranny.*
> - Alexander Solzhenitsyn

American liberties were foundering before the War on Terror was used to elevate the executive branch above the law. In our book, *The Tyranny of Good Intentions* (2000, 2008), Lawrence Stratton and I documented the piecemeal erosion of what William Blackstone called "the rights of Englishmen," which are what we know as the Bill of Rights.

The English, after centuries of struggle, succeeded in making government accountable to law and in making law accountable to the people. Legal principles, such as *habeas corpus*, right to an attorney, prohibition against self-incrimination, no crime without intent, no retroactive law, were created as shields of the people against the government's use of law as a weapon. As a British colony, Americans inherited these legal protections, and they became a part of the US Constitution.

It is to these protections that individuals living within America, the UK, Canada, Australia, and New Zealand owe their prosperity. People secure in their person and their property are a productive force.

In my career as an economist, somewhere along the way I became aware that legal uncertainty could adversely affect the economy as much as economic uncertainty. I began to notice that property rights were being both contravened and created by regulators, acting both in the absence of statutory authority and in defiance of clear statutory language.

There is an old saying that "the road to Hell is paved with good intentions." One way a land of liberty can go to hell is by losing the law that protects liberty. An easy way to lose law is to allow those who enforce the law also to create it. Certainly, good intentions played a role in the destruction of law by regulators.

For example, in haste to protect wetlands, the Environmental Protection Agency created wetlands regulations, on the basis of an expansive interpretation of the 1972 Clean Water Act which forbids dumping into "the navigable waters of the United States." These regulations resulted in federal taking of private property. All of a sudden farmers' productive bottomlands became protected wetlands. The presence of certain weeds and soil composition turned developers' dry tracts into protected wetlands. Ocie and Carey Mills actually lost their liberty for 21 months when they were convicted by federal prosecutors for a "wetlands violation" for leveling a building lot for which they had a Florida permit. Wetlands, or the vast majority of them, are not navigable waters, and neither do weeds and soil-composition create a navigable water. On the basis of regulations devoid of statutory authority, people lost both the use of their property and their liberty.

In an effort to advance racial minorities and women, the Equal Employment Opportunity Commission created a regime of race and gender quotas despite the explicit prohibition of quotas by the 1964 Civil Rights Act. The quotas created property rights based on race and gender in employment, promotions, and university admissions. Thus, at the hands of the EEOC, the 1964 Civil Rights Act, which was intended to give statutory support to the 14th Amendment— equal treatment under the law—was used to subvert equal treatment with a system of preferences for "preferred minorities." [See Roberts and Stratton, *The New Color Line*, 1995.]

I noticed also that prosecutors were creating laws based on expansive interpretations of statutes, and that people were being tried for crimes that no one knew existed. Prosecutors were also creating crimes based on novel theories that a crime had occurred. For example, Benjamin Lacy, an apple-juice producer in Virginia, was indicted for a "conspiracy" to pollute a stream on his property because of a few mistakes the 73-year old had made in filling out monthly wastewater report forms over a multi-year period. The evidence showed that the stream was pristine, but Mr. Lacy was indicted and lost his life savings, on the basis of a prosecutor's theory that a few innocent mistakes were evidence of a conspiracy to pollute.

Legislators themselves lost respect for our legal tradition. They not only failed to rein in overreaching regulators and prosecutors, but added to the chaos themselves. In the War on Crime, Congress passed in 1970 the Racketeer Influenced and Corrupt Organizations (RICO) Act. A provision of this act permits prosecutors to freeze, prior to trial and conviction, the defendant's assets, thus depriving the defendant of the ability to pay attorneys, thereby increasing the chance that the defendant can be coerced into a plea bargain, regardless of the strength of the case against him.

In the 1980s, the War on Drugs created legislation that permits assets that "facilitated" a drug crime to be confiscated. Police and prosecutors have expansively interpreted this statute. If federal agents conduct a drug sting on your property, your property can be seized on the grounds that it facilitated the "crime," whether or not it involved your participation. Merely having $100 in cash on your person is sufficient for police to infer that the cash is "drug money" and can be seized by police. For example, on May 18, 2011, News Channel 5 in Nashville, Tennessee, reported that police were stopping motorists on I-40, searching for cash and confiscating motorists' money. Rival police jurisdictions have almost come to blows over which has control over what part of the interstate highway. [http://www.newschannel5.com/story/14643085/police-profiting-off-drug-trade]

My columns on how the law was being lost resulted in an invitation to give the 1992 Frank M. Engle Lecture at the American College in Bryn Mawr, Pennsylvania. From this lecture developed *The Tyranny of Good Intentions.*

In the US especially but also in the mother country itself and its former English colonies, the rights of Englishmen have been, by degree, set aside in the interest of what Thomas More, in "A Man for All Seasons," described as cutting down the law in order to better chase after devils.

Law was cut down in order to chase after drug dealers. More law was cut down in order to chase after alleged child abusers and S&L crooks. Environmental accidents were turned into crimes. Prosecutors gained the right to create new crimes that are not on the books by unique interpretations of statutes, to pay witnesses for testimony against a defendant, and to coerce a defendant into a guilty plea by piling on charges.

Today in the US, the land of freedom and democracy, 96 percent of all felonies are resolved with plea bargains. So few cases go to trial that the police seldom bother to investigate crimes. Instead, as in the Humphrey Bogart film, "Casablanca," they round up the usual suspects and pile on charges, until the suspect realizes that it is in his interest to reduce his prison time by making a deal with a false confession.

Before the onset of the 21st century, law had lost much of its ability to protect the innocent.

With the events of September 11, 2001, and the public's acceptance of the government's explanation that America was attacked by Muslim terrorists, the U.S. government's response was "the war on terror," which produced such police-state laws as the USA PATRIOT Act, the Military Commissions Act of 2006, and other legal abominations. Air travelers are now subject to being porno-scanned or sexually groped in order to board a commercial aircraft.

The "war on terror" was launched with invasions of Afghanistan and Iraq that are war crimes under the Nuremberg standard. The US military attacks on Afghanistan and Iraq were based on false pretenses. The ongoing wars and occupations have resulted in many times more civilian deaths than deaths of an alleged enemy. The American public accepts these illegalities and war crimes, because the public has been put into a state of fear of terrorism. Americans have forgotten the Founding Fathers' warning: that their own government is the greatest threat to their liberty. It is irrational to seek security in a police state that can arrest and hold you indefinitely without charges, torture you, try you on secret charges, and confiscate your assets. This is a much larger threat to Americans than a few stateless terrorists half a world away. A country that allegedly fights and dies for its values should not abandon its values because of fear of terrorists.

The illegal wars have now expanded. The US military routinely violates the sovereignty of Pakistan, Yemen, Somalia, and Libya. Most of the casualties of the military operations are women, children, village elders, and international law. Crimes against humanity are now routinely committed by the United States government and its NATO puppets.

The Bush/Cheney regime lost no time in turning the war against terror into a war against the American people. Compliant officials in the US Department of Justice (sic) wrote legal memos that exempted the executive branch from obeying laws against spying on Americans without warrants, against torture, against holding suspects indefinitely without presenting charges, against holding suspects without providing them with legal representation, and against lying in order to achieve an undeclared agenda. Elevating the president above the law creates a Caesar. The notion that the public can be made secure by removing the accountability of government to law is absurd.

Media propaganda against "suspects" became the *modus operandi* for conviction, not evidence presented at trial. A public, hyped with fear by the government and media, accepted the phony prosecutions as necessary acts of protection for the public.

The fraudulent terrorist cases that have been brought against American citizens are more absurd than an Orwellian version of Franz Kafka. For example, an American citizen, Syed Fahad Hashmi, who was studying for an advanced degree in London, allowed an acquaintance, Junaid Babar, to leave some socks and rain ponchos at his apartment. The US government claimed that the socks and ponchos were on their way to al Qaeda operatives and that Hashmi, by allowing these items to be kept in his apartment, had provided material support for al Qaeda.

The fact of the matter is that Hashmi was a defender of Muslim rights, which annoyed the authorities, and he was arrested on the word of Babar. The only evidence against Hashmi was the word of Babar, who was allegedly the person transporting the socks and raincoats to al Qaeda, but was not prosecuted in exchange for testifying against Hashmi.

It looks like a set-up to silence a critic. Faced with a 70-year sentence, and most certainly no fair trial, Hashmi made a plea in exchange for a 15-year sentence.

This is American justice [sic] today.

As the justice system crumbles, the power of the president increases. Obama began a war in Libya by violating the War Powers Act. Congress has relinquished its authority to declare war, but the War Powers Act requires the President to at least inform Congress before he starts another war.

Following in the steps of the Bush regime and the Republican Federalist

Society, Obama ignored the War Powers Act, on the basis of the unitary powers of the executive that the Bush/Cheney regime succeeded in creating. According to executive-branch claims, this power is not subject to Congress or the courts.

The Obama regime also claims the right to assassinate anyone, including American citizens, whom the regime considers to be a threat. In other words, the president of the United States has declared that he has the power to murder individuals without due process of law. When the Obama regime made this announcement, it was connected to the planned assassination of an American citizen who was described as an al Qaeda operative. Thus, insouciant Americans accepted the complete overthrow of the U.S. legal system, in order to achieve the death of a "terrorist."

The United States originated as a republic, but soon devolved into a democracy. Now the democracy has been supplanted by an oligarchy of money, and the oligarchs themselves are now confronting the rise of a Caesar. Thanks to U.S. Department of Justice [sic] legal memos written during the Bush/Cheney regime, the president, when at war, which is a presidential decision, is immune from US statutory law, international law, and the U.S. Constitution. According to the doctrine, the executive has unitary powers that transcend any legal or constitutional constraint on executive power.

In other words, the United States is a police state. This is why Caesar Obama can thumb his nose at the War Powers Act. This is why the Federal Reserve can violate its own rules, and print money without regard to the consequences, in order to finance the regime's wars of aggression.

The US invasions of Iraq and Afghanistan are expensive and illegal acts that create precedents for greater illegality and expense in the future. But the war against Libya and a likely intervention in Syria are reckless escalations as the U.S., under the cloak of Arab protests, is bringing itself into confrontation with China in Libya and with Russia in Syria.

China has large oil investments in eastern Libya. The purpose of the Washington-inspired armed rebellion in eastern Libya is to evict China from its oil investments, in order to deny China independent energy sources and delay China's rising challenge to U.S. economic power.

In Syria, the stakes are the Russian naval base at Tartus. If the Assad regime can be overthrown, Russia's naval presence in the Mediterranean can be terminated. Turning the Mediterranean, which borders Europe, the Middle East and North Africa, into an American lake has strategic advantages for US hegemony.

China and Russia are different level opponents than Iraq. By bringing three nuclear powers into confrontation, Washington has elevated the risk of nuclear war. Washington's reckless pursuit of hegemony threatens life with extermination.

If Congress could find the gumption to defend its constitutional prerogatives and impeach Obama for his violation of the War Powers Act, and if the American people could overcome their fear of terrorism and realize that the greater threat is a domestic police state, Americans would have a chance to rescue themselves and the world from Armageddon.

Against War
and the Police State

The Making of a Libertarian Radical

Anthony Gregory is Research Editor at the Independent Institute, a policy adviser for the Future of Freedom Foundation, and a columnist for LewRockwell.com. His writings have appeared in such places as Huffington Post, The Daily Caller, The Christian Science Monitor, Bloomberg BusinessWeek, The San Diego Union Tribune, The Dallas Morning News, The Sacramento Bee, Antiwar.com, Human Events, The Journal of Libertarian Studies, Counterpunch, The American Conservative, Liberty Magazine, Mises.org *and* Liberty and Power, *and have been translated into several languages. He got his B.A. in history at UC Berkeley in 2003, where he wrote his thesis on the 1993 Waco disaster. He sings and plays in a rock band,* The Melatones, *and is an Eagle Scout. He gives talks frequently and is now writing an Independent Institute book on habeas corpus, detention policy and individual liberty. He loves cooking, reading fiction, and watching television shows, and lives in Oakland, California, with his girlfriend and their maltipoo.*

Once as a young boy, I lost my wallet in the mall. A policeman named Officer Duffy found it and asked me how much was in it. I knew the amount down to the penny and so he returned it. For years thereafter I admired the police.

Another time long ago, playing with toy soldiers in the backseat, I told my father it was not fair that he got to live through a major U.S. war, and I hadn't. In an unusually firm admonition, my dad said war is nothing to wish for. It was as though I had inadvertently spoken an obscenity. And in fact I had.

My dad also told me of his fear as a young man of being drafted into the Vietnam War. He raised me with a deep respect for free speech and freedom of religion, teaching me about the Bill of Rights before I was in kindergarten. He told me about the problems of drug abuse, but explained why the drug war was a mistake. My mother, meanwhile, told me stories of Communist Korea, from which her family had fled, imparting an awareness of state power's horror at its worst.

I was nine when the first Gulf War began. I believed President George Bush when he said Saddam Hussein was a ruthlessly wicked man who ought to be deposed. My dad, who had voted for Bush, said this might be so, but there was no way to wage war without killing the innocent. That stuck with me forever: the idea that bombings killed children.

My elementary school, in support of the war, told us kids to come to class wearing red, white, and blue, and donning American flags. My father, upset at this indoctrinating, dug through a box of college stuff that was gathering dust in the garage and pulled out a peace armband from the Vietnam protests to wear instead. From then on, no major war would be waged without practically everyone around me knowing of my disapproval.

My first sense that the justice system was flawed also came in 1990. My mom was railroaded into paying a fine for gathering mussels in Monterey. The park ranger who ticketed her—and searched me, a nine-year-old boy—claimed she dug up many more than she had, and then later accused my mother of lying about what she was doing, when her imperfect English had merely caused some confusion. The main allegation was that my mom illegally collected mussels in a Marine Reserve. My dad's meticulous research found that the act was probably committed outside the Reserve's boundaries. The ticket was reissued with a modified location to match the charge, and the arraignment schedule was changed without notification and a bench warrant put out for my mom. The stress led my mother to plead no contest for the sake of her sanity and to save thousands in a protracted legal battle. It was a minor injustice, but I'll never forget my mom's frustration. For years she was afraid to return to Monterey.

I first heard of libertarianism when I was about seven. I think it was the Ron Paul campaign in 1988. Much later, with more understanding, I started calling myself a libertarian in the eighth grade. My dad once again converted me on a question of state violence. I had favored a tough response to the immigration "problem." My dad's argument was simple: If I'm a libertarian, I must side with the freedom of peaceful immigrants to cross the border. That's all it took.

My eighth grade history teacher was unusually conservative for the profession, but concerning America's wars, his views helped to radicalize me. He told the class that some historians believed FDR had advance knowledge of Pearl Harbor. He also explained that the Civil War was not merely a crusade to abolish slavery, but was tied up with the politics of taxation and the centralization of political power.

My brother, Duane, eight years my senior, was another early influence. He taught me the danger of government monopolizing weapons, a violation of human rights that entices all too many liberals and pacifists when it is called "gun control." He explained that oppression often leads to violence from the disenfranchised, and although such violence should be condemned, the root causes must be understood. But his biggest ideological impact on me was less direct.

Early on my brother harbored an admiration of authority. He dreamt for years of being a police officer, and was well on his way, taking training courses and gaining relevant experience as a private security officer at the mall, even climbing to the top position. (Yes, this was the same mall where, years earlier, Officer Duffy had reacquainted me with my wallet.)

During a training exercise, my brother was injured, which may have hurt his prospects as a police officer. More important, he began questioning whether the police community was really the right place for him. Five of his colleagues in the academy ended up joining the police force only to be arrested for serious offenses. In the years since my brother has become increasingly disillusioned with law enforcement, and one of his good friends, a former cop, frequently encourages me in my criticisms of law enforcement.

Strangely enough, being a Boy Scout made me much more anti-authoritarian. I followed the rules and did my duty well enough to earn the rank of Eagle, but I also opened my mind a lot during those years of camping and socializing with fellow adolescents outside of the government-school matrix, where I enjoyed endless discussions in politics, religion, and philosophy. My friend Scott Garner and I realized we were both on the libertarian path. I'd share literature with him. He convinced me to oppose mandatory uniforms in public schools. I still remember when we both came to oppose government control of abortion. We were both pro-life and personally socially conservative, but as we read critiques of state power we began abandoning our traditionally rightwing positions. I still keep in touch with him.

School also radicalized me, as I protested rules that seemed patently unfair. Students caught fighting were punished whether or not they started it. Teachers exercised too much authority over students and their property. I rarely got in trouble, but I hated seeing the "bad" kids disproportionately punished.

In high school, I lost even more confidence in the system, as I saw fellow students mistreated by the police. One day at lunch, my friends and I sat on the bleachers to watch some kids playing soccer. Several police officers approached us and demanded we relinquish our alcohol, of which we had none. Our bags and wallets were thoroughly searched—as though we had liquor stashed in our billfolds. This whole time I thought of Officer Duffy, finding my wallet in the mall and returning it. Yet here was a cop searching through my wallet, not to ensure it was mine, but to find something with which to get me in trouble.

It was a petty humiliation, but it was still obnoxious and offensive. We were all honor students and had shown no signs of suspicious behavior. I realized how much worse off we would have been if we had appeared more delinquent.

In 1999 President Clinton went to war with Serbia. I was 18 and had just registered for the Selective Service. I was also active in libertarian politics at the urging of my girlfriend at the time. Introduced to Antiwar.com by a man I met in the Libertarian Party, I began reading everything I could about Clinton's war. I spoke out against it in class every day, and wrote a piece for the school newspaper condemning America's actions in "Yugo-Nam."

But I was still not a peacenik in the way I am now. It was easy for a libertarian to oppose Clinton's war, because everyone on my side hated Clinton. The real test came after 9/11.

I was a history student at UC Berkeley. While it was an unusually easy atmosphere for protesting the war, much of my identity was invested in opposing the leftists and socialists on campus. At that point I still believed that the right was more pro-freedom than the left (many self-described progressives had supported Clinton's war). It was unsettling to me that the leftists were so much more reasonable than conservatives after 9/11.

The country was overcome by war fever, and even Berkeley wasn't spared. But my closest friends—Lewis Ames, Tony "Stony" Burke, Serenity Wang, Ethan Lee, Mason Guffey, Mike Rubin—were wholly unimpressed with the war propaganda. Our lifestyle had bordered between bourgeois and bohemian—a very typical tendency among college students—and we tended to reject conflict. We thought peace was obviously preferable to war. I still talk with these friends about the world's happenings.

I asked Kelly, the young woman I was dating, who had less rigid ideological commitments than mine, why she instinctively opposed the war, and she replied that she didn't think the U.S. could go over to Afghanistan, bomb a bunch of people, and everything would be OK. Ten years into this war, I wish this wisdom had won the day.

September 11, 2011, was a defining moment in my developing political philosophy and ideological identity. I had generally favored non-intervention. I saw such policies as the sanctions on Iraq, the one-sided support for the Israeli state, U.S. backing of apostate dictators, and troops on Muslim soil, as having incited the attacks, and I knew a full-blown war was an unacceptable response.

But I also believed that government had legitimate roles in national defense and policing. I respected anarchism, as good friends like Stony helped me see it wasn't just a philosophy for troublemakers and vandals. Yet I wasn't convinced that government had no proper military function.

I looked to libertarians I had admired for years for their reaction. Some institutions came out firmly in favor of U.S. military action. If defined narrowly enough, it was something I could support in theory—military strikes pinpointed against terrorists, commandos sent in to capture al Qaeda's leaders. Yet some "libertarians"—and many Americans—seemed to go way beyond this, advocating all-out war with one or more countries.

A few libertarians came out squarely for peace. Harry Browne, the 2000 Libertarian presidential candidate, for whom I had voted, published a bold article on 9/12 called "When Will We Learn?" focusing on the sins of U.S. foreign policy. He took a lot of grief for it, but it inspired many people like me, making it easier to oppose the war.

I soon found other libertarians taking the pro-peace, pro-civil liberties position. Lew Rockwell and the Mises Institute, L. Neil Smith at the Libertarian Enterprise, Jacob Hornberger at the Future of Freedom Foundation, Sheldon Richman, and David Theroux at the Independent Institute were among those who took an unambiguous position against war.

So I opposed Operation Enduring Freedom. When my friend Joe came to visit, he asked what I thought of the war. I said, "I'm against it." It felt very liberating to take that position, to distance myself from all that was happening to the innocent civilians and refugees in Afghanistan.

With the USA PATRIOT Act and Afghanistan war, Bush seemed much more interested in flexing power than protecting lives. The government appeared incapable of ethically responding to a foreign threat. It was failing in its one "legitimate" function. Now, suddenly, I realized that the idea that the government should be distrusted—except in war—was not just a paradox but a contradiction.

Meanwhile, I still had a soft spot for the cops even as I distrusted them. When a construction worker told me years before that he knew several girls who had been raped by police, I was a little surprised, but did not find it hard to believe. I was very much against the drug war, immigration controls, and civil liberties violations. But somehow I still took the old John Birch Society line: "Support your local police." As late as my freshman year in college I had even supported the death penalty—the power of the state to kill!

In November of 2001, I sat with Kelly in a pizza parlor and noticed a few police at the next table. Then it hit me. They didn't make me feel any safer. That was the moment I gave up on supporting the local police.

Some police want to be honest and protect people's rights, and some do good deeds on duty. But one cannot help but commit wrongs in such an immoral system. When your orders are unjust—jailing people for victimless crimes and intimidating the law-abiding—it is very difficult to act decently all the time and keep your job. Surely, so long as police must enforce such horrendous policies as the drug war, much of what they do has nothing to do with serving and protecting, regardless of the good intentions of some who join the force.

Around the time I lost faith in government police I also began reading Thomas Szasz, the great libertarian psychiatrist whose opposition to what he calls the "therapeutic state" and conventional concepts of mental illness helped form my current views on psychiatry and civil liberties. Szasz's work in challenging involuntary hospitalization helped usher in major reforms in the 1970s, after a long history of compulsory and brutal psychiatric commitment being the norm. The system is still far from perfect. Several times in the last ten years I have been confronted with the question of whether an acquaintance should be involuntarily held for evaluation in a process known in California as a "5150." Each time, including when I was somewhat afraid of the person, I felt that forced therapy was simply unacceptable. The civil liberties of those deemed mentally ill continues to be an area lacking the attention it deserves.

Afghanistan and the war propaganda concerning Iraq prompted me to read a lot about the history of U.S. foreign policy. I had remembered a piece by Jacob Hornberger challenging conventional wisdom on World War II. I read more by him, Ralph Raico, and others on it. If even the "Good War" could be questioned, then no war would be sacred. I'm now convinced that the mythology surrounding World War II is among the most important to challenge.

I read revisionist history on Pearl Harbor, criticisms of the Hirsohima and Nagasaki bombings, accounts of Japanese internment, the draft, and the economic costs of the war. I learned that the U.S. helped Stalin round up a million refugees. I realized that the Allies were not the unvarnished heroes they were made out to be and that U.S. involvement was not necessary to stop Hitler, whose fate was probably doomed the moment he decided to invade Russia. Moreover, the Axis atrocities, while every bit as horrendous as they are depicted in the conventional literature, were likely not curbed by the war, but might in fact have been exacerbated by the war.

In late 2002 I met Jeff Riggenbach, a journalist, author, and broadcaster who had been a member of the libertarian movement for decades. He became a major philosophical influence and an encouraging mentor in my writing. I might not be a writer except for his guidance. He was refreshingly unwavering in his opposition to Bush's wars. "How can dropping bombs from thousands of feet above ever be defense?" he asked me.

Even after 9/11, I had humored the idea of the U.S. bombing foreign nations if "it had to" in defense of the country. I found the bombings of Hiroshima and Nagasaki to be indefensible, and all U.S. wars in the 20th century to be unjust. But in theory, I could see a case for the U.S. unleashing its awesome weapons.

Reading Murray N. Rothbard's classic essay "War, Peace, and the State" made it impossible for me to see war the same way ever again. If I cared about individual rights, then I must oppose bombings, invasions, occupations, and other modern tools of war that inevitably kill and maim the innocent. Rothbard helped move me from an America-First position of opposing "nation-building" to seeing war itself as criminal. My dad had laid the foundation of this understanding when I was a kid. Reading Rothbard made me realize there were no defensible modern wars.

I will never forget what felt like a slow-motion run-up to the Iraq war. The United States was about to embark on a brutally aggressive attack, killing many thousands, and there was absolutely nothing I could do, even as I marched at antiwar rallies and wrote some of my first published commentaries. The Berkeley club I was in, the Cal Libertarians, hosted great antiwar talks by Justin Raimondo and Ivan Eland. That spring I was also writing my undergraduate thesis. My topic was the 1993 federal raid at Waco, where the Branch Davidians died in a horrendous fire at the hands of the FBI. Studying Waco and the press reaction, which was mostly pro-government, intensified my hatred of the police state. During the day I was reading about a government atrocity conducted exactly ten years before, and in the evenings I read and watched the news about the impending war with Iraq. Watching the bombings of Baghdad in March 2003 left me ill, angry, and depressed. Most modern wars are rationalized in terms of national security and humanitarianism, but from Shock and Awe and Abu Ghraib to the surge and continuing chaos, we have seen once again the truth behind the propaganda.

As the Iraq War began, I continued to question modern policing. A couple of my friends, very peaceful souls, got shot with rubber bullets at an antiwar rally. Soon after that, my now-deceased friend Mike Pelton was arrested, jailed for more than a day, and then released (in the rain, in the middle of the night, without his bike or ID)—all because he refused to sign a ticket for riding a bicycle in a dismount zone. His refusal was his legal right, he insisted.

In 2004 I began working full-time at the Independent Institute, whose founder and president, David Theroux, was among the few to resist the post-9/11 war hysteria. I began writing for Lew Rockwell, another consistent and vocal opponent of militarism. I met Scott Horton, who hosted an independent interview show on KAOS radio in Austin. He became my go-to guy on all questions of foreign policy. He now hosts Antiwar Radio. Through Scott I met Angela Keaton, who now works at Antiwar.com and whose indefatigable peace activism continues to inspire me.

I've been lucky to meet many others who encouraged my hardline antiwar view. Walter Block, who had been Rothbard's student for many years, applauded my articles criticizing pro-war libertarians. Jeff Hummel, a historian and economist whose history of the Civil War is among my favorite books, also reassured me that a radical antiwar position is the correct one. Karen Kwiatkowski, an Iraq war whistleblower, reinforced my notion that the peaceniks were the good guys. Meeting Daniel Ellsberg was also powerful in this regard.

Getting to know Eric Garris, webmaster for LewRockwell.com and the founder of *Antiwar.com*, has been especially valuable. We met at one of Riggenbach's monthly Beer Bust parties, hosted by Jeff and his wonderful wife, Suzanne, at their San Francisco apartment. Eric spent every day reading about war and had always seen the intimate connection between freedom and peace. I talk with him very often.

Robert Higgs, a historian and economist editing the Independent Institute's quarterly journal, might be my biggest intellectual hero on questions of government power. His work, along with Rothbard's, Hummels's and many others, showed me that war was the greatest cause of government expansion in U.S. history. Everything libertarians hate about Washington DC—the regulations, welfare programs, taxing schemes—has roots in warfare. War is indeed, as Randolph Bourne put it, "the health of the state." I now believe peace is the key issue in opposing state power.

Higgs has an unusual combination of traits: He writes clearly, his scholarship is airtight and respected, and he is unflinching in opposing state violence. His many books and articles on war and statism are mandatory reading. The personal correspondence I've had with him, and the few times I've met him in person, have been highlights of my life. No one burns with more outrage at injustice, no one cares more for the individual liberty of each and every forgotten victim of the state, than Bob.

My girlfriend, Nicole Booz, has probably been my biggest inspiration when it comes to my never-ending struggle not to overlook any injustices. She has fostered my anti-violence philosophy through stressing love and positive energy in her interests and the space we share. She is an incredibly nurturing and loving person, teaching preschool for the eight years we've been together. She loves to garden, taught me to love herbs and plants, got me to start cooking, and convinced me finally to have a puppy with her. She has taught me about a practice called "non-violent communication," encouraging me to become more pacifistic, not just in my politics but in my personal relations, although I do not always succeed.

I have come to hate violence in all forms, especially when it's institutionalized and socially accepted. Studying history and considering the moral issues involved, I now take an absolutist position against war. I see all wars in American history, including the Revolution, as unjust.

I've been working on a book for the Independent Institute on *habeas corpus*, which has made me more dedicated to civil liberties but also far more cynical that the state can ever be trusted to protect the rights of the accused.

So long as we have a state, we need to be jealous of our civil liberties. On a philosophical level, however, I have come to take a much more radical position. Reading about everyday police abuses and talking with great libertarians like Lew Rockwell have helped lead me to believe that modern police departments and prisons should simply be abolished, with community and market alternatives coming in to fill the void.

Prison in particular warrants far more attention. It is a totalitarian institution that needs to be completely rethought. Conservatives cheer mass incarceration, and even liberals are happy to see a white-collar criminal caged. I find the whole enterprise completely horrifying. I'm unsure what the best alternative is, but I have some ideas, guided by libertarian and other literature exploring civilized approaches to the provision of justice. Regardless, this should be debated and discussed openly and constantly, not shoved under the carpet as if the millions in America's jails and prisons—the largest inmate population in the world—were not human at all, not even worthy of the sympathy animals deserve. This will never be discussed in the presidential elections, nor will the drug war, police abuses, or militarism, beyond a superficial level. Ron Paul is saying some great things in the GOP primary about America's wars, but it's clear the establishment would prefer to minimize meaningful discussions of state violence.

I'm lucky that my adoption of the anti-police state, antiwar position has mostly been an intellectual endeavor. I've been stopped, searched, and detained by police, bullied by lying cops, and slowed down by airport security, but I am very fortunate compared to so many others. I've met veterans traumatized by war, immigrants living in fear of deportation, members of minorities constantly harassed by police, vagrants who've been treated as subhuman.

Some acquaintances told me of their community service under police direction. They were forced into the dangerous, degrading, and immoral work of going through the shanty-towns constructed by homeless people to destroy them, seizing what little property these poorest of Americans have. Every experience I've had and heard about strengthens my conviction that the enforcement arm of the state is the least trustworthy government agency.

To this day, virtually everything government does frustrates me, but I am always most appalled by the clear-cut violations of human dignity that occur in war and policing. I hold onto my economic principles very tightly, but I am particularly offended when civil liberties are under attack. Executions, police beatings and killings, and the spectacle of Americans arguing over whether Muslims should be allowed to build a mosque somewhere, are the kinds of incidents that most upset me.

When I read about Cory Maye, who was sentenced to death for shooting and killing a cop who had raided his home at night in a mistaken drug bust, I can't help but get very angry. (In his case, thanks largely to the journalistic efforts of Radley Balko, the story ends mostly well, as Maye is now out of prison.) I burn when I think of Omar Khadr, captured as a minor, abused for years at Guantánamo, and, as of now, still detained by U.S. authorities. I was very disappointed to see some of my liberal friends defend the brutal detention of Bradley Manning, the soldier accused of leaking information about U.S.

atrocities to WikiLeaks.

All war news bothers me. Every August, I'm disgusted to see anniversary op-eds defending America's war crimes in Hiroshima and Nagasaki. As much of the country applauded the anti-climactic and much-awaited killing of Osama bin Laden, nearly a decade after 9/11, I found the national celebration to be rather grotesque. Even the death of a mass murderer disturbs me.

As the state's armed enforcers become ever more brutal, as punishments become more draconian, wars widen, and the prisons swell, as the presidency grabs more power by the day, I become more confident that the state's powers to arrest, punish, and kill are the ones to oppose the most. The tendency of a militarized police state to expand is the greatest threat to freedom.

Even before the war on terror, the U.S. had bases in over a hundred countries and the world's largest military establishment by far. President Obama has only proven that the problem is thoroughly bipartisan, with his continuation of the Bush policy of detention without trial, his abuses of *habeas corpus*, and his drone assassination of American citizen Anwar Al-Awlaki (along with his son and others) without due process. Obama has normalized what were previously seen as Republican anomalies in policy, such as torture and indefinite detention.

At home, we have a hundred SWAT team raids a day, police departments have adopted battle rifles, tanks, and even drone weaponry, and cops in riot gear use flash-bang-grenades and tear-gas canisters at the first sight of any protester stepping out of line. About three thousand people have been killed by police on U.S. soil since 9/11—as many as died on that day. A cursory look at such sites as injusticeeverywhere.com, which documents over a dozen stories of police misconduct every day, illustrates the depth of the problem. Will Grigg, who used to edit the conservative *New American* magazine, has also become a great resource on these matters.

Corruption, waste, fraud, political abuse, inequity, bureaucracy and injustice were the sins that made me come to find big government such a threat to freedom and human life. But the clearest areas where this is so, and the areas where conservatives, and even some libertarians and liberals, often turn a blind eye, surround the questions of war and police power.

The child watching his brothers and mom blown to bits in their own home, all because they happen to live in a country the U.S. president has decided is the enemy.... The innocent Muslim businessman detained for five years without charge... The child soldier tried by military commission.... The young prisoner raped and beaten by his cellmate while the guard looks the other way.... The little girl shot by a SWAT team in her own home.... The eccentric forced to undergo psychiatric treatment and medication against his will.... The college enrollee whose life is ruined because he sold some ecstasy to an undercover agent.... The family ripped apart, half of them deported, because they were born on the wrong side of a line on a map.... The grandfather tased in a confrontation with police.... The sex worker forced underground and threatened with jail.... The young woman sent to prison because her drug-dealing boyfriend testified against her in a plea agreement.... The young man who never had a chance at a fair trial, sentenced to death for killing a cop....

These are the people with the least voice in our world, and I've come to believe that anyone who objects to the problems of government needs to realize it. Government is always dangerous, but the police and warfare state are where the violence actually comes down, to crack skulls and snuff out life. Any movement genuinely interested in stripping the state of its frightening power must keep focused on the nightstick, the prison cell, the bomber. This is where the most harm is done, and where the victims are the least able to fight back.

Since I was a small child, I have never again come across Officer Duffy, the cop who found my wallet and returned it to me. And I don't just mean I've never seen him in the flesh again. I mean also that I've never come away from any member of the state's enforcement apparatus with as positive an impression as I had in the mall over twenty years ago. There were many times I indulged in my nostalgia, searching for a mark of that kindness smiling behind a badge, but I am convinced now that this is a mistake. Is there humanity in the man wearing the uniform and badge? Surely there is. But the uniform itself, at least in our world, more often represents power and subjugation than virtue and protection.

Why Am I
a Peace Activist?
Why Aren't You?

David Swanson

David Swanson is the author of War Is A Lie *and* Daybreak: Undoing the
Imperial Presidency and Forming a More Perfect Union. *He is Co-Founder of*
WarIsACrime.org *(formerly AfterDowningStreet.org); an organizer with
RootsAction.org; creator of ProsecuteBushCheney.org; Washington Director of
Democrats.com; and a board member of Progressive Democrats of America,
the Backbone Campaign, Voters for Peace and the Liberty Tree Foundation for
the Democratic Revolution. He was the press secretary for Dennis Kucinich's
2004 presidential campaign, media coordinator for the International Labor
Communications Association, and worked three years as communications
coordinator for ACORN, the Association of Community Organizations for
Reform Now.*

More than any other description, except for perhaps husband and father, I
have been for the past six years a peace activist. Yet I hesitate on the question
of how to tell my personal story of experience with war. I recently visited
Afghanistan briefly, in order to speak with people who have experienced war.
I've spoken with many U.S. soldiers and non-U.S. victims of war. But I have
no personal experience of war. (Being in Washington, D.C., on September 11,
2001, doesn't change that; by the time a crime had been transformed into a war,
the war had been moved elsewhere.)

I know a Vietnam veteran who opposed that war, but grew so tired of being
told he wasn't qualified to do so that he joined up. Once he got back, and for
decades since, he's been opposing wars with the benefit of the aura of someone
who knows war. I don't have that, and I certainly do not want it. I value war-
opposition by those who have known war, but I value other war-opposition as
well. I also imagine we can all spot the fatal flaw in any proposal that would
have people experience wars before they could oppose them. In 2006, a
congressional candidate and Iraq veteran in Ohio who was speaking on a panel
with me urged requiring military "service" for all politicians, so that they could
oppose militarism with greater knowledge of the military. Raise your hand if
you think that would work.

So, the obvious question is probably how I became a peace activist. To my
mind, however, the question has always been why anybody is not. I understand
there are not a lot of job openings for professional peace activists, but there are
unlimited part-time volunteer positions.

When I was a kid growing up in Northern Virginia, in a family that had no
one in the military and no one opposing the military, we had a guest come to

visit. He very much wanted to see the U.S. Naval Academy in Annapolis, Maryland. So we drove him over there and showed him around. He was quite impressed. But I became physically ill. Here was a beautiful sunny town full of people enjoying life... and people being trained to murder other people in large numbers. To this day I cannot imagine why I need a particular explanation for finding that unbearably revolting. I want to hear an explanation from someone who doesn't find it so.

Oh, they'll tell us, we all find war to be troubling, but being a grown-up means having the stomach to do what's needed to prevent something worse.

The thing is, I never much trusted grown-ups. I wasn't revolted by the idea of war for myself, while willing to let others engage in it. I refused to take it on faith that such a horror as war could be justified—for anyone. After all, like all kids, I had been taught to work out problems with words rather than fists. I had been told that it was wrong to kill. And, like almost all people, I was viscerally inclined to resist the idea of killing anyone. If I was going to accept that in some cases it was right to kill lots and lots of people, and that it was right to always be training and building a huge war machine just in case such a situation arose, then someone was going to have to prove that claim to me.

In my experience, common wisdom was often wildly wrong. A huge industry of churches was maintained on Sundays to promote ideas that my parents (along with most people) took seriously, but which struck me as utter nonsense. The idea that war was peace came to seem to me so nonsensical on its face, I'd only believe it if offered proof. Yet all such thinking was in the back of my head. I never thought I'd work as a peace-activist, until the moment I found myself doing so at age 35. It took me years—traveling, studying, dropping out of architecture school, teaching English in Italy, picking up a Master's in Philosophy at the University of Virginia, and working as a reporter and a press person—before I found my way.

I became an activist in my late 20s on domestic issues of criminal justice, social justice, and labor rights. I became a professional activist at age 30 when I went to work for ACORN, the association of community groups that scared so many powerful people that it was slandered in the media, defunded, and destroyed several years later, after I had moved on. I protested the first Gulf War and the build-up to a 2003 war on Iraq. But I became something of a spokesperson and writer against war when I worked as press-secretary for Dennis Kucinich's presidential campaign in 2004. He made peace the number one issue in his platform. We talked about peace, trade, and healthcare—and not that much on trade or healthcare.

In 2005, I found myself working on a campaign to impeach and prosecute President George W. Bush for lying the nation into war. Congressman Dennis Kucinich introduced 35 articles of impeachment (selected from drafts of many more). I later published the articles as a book, with additional material from former federal prosecutor Elisabeth de la Vega and me on how to prosecute Bush for his crimes. The titles of the 35 articles tell the story:

Article I Creating a Secret Propaganda Campaign to Manufacture a False Case for War

Against Iraq.

Article II Falsely, Systematically, and with Criminal Intent Conflating the Attacks of September 11, 2001, With Misrepresentation of Iraq as a Security Threat as Part of Fraudulent Justification for a War of Aggression.

Article III Misleading the American People and Members of Congress to Believe Iraq Possessed Weapons of Mass Destruction, to Manufacture a False Case for War.

Article IV Misleading the American People and Members of Congress to Believe Iraq Posed an Imminent Threat to the United States.

Article V Illegally Misspending Funds to Secretly Begin a War of Aggression.

Article VI Invading Iraq in Violation of the Requirements of HJRes114.

Article VII Invading Iraq Absent a Declaration of War.

Article VIII Invading Iraq, A Sovereign Nation, in Violation of the UN Charter.

Article IX Failing to Provide Troops With Body Armor and Vehicle Armor.

Article X Falsifying Accounts of US Troop Deaths and Injuries for Political Purposes.

Article XI Establishment of Permanent U.S. Military Bases in Iraq.

Article XII Initiating a War Against Iraq for Control of That Nation's Natural Resources.

Article XIII Creating a Secret Task Force to Develop Energy and Military Policies With Respect to Iraq and Other Countries.

Article XIV Misprision of a Felony, Misuse and Exposure of Classified Information And Obstruction of Justice in the Matter of Valerie Plame Wilson, Clandestine Agent of the Central Intelligence Agency.

Article XV Providing Immunity from Prosecution for Criminal Contractors in Iraq.

Article XVI Reckless Misspending and Waste of U.S. Tax Dollars in Connection With Iraq and US Contractors.

Article XVII Illegal Detention: Detaining Indefinitely And Without Charge Persons Both U.S. Citizens and Foreign Captives.

Article XVIII Torture: Secretly Authorizing, and Encouraging the Use of Torture Against Captives in Afghanistan, Iraq, and Other Places, as a Matter of Official Policy.

Article XIX Rendition: Kidnapping People and Taking Them Against Their Will to "Black Sites" Located in Other Nations, Including Nations Known to Practice Torture.

Article XX Imprisoning Children.

Article XXI Misleading Congress and the American People About Threats from Iran, and Supporting Terrorist Organizations Within Iran, With the Goal of Overthrowing the Iranian Government.

Article XXII Creating Secret Laws.

Article XXIII Violation of the Posse Comitatus Act.

Article XXIV Spying on American Citizens, Without a Court-Ordered Warrant, in Violation of the Law and the Fourth Amendment.

Article XXV Directing Telecommunications Companies to Create an Illegal and Unconstitutional Database of the Private Telephone Numbers and Emails of American Citizens.

Article XXVI Announcing the Intent to Violate Laws with Signing Statements.

Article XXVII Failing to Comply with Congressional Subpoenas and Instructing

Former Employees Not to Comply.

Article XXVIII Tampering with Free and Fair Elections, Corruption of the Administration of Justice.

Article XXIX Conspiracy to Violate the Voting Rights Act of 1965.

Article XXX Misleading Congress and the American People in an Attempt to Destroy Medicare.

Article XXXI Katrina: Failure to Plan for the Predicted Disaster of Hurricane Katrina, Failure to Respond to a Civil Emergency.

Article XXXII Misleading Congress and the American People, Systematically Undermining Efforts to Address Global Climate Change.

Article XXXIII Repeatedly Ignored and Failed to Respond to High Level Intelligence Warnings of Planned Terrorist Attacks in the US, Prior to 911.

Article XXXIV Obstruction of the Investigation into the Attacks of September 11, 2001.

Article XXXV Endangering the Health of 911 First Responders.

The full articles and documentation are available at: http://warisacrime.org/busharticles.

Working on this project meant working closely with and becoming a part of the peace movement, even while engaged in something less than peaceful: seeking to put someone on trial and imprison him. I immersed myself in online and real-world activism, organizing, educating, and protesting. I strategized, lobbied, planned, wrote, protested, went to jail for protesting in or sitting in congressional offices or the street in front of the White House, did interviews, and pressed for peace.

Needless to say, we did not impeach Bush. And (I wish it were needless to say) when it comes to abusing power, Obama has proven to be worse than Bush was. But we did educate the public about war lies, thereby turning people against the war on Iraq, and later against the war on Afghanistan. Opposition to attacking Iran, which has thus far prevented it, has grown out of rejection of lies closely resembling those told about Iraq. A new war on Libya became unpopular faster than any previous U.S. war.

There are downsides to, and even seeming hypocrisy in, the peace movement. We don't always behave peacefully toward each other. We don't always share the same vision. Some groups favor peace when doing so helps a particular political party, and are otherwise very accepting of war. Some honestly think particular wars are crimes but deem others to be justified. Some try to work with corrupted insiders. Some try to bring pressure from outside the halls of power. Some try, with great difficulty, to bridge some of those gaps.

But my peace movement experience overall has been incredibly positive. I've made good friends who I see a handful of times a year, on stages or in streets, and as often as not in police vans. The fulltime peace activists, most of whom have other fulltime paid employment, and serve no particular organization, but hold the movement together with their spirit and reliability: these are people with more great stories than any writer will ever get onto paper or computer screens. These are the people for whom, outside of my family, I am most grateful. If any of them had ever been visible in the way military recruiters and toy soldiers are visible, perhaps I would have found my way to the peace movement sooner.

My focus or approach may evolve, but I cannot imagine ever leaving. In 2009 and 2010, I wrote two books, the second one on the question of whether any war had ever been justified. The title is a giveaway of the conclusion I reached: "War Is A Lie." And it isn't just any lie. It is the justification of the worst thing anyone has ever devised. Ending it now is no longer just a question of making the world more pleasant, but a question of survival. Weapons proliferation, blowback, economic collapse, environmental collapse, political collapse... choose your poison; war will destroy us in one or more of these manners, unless we put an end to it. Why in the world would anyone not want to?

Blessed Are
the Peacemakers

Jeff Taylor

Jeff Taylor is a political scientist and author of Where Did the Party Go?:
William Jennings Bryan, Hubert Humphrey, and the Jeffersonian Legacy.

My movement toward peace came in fits and starts. My childhood coincided with the rise of the Vietnam War. The U.S. government began direct military attacks in Vietnam the year after I was born. By the late 1960s, I was conscious of filmed footage of the war on the evening newscasts.

My parents were typical Middle America citizens—far from the hippies and anti-war longhairs demonstrating in the streets. My dad was a law-and-order guy, but he was also an anti-establishment guy, who distrusted politicians and derided Tricky Dick. He had inherited a common-sense, agrarian populism from his father, and this extended to the war. I don't recall him ever saying a supportive word about the war, or ever casting it in moralistic terms. Like Governor George Wallace, whom my dad supported in 1968, he probably thought we ought to either go all-out and win the war, or get the hell out and bring our troops home.

By 1972, I was definitely opposed to the Vietnam War. I viewed it as a waste of American lives. I don't remember being inspired by any contemporary anti-war activists, but I was one of only two students in my sixth-grade class to favor McGovern over Nixon, partly because of the war issue.

I wasn't a pacifist, though. A typical American boy, I grew up playing with toy soldiers and armaments, playing Army with my neighborhood friends. A devotee of American history, I loved the war narratives, going back to the American Revolution. I was also attracted to the pageantry and splendor of European royalty, including the conquerors and empire-builders. I had a fantasy life in comic-book drawings that my friend Paul and I drew, and my job was U.S. Navy admiral of the fleet until moving to Britain to become a duke and, eventually, invading the backward country of Sierra Leone so I could become king. (Obviously my dislike of the war was coming from practical populism, not pure principle.)

While I was a McGovern booster in the fall of '72, Hubert H. Humphrey had been my first choice for president earlier in the year. By this time, HHH was a vocal, if opportunistic, opponent of the war. A couple years later, I shifted from liberal Democrat to conservative Republican (retaining partisan independence: I also liked conservative Democrats like Wallace).[1] My seemingly erratic course made some sense, since I remained a populist. There were similarities between what right-wing populist George Wallace and left-wing populist Fred Harris were saying in 1975.

Having become more aware of the evils of totalitarian oppression—

especially Communism—I liked the strong anti-Communist stance of Governor Wallace and Governor Reagan. Yet I had not bought into the bipartisan Cold War consensus. Listening to the new syndicated radio commentary program of my new hero, Ronald Reagan, I was angered by his defense of the Vietnam War as a noble cause, commenting on tape afterwards that I completely disagreed and that the honeymoon was over. Even so, my marriage with the incipient New Right continued. Reading *Conscience of a Conservative* by the hawkish Barry Goldwater inspired me to wonder why we didn't just nuke the Soviets and free the enslaved masses behind the Iron Curtain. Not a carefully-thought-out plan, but my zeal was well-intended. I remember talking with Grandpa Crowder one day about his time in the Navy during World War II. I remember thinking I'd rather be in the Navy than the Army or Marines because it would be safer. I felt a tinge of shame because of my cowardly line of thought, but self-preservation is a strong instinct.

In explaining my embrace of a nonviolent ethic, I've sometimes said that when I became a Christian I was naive enough to take the New Testament teachings on peace literally, which turned me into a pacifist. There's truth to this thought; in actuality, the change was more complex and less immediate. It was a gradual process by which I arrived at a consistent valuing of God-given life. Still, it is true that my Christian faith was moving me out of conservative Republican politics, about the same time Jerry Falwell and Pat Robertson were leading millions of other Bible-believing Christians into that camp.

I was raised in the Congregational Church. I took some satisfaction in the fact that ours was the church of the Pilgrims. My mother and grandmother were examples of Christian piety. Belief in God and reverence for Christ were parts of my life from my earliest years, but I had never read the Bible myself, and I did not understand what it meant to personalize and internalize Christianity. I was sincere in a limited sense but my identity as a "Christian" had little effect on my daily life. I had little sense of my own sinfulness and my interior life did not include fellowship with God. As I was preparing for my senior year in high school, I understood the reality of spiritual things and felt my own need for a Savior. That was my conscious conversion from a God-fearing cultural Christian to a God-knowing personal Christian.

A year later, during a meeting at a Bible conference, I committed myself to the lordship of Christ. At that point, I began reading the Bible from cover to cover. Like a sponge, or a newborn babe, I thirsted after the pure milk of the Word. I remain a theologically conservative/orthodox Christian. I know the Bible to be accurate. Scripture should be our primary guide for thought and practice. By the late 1970s—before reading the Bible myself—I had developed a keen sense of the struggle between good and evil by reading two Christian authors: Alexander Solzhenitsyn and J.R.R. Tolkien. The question was, How should those with a sense of justice and morality oppose evil in the world?

In November, 1979, one week after the American embassy was seized in Tehran, I wrote a paper for my freshman Western Man course at Northwestern College, entitled *Is War Wrong?* My journal entry explains: *"Did a 9-page paper rather than the 3-4 required. Learned a lot from the paper and felt I couldn't end it prematurely without resolving it for myself one way or the other."*

I had already read through the New Testament for the first time but I didn't have a specifically Christian view of war prior to writing the paper. In the end, I put myself in the Just War Theory camp... although I didn't know it was called that. I primarily cited Scripture. The non-biblical sources quoted were mostly those with whom I was familiar at the time: Protestant chiliasts and dispensationalists, rather than Roman Catholics like Augustine and Aquinas.[2] It was a sincere but misguided effort. To paraphrase Dooyeweerd, I was using the Christian religion as "a decorative superstructure" atop a nationalistic ideology that was "at bottom and in essence" pagan.[3]

On January 23, 1980, I chronicled, *"This afternoon wild rumors of us going to war against the USSR and Carter reinstituting the draft spread, causing minor hysteria. He ended up announcing reinstitution [of draft] registration, during his State of the Union address (the jerky guy!)."* While recognizing the validity of war in theory, I was not eager to be sent overseas to fight Soviets or Iranians. I was already a Reagan '80 supporter but was gratified when Governor Reagan came out in opposition to draft registration. (One of the many promises he neglected to act upon after his election.)

I retired from politics in early February, 1981. I was influenced by deeper reflection on the New Testament, by Christ-Against-Culture theology, by Francis Schaeffer's warning about confusing loyalty to country with loyalty to Christ, by disillusionment with the pragmatic Reagan administration, and by disgust with the hypocrisy of campus leaders whose sociopolitical pronouncements seemed more grounded in liberalism than Christianity.[4] I explained my withdrawal in this way: "Politics *cannot* solve the problem—sin and man's lostness.... Conservatism *cannot* be equated with Christianity." My apolitical, Christian anarchistic period peaked in November, 1984, when I chose to not vote in the presidential election. By the time I became sociopolitically reengaged the following year, my location on the American ideological spectrum had moved from Right to Left. (My populism remained a constant, which accounted for the ongoing "conservative" tilt of some of my positions on cultural/moral issues.)

Part of my new, or recovered, left-wing orientation began in my college years and peace played a major role in this. Inspirations for my anti-war stance were primarily Christian, including anti-worldly dispensationalism but branching out beyond that school of theology, as well (e.g., Jesus People variant of the 1960s Counterculture and the Anabaptist movement of the 1500s). Ironically, the establishment of Northwestern College, with its constant drumbeat of "social consciousness," did little to move me in the direction of peace. Proclaiming that "Christ is lord of all life"—a noble and accurate Reformed, and more importantly Christian, concept—college and denominational leaders encouraged students to join the Church's interaction with the World. It seemed to me, however, that the resulting interaction more often than not made the Church more worldly rather than the World more Christian. This National Council of Churches/World Council of Churches approach—administered by a self-satisfied, economically privileged, socially elite, theologically apostate bureaucracy in New York City, not only blurred the lines between the World and the Church but actively embraced the World, in contradiction to the teachings of Christ and his apostles.

I was moved by strains of Christianity more traditional and more radical. I learned of Tertullian, the 3rd-century father of Latin theology, in one of my classes, and eventually read of his objection to a disciple of Christ serving in the army of Caesar. A different class exposed me to the Lutheran martyr Dietrich Bonhoeffer, where I was struck by his literal interpretation of the Beatitudes, including "Blessed are the peacemakers." In another class, we had a guest speaker who was a Mennonite. I found his testimony compelling despite having some intellectual reservations. I remember history professor Ron Nelson, a tragic victim of gun violence a few years later, giving gentle encouragement to this alternate side of the Protestant Reformation. My brief classroom encounter with the Peace Church tradition bore fruit down the road as I became a reader of John Howard Yoder, especially his book *The Original Revolution*.[5]

Bonhoeffer and Yoder rejected the NCC/WCC approach of the spiritually-compromised "liberal" church, with its simultaneous platitudes of "peace and justice" and complicity with the worldly power structure that practices war and injustice. It's the old problem of Riverside Church, standing up for the downtrodden while being funded by the Rockefellers or the Episcopal Church, fancying that it has a prophetic voice while being populated by the cream of wealth and respectability and being pulled along by every trendy cause of the American upper class.

Chris Hedges points out that the modernist institutional church "seeks to protect its vision of itself as a moral voice and yet avoids genuine confrontations with the power elite." He gives an example: "In a typical bromide, the National Council of Churches... urged President George W. Bush to 'do all possible' to avoid war with Iraq and to stop 'demonizing adversaries or enemies' with good-versus-evil rhetoric, but, like the other liberal religious institutions, did not condemn the war." Lacking a sure foundation of spiritual reality and biblical truth, such self-styled religious progressives don't believe in "good-versus-evil" in any context, so they have little to offer beyond empty platitudes amounting to little more than "Be nice to one another." That's not exactly the pure or complete Gospel of Jesus Christ. As Davidson Loehr, a Unitarian-Universalist minister, observes, "By bringing 'heaven' down to earth with the Social Gospel, religious and political liberals lost any framework that could critique the things they happened to believe. Individual rights have to be balanced by our responsibility to the larger wholes. But why? In the name of what? Few seem to know or care."[6]

Late in my junior year as a college student, in April-May 1982, I discovered two important books: *Fundamentalism and American Culture* by George Marsden and *Discovering an Evangelical Heritage* by Donald Dayton. Both linked anti-war sentiment to evangelical ministers whom I respected. Dayton mentioned that a biography of D.L. Moody published in 1900 described how the future evangelist "could not conscientiously enlist" in the Union army during the Civil War. As Moody explained, "There has never been a time in my life when I felt I could take a gun and shoot down a fellow human being. In this respect I am a Quaker."

Marsden referred to A.C. Gaebelein, a dispensationalist preacher and consulting editor of *The Scofield Reference Bible*. Gaebelein was editor of *Our Hope* magazine, which published an editorial after the U.S. entered World War I, asking the question "Should a Christian Go to War?" Samuel Ridout replied, "The very question well-nigh answers itself." According to Ridout, Christians should serve but not fight: "There are lines of duties as clerical, ambulance service on the field of battle, ministering to the wounded and dying in the hospitals—ministering *Christ*, as we minister to the body."[7]

The approach of Moody and Gaebelein anticipated that of Watchman Nee, one of my favorite authors. Addressing fellow Chinese Christians in 1940, during World War II, Nee said, "*We must know how to pray. It must be possible for British and German, Chinese and Japanese Christians to kneel and pray together, and all to say Amen to what is asked. If not there is something wrong with our prayer.... In the last European war there was much prayer that dishonoured God. Let us not fall into the same error. The church must stand above national questions and say, 'We, here, ask for neither a Chinese or a Japanese victory, but for whatever is of advantage to the one thing precious to Thee, the testimony of Thy Son.'*" Nee preached and practiced the scriptural injunction "Love not the world" (I Jn. 2:15-17), by following He who speaks to us of the Kingdom of God (Lk. 9:11). During my college years, he was of great influence on my thinking, as was the *Scofield Reference Bible*, which noted that the present world system (*kosmos*) is in rebellion against God, dominated by Satan, and organized on the basis of the "cosmic principles of force, greed, selfishness, ambition, and pleasure."[8]

One of my favorite singer-songwriters, associated with the charismatic Jesus Movement and the rise of Contemporary Christian Music, was Larry Norman. While recording with a secular label in the early 1970s, Norman asked, "Do you really think the only way to bring about the peace is to sacrifice your children and kill all your enemies?" The Vineyard Church, a young denomination partly born in Norman's living room in Hollywood, played a key role in the conversion of rock superstar Bob Dylan, about the time I was experiencing my own conversion. My love of born-again Dylan led to my eventual discovery of his prodigious back-catalog, including anti-war folk songs like "With God on Our Side." Joan Baez—Dylan's sometime collaborator—sang "Heaven Help Us All," a song which helped inform my social conscience.[9]

While I read and listened to these figures mostly for spiritual sustenance, there was a cumulative effect derived from the portions of their works that touched on sociopolitical topics, including war. *Prelude to the End of This Age* was a booklet I self-published for my NWC friends, in early 1981, explaining my retirement from politics. I issued a lengthier *Prelude Part Two* in January, 1982, as my response to Francis Schaeffer's *A Christian Manifesto*. My apolitical approach had been influenced by his writings of a decade before, but he was now issuing an intellectual call to political arms which helped spawn the Religious Right. I agreed with Schaeffer on the heinous nature of abortion, but I disagreed with his new approach.

I brought up my views on war in my chapter on unequal yoking: "I will show you six historical examples of Christians uniting with unbelievers in a common purpose. Not just any common purpose, mind you, but in *warfare* (worldly, not spiritual)!... A Christianity which has to be maintained by the sword is a Christianity not worth maintaining.... Bear in mind that they weren't yoked together for something like helping the poor or caring for orphans—but for bloodshed!... When we studied these conflicts in a European history class, I was aghast. I thought, 'How could these people have been *Christians*?' It was hard for me to conceive of Christians killing people. It still is."

In my ongoing effort to explain myself, I wrote *I Am Not a Conservative* in late 1984/early 1985. I began writing two days before the presidential election—an election I would sit out because of my Christian apoliticality. One section deals with U.S. foreign policy: "Unlike conservatives, I am not worried about having a 'strong national defense.' If the United States government wishes to be militarily superior to the Soviet Union that's the government's business. I'm not interested in promoting (or opposing) such a policy.

I have no love for nuclear bombs. I understand why the government feels a need to have them, and I understand why conservatives oppose unilateral disarmament, but I think the whole thing is a shame (wasting money on weapons of destruction when it could be spent on keeping people alive—for instance, the millions in Africa who are dying of starvation, malnutrition, disease).

I could be called a 'pacifist' in one way, in that I would not be able to kill people in a war. If I were drafted I would either try to work as a medical person, or I would leave the country, or I would go to jail. I could not carry a gun and shoot people. For me killing people would be violating the commandments Jesus gave. I know many Christians use casuistry to justify participation in combat... this may be okay for them, but I could not in good conscience try to kill people. Why would I want to kill a creature who—like me—has been made in the image of God?"

The book goes on to quote from the Schleitheim Confession of the Anabaptists, make mention of the Quakers, and quote Roman Catholic mystics Blaise Pascal and François Fénelon. A long quotation from mystical Anglican minister William Law is included, as well as a reference to American statesman William Jennings Bryan and his pacifistic debt to Russian novelist and social philosopher Leo Tolstoy. The conclusion of the book quotes Bob Dylan's "Masters of War"—an old folk song I heard for the first time on his new live album, 21 years after it was initially recorded.[10] The new rock-arrangement drove home Dylan's outrage at the Merchants of Death / Military-Industrial Complex / Masters of War, thanks to the slashing fuzz guitar of Mick Taylor, formerly of the Rolling Stones.

For the rest of the 1980s, I immersed myself in the best of the non-Marxist, libertarian Left. This included a number of activists and intellectuals who stood for peace (*e.g.*, Jefferson, Schweitzer, Tolstoy, Gandhi, Jeannette Rankin, A.J. Muste, Oswald Garrison Villard, Dorothy Day, Thomas Merton, Dwight Macdonald). I joined the Green Party, which has nonviolence as one of its Four Pillars and Ten Key Values, and eventually identified with the Friends United Meeting variety of Quakers. Contemporary peace-and-justice public intellectuals like Ralph Nader, Cornel West, and Andrea Dworkin also inspired me. Becoming a father deepened my personal understanding of the precarious and precious nature of life.

My theology has always been wide and irenic, within the boundaries of evangelical orthodoxy. To borrow wording from Whitworth University, I recognize the Bible to be "the inspired and trustworthy record of God's self-disclosure and our final rule for faith and practice." This does not mean I cannot work with modernistic Christians or with non-Christians. Since the mid 1980s, many of my friends, heroes, and favorite authors have been agnostics, atheists, unorthodox Christians, or adherents of other spiritualities.

I have a consistent life ethic, meaning opposition to war, abortion, death penalty, hunting, and meat-eating. I joined Feminists for Life of America because I was not just anti-abortion but pro-life and pro-woman. I became an ethical vegetarian and joined PETA. Still, growing up close to farm life, actually knowing hunters, and being around guns since infancy have kept me from the self-righteousness often exhibited by devotees of animal rights. Life is more complicated than PETA lets on, and its Hollywood tactics—using nude supermodels and shoving a pie into the face of the Iowa Pork Queen—aren't making many converts in the Heartland.

I'm not pushy about my views on reverence for life with regard to all of God's creatures. It's more of a personal thing for me. I don't even like to kill bugs—even seemingly ugly and scary bugs—so I usually remove them from the house rather than destroying insect life. Dear to me is the vision of the coming millennial Peaceable Kingdom, described by Isaiah and other Hebrew prophets and painted by the Quaker artist Edward Hicks. Someday the harmony of Eden will be restored as the King reigns over all—humans, animals, and all of creation.

When Jesus said, "Blessed are the peacemakers," he did not provide a loophole ("...and the warmakers who are motivated by justice or love"). With that kind of thinking, we move into the Orwellian territory where "war is peace." Paul wrote, *"Bless those who persecute you; bless and do not curse them.... Repay no one evil for evil... Beloved, never avenge yourselves, but leave it to the wrath of God; for it is written, 'Vengeance is mine, I will repay says the Lord.' No, 'if your enemy is hungry, feed him'... Do not be overcome by evil, but overcome evil with good."* (Rom. 12:14-21) Basically, it's a reiteration of the Sermon on the Mount principles. In contrast to the weapons of "worldly warfare," Paul told believers, *"We are not contending against flesh and blood, but against the principalities, against the powers..."* (II Cor. 10:3-4; Eph. 6:12)

Just War Theory is often used as a giant loophole, for both politicians seeking divine sanction for war and Christians seeking to evade the teachings of Christ. It is better than endorsement of all war, but its application is so subjective that it ends up being rather meaningless. It has more commonly been used to excuse and promote war than to avoid or oppose war, which makes sense since it was devised as an alternative to pacifism. Every government is going to claim to be acting justly, and every Christian who wants to support the war is going to believe it.

Just War was a scholastic import into Protestantism, via Luther and Calvin, from the Roman Catholicism of Augustine and Aquinas. While there are philosophical and theological arguments in its favor, the theory lacks any clear biblical basis in the New Testament. Just War Theory tries to strike a middle ground between unbridled militarism and consistent pacifism. It's a sort of amber stoplight: *proceed with caution.* More often than not, however, it acts as a green light, rather than a red one. In fact, has there ever been an instance when a national government decided to *not* go to war because of Just War Theory? You may be a Christian—or non-Christian—who does not embrace pacifism. That's okay. The perfect need not be the enemy of the good. If we're honest with ourselves, most of us can agree that most of the wars in which we have been involved during the past century have been unjust wars of aggression and greed, having more to do with empire and monopoly than with national defense or humanitarian crusades.

As Americans, we can oppose the bad foreign policies for which the troops are serving as pawns without despising the good personal qualities that often motivate and are often exhibited by the individuals in uniform. In other words, we can recognize the fictional and manipulative nature of the "fighting for our freedom" cliché while honoring the patriotism, bravery, and sacrifice of combat veterans. For example, I can reject the Vietnam War, while respecting Colonel George "Bud" Day USAF and Major Ed "Eagle Man" McGaa USMC.

Horrible hypothetical acts are timeworn red herrings used against the principle of nonviolence. Example: Should one sit idly by and watch a woman being raped or a kid getting beat up on a playground? Response: When was the last time a U.S. war was triggered by either of those events? Those are crimes, not acts of war. If a horrific crime occurs against you or your loved ones, I think God will understand and forgive if you violate the command to love all— even a criminal, even an enemy—in your response. It is a very human response to want revenge or to use force in defense of those we love. Objectively, it is a moral failure, but it is understandable and I'm not going to sit in judgment. But those cases have nothing to do with war; nothing to do with men in offices thousands of miles away cold-bloodedly plotting to attack complete strangers who have done them no personal harm; nothing to do with enlisted men who then go out to kill complete strangers who have done them no personal harm. We're not talking about neighbors rallying with their guns, to defend themselves and their families from violent invaders on a personal level. We're talking about professional soldiers, impersonally killing people because our government has a quarrel with their government. That is not part of Christ's program.

The argument that Christ's disciples can use force in defense of others, if not in defense of ourselves, is untenable. Neither Jesus nor Paul provided us with that loophole. Jesus said, "Greater love has no man than to lay down his life for his brothers." That is self-sacrificial (suicidal) love, not homicidal love. Laying down your life for those you love is not the same as taking someone else's life. When Peter tried to do this very thing in the Garden of Gethsemane, in defense of Jesus, the Master rebuked him and healed the ear of his enemy's servant.

One might say, "But Jesus knew he had to be arrested and crucified for God's plan to be achieved." True enough, but Christ did not say, "You do not know what you are doing; the Son of Man must be taken away like a sheep to the slaughter..." Instead, he gave another blanket condemnation of violence: "He who lives by the sword shall die by the sword." That's not a good recruiting slogan for the military. It is a good piece of wisdom from the Lamb of God and the Lion of Judah. Most Americans call themselves Christians, not Martians. Instead of honoring the god of war, we should follow the Prince of Peace.

---

[1] Wallace's populism appealed to me. His racism held no appeal. Bear in mind that this was 1974, not 1964. Moving to Alabama in recent years has given me a different perspective on the back story.

[2] Interestingly enough, I did quote a Just War explanation by the Christian Reformed Church, a more conservative Dutch Calvinist denomination in comparison to the Reformed Church in America (sponsor of NWC) and sponsor of neighboring Dordt College. A hero of the CRC, and deservedly so, is Abraham Kuyper, the great Reformed theologian and statesman in Holland. Kuyper presumably believed in Just War but in 1916 he sounded much like W.J. Bryan—his favored candidate for U.S. president in 1900—when he criticized American leaders for their pro-war influence: "Everyone in America—women included—is now at work to insure that bombs and howitzers can be sent by the shipload across the ocean, and to get rich by this trade. And this despite knowing that soon a human life will hang by such a bomb or shell.... America *can* organize a force for peace against the power of war. But it stays home.... And all this for the love of money." – James D. Bratt, ed., *Abraham Kuyper: A Centennial Reader* (Grand Rapids, Mich.: Eerdmans, 1998), 3, 291.

[3] Herman Dooyeweerd, *The Crisis in Humanist Political Theory: As Seen from a Calvinist Cosmology and Epistemology* (Grand Rapids, Mich.: Paideia Press, 2010), 162.

[4] For Christ Against Culture, see: H. Richard Niebuhr, *Christ and Culture* (New York: Harper & Row, 1956), 45-82. I learned of the Niebuhr model in a college class. Schaeffer's warning was in the context of the late 1960s: "In the United States many churches display the American flag. The Christian flag is usually put on one side and the American flag on the other. Does having the

two flags in your church mean that Christianity and the American Establishment are equal? If it does, you are really in trouble. These are not two equal loyalties.... If by having the American flag in your church you are indicating to your young people that there are two equal loyalties or two intertwined loyalties, you had better find a way out of it.... Equating of any other loyalty with our loyalty to God is sin." – Francis A. Schaeffer, *The Church at the End of the 20ʰ Century* (Downers Grove, Ill.: InterVarsity Press, 1970), 82-83.

[5] Leonard Verduin, *The Reformers and Their Stepchildren* (Grand Rapids, Mich.: Eerdmans, 1964); Dietrich Bonhoeffer, *The Cost of Discipleship*, rev. ed. (New York: Collier, 1963), 126-27; John Howard Yoder, *The Original Revolution: Essays on Christian Pacifism* (Scottdale, Pa.: Herald Press, 1971).

[6] Chris Hedges, *Death of the Liberal Class* (New York: Nation Books, 2010), 21, 22, 163. The anemic request put forth by disciples of the bureaucratic Mush God(dess) that we "Be nice to one another" has an unstated exception: We may be self-righteously scornful toward politically incorrect groups such as evangelical Christians, anti-abortionists, traditional moralists, conservative Republicans, etc.

[7] Donald W. Dayton, *Discovering an Evangelical Heritage* (New York: Harper & Row, 1976), 134; George M. Marsden, *Fundamentalism and American Culture: The Shaping of Twentieth-Century Evangelicalism, 1870-1925* (Oxford: Oxford University Press, 1980), 144. Unfortunately, *Our Hope* eventually succumbed to worldly jingoism, enthusiastically embracing the war as a righteous cause.

[8] Angus I. Kinnear, *Against the Tide: The Story of Watchman Nee* (Fort Washington, Pa.: Christian Literature Crusade, 1973), 117; Watchman Nee, *Love Not the World* (Wheaton, Ill.: Tyndale House/CLC, 1978); C.I. Scofield, ed., *The Scofield Reference Bible* (New York: Oxford University Press, 1917), 1342. C.S. Lewis was no pacifist (one of his wartime talks was entitled "Why I Am Not a Pacifist"), but he recognized the power that God allows Satan to exercise in the world during this age: "Enemy-occupied territory—that is what this world is. Christianity is the story of how the rightful king has landed, you might say landed in disguise, and is calling us all to take part in a great campaign of sabotage." – C.S. Lewis, *Mere Christianity* (New York: Macmillan, 1960), 51.

[9] Larry Norman, "The Great American Novel," *Only Visiting This Planet* (MGM/Verve Records, 1972; Street Level Records, 1978); Bob Dylan, "With God on Our Side," *The Times They Are A-Changin'* (Columbia Records, 1963); Joan Baez, "Heaven Help Us All," *Blessed Are...* (Vanguard Records, 1971).

[10] Bob Dylan, *Real Live* (Columbia Records, 1984); Bob Dylan, *The Freewheelin' Bob Dylan* (Columbia Records, 1963).

Fortunate Soldier

Joey B. King

Joey King was a Distinguished Military Graduate from Tennessee Tech University in Cookeville. He graduated from the following Army schools: Airborne, Ranger, Pathfinder, Air Assault, Infantry Officer's Basic Course, Jungle Expert, and the Infantry Officer's Mortar Platoon Officer's Course. He served with the 82nd Airborne Division and the Airborne unit in Vicenza, Italy. He was a platoon leader and company executive officer. He resigned from the active army in July, 1987, and later resigned from the Reserves. Since leaving the Army, Joey has been active in various causes including the Buddhist Peace Fellowship, Truth-in-recruiting, Gandhi-King Conference on Peacemaking, Veterans Day Parade, Stop the Bombs, and the School of the Americas Watch. He also participated as an international election observer in El Salvador in March 2009. Joey is chair of Veterans for Peace of Middle TN and a member of the Veterans for Peace National Board of Directors.

A few years ago, I attended the Gandhi-King Conference on Non-violence in Memphis, Tennessee. One of the guest speakers made me aware of something I had not considered previously: there is a difference between peace and non-violence. As the speaker pointed out, every military person claims to be "pro-peace" because soldiers pay a high price in times of war. There are even "peacemaker" pistols and missiles. Until that time, I had assumed peace and non-violence to be two names for the same concept.

For all practical purposes, peace is often used to describe the absence of hostilities between states or groups. Peace is a state of no war. Non-violence, on the other hand, is far different, because it is *both* a state of being *and* a means to achieve that state. Non-violence is both a personal choice and a tactic used to achieve social change.

Unfortunately, English is a poor language for expressing the concept of non-violence. Instead of non-violence, I prefer the Sanskrit term, *ahimsa*, because it has a far deeper meaning.

As a member of Veterans for Peace, I often get asked how I went from being an airborne ranger to a Gandhian pacifist. Most people assume that one grand event changed my life instantly. It was not like that with me. It was more of a step-by-step process. This is my personal journey to *ahimsa*.

During my junior year in high school (1979), Iranian students took American diplomats as hostages and held them at the U.S. embassy in Tehran for 444 days. In 1980-81, my age-group became the first to be subjected to the re-instituted US Selective Service System. My mother suggested that I join college ROTC, since the U.S. was almost certainly going to war with Iran, and it would be better to go into the Army as an officer. That scenario may sound far-fetched 30 years later, but it was a real possibility then.

In those days, college students could take one hour of ROTC in lieu of physical education during their freshman and sophomore years. There was not an obligation for military service until the junior year. I really enjoyed my classes, and I decided to enroll in ROTC advanced courses, which obligated me to three years of active duty service and three more of Individual Ready · Reserve (IRR) service. (Today, I believe the total commitment is eight years.)

As the Iranian hostage crisis was coming to an end, the civil war in El Salvador heated up. President Ronald Regan convinced me that communism was infiltrating the U.S. from Central America and the Caribbean. I dedicated about five years of my life, preparing to kill "communists" in El Salvador and elsewhere. Thankfully, that situation never materialized.

I graduated college in December, 1984 and entered the Army as an infantry officer. After graduating from Ranger school, I was assigned to the 82nd Airborne Division at Fort Bragg, North Carolina as a platoon leader in the late summer of 1985. I was there for a little under a year. My opinion of the Army soured pretty quickly. My second battalion commander was horrible. Looking back, having such a horrible battalion commander was fortunate, because it opened my eyes to how bad the Army could be. I decided I would leave the Army after my first tour. I was transferred to the airborne unit in Vicenza, Italy in May of 1986, and honorably discharged under an early-out program in July, 1987. (President Ronald Regan had decided there were too many junior officers in the Army, and I was more than happy to relieve him of one Lieutenant.)

It was the right decision for me. I never served a single day in combat, and I consider myself to be the luckiest human on earth.

I was still obligated to serve in the Individual Ready Reserve (IRR) until December, 1990, but at about that time, the first Iraq war erupted. The Army delayed my discharge for two years. In my resignation statement from the IRR, I said (in part): "I am resigning because of a personal conviction that war is an unacceptable means of resolving differences among nations." That statement is a far cry from *ahimsa*, but it was a step in the right direction.

I joined the Libertarian Party (LP) in November, 1991 and remained a member until about 2003. As part of joining the LP, one must sign a pledge that states: "*I certify that I do not believe in or advocate the initiation of force as a means of achieving political or social goals.*" (Again, not *ahimsa*, but another step in the right direction.)

As I became more involved with libertarianism, I would hear my fellow libertarians mention the concept of Non-Initiation of Force (NIF), also known as the "Zero Aggression Principle" (ZAP) or the "Non-Aggression Principle" (NAP). In "Libertopia," ZAP means that one should not initiate force, but one was within one's rights to retaliate in self-defense.

After a decade of reflection on libertarianism, it became obvious to me that the LP's statement of non-initiation of force was too limited. By that, I mean it is dependent upon how one defines and responds to force or aggression. For example, can animals, insects, and the environment be aggressed against? If the answer is, "yes," then who speaks for animals, insects, and the environment when they have been aggressed against?

We cannot prevent force from being initiated upon us; we can only control our *response* to it. Mohandas Gandhi said, "An eye for an eye leaves the whole world blind." The Reverend Martin Luther King Jr. said that violence only leads to a never-ending upward spiral of violence.

As time went along, I began to think back from a violence/non-violence prospective on some of the American "heroes" I had studied:

- George Washington committed genocide against Native Americans in New York, and owned slaves.
- Thomas Jefferson was a slave-holder and kept his own bi-racial children in bondage.
- Andrew Jackson slaughtered Native peoples, held slaves and participated in multiple duels.

Clearly, all three were violent men who profited monetarily from violence. The same is true of most American "heroes." Today, their defenders try to make the argument that these men were just part of the culture they lived in, but that argument falls short. (The Amish, Mennonites, and Quakers of the same era were anti-slavery, and did not commit genocide against the Indians.)

What does that say about an American culture that still worships their behavior today? When viewed from the prospective of violence and non-violence, the Reverend Martin Luther King Jr. is perhaps our greatest American hero.

Turns out, I wasn't the first one asking these questions, of course. I was just looking in the wrong direction for answers. I was looking "West" when I should have been looking "East." In January 2004, I started a yoga practice. My teacher explained the concept of *ahimsa* in the spring of that year, and I immediately found my answers. *Ahimsa* is as close to zero aggression as has ever been conceived by humans, and it has stood the test of time (in the form of practice) for well over 2500 years.

I know I am generalizing here, but one other significant difference I found is that western philosophies tend to be long on analysis and short on solutions. That tends to be the exact opposite of eastern philosophies. When I starting reading more Buddhism, Yoga texts, Jainism, Gandhi, and Thich Nhat Hahn it became clearer. These major eastern philosophies spend a great deal of time explaining and practicing the tenets of non-violence.

For example, the founder of the Jain sect, Mahavira, recommended to his followers:

"Do not injure, abuse, oppress, insult, enslave, torture, torment, or kill any creature or living being."

Take a moment and re-read Mahavira's words. It could be argued that those 16 words comprise the most ethical sentence ever written. No wonder it has stood the test of time for 2500 years.

Devout followers of Jainism do not step on insects, nor do they eat onions (because one must kill the whole plant to eat the onion). That sounds extreme to most individuals, I understand, but it shows how serious they are about non-violence. To get another glimpse of Jain views on *ahimsa*, look at the vows, consisting of four (sometimes five). These vows are also common to Yoga, Buddhism, and Hinduism:

- *Ahimsa* (including non-violence to self)
- Truth
- Non-attachment
- Non-Stealing

It is important to note that these are not "commandments" in the western sense, but rather ideals to strive towards. The last three vows essentially relate to non-violence (*ahimsa*). Here's how:

Falsehood is a form of violence to both the listener and the speaker. All of us can think of some form of violence that has resulted from falsehood. As a US Senator once said, "truth is the first causality of war." Russian Nobel Prize winner Alexander Solzhenitsyn believed that lies are a necessary pre-condition of all nation-state violence. How else could they convince us that "the other" is evil?

Non-attachment concerns greed (attachment to things) and ideas; both of which are forms of violence. Greedy people can quickly lose sight of the importance of living things. If the mind changes from a "people-first" mentality to a "things-first" mentality, individuals may choose to employ force against other individuals. The slave-based sugar oligarchies of the colonial era are a prime example of this phenomenon. During the European colonial period of the Americas, immeasurable violence was unleashed to maintain profits and keep up with European demand for sugar. In modern times, oil companies have killed activists in Nigeria and laid waste to native lands in Ecuador.

There is a story from Greek antiquity. The Cynics were ancient renunciates, those who have renounced lay-life. The person we usually study from this movement is Diogenes. There is a famous dialog between him and Alexander the Great. Alexander's army came through and Diogenes asked about Alexander's plans. Alexander answered that he wanted to conquer Greece.

"Then what" asked Diogenes. Alexander replied that he wanted to conquer Asia Minor. Again, Diogenes asked, "Then what?" Alexander replied that he would be conquering the world. "After you conquer the world, what will you do?" Diogenes asked. "I will rest," replied Alexander. Diogenes quickly asked, "Why not rest now, and save yourself all that trouble?"

After finding my answers by looking eastward, I came to realize that my goal is liberation. I also found a means to achieve it. I accepted that one can only change oneself, and one can only change oneself now. This is also known as "one-ness" or "ego-less-ness." Ideas like "utopia," "heaven," "global change," "worker's paradise," "revolution," and "hope" are really delusions of the ego. All offer the false notion of an improved future state, based on the actions of others. Liberation comes only in the here and now, and is achieved individually. I chose to change through *ahimsa*. Society may or may not follow. All that any of us can do is change ourselves and hope our actions influence others.

I do not intend to discourage people from joining peace groups, but one must be satisfied if the only one changed is oneself. The Buddha said, "Better the man that conquers a thousand men is the one who conquers one, himself." He also said, "Peace comes from within, do not seek it without." Meanwhile, contemporary thinker Eckhardt Tolle says the only time we can exist in is "the now."

One important thing I have learned through my yoga practice is to be patient with myself. Contrary to popular myth in the U.S., goals are really not important. They are just masks for ego. Three of the most prominent ways I have found to practice *ahimsa* are through yoga, vegetarianism, and activism. There are also three main reasons in which people convert to vegetarianism: environmental, health and morality. I converted for all three reasons:

- A vegetarian diet has a far lower carbon-footprint and environmental impact than does a meat-eating one. Outside of transportation, meat-eating is the number one carbon producer for the average American.
- From a cardiovascular stand- point, it is far better to go vegetarian.
- Finally, I do not harm other beings. It became impossible for me to justify the killing of other creatures unnecessarily.

My peace activism has taken many avenues. Currently, I serve on the national board of Veterans for Peace. My experience has shown that I have a certain amount of "street-cred" when someone knows I am a member of Veterans for Peace. This is probably because the militaristic culture of the United States puts soldiers on such a pedestal that they give more credence to me than a life-long Quaker.

Deep non-violence also has many personal benefits, ranging from a lower heart rate to an enhanced peace of mind. I spent five years of my young-adult life training to kill Central American "communists." What a horrible waste of time!

M.K Gandhi said, "The state represents violence in a concentrated and organized form. The individual has a soul, but as the state is a soulless machine, it can never be weaned from violence to which it owes its very existence."

The individual can also choose to participate in "concentrated and organized" violence, or one can choose not to participate. In 2004, I chose "conscientious non-voting." For the first time since I was 18, I sat out the election. (Conscientious non-voting can be differentiated from apathetic non-voting, in that I *do* give a damn.)

One of the reasons for my choice is that the very act of participating in elections is a participation in "concentrated and organized" violence. Although

I am not a Christian, I share this view on non-voting with the Anabaptist Christian sects (Amish, Mennonite, Hutterite and Dunkard), from their reading of Jesus' *Sermon on the Mount*. The Christian Anarchists, Leo Tolstoy, Ammon Hennacy and Dorothy Day also share this view. On Election Day, Ammon used to say he did vote; he just chose not to assign responsibility to someone else at the ballot box. He voted with his body every day, instead.

I have not, as of yet, chosen to avoid paying war-taxes. If I choose to do that at some point, the only route for me would be voluntary poverty. Gandhi, Tolstoy, and countless Buddhist monks have chosen this route.

I think it is equally important to choose non-violence in our everyday purchases. Non-participation as a form of resistance is an option. Bartering, buying used goods at a thrift store or planting a garden are acts of resistance.

Gandhi has become my guide. Most Americans don't realize it, but he led massive non-violent movements in South Africa before moving back to India. I still use his guidelines today when instructing others on how to behave at an action. These guidelines take into account the three aspects of non-violence: speech, action, and thoughts.

This is the pledge to nonviolence signed by marchers with Mahatma Gandhi in 1921:

1. A civil resister will harbor no anger.
2. A civil resister will suffer the anger of the opponent.
3. In so doing, a civil resister will put up with assaults from the opponent, never retaliate; but he will not submit, out of fear of punishment, to any order given in anger.
4. A civil resister will voluntarily submit to the arrest and he will not resist the attachment or removal of his own property.
5. If a civil resister has any property in his possession as a trustee, he will refuse to surrender it, even though in defending it he might lose his life. He will never retaliate.
6. Non-retaliation excludes swearing and cursing.
7. A civil resister will never insult his opponent, nor take part in the newly coined cries contrary to the spirit of nonviolence.
8. A civil resister will not salute the Union Jack, nor will he insult it or its officials, English or Indian.
9. If anyone insults an official or commits an assault upon him, a civil resister will protect such official or officials from the insult or assault at the risk of his own life.

In this manner, these brave, non-violent disobedients freed themselves and their communities from the tyranny of the British government.

I do some truth-in-military-recruiting work every year with high-school students. One of my partners in that endeavor tells me that he keeps coming back every year to change one young person's mind about the military. He may never know for sure if he has changed a young person's mind, but that thought drives him. It drives me too. It does not conflict with my here-and-now philosophy. My actions may positively influence someone else; if they don't, then that is something with which I must live.

Conclusion

Soon after the U.S. invasion of Iraq in 2003, I joined Veterans for Peace (VFP). Since then, it has been my primary outlet for activism. Through VFP, I worked as an international election observer for the 2009 El Salvadoran Presidential election. While I don't believe that voting is the ultimate solution, it is certainly preferable to a twelve-year civil war, as they suffered in El Salvador.

Most importantly, I was able meet the people I had previously wanted to kill. That is powerful. They are honest individuals for the most part. My government and the El Salvadoran government told me "communists" were everywhere in the 1980s. Declassified internal documents from both governments reveal that they viewed 90 percent of the El Salvadoran population as "the enemy." Most people would call that "a majority."

As I said in the beginning, English is a poor language to convey the true meaning of non-violence. Given the 500-year history of European colonialism, I suspect that other European languages are equally ineffective. My wish is that my personal story might provide someone an incentive to explore *ahimsa* as a way of life, and to realize the difference between peace and non-violence. I have not achieved perfect *ahimsa*. That is humanly impossible. But, as I strive, I am certainly better for it, and, likely, others are too.

Nigeria:

A Case for Peace

Fiyinfoluwa Elegbede

Fiyinfoluwa Ebenezer Elegbede is a writer and blogger in Nigeria. He is involved with a number of Small and Medium Enterprises as volunteer development consultant and as a business partner. He interned at the Directorate of Public Relations, University of Agriculture, Abeokuta. He presently studies at the Nigerian Institute of Public Relations majoring in Peace Studies and Conflict Resolution at the National Open University of Nigeria–Abeokuta Study Campus, Ogun State. An avid volunteer, Fiyinfoluwa has volunteered in such notable projects and activities as the Enhancing Nigeria's Response to HIV/AIDS program, as a Venue Outreach Staff (VOS); AGABUS Palliative Care Centre, as Development Consultant; African Liberty Students Organisation, as Outreach Assistant; and the Dele Momodu 2011 Presidential Campaign Organisation, handling Social Network Publicity. Fiyinfoluwa is at present the Outreach Assistant of AfricanLiberty.org, an Atlas Economic Research Foundation Global Initiative and platform for sharing and disseminating practical ideas of liberty and bringing African voices to a wider world, working with African media to disseminate policy ideas for a new century of peace, freedom and prosperity of the African continent.

The role played by peace in the socio-economic development of the many developed and developing nations of the world cannot be overestimated. However, issues such as military interventionism, police state abuses, human rights infringements and domestic violence have continued to erode the beauty of a peaceful society, and its attendant contribution to the development of a nation. Let's look at the role of military interventionism, and its consequent abuse of the rights of a citizenry, as a barrier to the development of any sovereign state, using the example I know best: Nigeria.

During pre-colonial Nigeria, most Nigerians regard the military as an instrument fashioned by an alien authority for the purpose of destroying the political independence of the various ethnic groups and their cherished ways of life (Ojukwu, 2003). This assertion and fear was made manifest in the post-colonial period, when military interventionism was the order of the day, consequently adversely affecting the growth and development of the region.

One event from my pre-teen years has refused to leave my memory since: the 1993 post-election riots, the first time I ever experienced any form of rioting. The morning of that fateful day was a splendid one. We had had to sing *"Rain, rain go away / Come again another day / Little children want to play."* This was due to the rainfall outside, although it had no negative effect on our classes. The unusual sight of military vehicles, moving at faster than ordinary speeds makes for a frightening scenario, especially when coupled with the flames of burning tires all around the adjourning streets leading to my home. (I later learned this was a show of solidarity for the cause of the rioting, as well as a risk of damage to such vehicles from the angry rioters) Being just about eight years old at the time, I remember having to dedicate more of my time to protecting my younger brother, who was a couple years younger, from walking into the path of these high-speed vehicles and the angry rioters.

This was my first experience of the negative effects of military intervention, and by extension, of the disruption of peace in Nigeria.

Many years earlier, back in 1966, certain aggrieved junior officers of the Nigerian military, led by Major Chukwuma Kaduna Ezeogwu, had violated the British tradition (according to Robin Luckham) of military subordination to civilian direction, seizing power in a bloody *coup d'état* that witnessed the death of the then-Head of Government, Alhaji Sir. Tafawa Balewa, along with Sir Ahmadu Bello, Prime Minister of the Northern Region; Chief Akintola, Prime Minister of the Western Region; and Chief Festus Okotie-Eboh, the federal finance minister. This effectively marked the beginning of more successful bloody and bloodless coups, until that of August 27, 1985, which saw the ascension into power of the incumbent (as of 1993) Head of The Armed Forces Ruling Council (AFRC), General Ibrahim Badamosi Babangida. He was popularly referred to as "Maradona" (because of his widely acknowledged manipulative skills at achieving self-serving aims and objectives, at the expense of everyone else).

However, after many tactical delays and a prolonged stay in power, he agreed to return to civilian rule, with the creation and imposition of two new political parties, the National Republican Council (NRC) (led by Bashir Tofa from northern Nigeria) and the Social Democratic Party (SDC) (led by Chief Kashimawo Olawale Moshood Abiola, from the southwest), Both were wealthy businessmen. This imposition of a new regime, provoked widespread criticism.

However, the June 12, 1993 election, widely believed to have been decisively won by the SDP-led late Chief Kashimawo Olawale Moshood Abiola was annulled by the then-IBB military regime. This spurred violent protests that witnessed the loss of many lives and massive destruction of property,, consequently dashing the hopes for a return to civilian rule in Nigeria. It also marked another elongated and highly oppressive five-year military tenure, under Gen. Sani Abacha, a former Chief of Staff to the IBB regime.

It is worth noting that the legitimate basis for military intervention in the internal affairs of a sovereign state—putting down internal aggression, matching the intensity of that aggression (*e.g.*, Ajagun and Odion, 2010)—has never been a pivotal issue in the military interventions in Nigeria. Rather, such excuses as "sconomic mismanagement," "corruption," "poor discipline," "maladministration," "political violence," "disunity" and "ethno-regional politics" have been the chorus of most military interventionists, as an explanation for their actions, many of which they have aggressively orchestrated in their fearful reigns of terror. The military, particularly under the

Babangida and Abacha administrations, has transformed corruption from an uncivil act by public officials into a *raison d'etre* of the Nigerian State.

In all, Nigeria has witnessed a total of five *coup d'états* involving changes of government, as well as two more against civilian governments; there has been a total of thirty years of military rule between its independence in 1960 and the present, with no viable socio-economic merits to show for it, and a stifling of the development of democracy. What has been witnessed by the Nigerian State through these thirty years has been State Aggression and Oppression, massive Human Rights Abuses, Economic Degradation and large-scale Corruption. Tthere has also been a Civil War, Meanwhle, extrajudicial killings have led to more domestic wars between tribes; a rise in corrupt politicians; election violence; and a non-peaceful state. It is important to state that the military has had neither the inclination nor the opportunity to play a primary political role in the establishment of strategic ends; theirs is a secondary, though inevitable responsibility (Ojukwu 2003).

Military rule in Nigeria has negatively impacted the Nigerian society, by generalizing authoritarian values which are both anti-social and destructive of politics, leading to a decline in civility and a rise in violence in social interaction. This was evident in the post-military democratic government era of former Nigerian president, Chief Olusegun Obasanjo, a retired army general himself, who to date remains plagued with condemnations from the local populace, of engaging in do-or-die politics, a reminder of the military's style of absolute concentration of power in a single hand.

Police-state abuses are yet another element of infringement on the peaceful co-existence of a nation state. Not long ago, Nigeria witnessed what seems to be a real and genuine anti-corruption effort, led by then-Chairman of the Economic and Financial Crimes Commission, Mr Nuhu Ribadu, under the civilian regime of former Nigerian President, Chief Olusegun Obasanjo.

This effort involved the largest seizure of stolen public funds in Nigerian history, and was heralded by both local and international observers. However, a turn of events later unfolded when, after the election of a new president in the 2007 general elections, the late Alhaji Musa Yar'adua, the anti-corruption czar was summoned for questioning, and consequently demoted in police-rank (although a court of law later reversed his demotion).

He was vaguely accused of "selective" victimization of politically exposed persons (PEP), who were not allies of the administration during his reign. It came as no surprise as revelations kept flowing in on how the police was used, under instruction from the then-head of state, to clamp down and arrest persons suspected of corrupt practices. The anti-corruption agency was accused of being used manipulatively, punishing those considered to have gotten on the wrong side of the then-president. Hence, the explanation for his (Nuhu Ribadu's) ordeal at the beginning of a new administration, ironically parading allies who at one time of another had been allegedly victimized by his immediate predecessor's regime. Things did not go well with the anti-corruption czar; rather than been rewarded for his exploits at fighting corruption in the country, he was first sacked as head of the anti-corruption agency, and (more unexpectedly?) later demoted in rank as a police officer.

Such accusations of the use of the Police by the state, to actualize personal non-state interests, are a common phenomenon in Nigeria. At lower levels of police abuse in the Country is the rising level of unwarranted arrests by police officers, after receiving any form of complaint from one aggrieved person toward another. These arrests would have been applauded as a means of upholding a peaceful and crime-free society, but for the original intention of the police after such arrests. The police were carrying out arrests, based on trivial complaints, whereby those arrested, found either innocent or guilty after interrogation and questioning, would not be allowed to leave the counter without meeting an "unofficial" condition of bail.

There is a widely spread saying, excessively re-affirmed by the Police boss at the State Police Headquarters, that "bail is free." However, this bail is not and never has been "free" for the poor average Nigerian finding himself in police nets for one reason or another. Whether found guilty or innocent, the police will demand amounts of money from the arrested, claiming payment for policing services rendered, for the pre-trial night spent at the police station, behind a counter or in a cell, and so forth—which you are made to understand are not free.

Another popular saying, that "the police are your friends," is another thing considered to be a mere slogan by those same police officers, who will lure you to the station gate before initiating force and slamming you in the face, so that you'll know who your true friend is when you enter the police station after being arrested. Then, you will be advised to call those who will sort out your Bail Fees, your true friends.

In Nigeria, resisting arrest, even without an arrest warrant, complicates your argument for innocence with the typical Nigerian police. It is best advised that you submit to the arrest-attempt, even if the police produced no arrest warrant, as efforts to challenge the authority to arrest you without such warrant might only work for the "big men" in the society. On your part, you will be considered as stubborn and uncooperative, and might be subjected to unpleasant treatment at the police station. These uncivil acts do not promote a peaceful society; rather, they erode what remains of a peaceful and civil society, providing a virtual case-study of the Nigerian State.

You find the police at checkpoints demanding twenty-*naira* tips from motorists; those who fail to comply will be made to go through unnecessary delays and questioning. Such questioning involves a request for your driving and vehicle licenses, as well as other precautionary material in the vehicle, such as a fire extinguisher. These requests are in no way the proper function of the police, unless the vehicle in question is similar to one already reported missing. They supposedly man these checkpoints to stop and search suspicious motorists, who could be criminals, or even terrorists. Instead, refusing to pay a simple twenty-*naira* bribe when it is demanded might place the refusing motorists in the position of suspicion of being a criminal and terrorist. These actions are totally uncalled for by a state agency given the responsibility of maintaining law and order in the state. (I would also say that in Nigeria today, you can pay the police to not only enforce arrests, but also to torture those you personally consider to be offensive to your personal self, regardless of your status in the community—as long as you have the cash to throw away.)

Civil violence and domestic wars have immensely and negatively distorted the growth of a peaceful state, a precursor for socio-economic development. A Civil War is development in reverse with immense economic losses (Collier, 2007). Wars between tribes, terrorist acts by an aggrieved sect, and post-election violence have all characterized the slow growth and economic development in the Nigerian State. Recently, the incumbent Head of State, Dr. Goodluck Jonathan, affirmed his fears that unless Peace is restored in Nigerian, his economic policies for national growth and development might never take root, let alone their ever coming to fruition.

Nigeria has witnessed a lot of tribal wars, affecting trade and the movement of persons from one tribal region to another. More disheartening is the recent spate of terrorist acts by various sects within the country. Throughout the present regime of Chief Olusegun Obasanjo, he has to deal with several religious and ethnic wars, having at times to declare a state of emergency in some states. In recent years, the nation has witnessed several kidnappings and destructive activities by aggrieved youths in the Niger Delta, many of whom later dropped their arms and embraced the Amnesty Programs initiated by the administration of the late president, Umaru Musa Yar'Adua.

However, more recently and to date, there are classical terrorist activities by a northern-based religious sect, who call themselves Boko Haram (Western Education is a Sin). This sect has murdered hundreds of thousands of innocent Nigerians, and set notable buildings on fire, including the Nigerian Police Headquarters and the United Nations Building in Abuja. The activities of these sects have effectively called into question the dedication of the Nigerian government toward the security of the lives and property of its citizens. It should be noted that these sects have effectively limited the movement of the President, even within the Nation's Capital, and restricted celebrations of the annual Independence Anniversary within Aso Rock, the seat and residence of the Government, as well as much of the usual pageantry around Abuja, the nation's capital.

In all, only a couple of arrests have been made, including that of an incumbent Senator in the Upper Legislative Arm of the National Assembly, who is accused of sponsoring the activities of the dangerous sect. The activities of similar groups, evolving from one level to another, have largely contributed to making Nigeria an Investment- Risky Nation. In the State of Bornu, where these Boko Haram sects are said to be headquartered, there have been mass relocations to neighboring areas, for fear of being caught unawares in the regular bombings with human casualties that were for some time a daily activity. These activities have impeded the growth and development of the State through government programs and trade activities. (Such a State is by no means on my current list of places to visit.)

Election violence has gained a reputation as the most predictable event in Nigeria of today. Ranging from Local Government elections to the Presidential ones, lives continue to be lost, due to rioting in the wake of elections, even before results have been announced. The high point of this came after the recent presidential elections, when five youths currently serving in the mandatory post-college National Youth Service Corps program were brutally murdered in cold-blood by angry election protesters. Although the government honored these young Nigerians with financial rewards to their families, the event called into question the viability of the program, with many prominent Nigerians calling for its scrapping.

Speaking of Human Rights Abuse and Infringements, there are loads of such abuses in the day-to-day activities of the ordinary Nigerian citizen. Human Rights are a moral entitlement, and much more than a want or desire (Ashford, 2011). The case for human rights in Nigeria is likened by oppressive governments to similar claims from western governments and their citizens. Hence, the respect for human rights in Nigeria and Africa at large has been consciously and dangerously replaced with the imposition of governance through abuse by state agents. This has been helped in no small means by a poor and corrupt judicial system, as well as complicated rules for seeking justice and expressing one's right to life, liberty and property, respectively.

While it is no crime to be governed, the actions of (suppressive) governance and the agents of the state have made possible the erosion of basic human rights, most especially to the abuse of power. As Lord Acton said, "Power tends to corrupt, and absolute power corrupts absolutely." This is no doubt the case with respect to human rights in a typical Nigerian state, where powers and bureaucracy dictate what rights exists, and to who this right is due.

There are regular stories of persons sustaining permanent body injuries, public embarrassment and other forms of suppression, from state officials who take the law into their own hands, dishing out on-the-spot punishments to those they consider as domestic offenders, or intrusive on their own peaceful states of mind.

An example that readily comes to mind is that of a Naval Officer and another Nigerian citizen (names withheld) of equal human rights: "On the third of November, 2008, on Muhri Okunola Street, Victoria Island Lagos, the traffic was chaotic. A young lady (name withheld) driving home from work didn't move her vehicle out of the way of a military convoy on time, resulting in severe beatings by armed Nigerian Navy men. The convoy consisted of a Naval officer's saloon car and his pilot truck, consisting of six armed bodyguards, who not only mercilessly beat up the lady motorist in question, but also stripped her naked. The bodyguards also physically beat up several Price Waterhouse/Coopers staff, and destroyed cameras that were filming the event as it unfolded." However, another video clip, recorded on a personal camera, proved pivotal in securing justice through the courts. This was notable, as several other similar attacks went unpunished and received no such publicity.

Taking that as an example of citizenry, a more prominent instance of Nigerian human rights abuse is the denial of the rights to franchise to the present Governor of Bayelsa State. He was said to have stepped on some toes of the powers that be, being from the home state of the incumbent President, and thereafter was relieved of his right of nomination for primaries of his own party where he is presently the governor. He cried wolf, but the National Secretariat of the party came out and declared that his nomination for party governorship primaries was a party matter.

Hence, if such abuse can be perpetrated, even among those who hold power, what more can be said for the average Nigerian? The history of rights abuse in Nigeria transcends the abuse of the immunity and legitimate powers conferred on state agents by virtue of their offices, extending to unconsolidated property rights and its abuse, such infringement of privacy rights being among the other forms of domestic violence.

However, above all this, there is one common element: the superiority and supremacy of peace and peaceful co-existence, as a vital ingredient for achieving growth and development. All the cases cited show, rather explicitly, that violence, war, military interventionism, human rights abuse and state police abuse all constitute a hindrance to peace and consequently, to any meaningful development taking place.

We must embrace Peace, rather than conflicts. We must acknowledge the relevance of a peaceful state as a precursor to achieve any meaningful development. Most importantly, we must realize that our liberty is best achieved when we respect the rights of others to life, liberty and the pursuit of happiness.

Peace Is
Not for the
Faint-hearted

John Grant

John Grant is a writer-photographer living outside of Philadelphia. He has worked with Veterans For Peace and the Philadelphia Peace Movement for three decades. He writes for the on-line publications This Can't Be Happening *and* In the Mind Field.

I was raised in the late 1950s, not far from Homestead Air Force Base, the huge Strategic Air Command base just north of the Florida Keys. Some nights we could hear a low roar as dozens of the eight-engine B52 bombers warmed up together. Outside the base gate, there was a huge billboard that declared:

PEACE IS OUR PROFESSION

My father was a conservative WWII Navy veteran, who had been the captain of a PT boat in the Solomon Islands and in the island-hopping campaign through Peleliu and Okinawa headed toward Japan. He told me and my two brothers he had been scheduled to drive his PT boat into Tokyo harbor for the final invasion of Japan. Questions about the need for the atomic bombs didn't carry much weight with my father. He was certain they had saved his life. They were also a natural bookend to Pearl Harbor, since "the bloody Japs" had started the war.

Still, as conservative, racist and belligerent as my father could be, he always laughed and shook his head at the sign outside the Homestead AFB gate. To him, it was an insult to the English language.

Every bit of knowledge and experience I've accumulated in my life since then has reinforced this idea, that the last thing SAC and the U.S. military is about is "peace." As my father's rebellious middle-son, I agreed with him on the SAC sign and would grow to see the United States military as only interested in "peace" as a propaganda stand-in for domination, as in "peace is when you have someone by the throat and they can't hurt you." I'm not a pacifist, so I can't say that violence—or its ultimate collective expression, war—is never necessary; it should be clear, however, to anyone not befogged by propaganda, that what our Pentagon and military does is far from making peace.

Our military is the largest item in the federal budget—over 50 percent of the budget—and what it does is plan for war and make war; once it has begun to make war, it keeps on planning for more war, until it feels like we're on a runaway train.

My first inkling that I was rebelling against the great myth of American War was my 10th grade term paper on D-Day. I went through all the encyclopedia articles and read parts of books, but what really got me was the correspondent Ernie Pyle's account of the day after D-Day, when the smoke had cleared on Omaha Beach.

I ended the paper dealing with the various battles and deployments of forces simply by quoting Pyle's elegiac account of a stroll on the beach after the battle, with wreckage and death everywhere. Mrs. McConnell, my English teacher, really liked me, and the ending of the paper must have struck an emotional chord. (This was 1963, and as I look back, I imagine she was quite "liberal" politically.) She gave me an A++ and wrote "Bravo!!" on the last page. It took me many years to realize how important that positive comment was for me in my life. She had recognized something in me that has turned out to characterize much of my life.

I was not a popular kid, played no athletics and had a real recalcitrant streak that included smoking in the boys' room and the rest. At the time, I was reading Hemingway and Steinbeck. I read the French militarist Jean Larteguy's novel *The Centurians* about the French in Indochina and Algeria. I loved Graham Green's *The Quiet American* about an early CIA agent mucking things up in Vietnam. What I loved was the exotic colonial atmosphere, and as I look back, I think Greene would roll in his grave if he knew his magnificent anti-American novel actually made this kid want to go to Vietnam.

I'm not sure whether it was intentional or not, but my father effectively dashed any romantic notions I might have had of war, as glorious or in any way elevated. One memorable lesson was the prized trophy he showed me and my two brothers that he had brought back from the island of Peleliu—a 14-inch-long fibula lower leg bone he had cut from a Japanese corpse and cleaned up by letting little fish clean it as it dangled below the boat on a rope. He'd then soaked it in diesel fuel. Always the wit, he attached to it a manila tag that said "Made in Japan," then sent it home to his mom, addressed to her cocker spaniel, Ink.

I joined the Army seven days after my high school graduation, to get out of the house and away from my father, since we were by then at each other's throats. I was ready to "see the world" (that era's military-recruitment version of "be all you can be"). I became a radio direction-finder in intelligence, and was sent to Vietnam, ending up in the mountain town of Pleiku in the Central Highlands. I was a wide-eyed 18-year-old kid in the middle of a massive military intervention. It was the adventure of my life.

I was not in the infantry, and my year in Vietnam was a real-life exposure to all the foreign, exotic things that had intrigued me in Larteguy and Greene. Certainly, I could have been killed or wounded, which was true for anyone there; the reality of death and mortality was never far away. It helped that I was so young, and so very naïve. Looking back, I seem to have been a bit charmed with the luck of the innocent.

I was part of a small team that fanned out and triangulated the bearings of radio broadcasts sent out by North Vietnamese radio operators. In that role, I moved around a lot in the highlands, and if we were in a dangerous area we were always protected by a squad of grunts. I witnessed B52 raids that literally shook the ground. I spent time at two Special Forces camps. Several times, I hugged the dirt in a bunker as mortars crunched outside. I was never shot at.

I flew in open-doored Huey choppers, over the snake-like Se San River glinting in the chill dawn light, an incredible sight I will never forget. And—confession—I had sex at any opportunity I could, with some of the loveliest young girls in the world, for five dollars in bars and at laundries along the roadways. This last is one of the dirty little secrets of Vietnam. We were kids with dollars burning holes in our pockets, and the Vietnamese would do anything to get them.

Compared to some of my friends who suffered serious wounds and some who had to kill Vietnamese (and, of course, the millions of Vietnamese who suffered the most), my duty was easy; I chalk up my year in Vietnam as one hell of an education. It feels like I was part of a huge gang with all the worst attributes of what people say about American tourists—except, instead of cameras, we had loaded guns. We ran the gamut of human strength and weakness, good and evil.

I came home and submerged. I went to Florida State University on the GI Bill, where it never dawned on me to join the protests. I just stood on the sidelines while furious FSU students surrounded the ROTC building on campus. The local sheriff had deputized a hundred local good ol' boys, who wore jeans and helmets with plastic visors and billy clubs and bats in their hands. After I graduated, as the war was finally ending, I moved to Temple University in Philadelphia to pursue a Masters degree in journalism.

A Political Education in Central America

As the 1980s arrived and Ronald Reagan became president, Central America was in political turmoil after a long and brutal history of land expropriation and repression of the poor by oligarchies and the militaries used to keep them in power. Anastasio Somosa, the gangster dictator of Nicaragua, had been overthrown in 1979 by a rag-tag revolution that called itself the Sandinistas, after Augusto Sandino, a famous rebel who had fought U.S. Marines in the 1920s. The Reagan administration quickly mobilized an army of thugs and remnants of the hated Somoza *Guardias* and called them the Contras, for counter-revolutionaries. US ambassador John Negroponte oversaw this war from his post in Tegucigalpa, Honduras, directly north of Nicaragua.

In neighboring El Salvador, the repression was wide-spread and ruthless, leading to the 1980 murder of Archbishop Oscar Romero as he was saying mass. In Guatemala—the heart of darkness in Central America—rebellious Mayan elements were massacred by the military by the thousands. Various rebel armies grew out of this repression, most notably the Farabundo Marti Liberation Army (FMLN) in El Salvador. With the US government fueling the flames by providing the region's governments with large amounts of military aid, war spread throughout Central America.

It was travel to Central America during these years that, like Paul on the road to Damascus in Acts 9:18, caused the scales to fall from my eyes. Armed with a new-found sense of journalistic mission and a self-taught love of black-and-white documentary photography, I made a total of ten trips to Central America. The first was in the summer of 1984. I went with five union men from Philadelphia to Tegucigalpa, Honduras. By the second day there, we were all arrested and deported for meeting with labor leaders, who wanted to tell us stories of the murders and disappearances of their fellow workers and leaders. On other trips, as I listened to people tell heart-wrenching stories of things that had been done to them, their relatives and their friends, an entire history opened up for me. It was one-on-one, human story-telling, and it had nothing to do with the charge of communism and everything Ronald Reagan (and even Pope John Paul) said to demonize the politics of the poor in Central America. To me, it was not an East-West Cold War struggle; it was a North-South struggle, between those in power and those they oppressed and harmed.

I helped set up a sister-clinic relationship with a clinic in *La Trinida*, Nicaragua, that had been shot up by Contra thugs. I found a spent bullet in the wall, and used to show it off when I spoke back home. I made a number of trips into the FMLN rebel zones of El Salvador, one where I spent Christmas in the Chalatenango village of San Jose Las Flores. Maybe a hundred guerrillas came down from the hills to celebrate the holiday that featured a torch-lit procession of Mary and Joseph looking for shelter and, later, dancing to the Rolling Stones on a boom box.

I'll never forget meeting a woman who told a story about searching for her disappeared daughter, only to find her young body skinned in a dump. In a chapel in the Jesuit University of Central America in San Salvador, black-and-white drawings of bodies in such scenes line the walls of the sanctuary.

One morning in the 1990s, the sole survivor of the notorious 1981 El Mozote massacre in the department of Morazan cooked me and a friend breakfast. A brigade trained by the United States government at the School Of The Americas at Fort Benning, Georgia, was responsible for the massacre, where hundreds of defenseless civilians, including children, had been murdered. I was there to photograph Argentine forensic anthropologists, as they painstakingly exhumed the bones of men, women and kids slaughtered in a chapel; next, at a morgue in San Salvador, I photographed pathologists trying to make sense out the collection of human bones.

My father listened to my stories from Central America, but there was no way to affect his love for Ronald Reagan. The one thing he and I saw eye-to-eye on was religion. He taught physiology at the University of Miami Medical School, and he would have nothing to do with religion; I followed him on that path. *God? You gotta be kidding. A wise old deity floating somewhere "out there" who somehow knew everything you thought and did? No way.* It seemed too clear to me that religion was something in the mind, something that very Earthbound people came up with out of their imaginations when confronted with the great unanswerable mysteries of life. Too often what their deity was saying lined up exactly with the oppressive social consensus of the times. That was certainly true with the Catholic Church in Central America.

During my trips to Central America I encountered Liberation Theology and the notion—known as "the preferential option for the poor—that, beyond his spiritual existence, Jesus Christ had been a political activist, advocating for the poor against the imperial forces of Rome. This was, certainly, a simple-minded understanding of the Theology of Liberation. But as I met poor people who found strength in the movement, it moved me as well. It made me recall the one time I attended any kind of church.

Before my family moved to Florida, we had lived in a small town outside New York City. My father was trying to enter the corporate world in a pharmaceutical company, so to keep up his corporate image, he broke down and sent his kids to Sunday School. I recalled pictures in books of a kindly Jesus in sandals. As I looked back, that kindly, compassionate figure was the same Jesus I felt I was encountering among the suffering poor in Central America. These connections didn't alter my atheism, but it gave me a whole new appreciation for suffering and its connections to the spiritual urge in all human beings. The Catholic hierarchy in places like Central America was telling the poor not to rock the boat politically; be good and you will find paradise in the next world. The liberation theologists were saying, no way; you can struggle for a better life here and now, in this life. And, against conservative Catholic wishes, the spiritual and historic Christ was enlisted in that struggle.

There was certainly an element of leftist tourism about some of the trips I took to Central America, especially the ones connected to a tour. There was the time in Esteli, Nicaragua, when Sandinista President Daniel Ortega drove by in a jeep with Vice President and novelist Sergio Ramirez sitting in the passenger seat. I'd read Ramirez's novel *To Bury Our Fathers*. We waved, and they waved. There was the evening I had beer and *papusas*—a delicious stuffed tortilla famous in El Salvador—at the home of the Lutheran Bishop, Medardo Gomez. Two weeks earlier, he had been snatched off the street by what he feared was a death squad. They had only roughed him up to terrify him, then thrown him out of the car. Instead of being silent, which is what they wanted, he said he was determined to do the exact opposite: To make as much noise as he could, and go as public as he could, about the abduction and everything else he was fighting for. It was one of the best, most counterintuitive lessons I learned about the rough and tumble of politics.

Like my year in Vietnam, all those trips and the many photographs of people I took added up to an incredible education. As a white, middle-class man, I learned what it meant to be third-world poor, powerless and kicked around; I also learned how not to give up, and how to speak to power. I think I learned humility as an American—as well as how very lucky I was. When I got home, I took this message anywhere I could find an audience. I threw myself into the darkroom to print and mount gallery exhibits of 16 x 20 black-and-white prints.

Traveling around Central America, stumbling through conversations in my bad Spanish, it all seemed important, and I was sure once I got home I would use my photographs and my skills as a journalist to enlighten everyone so they, too, would begin to understand what I had come to understand. But at the end of a trip, when I actually got home, it seemed only a matter of hours before I was overwhelmed by the speed and the cacophonous nature of our culture, and what the Romans called the distractions of "bread and circus." Everything that had made such sense in a rebel zone of El Salvador was quickly swamped. Some people I told stories to would sneer that I had been brainwashed, that somehow because I traveled to Central America I understood less than they did—because they watched television.

It all had something to do with what the Salvadoran guerrilla politician Guillermo Ungo was getting at when he said, "El Salvador is a very tiny place, unless, like I have done, you walk it from end to end." Once, as the war was coming to a close, a friend and I were on our way to San Salvador and recognized Ungo sitting in a chair in the Miami airport. He was waiting for the same flight we were going on. I said hello in my pathetic Spanish, and we stumbled around a bit in Spanish. He smiled and wished us a pleasant visit to El Salvador.

Since those years, the world has changed. The FMLN guerrilla party in El Salvador elected a president, Mauricio Funes, and in June, 2009 I went to San Salvador for his inauguration.

Keeping the Peace Movement Alive

The political reality we are all living in seems wrapped up in the fact the good times, that began with the end of World War II and became the rising affluent tide into which I and other Baby Boomers had been weaned, are in decline. And as the glory of that post- WWII period declines, obversely, our expectations seem to be rising. Culturally, many of us have bought hook, line and sinker the notion of American Exceptionalism, which when linked with the deeply entrenched realities of American Militarism, add up to a tragic dilemma. Given the extent of our military, and the power of the military-industrial-complex (of which President Eisenhower warned the nation as he left office in 1961), it has become a national reflex to see international problems in terms of military solutions. In the same way, domestic problems, like our huge demand for drugs, are seen in terms of police, courts and prisons.

We're at war in Iraq, Afghanistan/Pakistan and now Libya. Add to that The Drug War, which is no longer a metaphoric "war" and has been growing horrifically in violence, especially across the border in Mexico. It now has filled our domestic prisons to the max, and the need for new prisons is a perennial budget item that finds little opposition.

In such a climate, many see peace as impossible. It is shrugged off as folly, an idealistic vision associated with naiveté. For some, being a "peace activist" is like confessing you still believe in the tooth fairy. Inside the peace movement, it breeds a kind of why-bother demoralization. Some people say, "If only we had the draft, then there would be people in the streets and our wars would be ended." The media is blamed; everything would be better if only the media would stop taking the government-corporate line and cover events from the people's vantage point.

In *Shock Doctrine: The Rise of Disaster Capitalism,* Naomi Klein takes this all up a notch. She defines "disaster capitalism" as "orchestrated raids on the public sphere in the wake of catastrophic events, combined with the treatment of disasters as exciting market opportunities." That is, there's great opportunity to be had for those brilliant and ruthless enough to reap the whirlwind.

We understand this, and then realize it's only a matter of time before those enamored with this process make the next logical leap: If chaos leads to change, why should those who have done the planning, and who have the resources needed to manage that change, wait passively for chaos to break out. If you can, why not set off and encourage that fertile chaos?

There's truth in all of the above. We are, indeed, living in the condition Eisenhower warned about, and the forces of crony capitalism and militarism do, indeed, take advantage of chaos to pursue their ends. And these forces only seem to get stronger.

So what is a poor peace activist to do? Gandhi's answer was The Truth Force or *satyagraha*, a version of the old saw, *the truth shall set you free.* In my 26 years in the peace movement, I've distilled the struggle down to a stand-off between Power and Truth. In the short run, Power usually wins hands down, running over Truth with a tank and leaving it like road kill. This is the peace movement's current condition: a demoralizing low point that provokes many to flee the cause of peace and find comfort amongst the tanks. As I see it, it's an existential condition that has to be accepted and seen as a beginning point, the point where one scrapes oneself off the roadway and gets to work.

I recently heard Ralph Nader speak at a veterans' anti-war rally in front of the White House. He's a man who has been an activist for progressive change for more years than many peace activists have been living on the Earth. He has survived all the ups and downs of the movement. His recommendation was the oldest and most simple advice one could ask for: "We've got to dig deeper into our communities," he said.

For me, that is more and more the challenge. Our communities may be saturated with corruption, and less than sensitive to the notions of peace and justice we in the peace movement have come to assume as natural law. But, as I think is Nader's point, it's time to move beyond a sense of righteousness. Pragmatism is what's needed. Maybe it takes developing a richer sense of humor, maybe a willingness to calmly listen to someone who may seem offensive, before finding the courage to engage that person in a discussion about what you have in common. Sometimes we can be surprised at what we have in common with people. But we can't be chumps, either. If we're advocating for peace, we need to be tough and, if necessary, in the spirit of Gandhi, take a blow. And, if it comes to that point, physically defend ourselves. That may not be perfectly Gandhian, but even Gandhi had moments that were not entirely "Gandhian."

In my case, I find strength in places like the poetry of Walt Whitman, a great American who purged all the pretense from himself and faced life as it came at him—and loved every second of it, never losing the joy, beauty and wonder of it all. In that spirit, I teach creative writing in the Philadelphia Prison. I read things on the left and the right. I love history. I work with Veterans for Peace, and do my best to organize people to end our wars and find a better way. I keep up on veterans' issues like Post Traumatic Stress Disorder.

Sharing a laugh is one of the things I most enjoy. I currently write for two on-line publications. I made a documentary film, and I still use my camera. I try to listen better; but, then, I also feel I'm getting too old to shut up. Reporting, analyzing and writing is where I take my stand, where I have ended up after scraping myself off the roadway.

Why Peace? Because the struggle for peace is so much more enjoyable and rewarding than surrendering to the death-obsessed culture of war. And, because the peace movement has become my family. The point is to keep on keepin' on, and to love life—and to give as good as you get. Organize and be ready to fight. As deceased World War II veteran Gene Bloomfield, a beloved friend, used to tell me with a grin: "Don't let the bastards get you down."

U. S. Foreign Policy
and Military Interventions

John H. Johns

Brigadier General Johns served 26 years as a combat arms officer, retiring in 1978. He served in command positions up to Assistant Division Commander of the 1st Infantry Division and held numerous staff positions, including 8 years on the Army General Staff, culminating his career as Director, Human Resources Development. After retirement, General Johns served for 14 years as a professor of political science at the National Defense University, where he taught core courses on National Security Strategy and National Security Decision-making. He also taught elective courses in Ethics, National Security Studies on Latin America, Leadership, and Government/Business Relations. General Johns is a graduate of the Army Command and General Staff College, the National War College, and the Industrial College of the Armed Forces. He has masters' degrees in psychology (Vanderbilt University) and international relations (George Washington University), and a doctorate in sociology (American University).

Professor Andrew J. Bacevich recently declared in the April 03, 2011 edition of *Newsweek: "Despite the Libyan intervention, the era of Western meddling in the region is coming to an end."* Perhaps he has seen new evidence of a learning curve since he published his 2010 book, *Washington Rules: America's Path to Permanent War.* Let us hope that his latter view is correct. Otherwise, we may be writing the next chapter for a revised edition of Paul Kennedy's *The Rise and Fall of the Great Powers.*

Historical Context

All great powers have had an element of imperialism in their foreign policies. More often than not, these policies have been cloaked in moralistic terms. Before I turn to our current policies in the Middle East, let me explain why many in the world may see our current policies as imperialism, or neo-colonialism.

In the case of United States imperialistic policies, the last hundred years has largely been under the ideology of "Wilsonian Idealism." One can argue, however, that the history of American foreign policy during the period from the 1890s until the present has been one of economic and military imperialism. In a penetrating account of American intervention in foreign countries, Stephen Kinzer's book, *Overthrow: America's Century of Regime Change from Hawaii to Iraq* (2006), summarizes the quest for worldwide economic and military hegemony, which began in 1893 with "regime change" in Hawaii. The fact that our first viceroy to Hawaii after the overthrow of Queen Liliuokalani was

Stephen Dole—and the establishment of Pearl Harbor—suggests the rationale for that intervention. During the following twenty years, the U.S. waged a concerted strategy to control the Caribbean and Central American regions for a combination of ideological, economic, and military purposes. In addition, the Philippines were added to the U.S. sphere of control. Reportedly, one of the major reasons for the Spanish-American War was to open markets for U.S. business, but one can argue that another goal was empire building. It is not easy to separate the two goals.

These activities were cloaked in moral terms of bringing the "blessings of freedoms" to the liberated people of these countries, but few or no nation-building activities were attempted in these liberated countries. Essentially, the U.S. engineered the regime changes to establish military bases and to gain economic access. In his book *All the Shah's Men: An American Coup* (2003), Kinzer describes how we are still suffering the consequences of the 1953 overthrow of the democratically-elected government of Iran, in order to have access to cheap oil. Arguably, this act is an important ingredient leading to the terrorism in the Middle East today. In early 2008, I participated in a nation-wide tour with Kinzer titled "The Folly of attacking Iran." This was a time when many "hawks" were beating the drums to attack Iran. Fortunately, cooler heads prevailed.

The "Cold War" was largely framed in terms of a moral crusade against "Godless Communism" versus "The Free World." This revived the passions of Wilsonian Idealism and provided the rationale for a series of military interventions through the 1970s. A few international experts warned against the moralistic tone of U.S. policies. In the late 1940s, the former ambassador to Russia, George Kennan, argued for a pragmatic approach toward Russia. More than 35 years later, he wrote:

> *"We must be careful about what might be called the histrionics of moralism at the expense of its substance. By that is meant the projection of attitudes, poses, and rhetoric that cause us to appear noble and altruistic in the mirror of our own vanity, but lack substance when related to the realities of international life."* - "Morality in Foreign Affairs," *Foreign Affairs*, 1985.

Another pragmatist, Hans Morgenthau, wrote in similar terms.

"Nations no longer oppose each other...within a framework of shared beliefs and common values, which imposes effective limitations on the needs and means of their struggle for power. They oppose each other now as the standard bearers of ethical systems, each of them of national origin and each of them claiming and aspiring to provide a supranational framework of moral standards which all the other nations ought to accept and within which their foreign policies ought to operate...Thus the stage is set for a contest among nations whose stakes are no longer their relative positions within a political and moral system accepted by all, but the

ability to impose upon the other contestants a new universal political and moral system recreated in the image of the victorious nation's political and moral convictions." - *Politics among Nations*, New York, Knopf, 1978.

Vietnam as Prologue

I was first introduced to the subject of military intervention in 1960 when, fresh out of graduate study in psychology, I was assigned to the U.S. Army Special Warfare Center at Fort Bragg, N.C. The focus at that time was the emerging conflict in Vietnam. It was apparent to many of us at the Center that the real problem was not primarily military, but the building of political support for the government of South Vietnam. Consequently, the Special Warfare School soon developed a new course, labeled "Counterinsurgency." A central component of the concept of counterinsurgency was the requirement to build a sense of nationhood among the people. From this grew the concept of "nation building," which involves the strengthening of political, economic, social, and judicial systems that bring stability to a country.

I must admit that I was rather naïve about the ability of U.S. military power to "build a nation." I was assigned as the senior advisor to the Vietnamese Psychological Warfare School (later the Political Warfare School) in 1962. I quickly realized that it was rather presumptuous of my fellow advisors and me to be telling the Vietnamese officers how to build the institutions necessary to gain the allegiance of their people. As I gained some insight into the political dynamics of the situation, I concluded that we were, in essence, trying to export our value system to a culture that did not necessarily share the particular institutions that reflected those values. In short, our policies reflected "Wilsonian Idealism."

When I returned from Vietnam and was assigned to the Army Staff, I had an opportunity to write several studies and work on ad hoc groups formulating doctrine for military interventions involving counterinsurgency and nation building activities. One of the major studies was *Nation Building: Contributions of the Army* (NABUCA). That study, which was distributed by the Army Secretary as policy guidance for the development of doctrine and curricula in Army schools, recommended that we not attempt to export our political and economic systems to cultures that may not be compatible with the ideologies underlying those institutions. I later served on a committee that inserted that recommendation into the Civil Affairs manual. The study also suggested that large-scale U.S. combat forces were inappropriate for conducting counterinsurgency; our role should be limited to an advisory one.

During my tour on the Army Staff, I also served on a study group that led to the establishment of a career field now know as the Foreign Area Officers' (FAO) program. This career field built on the former Foreign Area Specialty Training (FAST) program that was focused on the intelligence function. The new program was designed to develop a cadre of officers educated in the functions of not only intelligence functions, counterinsurgency and Nation

Building as well. Those officers would also be educated in the specific culture of areas in which they would operate. These specialists would be deployed as advisors to elements of the local military. The Army Chief of Staff, General Harold K. Johnson, said he envisioned a cadre of some 6,000 FAO members. Many of these would be in the reserves, where they could maintain their skills and be called up as needed.

It is interesting to note that when the Army Secretary wrote the letter of transmittal for NABUCA, he asked that it be "close hold" because other agencies such as State, AID, CIA, and USIA might accuse the Army of encroaching on their turf. The doctrine as outlined in NABUCA in fact cited the need for an integrated effort of all U.S. agencies in Vietnam, but focused on the U.S. Army's role. There were attempts in Vietnam to coordinate the roles of our military with civilian agencies, but the fact is that our civilian agencies have never developed a cadre of people trained to do the functions of counterinsurgency and nation building. This short coming still exists.

The less-than-total victory of the Vietnam conflict dampened the fervor of the more jingoistic and chauvinistic elements of our society. They were disappointed that the conflict had not produced "total victory." The War Powers Resolution of 1973 was an attempt to curb the power of future presidents to rush to war. As we know, that act has had no real effect on those powers. The backlash did, however, lead to the end of the military draft, which has had important implications—not all intended.

Revival of Imperialistic Policies

The neo-conservative movement in the late 1970s and 1980s rekindled the lust of those who believed in the manifest destiny of America to transform the world in its image. In a general sense, the neoconservatives told the world that American/Western values are the values that should be adopted throughout the world. And, it must be admitted, these values are sacred to a majority of Americans. In fact, it is often considered unpatriotic to question the universality of individualism, liberal democracy, and free enterprise. This is sometimes referred to as "American Exceptionalism." Some went so far as to declare that these values represent "the end of history." Francis Fukuyama wrote in "The End of History," in *The National Interest*, Summer, 1989: "We may be witnessing . . . the end of history as such: that is, the end point of mankind's ideological evolution and the universalization of Western liberal democracy as the final form of human government." He added capitalism to that list of values.

The quick and relatively painless 1991 Gulf War bolstered the stock of the neoconservative's Pax Americana approach, but some warned against this exuberant policy. In his 1996 book, *The Clash of Civilizations: Remaking of World Order*, Samuel P. Huntington warns those who assume the Western World values and doctrine represent a universal civilization "…generally share beliefs in individualism, market economies, and political democracy…" He rejects the notion that these beliefs are shared outside the West and warns,

"[O]nly naïve arrogance can lead Westerners to assume that non-Westerners will become 'Westernized' by acquiring Western goods." Above all, he warns against the notion that the West can impose its values on the non-Western world: "...Western belief in the universality of Western culture suffers three problems: it is **false**; it is **immoral**; and it is **dangerous**." That it is false is the central thesis of his book. It is immoral he says because what would be necessary to bring it about. It is dangerous because it could lead to a major intercivilizational war between core States that could lead to the defeat of the West. (Pp. 310-311).

Notwithstanding these warnings, we have continued to base our foreign policy on Wilsonian Idealism—recently aided by what some have called "muscular militarism." The leading paragraph to the 2002 National Security Strategy set the stage for our Iraq policy:

"The great struggles of the twentieth century between liberty and totalitarianism ended with a decisive victory for the forces of freedom—and a single sustainable model for national success: freedom, democracy, and free enterprise...These values of freedom are right and true for every person, in every society—and the duty of protecting these values against their enemies is the common calling of freedom-loving people across the globe and across the ages."

It is interesting to note that Fukuyama has had second thoughts after our Iraqi venture.

"Outside powers like the US can often help in this process by the example they set as politically and economically successful societies. They can also provide funding, advice, technical assistance, and yes, occasionally military force to help the process along. But coercive regime change was never the key to democratic transition." - Francis Fukuyama, "The History at the End of History," *The Guardian* (London), Apr. 3, 2007.

Current Policy

The United States is facing a threat unlike any we have faced in the past. We are sailing uncharted, perilous seas. There are indications that we may not have accurately identified the nature of this threat, and may be solving the wrong problem. Indeed, the phrase "War on Terrorism" is a misnomer that could indicate that we are on the wrong path. As will be discussed below in more detail, terrorism is a means of violence for political ends; the ultimate purpose is to influence political decisions of adversaries. If we focus too narrowly on the violent acts—the symptoms—we will miss the target and exacerbate the problem.

The September 2001 terrorist attacks arguably signaled the greatest threat to the United States' national security since World War II. It was important for the U.S. to correctly identify the threat and craft the appropriate foreign policy and national security strategies to counter that threat. I would argue that the

U.S. neither defined the nature of the threat accurately, nor adopted the correct response to the actual threat. As a consequence, the U.S. has found itself mired in the wrong wars, in the wrong places, and at the wrong times. Moreover, the U.S. has become engaged in a series of seemingly endless military ventures by conducting counterinsurgency operations, refereeing civil wars, and attempting to accomplish nation building all at once. In the name of the "war on terror," these actions have increased the threat by abandoning the moral high ground, which is at the heart of the battle of ideas, as I will explain below.

"Support for the United States has plummeted. Polls taken in Islamic countries after 9-11 suggested that many or most people thought the United States was doing the right thing in its fight against terrorism; few people saw popular support for Al Qaeda...by 2003, polls showed that 'the bottom has fallen out' of support for America in most of the Muslim world." - 9-11 Report

President Bush had described the problem in rather simple moralistic terms: "They hate us because we are free"; it is a war of "good versus evil." This simplistic answer appealed to Americans; it was less persuasive to the many other audiences. There is growing evidence that our use of military force around the world has done little to reduce the number of radicals who use terrorism as their weapon of choice.

Indeed, the growing recruitment into the radical ranks reflects a losing battle for the hearts and minds of the population from which these recruits come, primarily, from the Islamic world. A June 2004 Zogby poll taken in Arab States found negative views of the United States as follows: Egypt 98 percent; Morocco 88 percent; Saudi Arabia 94 percent; UAE 73 percent. The major reasons cited all involved unfair foreign policy, e.g., support of Israel and the Iraq war.

The same survey showed the most admired people to be: 1) Jacques Chirac; 2) Gamel Nasser, the martyred president of Egypt, 3) Hasan Nasrallah, the Hezbollah leader; and 4) Saddam Hussein and Osama bin Laden (tie). Other polls showed the unfavorable view of the United States existed throughout the world, including Europe.

I spent a good portion of my military career in what was then called "Psychological Operations." In essence, the goal is to persuade a given audience that your side has the moral high ground. It seems obvious to me that the United States has failed to get its message across to many parts of the world. Part of the problem is our product. As Huntington argued, we cannot assume that the rest of the world wants our political and economic systems, especially if they are exported through the barrel of a gun. Raising the decibels on our message by moralizing based on a belief in "American Exceptionalism," as Morgenthau and Kennan warned, is not effective. Assuming that our foes hate us because we are free buries our heads in the sand.

The first step we must take is to recognize that the so-called war on terrorism is a war of ideas more than it is a war to be solved by military force. I believe that our operations in Iraq, Afghanistan and Pakistan are counterproductive, for several reasons: 1) Counterinsurgency and nation building conducted by U.S. combat forces are impossible missions; those activities must be done by locals; 2) operations such as Vietnam, Iraq, and Afghanistan are perceived as neo- colonialism; and 3) there will inevitably be atrocities, to include torture. Consequently, these operations erode our moral authority.

Our fundamental strategies of counterinsurgency and nation-building activities undertaken in Iraq and Afghanistan (and Vietnam several decades ago) are doomed to failure. The unfavorable conditions in all those situations put this kind of effort in the class of "mission impossible." Nation-building efforts have the best chance of success in countries that have stable institutions and little or no active insurgency movements. In the wake of 9-11, our current rationale for intervention is to prevent havens for terrorists. While weak and failing States may be breeding grounds for insurgency movements and havens for terrorists, nation building is a long and difficult process, even under the most favorable conditions. The problem is magnified when that process attempts to export the United States' values (i.e., democracy and market economies) through the barrel of a gun.

In addition to the fundamental flaws in our military strategy, equally important is the economic costs of conducting these operations. In the summer of 2008, the National Intelligence Estimate listed the economic situation, not terrorism, as the greatest threat to U.S. national security. Our military leaders have echoed that view. This poses the question: are we providing the material for a new chapter in Paul Kennedy's book, The Rise and Fall of the Great Powers? In that 1987 classic, Kennedy makes a persuasive case that all great powers have fallen because they went bankrupt trying to exercise hegemony over large portions of the world. One can easily conclude that the United States is repeating that mistake.

In his 2010 book, Washington rules: America's Path to Permanent War, Professor Andrew Bacevich makes a compelling case that the American political ethos has condemned the United States to a state of permanent war. He provides the background to this conclusion in a series of books focused on American Imperialism and the emphasis on military power as the principal element of foreign power. This dismal conclusion comes at a time when the country faces an economic crisis that threatens to bring the nation to its knees. It may be that the United States is now providing the material for the next chapter of Kennedy's book, or we can hope that Obama follows the proposal of Chalmers Johnson in his 2010 book Dismantling the Empire, to wit, Obama must begin to dismantle the empire, before the Pentagon dismantles the American dream.

Morality and National Security

One of the most underrated elements of national power is a nation's moral standing in the international community. Every country reserves the right to protect physical security, even if it entails the violation of international norms. Flouting these norms, however, should be rare and only done after carefully weighing the costs. It has become popular in some circles to dismiss the United Nations and other international institutions as debating societies that serve irresponsible demands of Third World countries. Admittedly, working toward international moral order based on shared values requires a great deal of patience. It is difficult to achieve agreement on other than abstract values and rules that lend themselves to a wide variety of interpretations, but the effectiveness of these moral concepts depends to a large measure on the voluntary response to world opinion, usually expressed through the international institutions involved. By engaging in unilateral activities, the United States has gained the reputation of being arrogant.

In addition to unilateral policies, the commission of atrocities and torture by the U.S. military has eroded our moral stature. The revelation of widespread torture of prisoners in Cuba and Iraq justifiably shocked the world community, including the American people. The stark photos of the degradation of the prisoners left little need for words to convey the implications for world opinion. The damage to our moral standing in the world—and support for our "war against terrorism"—was profound. More damaging than the acts themselves was the revelation that officials at the highest levels had approved these acts as legitimate interrogation techniques.

Polls in 2004 showed that the American public shared the outrage of this moral breakdown and violation of the values we present to the world in our effort to promote human rights and dignity. Within a year, however, the outrage had diminished considerably, and there was little public pressure to take action to remedy the conditions that had led to these acts. A 2005 poll showed that less than 40 percent were bothered a "great deal" by the use of torture.

It is inexcusable to ignore the role of the systemic climate established by the policy makers and the apparent acquiescence by the chain of command. When policy documents waive international laws, the people on the ground have the burden to reject that policy. In my view, the behavior of these senior officials represents more serious violations than those at the end of the process. The recent resistance to closing Guantanamo Bay is an indication that we have forgotten the costs of these actions.

During the 2008 presidential campaign, a group of retired officers, led by General Joseph Hoar, USMC, Ret., and General Charles Krulak, USMC, Ret., conducted a "Campaign to Ban Torture." The group met with most presidential candidates, to recommend that torture be banned and that the facility at Guantanamo Bay be closed. All Democrats and two Republican candidates, Huckabee and McCain, agreed with these recommendations. With 19 of those officers in the Oval Office on 22 January 2011 in attendance,

President Obama signed directives to accomplish those recommendations. Unfortunately, political reality has prevented the closure of Guantanamo.

The most critical aspect of this scandal, especially in terms of immediate implications for our national security, has to do with the international community. The conduct of torture itself, and the way we have handled it, has the potential for long-term damage to our war against those who are using terrorism as their primary means of violence. Terrorism is not new; nations as well as non-state actors have used it. When used by non-state groups such as those now confronting us, those groups depend on at least tacit support from the societies in which they operate. That support depends in large part on how those groups are perceived in regard to the justness of their cause and that of their adversaries, rather than on the acts of terrorism themselves. In this sense, the war against terrorism is a war of ideas, with emphasis on who holds the moral high ground. From all accounts, we have been losing this war and the torture of prisoners was, and continues to be, a significant factor. How the international community perceives our reaction to it is critical in this war of ideas.

The fundamental flaw in our treatment of torture, it seems to me, is the clear disdain of some administrations, and elements of the public, for international norms of conduct. Unless our body politic, including the public, develops a greater respect for responsible membership in the international community, we will find it difficult to regain the moral high ground. Without that moral status, the war on terrorism will be unsuccessful. The rules regarding torture, like other international protocols, are a set of principles and norms designed to serve the interests of the entire world community. At times, conforming to these rules may cause inconveniences. To dismiss them in a cavalier manner, as the Bush administration—particularly Vice President Cheney—did, was a breach of trust. Trust is a precious commodity, hard to earn, easily squandered, and when lost, very difficult to regain.

Conclusions

The comments in this essay should not be taken to infer that I am an isolationist. The United States is still the most powerful nation in the world, economically and militarily. It has an obligation to use its influence to maintain a peaceful and just world community. Likewise, my criticisms of our conduct in global affairs should not be taken as "blame America first." Some tend to label any introspection regarding our foreign policy and actions as unpatriotic. In my view, the refusal to make an honest examination of policies is unpatriotic. I consider myself to be a patriot who wants the best for my country and its people. While my moral compass includes the welfare of all people, present and future, my obligation is first to this country. However, I believe the best way to achieve this outcome is to adopt a pragmatist approach to foreign policy, one that tempers idealism with the realities of an interdependent world where conflicts must be resolved by win-win strategies, rather than win-lose where winner takes all. The latter strategy more often than not results in lose-lose consequences.

All great powers have practiced imperialistic policies and that is to be expected. One should not be too quick to judge such policies as selfish pursuits of hegemony. It is natural for nations to believe in the primacy of their particular values and conclude that policies that advance those values and interests are for benevolent reasons. Such beliefs in "exceptionalism," however, can often stem from misguided notions and self-righteous arrogance.

It is difficult to evade the sociocentric nature of viewing the world and respect the view of other participants in the international system. But pragmatism dictates that wise leaders do that. In a 14 January 2011 op-ed in the *Washington Post*, "Avoiding a U.S.-China cold war," Henry Kissinger observed: "Each assumes its national values to be both unique and of a kind to which other peoples naturally aspire. Reconciling the two versions of exceptionalism is the deepest challenge of the Sino-American relationship." He warned that if both China and the United States adopt policies based on a view of their own exceptionalism, it will lead to gridlock (and a lose-lose outcome?).

There are influential elements in our foreign-policy process that advocate some of the dysfunctional characteristics I have mentioned. The belief that our values are best for the all societies and that we have a moral duty to export those values seems to me to be rather arrogant. Even if we continue to espouse our values, from a pragmatic standpoint, we should seek better ways to export them. The over-reliance on military power is, in my view, counterproductive. For reasons that I explain above, repeated excursions to put down insurgencies and build nations are not only futile, but they end up alienating the world and draining economic resources that can be best used for other purposes.

In general terms, I suggest the United States foreign policy be based on the following principles:

1. Work through international institutions as much as possible in conducting foreign policy. This is a pragmatic necessity. No nation can exercise hegemony—economically, culturally, or militarily—and we need to recognize that. Sovereignty is no longer sacrosanct. Emphasize "soft power," rather than military muscle. "Militarism" must be curbed.

2. Limit interventions in troubled nations to the advisory role; avoid the use of U.S. military forces to attempt to do what only can be done by indigenous people, specifically counterinsurgency and nation building. Moreover, do so knowing that there will inevitably be "collateral damage" and atrocities, regardless of how well-led and -trained our troops are.

3. Develop a National Advisory Corps to deploy, to aid nations in need of building institutions. This cadre could be patterned after the Army's Foreign Area Officer program, with each agency focusing on its respective functional area.

4. Beware of self-righteous arrogance that blinds us to understanding how others in the world view our policies and actions. Jingoism and chauvinism are deadly enemies.

5. Abide by international norms except in dire situations. As some have argued, "the norm is mightier than the sword."

Our leaders must understand the realities of today's international system; the era of U.S. dominance that allowed a unilateral approach to foreign policy has ended. While it may be frustrating to work through international institutions to achieve our goals, it is a necessity. Surrendering any degree of sovereignty—military, economic, or political—is painful. It is best done before it is forced on us. We are not alone in this process; Europe is wrestling with the same process. The history of mankind has been, out of existential necessity, the evolution of the establishment of common institutions to promote cooperation toward achieving common goals.

Biology of Peace

Mazin Qumsiyeh

Professor Mazin Qumsiyeh teaches biology and does research at Bethlehem and Birzeit Universities in occupied Palestine. He previously served on the faculties of the University of Tennessee, Duke and Yale Universities. He is now president of the Palestinian Center for Rapprochement Between People and serves on the board of Al-Rowwad Children Theater in Aida Refugee Camp. His main interest is media activism and public education. He has published over 200 letters to the editor and 200 op-ed pieces and been interviewed on TV and radio extensively (local, national and international). Mazin has published several books, including Sharing the Land of Canaan: Human Rights and the Israeli/Palestinian Struggle *and* Popular Resistance in Palestine: A History of Hope and Empowerment.

I grew up under Israeli occupation, a brutal military occupation accompanied by "colonization" (land theft). My family suffered, though not as much as other Palestinian families. It is hard to describe how much the occupation invades every aspect of one's life here: from eating and drinking to education and from healthcare to travel, from economy to freedom of religion. The antithesis of all of this repression, violence, occupation, colonization and war is, of course, peace. I was thus captivated by peace as a concept, a dream, a hope. Sometimes I was thinking of peace in terms of a state of external calm and lack of disturbance. In other times, I thought peace was related to freedom from repression. Now, I think of peace as being an inner peace, that only comes from acting on what we believe and freeing our minds of the bondage acquired from external sources.

In the Buddhist traditions, we are asked to seek, to have "joyful participation in the sorrows of this world." I was reminded of this when I was held on July 27, 2011, along with some Israeli and Palestinian activists, in the Israeli military compound at Atarot. This was after being attacked by Israeli soldiers for participation in a peaceful demonstration in the village of Al-Walaja. This beautiful village in the West Bank is slowly being depopulated of its last remaining citizens. Simple and beautiful slogans are hard to apply here, as a wall will encircle the remaining houses of the village, cutting the inhabitants off from their livelihood and forcing them to leave.

How can we even begin to comprehend the sorrow that has engulfed the land of Canaan in the past few decades? The sorrows of the native inhabitants are so horrendous that it sometimes seems unreal. Of 11 million Palestinians in the world, 7 million are refugees or displaced people. The 5.5 million natives who remain inside the country (many displaced) are restricted now to shrinking concentration areas, amounting to only 8.3 percent of the historic land of Palestine.

According to the latest survey of the Palestinian Central Bureau of Statistics, some 26.2 percent of families live in poverty and 14.1 percent live in deep poverty, for a total of 40.3 percent living in poverty or deep poverty in the West Bank and Gaza. The situation in Gaza is worse than in the West Bank with 1.5 million people, most of them refugees squeezed in an arid part of Palestine, besieged, blockaded and denied even basic living necessities. This, the worst post-WWII horror inflicted on a people, indeed portends so much suffering. So how can we have personal peace, let alone joyful participation, when we suffer so much?

On a personal level, I have lost many colleagues and friends. Just in the last year alone, I have lost friends who practiced nonviolence and strove to peace: Juliano Mer Khamis, Vittorio Arrigi, Bassem and his sister Jawaher Abu Rahma. I lost many other friends and relatives to illnesses that seem to be increasing in our population. Cancer and heart disease have claimed the lives of many of those: my two brothers-in-law and four dear friends and fellow activists. All such losses certainly make deep scars that reach to the soul. Even routine difficulties in life stir us and disturb us, leaving us a little further from peace. So how can we aspire to peace while our own souls are still far from peace? I believe our internal turmoil is mainly due to a lack of understanding of human nature and the trajectories of history.

To understand humans and what drives us, we have to understand our biology, especially our early development. I taught developmental biology and researched how things could go wrong in early development. We all start as a zygote, a single cell which is the result of the union of the sperm nucleus with the egg nucleus inside the cytoplasm of the egg. That primal cytoplasm is a soup containing codes for proteins that allow the early embryo to get its initial organizational structure, even before the code in the nucleus of the zygote starts to shape the future of the individual. In a sense then, we all depend far more on "stuff" we get from our mothers than stuff we get from our fathers. In developmental biology we know that axis formation (having three dimensions: anterior-posterior, dorsal-ventral, left and right) comes from the cytoplasm of the egg from our mothers. In essence, without that initial material we get from our mother, we would simply be a round blob.

But the miracle of developmental biology is that the joining of 23 chromosomes from the sperm with 23 chromosomes from the egg makes one nucleus. There are already endless genetic possibilities for those maternal and paternal chromosomes. This is because the process of producing sperm and eggs, called *meiosis*, not only reduces the chromosomes by half (from 46 to 23), but creates myriad opportunities for having very different sets of genetic variation, through recombination and chromosome segregation. That is why no two sperm and no two eggs are the same. That is why no two siblings are the same (except of course identical twins, which come from the same zygote).

The first cell divides to become 2, 4, 8, 16, 32, 64 cells. That early embryo implants itself on the uterine wall and the interspersing of embryonic and maternal tissue forms a placenta. This remarkable structure is where nutrients are supplied to the embryo, and oxygen and $CO2$ are exchanged. Many embryos are lost along the way because they have genetic codes that affect these developmental processes. Some 15-20 percent of recognized pregnancies end-up spontaneously aborted (a natural selection process). Harmful mutations are the price that our species pays for possibilities of useful mutations. Mutations are the natural substances upon which natural selection operates. Useful mutations survive and travel to the next generation. That simple idea (developed and spread by Charles Darwin) revolutionized our understanding of biology and in turn has advanced a wide range of fields, from environmental research to medical studies.

The embryo developing in the uterus is, of course, subject to its environment. Both harmful and beneficial stimuli shape its very existence and future. That is why pregnant mothers are told to stay away from harmful materials (alcohol, tobacco and other drugs) and maintain a good diet. (Many Palestinian mothers delivered babies with blindness in the few years following the Nakba of 1948, because of vitamin-E deficiencies in the refugee camps.) Some scientific studies also suggest a child's brain development may be susceptible to nutritional food and toxin-free air and the absence of other harmful things. There are data that show that even music and the mother's good mood influences the mental capacity and development of the child she is carrying. Needless to say, women in war zones do not produce the healthiest babies. This is why the impact of a military occupation is not just on the adults and children around but on future generations.

After birth, education from society may create tribalistic racist notions (e.g., Nazi Germany... or Israel today). Challenging these notions of superiority and striving for common good is possible, but it requires shedding some of the educational baggage that nationalistic and militaristic societies use to saturate young minds. At one level, this is more difficult today than in the past: Modern warfare is much bloodier than ancient warfare, but it is conducted from a distance.

Soldiers no longer come home to wash off the blood of their enemies from their clothes and swords. They come home with images of the tools that they have used to destroy enemies from a distance. The faces of their enemies are not familiar to them, only outlines in gun sights or on computer screens. The facial distortions and agonized screams of those killed do not reach the killers. Some of these killers like to pretend they do not imagine these things. They want to cling to the elements of their humanity. They may go back home, and even help an old lady cross the street or pass a candy to a child. But deep in their psyches, these killers know that they have destroyed a human being just like them, with flesh and blood, with feelings, with people who loved him or her.

On the other hand, the development of the internet and of methods of social communication allow a closeness of the human family in new and incredibly positive ways that promote social transformation towards peace and human rights. From the organizing against the World Trade Organization and International Monetary Fund in Seattle, to Tunisia and Egypt, people are finding their voice. Here in Palestine, we have had a vibrant activist community for decades. Increasingly, Israeli and international activists join hands with native Palestinians in our struggle for peace with justice.

After 20 years of fruitless negotiations between colonizer and colonized, occupier and occupied, even Palestinian elites have come around to see the power of the people. Engaging in international diplomacy while doing popular resistance is seen as critical in increasing the pressure to arrive at a just resolution. If the Israeli government remains intransigent and continues to build colonial settlements on Palestinian lands, the only remaining option will become adopted by more and more people: a push for a single democratic state throughout historic Palestine. That outcome may already have been guaranteed by the relentless expansionist Zionist project. By making a two-state option impossible and forcing us into close contacts, we (Palestinians and Israelis) are developing joint strategies to work for peace, even as walls are erected on our land.

What is remarkable is that humans of different backgrounds are coming to regard peace as personal, and to regard politicians as "behind the times." All humans have behaviors that trace back to our ancestral primates. From sex to feeding to self-protection to ambition to control of space, we as a species are driven by these deep-rooted innate behaviors. To what extent we can control our behavior in a positive fashion determines our humanity. Governments endeavor to maintain the status quo of control over individuals and the manipulation of conflicts for their benefits. Yet, the achievements by individuals working together towards freedom, peace, and self-government are a testimony to the power that resides in us.

We learned from the civil rights movement in the US, from ending apartheid in South Africa, from the freedoms achieved in Eastern Europe, and from the Arab Spring. I believe the main reason this world functions (and the main reason we remain optimistic) is that good people are everywhere, endeavoring toward inner peace and extending it by deeds to achieve peace in our societies. This happens despite the push-back from governments who are happy with the status quo. Without this "people power," we would have endless wars and endless repression and injustice. With it and with human cultural evolution speeding up, we indeed look forward to a day when no human life is lost in useless wars and conflicts, and all individuals are free from state aggression. It is up to us to work to accelerate the trend in history.

Finding Peace through the Veils of War

Jon Turner

Jon Turner is a father, partner, poet, and veteran. He actively seeks peace while learning to maintain a balance in his own life. He served four months in Haiti and two tours in Iraq as an infantryman with the Marines, receiving a Purple Heart. Jon has been diagnosed with Post-Traumatic Stress and endured two traumatic brain injuries from explosions. He is actively involved with Warrior Writers, Revolutionary Poets Brigade, Seven Star Press and makes paper from his military uniforms, in order to creatively process the wartime experience for himself, his family and friends. Jon has obtained his level 3 Reiki certification, completed a plant spirit healing apprenticeship and, in 2012, will be attending herbalist school to help veterans and their family members heal with natural medicine.

Each time I look at war I feel differently about it. What I have noticed about war is that it is not one fixed emotion. There is no real way to describe the situation aside from confusion. Everything that happens leading up to, during and afterward has such a profound effect on one's soul, that often what is left is misunderstanding and confusion for the duration of life. What I have seen—from old-timers, the new birds, and all in between—is almost a false love for the event, the disillusionment of feeling what happened as being right.

The media's portrayal of war, I believe, has been one-sided and vague. Since September 11, 2001, American media has repeatedly victimized this country, and gotten so caught up in drama that it fails tremendously at capturing the whole story. During the ten-year anniversary of 9/11 this year, all headlines read something along the lines of "Remembering That Day." It is unfortunate that so many innocent people died, but I saw no stories talking about the two wars in which the U.S. government is currently engaged, the trillions of dollars spent on them, the millions of innocent lives that have been lost, the millions of families broken, the lack of proper care to the two million veterans who have fought overseas, or the many homeless veterans and veterans who have taken their own lives. I still am very confused by my war experience, as I feel most veterans are. Most are afraid to allow their true feelings to be expressed. Our culture is very judgmental, so I understand why they would not tell their story, but the emotions that matter most come from the individuals who have lived both sides of the story. It is beneficial to listen when someone tries to portray that experience.

I once listened to a Cherokee man speak of identities, and how taking on other personas throughout life can mislead us from our own true selves. We as humans learn from our families, our friends, our experiences and our interactions. However, it is easy to be influenced by others, if we lack solid understanding of our own selves. I believe that this issue of identity has played a large role in all wars.

New recruits, on the first day of training, are told to forget who they are, the things they enjoyed, and their memories and families. Their innocence is stripped away, to be remolded into a basically trained soldier, imbued with knowledge that completely counteracts all visions of peace. In other words, a recruit is taught to be angry; in some cases, those who already hold this emotion are allowed to express it freely. It is accepted and practiced within the realms of military life, as well as being highly encouraged in training and on missions. A recruit is taught to disassemble and assemble a weapon intended to take another life, and be okay with the decision. Each thrust with a bayonet: *KILL!* Each blow to the chest: *KILL!* Each step in cadence: *KILL! KILL! KILL!!* The notion of killing something is consistently stressed in practice throughout basic training, making it easier later on for the soldier to pull the trigger or drop the projectile when faced with those real life situations in a combat zone. An aggressive influence is drilled into your mind and bones during class, in conversation, in story or in actual event. If you live in a state of chaos or anger long enough, it will become your life. The act of destruction becomes muscle-memory, and war becomes a desire.

During my first tour to Iraq, we received mainly indirect fire (*i.e.*, mortar blasts and improvised explosive devices); the only large firefight my platoon encountered happened on April 2, 2005, at the tail end of the attack on Abu Ghraib prison. As we rolled near the west side of the compound just south of MSR Michigan, after hearing the 50-caliber rounds rip through the air for the last hour-and-a-half (on top of the explosions, cracks of gunfire and kicked up sand), everyone was excited. It is a feeling similar to losing your virginity, because you are about to do what everyone has talked about, what the movies and video games glorify. I'll tell you, there is no glory in a firefight. When you are close to death, the confusion is so great that you do not remember what has happened, until someone tells you or after years have passed. Explosions have a way of scaring your soul into not wanting to return.

April 2 was just a taste, though. It wasn't the real thing everyone was desperate to know. (This is a feeling similar to not being kissed by someone you truly have feelings for.) By the time we had gotten there, unloaded and set up position, the streets had been mostly cleared, and we were getting ready to head back in the wire. For those of us who deployed again, that excitement was still there, in anticipation of the heroic battles we would tell stories about to our grandchildren. Unfortunately, those wishes of battles came true, claiming the lives of 18 marines in my unit and issuing over 90 Purple Hearts. I received the medal for a piece of fragmentation, still lodged next to my jaw, from a mortar blast.

War to me had become a state of chaos with no boundaries, nothing to tell the difference between my own feelings and those of war itself. My life had become confusion, which I still deal with today over five years past. It remains difficult to find the separation between balance and chaos, when all you have been living in is confusion. Also worth mentioning are the number of lost souls, well into the thousands, still wandering because their lives were so abruptly ended. Those memories linger.

A peaceful death is one where the person preparing to pass is made aware of what might happen, feelings that might be had or visions that might be seen. A shaman or medicine man or medicine woman can assist in this transition from physical life into the next, using knowledge that has been kept and taught for thousands of years. The person ready to pass on has made peace with living, and after the breathing stops, is grieved for properly by family and friends, in a sacred ceremonial way which further assists the passing soul into the next path of life: becoming a spirit.

During tragic or sudden death, however, souls may be confused, lost and unable to pass smoothly; therefore, they might still be wandering the earth plane, and possibly attaching themselves to living humans, or even taking up residence in someone else's body. Because so many people have died and not been properly grieved for throughout the years, this is very common. But, with plant medicine and a shaman, the transition will properly occur, putting that soul at ease.

When you live in the midst of war, it becomes too easy for it to become your life, even after you have returned home. And without proper integration, sharing stories and having them understood and not judged, we are expected by our peers and our society, to become normal again. After all of my deployments and being released from the Marines, I lost a lot of hope in humans, for their not knowing or wanting to know what to do with returning veterans. Most people in bars, if they found out you had just returned home, will buy your drinks, but that really does nothing, except further disconnecting you from everything that should be addressed. The stories told on bar stools are often forgotten, and the loneliness and misunderstanding is still waiting for you in the morning. (You only hope you didn't get into too much trouble the night before.)

There had been too many times when I did not recognize being back in the states; I pulled knives on people, and called Indians "sand niggers" ; I completely disregarded interaction and conversation thinking about sand, and was completely hateful and obnoxious to strangers—who couldn't care less that I had just returned from war. All the while, I was going through every emotion at once, and having to run away enraged and screaming for my meds, because something was not right in my head. Everyone became the enemy. Every scenario was an ambush; once on the pills, I was dependent.

These are all common occurrences for returning veterans. The classes given to us before leaving Iraq were a joke; the chain-of-command had not yet accepted (and often denied) the troubles, drinking and drug abuse as being symptoms of Post-Traumatic Stress. It was a blessing that I was single, and the only person to take care of was me. I simply tried to forget that I had even enlisted.

At war, I found that only at night after everyone had gone to sleep (while not on post or patrol at the government center) would I find solace in myself waiting for the sun to rise. I would mostly listen to music with an attachment to memories of home, knowing that the last place I wanted to be was in Iraq, or even in the military. It took me three years to realize that this lifestyle was not one I wanted to be living, and I knew that it would take a long time to break off the layers and layers of armor, hiding the light within my heart.

I still do not know the turning point at which I knew that everything was a mess. It could have been many things—hearing my friend scream after a mortar landed on the back of his chair; seeing my other friend's head caved in from a sniper's bullet; or maybe just one too many explosions—but somewhere in July or August of 2006, there was a large shift in my beliefs and feelings about war, a shift that felt very familiar. I felt it. I knew it. From that point, I actively began to try to remember what it was to love something.

It is unfortunate to know that there are some soldiers who may never make this connection. The armor has been passed from generation to generation, because they never had a proper grieving process from previous battles. The families of returning veterans are left to wonder why it is that their soldier is so distant, so detached, and most likely just as confused, not knowing how to act or react. I have met and known many veterans who have been unable to share their stories with family members, afraid of how they might feel, or just cannot tell their stories, period. It is a hard feeling to have, knowing what you have been through, while people back home were carrying on with their lives, with no understanding of what it is to be at war.

Six years have passed now, and memories are still being unearthed. They have a way of coaxing you in and almost severing your connection to yourself. It's almost as if they want you to be lost again; the truth is, they wish to be honored and recognized as having actually occurred. It's like cleaning your closet: you need to go through everything, try it on, and get rid of what no longer fits. For so long my experience was suppressed; I tried to forget, through my own will (with the assistance of drugs and alcohol). In order to heal, however, the arising memories must be accepted and allowed to pass, an extremely difficult process.

When I go back to these events, I instantly notice not feeling like myself, knowing that at that time, my body and mind were in such a completely altered state of being. It's like you are thinking the thoughts of war: angry at everything, harnessing hate and aggression, speaking dirty thoughts, tasting contaminants in the sandy air. You have to separate yourself from those memories and look at them from a distance, so that you do not get sucked back in.

What has most encouraged my healing now is my family. I do not know where I would be, had I not met my wife Catherine (who worked for the organization hosting our art exhibition). She has walked along, by my side each step of the way, as I've revisited these battles. In a way, this war has become a part of her, from a different perspective that allows me to recognize the different patterns in my behavior and emotions. We sometimes joke that we are either silly or crazy in love, but we are both determined not to let our partnership fail. As difficult as it can be, what binds us together is love: for each other, our son, our dog, and both of our families.

The spark that flew between us when we first met was enough for me to say, "Fuck war, I've had enough!" Thinking back on that first connection gives me a better understanding of love and what it is capable of. I believe that if we can find a new focus, that has a positive impact on our lives, then we can turn this whole thing around. Sometimes we have to be a witness to horrible things, to get us to where we must be in order to play out our roles as humans; we have the opportunity, though, to feed the aggression and sorrow with understanding, to turn the soil and grow something beautiful.

It starts in ourselves, in our homes. It starts with patience and compassion. It starts with love.

Imagining a Healing
in the Broken-Middle
of Jerusalem

Marc H. Ellis

Dr. Marc Ellis is University Professor of Jewish Studies, Director of the Center for Jewish Studies and Professor of History at Baylor University. He has lectured around the world and published more than twenty books on the subjects of Jewish identity, the Holocaust, Israel and the Palestinians and Jewish-Christian relations. His most recent books include a third and expanded edition of Toward a Jewish Theology of Liberation, Reading the Torah Out Loud *and* Judaism Does Not Equal Israel. *Next year he will publish* Encountering the Jewish Future, *an exploration of the lives and thought of Elie Wiesel, Martin Buber, Abraham Joshua Heschel, Hannah Arendt and Emmanuel Levinas. Dr. Ellis' books have been translated into ten languages. Among other venues, he has lectured on Jewish and Middle East issues at the United States Holocaust Memorial Museum, the United Nations, the Carter Center and the Kennedy School at Harvard University.*

Why peace? Is peace the absence of war? Not necessarily. Can there be real peace without justice? Or when injustice and peace co-exist is peace just a cover for another kind of war? Can peace with justice bring the healing of broken histories? Are Jews and Palestinians condemned to broken histories or can they be healed—together?

I first experienced war in 1973. I was a college student studying in London when during a school break, I traveled to Israel. I visited Israel because years earlier my Hebrew school teacher had become angry with me when I asked him about his own visit to Israel right after the 1967 Arab-Israeli war. I had read a feature story in a monthly magazine that highlighted the latest Palestinian refugee crisis caused by war. The story also mentioned the origins of the Palestinian refugee crisis in 1948, when Israel was created. Those refugees were still displaced. Would these refugees experience the same fate?

Like most American Jews of my generation, I knew little about the state of Israel and almost nothing about the Palestinians. I knew of "the Arabs" as they were referred to—at least in the broadest and most negative of categories. Were "the Arabs" different than Palestinians or were they the same? Why were they refugees and would their condition alter in the near future? I wondered as well if we as Jews had any responsibility for their plight.

My questions were many, my ignorance clear. But instead of responding in a measured way when I mentioned Palestinians, my teacher flew into a rage. I couldn't understand his rage. I was determined to see the situation for myself and during my time in Europe the possibility came. I traveled to Israel in the month of October. During my stay, the Yom Kippur War began.

I remember the beginning of the war vividly. I was traveling through the Galilee when I heard sirens. At that very instant, the apartment buildings around me became full of Jews heading down the stairways. At first I thought it was a practice fire drill, as I often had in the schools of my youth. But then, since the stairways were full, it seemed that everyone was participating, willing and without complaint. People signaled me to join them. I was unsure. They were insistent. Soon I was in the basement with them, which I quickly realized was their bomb shelter. The war had begun.

This was Israel's war with Egypt, which followed on the heels of the 1967 war where Israel had defeated Egypt, Syria and Jordan. The October war was payback for Egypt's humiliating defeat in the 1967 war. Having taken Israel by surprise, early in the war Egypt advanced steadily, placing Israel in so much danger that then-Prime Minister Golda Meir pleaded for emergency shipments of armaments from the United States. I was unaware of the danger, though, for inside of Israel the war effort was concentrated and fluidly organized. Later, Israel reversed Egypt's advance and the war ended in a stalemate. Egypt's victory set the stage for Anwar Sadat's visit to Jerusalem and the Camp David Accords that followed. In a sense, peace between Israel and Egypt was established, though Sadat paid for this peace with his life. The region itself remained on war-like footing.

Years later, in the late 1980s and early 1990s, I traveled to Israel during another time of war. This war, which became known as the Palestinian Uprising (in Arabic, *Intifada*), came from within. It was a rebellion of the Palestinians on the West Bank and Gaza I had asked my Hebrew school teacher about. They wanted a state of their own alongside Israel.

During the Palestinian uprising, I visited wounded children in Palestinian hospitals. The hospitals were full of children who had been shot by Israeli soldiers. Many of the children suffered traumatic and life-altering injuries. Some were brain dead. They would live only days longer. I had started writing about the Israeli-Palestinian crisis and how it related to the Holocaust, Jewish history and identity and the future of the Jewish people in the early 1980s. Now I was face to face with that future. I saw the Jewish future in the dazed eyes of the children and in their parents' irreconcilable pain.

Surrounding the children's beds were symbols of Palestinian freedom, usually the colors and flag of Palestine, along with the framed picture of the child. I spoke with the parents about their children, about Palestine, about Israel and... yes, about their experience with Israelis. I heard difficult things, including how the Holocaust was used against their desires to be secure and free. Some Palestinians asked if the Holocaust really occurred, or whether it was propaganda to feed Israel's appetite for more and more land. Their feelings were bitter, and understandably so. At times, the historical record of Jewish suffering was denied or pushed aside. Could Jews who had suffered so much cause another people to suffer?

It was the same story I heard when years earlier I visited Gaza and sat in the homes of families whose sons had been killed by the Israeli military. The framed pictures of the children in the homes and in the hospital were also the same. They were pictures of "martyrs" for Palestine. In Hebrew school I had learned of the Jewish tradition of martyrdom. I wondered whether our history of martyrs had produced these new martyrs, and what that might mean for Jewish history. Could it be that my understanding of martyrdom had to expand, and that now our own martyrs and the martyrs we had created had become one?

History has strange arcs. When a people are violated, those that they violate become part of their history. Until the violation is reconciled, there is emptiness in the history of the conqueror, even and especially when the victors celebrate their victory. Israel has won the war against the Palestinians, but Israel's victory has brought dissension even among Jews themselves. By visiting the home of the Palestinian martyrs was I creating a bridge toward reconciliation between Jews and Palestinians?

The cycle of war continues, in the last years alone spawning an Israeli invasion of Lebanon and Gaza. As the underlying issues remain unresolved, more wars seem to be in the offing. There are those who think that the expansion of Israel has gone so far as to place even the two-state solution that the Palestinian uprising sought out of reach. Today Israel's power stretches from Tel Aviv to the Jordan River, with millions of Jews *and* Palestinians sharing—unjustly—the land.

Clearly Palestine has been conquered by Israel. With Palestinians increasingly surrounded and enclosed by the Wall, the situation continues to deteriorate. There is no end in sight.

For Palestinians, the desire to be free encompasses the need for justice for what they have lost. But even beyond the lost lands that became Israel, the settlement and occupation of the territory they had left deprives Palestinians of the ability to regroup, to start again, in short a future for themselves and their children.

Why then think of peace in Israel and Palestine? So the cycle of violence, displacement and atrocity can end. Even if the cycle was stopped through some kind of peace agreement, peace would only be the beginning. Peace can only take root if there is a promise of justice to come. A question is how justice in Israel-Palestine can be envisioned. But before that vision can be taken seriously, indeed as a prerequisite to peace and justice, a confession is necessary. Yes, in my experience of this seemingly endless war, and as a Jew, it seems to me imperative for Jewish Israelis and Diaspora Jews as well to confess that, in the establishment and expansion of the state of Israel, what we as Jews have done to the Palestinian people is wrong. No matter what Jews think of the need for a Jewish state, historically or in the present, the Palestinians have suffered tremendously. They are suffering today. Only the end of that suffering will bring a true peace to Israel, the Palestinians and the Middle East region itself.

The concept of justice is difficult to define in detail anywhere. Obviously, this is true in the Israeli-Palestinian case. What will happen to the Palestinian refugees I read about and subsequently experienced in the homes and hospitals in Gaza and the West Bank? Will they be repatriated to the whole land or part? Jerusalem is the geographic, cultural, intellectual and religious center of Israel-Palestine, of central importance to Israelis and Palestinians. Jerusalem is also central to Jews, Christians and Muslim around the world. For the purposes of peace and justice, is it best to divide Jerusalem, making West Jerusalem the capital of Israel and East Jerusalem the capital of Palestine? Or in order to give birth to a future beyond the tragedies of the past, would it be better to build a united Jerusalem, shared and governed jointly by Jews and Palestinians?

A shared Jerusalem would become a beacon of shared life for both peoples who physically live in Jerusalem and for those who call Jerusalem their spiritual home. Is a shared Jerusalem a realizable hope or a utopian fantasy?

An idea I had some time ago, in the midst of this ongoing war, might be worth contemplating. If Jerusalem is the middle of Israel-Palestine, to which both peoples are drawn, it is also broken, in that both peoples meet in Jerusalem with broken histories and psyches. For Jews, it is centuries of suffering, culminating in the Holocaust and now a new level of brokenness experienced in the dislocation and oppression of the Palestinian people. Palestinians have been broken by the establishment of the state of Israel and its subsequent expansion. They have also, too often, been isolated in the Arab world and beyond. Could Jews and Palestinians who live in Israel-Palestine and Jews and Palestinians in their respective Diasporas, meet in the broken-middle of Jerusalem to begin the healing of their individual histories?

Over the years and even more so today, I doubt whether Jews can experience a healing only by ourselves. It may be that the healing of Jews and Jewish history only occur in partnership with the Palestinian people.

Is this thought of a joint healing of Jew and Palestinian blasphemous? It seems that many Jews feel that way. However, increasing number of Jews—Jews of Conscience—feel the opposite. Many Jews of Conscience feel that a joint healing is the only way forward for Jews, the Jewish people and Jewish history.

For Jews of Conscience the war between Israel and the Palestinians has come home in a civil war among Jews. Jews who have different views of the Middle East situation are at each other's throats. It is difficult to imagine peace among Jews until there is justice among Israelis and Palestinians. To go that route, however, is to admit that Jews have violated the rights of others—as our rights have been violated in the past. This is difficult for Jews to admit because it throws our vision of ourselves into stark relief. Have we joined the ranks of the conquerors? Jews of Conscience believe we have. Jews of Conscience want a different face of Jewishness.

Why peace in Israel-Palestine? Just imagine what a united and peaceful Jerusalem would mean to Palestinians, to Jews and to the world. Would a truly shared Jerusalem preface the beginning of a justly shared planet?

Peace vs. Interventionism

Maulana Wahiduddin Khan

Maulana Wahiduddin Khan is an Indian Islamic spiritual scholar who has adopted peace as the mission of his life. Known for his Gandhian views, he considers non-violence as the only method to achieve success. Internationally recognized for his contributions to world peace, he has received, among others, the Demiurgus Peace International Award, the Padma Bhushan, the Rajiv Gandhi National Sadbhavna Award and the National Citizen's Award. A recent book, The 500 Most Influential Muslims of 2009 by Georgetown University, Washington DC, has named him "Islam's Spiritual Ambassador to the world." The Maulana has authored over 200 books on Islam, prophetic wisdom, spirituality and peaceful co-existence in a multi-ethnic society, the most recent being The Prophet of Peace: The Teachings of Prophet Muhammad; Jihad, Peace and Inter-Community Relations in Islam; *and* The Ideology of Peace. *These books not only offer a peaceful solution to the menace of terrorism, but also help individuals understand the concept of peace in Islam. The Maulana is an Islamic Spiritual Scholar and founder of the Center for Peace and Spirituality International.*

Human life on this planet earth is governed by the laws of nature. One law of nature is this: interventionism always fails to work, while non-interventionism always works. The history of mankind has proved the veracity of this well-known law. Scholars generally define peace as the absence of war, but this is a negative definition while peace is a positive phenomenon. According to my experience, a better definition of peace can be given in terms of opportunity.

Peace is the greatest concern of all thinkers and reformers. Scholars have developed an independent discipline called Pacifism. Pacifism means the science of peace. Numerous books and articles are published in different languages. One such book is the *Encyclopedia of Peace* but it is a fact that peace is a distant dream. No accepted definition of peace is available among scholars. Also, no scholar was able to develop an ideology of peace in terms of a practically achievable goal. Consequently, the question of peace only added to disturbing the peaceful atmosphere.

Peace For the Sake of Peace

There is basically one reason that people are not able to achieve peace. That is that these people have attached conditions to peace that are not directly related to peace. Some say we want peace, but we want peace with justice. Some say we want peace with human rights. This concept of peace has only contributed to making peace a goal that seems to be unachievable. As a result, people are confused as to whether peace is an achievable goal.

The simple answer to this question is that peace is definitely achievable, but it has to be seen in its true perspective.

The fact of the matter is that peace is always desirable for its own sake, and every other desirable state comes *after* peace, not along with it. Peace cannot directly give you justice or human rights. When one establishes peace for the sake of peace, this only opens the doors of opportunities, and by availing of these opportunities you can achieve all other targets. That is, other targets like justice and human rights are a result of your own effort and not the direct result of peace. So, the maxim I follow, when peace is the desired state, is: "*Ignore the problems, and avail of the opportunities.*"

Once people become tolerant and obtain peace for its own sake, what that actually does is open up opportunities—it creates favorable conditions, which enable people to strive for their ideals, eventually attaining justice, human rights and other constructive ends.

This happens due to the law of nature. When the individual refrains from making a controversial matter into one of prestige, this gives rise to serious thinking. This non-emotional thinking helps him to understand that if he were to walk out of the point of controversy he would find all other paths open to him.

So we can say that when we establish peace for its own sake, it opens the door to all kinds of opportunities, while intervening in situations only leads to violence or war, jeopardizes all the present opportunities and closes the door on all new opportunities.

The Benefits of Peace

It is a fact that all worthy feats in this world have been performed by peaceful endeavor. No great or noble task has ever been carried out by the power of violence. This applies equally to scientific discoveries and technological progress. Neither educational institutions nor research institutes have ever been established by violent means. Iron's conversion into machines was done by the power of peace.

Violence *per se* is destructive, and no constructive result can ever come from a destructive act. This is the law of nature and as such is immutable. Violence is against real human nature. Violence, the greatest of all crimes, is lethal to humanity. In spite of this, why do people engage in violence? The reason is that they take into account only present conditions, and lack the ability to see future prospects. Then such people find self-styled justifications for engaging in violence. Their version of justification appears to them to be based on logical argument, but in actual fact their arguments are fallacious. In defiance of all rational opinion, they adhere to the notion that, in their own case, for such and such reason, engaging in violence has become morally justified.

But, the truth is that any so-called justification for violence is invalid. Whenever an individual or a group engages in violence, they have at one and the same time the option of a non-violent or peaceful method. This being so, why should violence be resorted to at all? When the opportunity to achieve one's objective is available without having recourse to violence, why should everyone opt for violent methods? The truth is that violence must be in principle discarded absolutely and peace must be adopted absolutely. Therefore, man ought not to engage in violence on any pretext. He must adhere to a peaceful course of action in all situations.

Positive Status Quoism vs. Interventionism

The best formula of living a peaceful life, as opposed to interventionism, can be formulated in these simple words: *Positive status quoism*. That is, the peace-lover accepts the status quo to remove himself from the point of confrontation, to work in other fields where he may proceed with constructive action.

Instead of becoming embroiled in problems, he looks to the future and directs his energies towards the availing of opportunities. That is why the status quoism of a peace-loving person is indeed positive. Another name for this is "the peaceful method." I can say with certainty that the status quoism of a peace-loving person is not a form of inaction; it is rather a positive plan of action, in the real sense of the word.

One element of positive status-quoism is the "wait and see" policy. This means that whatever man is easily able to do at the present time should be done, while whatever he feels presents too many difficulties should be postponed until the situation seems more favorable.

It often happens that whenever faced with difficult situations or undergoing some bitter experience, out of sheer exasperation, one resorts to violence. But this kind of reaction is a result of deviation from nature. The truth is that the law of nature always favors those who adopt a realistic path. If such individuals or groups who stand by truth and justice do not act in an overly hasty manner and remain patient, such favorable conditions are ultimately produced for them that success will come to them on its own.

In most cases, failure awaits those who are so impatient that they act emotionally, without giving much thought to the repercussions. On the contrary, those who opt for the way of patience are destined to be successful.

When an individual adopts the path of patience, he is following the path of nature. And when he adopts the path of impatience, he deviates from the path of nature. And one who strays from the path of nature has no prospects of success in this world of God.

Flowers and Thorns

The fact is that life is full of problems. Even Prophets are not exceptions in this regard. Everyone including prophets have to begin in a situation where there are problems and unwanted situations. So, what to do? People generally are obsessed with their own desires and thoughts. So they take problems as obstacles, they try to remove the obstacles first.

Due to their obsession they fail to differentiate between peace and problems. They believe consciously or unconsciously that peace is a secondary matter; we first have to intervene and remove all the obstacles so that we may be able to achieve our desired goal. Unfortunately, this kind of methodology is against the law of nature.

According to the law of nature, in our world there are flowers, but there are also thorns. It is therefore a common experience for one who wants to engage in any positive activity to feel that there are obstacles in his way, perhaps by the very law of nature. This applies to the individual as well as to the entire nation. One way of addressing such a situation is for him to intervene and set about removing all obstacles from the path, and only then beginning to work towards his goal. This method is generally defined as "radicalism."

Radicalism greatly appeals to extremists or to those who are guided by their emotions. But it is impractical insofar as achieving any positive goal is concerned. While radicalism may be effectively used for the purposes of destruction, it is worse than useless when it comes to construction.

Once the path of radicalism has been chosen, not only does the prevalent system fall apart, but in the process of what are essentially ruinous activities, all those social traditions which had taken centuries to build simply fall to pieces. Then, as a result of bloodshed and violent confrontation, innumerable people fall victim to all kinds of afflictions. While experience shows that the method of radicalism is ideologically very attractive, in terms of its practical outcome, it is devoid of all merit.

Instead of radicalism, the peaceful method is that of avoiding confrontation with the status quo, and chalking out a plan for possible action within possible spheres. By temporarily accepting the status quo, we may then avail ourselves of current opportunities.

We can say that the method of radicalism invariably produces violence: on the contrary, positive status quoism fulfills its target by keeping the peace in society. While the former invariably aggravates the problem, the latter (by avoiding friction) proceeds smoothly, without creating any problems. If one is the way to perversion, the other is the way to construction.

Future-Oriented policy

To put it another way, positive status-quoism as against interventionism can also be thought of as a form of foresight. As a policy, it is in accordance with the natural law of "wait and see." There are times when each individual and community finds themselves in the kind of situations in which they begin to feel that they are faced with certain obstacles, which prevent their making any headway. In such cases, most people come—consciously or unconsciously—to regard such difficult circumstances as a permanent condition.

As such, they begin to wrestle with the circumstances in order to remove the hurdles. Fighting of this kind always proves futile, and only results in making things go from bad to worse. It should be remembered that difficult circumstances are never here to stay. They are always of an ephemeral nature. This being so, the easy solution to this problem is to ignore it, rather than unnecessarily wage war on the circumstances. This policy will preserve man's mental peace and whatever lies in store for him will in time become available to him.

Whenever man is confronted with any problem, he wants to intervene and solve it without delay. This is where he actually goes wrong. If he could just shelve his problems at least for a short time, he would find that solutions would present themselves which had nothing to do with combating circumstances head on or with coming into confrontation with opponents.

None of his problems would remain such for an indefinite period of time. In most cases violence takes place only because this principle, not being generally understood, is not applied in daily living.

De-Linking Policy

Positive status quoism can also be defined as a de-linking policy, which entails finding ways of peaceful action despite the existence of controversies. This means that, irrespective of confrontational state of affairs or other adverse circumstances, such strategies should be adopted as may prevent war being waged and violence taking place. Controversial issues must be set aside, so that present opportunities may be availed of in an atmosphere of peace.

In following this policy, two gains simultaneously accrue: the establishment of peace, notwithstanding the pernicious atmosphere created by controversies; and the optimization of work opportunities, despite the presence of problems. One great benefit of this de-linking policy—in that it is the most felicitous natural formula for the establishment of peace—is that conducive circumstances for result-oriented actions are no longer a matter of the past, but become an actuality today.

Positive status quoism is undoubtedly the most successful strategy for the construction of a peaceful life. The essential condition for the utilization of this strategy, however, is for man to develop the kind of positive attitude which will enable him to rise above his circumstances. Even in the most adverse situations, he should be able to weather all storms, as the big birds do in such times. His thinking should not be the result of prior conditioning. He should rather think out and plan his actions without any prejudice.

Those who are deprived often use a term to explain their condition—state aggression. State aggression is only a negative name for a natural phenomenon. In every state there are a number of political problems which are common to all. Some people are benefited by the political system, whereas others are deprived.

The fact is that no political system can establish ideal equality among people; this phenomenon arises out of people having different levels of capabilities. At one stage in modern history, certain socialist leaders wanted to establish equal economic distribution, but because economic equality is against the laws of nature, this was simply not possible anywhere in this world. The only solution for those so-called "deprived" persons is to enhance their abilities, rather than attempting to engage in the politics of opposition.

Conclusion

In this world of diverse interests, peaceful activism through positive status quoism, not interventionism, is the optimal base for the conception and implementation of constructive projects. Taking up this position may call for special virtues such as insightfulness as well as the capacity for the most superior type of planning. Thus it brings a two-fold benefit: first, no disturbance of the peace; second (and ultimately), the guarantee of success. This formula can thus be summed up: Avoid confrontation, adopt peaceful activism.

America's
Failed Intervention
in Iraq

Michael M. O'Brien

Michael O'Brien is a West Point graduate. He was an Infantry officer in the Army and left the service to work in commercial real estate in the Washington, DC area. He was the Real Estate Advisor to the Iraqi Ministry of Defense in Baghdad from July 2006 to September 2007. He is the author of America's Failure in Iraq: Intervention to Withdrawal 1991-2010. *His website is:* www.americasfailureiniraq.com.

I always supported a strong military and national defense establishment. This stemmed primarily from my father, who I admired more than any other person. The son of Irish immigrants who settled in Newport, Rhode Island, he was accepted to West Point during the Second World War, graduated in three years, and went to Europe. He remained in the Army and was assigned to Vietnam in its early stages. He finished out his career in the Pentagon amidst the anti-war conflagration.

Admiring my dad as I did, I wanted to follow in his footsteps and attend West Point too. Although my father wanted me to go there, he never pressured me. After graduation I was commissioned as an Infantry Second Lieutenant and off I went to my first duty assignment in the Canal Zone in Panama. I also served in Korea and Texas, and decided to resign my commission and enter private industry. The way I saw it, why bother working with people I had nothing in common with (I don't hunt or fish), to include officers I had no respect for, if I never made it to brigadier general. I served under some great officers, but also under many who had no integrity, and weren't very bright. I often asked myself what they would have been doing if they weren't in the Army. I knew the only way to make general was to be a "yes man," which I wasn't. My two brothers both graduated from West Point as well. My younger brother is a full colonel today.

The military culture I grew up in was a huge part of my family. We were typical of the nation in the post-World War II era. National defense was Priority Number One, and to question it was the same as declaring treason. It led us into Vietnam to fight the "threat of communism." It all sounded good back then when I was a kid. That's how I felt—until I went to Iraq in July 2006.

Operation Iraqi Freedom

I was never sold on our invasion of Iraq in 2003. It never made sense to me. Not being a fan of Colin Powell, I was less of one after his performance in front of the UN Security Council with his bogus 'proof' that Iraq possessed weapons of mass destruction (WMD). When he presented his 'evidence,' the best he could come up with was a recording of two Iraqi officers talking about a "weapon." That was it. But because of Colin Powell's popularity and prestige, the Security Council bought it hook, line and sinker.

I had worked for George W. Bush on his presidential campaign in 2000, and as a political appointee in the first two years of his administration. I was with the State Department on assignment to Dhaka, Bangladesh on September 11, 2001, and then on the staff of Tom Ridge at the Office of Homeland Security in the White House. I left the Bush administration in 2003, believing the president had our country on the right track. Though I had doubts about our invasion of Iraq, I went there as a Department of Defense contractor in July 2006, still believing George W. Bush knew what he was doing. I was the adviser to the Iraqi Ministry of Defense on all issues related to the basing (land, construction, facilities, etc.) for the new Iraqi Army.

It didn't take long for me to discover the real reason why I was in Iraq. It wasn't to assist the Iraqi Army or the Iraqi people. Rather, it was to be in Iraq, alive and not in a pine box, so my American employer could collect fees from the U.S. Government for my being over there. I started to figure things out the day I arrived, when my in-country manager told me and the others I was with that we would likely not end up doing the job we were hired to do. He said we might end up doing something completely different, telling us: "that's the way things are in Baghdad."

In addition, none of the Coalition (i.e., U.S. military) would listen to a word I had to say about the field I was the advisor for, even though they knew nothing about it themselves. The U.S. military was doing everything for the Iraqis, not caring what they said or wanted, or what I said either. That was bad enough, but they then proceeded to do things in violation of the new Iraqi Constitution, such as taking land without clear title. And the Iraqi Ministry of Defense was its client.

Within short order, I also began to see the effects of Paul Bremer's decision to disband the Iraqi security ministries, its Ministry of Defense and Ministry of Interior. Having only passing knowledge of this from news accounts before arriving in Iraq, it hit me like a brick wall when I got there. Not only had the United States invaded a country that posed absolutely no threat to our security (just as Vietnam had posed no threat), we essentially made up reasons to do it (*e.g.,* the WMD that were never found). Then we eliminated Iraq's ability to defend itself, based on the fantasies in Paul Bremer's mind. The result of these actions by the United States created an Iraqi government without its head (Saddam), and now without its arms and legs (its army and national police). We did this, for reasons that are known only to a handful of advisors to President George W. Bush, and maybe not even to Bush himself.

I found myself in Iraq, a contractor with no purpose to serve, other than to stay alive so my employer could collect fees. But I also found myself the citizen of a country that I had grown up thinking was the greatest in the world, only to be red-faced and embarrassed in front of the Iraqis I worked with every day. They would tell me they understood the U.S. needed to fight the global war on terror, but why did we have to pick Iraq to do it in?

The "military-industrial complex"

In time, the words of President Dwight D. Eisenhower, when he warned the nation in 1961 of the growing "military-industrial complex," began to make more sense to me. As a contractor in Iraq, I realized we had indeed arrived at the very point he had been telling us to avoid. I was now a small cog in that "complex" myself, and I didn't like it. I felt like I was being used as much as the Iraqis were. I decided to write a book about America's involvement in Iraq when I returned home.

Looking back to the Second World War my father served in, our nation depended on private industry to build the planes, tanks, rifles, boats and everything else the nation needed to fight the war, and to supply our allies. But what happened when the war ended? Did these companies, which had made money beyond their wildest dreams, simply go away quietly into the night? Not quite. Like a government bureaucracy, once they were entrenched, they weren't going anywhere. The money was simply too good.

And with good money comes the power to perpetuate the making of it. That power is exercised through the labyrinth of lobbyists and former generals and members of Congress who put profit ahead of the nation's best interests. For example, is it in the nation's best interest to fund a weapons system that isn't needed in the world we live in today? The answer would be no. But that is not what the company making it wants to hear, and it will do whatever it takes to get the contract to make it, or continue to make it. One good way to assure this happens is to hire the general who was in charge of the weapons system after he retires from active duty. He should have no problem stroking the right person in the Defense Department to keep the contract from being terminated. Sound farfetched? It's happening every day. But these generals are beyond reproach because, well, they're retired generals. We're supposed to accept that at face value.

This results in the US government awarding contracts for things it doesn't need, justified by perceived threats to our nation's security. In rare cases, our 'leaders' realize this and don't award the contract for the product. Maybe the defense contractor has fallen out of favor with its key supporters in Congress. Maybe its political contributions to those members have dropped off. It's all politics in Washington, with lobbyist and members of Congress scratching each others' backs. In the end, it's all about money. Peoples' lives are not the focus anymore. How many innocent civilians have died in Iraq since 2003, because of an invasion with no legal justification? Meanwhile, defense contractors have made billions. They take that money and contribute to the politicians who appropriated the funds, hire the retired generals who awarded the contract, and lobby politicians to continue prosecuting the war. What a system!

"Self Defense"

If defending our own security doesn't fit the bill, our national leadership can always decide to defend another country's instead. Even if the other country is halfway around the world, our leaders say defending its security is the same as defending our own. Case in point—Iraq. What does defending Iraq have to do with defending the United States? Nothing, but it sure sounds good. The defense establishment certainly doesn't mind. Any excuse for a war will suffice. As a result, U.S. lives and resources are expended for the profit of the defense contractor supplying the goods or services. The extent of this has gone way beyond providing rifles and tanks. Now it includes providing bodies too, only we call them "security contractors" (*i.e.*, homegrown mercenaries).

Let's look at Iraq with rational thought and logic. Was the Iraq government going to invade the United States in 2003 if we didn't invade Iraq first? No, it wasn't. Was the Iraq government about to invade a neighboring country in 2003 if we didn't stop it first? No, it wasn't. Then why did we invade Iraq in 2003 if neither of these reasons—which are the only legitimate reasons to invade another country—existed? Based on my experience in Iraq, it is difficult for me to come to any conclusions other than these: George W. Bush wanted to spin his spurs and show the world how tough he was, and Saddam Hussein was as good a target as anyone; he wanted to get even with Saddam for his attempt on his father's life; and neoconservatives on his staff with their own agendas got him to do what they wanted: start a war with Iraq.

When we look at the real winners of this invasion, the Iraqi people are not on the list. If they now have something that resembles a democracy, it's more dumb luck that anything else. To say we invaded to instill democracy there is an exercise in reverse logic—that was *not* the reason we were told for our invasion *before* it occurred. We were told it was to eliminate Saddam's weapons of mass destruction. The American people are losers as well. The real winners have been the corporations supporting the United States defense establishment in this venture: the CEOs and executives, the lobbyists for these companies, active duty generals getting more stars, and retired generals getting jobs at those same defense firms after they leave the service—the revolving door and crony system that is the modern day military-industrial complex.

Could it be said that nearly 5,000 American soldiers, and as many as 500,000 Iraqis, died so U.S. defense contractors could haul in cash? Not directly, but indirectly very much so. It all goes back to the Second World War and the establishment of companies that were literally too big to fail. Unfortunately, rather than re-tool themselves to make products that helped people, not just products for war, these firms remained in their original lines of business. This was far more profitable than competing in the marketplace. The only way to continue making these profits is to continue selling these products. And the only way to continue selling these products is to have continued warfare.

The War on Terrorism

Certainly the war on terrorism must be met with force. This, and any war, can only be won with superior manpower and technology to support it. We invaded Iraq without legal and moral justification. To do this we invaded with too few ground forces, but with a lot of tanks and guided bombs, which have a high profit margin. Soldiers are strictly overhead. The tank and bomb manufacturers did well, but our men on the ground didn't because there weren't enough of them to defend each other, much less mount a strategic offensive against the insurgency—that we created.

Because there were too few infantry soldiers, they suffered far more casualties than necessary. This was because Donald Rumsfeld went into Iraq on the cheap (I call it "Invasion Lite"), under the command of "Mr. Yes Man" himself, Tommy Franks. As a result we lost more soldiers than we should have. The Iraqi people suffered far worse, because too few American troops were there to defend them, especially after Paul Bremer took away Iraq's ability to defend itself.

The facts are these:

- The President of the United States invaded Iraq… for no valid reason.

- The Secretary of Defense executed the invasion… with too few infantry soldiers.

- The caretaker governor appointed by the President and the Secretary of Defense… disbanded Iraq's internal security infrastructure after we invaded.

- The President of the United States, the Secretary of Defense, and the military commander on the ground in Iraq… all failed to address the growing insurgency that developed (as a direct result of our invasion and occupation of Iraq, as well as the points mentioned above).

It's not hard to understand why many people around the globe dislike the United States. This perception has been created by the actions (mistaken or otherwise) taken by by our national leadership, not by the American people. As in many other countries, the people are not the ones who cause the problems, their leaders are. In the case of Iraq, the American people are suffering for our leader's failed intervention in the affairs of another country, an intervention that was illegal and unnecessary. We are now in the same situation as people in countries we used to look upon with disdain.

Throughout all this defense firms, like the one that employed me in Iraq, have continued to make huge profits. In addition, my firm was managed by two retired US Army 4-star generals, one a former Chief of Staff. They left the Army and went into defense contracting. They knew they could walk the halls of the Pentagon and get all the business they wanted. Even after they leave the service, no one is going to make a retired 4-star general wait outside the office. The crony system between the Pentagon and the "Beltway Bandits" housed in buildings in nearby Crystal City take the term "conflict of interest" to new heights.

The military-industrial complex is now calling the shots in U.S. defense policy. One could almost say it is telling the Pentagon, and even the White House, what to do. "The tail is wagging the dog." Taking it to the extreme, are these firms supporting the Defense Department, or is the Defense Department supporting these firms?

In an Orwellian way, this could be what Eisenhower envisioned when he gave that speech back in 1961. He was the Supreme Allied Commander in Europe during World War II, so he knew all about the need for defense contractors to support his mission. But then he became the president and could see that these same firms were still around, only now they were influencing U.S. defense policy. No doubt he didn't like what he saw. Maybe "Ike" feared the U.S. government would someday engage in war for war's sake. (By a twist of fate, the month he gave that speech in 1961, my dad was on his way to Vietnam, as one of the first U.S. advisors to the South Vietnamese Army.)

Because the military-industrial complex is so large, and has so much influence over our national leadership, our nation is getting involved in questionable conflicts we have no business getting involved in, and that have nothing to do with our national defense. There is always a seemingly plausible, but on closer scrutiny unjustified, excuse used to get the ball rolling for our next conflict.

But who is asking the question: why are we doing this? If the question is asked at all, it certainly isn't being asked by defense contractors. Their only concern is how many units of their product the government is going to buy. In the meantime, thousands of American soldiers, and innocent non-combatants in countries half way around the world, die as a result of bogus conflicts that have nothing to do with our own security. On top of this, the conflict (*i.e.*, the invasion) is poorly executed, making matters far worse.

Are money, power, and influence more important than peoples' lives, to include our own soldiers? Should we be more diligent and watchful of our government's war powers? I leave these questions up to the readers to decide. At least they might cause enough concern to begin the debate.

Peace through
Economic Freedom

Michael Strong

Michael Strong is the co-founder of Freedom Lights Our World (FLOW), Conscious Capitalism, and the Free Cities Institute. He is the lead author of Be the Solution: How Entrepreneurs and Conscious Capitalists Can Solve All the World's Problems *and* The Habit of Thought: From Socratic Seminars to Socratic Practice. *Prior to founding FLOW, Michael was an educational entrepreneur who created a series of schools based on Montessori, Socratic, and entrepreneurial principles, including a charter school ranked the 36th best public high school in the U.S.*

I have always been a non-violent, non-aggressive person who believes in, and lives, by the dictum "live and let live." Indeed, I've never quite understood why some people hate, attack, or want to control other people.

The biggest transformation in my worldview with respect to peace has come with the growing recognition that:

1. Capitalism, as long as it is based on mutually-beneficial voluntary exchange in which government does not play favorites, is one of the world's most powerful foundations for peace;

2. Many of those who are hostile to voluntary exchange as a force for peace often support acts of unilateral aggression by governments.

3. A widespread acceptance of state-initiated violence as "normal" is the real obstacle to a more peaceful world.

I'll provide a biographical account of this three-decades long transition from a progressive hippie-kid to a voluntaryist (*i.e.*, that we should allow, in Leonard Read's memorable phrase, "Anything That's Peaceful.")

My parents were uneducated people who moved to a farm in northern Minnesota in 1970 when I was ten. While they were not themselves hippies, it was the beginning of the "back to the land" movement, and many of our neighbors were hippies. When I was not milking cows or baling hay, I was reading *Mother Earth News* and the *Whole Earth Catalog* along with gobs of science fiction and classic novels. By 1978, we had run out of money on the farm, and we moved into a trailer house with my grandparents in Aspen, Colorado, so that my dad could bring in some cash.

Aspen was a much more cosmopolitan place than Minnesota, and as a young intellectual I began reading the *New York Review of Books* and *Harper's*. As a consequence, although my parents were apolitical, by the time I went to Harvard University, I knew that all decent human beings understood that government was for the most part a force for good, and capitalism was bad.

After one year at Harvard I transferred to St. John's, famous for its "Great Books" approach. I looked forward to going back to the very beginnings of western civilization and thoroughly studying everything, to see how and where things had gone wrong. I especially looked forward to reading Hegel and Marx sequentially, so that I could understand exactly where Marx was coming from.

Three years later upon reading Hegel I found myself profoundly disappointed by the obscurantism. Likewise, Marx did not impress me, but then neither did Adam Smith. I ended up writing my senior thesis comparing Marx and Smith, determining that they represented incommensurable paradigms, but without committing myself to either paradigm.

St. John's is unique among Great Books programs, in that it includes a close reading of the classic historical texts in math and science, such as the sequence: Ptolemy, Copernicus, Kepler, Galileo, Newton and Faraday, Maxwell, Michelson-Morley, Lorenz, and Einstein. This experiential approach to scientific paradigm-shifts (often one becomes emotionally attached to reading Ptolemy, only to have it all overthrown by Copernicus, etc.) had led me to a deep interest in the philosophy of science. I decided to study the economists at the U. of Chicago up close, to learn why they believed that free-market capitalism was beneficial rather than harmful.

I attended the U. of Chicago in the Committee on Social Thought. I quickly realized that despite reading voraciously in high school, a year at Harvard, and four years at St. John's, I knew nothing about economics. I was impressed by the mountains of empirical evidence the Chicago economists had amassed on the effectiveness of markets, and on the simple fact that people respond to incentives. But my most transformative experience took place deep in the bowels of Regenstein Library, while I was researching original sources for the claim that, under 19th century laissez-faire capitalism in Britain, the rich got richer and the poor got poorer.

I accepted that it had long ago been documented that 19th century laissez-faire capitalism had impoverished the working class while enriching the capitalists. Engels had documented it, Charles Dickens and other literary figures had documented it, and all of the history textbooks and history teachers had told us the simple morality tale: until the rise of the interventionist state, unregulated capitalism had run rampant, and people had suffered unnecessarily.

However, a Chicago economics professor (probably Stigler) had made this outrageous claim that in 19th century Britain the standard of living of the working class had steadily improved, prior to the introduction of progressive reforms. I went tracking down original sources to show him just how mistaken he was.

I remember just how shocked I was when I started digging into the empirical literature on the subject, only to discover that, by the late 1980s, the scholarly debate had become not whether, but by when and by how much, the standard of living of the working class had improved. It was clear to me that the predominance of evidence, and the predominance of informed scholarly opinion, said this: by, say, 1840 the standard of living for the working class was improving, and over the succeeding decades, the improvements became quite substantial.

At first I felt sick to my stomach: How could such a thing be true? Gradually, as I digested it over the weeks and months that followed, and saw how extensive the evidence was that capitalism had, in fact, benefited the poor, I became increasingly angry at the mainstream intellectual establishment. For me, this had been a fundamental moral fact; now I was beginning to realize how the entire premise on which I had rejected capitalism—the foundation from which I had built my morally and intellectually superior identity—was false!

That began a long process of re-evaluating everything, and beginning to take seriously economic arguments I had previously ridiculed rather than evaluated. Bit by bit, I began reading the revisionist histories of the 20th century, in which (instead of Teddy Roosevelt, Woodrow Wilson, and FDR being portrayed as a series of heroic figures fighting against the forces of reaction) I came to see each of them as arbitrarily increasing the extent to which the government attacked peaceful people, engaged in mutually beneficial exchanges, for no good reason. Thanks to an Institute for Human Studies summer seminar, I was introduced to Austrian economics and anarcho-capitalism, and was now ready to study these entirely fresh and fascinating arguments with an open mind.

As it turned out, at about the same time, I began training teachers in Chicago Public Schools to lead Socratic Seminars. While St. John's is best known for its "Great Books" program, all classes there are taught Socratically; there are no lecture courses. I had especially loved this aspect of St. John's; indeed, the leading reason I had transferred from Harvard was that I did not like being lectured at, even by famous people. I loved the intellectual autonomy of St. John's, where the professors were called "tutors" and were regarded as merely the most experienced learners in the class.

I so loved leading those discussions in Chicago, I accepted a full-time job in Alaska, training teachers to lead Socratic Seminars. Although at the time I expected to finish my dissertation, my Socratic work led willy-nilly to a fifteen-year career in education, starting in the public schools and then later creating a series of private schools and ultimately a charter school (ranked the 36th-best public high school in the U.S.)

One aspect of my career in education gave me an insight into peace that is rarely acknowledged: Public education is an act of brute-force colonialism. As a secular humanist intellectual, whose mission in life was to get kids to think for themselves, I often encountered hostility from fundamentalist Christian communities in Alaska. On one occasion, I had a mother tell me point-blank: *"Your questions cause confusion. Confusion comes from Satan. Therefore what you are doing is Satanic."* Initially, I simply dismissed these people, much as intellectuals celebrate Galileo against the "ignorance" of the medieval Catholic Church, or how the Scopes "Monkey" trial has been used to glorify the heroic defenders of evolution against the benighted evangelicals who refused to acknowledge the science of evolutionary biology.

Today, while my cosmology has become the same as Richard Dawkins', I don't regard it as necessary or appropriate to force my beliefs onto others. As a young intellectual, I remember being proud of the fact that I was not racist or sexist, yet I and many of my peers had made snide remarks about fundamentalist Christians. At one point I was hitchhiking in Alaska and was picked up by a fundamentalist Christian pastor, who had been attending a workshop on marital counseling. As we talked, I saw that he was clearly thoughtful and caring, and was struggling hard to find the best way for couples to find mutual happiness and fulfillment in their marriages. I immediately realized that my belief that such people were all anti-women was sheer bigotry, and gradually I saw how most intellectuals generally were bigoted towards such people. The dehumanization associated with such bigotry has allowed us to blithely consider it justifiable to forcibly impose our beliefs on their children, by means of government schools.

In 2004, I met John Mackey, the co-founder and CEO of Whole Foods Market. John and I quickly discovered that while we were both culturally from the left, and continued to be idealistic do-gooders, we had become intellectually convinced that the best way to solve world problems was by means of entrepreneurs and markets, rather than government. We created Freedom Lights Our World (FLOW), a non-profit dedicated to "Liberating the Entrepreneurial Spirit for Good," promoting entrepreneurial solutions to world problems.

Relatively early on, we realized that this was far too broad a mission for one small non-profit, so we decided to focus on particular programs, with a far narrower mission. The first such program we created was Peace through Commerce (PTC). It quickly became clear to us that the mainstream peace movement did not appreciate how economic freedom was one of the most powerful forces for peace on the planet.

I had been studying the Fraser Institute's annual "Economic Freedom of the World" reports, when the 2005 report came out with Erik Gartzke's article "Economic Freedom and Peace." Among other factoids, Gartzke's econometrics showed that economic freedom was fifty times more effective than democracy at reducing conflict.

I began conducting more research on the relationship between economic freedom and peace. There were many 18th and 19th century thinkers, including Montesquieu and Kant, who believed that trade between nations would reduce conflict. Richard Cobden and John Bright, the famous advocates of free trade who led the fight against the "Corn Laws," were also principled opponents of colonialism. It turns out that many of the 19th century classical liberals were principled opponents of colonialism, including the much maligned William Graham Sumner (VP of the Anti-Imperialism League), and the individual who first called attention to the injustice and horrors of King Leopold's Belgian Congo.

Sadly, these principled classical liberals lost their political influence in the late 19th and early 20th century, as Teddy Roosevelt transformed the U.S. into an explicitly imperialistic nation, while Lenin spawned an entire genre of writing accusing capitalism of being fundamentally imperialistic. After WWI, many intellectuals became cynical about western civilization and increasingly anti-capitalist.

By the end of the Great Depression, classical liberalism had nearly vanished as an intellectual movement. The newly liberated colonies in the 1940s, '50s, '60s, and '70s almost all created regimes, based on either Marxist principles or democratic socialist principles. The Cold War created an environment of mutual mistrust and hostility, in which the very idea of economic freedom was almost non-existent, and proxy wars raged around the world throughout the second half of the 20th century.

Sir John Cowperthwaite, who later became the Financial Secretary of Hong Kong, had been educated as an old-school classical liberal in Britain prior to WWII; he took up his first civil-service post in Hong Kong in 1941. As Financial Secretary, he set Hong Kong on a course of extraordinary economic freedom. In parallel, Lee Kuan Yew, the founding Prime Minister of a newly independent Singapore, found his country in a precarious state and in order to create a prosperous, independent nation, he likewise set Singapore on a path of extraordinary economic freedom. As a consequence, Hong Kong and Singapore have been the world's two most economically free entities for the past fifty years. They have also been the fastest growing entities, moving from roughly African-level poverty in 1960 to becoming two of the wealthiest regions on earth in fifty years.

Despite the ongoing intellectual influence of Marxism and Leninism, as well as the widespread intellectual sympathy for democratic socialism, by the 1980s the clear economic success of the four Asian tigers—Hong Kong, Singapore, Taiwan, and South Korea—had become hard to deny. This empirical phenomenon led in part to the Washington Consensus, a movement by the World Bank and the IMF that promoted economic liberalization around the world. Unlike the classical liberals, however, the mathematically trained economists who promoted the Washington Consensus failed to appreciate the importance of key market institutions such as property rights and the rule of law. Since the late 1990s, more sophisticated advocates of economic freedom have returned to the classical liberals' appreciation for property rights and the rule of law as essential prerequisites to the functioning of a market economy.

It is important to understand this history, because while the anti-globalization movement was right to call attention to abuses of power by the World Bank and IMF (multinational organizations should not be dictating the economic policies of sovereign nations), as well as to failures of the Washington Consensus, they are tragically wrong to be against globalization *per se*. Every nation that has become prosperous has done so by means of a commitment to global trade. Singapore became exceptionally prosperous by deliberately courting the much-maligned multi-national corporations. The problem with the Washington Consensus was not that it promoted economic liberalization and globalization, but that it coerced nations into a one-size-fits-all approach, neglecting local situations and the importance of the legal institutions required for a capitalist society to function properly. Hernando de

Soto, co-chair on the U.N. Commission on the Legal Empowerment of the Poor, likes to point out that because most of the world's poor do not have access to their nation's legal system, when we create a free trade agreement with a poor nation we are really only creating an agreement with the seven-percent or so of the population that is actually functioning within the legal system of the state.

That said, when a country has a properly functioning legal system, economic freedom becomes a powerful force for peace. Despite Ireland's recent economic troubles, it remains one of the world's most stunning economic success-stories of the past twenty years. In 1990 it was, along with Spain, one of the poorest nations in Europe. By 2006, it was one of the richest nations on earth, with significantly higher income than the U.S. Even today, after the collapse, it remains roughly as prosperous as the U.S., and still much wealthier than Spain.

As Ireland moved from poverty to prosperity in the 1990s and 2000s, so too did Northern Ireland (they are, not surprisingly, major trade partners). Meanwhile, as unemployment rates plummeted in Northern Ireland, the discrepancy between Catholic unemployment and Protestant unemployment also fell from a 14 percent discrepancy in 1985 to a 3.5 percent discrepancy in 2004. The result: A ceasefire was signed between the Irish Republican Army and the government. After decades of violence, Northern Ireland became largely peaceful. Although various negotiators and political leaders were involved in the details of the ceasefire, the background story that is rarely recognized is the extent to which rising prosperity, which reduced the longstanding Protestant/Catholic unemployment differential, almost certainly provided the conditions within which the peace could be negotiated.

In a world in which bigotry towards Islam has become ubiquitous, in which many people believe that religious ideologies are the fundamental cause of violence, it is worth remembering the fact that Catholics and Protestants were involved in vicious, violent wars with each other, literally for centuries. And yet, as prosperity broke out across Europe, most recently in Northern Ireland, these fierce religious hatreds vanished in a world in which opportunity, hope, and prosperity seemed within reach to all. It remains to be seen whether or not the 2008 financial collapse and associated decline, in Irish and Northern Irish prosperity, will result in renewed violence. But regardless of what happens going forward, the decline of long-standing violence in Northern Ireland as a consequence of increased prosperity is noteworthy.

Most war fatalities in the past several decades have been civil war fatalities, and most African nations have experienced one or more civil wars since independence. In fact, the Congo wars alone have resulted in more fatalities than any war since WWII. If one cares about peace, one should care first and foremost about Africa. Yet what almost no one seems to realize is that African nations have the most highly regulated economies of any region on earth. If one looks at the bottom twenty nations on either the World Bank's Doing Business ranking or the Cato Institute's Economic Freedom Index most of the nations at the bottom are African (along with Venezuela and Myanmar).

Take Rwanda, for instance. Although the 1994 genocide may be accurately understood as the result of decades of carefully cultivated Hutu extremist ideology (which was as intellectually sophisticated in its development and diffusion as was the Nazi ideology), there again one can identify an invisible substratum of economic oppression. The Hutu regimes that controlled Rwanda from independence to 1994 were socialist regimes that were almost Stalinist in their extreme control over the economy. Rwanda was thus one of the least economically free nations on earth (to this day neighboring Burundi is near the very bottom of the economic freedom indices).

Happily the current President of Rwanda, Paul Kagame, has made Rwanda one of the most improved nations on earth on the Doing Business ranking. He is doing everything he can to promote entrepreneurship and to create a legal environment within which entrepreneurs can flourish. May he succeed (For readers who want to help: I am actively seeking partners to work with several Rwandan entrepreneurs in for-profit enterprises. If you want to help create lasting peace in Rwanda, "be the solution" and help them succeed).

At the end of the day, the Hutus and Tutsis in Rwanda are not so much different from the Protestants and Catholics in Northern Ireland. When ethnic or religious groups find themselves competing for the same piece of a tiny pie, it is all too easy for entrepreneurs of hatred to rally people to their cause. Conversely, when the pie is growing rapidly, when everyone realizes that it is possible to improve their lives by means of hard work, young men want to work to get ahead and their families (and girlfriends and wives) insist that they work to contribute to the family.

Every low-income nation with large numbers of unemployed males and competing ethnic or religious groups is at risk of violence. Until and unless we create the conditions for prosperity in poor nations around the world, they will continue to collapse into violence. Secure and transferable property rights, rule of law, and economic freedom are the essential preconditions to prosperity. Every nation that provides access to those institutions to all of its citizens is prosperous, every nation that does not is poor. It is that straightforward. Nations that provide opportunity, jobs, and hope for their citizens rarely experience civil conflict; they do not frequently collapse into systemic violence or civil war.

While internal economic freedoms alone do not prevent violence due to nation-on-nation aggression, if the governments of each nation simply focused on providing secure property rights and a fair criminal justice system, there would be hundreds of thousands fewer violent deaths around the world each year. In a world in which nation-on-nation aggression seems to be declining, and is likely to continue to decline as trade ties deepen, we'd be well on our way to a more peaceful world.

Meanwhile the mainstream peace movement is almost 100 percent focused on promoting social justice, which typically implies reductions in economic freedom. Global multi-lateral institutions mostly promote democracy, with a social justice agenda attached. While it is theoretically possible that promoting social justice and democracy could reduce crony capitalism and increase economic freedom, in practice very few mainstream peace advocates had any awareness of these issues.

In the early stages I was very excited by our Peace through Commerce project, thinking that we could get to the Dalai Lama and major leaders of the global peace movement and get them to advocate for a real, effective path to world peace based on an understanding of the key role of economic freedom. But as we worked at selling this concept to diverse audiences, we found a striking degree of ideological intransigence. Mainstream peace groups were reluctant to partner with us, and individuals in the peace movement seemed to dismiss our arguments and explanations. Although we didn't get to the Dalai Lama, other major spiritual leaders, listened politely to us and then went back to the sources they trusted.

We did partner with the Association to Advance Collegiate Schools of Business (AACSB), which had independently created a "Peace through Commerce" program, focused on ways in which conscientious and responsible corporations could serve as a force for peace. Although their program did not emphasize economic freedom, they saw our program as an important and legitimate complement to theirs, and co-sponsored an event at George Washington University. This conference content was later repurposed for an e-conference through the World Bank Institute and conference papers were published in a special issue of the Journal of Business Ethics (my contribution is titled "Peace through Access to Entrepreneurial Capitalism for All").

We also struggled to obtain funding for the program. While John Mackey and other donors had provided funding for basic operations, if we were to expand the program, we needed significantly more funding. We tried to persuade corporations to support the program, but they said that if it was the slightest bit controversial they couldn't fund it. (In order for corporations to get public relations mileage out of their philanthropy, it has to be perceived as completely mainstream and positive.)

Finally, we had begun to get traction from some leading women philanthropists for a related program, Accelerating Women Entrepreneurs (AWE), which promoted women entrepreneurs and economic freedom in the developing world. Our pitch was that if micro-entrepreneurship was good for women, how much better would it be if developing world women were running $5 million or $50 million businesses? Our materials showed how this program could also result in peace through the diverse content we had accumulated for our Peace through Commerce program.

And then John Mackey's *WSJ* op-ed arguing against Obamacare came out, and the women philanthropists, who had come from the progressive side, insisted that they could not work with us, because of that. They further argued that they could not cite the Fraser Institute economic freedom data, since it was a right-wing think tank that accepted money from tobacco companies. They led a movement to spin off AWE into a separate organization. Later those women left. AWE survives, now integrated with PTC as a separate organization that sells products from Palestinian women, while continuing to educate the world on the economic freedom message. Overall, though, I have been more than disappointed by progressives' openness to introducing economic freedom into their "peace" movements.

The one significant exception consists of human-rights advocates who had actually worked on the ground in country, many of whom understood firsthand that, without opportunity, jobs, and prosperity, human-rights abuses would continue, regardless of NGO activism. Many of those became strong advocates of indigenous entrepreneurship as a path to creating jobs and prosperity (anyone who promotes entrepreneurship on the ground in a developing nation soon becomes aware of the pervasive obstacles to economic freedom).

The motto of FLOW had always been "Criticize by Creating." In the course of researching how to increase economic freedom in the developing world, and consequently reduce poverty and conflict, Mark Frazier had introduced me to the free zone movement. He pointed out that in a successful free zone land values increased 50 times, 100 times, even more. In addition to being a tremendous for profit opportunity when it worked, Mark showed me that in order to increase the probability that a free zone would be successful, as well as to support the poor, one could finance community trusts, using the land-value gains of successful free zones. This led to a 2007 paper we co-wrote on "Women's Empowerment Free Zones," in which free zone land-value gains would be devoted to financing community trusts for women and children.

Around the same time I met Jane Goodall at a dinner at John Mackey's home, and tried to interest her in the concept of a free zone where land-value gains would go to a fund to save the chimpanzees. (More importantly, it is perfectly clear from the information at the Jane Goodall Institute that the real reason chimpanzees are threatened with extinction is habitat depletion, due to poor people cutting trees for firewood and bushmeat hunting, killing chimps to eat. Both of these problems could be solved more effectively by free zones in Tanzania and nearby nations, in which poor people could get good urban jobs and leave behind that subsistence lifestyle.) Goodall listened to me politely, then suggested that I contact the Executive Director of the Goodall Institute. I did, and he understood the logic and was somewhat sympathetic, but he ultimately never followed up.

After PTC and AWE split off, John decided that his primary interest was in Conscious Capitalism (CC), a third program we had created. As I continued to work within the CC movement, I became increasingly interested in free zones, and free cities, as a path to global peace and prosperity. Patri Friedman had launched the blog "Let a Thousand Nations Bloom" promoting the idea of creating new governments as a way to work around the problem of encroaching statism. I began blogging there, gradually developing my thoughts on how free zones and free cities could lead to new enclaves of freedom, prosperity, and peace.

One of Patri's arguments that I found most compelling was that the two words "Hong Kong" had done as much for the freedom movement as had all of his grandfather's works. It seemed better to get to work on creating a peaceful, prosperous future for all, rather than spend too much time trying to persuade people who would not budge.

In the meantime I had co-written an article on the Dubai International Financial Centre (DIFC), focusing on the fact that the DIFC had hired a retired British commercial law judge to administer British common law on the 110 acres of the DIFC, as a means of importing world-class financial law into Dubai (which is otherwise under Sharia law). I had also met (through our AWE program), and then married, Magatte Wade, a Senegalese entrepreneur, and she and I were now discussing how to make Senegal prosperous, by means of creating a free city with its own legal system within the country.

Bob Chitester introduced us to Paul Romer, who was preparing a TED talk, in which he introduced the concept of Charter Cities. We scheduled a visit with Romer to come to Senegal to promote the concept, but it didn't work out. We went on to meet with several government ministers, who were enthusiastic and said the president would love it, but we did not get to meet with the president.

I met Kevin Lyons after speaking at the 2009 Seasteading Conference. Kevin and I have since been working together on promoting Free Cities around the world. Most recently we have begun working with the government of Honduras to create a real Free City on the ground in Honduras.

When I began working on FLOW in 2005, it had appeared to me as if the case for creating a world without aggression had been well established, but that too few people were aware of that case. Much of the problem had to do with the fact that capitalism and free markets had been "branded" right-wing. John and I thought that all we had to do was to re-brand capitalism and bring out the humane elements, and we would create a groundswell of support for a peaceful, prosperous world that works for all.

In some ways, the Bush presidency worked against us, insofar as he used the rhetoric of "free markets" but practiced violent aggression abroad and imposed coercive measures on the economy at home. But, we consistently spread the message that Bush's "free markets" were not at all about freedom, and that mainstream libertarian organizations such as the Cato Institute were repudiating him and the Republican leadership that supported him.

The crash of 2008 and the Obama presidency have made everything much worse. The crash has been used by every progressive pundit as an opportunity for ideological revenge on the Reagan revolution, along with the unanimous chorus in the mainstream media that "deregulation" had brought this upon us. This is not factually accurate, of course, but it has bolstered justifiable anger, at a financial system in which taxpayers were forced to bail out bankers who made bad decisions. This has allowed partisan passions to replace dispassionate analysis. (As long as government subsidizes financial risk—via bailouts, Fannie/Freddie, FDIC, the "Greenspan Put," etc.—we will see periodic financial crises in which taxpayers are forced to give their money to some of the richest people in human history.)

Meanwhile, Obama has been the perfect "anti-Bush" symbolic figure: a handsome, articulate, charismatic African-American who promised "Hope and Change" from the rightfully loathed Bush administration. Sadly, although all of my progressive friends had uniformly rejected Bush's policies of starting and continuing wars, none of them seem to have noticed Obama perpetuating the wars, and even adding additional ones. We are killing hundreds of children with drones, in countries where we are not even at war… and, again, no one notices.

My work on Free Cities in Mexico and Central America has called my attention to the drug wars there, in which thousands of people are dying. Again, no one pays attention. Earlier I remember hearing Superior Court Judge James Gray explaining how the leading lobbyist for "three strikes and you're out" in California was the prison worker's union (it also turns out that most prison-rapes are prison-workers raping prisoners). In some inner city African-American communities, four out of five young males can expect to be caught up in the criminal justice system in their lifetimes. And, as Radley Balko continues to document, innocent Americans are constantly being imprisoned, maimed or killed in their homes, due to the War on Drugs. And no one notices.

When I point out to my progressive friends the fact that, even under a "progressive" president, the U.S. is involved in countless illegal wars of aggression, while causing the deaths of many thousands of people and devastating inner-city communities in the drug wars, they try to excuse these incidents, or fall back on "the Republicans are even worse." The fact that they are caught up in a binary political universe itself perpetuates the problem.

Several years ago I saw an article in a magazine, titled "The Biggest Crime You've Never Heard Of," about the Union Carbide disaster in Bhopal. That article strikes me as emblematic of just how out of touch some people are with reality. Yes, Bhopal was a bad thing, but my sense is that far more people are aware of Bhopal than are aware of the Stalinist and Maoist murders.

Or, if one disagrees with that assessment, consider the fact that Josip Tito, the "good" communist, is estimated to have killed a million people. Who is aware of this? Or that the French government actively supported the extremist Hutu government right up to and during the Rwandan genocide. Or consider the many thousands of people killed in the drug wars around the world. Or the Native American genocides, or the other acts of U.S. government imperialism documented by Chomsky. And on and on and on.

The routine crimes of governments itself are strangely invisible.

Why can't we just let people choose their lives voluntarily? What if we were to work together towards a world in which we all agreed that aggression was illegitimate? Imagine a world in which each of us is free to create without fear of aggression, in which we all agree to allow people to make voluntary agreements with one another, and in which we all feel an immediate abhorrence towards (and work effectively together to halt) those who initiate acts of violence.

You may say that I'm a dreamer
But I'm not the only one
I hope someday you'll join us
And the world will live as one

I'm still with John Lennon, except now I realize that "possessions," and respect for the possessions of others, combined with a willingness to let people do "anything that's peaceful," is the solution, rather than the problem.

----

[1] Taken from Honaker, J., 2004-04-15, "Unemployment and Violence in Northern Ireland: a missing data model for ecological inference." Paper presented at the annual meeting of The Midwest Political Science Association, Palmer House Hilton, Chicago, Illinois Online <.PDF>. 2008-09-15: http://www.allacademic.com/meta/p83125_index.html

From Guernica to Fallujah

Pepe Escobar

Pepe Escobar is the roving correspondent for Asia Times. *His latest book is* Obama does Globalistan.

Note: As a foreign correspondent, I've seen my share of wars, from Kashmir and Sierra Leone to Afghanistan and Iraq, and was faced with immense human suffering and distress in Cambodia or sub-Saharan Africa. I've been deeply touched by the people I met in Afghan refugee camps in Pakistan and Iran. And I've been blessed to meet remarkable Sunni and Shi'ite Iraqis—trying to survive Shock and Awe and its aftermath. Although I was not physically present at the siege of Fallujah immediately after the 2004 US presidential election, for me this is the graphic post-modern answer to the question "Why peace?" (*This article was originally published by* Asia Times Online *on December 2, 2004.*)

> *"It's difficult to believe that in this day and age, when people are blogging, emailing and communicating at the speed of light, a whole city is being destroyed and genocide is being committed—and the whole world is aware and silent. Darfur, Americans? Take a look at what you've done in Fallujah."*   - Female Iraqi blogger Riverbend

The Fallujah offensive has virtually disappeared from the news cycle. But history—if written by Iraqis—may well enshrine it as the new Guernica. Paraphrasing Jean-Paul Sartre writing memorably about the Algerian War (1956-62), after Fallujah no two Americans shall meet without a corpse lying between them: the up to 500,000 victims of the sanctions in the 1990s, according to United Nations experts; the up to 100,000 victims since the beginning of the invasion of Iraq, according to the British medical paper *The Lancet*; and at least 6,000 victims, and counting, in Fallujah, according to the Iraqi *Red Crescent*.

The new Guernica

Fallujah is the new Guernica: The residents of the Basque capital in 1937 were resisting the Spanish dictator Francisco Franco; Fallujah in 2004 was resisting the dictator Iyad Allawi, the US-installed interim premier. Franco asked Nazi Germany—which supported him—to bomb Guernica, just as Allawi "asked" the Pentagon to bomb Fallujah. Guernica had no air force and no anti-aircraft guns to defend itself—just like Fallujah. In Guernica, as in Fallujah, there was no distinction between civilians and guerrillas: the order was to "kill them all." The Nazis shouted, *"Viva la muerte!"* ("Long live death") along with their fascist Spanish counterparts before bombing Guernica.

Marine commanders said on the record that Fallujah was the house of Satan. Franco denied the Guernica massacre and blamed the local population—just as Allawi and the Pentagon deny any civilian deaths and insist "insurgents" are guilty—after all, they dared to defend their own city, hiding inside their hundreds of formerly intact mosques.

Fallujah has been reduced to rubble, and thousands of civilians have died. But *Asia Times Online* sources in Baghdad confirm that according to residents, the southern—and larger—part of Fallujah is still controlled by the resistance; the Americans control only the north and some eastern spots. Small groups made up of five to 20 mujahideen still conduct hit-and-run attacks. More than 15,000 refugee families may be living in sordid makeshift shelters around Fallujah—not to mention the upwards of 200,000 residents who escaped the city before it was leveled.

Talking to *al-Jazeera* television network this past weekend, Sheikh Abd as-Salam al-Kubaysi, chief of the public relations department of the powerful Sunni Association of Muslim Scholars (AMS) confirmed that "until now, more than half of Fallujah is in the hands of the resistance." Al-Kubaysi added that "the Americans are entrenched in Fallujah but cannot get out and on to any street or alley in more than half the city, whether that be in Jolan, Shuhada or the industrial zone, or Nazal, or in many places."

Dr al-Kubaysi is an unimpeachable source. A native Fallujan and university professor of Islamic Sharia, he represents the AMS outside Iraq and lived in Fallujah until before the invasion of Iraq. AMS clerics in Baghdad also confirm Iraqi *Red Crescent* estimates, via its spokesman Muhamad al-Nuri, that more than 6,000 people—mostly civilians—may have died. Nuri confirms, "bodies can be seen everywhere and people were crying when receiving food parcels. It is very sad, it is a human disaster."

Another Halabja?

Fifteen years ago in Halabja—at a time when Washington was an enthusiastic supplier of chemical weapons to Saddam Hussein—thousands of Kurds were gassed. Even the US Central Intelligence Agency has disputed Saddam's responsibility, blaming Iranians instead. Assuming Saddam did it, and did it deliberately, the US may have done the same thing in Fallujah. As *Asia Times Online* has reported, Fallujah doctors have identified either swollen and yellowish corpses without any injuries, or "melted bodies": victims of napalm, the terrifying cocktail of polystyrene and jet fuel.

Our sources confirm testimonies by residents who managed to escape the Jolan neighborhood of bombing by "poisonous gases." A resident called Abu Sabah told of "weird bombs that smoke like a mushroom cloud... and then small pieces fall from the air with long tails of smoke behind them. The pieces of these strange bombs explode into large fires that burn the skin even when you throw water over them." This is exactly what happens to people bombed with napalm or white phosphorus. The UN banned the bombing of civilians with napalm in 1980. The US is the only country in the world still using napalm.

Upwards of 250,000 Fallujans at least had the chance to escape: instead they became Fallujah refugees. Practically not a single word from them about the massacre is to be found in US corporate media. This is yet one more extreme, bitter irony of the war: President George W Bush and the neo-conservatives invaded Iraq based on "intelligence" supplied by five-star refugees like Ahmad Chalabi and Allawi—but refugees nonetheless.

The counterinsurgency blueprint

The defining image of Fallujah—for Iraqis, for the Arab world, for 1.3 billion Muslims—is the summary execution of a wounded, defenseless Iraqi man inside a mosque by a marine. This execution, caught on tape, suggests "special" rules of engagement were applying. Marine commanders have been on the record telling their soldiers to "shoot everything that moves and everything that doesn't move"; to fire "two bullets in every body"; in case of seeing any military-aged men in the streets of Fallujah, to "drop 'em"; and to spray every home with machine-gun and tank fire before entering them. (These 'rules' are all confirmed by residents of Fallujah who managed to escape.)

The counterinsurgency blueprint in Iraq is a 182-page field manual distributed to each and every soldier and issued in October by the Pentagon. It's very enlightening to confront its provisions with the reality on the ground in Fallujah—and also take into consideration the fact that the rules of engagement became even "looser."

Counterinsurgency missions must achieve the end state established by the president. All leaders must keep in mind the purpose of their operations and the criteria of success used to assess them. Achieving success in counterinsurgency operations involves accomplishing the following tasks:

- *Protect the population.*
- *Establish local political institutions.*
- *Reinforce local governments.*
- *Eliminate insurgent capabilities.*
- *Exploit information from local sources.*

By any standards, the whole mission was a political disaster. Fallujah's population was not protected: it was bombed out of the city and turned into a mass of thousands of refugees. Political institutions were already in place: the Fallujah Shura was running the city. No local government can possibly run a pile of rubble to be recovered by seething citizens, not to mention be "reinforced." "Insurgent capabilities" were not eliminated; the resistance dispersed around the 22 other cities out of control by the occupation, and spread up north to Mosul; and the Americans remain without intelligence "from local sources" because they antagonized every possible heart and mind. All this to achieve the "end state" established by Bush.

On armed action:

This course favors violence rather than mass mobilization and normally results in an inverted pyramid, with the combatants themselves the bulk of the movement. This was the approach taken by [Fidel] Castro in Cuba during the 1950s and may be an approach some insurgents in Iraq have taken against the post-Saddam government, although some efforts to mobilize have been reported.

Wrong. The combatants are not "the bulk of the movement"; they are an armed vanguard representing the widespread Sunni struggle against the occupation. Whole cities are mobilized against the occupation. Whole sectors of Baghdad—for the first time since April 2003—are totally out of the Americans' control. (Many in the Sunni triangle told this correspondent in 2003 they were at the tipping point of joining the armed resistance. They've already crossed the line long ago.)

Security of the populace is an imperative. This is security from the influence of the insurgents initially. The population is then mobilized, armed and trained to protect itself. Effective security allows local political and administrative institutions to operate freely and commerce to flourish.

Sunnis simply don't trust US-trained security forces, period: they are identified as collaborationists, just as in Nazi-occupied France, or in Algeria fighting French colonialism in the early 1960s. The resistance has widely infiltrated the US-trained Iraqi forces. Additional proof is that hundreds deserted and joined the resistance immediately before the Fallujah offensive.

As quickly as possible, though, HN [host nation] military and police must assume the primary combat role. A long-term U.S. combat role may undermine the legitimacy of the HN government and risks converting the conflict into a U.S.-only war. That combat role can also further alienate cultures that are hostile to the U.S. On the occasion when the threat to U.S. interests is great and indirect means have proven insufficient, preemptive U.S. combat operations may be required. Direct use of U.S. combat forces in counterinsurgency operations remains a policy option for the president, and army forces provide it when required.

The majority of Iraqis know this has always been a US-only war; they have been "alienated" for a long time now, if not downright hostile. Fallujah was indeed a 'preemptive US combat operation," so this means an indigenous resistance was a "great" threat to US interests; this also means, according to the Pentagon itself, that the responsibility for the Fallujah massacre is ultimately Bush's.

Excessive or indiscriminate use of force is likely to alienate the local populace, thereby increasing support for insurgent forces.

The Pentagon describes Fallujah, even before it happened:

The American way of war has been to substitute firepower for manpower. As a result, US forces have frequently resorted to firepower in the form of artillery or air any time they make contact. This creates two negatives in a counterinsurgency. First, massive firepower causes collateral damage, thereby frequently driving the locals into the arms of the insurgents. Second, it allows insurgents to break contact after having inflicted casualties on friendly forces. A more effective method is to attack with ground forces to gain and maintain contact, with the goal of completely destroying the insurgent force. This tactic dictates that military forces become skilled in pursuits. The unit that makes the initial contact with the insurgent force requires rapid augmentation to maintain pressure against the fleeing force, envelop it, and destroy it. These augmentation [reaction] forces should be given the highest priority.

The "American way of war" once again messed up in Fallujah, whatever the method. "Massive firepower" indeed caused widespread "collateral damage"; and reaction forces failed to "maintain pressure against the fleeing force." The resistance is reorganized all over the Sunni triangle, as well as in Mosul, and still controls at least 60 percent of destroyed Fallujah itself.

The successful conduct of counterinsurgency operations relies on the willing support and cooperation of the populations directly involved. Greater priority and awareness is needed to understand the motivations of the parties involved in the conflict and the population as a whole. The understanding of the background and development of the conflict into which US forces are intervening is of particular significance. This requires a detailed understanding of the cultural environment and the human terrain in which the U.S. forces will be operating and thereby places a heavy reliance on the use of HUMINT.

HUMINT, human intelligence, was the first casualty in Fallujah. When you have marine commanders justifying an attack on a whole city because it is the house of Satan, any "detailed understanding of the cultural environment" had already been buried in the desert sands.

Failure to recognize, respect, understand and incorporate an understanding of the cultural and religious aspects of the society in which US forces are interacting could rapidly lead to an erosion of the legitimacy of the mission.

In fact, this whole scenario started playing out as early as April 2003, when the resistance movement was born at the Abu Hanifa Mosque in Baghdad and when marines opened fire on a peaceful demonstration in Fallujah.

The mission of PSYOP [psychological operation] is to influence the behavior of foreign target audiences to support U.S. national objectives.

PSYOP accomplishes this by conveying selected information and advising on actions that influence the emotions, motives, objective reasoning, and ultimately the behavior of foreign audiences. Behavioral change is at the root of the PSYOP mission.

The record shows that the majority of world public opinion does not support "US national objectives" in Iraq, regardless of whatever extensive PSYOPs they have been subjected to.

Deny insurgents access to the population and resources. Deny the enemy the ability to live. Cut them off from food, water, clothing -- everything. Identify and prioritize population sectors and resources to be secured and protected. Unify and coordinate all civil and security forces and assets within the community with special attention given to around-the-clock security, intelligence collection, PSYOP and civil affairs. Include HN forces in security-related plans and operations to the maximum extent possible. Mobilize, arm, and train the local population to provide their own local community security. Structure security force activity and actions to lead to the populace overtly picking a side. However, these activities and actions must not be abusive. Establish leverage. Use advice, equipment, and money to attempt to change people's attitudes and behavior positively.

This is the same old "starve the water and the fish will die" tactic, already analyzed in a previous article (*Counterinsurgency run amok*, Nov 18, 2003). Once again it has been an abject failure, as the 'fish' keep breeding, the 'water' is no less than the whole Sunni triangle, and nobody is able to identify a single tangible benefit of life under occupation.

Typical objectives for a population and resources control operation include the following: Sever any relationship between the population and insurgents. Identify and destroy insurgent support activities within the community. Identify and destroy insurgent organizational infrastructure. Identify and eliminate the insurgent political apparatus (communications). Institute harsh penalties for those caught supporting the insurgents. Create a secure physical and psychological environment for the population, one in which people are free to go about their business and prosper without worrying about insurgents taking their freedom and prosperity from them. Counteract enemy propaganda. Conduct a national IO campaign strategy with interagency planning and resources that distributes its message and is responsive to current events to ensure relevancy.

The cumulative US failure is due to well-known reasons: cultural insensitivity; no local human intelligence, because hearts and minds have been alienated by a "circle the wagons" mentality; and total incapacity of creating "a secure physical and psychological environment for the population." Moreover, counterinsurgency "experts" have no definitive weapons against the democratization of high technology. A marine can call an air strike with a satellite phone? The resistance replies with thousands of engineers, technicians and mechanics able to rig thousands of cellular phones and remote-control doorbells to set up ambushes and booby traps.

Regardless of the legal status of those persons captured, detained or otherwise held in custody by US soldiers, they receive humane treatment until properly released. They are provided with the minimum protections delineated in the Geneva Conventions.

Compare it with Abu Ghraib prison, where serious abuses took place. And compare it with the leveling of a whole city in order to "save it."

The facts of the occupation

The "success" of US counterinsurgency efforts can also effectively be measured against the occupation record so far:

- Dead Iraqi civilians are estimated to be anything from 15,000 to 100,000 (the British Lancet report). Johns Hopkins University is 90 percent certain there are more than 40,000 dead civilians.
- The resistance was around 5,000 strong in late 2003. Now it is at least 20,000 strong. Some British generals put them at 50,000 strong—and counting.
- Of the US$18.4 billion in Iraqi reconstruction funds, Washington/Baghdad has spent only $1.7 billion. Our Baghdad sources confirm the capital has degenerated into a giant, hyper-violent slum, getting worse by the day. There's 25 percent less electricity now compared with Saddam-times in early 2003, 66 percent less in Baghdad.
- At least 400,000 Iraqi children suffer from chronic diarrhea and have almost no protein, according to a UN development report. Sixty percent of rural Iraqis and 20 percent of urban Iraqis are forced to drink contaminated water.
- According to a Gallup poll—taken before the Fallujah massacre— only 33 percent of respondents thought their lives were better than before the war. Ninety-four percent said Baghdad was more dangerous. Sixty-six percent believed the occupation could degenerate into a civil war. And 80 percent wanted the occupation over right after the January 30 elections.

One thousand Guernicas

What Americans and US corporate media seem incapable of understanding is that counterinsurgency operations—however massive and deadly—simply are not enough to break the back of wars of national liberation. The Fallujah offensive was a typical demonstration of the power of which Washington "chicken hawks" are fond. But if they had read their Che Guevara (*Episodes in the Cuban Revolutionary War*) and their General Vo Nguyen Giap (*Writings*) of the Vietnam resistance correctly, they would have seen that instilling fear and terror is useless as a strategy of capturing hearts and minds.

No wonder the majority of Sunnis (the "water") keep supporting the resistance (the "fish") with weapons, cash and shelter, and are inclined to boycott the elections. Much more than grieve over the dead and the rubble to which Fallujah was reduced, they took note of two very important facts. Not a single government agency, be it American or Iraqi, offered any kind of assistance to the 200,000-plus residents who in a flash were turned into refugees: instead they turned off water and electricity in the city. And the UN High Commissioner for Refugees was nowhere to be seen—nor were any other representatives of the "international community."

The real story of what happened to Fallujah is being told by these 200,000-plus new refugees, and a few lucky hundreds who managed to escape during the battle. They are the Picassos who will paint the new Guernica for future historians. As soon as these thousands of refugees return home, so will the bulk of the resistance: after all they are residents of Fallujah themselves, enjoying total local support; and they will certainly attack any US-trained kind of force left behind to protect whatever US-installed puppet government is put in place.

So the Americans may leave the "house of Satan," and then the Fallujah *mujahideen Shura* (council) that was running the city since last April inevitably will be back to power; or the Americans may stay in Fallujah, and the resistance will continue to wreak havoc in a string of other cities in the Sunni heartland. The result will be the same: the new Guernica sacrificed for nothing.

Nothing? Not really. The ironclad, not-so-hidden neo-conservative agenda for the Middle East is the balkanization of the Arab world—serving the interests of their allies, the Likud Party in Israel. The neo-cons want the Middle East to fracture along ethnic and tribal lines. They want Sunni against Shi'ite. They want civil war in Iraq. They want chaos, as in "the empire of chaos" as formulated by stellar French scholar Alain Joxe. Israel Shahak's *The Zionist Plan for the Middle East* details that to survive, Israel must become an imperial regional power by balkanizing all existing Arab states. In this scenario, a major counterinsurgency operation like Fallujah, the new Guernica, may have been the first. It certainly won't be the last.

Eminent Domain,

Intervention and "Redevelopment"

Robert McNamara

Robert McNamara, a 2006 graduate of the New York University School of Law, is a staff attorney with the Institute for Justice.

Bill Brody bought his piece of the American dream in 1996. Bill's dream, though, probably didn't look like yours. Bill's dream was a dilapidated multi-level set of interlocking buildings on Main Street in Port Chester, N.Y.; where anyone else would see a disaster, Bill—who, like his father, owned his own lumber business—saw an opportunity. Bill believed in Port Chester's Main Street, and he believed in himself.

And he was right. Over the next few years, Bill spent countless hours and thousands of dollars completely renovating the building from top to bottom, frequently making the repairs by hand. Just as he finished, the Village of Port Chester announced that it would be taking his newly restored property through eminent domain, so it could be handed over to a private developer and turned into a parking garage for a Stop'n'Shop.

What's Bill Brody doing in this book? When I was asked to contribute an essay to a volume entitled "Why Peace," I was a little surprised. I'm a constitutional lawyer by profession. I like peace, of course, but I don't have any expertise in international relations, just-war theory or any of the other things I'd expect to see in a book like this. But when the topic was phrased as "peace and nonintervention," I immediately thought of Bill, who was one of my first clients as a young attorney, and of the many, many others like him. I thought, in other words, of the inability of people with power to leave well enough alone.

The story of Bill Brody—and so many others like him—is ultimately a story about redevelopment, and the inability of local officials to simply get out of the way of people who are trying to improve their neighborhoods. The Village of Port Chester wanted to take Bill's property in the name of "redevelopment"—Village officials thought the downtown area wasn't nice enough, and their solution was to seize property from ordinary people and hand it over to a private developer to build a shopping center.

Of course, Bill also originally thought his own building wasn't nice enough. But his solution didn't involve confiscating anything—instead, he just *made* it nicer, refitting the heating and air-conditioning system, installing a new marble lobby, and refitting the property throughout. This, however, didn't count as "redevelopment" in the eyes of government officials. The only thing that would count as redevelopment was tearing out the whole neighborhood, root and branch, to make way for the Village's chosen private developer.

The ironies don't stop there. The Village's agreement with its chosen private developer didn't just give the developer the right to have property taken

486

from others through eminent domain. It also waived or changed a whole host of rules about development in the area, like zoning restrictions on what people were allowed to build. Apparently, prior to entering into an agreement to seize private property for private profit, none of the Village authorities thought that relaxing these same restrictions might have helped people already on the ground—people like Bill—improve the buildings in the area.

Bill's story is not unique—not only do state and local governments use the power of eminent domain to seize private property in the name of redevelopment, they frequently use that power to seize property whose owners are *actually engaging* in redevelopment. In National City, California, for example, Carlos Barragan, Jr., and his father run a nonprofit gym called the Community Youth Athletic Center. The CYAC is a boxing gym, providing training to local at-risk kids, but it also provides a lot more: mentoring, tutoring, help with homework, etc.. As the people who run the CYAC like to say, the boxing is just a hook—it's a way to bring kids in, to expose them to the tutoring, mentoring, and discipline that the CYAC's programs offer. And the CYAC is a roaring success: instead of joining gangs, the CYAC's kids graduate from high school; they become firefighters or police officers; they go to college.

By any reasonable measure, Carlos and his colleagues at the CYAC are engaged in real community redevelopment—every day, they make their community better by helping kids improve their performance in school and in life. But that kind of "redevelopment" isn't what the government of National City has in mind. Their kind of "redevelopment" involves seizing the CYAC's gym (and a number of other local properties), in order to make room for luxury condos built by a local private developer. While the CYAC has thus far—with the help of the Institute for Justice—managed to keep its property safe by prevailing in the courts, the city government's grand plans still hang over their heads.

The stories are legion. Ordinary people working hard to improve the communities they live in are met not with the praise and acknowledgement they deserve, but with an implacable government bent on kicking them off their own property. Armed with what courts have called the "despotic power" of eminent domain, local and state officials seem committed to tearing out neighborhoods root and branch to make way for their own personal visions of redevelopment—no matter how much redevelopment the private sector is already managing on its own.

This is tragic. It is morally wrong. But—perhaps most infuriatingly—it is completely unnecessary.

Destroying neighborhoods in the name of redevelopment accomplishes one thing: It destroys neighborhoods. What it does *not* do is result in redevelopment—indeed, it impedes it. As independent developer Doug Kaplan writes in his report, *Simplify, Don't Subsidize*, a publication of the Institute for Justice, the primary obstacle to development is actually local government. Kaplan argues that—just as the Village of Port Chester should have realized that loosening its zoning laws would be a better way to encourage development than stealing Bill Brody's property—local governments looking for new development are best served by getting out of the way.

The mere fact that local governments' deals with private developers almost always include (in addition to promises of eminent-domain abuse) provisions reducing tax burdens, or lessening requirements for zoning or permitting, is evidence that eminent domain isn't what's missing from the private-development picture. "If cutting taxes, reducing fees and streamlining regulations benefits government's public/private partners, then think what miracles could occur if government did the same for everyone," Kaplan writes. "Do less to us, and watch us have fun taking care of the rest."

And it's not just private developers who feel this way. Former Anaheim Mayor Curt Pringle, in an Institute for Justice publication entitled *Development Without Eminent Domain*, describes how Anaheim's city government revitalized its downtown area without abusing eminent domain. By providing what Pringle calls a "foundation of freedom"—basically, by *not* doing the things local governments usually do to impede development—the city allowed its downtown area to transform into a vibrant center of housing, retail, and restaurants that is the envy of other California cities.

Anaheim's story is just an anecdote, but it's a symptom of a broader trend: It just isn't true that cities need to use eminent domain to foster new development. As my colleagues Dick M. Carpenter II, Ph.D., and John K. Ross demonstrate in their report *Doomsday? No Way*, preventing the government from abusing eminent domain does nothing to hinder economic development. Defenders of eminent-domain abuse have long argued that restraining the government's abuse of this power would prevent important large-scale economic development. So when dozens of states began reforming their eminent-domain laws to rein in abuse, in the wake of the Supreme Court's 2005 decision in *Kelo v. City of New London*, Carpenter and Ross saw an opportunity. Looking at key indicators of economic development in states that adopted eminent-domain reforms, they conclusively showed that those reforms did literally nothing to hinder development. When hauled into the clear light of statistical analysis, the claims of the defenders of eminent-domain abuse look different. They look false.

But it isn't just that intervention through eminent-domain abuse is *unnecessary* for development. It's that it doesn't work. American legal history is full—overfull—of stories about local governments drawn in by promises of redevelopment that turn out to be mostly or entirely false. It is all too easy for government officials to put their faith in grand promises of what *could* exist, if they are only willing to destroy an existing neighborhood. It is also all but impossible for property owners (constrained as they are by reality) to convince the government that the existing development is better than the development that exists only in someone's imagination.

This temptation to destroy existing properties in pursuit of imaginary future wealth may be understandable, but giving into it is tragic. Until 2005, the iconic case of eminent-domain abuse folly was the destruction of the Poletown neighborhood in 1981. Poletown, a vibrant, racially integrated area of Detroit, was swept away by eminent domain, to make room for a promised General Motors plant. The destruction was accomplished easily enough, but the plant itself never managed to employ even half as many workers as the original rosy promises had suggested.

But the disaster of Poletown was eclipsed in 2005 with the destruction of the Fort Trumbull area of New London, Connecticut, in the wake of the United States Supreme Court's disastrous decision in *Kelo v. City of New London.* There, the New London Development Corporation used eminent domain to seize a working-class neighborhood in the name of the higher tax revenues that would be brought by an imagined complex of expensive condominiums. Although the Supreme Court endorsed the idea that government could take property from one person and transfer it to another private owner, with no more justification than imagined future tax revenues, the practical outcome of the case was predictable. The Fort Trumbull neighborhood was razed, and in its place the New London Development Corporation built—nothing.

As of this writing, some six years after the *Kelo* decision was handed down, the working-class neighborhood has been replaced by an empty field, full of weeds, birds, and feral cats. (The Institute for Justice, which represented the property owners in the case, raised private funds to move the little pink house that belonged to Susette Kelo, which had become a national symbol of eminent-domain abuse, across town, to install it on a new foundation. With the completion of that move, IJ has engaged in more construction in New London after the *Kelo* decision than the New London Development Corporation has.)

What lessons can we draw from the American struggle with eminent-domain abuse? A few key points present themselves. First, it is all too easy for public officials to overlook real progress being made by people already on the ground. Second, it is impossible for reality to compete with imagination: When local officials measure the development they *imagine* against a neighborhood as it exists in the real world, they are all too often seduced by the unrealistic vision they've conjured in their minds. And, finally, when the two previous points work in combination with the absence of a check on the exercise of power (as the United States Supreme Court unfortunately failed to check the abuse of power in *Kelo*), we will almost inevitably see government officials engaging in catastrophically failed efforts at redevelopment, destroying existing communities in pursuit of an unattainable vision of perfection.

While the tide is turning against eminent-domain abuse in the United States—43 different states have changed their laws in response to the Supreme Court's decision in *Kelo*—the change has come too late for many property owners, including Port Chester's Bill Brody, whose building was destroyed before a court could declare the taking unconstitutional. (Bill has, however, received a full apology for the unconstitutional taking from the Village of Port Chester, which has also named a street in his honor.)

At minimum, we should not allow the lessons of decades of ill-fated intervention in the name of "redevelopment" to go ignored. The lessons of eminent-domain abuse are simple: Government power, unchecked, will be abused—and government efforts to create will, all too often, only destroy.

Occupying Iraq,
State Department-style

Peter Van Buren

Peter Van Buren has served with the Foreign Service for over 23 years. He received a Meritorious Honor Award for assistance to Americans following the Hanshin earthquake in Kobe, a Superior Honor Award for helping an American rape victim in Japan, and another award for work in the tsunami relief efforts in Thailand. Previous assignments include Taiwan, Japan, Korea, the UK and Hong Kong. Peter volunteered for Iraq service and was assigned to ePRT duty 2009-10. His tour extended past the withdrawal of the last combat troops. Peter worked extensively with the military while overseeing evacuation planning in Japan and Korea. This experience included multiple field exercises, plus civil-military work in Seoul, Tokyo, Hawaii, and Sydney with allies from the UK, Australia, and elsewhere. The Marine Corps selected Peter to travel to Camp Lejeune in 2006 to participate in a field exercise that included simulated Iraqi conditions. Peter spent a year on the Hill in the Department of State's Congressional Liaison Office. Peter authored the book We Meant Well: How I Helped Lose the Battle for the Hearts and Minds of the Iraqi People *and maintains the blog* WeMeantWell.com. *Born in New York City, he lives in Virginia with his spouse, two daughters, and a docile Rottweiler.*

Way out on the edge of Forward Operating Base Hammer, where I lived for much of my year in Iraq as a Provincial Reconstruction Team leader for the U.S. Department of State, there were several small hills, lumps of raised dirt on the otherwise frying-pan-flat desert. These were "tells," ancient garbage dumps and fallen buildings.

Thousands of years ago, people in the region used sun-dried bricks to build homes and walls. Those bricks had a lifespan of about 20 years before they began to crumble, at which point locals just built anew atop the old foundation. Do that for a while, and soon enough your buildings are sitting on a small hill.

At night, the tell-area was very dark, as we avoided artificial light in order not to give passing insurgents easy targets. In that darkness, you could imagine the earliest inhabitants of what was now our base looking at the night sky, and be reminded that we were not the first to move into Iraq from afar. It was also a promise across time that someday someone would undoubtedly sit atop our own ruins and wonder whatever happened to the Americans.

From that ancient debris field, recall the almost forgotten run-up to the American invasion: the now-ridiculous threats about Saddam Hussein's weapons of mass destruction; Secretary of State Colin Powell lying away his own and America's prestige at the U.N.; those "Mission-Accomplished" days when the Marines tore down Saddam's statue and conquered Baghdad; the darker times as civil society imploded and Iraq devolved into civil war; the endless rounds of purple fingers for stage-managed elections that meant so little; the Surge and the ugly stalemate that followed… all fading to gray as President George W. Bush negotiated a complete withdrawal of U.S. forces from Iraq by the end of 2011, and the seeming end of his dreams of a Pax Americana in the Greater Middle East.

Now, with less than seven months left until that withdrawal moment, Washington debates whether to honor the agreement, or—if only we can get the Iraqi government to ask us to stay —to leave a decent-sized contingent of soldiers occupying some of the massive bases the Pentagon built, hoping for their permanent occupancy.

To the extent that any attention is paid to Iraq back here in Snooki's America, the debate over whether eight years of war entitles the U.S. military to some kind of Iraqi squatter's rights is the story that will undoubtedly get most of the press in the coming months.

I did not go to Iraq with the intent of writing a book; I planned nothing more than a few emails to my wife, reminding her to pay the mortgage each month. But almost from Day One, extraordinary things began to happen around me, and I realized that the version of Iraq in general that was available back home (in particular of our reconstruction efforts) had nothing to do with the HD/3-D version I was experiencing. I remained ambivalent about the idea of a book until about two months into my tour, on what I call Judgment Day.

That was the day I was called into the Embassy for a come-to-Jesus session over canceling the I-guess-now-infamous Sheep for Widows project, as is outlined in my book. People had complained. My boss s l o w l y laid out my many faults (a common State Department habit left over from a lifetime of d e a l i n g with f o r e i g n e r s). His boss had political ambitions, so most of his sentences were guarded passive-aggressive barbs, consisting of the words *mandate, robust, empower* and *team building*. The two men spent an hour reviewing my performance as failing to meet their unillustrated standards, concluding that I should not bite the hand that fed us.

Their words were officially correct and carefully chosen, but what was unspoken was clear enough: *"Stop making a fuss. No one cares about the money, we have lots of money, and not spending it angers people. We all know we are not going to really change much in Iraq, so just do your year in the desert. Don't bring us down with you. We all have careers to consider."* (They were right. My boss ended up working as a contractor-advisor for the Army for big bucks, and his boss was appointed Ambassador to Syria. All I got was this lousy T-shirt.)

And there it was, the whole thing plain as day. I was right about being wrong. There was no point other than to spend money, maybe get ourselves promoted. It was at that point I realized that I needed to tell this story.

How this won't end

Even if the troops do finally leave, the question is: Will that actually bring the U.S. occupation of Iraq to a close? During the invasion of 2003, a younger David Petraeus famously asked a reporter: "Tell me how this ends."

Dave, it may not actually end. After all, as of October 1, 2011, full responsibility for the U.S. presence in Iraq was transferred from the military to the Department of State. In other words, as Washington imagines it, the occupation won't really end at all, even if the landlords are switched.

And the State Department hasn't exactly been thinking small, either, when it comes to its future "footprint" on Iraqi soil. The U.S. mission in Baghdad remains the world's largest embassy, built on a tract of land about the size of the Vatican and visible from space. It cost just $736 million to build — or was it $1 billion, depending on how you count the post-construction upgrades and fixes?

In its post-"withdrawal" plans, the State Department expects to have 17,000 personnel in Iraq at some 15 sites. If those plans go as expected, 5,500 of them will be mercenaries, hired to shoot-to-kill Iraqis as needed, to maintain security. Of the remaining 11,500, most will be in support roles of one sort or another, with only a couple of hundred in traditional diplomatic jobs. This is not unusual in wartime situations. The military, for example, typically fields about seven support soldiers for every "shooter." In other words, the occupation run by a heavily militarized State Department will simply continue in a new, truncated form—unless Congress refuses to pay for it.

It would better serve America's interests to have an embassy sized to the message we now need to send to the Middle East, and it shouldn't be one that shows boastful conquest.

A place to call home

After initially setting up shop in a selection of Saddam Hussein's Disneyesque palaces (in one of the dumbest PR moves of all time), plans were made to build an embassy worthy of the over-the-top optimism and bravado that characterized the invasion itself. Though officially photos of the inside of the Embassy compound are not allowed (for "security" reasons), a quick Google search under "U.S. Embassy Baghdad" turns up plenty, including some of the early architectural renderings of the future gargantuan compound. (Historical minifact: back in 2007, TomDispatch first broke the story that the architect's version of the embassy's secret interior was displayed all pink and naked online.)

The blind optimism of that moment was best embodied in the international school building stuck in one corner of the embassy compound. Though a fierce civil-war-*cum*-insurgency was then raging in Iraq, the idea was that, soon enough, diplomatic families would be assigned to Baghdad, just as they were to Paris or Seoul, and naturally the kids would need a school. It may seem silly now, but few doubted it then.

Apartments were built, each with a full set of the usual American appliances, including dishwashers, in expectation that those families would be shopping for food at a near-future Sadr City Safeway and that diplo-tots Timmy and Sally would need their dinners after a long day at school. Wide walkways, shaded by trees and dotted with stone benches—ultimately never implemented—were part of the overall design for success, and in memory now serve as comic rim-shots for our past hubris.

In la-la land they may have been, but even the embassy planners couldn't help but leave some room for the creeping realities of an Iraq in chaos. The compound would purify its own water, generate its own power, and process its own sewage, ensuring that it could outlast any siege and, at the same time, getting the U.S. off the hook for repairing such basic services in Baghdad proper.

High walls went up rimmed with razor wire, and an ever-more complex set of gates and security checkpoints kept creeping into the design. Eventually, the architects just gave up, built a cafeteria, filled the school building with work cubicles, and installed inches-thick bulletproof glass on every window. The embassy's housing for 4,000 is, at present, packed, while the electrical generators run at capacity 24/7. These need to be upgraded and new units added very soon, simply to keep the lights on.

And now, the embassy staff in Baghdad is about to double. One plan to accommodate extra personnel involves hot-bunking—sharing beds on day-and-night shifts as happens on submarines. The embassy will also soon need a hospital on its grounds, if the U.S. Army truly departs and takes its facilities with it. Iraqi medical care is considered too substandard and Iraqi hospitals too dangerous for use by white folks.

You and whose army?

A fortress needs guards, and an occupier needs shock troops. The State Department's army will be divided into two parts: those who guard fixed facilities like the embassy, and those who protect diplomats as they scurry about trying to corral the mad Iraqis running the country.

For static security, a company named SOC will guard the embassy facilities for up to $973 million over five years. That deflowered old warhorse Blackwater (now Xe), under yet another dummy corporate name, will also get a piece of the action, and of the money pie.

SOC will undoubtedly follow the current security company's lead and employ almost exclusively Ugandans and Peruvians transported to Iraq for that purpose. For the same reasons Mexicans cut American lawns and Hondurans clean American hotel rooms, embassy guards come from poverty-stricken countries and get paid accordingly—about $600 a month. Their U.S. supervisors, on the other hand, pull down $20,000 of your tax dollars monthly. Many of the Ugandan and Peruvian guards got their jobs through nasty intermediaries ("pimps" and "slavers"), who take back most of their meager salaries to repay "recruitment costs," leaving many guards as little more than indentured servants.

Long-time merc group Triple Canopy will provide protection outside the embassy fortress, reputedly for $1.5 billion over a five-year span. The overall goal is for State to have its own private army in Iraq: those 5,500 hired guns, almost two full brigades worth of them. The Army guards Fort Knox with fewer soldiers; my Forward Operating Base made due with less than 400 troops, and I slept comfortably.

The past mayhem caused by contracted security is well known, with massacres in public squares, drunken murders in the Green Zone, and the like. (Think of the mercs as what the Army might be like without its NCOs and officers: a frat house with guns.)

Most of them are Americans, though with a few exotic Brits and shady South Africans thrown in. They love 5.11 clothing and favor fingerless leather gloves. (Think biker gang or Insane Clown Posse fan boys.)

Popular is a clean-shaven head, with no moustache but a spiky goatee teased straight out. You know the look from late-night convenience store beer runs. They walk around like Yosemite Sam, arms out as if their very biceps prevented them from standing straight. They're bullies of course, flirting inappropriately with women and posturing around men. Count on them to wear the most expensive Oakley sunglasses and the most unnecessary gear (gold man-bracelets, tactical hair gel—Think: Jersey Shore rejects.)

Aggressive tattoos on all exposed skin seem a prerequisite for membership in Club Merc, especially wavy inked patterns around the biceps and on the neck. They all let on that they were once SEALS, Green Berets, SAS, or Legion of Doom members, but of course they "can't talk about it." They're not likely to disclose last names, and tend to go by nicknames like Bulldog, Spider, Red Bull, Wolverine, or Smitty.

If arrogance was contagious they'd all be sneezing. All Aryan, all dudely, and now all that stands between those thousands of State Department personnel and Iraq. Oh yes: the seersuckered and bow-tied diplomats are supposed to supervise the mercs and keep them on the right diplomatic path, kind of like expecting the chess club to run herd on the football team.

With the U.S Army departing in whole or in part by year's end, most of the array of Army air assets State used will need to be replaced. A recently released State Department Office of the Inspector General's (OIG) "Report on Department of State Planning for the Transition to a Civilian-led Mission in Iraq Performance Evaluation" explains that our diplomats will, in the future, have their own little Air America in Iraq, a fleet of 46 aircraft, including:

- 20 medium lift S-61 helicopters (essentially Black Hawks, possibly armed);
- 18 light lift UH-1N helicopters (new models of 'Nam era Hueys, possibly armed);
- Three light observation MD-530 helicopters (Little Birds, armed, for quick response strike teams… er, um, observation duties);
- Five Dash 8 fixed-wing aircraft (50-passenger capacity to move personnel into the "theater" from Jordan).

The OIG report also notes that State will need to construct landing zones, maintenance hangars, operation buildings, and air traffic control towers, along with an independent aviation logistics system for maintenance and fueling. And yes, the diplomats are supposed to supervise this, too, the goal being to prevent an Iraqi from being gunned down from an attack helo with diplomatic license plates. What could go wrong?

How much?

At this point, has cost started to cross your mind? Well, some 74 percent of embassy Baghdad's operating costs will be going to "security." State requested $2.7 billion from Congress for its Iraq operations in FY 2011, but got only $2.3 billion from a budget-minded Capitol Hill. Facing the possibility of being all alone in a dangerous universe in FY 2012, the Department has requested $6.3 billion for Iraq. Congress has yet to decide what to do. To put these figures in perspective, the State Department total operating budget for this year is only about $14 billion (the cost of running the place, absent the foreign aid money), so $6.3 billion for one more year in Iraq is a genuine chunk of change.

Which only leaves the question of why.

Pick your forum—TomDispatch readers at a kegger; Fox News pundits following the Bachmann bus; high school students preparing to take SATs; unemployed factory workers in a food-stamp line—and ask if any group of Americans (not living in official Washington) would conclude that Iraq was our most important foreign policy priority, and so deserving of our largest embassy with the largest staff and largest budget on the planet.

Does Iraq threaten U.S. security? Does it control a resource we demand? (Yes, it's got lots of oil underground, but produces remarkably little of the stuff.) Is Iraq enmeshed in some international coalition we need to butter up? Any evil dictators or WMDs around? Does Iraq hold trillions in U.S. debt? Anything? Anyone? *Bueller…*?

Eight disastrous years after we invaded, it is sad but altogether true that Iraq does not matter much in the end. It is a terrible thing that we poured 4,459 American lives and trillions of dollars into the war, and without irony oversaw the deaths of at least a hundred thousand, and probably hundreds of thousands, of Iraqis in the name of freedom. Yet we are left with only one argument for transferring our occupation duties from the Department of Defense to the Department of State: something vague about our "investment in blood and treasure."

Think of this as the Vegas model of foreign policy: keep the suckers at the table throwing good money after bad. Leaving aside the idea that "blood and treasure" sounds like a line from "Pirates of the Caribbean," one must ask: What accomplishment are we protecting?

The war's initial aim was to stop those weapons of mass destruction from being used against us. There were none, so check that off the list. Then it was to get rid of Saddam. He was hanged in 2006, so cross off that one. A little late in the game we became preoccupied with ensuring an Iraq that was "free." And we've had a bunch of elections and there is a government of sorts in place to prove it, so that one's gotta go, too.

What follows won't be "investment," just more waste. The occupation of Iraq, centered around that engorged embassy, is now the equivalent of a self-licking ice cream cone, useful only to itself.

Changing the occupying force from an exhausted U.S. Army that labored away for years at a low-grade version of diplomacy (drinking endless cups of Iraqi tea) to a newly militarized Department of State will not free us from the *cul-de-sac* we now find ourselves in. While nothing will erase the stain of the invasion, were we to really leave when we promised to leave, the U.S. might have a passing shot at launching a new narrative in a Middle East already on edge over the Arab Spring.

Embassies are, at the end of the day, symbols. Sustaining our massive one in Iraq, with its ever-lengthening logistics and security train, simply emphasizes our failure there, along with our stubborn inability to admit that we were wrong. When a country becomes too dangerous for diplomacy, like Libya, we temporarily close our embassy. When a country becomes dangerous, but U.S. interests are still at stake, as in Yemen, we withdraw all but essential personnel. Similarly, in Baghdad, what's needed is a modest-sized embassy staffed not by thousands but by scores—that is, only the limited number of people necessary to make the point that it is no longer an extension of a failed occupation.

Nothing can change the past in the Middle East, but withdrawing the troops on schedule and downsizing our embassy radically, to emphasize that we are no longer in the business of claiming more space for the American empire, might very well help change the future.

What Works
in the Face of Oppression

Matt Kennard

Matt Kennard graduated from the Journalism School at Columbia University as a Toni Stabile Investigative Scholar in 2008. He now works for the Financial Times *in London. He has written for* The Guardian, Salon, The Comment Factory *and the* Chicago Tribune, *among others. In 2006 he won the Guardian Student Feature Writer of the Year Award. His book,* Irregular Army, *is being published by Verso in 2012*

I have just spent two weeks volunteering in Palestine, and what I saw over there pressed home to me how important it is for concerned citizens to make the journey to the Occupied Territories to make their presence felt. During the December-January Israeli attack on Gaza, the sickness many people felt about the massacre was compounded by a feeling of helplessness. But there is a way to help out and attenuate the crimes of the occupation: what you realize in Palestine is that just having a foreign passport instantly civilizes the Israel Defense Force (IDF) when they are in your presence.

I was working with the International Solidarity Movement, which was set up in 2002 by Huwaida Arraf and her boyfriend Adam Shapiro to bring internationals sympathetic to the Palestinian cause to witness and combat Israeli repression during the Second Intifada. Since then it has achieved a fair degree of infamy—like any organization which tries to protect Palestinians it has been traduced as "terrorist-supporting," "anti-Semitic" and all the rest.

There are even a couple of organizations online set-up exclusively to libel and destroy the ISM: Stoptheism.com tries to expose its activists and says the ISM represents "Hamas, and other terrorists under Yassir Arafat"; and the Committee for Accuracy in Middle East Reporting in America states that "ISM encourages members to place themselves in dangerous situations to protect terrorists or their homes."

But after spending about an hour with the ISM in the West Bank you realize all these calumnies are baseless propaganda. From the start of my time there, I was impressed by the integrity and professionalism of the organization. The ISM runs a two-day training weekend in London, which instills in prospective volunteers the ethos of non-violence and the Palestinian-led *modus operandi* (i.e., everything we do has to be ratified by a Palestinian council). When you arrive in Palestine you have another two days of training, which takes you through the history of non-violent resistance in Palestine and the specifics of how to deal with violence from the IDF.

497

When I was there I met inspirational activists from Scotland and the Czech Republic, who had spent months living with families in East Jerusalem being illegally evicted by an Israeli settler company. This was not glamorous stuff; it was staying up all night and sleeping on a thin mattress in a single room together, day after day, month after month. I also met activists from Sweden who were manning checkpoints to make sure that no Palestinians were physically abused.

I had my own experience of this on the way out of Nil'in, for the Friday demonstration against the annexation wall. I saw an IDF soldier kicking a Palestinian man at a checkpoint at the edge of this Palestinian village. I got the taxi to stop, and got out and just watched. I don't know what effect it had, but you could see a change in the eyes of the soldiers when they saw my camera pointing their way.

There was a group of activists from Italy who lived in Hebron, which is a particularly disturbing example of the occupation in the West Bank, since settlers have occupied the downtown market which is now closed down because of the harassment the settlers gave the Palestinians living there. When you walk down the now-defunct market there is grating overhead, and caught in it are all sorts of projectiles, bricks and debris. The settlers in Hebron are famous for their extremism. They celebrate the anniversary of the 1994 Hebron massacre by Baruch Goldstein, and the presence of the 500 of them in Hebron makes downtown a militarized zone. In Hebron, ISM volunteers escort Palestinian kids to school, to protect them from the settlers, who have been known to shoot at them wildly from their rooftops.

The courageous 22-year-old ISM activist Tom Hurndall was killed doing work like this in Gaza in April, 2003. He was moving Palestinian children out of the line of fire of IDF snipers and was shot in the head, despite having international signs. Hurndall's death shone the media spotlight on the conduct of the IDF in the Occupied Territories, only because he was British— Palestinians are shot with appalling regularity.

And that is why the ISM activists are so brave: they are putting their lives on the line, solely because they know they are worth more in the eyes of the IDF. It is also why the Israeli authorities try to keep out the ISM, by blacklisting anyone they suspect of being involved. Many ISMers have been slapped with a 10-year ban from entering Israel, even though the ISM is a completely legal organization in Israel.

I went to the non-violent Friday demonstrations in Bil'in and the nearby Nil'in on alternate weeks. Again the local villagers say that even though those among their ranks have been killed at an alarming rate in the past year (two in Bil'in, five in Nil'in, including a 10-year-old with a live shot to the head) it would be much worse if the internationals didn't turn up. Recently, U.S.-citizen and ISM activist Tristan Anderson was rendered a vegetable by a high- velocity teargas canister. While I was in Nil'in, the IDF were aiming right for us as we stood on the side of the verge. The only thing the IDF are up against at these demonstrations is stones in slingshots, more a symbolic act than anything else.

On one Friday, a Palestinian man was killed with a live round. "We always ask internationals to please come, because they are even more brutal when it is just us Palestinians," said the leader of the demonstration.

There are definitely dangers to volunteering in occupied Palestine, but it is a highly effective way of helping the Palestinians resist oppression, and because of our passports those risks are a smidgen of those faced by any Palestinian who raises so much as a finger of resistance. My stay was short, and I did nothing compared to the brilliant and inspirational activists—who range from teenagers to pensioners—who have spent far longer and risked far more. But it is clear that through the solidarity of internationals, Israelis and Palestinians the occupation can be fought. There are more losses than gains, and ISM and Palestinian activists will continue to be lost, but as George Orwell concluded in his *Looking Back on the Spanish Civil War*, where he had fought against General Franco's fascists, "I believe that it is better even from the point of view of survival to fight and be conquered than to surrender without fighting." In this sense, "fighting" doesn't always have to be violent.

Being in Palestine helped me understand how the truth about what our governments do in our name is invariably distorted in the media. That disconnect between the truth and what we digest is vital to keeping the domestic culture's passive acquiescence to the great crimes being done in our name. The powers that be are aware that if people knew the truth they would push them to stop the atrocities, like the massacre of Gaza in 2009-2010; or the massacre in Iraq which began in 2003 and endures until today.

It is really a faith in the innate goodness of humanity—who will react, when presented with facts about aggression and injustice—that drives me to try to highlight what is going on to captive people all over the world.

From Statism
to Voluntaryism

Pete Eyre

Pete Eyre grew up in the Midwest US, spent time in the libertarian think tank world of DC, and now works to advance the voluntary society one mind at a time through on-the-road projects such as CopBlock.org *and* LibertyOnTour.com. *When not on tour he calls the growing liberty community in the shire, 'home.'*

"Love it or leave it," read the text flanking the American flag on my left bicep. It was the second tattoo I got after turning 18. Today a black circle covers the text and an "A" covers the flag—a visible representation of my journey to embracing the ideas of liberty.

My paradigm shift didn't happen overnight, but was due to a multitude of influences: conversations, books, videos, and—most importantly—life-experiences and self-reflection. Like many, I had pretty much bought into the Statist Quo peddled by gun-run schools and the mainstream media. I believed the American structure of government (with its "checks and balances" and "proportional representation") to be the best system devised. Sure, flaws existed, but mechanisms also existed to bring about improvements. At least that's what I had been told....

Like many from my suburban high school, the next chapter in my life was spent at college. I majored in law enforcement, believing it to be a vehicle through which I could help my fellow man. I became heavily involved with organizations on campus and helped bring in speakers from various law enforcement agencies. I was awarded scholarships to help cover my costs to attend conferences. I went on tours of prisons, did ride-alongs in dozens of cities and spent a summer interning with the St. Paul Police Department.

In that latter role, after having accompanied a number of individuals wearing badges on "buy-bust" operations (where drugs or sex was solicited by plainclothes officers cruising around in seized vehicles, complete with transmitters in the trunk so those of us in trailing vehicles could know when to swoop in), I questioned whether the effort was worth it. I pointed out the number of people involved, the lack of a victim, and the fact that those arrested were processed and soon released. I was told "It's just a job, you can't think of it that way." "*Why would one choose to use time in such a way?*" I thought to myself.

Before another such operation we were advised to "be careful"—due not to threats from others, but to the large number of cameras downtown that would record their actions. Another time a K9 officer told me how he and his colleagues compared pictures of the bites their dogs do to "suspects," noting that fat and muscle tear differently. Later, while eating lunch at a Subway restaurant with a handful of officers, I was told a story about how one man

500

present had recently responded to a call, thrown his vehicle into "park" and run full-speed toward the "suspect" before kicking him in the head... because he had allegedly tried to swallow a substance deemed "illicit" under the law. The cop added that it was a good thing I wasn't from the ACLU. That idealistic "serve and protect" veneer was starting to erode.

Drug policy was the issue that caused me to become more liberty-oriented, since related legislation and its enforcement seemed to do the opposite of stated goals. But it wasn't until I read *Why Our Drug Laws Have Failed and What We Can Do About It: A Judicial Indictment Of War On Drugs* by Judge James Gray that I had a robust framework with which to better communicate against the harmful policies that existed. Though today I go farther in my prescription than does the author, it was key for me at the time:

> *This issue, like all others, boils down to property rights. You own yourself, or to put it another way, you have property in yourself, and thus have the right to ingest whatever substance you choose. If you aggress upon the equal negative rights of another, you are personally responsible, whether you were stone cold sober or high as a kite. It violates your natural rights when another person uses force to restrict or deny you such choice, even when done under the guise of "protecting you." And accompanying such misguided policies as the war on (some) drugs are perverse incentives and unintended consequences.*

> *Prohibition doesn't work. When a good or service is in demand, entrepreneurs will supply it. The artificially high price created by criminalization incentivizes more theft to support habits. The "illegal" status of certain substances means disagreements between parties aren't remedied through arbitration but through violence. What right does a group of people hundreds of miles away have to steal your money, then use it to buy planes and chemicals to spray the fields of a stranger thousands of miles away? What right do some individuals have to cage another individual who chooses to ingest a substance others have deemed "illicit?" None. When there's no victim there's no crime.*

During one summer-break my brother and I spent a week exploring New York City. We found ourselves in the Strand Book Store. I asked a clerk for the "libertarian section" (which wasn't too extensive) and left there with *The Libertarian Reader*, a collection of writings by liberty-oriented thinkers. One essay, Herbert Spencer's *The Right to Ignore the State*, offered an alternative to both the work-through-the-system and the outright-revolution perspectives, proffering instead an evolution that occurred on the individual level, one mind at a time. Such an idea, simple as it was, had enormous implications for my personal development.

When I was in grad school a girl noticed my shirt, which had "End the drug war" written boldly across the back, and told me I had to meet her friend. I did; he was involved with the College Libertarians and soon I was as well, seeing it as an avenue to endeavor toward peaceful interaction amongst individuals. Our meetings, though scheduled for an hour or two, often went on much later, prompting me to refer to them as "mind sex," since they were so stimulating. I still remember the first time our faculty advisor advocated that education be provided without governmental oversight. At the time I hadn't really questioned state intervention in education, but his lone comment helped me take my views (that the initiation of force is wrong) to their logical conclusions, applying them to all goods and services. Our group did outreach on campus, screened movies and discussed the ideas presented afterwards, and debated those involved with political organizations.

By the time I graduated, I had written off working for any federal law enforcement agency, since I couldn't support any of their missions. I had begun the interview process with the Seattle PD, NYPD and LAPD, and had a job lined up at a private surveillance company that paid well and provided me a vehicle; however, my life took a completely different direction when I learned that my application to intern at the Cato Institute had been accepted. I didn't know anyone in Washington, DC and the stipend was meager, but I knew it was an excellent opportunity. There I was, surrounded by some of the brightest minds, both in-house and among the many speakers and panelists I was able to observe. I primarily worked with the Foreign Policy & Defense area, but when I had time I also helped the Constitutional Studies folks. Needless to say I learned a lot and, for the first time in my life, I felt as if I had a solid grasp on economics.

That summer I was fortunate to be part of the Koch Summer Fellow Program, aninternship program facilitated by the Institute for Humane Studies (IHS), which is a top-tier organization that expands the freedom movement through seminars and scholarships for college students. This experience further increased my grasp of and affinity for the ideas of liberty and their universal benefits for peace and prosperity.

After this, I was hired by IHS and spent over two-and-a-half years becoming more versed in liberty, both through our programs and my interactions with my many awesome colleagues. It was there that I first read Bruce Benson's *The Enterprise of Law*, Ed Stringham's *Anarchy & the Law*, and other stellar books. In my last role at IHS, I traveled to different cities and connected with liberty-oriented students at their colleges and universities, helping to provide them with resources and network them with others in their area. Looking back, this position was instrumental in the tactics I now utilize.

In early 2008, I left IHS for Bureaucrash. It was a tough decision as I loved both the mission and my colleagues. However, I felt it was a logical progression for me, since I tended to be the most activist-oriented person on the staff, Bureaucrash's mission (at that time) was principled and the use of and leveraging of new media was paramount in the new position. The launch of a social networking site facilitated the connections of many individuals I now consider as good friends, as well as some of the most effective activists around.

Another idea implemented was the "Revolution In a Box," a collection of literature and other resources from a diverse array of libertarian organizations which was sent free to individuals who requested it, so long as they also indicated that they'd utilize the contents and share them with others. The success of this resource from inception to execution was due to its crowdsourced nature. Organizations who thought it worth their investment sent books, flyers, stickers, and DVDs for inclusion, and individuals volunteered to assemble the packages.

In early 2009, I left the think tank world of DC to hit the road with Jason Talley through Motorhome Diaries (MHD). We wanted to take our message "from K St. to Main St." by "searching for freedom in America," pointing cameras at those advancing the broad freedom movement. I left my salaried position, sold my motorcycle, stereo and most of my books, gave away other items to friends, and split the cost of a 30-foot RV with Jason.

A week into the project Adam Mueller (Ademo Freeman) sent us an email, indicating his interest in helping with the project. He became MHD's third crew member. We were just three guys with an idea and the desire to help spread the ideas of liberty. There was no instruction manual; we learned every day. After seven months we had spent time in 41 states, met thousands of people and uploaded almost two hundred videos to our YouTube channel. People opened their homes, donated money, and assisted us in countless ways, which only reaffirmed my belief that it's preferable to live in a society where force isn't legitimized for some.

For instance, about a month into the tour, while traveling from New Orleans to Nashville, we were stopped in southeast Mississippi by James Atkins of the Jones County Sheriff's Department. Atkins claimed to be unfamiliar with the temporary paper license plate tags then on the RV. A couple of hours later Jason, Ademo and I were in a cage. Fortunately, prior to being handcuffed Jason used his phone to Tweet a picture of the stop. Friends from hundreds, even thousands of miles away spearheaded a campaign to get our release. That night we were surprised to see Allison Gibbs, who had flown in from DC, accompanied by a local friend, appear with bail money. Since we hadn't been informed of our charges (let alone able to make a call), we had been in the dark about all the activity going on behind the scenes. We later learned the jail had received 300-500 phone calls, from people who didn't appreciate the actions of those with badges who had incarcerated us. The outpouring of support was impressive to say the least.

Later in the year we were prevented from attending three meetups and an event at which we were to speak, because it was north of the arbitrary political boundary between the United States and Canada. After searching our RV and discovering Alliance for the Libertarian Left literature (which the individuals wearing "Canada Border Protection Services Agency" badges claimed was "heinous propaganda") they cited our arrest in Jones Co. as rationale for not allowing us the freedom of movement. Before we left their facility (where we had been searched, questioned and detained for an hour), one woman with a badge told me, "I don't want to see my name online. I'm just doing my job!" She was apparently aware, after poring over our website, that holding individuals personally responsible for their actions was our *modus operandi*. I made it clear that yes, she and each of her colleagues who had violated our rights were responsible for their actions, and that a piece of paper didn't grant them immunity.

The next year I bought Jason out of his half of the RV (dubbed MARV, the Mobile Authority Resistance Vehicle), and Ademo and I founded Liberty On Tour (LOT). We spent a few months in Keene, NH doing logistics, then criss-crossed the country to "advance the voluntary society."

> *Voluntaryists advocate that all interactions, including the provision of all goods and services, be consensual. It's essentially a live-and-let-live philosophy, recognizing that the granting of arbitrary authority based on a title or badge is not ideal. Throughout history it has been this granting of extra privileges to others—to do things admittedly wrong for you or me to do—that has caused war, famine and misery. RJ Rummel coined the term* democide, *or death by government. Yes, a voluntary society won't be a utopia, but it will be a much more peaceful and prosperous society than now exists, since individuals will be left to pursue their own passions. Those who harm others will be more quickly held accountable.*

> *To put it simply, bad ideas have bad consequences and good ideas have good consequences. Advocating a move from the Statist Quo to a voluntary society means replacing the bad idea of a "legitimate" monopoly on the use of force, top-down control, and one-size-fits-all solutions with the good idea of consensual interactions, decentralization and a plurality of choices.*

Ademo's and my emphasis was on ideas, communication and activism. We hoped to cover and participate in activism and, if needed, be the catalyst. We collaborated with point-people on the ground for each stop, so that we could have a bigger impact.

Just prior to hitting the road with LOT, we traveled an hour south to Greenfield, MA, where a few friends had been arrested. Our goal was to post bail and return, yet we were kidnapped and caged and charged with a number of felonies and misdemeanors, since we had sought to document our interactions with those wearing badges through the lens of a camera. These rights-violations have only been exacerbated through the arbitrary court processes in the year since, yet our perspective (that it was those wearing "Greenfield Police Department" badges who were in the wrong!) has not wavered. Like the Institute for Justice, we've sought to win in the court of public opinion.

I have engaged in conversation all those who have kidnapped and caged me, pointing out that their actions violate my rights since I am always peaceful and never violate either person or property. Some wearing badges just laugh and treat me more roughly. Others ignore me. But some do seem receptive. When the door to my cage was about to be closed in Greenfield, one man replied to me, "I'm with you more than you know." "Why not quit your job then?" I asked. He responded "My family wouldn't understand." I told him that he ultimately had to do what he knew was right. And that if his family loved him, they would seek to learn why he took such actions—which admittedly were a dramatic change from the couple decades he'd likely already spent in that capacity.

Ademo's arrest in Las Vegas in late August, unfortunate as it was, further demonstrates the usefulness of being transparent and striking the root. After doing a story on the local Food Not Bombs chapter, we decided to stop by Weedz Alternatives, as we heard its owner had been harassed by those with badges since his shop sold synthetic marijuana. Soon after we returned to MARV, which was parked in a gravel parking lot nearby, there was a loud rap on the door. Looking out we saw three individuals wearing "Las Vegas Metropolitan Police" badges. We were told there was a federal building nearby and they considered our vehicle to be suspicious.

An hour later, despite calm conversation from our end, Ademo was being taken away in the back of a squad car. Portions of the interaction and future updates were streamed from my phone using Qik. Without question this objective video evidence meant increased support, since it was clear Ademo had done nothing to deserve his treatment. A day and a half later (thanks to hundreds of phone calls, media coverage, a protest, and Ademo's refusal to post bail), he was released and his charge dismissed. The support—by those both on the ground in Vegas and outside the area—was tremendous. It made all the difference.

Between the MHD and LOT journeys, Ademo had founded Cop Block, after being constantly harassed by those wearing badges in his sleepy Wisconsin town just north of Milwaukee. I soon joined him and now a dozen others round off the team, doing everything from writing to editing to creating podcasts and website work. Our tagline ("badges don't grant extra rights") has found enormous traction since virtually everyone has had a negative interaction with those who purport to "protect and serve." Daily we receive messages from people supporting our projects and inquiring how they can get involved.

Police departments have become more militarized: the uniform color has switched from blue to black, AR-15 rifles and submachine guns are standard issue, armored personnel carriers (bought for next-to-nothing thanks to Department of Defense surplus hardware program) are more commonplace, taser usage is up and detainment policies and lengths are more oppressive. Asset forfeiture programs incentivize the stealing of cars, cash and other property, placing the burden on the individual to prove it wasn't obtained "illegally." So much for innocent until proven guilty. Meanwhile, the mainstream media toes the government line, refusing to question policies or double-standards. If you're unjustly arrested, you can bet your name and information will appear in print. If someone wearing a badge commits some egregious action, they'll usually receive a paid vacation with their identity protected. This not only doesn't meet the mission statement of many departments (which emphasize integrity, communication, and community relations), it exacerbates the "us vs them" mentality, creating more tension and hostility, based simply on where one is employed.

While on the road with LOT's Free State Friendship Tour, I was one of eight arrested when doing a pro-police accountability rally outside the Manchester Police Department. My camera and phone were stolen from me. I implored my captors to think about their actions. One gentleman (whom I'd spoken to for over an hour prior to being arrested) later stopped by the fingerprint room and asked me who my favorite authors were; this was a significant change, because earlier when I'd offered him a DVD with some related videos he'd turned it down. For whatever reason—maybe the passage of time allowed him to chew on our previous conversation, or perhaps he felt more comfortable discerning such information when not around lots of others—I told him, Carl Watner and Larken Rose. "Watner and Rose, I'll remember that" he replied....

Through Bureaucrash, Motorhome Diaries, Liberty On Tour and Cop Block I've had a hand in creating hundreds of videos. I've been fortunate to meet individuals I consider among the smartest minds and best communicators around. I've heard from many others their own stories about how they came to embrace the peaceful ideas of liberty. At the same time, I've unfortunately seen more people being intruded upon, by those who believe they have the right to do immoral things, because they're so commanded by a boss or text on paper. In sum, more people are waking up, thinking for themselves and acting accordingly, which sometimes means not abiding by arbitrary man-made legislation.

Today I posit that any system that allows for arbitrary authority to be failed from the start. If it's wrong for me or you to do then it's wrong for another to do, regardless of their title or the patches on their costume. I'd never been kidnapped by those wearing badges prior to hitting the road. Two and a half years later it's happened five times. It seems that those who purport to "serve and protect" would rather harass and intimidate, especially when you're questioning their claimed authority. With the exception of charges levied against me in Manchester, NH for which I'm still waiting to hear the judge's ruling, thus all charges I've faced have been dropped (or in the case of Greenfield, found "not guilty" by a jury).

Voltaire noted that *"It is dangerous to be right when the government is wrong,"* and Thoreau concluded that *"Under a government which imprisons unjustly, the true place for a just man is also a prison."* But who or what is this amorphous entity known as "government," that which Bastiat called "the great fiction"? It's just an association of individuals. To bring about a freer more peaceful society, one cannot continue to grant legitimacy to the bad idea of government, which claims that certain people have the "right" to do things that are wrong for others. Can individual actions be categorized differently, based solely on the actor's place of employment? Can an action be just for one person but unjust for another? Of course not. We're each personally responsible for our actions.

Those who seek to control others thrive when information is censored. The Internet has been an important tool, allowing us to bypass the gatekeepers of yesteryear to share ideas and tactics and establish connections that permeate the real world. Today activists worldwide are collaborating.

At the end of the day, today's State, that we allow to obstruct and burden innocent individuals (who have done no harm to others) and advance the interests of some other individuals (those best able to curry government's favor) at a cost to the rest of us, is just a bad idea, and ideas can be unlearned. I've found the surest way to facilitate this is to establish personal connections with individuals, and encourage them to think for themselves, taking their views to their logical conclusions and demystifying the language surrounding actions done by State agents (taxes are theft, arresting peaceful individuals is kidnapping, etc.). As I tell those who are still on the fence, if we don't act now, just imagine how hard it will be for the next generation.

Or, as Voluntaryist author and thinker Carl Watner says, "*If one takes care of the means, the end will take care of itself.*" To realize the freer more peaceful society, we must live it and not be afraid of those who thrive on fear and scare tactics. The liberty-oriented community is growing. More are engaged in unschooling, agorism and civil disobedience. I'm optimistic about the future.

Freedom is Necessary
to Good Health

Robban Sica

Robban A. Sica, M.D., graduated from the University of Toledo and the Medical College of Ohio. She has been practicing integrative medicine for over 26 years and founded an integrative multi-specialty private practice of natural and alternative medicine, The Center for the Healing Arts, PC in Orange, CT. Robban successfully integrates into practice holistic medicine, anti-aging, natural hormone replacement and endocrine problems, nutrition/vitamin supplementation including natural alternatives to medication, allergies and environmental medicine, heavy metal detoxification, chelation therapy, and treatment of chronic illnesses. Certified in both Longevity Medicine and Clinical Metal Toxicology, she is President of the International College of Integrative Medicine (www.icimed.com) and secretary of the Alliance for Natural Health-USA (www.anh-usa.org), dedicated to preserving the right of practitioners to freely practice integrative therapies as well as patients to choose what form of treatment they prefer.

> *"The only freedom deserving the name is that of pursuing our own good in our own way, so long as we do not attempt to deprive others of theirs, or impede their efforts to obtain it. Each is the proper guardian of his own health, whether bodily or mental and spiritual."*
> - John Stuart Mill

The freedom to choose what type of healthcare and which health practitioner you want to see is in grave danger today. Most people are not aware of the many useful therapies and cures that have been suppressed by state aggression and, in some cases, eradicated. How did we get to this sorry state of affairs? And why am I so passionate about getting the public to wake up and realize what freedoms are being taken away that could cost them their quality of life—and even their lives?

I pursued the study of medicine, not only as an intellectual pursuit but also from the heart. My motivation was simply to help others live happier, healthier, more fulfilled lives. Treating the whole person seemed like an obvious necessity to practicing good medicine. Educating patients regarding preventive strategies, as well as correcting underlying imbalances that lead to illness, seemed equally essential to promoting good health. I quickly realized though that these ideas simply did not fit in the conventional medical world. I almost dropped out of medical school in my third year, but then I discovered holistic approaches that better fit how I felt I could help my patients. So after my first year of residency, I veered off the beaten path to study mind-body medicine and other alternative therapies, gradually integrating them with what I had learned in my conventional training.

Even once I was in practice, I continued to evaluate new information and treatments, searching for fundamental ways to impact the underlying causes of illness. When I started reading the research on chelation therapy, I was compelled to study this treatment. After careful review, I decided to offer this non-toxic intravenous treatment to my patients suffering with cardiovascular disease or heavy-metals toxicity. According to the FDA in 2008, both forms of EDTA, the drug used in chelation therapy, have been associated with a total of only 11 deaths in over 25 years, and half of those deaths were caused by administering the wrong form of the drug. This is an extremely safe track record compared to other drugs. Although aware of the controversy surrounding chelation, I did not fully believe in the conspiracy theory that there had been deliberate attempts to suppress this and other treatments. I was wrong.

For a number of years I went quietly about helping my patients, by utilizing an integrative approach and seeing the dramatic improvements in patients who could not find help in the conventional medical world. But one day I received a letter from the state medical board investigator, wanting to know "in what context" I was using chelation therapy. There had been no patient harmed or any complaint against me. The investigator simply saw on a website that I performed chelation therapy. That investigator later filed charges against me for "violating the standard of care" by performing this therapy, despite the fact that this so-called 'standard of care' does not exist in any codified form for medical treatments. The medical boards simply hire an "expert" who is in agreement with their opinion, and claim that opinion to be the "standard of care." Imagine being accused of breaking an unwritten law, when your only crime is making people healthier! Because chelation therapy was the treatment that facilitated my own recovery from nearly disabling chronic fatigue syndrome caused by heavy-metal toxicity, I simply could not allow this treatment to be suppressed. I felt patients who needed it had a right to receive the therapy.

I talked to a considerable number of doctors (and other practitioners) who had been persecuted by their medical boards for practicing alternative medicine. During their administrative hearings, these healers had faced a blatant disregard of due process, frequently resulting in censure, restriction, or loss of license. I knew that I would not receive justice in the administrative process. Since the best defense is often a good offense, my attorney and I chose to file a federal lawsuit in 2004 against the state for due process violations in my case. During the long, expensive, and arduous battle that ensued, I became increasingly aware of just how deep the conspiracy is to eradicate all forms of healing, except drugs and surgery. Although I ultimately survived this attack and successfully set a new precedent to allow the practice of chelation therapy in my state, the experience impelled me to join the health-freedom movement, which is dedicated to protecting the rights of practitioners to practice and consumers to choose among healthcare options. This journey pointed me in a new direction, blending my libertarian roots with my philosophy of healing.

"The efforts of the medical profession in the US to control...its job it proposes to monopolize. It has been carrying on a vigorous campaign all over the country against new methods and schools of healing because it wants the business...I have watched this medical profession for a long time and it bears watching." - Clarence Darrow, (1857-1938)

A package arrived in the mail one day as a gift from another physician in the Midwest who had also been persecuted by his medical board. Inside the package was a copy of P. Joseph Lisa's book, *Assault on Medical Freedom*, which would become a particular turning point for me. This outstanding book, published in 1994, provides an essential foundation of understanding how pharmaceutical-based medicine achieved and maintained supremacy over homeopathy, osteopathy, chiropractic, naturopathy and a host of other alternative medical systems.

Lisa, while doing research for a different book in the archives at the AMA headquarters in Chicago, had come across some shocking evidence. Since 1847, the American Medical Association (in collusion with the pharmaceutical industry, federal agencies, state medical boards, and private organizations) has systematically acted to suppress medical innovation and natural non-toxic therapies, in an effort to block competition to a solely drug-based medical system. In 1964, the AMA established the Coordinating Conference on Health Information (CCHI) comprised of non-governmental members (including the AMA, American Cancer Society, American Pharmaceutical Association, Arthritis Foundation, and Council of Better Business Bureaus) and governmental members (such as the Food & Drug Administration, Federal Trade Commission, US Postal Service, Office of Consumer Affairs, and the National Health Council).

Lisa uncovered the minutes of these clandestine meetings, documenting the CCHI's purpose and plan: to investigate and suppress targeted alternative treatments, modalities, services, products, manufacturers, and practitioners. Some of the special targets identified in their meetings included: chiropractic, cellular therapy, acupuncture, homeopathy, naturopathy, vitamin therapy, chelation therapy, and all alternative cancer treatments and modalities. Each member organization had its priorities of what treatments they wanted to eradicate and each agency had its own role to play out in accomplishing their shared objectives. For instance, "The US FDA would inspect, seize, send Regulatory Letters, and get injunctions against and prosecute targets given to them in the form of priority targets from the AMA and other medical vested-interest groups in the CCHI." (*quoted from CCHI meeting minutes, PJ Lisa,* Assault on Medical Freedom, *pg 34)*

"The thing that bugs me is that people think the FDA is protecting them. It isn't. What the FDA is doing and what the public thinks it is doing are as different as night and day." - Dr. Herbert Ley, Commissioner of the FDA, *San Francisco Chronicle*, 01/02/70.

These conspirators have been extremely effective in controlling cancer treatment by wiping out any competition to radiation and chemotherapy. For many years, "approval" of cancer treatments has been dictated and administered by such entities as the FDA, the AMA, and the National Institutes of Health (NIH); only certain therapies receive their blessing. Effective, inexpensive, and non-toxic alternatives have been deliberately suppressed. Most often, these natural treatments cannot be patented so monopoly status cannot be achieved in order to achieve the desirable profits from the treatment. When one of these breakthrough therapies was successful enough to become a threat to the profits of the "approved" therapies, then governmental agencies and prestigious private organizations deliberately misrepresented, discouraged, harassed, sued, ignored and suppressed, until their originators were bankrupt or worse. Many of these therapies have disappeared and are no longer available.

Meanwhile, the federal National Cancer Institute (NCI, which is part of NIH) and the "nonprofit" American Cancer Society have diverted billions of taxpayer dollars and charitable donations away from preventative strategies, discrediting them as useless, while heavily promoting increasingly staggeringly expensive drugs that are largely ineffective in the long term. But the conflicts of interest are rampant, with both the NCI and ACS tied extensively to the cancer-drug industry on both institutional and personal levels. Worse yet, the ACS receives funding from and shares a public relations firm with the chemical, fast-food, beverage, and tobacco industries. Any public education program that might point to the environmental and/or nutritional causes of cancer would be rapidly squelched.

How natural, non-toxic cancer prevention and cures have been marginalized and forgotten is a sad chapter in human history. I cannot even describe the deep sadness I felt while reading books such as Dan Haley's *Politics in Healing*, Dr. Samuel Epstein's *Cancer-Gate: How to Win the Losing Cancer War*, and Brian Peskin's *The Hidden Story of Cancer* for all the victims, both patients who have unnecessarily died of cancer and healers victimized by these medical-political machinations.

> *"Despite the fact that a predicted 350,000 persons in the US will die of cancer this year, the cancer bureaucracy keeps a closed mind...the basic issue is not the efficacy of Laetrile, but the infringement of freedom in what amounts to a life and death question."*-- US Congressman Philip M. Crane, Congressional Record, 1975.

The cancer death toll has grown in the three decades since Congressman Crane issued this warning (to over 570,000 in 2005) while costs have spiraled out of control, with very little improvement in outcomes. According to Leonard Saltz of Memorial Sloan-Kettering Cancer Center, the average total cost of cancer drugs for patients with advanced colorectal cancer in 1996 was $500, resulting in an expected survival of 11 months. Just 10 years later in 2006, the total cost of the course of cancer drugs rose to $250,000, but expected survival only improved to 24 months. (Reference: "Prices Soar for Cancer Drugs," Liz Szabo, 7/10-11/2006, *USA Today* (Internet version).

Ironically, the very success of this monopolization of medical care has led to our current healthcare crisis. The fact that medicine is the most highly regulated of all sectors of industry opens the door for manipulation by special interests in the market, determining which treatments are endorsed and which are not. The pharmaceutical industry spends millions of dollars on more than one thousand lobbyists on Capitol Hill to maintain the expensive drug based model. Non-drug innovative treatment is suppressed.

"Drugs are the fastest growing part of the healthcare bill," states former editor of the *New England Journal of Medicine*, Marcia Angell, MD, in her landmark book, *The Truth about Drug Companies: How They Deceive Us and What to Do About It.* Dr. Angell personally witnessed, during her two decades as editor of the *NEJM*, the change in the pharmaceutical industry, from "its original purpose of discovering and producing new drugs" to "a marketing machine to sell drugs of dubious benefit." In her own words, "this industry uses its wealth and power to co-opt every institution that might stand in its way, including the U.S. Congress, the Food and Drug Administration, academic medical centers, and the medical profession itself." This outspoken proponent of medical and pharmaceutical reform demonstrates clearly how which topics are chosen for research and what is published in the journals (relied upon as objective data by physicians) is controlled by Big Pharma.

This overwhelming industry influence has corrupted federal agencies, medical institutions, and universities, while hoodwinking the American public into paying for most real research with tax-dollars and donations. This two hundred billion dollar industry exerts its control by using advertising dollars to dictate what journals publish, by giving lucrative contracts to ex-FDA and other agency officials with current contacts within the FDA, and by making generous grants to universities and consulting contracts to influential physicians. Most especially, the pharmaceutical industry sends well over a thousand lobbyists and billions of dollars to Washington DC, more than any other sector of the economy, assuring that your senators and representatives are more responsive to their demands than to the needs of their constituents—*i.e.* YOU and your health!

Our current disease-care system is unsustainable. Each year medical care eats up a greater percentage of our gross national product. Every year, medical insurance costs become increasingly prohibitive for many. Yet research has shown that although the U.S. healthcare system is by far the most expensive in the world, it has some of the poorest outcomes. Just one documented example is a study published in 2003, which showed that U.S. per-person healthcare expenditures were double that of virtually all 30 industrialized nations, while ranking in second-to-last place in healthy life-expectancy. (Reference: *Overdosed America*, John Abramson, M.D., Harvard Medical School professor).

> *"If people let the government decide what foods they eat and what medicines they take, their bodies will soon be in as sorry a state as are the souls who live under tyranny."* - Thomas Jefferson

According to research, more and more Americans are turning to complementary and alternative methods for prevention, to sustain health and when conventional medicine fails. (References: Eisenberg, *NEJM*, January 1993. *JAMA,* July 1997; Astin, *JAMA*, Nov. 1998.) These studies document the free market still operating in healthcare, despite extensive regulation and manipulation. People are simply voting with their feet and their out-of-pocket dollars for therapies not covered by their insurance.

What is desperately needed for our health and our economy is a new healthcare paradigm that embraces treating the whole person with treatments that truly address the underlying problems, not just palliate the symptoms, forcing the patient to take multiple, expensive drugs year after year. We need access to all treatment modalities. Integrative medicine provides that paradigm. By addressing the deficiencies, imbalances, toxic exposures, and stressors that led to the illness, health and wellness can be restored, preventing illness and improving quality of life. But this change will not occur unless Americans stand up for their undeniable right to choose.

There is a strong precedent for the overwhelming success of such a grassroots movement. In 1994, faced with losing the freedom to purchase nutritional supplements, Americans sent more letters, faxes, petitions, and phone calls to Congress than on any other bill in the history of our country. This record still stands to this day. The result was the enactment of the Dietary Supplement Health and Education Act of 1994. While the FDA continues to erode the protections provided by DSHEA, the fact stands that we have the support and numbers to prevail, once the public understands what is at stake, namely, their life and their health.

"Unless we put medical freedom into the Constitution, the time will come when medicine will organize into an undercover dictatorship to restrict the art of healing to one class of men and deny equal privileges to others; the Constitution of the Republic should make a special privilege for medical freedoms as well as religious freedom."
- Benjamin Rush, M.D., Physician, signatory of the Declaration of Independence

Dr. Rush advocated for medical freedom to be included in the Bill of Rights. Unfortunately for us (and for the millions that have suffered and died due to suppression by the state of innovation in medicine), he did not prevail. It is time that we correct that gap in our Bill of Rights. It is time that we take back control of our health!

"In a free society men and women should not be prevented by Government from seeking medical remedies which they believe will be effective. Freedom of choice must be brought to bear upon the U.S. medical practice." - US Congressman Philip M. Crane, *Congressional Record*, 1975.

The International
March for Peace
in Central America
December, 1985-January, 1986

Blase Bonpane, Ph.D., is the Director of the Office of the Americas and a
Senior Research Fellow at the Council on Hemispheric Affairs in Washington,
D.C. He has led fact finding delegations and worked on the ground for peace
in Nicaragua, El Salvador, Guatemala, Honduras, Costa Rica, Panama, Peru,
Ecuador, Colombia, Mexico, Cuba, Japan and Iraq. He received the
Distinguished Peace Leadership Award from the Nuclear Age Peace
Foundation and numerous other commendations recognizing his commitment
to peace and justice, including several from the American Civil Liberties Union
and a Certificate of Commendation for his pursuit of peace in Central America
by the City of Los Angeles. His autobiography, Imagine No Religion, *was*
released in October of 2011. His previous books are: Civilization is Possible,
Common Sense for the Twenty-First Century; Guerrillas of Peace on the Air;
and Guerrillas of Peace: Liberation Theology and the Central American
Revolution. *He currently hosts the radio program* "World Focus" *in Los*
Angeles on Pacifica *network station KPFK. The Blase Bonpane Collection has*
been established at the Department of Special Collections of the UCLA
Research Library (Collection 1590).

The Central American Solidarity Movement spearheaded by The Office of the Americas had sent thousands of U.S. citizens to witness the Contra War in Nicaragua. This mercenary army was sent by the US government to overthrow the Sandinista Revolution. These paid killers were told not to attack the Sandinista Army but rather to attack liberation theologians, social workers, and any community supporting the Sandinistas.

As direct witnesses to this slaughter which led to the death of 40,000 citizens in Nicaragua we worked together with internationals to form the International March for Peace in Central America. This march was inspired by the Freedom Riders of 1961. Today it is not unrelated to the project of the Freedom Flotilla to Gaza.

We believe that the International March from December of 1985-January of 1986 had a direct impact on the uncovering of the Iran-Contra Scandal, August 20, 1985-March 4, 1987. This scandal involved the US government and the facilitation of the sale of arms to Iran which was under an arms embargo. The funds from these sales were used to support the Contra Mercenaries in violation of the Boland Amendment passed by the U.S. Congress. The Iran-

Contra scandal came to full view by November of 1986.

Reflecting on the International March for Peace in Central America, I cannot help but recall the Book of Exodus. After fleeing the oppression of Egypt, Moses was confronted by people who missed Egyptian food. Like us, they complained. They set out, not knowing where they were going. In similar fashion, our day-to-day insecurity led to anxiety. We made no attempt to claim this as the best march in Central America. It was the only march in Central America. It was a hope for nonviolent change. Success does not depend on how far we walked, but rather on the fruits of our walk. I wanted to avoid a "can-you-top-this atmosphere."

Our principal unity had to be on the objectives of the march, rather than on how, or where, we marched. There were constant differences of opinion. Some of the young people wanted to log-in more kilometers a day. Often, it was not possible to walk even five kilometers a day because of the armed conflicts and rigid opposition to the march in Costa Rica, Honduras, El Salvador and Guatemala. Many times it was necessary to repeat the axiom of Jesus, "Sufficient for the day is the trouble thereof." Calm and confidence were essential to combat anxiety and disaster.

I felt that every step of the march was on my shoulders. I knew that if I lost personal control at any moment it would be disastrous for the unity of the march. I found it necessary to debate other members of the directorate publicly. I had to ask people not to be so in love with their idea of the march that they would refuse alternative plans. I believe that what an individual wants to do is not necessarily the best thing for the group. Many great actions of history have required waiting. Milton said, "They also serve who only stand and wait." Gandhi, Martin Luther King, and Nelson Mandela knew when to wait. It is much harder to endure conflict than to attack.

One member of the directorate—whom I quickly understood to be totally out of sync with the peace movement—came up with a bizarre idea to get us to El Salvador. His proposal: take motorized canoes from Potosi, Nicaragua across the Gulf of Fonseca and land at the Salvadoran town of La Union. The Gulf is a convergence of El Salvador, Honduras and Nicaragua. U.S. warships frequently patrolled this area.

I personally opposed this proposal. It would have been an intrusion into one of the most strategic areas of the Central American conflict. In spite of my apprehension and the fact that the proposed action was planned for media purposes, a substantial number of marchers, especially the Danes, proceeded north on the way to Potosi. I kept thinking of the Gulf of Tonkin. Lyndon Johnson had used the Gulf of Tonkin as a contrivance just to get troops to Vietnam. We did not need to become part of a contrivance for the U.S. to send even more troops to this conflict.

Fortunately, the Nicaraguan government was alerted, and the dissident group received a plea from the Sandinistas to cease and desist. The government spokesperson told them that the Salvadorans would not permit the launches to land at La Union and that any such action would be taken as a provocation by Nicaragua. Nicaragua simply did not need more accusations of aggression as it bled from Reagan's war. The Danes reluctantly returned to the body of the march undaunted by having nearly created an international incident which could have been used against Nicaragua. Such adventurism always required urgent attention.

This same member of the directorate also called me a liar. When I called ahead to Costa Rica to tell them we were assembled and ready to proceed to their peaceful land, the spokesperson at the Quaker House in San Jose said, "Please listen, you have a member of the march who was arrested in Costa Rica some years ago. He is not welcome. The authorities here will pick him up and the march will be discredited. Please tell him to proceed to Nicaragua by air and rejoin the march there. He must not come to Costa Rica." I thought that message would be easily related by the individual named by the Costa Ricans. His response, however, was rage. He screamed that there was no such phone call from Costa Rica, and that I was doing this to keep him out of the leadership of the march. In his view, my intentions were subversive and paternalistic. He then got hopelessly drunk. This thorn in the side remained agitated, provoked, annoyed and disruptive for the duration of the march. What ultimately shocked me and taught me about the power of demagoguery was that some marchers looked to him as a legitimate leader.

During our seven-day vigil on the Honduran border, some of the participants from other nations were conspiring to simply march in defiance into the arms of the battle-ready Honduran Cobra Special Forces. In their view, such defiance was a sign of fortitude. They believed that the armed Honduran forces would not open fire. I did not share their enthusiasm. We were in a war zone.

Despite such tensions and conflict among the marchers, the contemplative heart of the march were the Buddhist monks. Their constant chants, drums and prayers served as a unifying element. For several days in Managua they chanted from sunup to sundown. They prayed through several days at the destroyed Cathedral of Managua, not eating or drinking.

One of my happiest recollections of the march was the chance to spend several hours with Rigoberta Menchu.[1] Here is my translation of her words that I taped as we sat together that blessed day. I write her words here in poetic form to represent the rhythm of her speech. A linguistic scholar told me that this great woman, who would soon receive the Nobel Peace Prize, actually speaks in verse. When I met her, she had only recently learned Spanish.

> The new president will make demands,
> But his demands will not be permitted.
> The military is going to select the Minister of Defense,
> Not the president.
> Power has been militarized.
> Our men are mobilized into Civil Patrols.
>
> A special *cedula*[2] awaits
> Members of the fundamentalist churches.

People of Nahuala have become fundamentalists.
People who used to be Catholics.
Why have they changed religions?

Because they are allowed to go further from the village
To look for firewood if they have a fundamentalist *cedula*.

People are forcibly acculturated.
They build highways.
They grow wheat instead of corn.
We are now living in total misery.
The new government will change names
But not reality.

We lack salt.
Salt is sold in pinches.
It costs three or four *Quetzales* per pound.
No one buys a pound,
So it is sold in pinches rather than pounds.
We are losing our culture.
There is no other way to preserve our lives
But to lose our culture.
Our people are prisoners in Chiapas.
We lack water.
Those in Campeche have it better.

Do you know that two thousand people died in Alta Verapaz
Rather than to give in to the army?
The army was going to put them into open prisons.
They refused.
This was not the only massacre.

They use certain churches to oppress us,
The Mormons.

A woman told me recently that she could no longer
Make *huipiles*[3].
But now that we cannot make *huipiles*,
We must make history instead.
After we make our own history,
We will make *huipiles* again.

Perhaps we are guilty of triumphalism.
We thought victory was right around the corner,
But this is not the case.
We must remember the slogans of

Grupo Apoyo Mutuo.[4]
To die honoring the names of our beloved.
They took them away living.
We demand to see them living.

The risk is very great,
Grupo Apoyo Mutuo is an obstacle to the new government,
And the new government might strike out at them.

I know my parents are dead and I am very proud of them.
But in my dreams I see my brothers and sisters.
I do not think they are dead.
Many times I dream they are alive.
They were captured by the army,
Taken away by night.
I really don't know if they are dead or alive.

And now I live in airports,
An international diplomat for the indigenous people of Guatemala.
I do not have a family, a house, a roof.
I do not have a country,
But hundreds of families are supporting me.

I have hope we can arrive.
We can have greater joy.
Drugs take people away from the realities of life,
But I have a vision of great change in the world.
People must make history.
I am disturbed by the level of ignorance in the United States.
I am disturbed by the degree of unconsciousness in the United States.
Your culture wants people to say, Oh, I didn't know that."

Rigoberta is the personification of the indigenous militant nobility that is sweeping through the Americas. Her words remain as an accurate account of what was happening in Guatemala at that time.

I often wondered about being in a position of authority. As a white male over fifty and a U.S. citizen, for many my status represented everything that is wrong with the world. The U.S. group especially marched with the weight of U.S. imperialism on our backs. Yet, I found that the more I was engaged with the marchers and the local people, the more this burden was overlooked.

The Danes and the Spaniards were aggressive, defiant, fearless, adventuresome, and ready at the proper moment to give a completely united front. Most of the Europeans were antireligious. At the beginning of the venture they had no concept of Liberation Theology. They did, however, come to respect the spiritual power of the Japanese Buddhist Monks. For instance, the dauntless Danes marching defiantly up to the Honduran Cobras, who were ready to kill them. All the while, they sang in Danish the "Ode to Joy" from Beethoven's Ninth Symphony. The image of these tough hard-drinking people will remain forever in my memory.

Some of the more pious, obedient and thoughtful marchers simply could not take the strain and left the march. The Canadians, who were particularly religious, often got fed up with the attitude of the more flamboyant types, such as the Danes and Spaniards who could sing all night, joke at everything and pay no attention to the needs of others who might have to sleep. Perhaps they could be categorized as thoughtless and selfish. Ironically, in spite of their constant complaining and all-night revelry, these thoughtless and selfish people were making history. They were able to persevere through the march simply by being themselves, while the more pious and obedient types were compelled to leave the march. It was as if the constant complainers were actually energizing their ambition to continue. By constantly reaffirming who they were and by being themselves, the Danes and Spaniards were able to go on. Even today I wonder: What would we have done if the Danes and Spaniards had stopped complaining?

The women complained less than the men did. How great women can look even without makeup, laundry facilities, water, and fancy clothing. Their femininity seemed enhanced along with their courage. I remembered the hymn, "How beautiful the feet of those who preach the gospel of peace," and reflected, not only the feet, but the whole person. They seemed to glow with an authentic spirituality that was not pietistic, that was not self-righteous and not sectarian. It was whole. Some of them had endured such harsh conditions before. For instance, the British women had served at the Greenham Common antinuclear demonstrations.

Occasionally one of the women would understandably become hysterical. The male members responded with their own version of hysteria: they became more macho and louder in an attempt to cover up the very real fear in carrying out the march. The constant exhaustion and threatening atmosphere began to take a toll on everyone.

At times the marchers looked to me like children, angry at their father. Apparently, I was the father figure. I frequently heard, "We're going to live our own life, this is our project and we're going to do it our way." It was necessary to point out time and again that the most dangerous acts were not necessarily the most effective and that sometimes the most dangerous acts were the most selfish. Even though I was often met with resistance by the young marchers, I considered my role as "father figure" necessary.

For instance, one young marcher was desperately ill; he became partially deaf and remained behind in Esteli, Nicaragua to rest and get some medicine at the local hospital. This was not sufficient. I came down from the Honduran border, went to his sickbed, got him up and put him into a cab bound for the Military Hospital in Managua. In obvious pain he shouted, "I don't want to go to the military hospital, I'm a pacifist." I countered, "You are going to the military hospital." In Managua, the efficient Nicaraguan doctor at the military hospital carefully diagnosed a mastoid infection, gave shots, medicine and a series of future appointments. The young man improved rapidly.

Ultimately, the International March for Peace in Central America was just the beginning. Our march had no historical precedent. Several nations came together as a family to observe areas of conflict and to petition for a peaceful settlement. Afterwards, many of the marchers stayed in Central America or returned later to do volunteer work. This was an incipient international solidarity movement which has now evolved globally.

Jorge Illueca's prophecy that our march would significantly influence Central American peace negotiations became a reality. Illueca was the senior Panamanian statesman and pillar of the Contadora peace process who spoke on the first day of our march in Panama. On that day, he said: "The march of these messengers of peace will light a flame of hope in the region and will contribute to creating a climate to stimulate and revitalize the Contadora negotiations." On February 10th 1986 his prophecy was fulfilled. All eight foreign ministers present at Caraballeda, including Mexico, Panama, Venezuela, Colombia, Peru, Brazil, Uruguay and Argentina, representing 85 percent of the people of Latin America, presented themselves to Secretary of State George Schultz in Washington, D.C., with the following demands:

- A permanent solution to the Central American conflict must be Latin American. It must not be considered part of the East-West conflict.

- Self-determination, non-intervention and respect for territorial integrity.

- Observance of human rights.

- Suspension of international military maneuvers.

- Formation of a Central American Parliament.

- Reestablishment of conversations between the United States and Nicaragua.

- No political, logistical or military support for any group intending to subvert or destabilize the constitutional order.

It was as if the Foreign Ministers could have taken these slogans directly from the banners of the International March for Peace in Central America. We believe that our constant support for Contadora as the avenue to a peaceful settlement prepared the way for the bold proposals of the meeting at Caraballeda in Venezuela on January 11th and 12th of 1986.

It was my hope that the relationship between malicious U.S. military adventures in Central America and the dismal domestic conditions in the United States would now be more obvious to U.S. citizens.

In the wake of the march the Costa Rican Association of Jurists also demanded of President Monge that Costa Rica Libre be dissolved because of its attack on the International March for Peace In Central America. The revulsion of the citizens of that country at the conduct of Costa Rica Libre's attacks on our march was so great that it appeared to tip the scales away from the pro-war candidate and lead to the election of the more progressive Oscar Arias.

The presence of peace marchers with the indigenous people of Guatemala as well as with the peasants of El Salvador and Nicaragua had a strategic value in protecting these people from attack. Peter Holding, an attorney from Australia and a member of the march identified the forced recruitment of Miskito Indians in Honduras for service in the Contras. He judged the Honduran judiciary to be non-functional and declared Honduras to be a de facto military dictatorship.

The people of Central America now understand that they can call on the international peace community to accompany them in times of struggle. I am extremely grateful to the people of the United States and the rest of the world who contributed their time, their efforts and their money to support this march. We believe we made an impact for peace in Central America. Central America certainly made an impact on us. We will let history make the final evaluation.

---

[1] Please read her book, *I ... Rigoberta Menchu: An Indian Woman of Guatemala*, Verso Press, London, 1984.

[2] Internal Passport

[3] Hand-woven blouses

[4] In English, "Mutual Help Group." This is a women's group in Guatemala that demands accountability of those who have disappeared and have been illegally detained by Guatemalan security forces.

Power vs. Force

*Steve Trinward was an SDS peace activist in the 1960s, a Libertarian Party
member/activist (even an LP-endorsed State Senate candidate once) in the
'70s, and a features journalist (covering war, draft and nuclear protests, etc.)
in the early '80s. He returned to LP activism from 1995 to 2004, working with
several candidates and issue-campaigns, culminating in a term serving on the
Libertarian National Committee, before returning to the political sidelines.
He's been a libertarian (and more recently, an anarcho-syndicalist) the whole
time. Steve has been an Associate Editor at* Rational Review News Digest *since
its inception in 2002; a freelance writer and editor for over 30 years; and an
outspoken advocate for peace and liberty through it all. He has been published
in a broad variety of venues, both print- and Internet-based, including* New
Age Magazine, Sierra Times, The Boston Phoenix, Rational Review, Liberty
for All, Nashville City Paper, Free Market News Network, Strike The Root,
WeRock Network, MethodsofHealing.com... *and* Inside Pool. *He also had an
essay included in* Why Liberty, *the previous book in this series. Steve currently
lives in Nashville, Tennessee, writing articles and songs, editing books
(including the one you hold in your hands) in a variety of genres, and working
on a book/CD project, entitled "Living Liberty," as well as on his own
memoirs.*

Preface: I get writing ideas in a variety of ways. This one comes from a lesson
a minister, presented on Groundhog Day, 2003, whose title I have even
appropriated for this piece. As a songwriter, I know the value of crediting co-
writers, so I eagerly acknowledge the work of the Rev. Dr. Mitch Johnson of
Religious Science of Nashville (now known as *Center for Spiritual Living
Nashville*[1]), without whom I'm not sure I could have formed this set of ideas.
Dr. Mitch describes his congregation and its doctrine as "freewill, holographic,
scientific panantheism." While preparing his presentation, Dr. Mitch came
across a book by Dr. David Hawkins, with the same title as his speech (and this
essay)—thus affirming that there are indeed "no accidents in Mind." (*The
lesson also contained quotations from the Hawkins book, as well as from
sources as diverse as the Bible, Deepak Chopra, Ralph Waldo Emerson and
Carl Jung; some of them are used here.*)

I have always had a problem with the word "power." It brings up for me
images like "might makes right"—which never seemed quite, well, right to me.
In the '80s and '90s, people talked about 'power lunches' and 'power ties';
neither of which I really wanted much to do with—I prefer a more leisurely
form at lunch, and I rarely wear ties (except, when one is expected, my
favorite: a John Lennon "Imagine" model, with piano-key blocks and lyrics
running down the middle).

I also firmly believed that an individual's proper relationship to "power" was confined to being its sworn enemy, but I have come to respect Power a lot more in recent times, and the Sunday lesson referred to above has only solidified that. Stated simply: ***Power is fine, and a good thing; it's Force that I detest and despise!***

Quoting from Dr. Mitch's lesson: "I have come to understand that true spiritual power arises from the meaning—the value, the life-enhancing qualities, the joy, the love—that we give to that which we want to create. In other words, this thing [we] want to experience or create … gives to all of life—not just you or me. It will bless the world, if you will…" He notes that the question to ask about a goal or intention is this: "Will this thing I want to create bless the whole world, or not? If it's a NOT, it won't come from true Power, it will come from Force!" He then cites the Hawkins book, finding more ammunition for his thesis:

> *"On examination, we'll see that Power arises from meaning. It has to do with motive; it has to do with principle. Power is always associated with that which supports the significance of Life itself. It appeals to that part of human nature that we call 'noble'… This contrasts with Force, which appeals to that which we call 'crass'. Power appeals to that which uplifts, dignifies and ennobles. Force must always be justified, whereas power requires no justification. Force is associated with the partial; power, with the whole. If we analyze the nature of force it becomes readily apparent why it must always succumb to power. This is in accordance with one of the basic laws of physics, because force automatically creates counter-force, and its effect is limited by definition.*

> *"Power on the other hand is still. It's like a standing field that doesn't move, Gravity itself, for instance, doesn't move against anything; its power moves all objects within its field, but the gravity in itself does not move. Force always has something to move against. Power gives life and energy; force takes these away. We notice that power is associated with compassion, and makes us feel positively about ourselves. Force is associated with judgment, and makes us feel poorly about ourselves…"[2]*

*   *   *

Okay, my turn. What I take from all of this is a very clear congruity between those sentiments and what true human rights are all about: a view of reality based on the essence of human Liberty, self-responsibility and voluntary action. I often note that the founder of Religious Science, Ernest Holmes,[3] did not set out to create a church, but a movement for consciousness-raising. (*And in all likelihood he was made aware not only of the potential for proselytizing his ideas, but of the tax benefits of adopting the former format, and so thus allowed his teachings to be couched in those terms—one more example of why income taxes should be abolished, as a distortion of good intentions!*)

To me, the key passage in this is that second paragraph, and the part about

Force requiring "justification—whereas Power is its own best witness. Exerting power, in the sense of using one's personal energy and intention toward a goal of higher-minded purpose, requires no apologies or explanations. Exacting force against an object—or worse yet, another human being— requires that any but the most callous totalitarian must first show good cause for the action (and even then, the action remains suspect until proven clearly to be necessary).

Then too, there is the affirmation that Power "*appeals to that which uplifts, dignifies and ennobles...*" When we look at Power as a manifestation of seeking a higher good—not the greater good of the many, at the expense of the few, but a truly larger purpose, in which the world of scarcity and win/lose gives way to one of abundance and win/win conditions. Seeking to maximize Liberty is clearly one of these higher purposes—perhaps the only real one, since the very nature of Liberty is that we can only possess it to the extent that we equally grant others the same autonomy of action sought for ourselves.

Then there is the association of Power with a unifying oneness, whereby all are treated as equally entitled (whereas Force is restricted to partial, at best dualistic, status). Force requires that there be some barrier or obstacle to push against—some Other that is not part of the force itself. Power issues from, and grows out of, a Unity of energy, and requires no such Other to work against, since it does not oppose, but merely radiates outward in harmony. Once again, this is displayed in such elements of Liberty as the Bill of Rights of the U.S. Constitution, which might better be defined as a "Bill of Restrictions on the Application of Force": each amendment is stated in terms like "Congress shall make no law" or "shall not be infringed"—showing not what latitude is allowed by some fiat (force), but how Liberty may not abridged, for ANY purpose.

Finally, in this one richly textured paragraph from Hawkins, there is the declaration of the supremacy of Power: "*If we analyze the nature of force, it becomes readily apparent why it must always succumb to power. This is in accordance with one of the basic laws of physics, because force automatically creates counter-force, and its effect is limited by definition.*" Here more than anywhere else is acknowledged the rightful ranking of these two elements, as the limitlessness of Power (which neither seeks nor has an adversary) outweighs the finite dimensions of Force.

Back to Dr. Mitch: "This sounds an awful lot like: Force is Judgment, and Power is Love," he says, noting that Hawkins himself arrives at the same conclusion later in the book. He then cites an oft-misused Biblical quote: "The teacher Jesus said something very interesting: *'Resist not evil.'* Now what I think he meant was this: We also know (from spiritual practice) that, *'what we resist... persists'*—And why? Because we give it the energy of our attention and emotion." He refers to high school physics: *for every action there is an equal and opposite reaction*, and concludes, "So resisting is in the nature of Force, rather than of Power.

"Now notice," he continues, "how similar to Eastern martial arts this is:

They teach you never to stand against a blow—to resist it, like a rock—but to bend with it, like a tree with the wind, and roll with it; you give it nothing to smack down. In like manner in our lives, we have to stop seeing people, situations and events as enemies to overcome, to force into submission and to our will. Because as we have come to see, there are no real enemies, except our own negative beliefs about who we are and what we can do."

ME: The thing that strikes me most about the lesson is how smoothly it fits with my own thoughts about resistance and battle, and the amount of energy one must expend, when treating the world as an adversary and not a companion and life-partner.

True, there may come a time when the only course open is direct struggle with the forces of tyranny; in truth, far too many of our compatriots have already fallen in such battles for self-determination and Liberty. Back in the early 1970s, Karl Bray went to prison for his convictions (preferring to do time, rather than submit to paying an income tax he saw as both illegal and immoral—and believing that the Fifth Amendment protection against self-incrimination actually meant something). While serving his sentence (peaceably, I might add) he died, under very suspicious conditions, after suddenly contracting cancer, despite no prior indications, symptoms or verifiable causes. (The Karl J. Bray Memorial Award for Activism is presented in his honor by the Libertarian Party of California to outstanding liberty activists in that state.)

He was only the first of several whose deaths were clouded with unanswered questions. During the early 1990s, the twin tragedies of Ruby Ridge, Oregon and Mount Carmel, Texas, woke many liberty-lovers out of their slumbers. In the former case, Bureau of Alcohol, Tobacco and Firearms officers entrapped Randy Weaver in a gun-dealing scam, attempting to force Weaver into becoming their informant (not because they suspected him of any wrongdoing). When he refused, a group of ATF thugs along with some from the Federal Bureau of Investigation) attacked him and his family, in the process murdering his wife, son and dog. This was followed by months of siege on the remaining family-members, before finally Weaver surrendered. (The FBI agent who shot his family got a commendation instead of a jail-sentence.)[4]

About the same time (1992-93), the Branch Davidians, a group of religious zealots under the leadership of David Koresh, were besieged in Texas for months by FBI agents and other aggressors, and then attacked and burned in their dwelling, using flamethrowers and other weaponry, by those same agents. In both cases, the victims were not being aggressive in any way, except to defend their right to live peaceably under their own way of life. (Meanwhile, that same FBI agent who murdered the Weavers was also present at this fiasco, and got another commendation for his bloodletting.)[5]

All of this should have reminded us of the fearsome Force that could be brought to bear, by a government bent on imposing its way at any cost. Instead, these and other outrages have mostly been forgotten by most Americans, in favor of the latest celebrity scandal or (worse yet) the latest fear-inspiring tactic perpetrated by our own government. The adage, "history doesn't always repeat itself, but it often rhymes," could be a wise watchword for those times, and those since then.

The real terror has continued, in many cases over the same issue: personal use of a controlled substance with proven medicinal properties, by those who have done nothing to harm anyone else in the process. Two examples are more than enough to make the case:

- In 2000, Peter McWilliams—a gentle, compassionate, self-help and inspirational writer, with multiple books about personal growth and healing on the best-seller lists—was basically murdered, by a system of "justice" that would not even uphold the laws (Proposition 215) already passed via legitimate citizen initiative. He had contracted both AIDS and non-Hodgkins lymphoma, and treatment for both was only manageable if he ingested cannabis to offset the nausea the prescribed medications brought on; without this to settle his stomach, he merely vomited the pills before they could have any effect at all.

  Nevertheless, the state of California where he resided chose to persecute and prosecute him for attempting to stay alive. While under home-arrest with an ankle-bracelet, for the use of this "illegal" herb (despite the prior passage of Proposition 215, legalizing cannabis for medical uses), he was prevented from using cannabis (except in the form of synthetic marinol capsules, which were nearly impossible for him to digest in his condition). Peter was found dead in his home by his housekeeper, having choked on his own vomit.[6]

- Another case, involving this same "illicit substance," is that of Steve Kubby (whose story is outlined in greater detail elsewhere in this book). This man has suffered for most of his life from a rare type of adrenal cancer, for which most medical authorities had signed his death-warrant decades earlier. He discovered, almost 30 years ago, that the medicinal qualities of marijuana served not only to mitigate the ravages of his condition, but actually restored him to fully functioning health. He became a poster-boy in the struggle to legalize marijuana for medicinal use, and was instrumental in the passage in 1996 of Proposition 215 in California, the first medical-marijuana statute in the U.S.

  However, the powers-that-be were now determined to stop him; they raided his home, found his "grow-room" (which under Prop. 215, was perfectly legal, as both he and his wife were official cannabis patients), and charged him with "possession for sale" and other spurious offenses. When his case was brought to court, a jury of his peers emphatically acquitted him, but the lawdogs were not done: they raided his home again, as well as that of an associate, and turned the discovery of a peyote-button and a marijuana-roach into a set of trumped-up administrative charges, and yet another impending trial.

Steve finally had to emigrate to Canada for a time, to find some release from California- and Federal-court harassment, over his personal use of something that was literally keeping him alive.[7] (Even after it was all over, having battled through challenges that broke up his marriage and divided him from his children for some time, Steve has continued to campaign for legalizing marijuana in California, including the current fight to "regulate marijuana like wine" now in progress and on the ballot for 2012.)

Even when someone is not ingesting marijuana—or any other "controlled substance," for that matter—the War on (Some) Drugs continues to have its "unintended consequences." This is due, not only to those caught in the direct crossfire of agent-vs.-drug-dealer shootouts, but also to misdirected raids on unsuspecting and innocent households (often warranted, at most, on the basis of a single informant's say-so).

The headlines still show up almost daily: in Atlanta, GA, in 2006, an elderly woman was attacked in her own home, by drug-warrior cops at the wrong address;[8] in Florida in 2008, an elderly man, seeking to chase away drug gangs, raised a weapon to scare away some men standing on his front lawn, not knowing they were drug-war agents, who pulled their own guns and killed him;[9] a Georgia pastor in 2009, after giving his last few dollars to help a parishioner in need, was accosted at the ATM while trying to refill his pockets, by drug-warriors in plainclothes, and when he tried to jump back into his car and flee (from what appeared to him to be a gang of thieves), they shot him to death, claiming he was a drug-dealer.[10] The list goes on, building each day with more outrageous and horrifying tales (*to confirm this quickly, just Google "drug war collateral damage"*).

Meanwhile, there are other tragedies, where lives are not ended, only turned into endless nightmares. For just one example, in Mississippi, back in 2001, local police raided the wrong house, once again looking for drugs. Cory Maye, a single-parent black man in his twenties, was invaded at gunpoint in the middle of the night.[11] Thinking he had been attacked by some gang or robbers, he shot back, killing one of the officers, defending himself and his baby daughter against the invaders. Problem was, the cop he shot was the son of the local police chief. A court-appointed lawyer, a mostly white jury and a zealous prosecutor combined to not only convict him of first-degree murder, but recommend and get the death penalty. Only after many years, with the significant help of one crusading journalist (Radley Balko), did Mr. Maye's case come up for serious review; in this instance, the news was good: a new trial was granted and he became a free man at last—after serving ten years in prison for defending against the attackers.[12]

With all of this to spur us on to direct confrontation, sometimes it's a wonder we're not all out in the streets, waging the revolutionary battles—like those brave Hungarians of the 1950s, dropping their tin pie-plates in front of the Soviet tanks, in hopes they would be taken for unexploded landmines. As I've noted, in one of my own songs, "Living Liberty":

Some people say the American dream has died
Slain on an altar of hatred, greed and fear
Some say it's time to take up arms
And fight for what's left of our rights
'Cause Armageddon time is drawing near... [13]

But what would be the point? The effort would be futile, scattershot and ultimately suicidal, given the present pro-war, pro-administration context of America in general. Martyrdom is for those who have given up all hope, and seek merely to leave a message or a battle-cry for the next wave of warriors. (Besides, as I go on to say, in that same song:

I think we still have a chance to turn this train around
With simple truths, built on solid ground:

   Walking in peace, choosing freely
   Hurting nobody along the way
   Standing in truth, sharing willingly
   Living Liberty, day by day... [14]

Back to Dr. Mitch again, this time on the use of "force" in getting your way. (In this case, he seems to be talking mostly about corporate ladder-climbing, but the premise is the same):

"I saw a Success seminar once that advertised this way: *'Smash the wall that blocks your path, by the projection of your Will!'* And I thought, hmm... That means first, there's a wall, a barrier, something against which I have to struggle and smash. And then, second, I've got to smash it and destroy it, to run over it. And third, I have to somehow summon all the energy and the fight and the weaponry I can bring, and the armor and the Will to do this! But do I really have to batter down doors in order to achieve my personal goals? Do I have to become stubborn, and grit my teeth, and be very willful and ... keep on pushing, despite the pain? Yes, you *can* create through will power, but ... it takes a lot of energy, and time and trouble, to keep an idea going and hold it together. Many successes have been created this way, but the price of that success is very high, in physical and mental well-being, when you have to force it."

ME: How much better would it be, if we just continued to rise above it, carrying on as best we can, knowing that in the long run we will prevail and succeed? How about if we use the *negative* energy that we get from the anger and rage these injustices bring up for us ... to create something *positive* around us? How about if we open our hearts to a bigger vision, of community and voluntarism and freedom—even if it's just among those with whom we live and work and love, those closest to our hearts and minds, and nearest to our vision of Liberty... and Peace... and Love?

528

Mitch: "A much saner approach to Power, to God, is to be willing to have it happen through you—and yes, there are times when you have to keep on keepin' on, even when you don't feel like it—but we use our Will to keep our minds on course, not to create with. An infinite, correlated intelligence and Love figures out the best way to do it, to be the greatest blessing to us, and the greatest blessing to all of Life. I'm not saying don't be persistent or determined. I'm saying, *'Be persistent and determined, without Fear or Force!'* . . . True Power comes from loving what we do, rather than forcing ourselves to do something that we really don't want to, and don't like."

ME: And once again, if we are going to succeed with this "revolution of ideas," it will be because we have come from what is highest and best within us, and the desire to bring Liberty to ALL people—not just from some "gimme mine" or "tit for tat" backroom deal, that puts one pressure-group in the driver's seat until the next one gains the favor of the King and his Court. It bears remembering that liberty is only truly a value to you if you're willing to grant it others—including (most especially) those who are unlike you in their beliefs, cultures and ways, so long as they behave peaceably.

Mitch: "The important point here is, Power, as we are talking about it, is spiritual Power. It's Love, really. If you are ever going to create a life, a city, a world free of enemies, free of poverty, free of obstacles to Good... then we have to free ourselves from Fear! Carl Jung said: *[T]hat I feed the hungry, forgive an insult and love my enemy—these are great virtues. But what if I discovered that the poorest of beggars, and the most impudent of offenders, are all within me, and that I stand in need of alms of my own kindness, that I myself am the enemy who must be loved.* Think of it like this: We can't generate Love from human Fear. Fear can only create Fear. Religions, nations, whole civilizations have crumbled, because someone was trying to force some kind of [what they considered] good into being on other people. That's that, *Oh, I'm gonna kill you for your own good!*"

ME: Yeah, *"We have to destroy the village in order to save it..."* The repetitions of history, from back when I was just beginning my libertarian journeys, echo eerily in the present context about "rebuilding Iraq" (while it still stands, before its impending destruction). The more I read and the more I see and hear, I become more cynical about the 'real reasons' given for war in the first place. Whether it's "Remember the Maine" (false excuse for Spanish-American War), Tonkin Gulf (bogus cause for accelerating Vietnam), the Lusitania (WWI), Pearl Harbor (real, but manipulated by FDR and his cronies to enter WWII), Weapons of Mass Destruction, "getting Osama" (Afghanistan) or some other false-flag effort... war has never been about what the powers-that-be claimed it was. The sooner we fully realize this and take it to heart, the sooner we can embark on the evolution to a species of humanoid who does not need to fight in order to justify our being.

A closing comment from Mitch: "As the Bible states, *Perfect Love casteth out Fear.* Only Love can create more love, and Love… is Power. Fear, on the other hand, is based on simple, five-sensory, *it's-out-there-and-it-might-be-out-to-get-me* information. But who we are, and what we are, are so much more than anything we might fear."

ME: As we say in unison at the Center, to close each prayer-treatment: "*…And so it is…!*" Beyond that, I'll close with the full lyric from another song I've written, one that more directly addresses this issue of why peace, and what the idea of non-aggression really means:

DON'T START WITH ME
©2011 *trin*SONGS [ASCAP]
Words & Music by Steve Trinward

Your Daddy's great-granddaddy met the Yankees at Bull Run
And Grandpa fought the war to end all wars
Your family's always ready when fighting's to be done
Standing tall to soldier for the cause
And now we've gotten one more plea from the reigning Commander in Chief
But maybe it's time to change those old beliefs

    DON'T START WITH ME and I won't start with you
    Let's let it be … I know you want it too
    We can have peace and love and freedom, and agree to disagree
    Pick your battles … but if you must make enemies
    DON'T START WITH ME

It's more than just a question of armies laying down guns
There's violence in every naked ape
The bloody thirst for vengeance… the need for Number One
To win it all whatever cost it takes
So how about we make a deal to talk it over instead of a fight
We'll blaze a new trail where might does not make right

    DON'T START WITH ME and I won't start with you
    Let's let it be … I know you want it too
    We can have peace and love and freedom, and agree to disagree
    Pick your battles … but if you must make enemies
    DON'T START WITH ME

        If nobody strikes the first blow … nobody needs to defend
        Isn't that a wiser way to live?[15]

----

[1] http://nashvillecsl.org/ I often refer to this (and its brother-center not far away at http://mccsl.org) as "my libertarian church."

[2] http://www.veritaspub.com/powervsforce.htm

[3] http://www.scienceofmind.com/about-holmes. Track down some of his writings to see a spiritual interpretation of liberty like few others.

[4] http://en.wikipedia.org/wiki/Randy_Weaver

[5] http://www.carolmoore.net/waco/. Carol's book is the definitive work on the subject of this tragedy.

[6] http://www.mapinc.org/drugnews/v00/n948/a03.html

[7] http://en.wikipedia.org/wiki/Steve_Kubby

[8] http://en.wikipedia.org/wiki/Kathryn_Johnston_shooting

[9] http://reason.com/archives/2009/01/23/the-drug-wars-collateral-damag

[10] http://www.freerepublic.com/focus/f-news/2800014/posts

[11] http://reason.com/archives/2006/10/01/the-case-of-cory-maye

[12] http://www.huffingtonpost.com/2011/07/31/homecoming-from-death-row_n_914470.html

[13] From "Living Liberty," words & music by Steve Trinward, © 1998, 2011 trinSONGS [ASCAP]. All rights reserved.

[14] *ibid.*

[15] "Don't Start With Me," words & music by Steve Trinward, © 2004, 2011 trinSONGS [ASCAP]. All rights reserved

Spain: A History of
Liberties Foreclosed by
the Imperatives of Empire

Thomas Harrington

*Thomas Harrington is Associate Professor of Hispanic Studies at Trinity
College in Hartford, CT where he teaches courses on 20th and 21th Century
Spanish Cultural History, Literature and Film. His areas of research expertise
include modern Iberian nationalist movements, Contemporary Catalonia, and
the history of migration between the peninsular "periphery" (Catalonia,
Galicia, Portugal and the Basque Country) and the societies of the Caribbean
and the Southern Cone. He is a two-time Fulbright Senior Research Scholar
who has lived and worked in Madrid, Barcelona, Lisbon, Santiago de
Compostela and Montevideo, Uruguay and speaks Spanish, Catalan, Galician
and Portuguese.*

Over the last decade or so, the term "empire" has begun to gain a much
stronger presence in our public life. People like Robert Kagan, Fareed Zakaria
and Niall Ferguson—darlings of a "strategic-thinking" establishment that until
quite recently viewed any application of that word to the US as clear proof of
one's unfitness to be taken seriously—now breezily invoke it to describe the
America's posture in the world.

Much as I hate to admit it, the change of rhetoric instituted by these media-
sustained paladins of a so-called "muscular" or "pragmatic" approach to world
affairs appears to have given many other writers—and, perhaps more
importantly, their editors—the courage to openly explore the long-present, if
systematically ignored, hegemonic imperatives of US life. One of the more
common ways of doing so has been through the technique of historical
comparison. Emblematic in this regard is Cullen Murphy's generally
thoughtful, *Are We Rome?*

I cannot say that I have read all that has recently been published in this
emerging genre of comparative imperial studies. But I have kept a close
enough eye on the books and articles appearing in this vein to note one very
curious thing: the near total absence of comparisons between the US and one of
the largest and more influential empires of modern history, that of Spain.

In seeking to locate the present-day US in the broader flow of time,
American writers (and Brits like Ferguson who spend a lot of time among us)
recur again and again to the examples of Rome and Great Britain. Indeed,
reading this new corpus of writings, one is left with the clear impression that
these are the *only* imperial trajectories containing any element of "pedagogical
value" for present-day American readers.

And this, despite the fact that for more than four centuries in the not terribly distant past (1492-1898) the Spanish Empire exerted an enormous cultural, economic and geopolitical force upon the world. The absence of the Spanish example in our current discussions of empire becomes even more remarkable when we consider just how deeply intertwined its history was with that of the US during the last two centuries of its existence, and just how much its demographic and linguistic legacies continue to influence the course of daily life in this country.

Why is the history of Spain and its empire so absent from our collective historical gaze? What, if anything, does its long history of hegemonic enterprises have to teach us? More specifically, what can we learn from the Spanish experience about the problem of generating and sustaining liberty under imperial conditions?

But before getting into all that, it would probably be helpful to discuss, albeit in a necessarily oversimplified way, what exactly we are referring to when we speak of the Spanish Empire.

The Creation of Imperial Spain

Modern Spain came into being with the merging of the Castilian (comprising mostly of the Western and Southern lands of the present state) and Aragonese (made up of the lands stretching from the mid-Pyrenees east to the northeastern-most section of the country's Mediterranean coast) crowns in 1479. The event took place against a backdrop of intense civil strife. For more than seven centuries the various Christian kingdoms of the Peninsula (including Portugal and numerous other entities later absorbed into either Castile or Aragon) had been engaged in an intense battle to purge "their" territories of the cultural and religious influence of the Arabian and Berber Muslims who had begun invading and colonizing the Iberian Peninsula at the beginning of the eighth century A.D.

The zeal to purify the land was extended to include the Jews whose families had either arrived in Roman times or had accompanied the Muslims invaders into the Peninsula. As this marathon exercise in ethnic and religious cleansing, known as the Reconquest, came to a "successful" close in the 1400s, numerous conflicts broke out among the "victorious" Christian potentates.

The aforementioned dynastic fusion, made possible by marriage of Ferdinand of Aragon to Isabel of Castile in 1469, led to a considerable diminishment of these tensions. At the time of the marriage, the ambitions of the strategic thinkers in the court did not appear to stretch much beyond the goal of effecting a durable pacification of the Peninsula, something that would, in turn, allow each of the co-equal monarchs—though they functioned as one in numerous matters, each had considerably more power than the other in their "home" turf—to pursue the longstanding interests of their respective kingdoms.

In the case of Ferdinand this meant reinforcing Aragon's long and successful commercial engagement (aided by its strong influence over Sicily and Sardinia) with the other commercially-minded peoples (e.g. Greeks and the Maghrebis of Algeria and Tunisia) of the Mediterranean. For Isabel, the challenge lay in consolidating her kingdom's potentially very rich agricultural and livestock-raising economy.

These relatively modest ambitions were altered by two key events:

The first was the marriage of Ferdinand and Isabel's daughter, Joana, who was (already being groomed to administer the two kingdoms of her parents as one) to Philip of Hapsburg, son of the Holy Roman Emperor Maximillian, which is to say, the son of a man who exercised effective control over the territories which make up today's Holland, Belgium, Germany and Austria, as well as healthy portions of France and northern Italy.

Though the marriage was wildly unsuccessful on the personal level, it had revolutionary effect on the course of Spanish and world history. Because he predeceased his father, Philip never gained full power over all of the territories theoretically subject to his control. However his son did. From 1516 until his death in 1558, Charles I ruled over a unified monarchy whose dominions stretched, albeit with notable gaps in France and Italy, from Gibraltar to Vienna, and for a time, as far east as Budapest.

The second key event was Isabel's decision to finance a maritime expedition to "the Orient" under the leadership of a Genoese mariner and long-time servant of the Portuguese crown (at the time Europe's unparalleled leader in naval technology and, not coincidentally, the colonial exploitation of African and Asian wealth) named Christopher Columbus. Columbus' "discovery" of America led to an extremely rapid and widespread colonization of much of the western world. By the middle of the 16th century Spain could speak (in addition to all of the European territories mentioned above) of having effective control over much of the Carribbean, large swathes of what is now the US Southwest as well as the important population centers of today's México, Peru, Ecuador and Bolivia.

In 1565, the Spaniards began their three-century domination of the vast Philippine Archipelago in East Asia. And owing to a dynastic merger in 1580 with Portugal, the huge holdings of the empire directed from Lisbon, which by then included Brazil, the coastal areas of today's Angola and Mozambique and myriad military-commercial outposts on the coasts of Africa and South Asia (e.g. Cape Verde Islands, Mombasa, Madagascar, Hormuz, Goa, Sri Lanka, Macau), also came under control of the Spanish Hapsburgs! This, while the Spaniards were steadily increasing their "hard" dominion over Central and South America through military expeditions south (from the Andes) to Patagonia and north toward today's Colombia and Panamá.

I hope the picture is coming into focus. Looking at a map of the world from 1600, we would see the Spanish presence, or perhaps more accurately, the presence of people working at the behest of, or in cooperation with, the Spanish Hapsburgs, all over Europe, America, Africa and Asia. Its dominions were obviously much grander than those of Rome at its zenith and quite comparable with, if not superior to, those of Great Britain at the height of its power in the 19th century.

Indeed, if we accept the ability to impose one's language on others as a key barometer of imperial strength, we would have to conclude that Spain was a much stronger "civilizing force" (yes, I realize it is a very problematic term) in its moment, than Great Britain ever was during its time of unquestioned hegemony. As anyone who has traveled to India or Pakistan can tell you, English remains (despite the widespread impression to the contrary in the US) a language that, despite its official status, is spoken fluently by a relatively small segment of the population in those places. Contrast that with the situation in Central and South America where, outside of certain recognizable pockets of indigenous culture (and of course, Brazil), Spanish clearly dominates everyday communication. And to the extent to which we want to view Portugal and its holdings as part of the great Spanish imperial experience (the dynastic merger mentioned above lasted from 1580 until 1640) we would have to also speak of the relatively impressive degree of Portuguese linguistic penetration achieved in Brazil, Mozambique, Angola, and for a considerable amount of time in Goa and Macau.

So why don't most Americans know this? Or if they know it, why do they tend not to bring it up when they deign to philosophize about the fate of empires?

The Black Legend

A chief reason can be found in what historians of the Hispanic world refer to as the "Black Legend"—that is, the strategically orchestrated demonization or disqualification all things Spanish, especially the country's comportment as a colonizing power in the Americas. The forces that gave rise to Spain's imperial expansion were derived from a largely pre-literate cultural matrix. Accordingly, written propaganda aimed at "selling" the enterprise to the so-called masses of Europe, played a relatively small role in the country's imperial push.

However, by the time the British, Dutch and various of the German principalities under Hapsburg control began to challenge Spanish control of the world system in the late 16th and early 17th centuries, print culture was becoming quite firmly established in Europe, especially in its northern regions. And these insurgent powers, especially the British, wasted no time in using it to wage information campaigns against their great geopolitical nemesis to the south. Over the ensuing decades these early practitioners of "perception management" successfully crafted and deployed an image of a "savage," "cruel" and "bloody" Spain, of a "dark" and "violent" race that callously disregarded the humanity of its Amerindian subjects.

The Imperial Spaniards, of course, possessed all of these horrible traits in abundance. But what imperial power does not? Does anyone really think the British conquered and despoiled the lands they conquered and despoiled by being gentle, kind and considerate? But I am willing to guess that most readers of this article would, if told that they must assign those adjectives to either the Spanish or the British imperial legacy, would, owing to the lasting legacy of the Black Legend, be much more inclined to apply them to the former than the latter. And this despite the fact (made abundantly clear when we compare the historically high levels of miscegenation—a pretty good indicator of ultimate human value one assigns to "the other"—in the Hispanic world with the historically low levels found in North America and Australia) that the penchant to segregate and/or assassinate non-European natives appears to have been much, much stronger among the sons and daughters of the British Isles than the children of Iberia.

As the number of "fresh" Spanish conquests began to wane, and with it, the size of the country's relative geopolitical advantage over the emergent powers of the European north, the promoters of the Black Legend began to shift their rhetoric from an emphasis on Spain's "cruelty" and "bloodthirstiness" to one centered on the empire's "backwardness" and beholdenness to Catholic "superstition." This change of tone coincided with an effort to paint the defeat of the Spanish Armada by the British in 1588 as the effective "end" of Spain's run as a leading power on the world stage.

While 1588 was obviously an important moment of change for the Spanish Empire and the overall geopolitical history of early Modern Europe, it was by no means the end of the line for Spanish might. During the 17th and part of the 18th century Spanish troops were still very widely deployed across the European continent and quite actively engaged in struggles against a broad slate of real and perceived enemies. And in America, Spanish bureaucrats, working within a vast and elaborately organized vice-regal system would minister to the affairs of state, and within the narrow confines of their undemocratic and colonialist view of life, to the needs of the continent's people, for another 250 years in México, Central America and South America, and for another 310 years in Cuba and Puerto Rico!

Was this bureaucracy corrupt and inefficient by today's standards? In all probability, yes, but here again we must look at the results. Whatever its faults and shortcomings, and I assure you there were many, Spain managed to spread the key tools of its culture (language, religion, literature, art and urban-planning) over a truly vast realm with a degree of uniformity--demonstrated by the quite exceptional degree of mutual intelligibility enjoyed today by Spanish-speakers from different countries and widely dispersed geographical areas—seldom, if ever, seen in the history of the world.

But perhaps the most damaging of the "truths" (at least in terms of its influence on future historians and commentators) spread by the northern shapers of the Black Legend is the idea that the Iberian peoples never truly participated in three trends or movements widely portrayed as being necessary precursors to the development of modern democratic governance: a) feudalism, which is to say, the development of a contractual relationship between the lord and his agricultural workers; b) the Renaissance; and c) the Reformation.

In other words, according to this view, the Spaniards and their numerous cultural offspring in America effectively "lacked the goods" to become anything more than the autocratically inclined and Caudillo-addicted peoples we all "know" them to be today.

When we apply a closer and less blatantly ideological focus to the historical record, a much different and more complex picture emerges. We can see that the peoples of the Iberian Peninsula were not terribly different than other Europeans when it came to recognizing the cultural centrality of the individual, the value of laws and the pursuit of well-organized political liberty.

Indeed, during certain moments of history, they were among the continent's leaders—at least conceptually—in these fields. But time and time again, the need to make war and defend the prerogatives of Empire, which is to say, the "right" of social elites to form armies in order to rob other peoples at the point of a gun, foreclosed the further development of social movements related to these ideas within the society.

A History of Liberty Foreclosed by the Imperatives of Empire

In the Anglo-Saxon rendering of the march of human liberty, 1215 has an exalted status as it was the year in which King John of England signed the *Magna Carta*, a document that subjected his heretofore arbitrary and absolute royal powers to certain limitations, especially in the realm of punishment for alleged offenses against the society.

But more than a hundred years before, in the Catalonian territories of Spain, Count Ramon Berenguer I (1023-1076), the effective monarch of the region, accepted the imposition by a restive noble class of numerous of written stipulations regarding the exercise of power within his realm. These collected fragments of Roman law, Visigothic law and brand new Catalan statutes, known as the *Usatges*, would be constantly updated over the ensuring decades and centuries until being adopted in the second half of the 13th century by *Jaume I*, the king of Aragon as the basis for a constitutional regime that had clear and theoretically enforceable limits on the exercise of royal power. During the beginning of this period, as the great Catalan cellist Pau Casals reminded the world in his famous 1971 speech before the UN, the Catalan gentry also established a mechanism, known as the *God's Peace and Treaty*, for *peacefully* arbitrating disputes between them!

Not surprisingly, Catalonia-Aragon enjoyed an extraordinary burst of vitality over the next two centuries, especially in the realm of commercial activities in the Mediterranean. While it would be an exaggeration to characterize this as an era of total peace, it can be said that the armed struggles of this time were carried out against peoples that, owing to their general geographical proximity to Aragonese possessions, could be reasonably construed, or presented as legitimate struggles of self-defense.

When Aragon became conjoined to Castile in 1479, it was not clear which, if either, of the kingdoms would emerge as dominant over the other. That said, there is, looking back, reason to believe that had things stayed as they were at the time, Aragonese customs, forged by a relatively advanced commercial economy and incipiently modern social regime rooted in a stable system of laws, might very well have gradually come to dominate the new polity.

But the "discovery" of America by Columbus in 1492 and the dynastic merger with the Hapsburgs, changed all that. From this time onward, Spain was a country where Castile's (as it was Isabel and not Fernando who had underwritten Columbus, her kingdom held near exclusive title to, and responsibility for, the new American realm) need to maintain and expand the American Empire, and the conjoined state's need to insure control over the lands traditionally controlled by the Hapsburgs in Northern Europe, came to dominate most facets of peninsular life.

It was not long before the subjects of the realm began to express their irritation in the new Imperial reality. In 1520, the governance councils, or *Comuneros*, of a number of large Castilian cities banded together to reject the new taxes levied by the crown (needed to pay for the bribes necessary to insure Charles's elevation to the post of Holy Roman Empire and the troops in America). The idea was to create an autonomous federation of city-states wherein peace and commerce would dominate, and where armed force would only be employed where in clearly defined cases of *local self-defense*. In keeping with that vision, the *Comuneros* formed militias designed to protect their innovative governance project against royal encroachment.

The result? A bloody and absolutely pitiless government assault on the secessionists in the spring of 1521. The crown had spoken quite eloquently: It would not permit mere subjects of the government, those that it regularly conscripted into its armies and taxed as it saw fit, to exercise local sovereignty and question the prerogatives of its imperial march to glory.

The scenario would be repeated from time to time over the next century as the spendthrift empire, showing clear signs of sclerosis, fought to maintain it hegemony in an ever-more competitive Europe. In 1640, as Spain was involved in an intense conflict with France as part of the Thirty Years War as well as serious (not to mention bloody and costly) challenges to its rule in the Netherlands, King Philip IV's main counselor, the Count of Olivares, acting over the pointed warnings of Catalan-Aragonese representatives to the court, broke longstanding custom by ordering the forced quartering of royal troops in Catalan villages and towns.

The commercially-minded Catalans, who had long chafed at the attempts by the unified crown with its seat in Castile to engage them and their considerable resources in foreign wars that they knew would only deplete them, erupted in rebellion. Allied with the French, the Catalans managed to achieve a military stalemate against the Spanish Empire for nearly a decade, a period during which they revived their culture and their *real* organs of self-government. But when the Peace of Westphalia of 1648 ended both the Dutch Rebellion and the Thirty Years War, Madrid was free to turn up the heat against it "fellow countrymen" in Catalonia. The culminating moment of the attack was the brutal siege of Barcelona of 1651-52 in which the population of the Catalan capital was literally starved into surrender.

For Spain, the cost of its imperially-induced brutality against its own subjects would be steep. Catalonia was nominally returned to the fold, but it "came back" impoverished and with a bitterness and distrust toward Madrid that really has never been expunged. It also came back much smaller as its centuries-long control of territories on the north side of the Pyrenees around Rousillon and Perpignan were ceded to the French crown under the Peace of the Pyrenees in 1659. And perhaps most significantly, the government's mistreatment of its own people in the name of war led to Madrid's loss of effective control over Portugal and its sprawling overseas empire.

As we have seen, Portugal was joined to Spain in 1580 through a dynastic union. However, large sectors of the Portuguese population, including the nobility never really accepted the idea that Madrid could or should effectively direct their destiny as a nation. So, when Catalonia rose up against Madrid in 1640, a group of Portuguese nobles under the direction of the Bragança family did as well. This meant that an already grossly overstretched Spain had, in effect, to choose between retaining control over Portugal or over Catalonia. As we have seen, it chose Catalonia, and as a result, Portugal re-acquired the sovereignty lost some six decades before.

I do not think that the all-too-familiar self-defeating dynamics of compulsive imperial war-making could be made any clearer. By 1620 Spain was, with its recent and present wars in America, Holland, Germany, Italy and in various points in the Mediterranean owing to ongoing confrontations tensions with the Ottoman Empire, already blatantly in the throes of what we would today call "Imperial Overstretch." At this point, representatives of its most commercially and socially advanced area, Catalonia, sought to curb Madrid's seemingly insatiable appetite for war. Rather than listen to their pleas, however, the empire decided instead to "teach them a lesson" in 1640 about the need to "support the troops" more vigorously. The result? Two more decades of brutal war, the only clear results of which were to foment internal bitterness, diminish geopolitical power and greatly deplete the national treasury.

One of the key tropes of the Black Legend, mentioned above, is the idea that Spain's iron embrace of the Catholic Church (or vice-versa) effectively condemned it to a secondary place in the European concert of nations at a key moment of the continent's developmental history. The underlying idea here is that it was the Renaissance, and perhaps more importantly, the Reformation, that paved the way for the peoples of the north to develop the traits we commonly associate with modern social development: capitalism, industrialism and, finally, parliamentary democracy. Since Spain never really participated in these movements, owing to the unbreakable grip of a deeply hermetic and essentially medieval church, the story goes, it never really stood a competitive chance against Great Britain and the Netherlands as the high modern era dawned.

To paint the Iberians as a people who "missed" the Renaissance is, like the argument about their not participating in feudalism, to conveniently forget a number of very salient facts.

Perhaps the most important of these is that the Renaissance might very well never have taken place, or certainly would have been greatly delayed in developing, were it not for Spain!

Implied in the name of the movement is the idea of re-birth, and more specifically, the re-birth after several hundred years of "darkness" of the enlightened and humanity-centered (as opposed to God-centered) ideals of the classical eras Greece and Rome. So, a key question becomes, how did the texts containing those ideals, written in Greek and Latin, make their way into a

European populace that, by the first years of the second millennium was, while maintaining Latin as a language of erudition, given over ever more fully to communicating in the vernacular?

Much of the credit can be given to Iberian kings, especially Alfonso X "The Wise" (1252-1284) of Castile for sponsoring the translation of numerous Greek, Latin, Hebrew texts, and with them, numerous Arabic treatises on scientific and technical matters (at the time, Arab scientific skills were well ahead of those of Christian Europe) into Castilian. From there, the ideas made their way into the other vernaculars of Europe, such as Italian. A similar, and many would argue, even more vigorous transfer of Classical ideals and Arab technical know-how began to take place in the Catalan sector of the Peninsula (always in much closer contact with Italy than Castile), during the mid-14th century under the leadership of Bernat Metge.

Should there be any doubt about the emergence on the Iberian Peninsula of a vital outlook of incipient modernity rooted in the drama of the individual human being before a complex, difficult and morally ambiguous world, one need only look at the novel (arguably the first in the world) *Tirant lo Blanc* written in Valencian Catalan by Joanot Martorell in the mid 15th century and published posthumously in 1490, or the generically-hybrid (part drama and part novel) *La Celestina* published in Castilian by Fernando de Rojas in 1499. Indeed, it is hard to think of any work written previous to the 20th century that conveys as powerfully and as starkly as the *La Celestina* the idea of a world where, for better or worse, God has, for better or worse, stopped watching actively over his human "flock."

Many of the questions which were to inform the launching of the Reformation were raised by the great Dutch Renaissance humanist and priest, Erasmus, before the religious war—rooted in the ideals of Reformation—swept across the European continent in the mid 1500s. In other words, Erasmus sought, along with numerous others, to find a way to reform a clearly decadent and corrupt Catholic church *from within*. His ideas were, at least for a time, well-known and quite enthusiastically professed in Spain by church leaders like Juan and Alfonso de Valdés, and Bishops Gattinara, Manrique and Fonseca. And one of his most effective and respected humanist colleagues on the pan-European level was the Valencia-born Joan Lluis Vives.

So what happened? Why, if it possessed most of the same humanistic and reformist impulses found in the future Protestant societies of the north did the Spanish process of change and modernization peter out?

Though the factors leading to this stagnation are many, a strong case can be made that it was the imperatives of Empire, especially the need to sustain wars on multiple fronts that, as much as anything else, inhibited the flowering of new and progressive social ideas in Spain.

Wars of Religion, or Wars of Empire?

According to most standard histories of Europe, the origins of the wars which rocked northern and central Europe in the years between 1550 and 1650 can be traced, in one form or another, to Martin Luther's decision to post his *95*

Theses, with their numerous complaints against the conduct of the Rome-based papacy, to the door of the Wittenburg Castle Chapel in the fall of 1518.

Like all historical interpretations, this one has its implied points of emphasis. For example, its mention of Luther's famous document draws the reader's attention to the theological reasons for the century of strife. And insofar as the narrative hints at the existence of geopolitical factors, the reader's gaze is directed toward the tensions between the "reforming" German principalities and Rome.

There is really nothing grossly incorrect about this emplotment (a term invented by Hayden White, to speak of the way historians "lay out" the narrative of history) of events. Of course the Reformation was a theological struggle. And it was clearly aggravated by long-simmering German political resentments toward Rome.

But as we know from more recent events, the official historical discourses about the origins of wars (*e.g.*, weapons of mass destruction, desire to curb Islamic terrorism) often leave out a number of very key motivations (Israeli geopolitical aims, the grand game of oil politics and, with it, long-term US pipeline and basing strategies) or reasons for the conflict. In the case of most accounts of the European religious wars of the 16th and 17th centuries available to US readers, studies which are grounded overwhelmingly in an Anglo-German view (with the occasional French-centered study) of the Old Continent, the Imperial "needs" of the Spain-based Hapsburgs are seldom given their due weight.

Let's take the matter of Religion. While the *theological imperatives* of the emerging Protestant movement were certainly real, a strong case could be made that they were only truly important (e.g. war-worthy) to the extent that they challenged the overall integrity of Madrid's dominant *geopolitical role* within Europe.

It has been said that when talking about the imperatives of the today's U.S. leadership class, it is nearly impossible to discern where its supposed interest in democracy ends, and its interest in its special variety of arms (and finance-driven crony capitalism) begins. There was a similar dynamic between Church and Empire in Spain.

To be a "good Spaniard" was—going back to the Reconquest—to be, necessarily a "good Catholic." Although there were sometimes turf skirmishes between them, the Church and the Spanish state worked hand in glove throughout the Empire in the pursuit of common goals. Indeed, it would have been next to impossible to conceive of the latter without the former.

Similarly, while the Papacy had, as always, some pretensions to being a supranational or transnational organization it was, not unlike the U.N. of today, heavily dependent on the funding and political cover provided by its most potent "national" backer, Spain, for its continued survival and effectiveness. This meant, in effect, that any attack upon the Church and its prerogatives was also viewed as an attack on the integrity of the Spanish Empire.

Viewed in this light, we can see the insufficiency of the "theological" and/or Germany vs. Rome framings of the Religious Wars mentioned above.[*]

He may not have been completely conscious of what he was doing, but when Luther made his famous complaints against "Rome" he was effectively aiming a dagger at the very heart of the Spanish Empire.

If it helps, think of it as being a bit like when Saddam Hussein, as president of a country with some of the world's largest oil reserves, said, in the Fall of 2000, that he would only accept payment for Iraqi petroleum in euros. With this seemingly innocuous statement about currency denominations, he sent planners at the Pentagon and State Department into a frenzy... and probably sealed his personal fate.

Why? Because to suggest that the world's largest known pool of oil would go on the market *in euros* was to call into question the role of the dollar as the world's reserve currency, and from there, the U.S. government's ability to continue to fund its huge deficits with semi-forced sales of its bonds to cash rich foreign nations such as China and Japan. Such a challenge to the underlying architecture of the US-led system could not go unanswered. And, as we all know, it did not.

And just as the U.S. tried several punitive techniques to re-assert its control over Hussein and his country in the decade or so leading to the invasion of 2003 (the currency announcement of 2000 was, as we know, the culmination of several decades on not so subtle challenges to Washington's "right" to use Iraq and its oil as it saw fit), the Spanish Empire sought to use its leverage over both the papacy and a number of German states—what we would today probably call "soft power" to suffocate, redirect and co-opt the rebellious energies unleashed by the publication of Luther's famous treatise. None of them worked.

So, in 1530, the Emperor Charles (Charles V of the Holy Roman Empire and Charles I of Spain) traveled to Augsburg with the stated intention of listening to the dissenting clerics and princes. He clearly hoped that his personal presence would compel them to "see the light" and work with him to generate a concerted response to the "Islamic terror" that was encroaching on the Empire from the East. However, Luther and his followers refused to renounce their critiques of the established order.

Faced with the recalcitrance of the Reformers, Charles did what imperial leaders tend to do with alarming regularity: he doubled down on the very policies that had alienated his would-be imperial collaborators in the first place. From this point onward, he and his immediate successors along with their numerous proxies would mercilessly target northern Protestants as "part of the problem" thus further complicating the already extremely complicated task of maintaining the integrity of his sprawling realm.

Indeed, within a few short years, the task of preserving the primacy of a clearly decadent Catholic Church through bullying, warfare and doctrinal intimidation became the new organizing principle of the Empire. Known as the Counter-Reformation, this highly organized attempt (marked by the convocation of the Council of Trent and the elevation of Jesuits to central role ecclesiastical affairs) to neutralize the inevitable rebellion against its own cruelty and greed, had much in common with today's US "War on Terror." In effect, Spain sought to forcefully undo a situation of its own making that, in all likelihood, could not have been reversed.

And like today's "War on Terror" the Spanish Empire's hopeless drive to reassert Catholic primacy in Europe and the world not only led to the senseless deaths of innocent soldier-peasants all across the Old Continent and throughout the Mediterranean but had profound effects on Spanish domestic life.

Remember that incipient culture of Renaissance Humanism and Erasmian Reformism mentioned earlier on? Well, it was quickly and harshly stamped out by the "you are either with us or against us" outlook of the captains of the Counter-Reformation. There was now no place in society for such stark and direct searches for the truth. Rather, Spanish creators and thinkers, aware that any deviance from for the official pro-imperial and pro-orthodox line could land them in trouble with authorities, re-directed their energies toward the creation aesthetically appealing, if ideologically opaque and obscure, artistic forms.

This desire to escape into the refuge of the "ornamental jungle" is the origin and quintessence of the Baroque, a sensibility that would dominate Spain's artistic life for the duration of the empire's lengthy decline. The singular genius of Cervantes, a convinced Humanist condemned to live at the height of the Counter-Reformation's heedless furor, lies in his ability to use humor and irony to point out the blatant absurdities of the fear-infused and fundamentally escapist Baroque mind.

Sadly, most of today's Americans know little of the Baroque and its origins. If they had a basic grasp of its ontology, they would, I suspect, see its discursive offspring all around us. They would see it, just to name a few of the hundred examples that could be given, in: a) verbose and supposedly "comprehensive" analyses of the current budget deficit that always manage to avoid the question of defense spending and the role of crooked financiers in creating it; b) the furious calls for Iran to dismantle its non-existent nuclear program which make absolutely no mention of the fact that our closest ally Israel has several hundred completely uninspected nukes aimed at the Islamic Republic; c) a government that lectures other nations on democracy and human rights while aggressively reducing both at home; and d) a President, who was elected on the slogan of "change," who has done less to break with his successor's policies than perhaps any opposition-party President in the history of the Republic.

As damaging as this calculated snuffing out of the country's incipient culture of modernity was Spain's reckless depletion of its national treasury through the persecution of war. The Spain of the 16th and 17th centuries lacked little in the way of the resources. This generally favorable circumstance was further bolstered by massive influx of ill-gotten gains (though it by no means legitimates them morally, it is true that the savage wars of depredation waged on the natives of America would "pay for themselves" well into the 18th century) from its American Empire. However, the European and Mediterranean conflicts waged almost non-stop between 1540 and 1650, and the aforementioned conflicts with Portugal and Catalonia waged between 1640 and

1668, turned Spain into a hugely indebted nation, dependent like the US today, on the willingness of one of its emerging geopolitical rivals (Holland) for the continuing survival of its financial system.

Though we can never turn back the clock on historical realities as large as the ones outlined above, it is nonetheless interesting to speculate about what might have happened had Spain not become entangled in a series of Imperial engagements at the start of the 16th century.

There is every reason to believe that, if it had been left to its own devices, the Aragonese part of the empire would have continued on a path to prosperity that would have paralleled (with its emphasis on manufacture and trade) that of the Italian principalities with which it had so much in common. And the program enunciated by the *Comuneros* in their rebellion against the monarchy gives us reason to believe that this fundamentally mercantile (as opposed to martial) form of social organization might very well have spread to the less-developed spaces of Castile in short order.

Had Spain not been obsessed with maintaining an empire it clearly would have been able to face the "challenge" of the Reformation with a much more flexible and equanimous spirit. Rather than seeing it, as today's fear-mongers like to say, as "an existential threat," its leadership class might very well have seen it as the force of intellectual innovation and much-needed reform that it really was. The fact that Erasmus, the movement's most illustrious precursor, was warmly welcomed by at least a part of Spanish clerisy in the years before 1530 suggests that such a path of evolution is not wholly beyond the realm of possibility.

Had Spain not been entangled in Imperial affairs it clearly never would have had the vast riches it stole from the Native Americans. But then again, it would have never lost that same booty in its century of European wars and against "unbelievers" and "heretics." And without those wasteful wars which, as I have suggested were as much or more about shoring up the architecture of empire as they were about theology, the Spanish government never would have found itself in the position of forcing the Catalans to quarter imperial troops against their will, a situation that led directly to nearly three decades of costly war between Madrid and Barcelona on one hand, and Madrid and Lisbon on the other.

Without these internecine conflicts provoked by the imperatives of empire, the Peninsula might, as the 19th and early 20th century Iberianists like to remind us, very well have evolved in a much more unified fashion, developing a system wherein each of the three major culture-nations (Catalonia, Castile and Portugal) played to their strengths (manufacture, agriculture and deep-water trade respectively) in the context of federal or confederal system.

Napoleon, Liberalism and the Drive to "Save" the American Empire

Spain's role as major player in European affairs came to a screeching halt in 1714, with the conclusion of the War of the Spanish Secession. In the ensuing century, using ideas and methods borrowed from the French Bourbons who now sat on the throne, the Spaniards rationalized their exploitation of

American wealth. This led to an unexpected uptick in Spanish economic fortunes as well as a fairly vigorous experiment in "enlightened despotism" during the reign of Charles III (1759-1788).

When Napoleon, purporting to bring the liberating ideals of the French Revolution to the Spanish people, invaded the country in 1808, the Spaniards became divided against themselves. The great majority, viewing the French as nothing more and nothing less than odious foreign invaders, organized armed resistance designed to expel them and bring back the old absolutist monarchy.

However, there was a small but very influential minority of courtiers (many of whom had imbibed the modern ideas of the *Encyclopédie* during the reign of Carlos III) who while they shared the armed rebel's (the term *guerilla* was coined precisely in this context) desire to end the occupation, believed that any future Spanish monarchy must have carefully delimited powers. In other words, they believed that Spain must evolve toward one form or another of truly representative government.

In the Fall of 1810 these "liberal" (the word was invented precisely to describe the forward-looking Spanish activists obsessed with liberty) partisans began meeting in southern Spain under the effective protection of the British navy. Sixteen months later they produced a document, the Constitution of Cádiz, which aimed to give the Spanish citizenry liberties that had seldom, if ever, been enjoyed under a monarchical system.

Writing a constitution was one thing. Making it the law of an occupied land was quite another. When Napoleon impulsively turned his attentions to Russia in the summer of 1812, the Allied (British, Portuguese and Spanish) fighters began to gain the upper hand against the French forces in Spain. There is solid reason to believe that their victory in the conflict (which finally came in 1814) might very well have led to the effective implementation of the new "liberal" constitution throughout the nation.

That is, had it not been for the imperatives of empire. By end of that same pivotal year of 1812, the rebellions of colonists in certain regions of the Americas had become too strong to ignore. So, Spain once again had to choose. Having just liberated themselves from foreign rule, would they opt for the liberty and democracy of the type conceived in Cadiz or would they seek to retain the long-held oppressor's "right" to continue controlling lands and peoples in America?

Once again, the leadership class of the country opted for the latter, pursuing a series of bloody and ultimately futile wars across the South American continent during the next decade and a half. By 1824, Spain had lost all its holdings in the South American continent to creole-led movements of national liberation, spending untold amounts of capital and human lives to do so.

Worse yet, the campaign to "save the empire" that could not possibly have been saved, facilitated the return, in a European era otherwise marked by a gradual but steady evolution toward constitutional monarchies, of absolutism in Spain.

In 1814, Fernando VII, a deeply ignorant man who had actively connived with Napoleon during the French occupation, is returned to the Spanish throne.

Like the Vietnam era draft-dodgers Bush and Cheney who reinvented themselves as super-patriots in the wake of September 11th, this cowardly plaything of the French invaders begins to present himself and a coterie of lackeys as the "true heirs" of Spain's grand imperial past.

Their answer for almost every challenge facing the country was to call for a return to the "traditional values" (martial Catholicism, Empire, Castilian supremacy, social hierarchy, preference for plunder over commerce) that they saw as having been the keys to Spain's past greatness.

One the monarch's first acts was to suspend the Constitution of Cádiz and throw its allegedly "frenchified" sponsors into jail (Yes, just like our own flag-waving yahoos, Spanish super-patriots of dubious comportment but big mouths loved to mock the French and any of their fellow countrymen who admired their social ideals.).

Never mind that the country was bankrupt, that much of the previously large empire was swiftly disappearing, that the Catholic Church had proven itself to be a major hindrance to citizen quality of life in most of the countries where it still held sway; nor that a group of their fellow countrymen, the world's first liberals, had generated a very advanced but still very sensible (in regard to acknowledging the weight of traditions) blueprint for the future course of the nation. They, the absolutists, had their story and they were sticking to it, regardless of the facts. And when the facts and the ideology came visibly into conflict, the solution was generally to ignore, and if that did not work, harass, imprison or exile the bearer of the uncomfortable facts.

The Empire as an Insatiable Zombie Presence in Spanish Life

In this way, the absolutist government of Fernando VII set in motion what historians often refer to as the "problem of the two Spains." This analytical schema holds that from the re-imposition of absolutism in 1814 until the defeat of the Second Republic in 1939 and perhaps beyond, Spanish political and social life was divided into two camps, the liberals and the traditionalists, each largely incapable of accepting the core validity of the other, and thus unable to work together in any way on the country's many problems.

While this paradigm is a useful tool for organizing the minds of newcomers to the study of Spanish history, it is not without its problems. The most glaring of these is that it often gives onlookers the clear, if wholly erroneous, impression (not unlike the carefully assembled "two-sided" debates in our own mainstream media) that the two groups were evenly matched in terms of their ability to implement their desired programs throughout the period.

A much more accurate way of viewing things would be to paint the 125 years between 1814 and 1939 one long era of reactionary politics that was occasionally punctuated by short, intense, but inevitably ephemeral (1820-23, 1835-37, 1854-56, 1868-70, 1931-36) liberal attempts to foment modernity. And in each of these brief historical moments, the need to "attend to the responsibilities of empire" curtailed, confused, or otherwise blunted genuine drives to re-define Spain along democratic lines.

Am I suggesting that the need to preserve empire alone induced the failure of these liberal efforts? Absolutely not. Each clearly had very complex domestic and intra-European dynamics of their own. Rather, I am suggesting that even as the Empire became greatly diminished in physical terms (after 1824 it had been reduced to nothing more than Cuba, Puerto Rico, The Philippines and a number of military outposts in today's Morocco and Algeria), it continued to exert an enormous and very real psychological influence in Spanish political and military life.

Emblematic in this regard is the so-called Glorious Revolution of 1868 and its immediate aftermath. In September of that year, a group of activists, led by a Catalan military officer (a rare breed!) named Prim, sought to effect a liberal revolution in Spain. Their ranks, which were comprised of everything from outright Republicans to fairly conservative proponents of constitutional monarchy, quickly forced the abdication Queen Isabella II. And no sooner had this occurred then a group of Cubans, led by Carlos Manuel de Céspedes, launched a war of Independence in Cuba.

Prim, who had spent much time in the colonies and who also knew Céspedes, quickly came out in favor of granting the island its freedom. Indeed, he spent much of the first two years of the revolutionary period actively exploring how best to go about doing this. However, in December of 1870, just days after he had installed a new constitutional monarch, Amadeo, (located through an arduous and nearly war-inducing pan-European search process) Prim was assassinated. To this day, rather amazingly, it is unclear who was behind the plot. However, it is not unreasonable to suppose that Prim's position on Cuba might have been one of the factors motivating his assassins and/or their handlers. What is absolutely clear is that his death greatly wounded the reformist movement and the cause of decolonization.

While the Revolution would hobble on for another four years, and would even assume the shape of a Federal Republic for eleven months following Amadeo's abdication in February 1873, the idea of giving up the colonies would never again be a core element of its program. In fact, in the most radical moments of the short Federal Republican period, the farthest President Pi i Margall would go was to speak of Cuban autonomy.

Prim's failure to "kill off" the empire during his moment at the center of the Spanish governmental system would have far reaching consequences. As the Constitutional Monarchists and Republicans fumbled in their efforts to reorganize the state according to modern tenets in the wake of his assassination, the forces of reaction gathered steam.

In late 1874, a coup ended the Republic and ushered in the restoration of the Bourbon monarchy. The conservative politician, Cánovas, working closely with the "restored" monarch, Alfonso XII, set up a political system designed to look like a democracy—complete with a system of two alternating parties—but that offered no possibility of a real give and take on any of the long-standing issues affecting the country. A key element of this effort was generating a new "civilizationist" rhetoric (as in Spain is nobly sharing its rich culture with the benighted people of the Caribbean and the Philippines) for justifying the continuation of the empire. In effect, Cánovas sought to gain a measure of social peace by placing the country's many roiling civic and conceptual conflicts (democracy or plutocracy, democracy or empire, lay or catholic, federal or centralist) in the social equivalent of cold storage.

Emblematic in this regard was the Peace of Zanjón (1878), which ended the war of liberation begun by Céspedes ten years earlier. However, beyond granting effective amnesty to the rebels, and freedom to the slaves that had fought in their ranks, the accord did virtually nothing to satisfy Cuban aspirations nor, for that matter, Imperial Spain's desire to shore up its tenuous hold on the "Pearl of the Caribbean."

It is thus not surprising that all of the above-mentioned issues, especially the question of Spain's colonial "vocation," should reappear with a renewed level of vehemence a short time later.

In 1895, Cuban fighters once again rose up against Madrid. Having lived for the last two decades in the Restoration's haze of trumped up and self-serving neo-traditionalist rhetoric, the Spanish Army thought, mistakenly, they would be able to make quick work of the rebels. When their initial attacks failed, they turned to brutal counterinsurgency measures, the most "innovative" of which was to "concentrate" the civilian population in prison camps to prevent them from acting as guerilla fighters. Besides providing humanity with the concept for, and the name of, one of the great scourges of the twentieth century, the "concentration camp," this policy proved highly counterproductive; it turned many otherwise indifferent and apolitical Cubans into seething partisans of independence. It also provided the United States, which had long coveted Cuba, with humanitarian pretext (sound familiar?) for entering into the conflict.

And enter it did. In the Spring of 1898, the US, using the still unexplained sinking of the *USS Maine* in Havana harbor as its *casus belli*, unleashed its burgeoning military power against the Spaniards. In four short months, the United States easily conquered all that remained (Cuba, Puerto Rico and the Philippines) of Spain's once sprawling empire. The country was now reduced, as the great philosopher Ortega y Gasset would say in 1920 commenting on the event, to its "peninsular nudity."

Long marginalized Spanish democrats hoped that a loss as embarrassing as this would awaken the Spanish elites to the need to finally abandon imperial thinking and embrace the long-delayed promises of liberty and democracy. They assumed, moreover, that a military establishment that had performed as poorly as the Spanish one had just performed, would have the good sense and grace to stop presenting itself—together with the Church with which it was closely allied—as *the* indispensable institution of national life.

They were wrong on both counts. While a number of important grass-roots movements of reform emerged in the first decades of the 20th century, the governing elites remained strongly devoted to old-style, top-down solutions. Worse yet, the Army not only did not accept the reality of its general decrepitude and pitiful performance in 1898, but began actively blaming other sectors of society for its problems.

Pioneering a technique that partisans of unbridled US military power would use to great effect in the wake of the Vietnam War, the brass of the Spanish Army (which was by far the best financed element of the government) argued that they had failed because they were "betrayed" by a political class who had not provided them with either the means or the operational autonomy to "get the job done."

In the decades following the war, a new generation of army and navy officers became wholly imbued with this ideology of victimhood. For them, Spain's loss of empire was not about the inevitable decline of a society that had refused numerous invitations to board the train of modernity, but rather the disappearance of the country's traditional values and diminished "will-to power." The shining star of this new cadre was a young Galician named Francisco Franco.

But how were they to prove their point? Well, by doing what all angry and emasculated males everywhere do: picking fights with people they believed could not possibly match them in physical strength. In the first quarter of the 20th century, the Spanish high command provoked confrontation after senseless confrontation with local chieftains in Morocco. However, things did not always go as swimmingly as planned, but, rather than use these defeats at the hands of the Moroccan irregulars as a cause for reflection, the Spanish brass responded with ever greater amounts of firepower and ever greater demands that the citizenry "get behind" the war effort.

But the Spanish people, especially the Catalans, had had enough. In the summer of 1909, a group of conscripts, waiting in Barcelona to board a troop ship bound for Morocco, began to riot. For a week they, and the many working class males that sympathized with them, terrorized the city—zeroing in on the possessions of the church and the upper bourgeoisie, two groups who they saw, mostly rightly, as being in active connivance with the imperial war machine. A number of the same elements rose up against the government again in 1917.

This popular rejection of senseless overseas adventurism only enhanced the military caste's sense of victimhood, and with that emotional state is always an accompanying sense of having a much clearer and truer vision of "reality" than anyone else. If the populace could not clearly perceive the "need" to fight senseless wars, re-subscribe to traditional codes of social and military honor, they would find ways to help them "see" more clearly. The most effective way of properly directing the gaze of the population to what they knew to be correct and necessary was to institute dictatorial rule.

In July 1921, Spanish forces were routed by the indigenous troops under the direction of Muhammad Ibn 'Abd al-Karim al-Khattabi, popularly known as Abdel Krim, in the Morroccan locality of Annual. The attack once again laid bare the intellectual bankruptcy of Spain's leadership class and the operational weakness of the armed forces. (Of course, these facts, though palpable to the great majority of the population, could not be admitted out loud.)

For two years following the defeat, the politicians in Madrid scrambled to find a solution to what they termed as a "national" crisis of confidence within the parameters of the very limited and constitutional regime designed by Cánovas. They could not do so. Finally, in September of 1923, General Miguel

Primo de Rivera, working openly with the support of the king and touting the need to avenge the defeat at Annual as one of his prime goals, staged a coup d'état. His remarks from the day of the takeover are, I think, quite indicative of the backward-looking caste of the Spanish reactionary mind: *"Enough of gentle rebellions that remedy nothing and damage the robust and virile discipline that we offer to Spain and to the King. This is a movement of men. He who does not view masculinity as his true nature, should wait things out in a corner as we prepare a great future for the Fatherland. Spaniards! Long-live Spain! Long-live the King!"*

The dictatorship designed by Primo lasted until 1931. In the spring of that year, the King, fearing he had lost the confidence of the people (largely because of his none too subtle support of the much-despised Primo) abdicated the throne. On the day following his departure, April 14th, a group of prominent civic leaders and intellectuals announced the formation of the Second Spanish Republic.

Over the next five years, Spanish republicans rushed to implement the democratizing changes they and their intellectual forebears had dreamed of instituting since 1810. For the conservative elements of the society, these reforms were far too much far too fast.

In July of 1936, a group of military officers led by Franco and backed by the church and the monied elites, launched a coup against the legally-elected government of the Republic. The insurrectionists expected a quick victory. But to their surprise, the government did not surrender. Backed, at least initially, by anarchist-led militias, the Republic and much of the citizenry fought back. However, the discipline and military might of the anti-government forces backed by the Church and the financial oligarchs, *as well as the* highly militarized fascist states of Germany, Italy and Portugal, proved too much for the Republic. On April 1st, 1939, the last Republican units surrendered to Franco.

The diminutive General with the high-pitched voice, who had earned his chops in the early twentieth century "demonstration wars" against the Moroccans, would rule Spain with an iron hand over the next 36 years. He would do so with the constant accompaniment of the iconography of the now-wholly inexistent empire. The main medium for recycling the image of the glorious past was the cinema.

Like Mussolini and Hitler the otherwise anachronically-minded Franco had an innate understanding of the power of this still relatively new medium. Beginning in the mid 1940s studios run by close friends of the regime began pumping out film after film centering on the country's glorious imperial past. Emblematic in this regard is *Locura de amor*, which tells the story of how unscrupulous foreigners from the Low Countries were really responsible for the famous mental instability of Ferdinand and Isabel's daughter Joana at the beginning of the sixteenth century. Another favorite story line, evident in *Últimas de Filipinas* and Franco's highly autobiographical (he actually wrote the script under a pseudonym) *Raza*, was that the Empire would have continued to prosper for many more years than it did if "the politicians" had only had good sense to leave the most serious affairs of state to the ever-incorruptible and always enlightened officer class of the military.

When, in the decade following Franco's death in 1975, Spain made a more or less successful transition to democracy, most references to Spain's imperial past suddenly disappeared from public life.

But just when it appeared that the ever-durable zombie force of empire had been vanquished forever, it appeared once again in the mid 1990s during the Administration of Prime Minister José María Aznar, a man whose father, like the fathers of many of the men in his cabinet, had been a loyal and devoted Francoist. Understanding that even the most rightward-leaning of their followers would find a full-blown defense of the *military* empire unpalatable, they chose instead to re-cycle the old trope about the wonders of Spanish *cultural* imperialism, which is to say, the ways in which Spain's imposed language and literature did so much to enrich the lives of the peoples they had conquered around the world. As part of the effort, they even produced a well-choreographed historical rehabilitation of the man who had dreamed up the concept, Cánovas! Implicit in this new (but simultaneously very old) rendering of history was the belief that Spain's "cultural children" in America should once again look to the mother country, the doting parent of the Hispanic "family" of nations, to guide them in matters of culture.

It is interesting to note that shortly after launching this new era of neo-imperialist rhetoric, Aznar effected the first major cutbacks to individual group right under Spain's still young constitution. Perhaps the most important of the "neo-imperialist" prerogatives that he arrogated to himself was the privilege to declare certain political parties illegal. And a few short years after that he, practically alone among the European leaders and in direct contradiction to the very clearly demonstrated desires of the Spanish electorate, decided to join George Bush's imperial crusade to bring democracy to Iraq at the point of a gun.

Conclusion

Though I studied European history in college, I graduated knowing precious little about the history of Spain. When during the course of my doctoral studies, I dug up my old college textbooks, I finally understood why. Spain was (outside of two or three fleeting references) nowhere to be found in my major course texts, one of which was putatively dedicated to "Europe from 1500 to 1815"!

As I would later find out, this tendency to "disappear" Spain, only the most important country in the world during this time-period, was not terribly uncommon. And, as I would come to understand, it obeyed a general northern European, and from there, American, drive to portray Spain as "different" from the other major European countries... and not in a good way. According to this view, Spain effectively lacked the cultural raw materials (Feudalism, the Enlightenment, the questioning of Roman orthodoxy) necessary to develop, as the northern nations eventually would, along modern and more or less democratic lines.

I have attempted to demonstrate that this view of things is not only highly inaccurate but betrays an Olympian disdain for the specifics of Spanish history. Spain had all of these key developmental elements and, in some cases, well before their supposedly more advanced European counterparts.

So what really happened?

I think I have shown that the biggest impediment to Spain's embrace of liberty, and thus peace, was not its cultural DNA, but rather the fierce attachment of its elites to the idea and practice of Empire and state aggression. Time and time again over the last five centuries important sectors of Spanish society sought to lead the country down a new path, away from the game of subjugation and plunder and toward a place of greater liberty for all. But each time their efforts were beaten back by what the traditionalist elites, who always portrayed the "urgent needs of empire" as paramount to all other social claims. And this, even when the empire largely ceased to be a palpable physical reality!

Perhaps Americans should keep this in mind as our own political elites dismantle what remains of a free and civilized life here at home while refusing to even put the question of empire, with its enormous financial waste and hard-wired need to curtail individual liberty, on the table for discussion.

Applying Local Lessons to Foreign Policy

Jason Ditz

Jason Ditz is the managing news editor at Antiwar.com. *His op-ed pieces have been published in newspapers and magazines across the country.*

My own path does not include the sort of epic twists and turns that would make a great novel. My first impulse in tackling the question of "why peace" was to avoid my personal experience entirely, because it is so extremely ordinary. I decided, however, that a very ordinary story might have value in and of itself, and might in its sheer lack of drama by worth considering.

For me the question of "why peace" is inexorably linked with the question "why liberty" and the answer to both is quite simple: governments simply cannot be relied upon to do ambitious things well, since their entire strategy at best involves wasting money, and often devolves into use of force and threats to impose their solution. There are few better examples of government ambition (and by extension, of violence) being taken to extreme levels, than a war.

But wars are so grand in scope, and so far removed from most of our day-to-day lives, that it can be difficult to see them clearly for what they are: government programs in their most raw form. It is therefore valuable to consider the more relatable, more local lessons before we draw our ultimate conclusions.

Rust Belt Lessons: Government Efforts to Save the Economy

My story starts in Saginaw, MI, in the 1980s. The city had been one of the many prosperous auto towns around Michigan, but by the 1980s many of the shops were closing or scaling back. The auto boom was over, the population in decline, unemployment and crime soaring. It is the epitome of a "rust belt" tale, and the same one you can find in countless cities and towns across the Midwest.

As with any town historically dominated by the unions, it is also pretty much universally Democrat, and even as the union's power faded local politics had no real party-line split; every man of political ambition was, as a matter of course, a registered Democrat. Still, electoral politics is just no fun without antipathy, and in Saginaw that was found along racial lines.

It sounds overly simplistic, but at the time it really wasn't. A city council was inevitably made up of nine Democrats, but the city is split down the middle by a river, and was so racially segregated, almost entirely along the basis of that river. Politics, then, was a question of which side of town (and by extension which race) had five seats, and which had four at any given time.

It is absurd looking back on it, but voters seemed to eat it up. Both sides had perfect "solutions" to the crumbling economy, which in both cases was to burden everyone with more taxes and increase spending, making life harder. Like any good government program, each faction had a perfect scapegoat, the other side of town and the other race, and a built-in set of patrons, who even if the plan didn't work were promised more favorable treatment than under the alternative regime.

Like any ambitious political program, it didn't really matter in the end which side won. Taxes would be raised and spending hiked; the economy would continue to worsen; and both sides could rehash their political agendas two years hence at the next election. For the average non-political person living in Saginaw, it really mattered little which side won. Sure, the snow might get plowed a bit earlier in my West Side neighborhood during a white regime, or an East Side regime might plant a bunch of flowers in front of the burnt-out remains of a once-prosperous downtown, but there was never any illusion of functionality no matter who was in power.

Indeed, the government's rare combination of coercion and incompetence was always on show, even though I never personally saw the overt violence. The city decided people weren't mowing their lawn regular enough, and suddenly was imposing forced mowing on people with tall grass, charging them an exorbitant fee for the "service." But government is bad at everything it does, and it wasn't long until they announced they were losing money on every lawn mowed, even though they charged almost 10 times what a private lawn-care company would. Faced with soaring costs, the mowing soon stopped, because the government simply couldn't afford it.

The government seems to be reliable in nothing so much as its ability to make things worse, and there are specific reasons for this: societies are built around voluntary interaction, and the government's non-voluntary role always perverts this system. But as a child I never really had to think so deeply about it, because the government's incompetence was so overwhelming and absolute as to be self-evident. There was never a reason to question if the government could do things right, because examples were myriad of them doing things wrong.

I think growing up in this environment was a great blessing to me. The illusion of functionality—and and worse, of the government's competence—exists in varying forms throughout the world, and largely involves a government taking credit for something good that happened that they had nothing to do with. A couple of decades earlier, Saginaw would've appeared functional, even though the same policies were largely in place. It was only once the auto industry stopped growing at a dramatic rate that the government's increases in spending needed a justification—when times are good most people simply don't want to rock the boat.

Which is amazing if you think about it. Government can grow at its leisure until a crisis hits, and then it can use that crisis to justify its further growth. The fact that things used to be a lot nicer serves as a great excuse for the government to keep making things worse.

The great thing was, this same passion play of endless failed politics was playing out at the same time on the state level, with many of the same problems. The state government's version was a bit more savvy, with Republicans from the west side of the state and Democrats from the east, and promises to big businesses and the poor being swapped out for the racial divide. Otherwise, though, it was remarkably similar, particularly in that both sides claimed to have the solution to returning Michigan to a former state of prosperity, even though that prosperity was largely in spite of, not because of, the political atmosphere.

The state's policy initiatives ranged from the absurd to the obscene, but were always destructive. The Democrats at one point envisioned "rescuing" the old car towns with something called the "Cool City Initiative," pumping money into crime-ridden neighborhoods to try to coax educated young people into moving there, with the assumption that jobs would follow. The Republicans, as they often do, seemed to grasp that the problem in those cities was crime, not lack of "coolness." Understanding the problem didn't mean having the answer, however, as their solution was to up the minimum sentences for consensual crimes like drug possession. Needless to say, crime remained, and remains, high in the cities despite a soaring prison population.

This similarity was especially true in results. Michigan can be counted on to swap from one party to another every so often, but either party is promising big government solutions, whether as massive welfare spending or massive subsidies for well-connected businesses. Either way, Michigan's economy reliably got worse and worse, and for the average person, it didn't really matter who was in office.

I remember quite specifically, when I was 10 years old, being taken to school (which was also a polling site) on Election Day. There was a UAW worker in the parking lot, haranguing people to vote Democrat, or the economy would face certain ruin. Even at age 10, it seemed pretty obvious to me that Democrats had been in power for years while things had gotten progressively worse; sure enough, when the Democrats won that election nothing changed. The city, and the state, continued their downward spiral.

When the Republicans took over four years later, again nothing changed, excepting the rhetoric. Failed programs were scrapped, other programs were put in their place, and those also failed. Fast-forward an election cycle or two, and the cycle can be repeated, with a new candidate who promises to have all of the answers but is likewise only another expert at spending other people's money unwisely.

The conclusion then was pretty obvious, and even as a young teenager I was able to piece together the reality that seemed to escape the voting public: big government solutions simply don't work, and no matter which side is in power, it doesn't benefit the ordinary person. Indeed, short of the loud ruckus they make during election seasons, which failing faction is in power is more or less transparent to the general public, and we only notice that those problems that were supposed to go away, X years ago when the last politician was elected, are still there.

If it weren't for those problems, people wouldn't bother to vote. Problems, therefore, whether government-created or just government-exacerbated, are the bread-and-butter of politicians—and how lucky for them that their own ineptitude ensures that there is no shortage of such problems?

But What Does That Have to Do With War?

Once we have concluded that big government solutions don't work, the argument against war becomes trivial, and the famous Randolph Bourne quote, "war is the health of the state," makes a lot more sense.

War is, in short, the ultimate expression of the ideal of government-as-problem-solver, and includes all of the same key interventionist features that failed city and state politics does. The enemy serves as the most pure scapegoat possible, with the antiwar faction always close behind. The public (which is usually assured that a war will "pay for itself") is positioned as the official beneficiaries, though surely arms dealers and the like are even better placed to reap actual rewards from the massive outlays of money associated with a war.

It seems incredible, then, that most of the people who understand that big government can't buy (or coerce) solutions to problems never seem to realize that a war, particularly of the modern, nation-building sort, is doomed to failure. If we cannot trust the government to improve the economy locally or reduce the crime rate, how can we possibly expect them to rebuild an entire foreign society in its own image with any measure of success?

The short answer, of course, is that they cannot. An offensive war will never produce benefits anywhere near commensurate with the expense to a society. That wars of this sort are fought at all is, on the surface, something of a mystery.

War certainly doesn't benefit the general public, which sees its money vanish into overseas adventures; nor does it benefit the combatants, who if they are lucky enough to come back from war unmaimed will still cope with psychological trauma. At best, they are rewarded with subsidized education, which they can then use to compete for jobs, in an economy which was itself battered by years of pointless conflict.

But they are fought, after all, and they do benefit certain people. Politicians can make a career out of shilling for wars, and can count on lucrative jobs as lobbyists for future wars after their retirement. Much as it is with the local problems, selling a government-imposed solution is far more important than the solution actually working.

And despite its costs, war seems to be an even easier sell to the voting public than economic programs are, perhaps a testament to the fear that can be mongered on a war's behalf. If the threat of economic ruin can induce people to vote for a plan doomed to failure, how much easier is the threat of death from on high as an inducement? Much easier, but only if used sparingly.

Fortunately, as with the economic solutions, politicians will, through sheer greed or foolishness, go to the same well a few too many times, until everyone can plainly see the futility of their promises. This is, of course, part of what is fueling the war exhaustion that shows support for the American government's recent conflicts plummeting in the polls, and which indeed every nation caught in a cycle of perpetual war has had to cope with.

Promises that the war is going well, repeated too often, ring hollow. Claims that some antiwar faction's lack of faith is to blame, when scrutinized, rest on the same assumption that the clapping of the audience in a Peter Pan play can bring Tinkerbell back to life. People may be gullible for a time, even shockingly so, but there is a cynicism embedded in the public consciousness that will inevitably find its way out.

War is the "health of the state" for key reasons: it empowers the state to expand its control over myriad aspects of day-to-day life; it also creates a massive outlay of money to dubious sources, which can be siphoned off to other ends. Most important of all, however, war can, like any good state solution, be depended on to create a whole new series of major problems, problems that in themselves will open up opportunities for more expensive, incompetent problem-solvers.

If a war creates shortages, the government will be quick at hand with a rationing system. If it spawns inflation, there will be bureaucrats ready to impose price-fixing schemes. Even if all it creates is public opposition, there will dependably be bureaucrats advocating for censorship and detention of the "seditious" peace activists. When the war is over, it will dependably create an influx of wounded soldiers, which will create opportunities for government health care schemes.

"Why Peace" Indeed?

Of course the very question of "why peace" is self-answering. Peace is rightly seen as a universally preferable situation, all things equal, and it is only by virtue of the machinations of various states that the *de facto* peace is so often derailed in favor of war.

Anything short of peace is going to require government meddling, and anyone paying close attention can see that this is inherently undesirable. Governments are bad at everything, and when given such broad powers over life and death, they can be counted on to make a huge mess of things.

In fact the nation-building endeavors that modern wars inevitably devolve into are themselves a way to ensure a war's open-ended continuation. A government can never claim victory without successfully installing a new puppet regime of some sort, and such a regime will need to tackle all of the problems of a ruinous military occupation. Tackling the problems of a destroyed nation is not so dissimilar from tackling the problems of a city or state facing economic turmoil, and we've all seen that the tools in the government's shed are not up to the task. Not by a long shot.

The more reasonable question is "why not peace?" and that answer inevitably folds back into the lessons of "why liberty" not being heeded. A big government will always find excuses to get bigger, domestically when they can, but eventually those excuses will spill over the border into open conflict with some other big government. To the extent that we lack liberty, we will eventually lack peace.

First, Justice:
Toward Peace in Palestine

Kathleen Christison

Kathleen Christison is a former CIA political analyst and the author of Perceptions of Palestine: Their Influence on U.S. Middle East Policy, The Wound of Dispossession: Telling the Palestinian Story *and (co-authored with her late husband Bill Christison)* Palestine in Pieces: Graphic Perspectives on the Israeli Occupation. *She writes frequently for the online newsletter* Counterpunch.org *.and lives in Santa Fe, New Mexico.*

The question posed is "why peace?" But the first question should more properly be "Why justice?" Why is it essential that justice precede peace, and why is peace without justice meaningless?

Peace alone is not an adequate alternative to violence and war. As the mere absence of war, it is an empty concept. Without justice first, peace is merely a benefit to the powerful, to those who can impose their own demands without giving to the powerless. Israeli commentator Gideon Levy, who writes for the newspaper *Haaretz* and spends most of his time in the occupied Palestinian territories witnessing the effect of the Israeli government's human rights violations on the Palestinian population living under Israeli domination, has observed that the Israeli media dehumanize the Palestinians, and that this dehumanization produces the odd reality that Israelis are able, even in the midst of conflict, to "live so much in peace with themselves."[1] Peace without justice benefits only those who can be satisfied with their own lot while the oppressed suffer.

Justice must also precede any reconciliation between parties in conflict. This concept was the basis and the very essence of the Truth and Reconciliation Commission that put a non-violent end to apartheid in South Africa. Nelson Mandela cautioned against regarding reconciliation—against regarding mere "peace"—as meaning parity between justice and injustice[2] (between the powerful and the powerless). Justice must first be done. Until the powerless have justice, and the powerful cease initiating force against innocents, there can be no peace or reconciliation.

The oppressed—whether they reside in South Africa, gather in Tahrir Square in Cairo, or cry out from Palestine—call for justice and freedom from oppression. They do not call directly for peace, because they know that justice for them will automatically bring peace, not only for them but for their oppressors as well. In Palestine, the people call out for justice rather than primarily for peace. In mosques and churches, Palestinian Muslims and Christians pray for justice and freedom, not first for peace.

The kind of peace proclaimed by South African Archbishop Desmond Tutu, the world's preeminent spokesman for justice for the oppressed, is a peace between human beings based on justice. "We are true witnesses," he proclaims, "if we are on the side of the weak, the powerless, the exploited."[3] We advance justice if we witness for the weak and powerless. Calling for a justice and peace that restore the humanity of the oppressor as well as of the oppressed, Tutu says, is "the only way we can ever be human is together." He is talking about peace in the spirit of *ubuntu*, the African philosophy that sees the individual as part of the whole of humanity, as one who uses his or her strength on behalf of the weak and the poor, who treats others as he or she would be treated, and who is therefore open to others and inextricably bound to the humanity of others. "The only way we can be free is together,"[4] Tutu says. A young Palestinian girl who lives in a refugee camp and has never tasted freedom, speaking in a film about what freedom means to her, knew intuitively what Tutu spoke about and knew the huge dimensions of freedom and justice: "If it's taken from us," she said, "we lose our link to humanity."[5]

* * *

It is perhaps naïve to talk about justice, in a world in which wars and the weapons to annihilate the human race proliferate however, if it seems impossible to end the wars and the militarism that society today appears to live by, one can at least strive for justice and true peace in small ways, hoping that victory in one area will create a spreading circle, reaching toward justice on a broader scale. If, as Desmond Tutu says, the only way to be free is together, and the only way to achieve justice is to achieve it for everyone, one can hope that justice here will bring justice there.

With regard to Palestine, Tutu has noted that simply because South Africans have achieved a measure of justice and freedom for themselves, they must not abandon the cause of another oppressed people. A *principled* commitment to justice by South Africans, he points out, means continuing to pursue justice and human rights for Palestinians—not forgetting others, not "walking over our ideals even while we claim we are on our way to achieving them," and not stopping at simply securing "a few deals for ourselves" and failing to work for others.[6] Thus might justice in one place ultimately lead to justice in another.

It took me quite some years, and a long period away from working as a government intelligence community bureaucrat, to recognize the moral emptiness of a U.S. foreign policy focused on a *realpolitik* pursuit of national security objectives, with no interest in any goal other than what might benefit the United States. I was a pragmatist, eager to do my supposed patriotic duty to the United States, and there was no room for the pursuit of justice in my rote pursuit of the policy prescriptions handed down to me. It was not until I had been away from government for years, had begun again to follow the Palestinian-Israeli situation, and had begun actually to witness the effects of U.S. policy on the Palestinian people, that I began to recognize the abysmal absence of any concept of justice in the implementation of policy in this critical area of the world.

I cannot tell this story without constant reference to my late husband Bill Christison, who accompanied me on this journey from pragmatic government bureaucrat to activist and witness on behalf of Palestine, and indeed who led me. He was my moral guide. He came to an appreciation of the need for justice before I did, and we began our frequent travel to Palestine, and our writing about it, together.

Our first West Bank-Gaza trip (in a series of trips that saw us travel there eight times in six years) came as a kind of epiphany. It was 2003, just as the U.S. war in Iraq was about to begin. We knew the situation in Palestine well intellectually, had been following and writing about the Israeli government occupation for years, and had visited East Jerusalem and Bethlehem briefly on previous occasions. But this was the first time we actually saw what the Israeli government does to Palestinians under occupation—saw the checkpoints at which Palestinians wait interminably for a teenage Israeli soldier to allow them to pass; saw the destruction of homes demolished simply because Israel wishes to be rid of non-Jews in its midst; saw the lush Israeli settlements built on expropriated Palestinian land; heard the racist views of Israelis who regard Palestinians as some unequal, unworthy species to be discarded and trodden under. It was the first time we actually witnessed the racist effects of Israel's exclusivist Zionist political philosophy.

We came to understand, because we saw, that Israel's occupation of the West Bank, Gaza, and East Jerusalem in 1967—an occupation that has now endured for almost 45 years—is not some passing phenomenon that will end when Israel and the Palestinians forge a peace agreement, but is a continuation of Israel's creation in 1948 as a Jewish-majority state with no room for non-Jews living in equality. In that year, having been allotted 55 percent of Palestine for a Jewish state by the United Nations partition resolution, the Israeli government expanded its control of the land to 78 percent by ethnically cleansing approximately 750,000 Palestinian inhabitants and razing over 400 Palestinian villages.[7]

The events of 1948 clearly demonstrated that Zionism, the movement that gave birth to Israel, is not merely an abstract political philosophy, but is an exclusivist ideology that has from its inception promoted the conversion of Palestine into a Jewish land, clearing it to the extent possible of non-Jews. When you are in Palestine, as we were repeatedly, it is impossible not to see this implantation of Jews across the whole land, not just inside Israel proper but also throughout the territories occupied in 1967. The Israeli-only settlements proliferating throughout these territories, the roads that criss-cross the territories and are accessible only to Israeli automobiles, the steady squeezing of Palestinians into ever-smaller cantons, the Separation Wall that winds in and out of the territories and further constricts Palestinian access to their own lands, and the striking permanence of these realities, all make it glaringly evident that Israel never intends to relinquish control of the territories, never intends to grant the Palestinians true independence and sovereignty, but rather is working toward the full integration of this Palestinian land into the Jewish state of Israel.

The injustice of this reality—the injustice that has gone unredressed for well over 60 years, that festers even though Israelis, as Gideon Levy says, "live so much in peace with themselves"—screams out.

The small effort that Bill and I made to bring the reality of these injustices to public attention in the United States began over two decades ago through our writing, but it was intensified when we began traveling regularly to Palestine and witnessing. What we saw was heartbreaking, a story of great, and continuing, loss. Not only were Palestinians dispossessed in 1948, rendered literally homeless and also stateless when the Israeli state was established in three-quarters of their homeland and Jordan took control of the remaining one-quarter, but their very existence was almost totally erased from public consciousness. Israeli Prime Minister Golda Meir explicitly denied their existence in an interview in 1969,[8] and Western policymakers and media have been complicit in the effort to ignore and push aside the Palestinians from the beginning. The widespread, worldwide silence about the Palestinians' fate applies equally to the approximately four and a half million Palestinians— descendants of the 750,000 dispossessed in 1948—who are registered refugees, many living in camps throughout the Arab world; to the more than one million Palestinians who live, because they are not Jewish, as second-class citizens in a state formally declared to be Jewish; to the approximately four million Palestinians who live uncertain and very precarious lives, without citizenship or any political rights, under Israeli occupation in the West Bank, Gaza, and East Jerusalem; and to the additional millions throughout the world, not strictly speaking refugees, but who live in some form of exile from their natural homeland.

When the Palestinians' story is told at all, it is told in fragments. Usually the Israeli government creates the narrative, and the world goes along. Palestinian citizens of Israel are usually regarded as a breed apart from their brethren in the occupied territories, most often called merely "Arabs" in an effort to deny their distinctness, lumping them with the mass of Arabs throughout the Middle East, and denying the reality that, together with Palestinians under occupation, they make up a single ethnic-demographic group in Palestine that will soon surpass Israel's Jewish population in numbers, or perhaps already has. West Bank/Gaza/Jerusalem Palestinians, including large numbers living in refugee camps, are regarded as having a separate identity from other Palestinians—so that their numbers will not appear to threaten Jewish numbers and, since they are living in a kind of national limbo under Israeli occupation, so that Israel will not have to give them political or national rights. The large numbers of Palestinian refugees scattered in camps in Lebanon, Jordan, and Syria also exist in a national limbo, separated from their homeland altogether and ignored by policymakers, peace negotiators, and human rights advocates in Israel, the United States, and throughout the international community.

If the Palestinians' presence in their homeland can be fragmented and denied any legitimacy, and their very identity denied, then their dispossession, as well as the ongoing human rights abuses perpetrated against them and the violations of international law carried out against them, can be dismissed and ignored. These crimes have all been "ruled out of the Western court" as having any legitimacy, as one Palestinian scholar observed years ago.[9] Because the Palestinians' fate is ruled out of the Western court, the world therefore forgets that there ever were Palestinians, that Israel is a colonialist power and a newcomer to the land of Palestine, and that Palestinians have an inherent right to resist their attempted annihilation. In this way, the world comes to believe that the Palestinians' resistance to their own existential destruction lacks any moral basis. This is the reality that Israel wishes to present to the world, a fiction in which Israelis are always innocent victims and Palestinians are not present or exist only as predators.

Virtually every action the Israeli government takes in the occupied territories is targeted at making the Palestinians disappear, either directly or by making life so miserable that many will leave. This remains true even 60-plus years after the ethnic cleansing of 1948. In the West Bank, because land continues to be confiscated for Israeli settlements and roads, Palestinians are squeezed into smaller and smaller areas and living space is fragmented into multiple disconnected segments. According to the United Nations Office for the Coordination of Humanitarian Affairs, based on an extensive study of land use in the West Bank, the Israeli presence in that territory—including settlements and outposts, settlement industrial zones, areas farmed by Israelis, Israeli-declared nature reserves, and Israeli military bases—covers 39 percent of the territory.[10] Because the entire West Bank constitutes only 22 percent of all of Palestine, this large Israeli presence restricts Palestinians to small, separated enclaves that together make up only 13 percent of their original homeland, and even here they still live under Israel's domination, with no way to control their own lives or future.

Israeli settlements throughout the West Bank and East Jerusalem, in all cases built on private or communally owned Palestinian land, represent the vanguard both of Israel's occupation and of Zionism's expansion throughout the territories, completing its advance across the entirety of Palestine.[11] Settlements are the centerpiece of the occupation; all other aspects of the Israeli presence revolve around them and are intended to guarantee their permanence and therefore the permanence of Israel's control. Israel's military presence in the territory is there to protect settlers and settlements. The Separation Wall is routed to link the major settlement blocs, inside Jerusalem and elsewhere in the West Bank, which include more than 85 percent of the nearly 500,000 settlers, to Israel. The 1,000-mile road network, on which Palestinian cars may not drive, connects the settlements to each other and to Israel. The hundreds of checkpoints and roadblocks throughout the West Bank, impeding free movement of Palestinians everywhere in the territory and ensuring their cantonization in non-viable segments of the land, are intended to prevent them from approaching the settlements and the Israeli-only roads. A rigorous system of permits controlling West Bankers' access to East Jerusalem, as well as movement elsewhere, further constricts Palestinian lives.[12] In this situation, preservation of any semblance of Palestinian nationhood, or even of a real Palestinian community, is virtually impossible, and this is precisely what

Israel intends. Israel wants the West Bank for itself, free of Palestinians to the extent possible.

Similarly, in East Jerusalem, Israel is advancing across the city, increasingly making this center of Palestinian political and economic life uninhabitable for Palestinians. Israeli authorities have been demolishing Palestinian homes for purely racial-ethnic reasons since 1967, and the pace of demolitions has recently increased.[13] Furthermore, in recent years, Jewish settlers have literally been pushing Palestinian residents from homes in the city on which the settlers have set their sights. This has occurred particularly in the Sheikh Jarrah neighborhood, where Jews claiming prior ownership have forcibly evicted Palestinian residents from homes they have occupied for more than 50 years. A similar process is occurring in Silwan, a neighborhood of approximately 50,000 Palestinians just outside the Old City walls where Israel is demolishing homes and evicting residents, in a questionable effort to excavate the supposed "city" where the biblical King David lived[14] and to build a related theme park. The ideological motive underpinning this project, which has the full blessing of the Israeli government, is to "prove" that Jerusalem is a Jewish, not a Palestinian, city.

The situation in Gaza is so very horrific that it almost defies description. Surrounded by a fence that has imprisoned its 1.5 million inhabitants since the start of the peace process in the early 1990s, Gaza has faced a strangulating economic siege imposed by Israel and supported by the international community, including the United States, since the Hamas election in 2006. Although the Israeli government withdrew its settlers and military troops in 2005, Gaza remains a territory under occupation since the Israeli government controls all entry to and exit from the territory, controls the import and export of all goods, controls the airspace and the seacoast, and repeatedly launches military attacks on the territory, including Operation Cast Lead, the three-week assault in December 2008 and January 2009 in which 1,400 Palestinians, the majority civilians, were killed and thousands of homes and other buildings destroyed.

The economic embargo of Gaza is deliberately intended to squeeze Hamas and punish Gazans by making them "go hungry but not starve," in the words of Egyptian officials who have helped the Israeli government maintain the blockade. According to the World Food Program, the numbers of Gazans who are "food insecure" (lacking access to enough safe, nutritious food) rose from 40 percent in 2003—an already horrifying statistic—to 61 percent in 2010, and another 13 percent are vulnerable to becoming food insecure. Unemployment stands at 45 percent, and 75 percent of the population depends on humanitarian assistance to meet basic needs; almost one-third of the total population are refugees from 1948.[15] Although the Israeli government contends that the siege and its repeated attacks on Gaza are in response to Hamas rocket attacks on Israel, in fact Israel's military, political, and economic assault on Gaza began well before Hamas was founded and any rockets were fired. The ratio of Palestinians killed in Israeli attacks versus Israelis killed by Palestinian rockets has consistently stood for years at about 100 to one.[16] This was also approximately the ratio during Operation Cast Lead.

Gaza is a place where the Israeli government has "warehoused" 1.5 million Palestinians, a term coined by Israeli anthropologist and activist Jeff Halper. It is a place where Palestinians live in an open-air prison, fenced in, fed or not as Israel chooses, and repeatedly bombed and shot at whenever Israel desires. This imprisonment, according to Halper, is a "static situation emptied of all political content...a permanent 'given'...a state of status quo."[17]

*   *   *

Talking about peace and investing energy in a Palestinian-Israeli "peace process" in the face of these continuing injustices make a mockery of peace. Discussing how Palestinians should compromise with Israel in order to achieve peace, without any attempt to redress the injustices done to them and the violations of rights perpetrated against them—without an effort to halt the political suppression, the physical confinement, the economic strangulation, and the psychological humiliation of an entire people—is a travesty of immense proportions. Only justice ended apartheid in South Africa, and only justice can end the horrific imposition of one people's wishes and demands on another in Palestine.

A woman in Austria, responding to an article of mine several years ago,[18] bemoaned the fact that the Western media and Western policymakers are blind to Israel's brutality toward Palestinians and lamented, "What is the worth of a civilization that has no eyes and ears for the suffering and agony of the people under Israel's bombs?"

I have had this *cri de cœur* posted above my computer for years. It reminds me every day that peace without justice stands as a huge failure of the human condition, a violation of the bonds that must hold humanity together.

---

[1] Itamar Eichner, "Israeli columnist: Media dehumanizes Palestinians," *YNet News* (March 15, 2011), http://www.ynetnews.com/articles/0,7340,L-4042816,00.html (date last accessed, March 16, 2011).

[2] Cited in Archbishop Desmond Tutu, "Israeli ties: a chance to do the right thing," *The Sunday Times* [of South Africa], September 26, 2010, http://www.timeslive.co.za/world/article675369.ece/Israeli-ties--a-chance-to-do-the-right-thing (date last accessed, March 9, 2011).

[3] Cited in Mike Nicol, introduction to *Believe: The Words and Inspiration of Desmond Tutu* (South Africa: Wild Dog Press, 2007), p. 22.

[4] Desmond Tutu, preface to *Ibid.*, no page number.

[5] Friends of the Jenin Freedom Theater NYC, video: "The Jenin Freedom Theater Today!" http://www.youtube.com/watch?v=pQGqmLyunm0 (date last accessed, April 7, 2011).

[6] Tutu, "Israeli ties."

[7] For the history of Israel's ethnic cleansing operation in 1948, see Ilan Pappe, *The Ethnic Cleansing of Palestine* (Oxford: One World, 2006).

[8] She told a British interviewer, "It was not as though there was a Palestinian people in Palestine considering itself as a Palestinian people and we came and threw them out and took their country from them. They did not exist." *Sunday Times* (of London), June 15, 1969.

[9] Walid Khalidi, "Introduction," in Walid Khalidi, ed., *From Haven to Conquest: Readings in Zionism and the Palestine Problem Until 1948* (Washington, DC: Institute for Palestine Studies, 1987), pp. xxii-xxiv.

[10] *The Humanitarian Impact on Palestinians of Israeli Settlements and Other Infrastructure in the West Bank* (Jerusalem: United Nations Office for the Coordination of Humanitarian Affairs, July 2007), pp. 70-71.

[11] Kathleen and Bill Christison, *Palestine in Pieces: Graphic Perspectives on the Israeli Occupation* (London: Pluto Press, 2009), p. 38.

[12] *Ibid.*, pp. 38-39.

[13] The Israeli Committee Against House Demolitions, an Israeli NGO, estimates that over 5,000 Palestinian homes, primarily in East Jerusalem, have been demolished since 1987 for "non-punitive" reasons—i.e., because the owners have failed to obtain residential building permits, which are almost impossible for Palestinians to obtain. See http://www.icahd.org/?page_id=5508 (date last accessed, March 26, 2011). The United Nations Relief and Works Agency has further recorded a substantial increase in demolitions in both East Jerusalem and the West Bank during the first few months of 2011. See "UN: Massive Increase in Home Demolitions," *Ma'an News Agency* (March 20, 2011), http://www.maannews.net/eng/ViewDetails.aspx?ID=369913 (date last accessed, March 26, 2011).

[14] Raphael Greenberg, "Shallow and Brutal Archaeology," *Haaretz* (October 8, 2009).

[15] Sara Roy, "Gaza After the Revolution," *Foreign Policy* (March 16, 2011), http://mideast.foreignpolicy.com/posts/2011/03/16/gaza_after_the_revolution (date last accessed, March 26, 2011).

[16] Christison and Christison, *Palestine in Pieces*, pp. 160-161.

[17] Jeff Halper, "The Palestinians: Warehousing a 'Surplus People,'" ZNet (September 8, 2008), http://www.zmag.org/znet/viewArticle/18750 (date last accessed, March 28, 2011).

[18] See Kathleen Christison, "Atrocities in the Promised Land: 'The Insane Brutality of the State of Israel,'" *CounterPunch.org* (July 17, 2006), http://www.counterpunch.org/christison07172006.html (date last accessed, March 31, 2011).

Peace and Liberty

Walter E. Block

Walter Block is a professor of economics at Loyola University New Orleans and a senior fellow of the Ludwig von Mises Institute. He is the author of Defending the Undefendable *and* Labor Economics from a Free Market Perspective.

As a libertarian, my perspective on peace and liberty is rather straightforward.[1] The essence of the libertarian philosophy is the non-aggression principle (NAP): one is required to respect the persons and justly owned property[2] of other people, and not engage in uninvited border crossings against other people. The libertarian is not necessarily a pacifist: he may engage in violence, but only of a defensive, not offensive, kind.[3] The NAP is of crucial importance, not only in domestic policy, but also in the foreign realm. Thus, the advocate of this political perspective is not "anti-war."[4] Rather, to be sure, while he opposes initiatory, or invasive, or imperialistic or offensive war, he is a *supporter* of *defensive* war.[5]

Why is this philosophy beneficial to the individual, and to the community? For several reasons. First, deontology, or rights. Libertarianism is the only perspective that allows the individual complete control of both his personal and professional life. In the former realm, anything between or among consenting adults is allowed, such as legalized gambling, pornography, prostitution, drug use (Block, 2008). In the latter, the person may engage in any *capitalist* act with any other consenting adult, and no economic imposition may be made upon him. This rules out taxes, statist regulation, government ownership, etc… The implication is *laissez-faire* capitalism, and the benefits thereof include prosperity and poverty reduction (Gwartney, 1976). In foreign policy, too, the individual and community are better protected. The U.S. presently militarily occupies some 150-200 other countries. Thus, we are in effect a trip wire; whenever anything untoward occurs, pretty much anywhere on the globe, our country is involved, willy-nilly. As Congressman Ron Paul said of the tragedy of 9/11, "they are over here because we were over there."[6]

Says Rothbard (1982), regarding the libertarian view of foreign policy:

"Does opposition to all inter-State war mean that the Libertarian can never countenance change of geographical boundaries—that he is consigning the world to a freezing of unjust territorial regimes? Certainly not. Suppose, for example, that the hypothetical State of "Walldavia" has attacked "Ruritania" and annexed the western part of the country. The Western Ruritanians now long to be reunited with their Ruritanian brethren (perhaps because they wish to use their Ruritanian language undisturbed). How is this to be achieved? There is, of course, the route of peaceful negotiations between the two powers; but suppose that the Walldavian imperialists prove adamant. Or, libertarian Walldavians can put pressure

on their State to abandon its conquest in the name of justice. But suppose that this, too, does not work. What then? We must still maintain the illegitimacy of the Ruritanian State's mounting a war against Walldavia. The legitimate routes to geographical change are: (1) revolutionary uprisings by the oppressed Western Ruritanian people, and (2) aid by private Ruritanian groups (or, for that matter, by friends of the Ruritanian cause in other countries) to the Western rebels—either in the form of equipment or volunteer personnel."[7]

The US and other states throughout history, unfortunately, have engaged in offensive violence, against individuals at home and abroad. The adverse effects this has wrought have been nothing short of monumental, and spectacularly horrendous. Take at-home first: Historians (Conquest, 1986, 1990; Courtois, et. al. 1999; DiLorenzo, 2006; Rummel, 1992, 1994, 1997) have estimated that the number of people murdered by their own governments in the 20th century amounts to almost 200 million—an astounding number,[8] given the widely held notion that these institutions are set up in order to *protect* their citizens. And this is to say nothing of the millions more of innocents, murdered in wars between states, such as World War I, World War II, the Korean "police action" of 1951, the Vietnam war, and the present U.S. undeclared wars in Iraq and Afghanistan.

At a time when the U.S. government maintains some 900 military bases, on the soil of about 150-200 different countries,[9] it is difficult to maintain the notion that this is all (or even mostly) for defensive purposes. Let us attempt to adopt a perspective that is not totally U.S.–centric, as articulated by our hawkish friends, the neo-conservatives. To wit, suppose some other country—China, Russia, Brazil—had established a similar number of military installations outside of its own borders. Would American analysts acquiesce in the notion that these expenditures were all, or even mainly, for defensive purposes? This seems unlikely, in the extreme.

It cannot be denied that it is the common belief among many U.S. citizens that America's aims are altruistic, not imperialistic, which is why so many don't object to the placement of our soldiers and sailors all over the world. But this is based on *magnificent* public relations emanating from Washington D.C., not on the facts of the matter. Imagine if our positions were reversed: we were citizens of China, Russia or Brazil. How would we then view placement of U.S. armies and navies? Or, let us ask ourselves how citizens of the rest of the world must interpret our actions. Altruism would be very far from the top of the list.

Then, there is the fact that U.S. military expenditures dwarf those of other nations.[10] According to this source[11] our nation spends 46.5 percent of world expenditures on weapons and soldiers, etc.; this is followed by China at 6.6 percent, France, 4.2 percent, UK, 3.8 percent, Russia, 3.5 percent. The next 10 countries, together, spend 20.7 percent of world armaments, for an average of 2.1 percent, and countries comprising the entire rest of the planet allocate a mere 14.7 percent of military spending. Again, were any nation other than the U.S. guilty of such massive investment in armaments, our conservative pundits would be likely gnashing their teeth at the hostile intentions of this other (hypothetical) country. Instead, we labor under the hubris of "American Exceptionalism" (Greenwald, 2009): we are blessed above all others by God, or by Nature, or by some such other elemental force: what applies to others does not at all pertain to us.

This libertarian position has been under attack, in very different ways, by scholars located on all sides of the political spectrum. Some on the right condemn libertarians who hew to the Rothbardian distinction between initiatory and defensive violence, characterizing the present U.S. stance as one of "defense," and maintaining that all those, such as Ron Paul, who wish to bring the troops home and engage them in defensive stances only, are "against defense." (For these individuals, the word "offense" has no meaning in the foreign policy context, at least as it might apply to the U.S. Limiting the US military to a very strong coast guard would be for them equivalent to pacifism, or surrender, or both.)

Consider the views of Randy Barnett, now a professor of law at Georgetown. He claims, *mirable dictu*, that the U.S. invasion of Iraq was justified, and on libertarian grounds.[12] For Barnett (2007), too, the distinction between offensive and defensive wars is elusive. Barnett has not fully taken cognizance of Ron Paul's analysis of the 9/11 World Trade Center bombing: "They are over here, because we were over there." Ron Paul and Rudy Giuliani debated over this very issue; the latter said he had never even heard of any such explanation.[13] States Barnett:

> *"Other libertarians, however, supported the war in Iraq, because they viewed it as part of a larger war of self-defense, against Islamic jihadists who were organizationally independent of any government. They viewed radical Islamic fundamentalism as resulting in part from the corrupt dictatorial regimes that inhabit the Middle East, which have effectively repressed indigenous democratic reformers. Although opposed to nation building generally, these libertarians believed that a strategy of fomenting democratic regimes in the Middle East, as was done in Germany and Japan after World War II, might well be the best way to take the fight to the enemy rather than solely trying to ward off the next attack."*

The difficulty is, Barnett does not take cognizance of who was the initiator. Yes, of course, if 9/11 was the opening scene of a war between the jihadists and the U.S., then, it must be conceded Barnett makes an important point. However, anyone even remotely familiar with the history of the Middle East knows full well that the Americans have been militarily active—in an offensive, not defensive manner—in that part of the world, for *decades* before the unhappy event of September 2001.

Another supposed leader of the libertarian movement is David Boaz, executive vice president of the Cato Institute. In Boaz (2010) this "libertarian" avers: "Suddenly, I find myself nostalgic for Bill Clinton. Back in 1996 ... we bombed a lot of countries, but didn't put American troops at risk." Who knew that the libertarian principle was to not put American troops at risk, while bombing innocent people? Did any of these countries that "we" bombed first attack us? Of course not. Did we murder innocent people abroad during the Clinton years? Without a doubt that is true. How, then, can a "libertarian" leader support any such goings on? It is rather difficult to reconcile this view with the NAP.

My experience with the left has also been less than fully satisfactory, albeit in a far different manner. When I first began work on this book (Four Arrows and Block, 2010), my co author was literally shocked to find that a person such as I, who opposes U.S. imperialistic war-mongering, could also embrace free enterprise. To his mind, the two are completely incompatible.[14] However, they are not only not incompatible, but, rather, are aspects of the same nonaggression principle. Both partake of the universal benefits of freedom.

What of the left's culpability in our foreign policy infringements? When Bush was engaged in unjustified wars in Iraq and Afghanistan, the "progressives" were gnashing their teeth, with (entirely proper) hatred for this imperialistic warmongering. Now that Obama has taken over this particular lemonade stand, however, doing nothing very much differently than Bush (or McCain) probably would have done, those "progressives" are eerily silent. I suspect that the main impetus of opposition on the part of liberals to this imperialism was not against it *per se*, but rather criticism of the persons responsible.

But Four Arrows is far from the only intelligent scholarly leftie to think that if you favor free enterprise you must support imperialist aggression.[15] Indeed, this viewpoint is endemic on this sector of the political spectrum. Thanks to Ron Paul, however, this opinion may well be in the process of change. For Congressman Paul is pretty much the only high-profile advocate of *laissez-faire* capitalism to take this stance. And, when people learn of this, and do a bit more research, they find out that there are a whole host of libertarians, headlined by Murray N. Rothbard, who take precisely this point of view. This is all to the good, if there is to be any left-right cooperation in battling foreign militaristic aggression on the part of the U.S.[16]

---

[1] This essay is inspired by Rothbard (1963).

[2] Based on homesteading. See on this Hoppe, 1993; Locke, 1948; Rothbard, 1973, 32;

[3] Browne (2005) starts off on the wrong foot by stating: "You're a libertarian because you abhor violence." No, libertarians do not at all abhor "violence," only *initiatory* violence. It is not until the very end of this essay that this author, properly, distinguishes between violence and its initiation.

[4] With all due respect to antiwar.com, this blog is misnamed. Since it is run by libertarians, it ought to be called something on the order of antiunjustwar.com.

[5] In Rothbard's view, there were only two justified, and, hence, defensive wars in U.S. history: the war of secession from Great Britain in the late 18th century, and the Southern war of secession from the North of 1861-1865.

[6] http://www.cbsnews.com/8301-503544_162-57340277-503544/ron-paul-9-11-prompted-glee-in-bush-administration/

[7] http://mises.org/rothbard/ethics/twentyfive.asp

[8] And this ignores highway fatalities which should be, but are not usually, ascribed to government. On this see Block 2006, 2009.

[9] http://www.thenation.com/article/157595/americas-empire-bases-20; http://www.japantoday.com/category/politics/view/2-congressmen-call-for-pullout-of-u-s-forces-from-japan; http://endoftheamericandream.com/archives/u-s-military-spending-is-out-of-control-12-facts-that-show-that-we-cannot-afford-to-be-the-police-of-the-world

[10]http://en.wikipedia.org/wiki/List_of_countries_by_military_expenditures; http://www.globalsecurity.org/military/world/spending.htm; http://endoftheamericandream.com/archives/u-s-military-spending-is-out-of-control-12-facts-that-show-that-we-cannot-afford-to-be-the-police-of-the-world

[11] http://www.globalissues.org/article/75/world-military-spending

[12] For a critique, see Block (2007), Richman (2008)

[13] Whereupon Paul offered Giuliani these four books in support of his claims: The 9/11 Commission, 2004; Johnson, 2004; Pape, 2005; Scheuer, 2004 (http://www.antiwar.com/blog/2007/06/02/ron-pauls-reading-list-for-the-farsighted/). It is not known that Giuliani ever condescended to read this material.

[14] During the course of our collaboration, Four Arrows acknowledged that this initial assumption of his was erroneous.

[15] Perhaps this equation of free enterprise at home coupled with a militaristic foreign policy stems from Bill Buckley, who encompassed both views. See on this Rothbard (1963).

[16] Two examples of left-libertarian cooperation, in addition to Four Arrows-Block (2010) are Radosh-Rothbard (1972) and Woods-Polnar (2008).

References:

Barnett, Randy E. 2007. "Libertarians and the War: Ron Paul doesn't speak for all of us " *Wall Street Journal*, July 17

Block, Walter. 2006. "Deaths by Government: Another Missing Chapter." November 27. http://www.lewrockwell.com/block/block66.html

Block, Walter. 2007. "Randy Barnett: Pro War Libertarian?" July 23; http://www.lewrockwell.com/block/block79.html; reprinted on http://antiwar.com/, 7/23/07

Block, Walter. 2008 [1976]. *Defending the Undefendable*. Auburn, AL: The Mises Institute

Block, Walter. 2009. *The Privatization of Roads and Highways: Human and Economic Factors*; Auburn, AL: The Mises Institute; http://mises.org/books/roads_web.pdf

Block, Walter E. 2010. "David Boaz is no libertarian," January 14; http://www.lewrockwell.com/blog/lewrw/archives/47525.html

Boaz, David. 2010. "Save America—Bring back Bill: Now I have a hazy memory of the Clinton years as a sort of Golden Age" *National Post*. January 12; http://network.nationalpost.com/np/blogs/fpcomment/archive/2010/01/12/save-america-bring-back-bill.aspx

Browne, Harry. 2005. "Why You Are a Libertarian" December 19; http://www.lewrockwell.com/browne/browne62.html

Conquest, Robert. 1986. *The Harvest of Sorrow*, N.Y.: Oxford University Press;

Conquest, Robert. 1990. *The Great Terror*, Edmonton, Alberta: Edmonton University Press

Courtois, Stephane, Nicolas Werth, Jean-Louis Panne, Andrzej Paczkowski, Karel Bartosek and Jean Louis Margolin. 1999. *The Black Book of Communism: Crimes, Terror, Repression*, trans. from French by Murphy, Jonathan and Mark Kramer, Cambridge, MA: Harvard University Press

DiLorenzo, Thomas. 2006. "Death by Government: The Missing Chapter." November 22; http://www.lewrockwell.com/dilorenzo/dilorenzo114.html

Four Arrows (aka Don Trent Jacobs) and Walter E. Block. 2010. *Differing Worldviews in Higher Education: Two Scholars Argue Cooperatively about Justice Education;* Rotterdam, The Netherlands: Sense Publishers

Greenwald, Glenn. 2009. "The NYT's definition of blinding American exceptionalism." May 8; http://www.salon.com/news/opinion/glenn_greenwald/2009/05/08/torture

Gwartney, James, Robert Lawson and Walter Block. 1996. *Economic Freedom of the World, 1975-1995* Vancouver, B.C. Canada: the Fraser Institute

Hoppe, Hans-Hermann. 1993. *The Economics and Ethics of Private Property: Studies in Political Economy and Philosophy,* Boston: Kluwer

Johnson, Chalmers. 2004. Blowback: The Costs and Consequences of American Empire, Holt; http://www.amazon.com/Blowback-

Consequences-American-Empire-
Second/dp/0805075593/ref=pd_bbs_sr_1/104-3659593-
2755132?ie=UTF8&s=books&qid=1180811841&sr=1-1/antiwarbookstore

Locke, John. 1948. *An Essay Concerning the True Origin, Extent and End of Civil Government*, in E. Barker, ed., *Social Contract*, New York: Oxford University Press, pp. 17-18.

Pape, Robert A. 2005. Dying to Win: The Strategic Logic of Suicide Terrorism. Random House; http://www.amazon.com/Dying-Win-Strategic-Suicide-Terrorism/dp/1400063175/antiwarbookstore

Polnar, Murray and Thomas E. Woods, eds. 2008. *We Who Dared to Say No to War: American Antiwar Writing from 1812 to Now.* New York, N.Y. Basic Books

Radosh, Ronald and Murray N. Rothbard, eds. 1972. *A New History of Leviathan*. New York: E. P. Dutton, http://mises.org/books/newhistoryleviathan.pdf

Richman, Sheldon. 2008. "A Bogus Libertarian Defense of War." *Freedom Daily*. January 23; http://www.fff.org/freedom/fd0710b.asp

Rothbard, Murray N. 1963. "War, Peace, and the State." *The Standard*, April, pp. 2-5; 15-16; http://mises.org/rothbard/warpeace.asp

Rothbard, Murray N. 1973. *For a New Liberty*, Macmillan, New York; http://www.mises.org/rothbard/newliberty.asp

Rothbard, Murray N. 1982. *The Ethics of Liberty*, Humanities Press, Atlantic Highlands, N.J.

Rummel, R. J. 1994. *Death By Government*, New Brunswick, NJ: Transaction

Rummel, R. J. 1992. Democide: Nazi Genocide and Mass Murder. Rutgers, New Jersey: Transaction Publisher.

Rummel, R. J. 1997. Statistics on Democide. Center on National Security and Law, University of Virginia

Scheuer. Michael. 2004. Imperial Hubris: Why the West is Losing the War on Terror. Potomac Press; http://www.amazon.com/Imperial-Hubris-West-Losing-Terror/dp/1574888498/antiwarbookstore

The 9/11 Commission. 2004. The 9/11 Commission Report: Final Report of the National Commission on Terrorist Attacks Upon the United States; WW Norton; http://www.amazon.com/11-Commission-Report-Terrorist-Authorized/dp/0393326713/antiwarbookstore

Tucker, Jeffrey. 1997. Book review of *Libertarianism—A Primer*. By David Boaz. New York: The Free Press, 1997. *Journal of Libertarian Studies*, Vol. 13, No. 1, pp. 109-120; http://mises.org/journals/jls/13_1/13_1_6.pdf

The War in My Life

Sumit Dahiya

Sumit Dahiya was born in India and made San Diego his home after his brother got stationed there with the United States Navy. He attended Florida State University to get his Bachelors in Finance and Economics. He is currently enlisted with the United States Army as a Field Artilleryman. He is currently working towards getting a Masters in International Relations from Troy University. He intends to attend Law School after being discharged from the Army. His interests include reading, writing, traveling, photography, cooking and listening to classical music.

It was around noon on a beautiful summer day in Kashmir. I was visiting my cousins. Their father was the Executive Officer in an Infantry Battalion based in Kashmir. The change of guard at the Quartermaster's building was taking place. I was in the parking lot across the building, admiring the beautiful scenery. The Pakistani Army outpost was a couple of football fields away from where I was. There is a saying about Kashmir in that part of the world: "If there is heaven on earth, it is right here." My reverie was broken by loud explosions. I turned around to see the Quartermaster's building in flames. The guards were running for cover. The familiar rattle of machine-gun fire erupted from all directions. The small Indian Army outpost in Kashmir had come under heavy mortar and small arms fire. I ran to the Military jeep grabbed a carbine and ran to take cover behind the two Indian Army soldiers who had been tasked with accompany me that day. War had come to me. I was twelve years old.

As I look back at my life, war and conflict have been its greatest highlights. My earliest memories are of watching Indian Army battle tanks on television, entering the Golden Temple to take out the "bad guys." The Golden Temple is the holiest site for the Sikh religion, located in Punjab state in North India. A Sikh holy man by the name of Sant Jarnail Singh Bhindranwale, who had a history of cozying up to the ruling Congress Party and then Prime Minister Indira Gandhi, had lost favor with India's ruling elites. He declared his support for the cause of an Independent nation of Khalistan that included most of Punjab. That's when he became a 'terrorist' according to the Indian Government. Sant Bhindranwale and his armed supporters took refuge in the Golden Temple under the belief that the Government would not send troops inside a holy site. They were highly mistaken.

Prime Minister Indira Gandhi ordered her military commanders to take out the 'terrorists' at any costs. In the summer of 1984 Operation Blue Star was launched. Over the next few days, hundreds of innocent pilgrims got caught in the crossfire and were killed. While the Indian Army suffered several casualties, the 'terrorists' were eventually killed by the Indian Army. This event was the beginning of one of the bloodiest insurgency movements in recent Indian history.

In October 1984, Prime Minister Indira Gandhi was assassinated by her Sikh bodyguards. Over the next few weeks and months thousands of innocent Sikhs were murdered in cold blood by activists associated with the Congress Party. Several individuals alleged to have led and directed the genocide against the Sikh community are now senior political figures in India.

Over the next few years, bomb blasts and terrorist incidents became part of our daily lives. If you wore a turban or gave any other indication of being a Sikh, you exposed yourself to abuse by the security forces. Many Sikh parents cut their children's hair shorter to save them from daily abuse and harassment. All public transportation systems had the following message stenciled: "Warning! Please look under your seat. If you see a strange object it could be a bomb. Raise Alarm!" From a child's perspective it is sad that I remember the warning verbatim. As a child growing up I was expected to remember songs, movies, cartoon sketches, poetry, etc. But I also took violent, conflict-related memories from my childhood into my adulthood.

In the late 1980s the separatist movement in the disputed North Indian state of Kashmir picked up. Now the Government gave us one more bogeyman to be scared of: The Muslims. If you were a Muslim or gave a remote appearance of being a Muslim, you were supposed to be the new "bad guy."

Besides the ones in Punjab and Kashmir, India has had several other small and big insurgency movements brewing in other parts of the country. In the far eastern states, people have very mongoloid features and traditions. They fail to see anything in common with their counterparts in the India. They have been fighting for autonomy for as long as India has been free from British rule. In other parts of the nation Maoist-inspired guerrilla movements are happening. Every few years the Hindu extremists feel the need to take care of the "Muslim Problem" in India. Sometimes it's a Mosque sitting on top of an ancient Hindu temple. Other times it is revenge for some Muslims having burned down a train full of Hindu pilgrims. As a coincidental consequence, Hindu extremist political parties then have a strong showing in the next elections.

In my senior year of secondary school, my time had come to become a part of a proud family tradition. Like other men, it was my turn to take the entrance exam for the National Defense Academy, India's premier Military College. Candidates are selected to be trained as Army Officers while attending college. I had mixed feelings about joining the Army: on the one hand I was enthusiastic about making my family proud; while on the other, I wanted to do something different.

The exam was split in two sessions, separated by lunch. The morning session was about mathematics and sciences and it went well. During lunch, while the other candidates were preparing for the afternoon session, I was contemplating whether I really wanted to do this. I found my answer when I saw a local train passing by. I had never been on one of those trains, and had always wanted to travel in them. So I ripped my examination ticket in half and boarded the train. I spent the rest of the day doing what I had always wanted to do; checking out New Delhi from the window of a local train.

I thought that once my mother found out that I had failed the entrance exam for National Defense Academy, she would give up all hopes on me. But, her hopes for me had only become even more exaggerated, after my brother had the smart thing by going to Engineering School and emigrating to the United States. I was happy that finally the men in my family were doing something different yet normal. I started working on what I always wanted to do in my life. I followed my brother to the United States.

My brother was deeply impacted by the events of September 11, 2001 and enlisted with the United States Navy. I stayed focused. I went to Florida State University and graduated with a degree in Finance and Economics. During my time as an undergraduate, I was highly influenced by the works of Austrian Scholars. I wanted to continue my education in Economics, so in 2007 I moved to San Diego to graduate degree at San Diego State University.

Around that time my brother got out of the Navy with severe physical disabilities, as well as mental and emotional issues. He would never be the same again. He felt like he was just a number, and the no one cared about the lower-enlisted ranks, as long as the numbers looked good. Due to the hazardous and physically challenging nature of his job in the Navy, he now suffered from back and skin-related issues. This caused stagnation in his career and he failed to see any purpose of carrying on with his service in the United States Navy.

Later on, he got married and had a family. But I remember him as a very different person. The military destroyed my brother. He would always tell me to never join the military. He went on to work in the Department of Veterans Affairs. As an active duty sailor and later as a Veterans' Affairs employee, my brother saw the side of the military they will never show in those "Be all you can be," "The few the proud," and "Army of one" commercials.

In 2009 I visited my family back in India and saw my grandfather, who I hadn't seen in a very long time. His affliction with Alzheimer's was starting to show. My grandfather is a highly decorated Second World War veteran who had gone on to command one of the most legendary armor battalions in the Indian Army. One evening I saw him wearing this traditional Muslim prayer hat. I had heard fragments of stories about that hat. Several military museums in India had requested him to donate it.

My grandfather had later become an army tank company commander during the 1965 war with Pakistan. After losing to him and his troops, a Pakistani colonel surrendered. The surrendering officer had turned out to be the legendary Pakistani Colonel Golewala. He had pleaded for leniency and placed his own prayer hat at my grandfather's feet, as a sign of respect and humiliation. My grandfather had taken the hat, and promised the Colonel it would never go anywhere below his own head. Although he is a practicing Hindu, he has since gone around wearing the Muslim prayer hat, leaving a lot of people amused.

As my grandfather recited the story in one piece for the first time, I felt the regret in his voice that none of his grandchildren had carried forward the family's legacy of serving in the Army. He felt that a family tradition built over hundreds of years was coming to an end. There I was back to square one in my life. Something I had run away from all my life was right there in front of me, mocking me and telling me it was about time.

I returned to the United States and, against my brother's repeated pleas, enlisted in the Army. After graduating from Basic Training I sent my grandfather a picture of me in my Class A uniform. Although I wasn't there to witness his pleasure, I could feel his pride from thousands of miles away. He had always had high regard for the United States Army. He worked with them during the fall of Berlin and later in Indo-China.

For all these years I had resisted the pressure to be in the military. But growing up in a military family, I always distinguished between the soldier and the mission. However questionable or politically motivated their missions were, the soldiers who I had known had taken pride in their service. They had lived their lives as legendary examples of courage, integrity and sacrifice. They were mostly good human beings who thought they were out there to do great things. But I was in for a surprise when I joined the United States Army.

Every day since I have been in the military, I have carried on me a copy of the United States Constitution. It has always been a matter of contention for a lot of other soldiers since the day a Drill Sergeant had asked me if I was crazy or something for going around with that document. Sometimes when it became really contentious, I held my ground, telling people that I carried it as part of my religious beliefs. However deceptive that may sound, I am very religious about the Constitution. I have always believed that it was this founding document that made our country so great and led us to be that shining city on the hill.

I have been surprised how out of touch other soldiers were with this document that I consider as the center-pillar of our profession. I had thought we had taken an oath to defend that Constitution. However, I have yet to come across a soldier who can halfway explain to me what it is about. From my understanding, even though we begin our military careers with an oath to defend the United States Constitution, such an oath has been reduced to just a formality. In the Founding days, such an oath was highly important, as the last and greatest defense of a nascent nation. Now, the soldiers take an oath to defend the Constitution, without even knowing what they are committing to.

I have developed a very strong impression that most people are in the military because of a paycheck and benefits. How can we trust such a mercenary military to have some honor, pride and integrity, and do the right thing when the Government continues to use us as a tool to achieve their narrow and shallow objectives in places around the world that have nothing to do with our true national interests?

In my opinion, we are involved in conflicts around the world, which could itself be classified as invalid from the Constitutional point of view. But very few individuals have shown the courage to question the legality of such missions. The "conscientious objector" clause in the military was created as a means to accommodate the views of those who think differently than the rest. But, in the current military, it is only the perfect means to attract all sorts of negative attention toward you, to the point where you are excluded from most promotions and career-development opportunities. You are nothing short of a leper if you question the missions handed down to the military.

I was assigned to a highly notorious Stryker Brigade based at Fort Lewis in Washington. When I first arrived here in the summer of 2010, bad things were about to be disclosed by the media. Soldiers from an infantry battalion were caught doing very bad things to local nationals, while they were deployed in Afghanistan. That is the most I can talk about what happened in Afghanistan, because of the media blackout enforced by my brigade. The media have been kept in dark about the case to such an extent that the brigade has since been renamed, though the media reports still refer to it by its old name.

Although I was shocked and saddened when I first saw what these soldiers had done in Afghanistan, I was not surprised. The heavy daily dose of subtle anti-Muslim propaganda that we receive from our leadership creates an impression that soldiers can get away with a lot of bad things, as long as "certain people" do not find out about it. The derogatory manner by which military personnel refer to local Afghan and Iraqi nationals as 'Hajis' sums up how we really feel for them. There are stories of how soldiers have fed pork as beef to local nationals; knowing that it was against their religious beliefs. Then there are stories of how every Afghan man is a homosexual and acts as such on Thursdays. To sum it up, there is an impression that all Afghans are godless homosexuals, and that it is acceptable to abuse their religious beliefs. It reminds me of how we were made to hate Muslims and Sikhs, in a very subtle manner, as we grew up.

On the other hand, the leadership puts on a show about winning hearts and minds. I think if there are hearts and minds that need to be won, they are right here at home in the military. The soldiers can start fixing their hearts and minds by learning about the United States Constitution, our history and traditions. How many soldiers even know why and when we are authorized to go to war? The Constitution only authorizes the military to go to war if it has been formally declared by the United States Congress. None of the conflicts in which we are currently involved have been formally declared as wars by the United States Congress.

As I look back at my life, there hasn't been a moment when there was any Peace. There has always been some conflict going on somewhere, and some friend or family-member has bled for it. One thing common in all conflicts is that they all involve some State authority. I wonder if there will be any conflict in the world, were it not in the interest of the State to maintain its monopoly on force and authority.

On the tenth anniversary of the September 11 attacks, NBC was running a segment on children who had been born after those attacks. They were talking about how these children have never known Peace. They may never know what it used to be like when you could watch the television without a mention of some United States service-member passing away in a faraway land that most Americans could not point out on the map.

Unfortunately the editor for that segment needs to look a little further back into our past 125 years. We are the greatest war-making nation the world has ever seen. We have quickly built a legacy of being at open or covert conflict with someone, somewhere on God's green earth at any given time. Sometimes it is about bringing an end to evil empires, other times it is to protect other godless heathens from their own Government. We support and endorse corrupt, tyrannical and autocratic regimes, while lecturing other nations on freedom and democracy. We ally ourselves with extremist nation-states that still practice some form of apartheid. And after all is said and done, we beat the drums of pride about how glorious our founding fathers and ideals were, and how we wish to share them with the rest of the world. Where did we lose sight of an America as it was envisioned by our Founding Fathers?

I am much older than the children born after September 11, 2001, but I have never seen Peace in my life. What about the children in Africa? I have still been fortunate to get a good education and have great life-opportunities. What about entire generations of people around the world living under conflict? Mankind has done everything from inventing the wheel to putting his fellow men on the moon. Our cultural, social, scientific and technological accomplishments are not been known to have been surpassed by any other known species in the entire universe. But we can never figure out something as basic, yet highly desirable, as Peace.

I believe that in order to bring Peace in the world, we can do small things here at home in America that will have a long-lasting impact. We need to get back to the kind of activism that came around in the days of the Draft. As long as we have a Government in Washington that refuse have a military strictly based on the Constitution, and going to war only as directed by the Constitution, private citizens must avoid military service. Parents must discourage their children from joining the military. Those who do volunteer for military service need to be highly educated in the area of United States Constitution. Service-members must be held to high standards and must be held accountable for unconstitutional actions.

I still believe in the nobility of military service. The stories of soldiers jumping from planes into machine-gun fire, charging onto beaches from amphibious vehicles, running into gunfire and jumping on grenades to save their battle-buddies will forever be legendary for the initiated as well as the uninitiated. But, are we really defending the Republic by shedding our blood? Just like there are countless others of valor in war, there are countless stories of how the men and women in Washington have only gotten richer and more powerful, as their families have become dynasties feeding off the military-industrial complex. War under its current design is not the answer for Peace.

I have a nephew who was born while I was in Basic Training, as the first-born of the next generation. The last time I was home in San Diego, I stared into his beautiful grey eyes and told my brother, "This is it! I am the last one in our family who will ever serve in the military." Our family has sacrificed a lot. The best way we can honor the family tradition of military service is by bringing it to a respectful end. When enough of us refuse to be a part of the State's aggression, my nephew will know what Peace is like. If not for us, maybe for the sake of future generations, it is about time we invented Peace.

The Masculinity of War

Kathleen Barry

Kathleen Barry, Ph.D., sociologist and feminist activist, is Professor Emerita of Penn State University. She is the author of five books. Her first, Female Sexual Slavery, *launched an international movement against violence against women. Her latest,* Unmaking War, Remaking Men: How Empathy Can Reshape Our Politics, Our Soldiers and Ourselves, *was published in 2011.*

Why peace? What happens to our concept of peace when we no longer limit peace to the absence of war, or see peace primarily as the end of state aggression and military and militia fighting? If we think of peace primarily as national and regional security, we hinder our discovery of different approaches to achieving lasting peace in our world.

When, however, we broaden and deepen our expectation of peace by taking it into the deeply personal and very intimate realities of our lives, we stumble upon human longing for it. That is where we find that for many, women in particular, peace from invasions and occupations are inseparable from intimate peace where the invasion is of one's body, mind and spirit. That violation— whether in bedrooms, workplaces, or on the streets where we walk—haunts women, not only in war zones but in "secure" states throughout the world.

The violence of war, whether or not you are its direct victim from a bullet or a bomb, controls your being, invades your body, shapes your emotions and powerfully frames your interactions with others. That is a cost of war rarely considered. That same internalization of masculine violence occurs for victims of rape, battery and sexual abuse, and because of that the United Nations finally has launched a global "Say no to violence against women" campaign. Masculine violence in war and in violence against women must be counted in the adverse effects of state aggression; it demands of us that eliminating both be combined in our plans for peace. That peace is not only the entreaty of peoples invaded and occupied, it is the quest of women around the globe, when their state is at war and when it is not.

Is rape not war? Or is it only relevant to peace when it is a strategy of war, a military aggression to harm women and humiliate their men? What of the personal terrorism of individual women all over the world who are subjected to rape? Would ending rape at home, on the streets, in war not open another path to peace? Would that be the same kind of peace that occurs, however tentatively, with the cessation of war? In searching for peace, can there be only an enemy of one in each invasion of the body?

Taking our question "Why peace?" to domains broader and deeper than ending war, I persist into the interiority of peace to ask, *How can we know what violence is when it is privatized and turned into individual dehumanization*? That is, when it has no context beyond one's body, when the war zone is one's self, when it is unspoken, when it is an undeclared war not by a state but by a rapist or a gang of them. Unlike war which is public, seen at least within the war zone, boasted and mourned, rape outside of war zones is usually an attack on one.

In the weeks, months, and even years after I was raped decades ago when I was in my early twenties, my heart desperately wanted peace, peace that would free me from the terrorizing memory, from everyday fears, peace that might allow me to regain something that had been lost to me, peace that is personal security. Combining the terrorism of violence against women, we might ask, *Is there any security in a state if personal security is regularly violated?*

Feminism has taken the unseen and unspoken of rapes, along with its enforced isolation and invisibility of women, into the public eye, to make the personal political. Almost instantly and spontaneously our isolation in pain and humiliation transformed our consciousness to the realization that rape is an act of power, that it must be addressed as a political issue. My own hunger for peace joined with a collective demand of women everywhere. Regardless of state boundaries and racial or cultural frameworks, we released ourselves and each other from haunting questions such as "Why me?" Together, our feminist consciousness forged a new awareness that power is sexual and gendered, and that it enforces female subordination through violent terrorism.

Understanding rape as a violation of personal peace reveals how terrorism, wherever or however it occurs, captures one's body seeking to suffocate one's self. For just as rape is a violation of personal peace and individual security, so is war. It is not only states that invade and occupy, those are the acts of aggression carried out in the masculinity of war. Just as I was initially alone when I was trying to peel off the crippling effects of masculine violence, so are women, men and children trying to regain clean water-supply, quiet homes, schools, healthcare—all of which crumble around them during war. So are people trying to protect their villages, overcome by depression, anxiety, nervousness and hyper-vigilance that the violence of war invokes. Those are the rape victim's burden too.

When I took up the subject of war from the perspective of how men are made expendable for it ("the soldier's sacrifice") in *Unmaking War, Remaking Men* (2011), I discovered the extent to which the masculinity of war *is* the masculinity of violence against women. It can begin with a good intention, that of protecting women, children, communities and the state. But even its first assumption, that women require male protection, is faulty. It is a pretext for male domination which ultimately turns back against women. It becomes the justification for war crimes in illegal wars such as U.S. wars against Iraq and Afghanistan from that initial faulty premise.

The protector role is an expectation of what I call core masculinity, which is both universal and socially prescribed for manhood. Men vary greatly in their individual responses to this social expectation of them: some reject it along with the violence required of them, while others take it on with macho vigor as a means of domination. And of course there are many gradations and variations in between. But the role as a social construction is a standard of manhood across cultures. Many men suffer challenges to their manhood when they do not engage in the macho roles laid out for them. Militaries rely on that core masculinity as an instrument of state aggression.

Take for example the thirteen-year-old Libyan boy who faced the camera behind the journalist somewhere in Libya with earnest almost innocence to say, "I'm going to kill Gaddafi." Of that he was certain, just as he was certain of what Gaddafi had done to Libya or to his family that showed in the pained and angry furrows on the brow of his otherwise youthful face. This was still in the early days of Libya's rebellion. If you were to empathize with him, you would see in him no doubt, no hesitation, no sense of glory, no macho and definitely no cold indifference. You could read on his face that the horror that was Gaddafi had to be stopped once and for all. He appeared neither indifferent to the fact that he might be killed, nor was there any evidence in his tone or demeanor that he was seeking glory or martyrdom. It appeared to be clear to him and his 16-year-old friend that they had to act—and to act like men as they headed off to the rebels' training camp.

That Libyan boy already knew his duty—to protect his family and his people. The revolution opened a space for him to take the action so that he could take his part in ending the harm, torture, massacres of Gaddafi's regime. More than likely, among the men who mingled in the background behind this boy and his friend with the same conviction and goal were recruiters, men who were bringing in boys from the streets and farms to prepare for armed resistance to Gaddafi. They, too, were fulfilling the requirements of core masculinity, acting on the aggression they had learned and the violence that is necessary to be a protector. The world of gender expectations combines with Gaddafi's vicious dictatorship to show them that there is no other way to settle issues.

This boy was acting from the same expendability of his own life that drove many well-intended young American men to enlist after the 9/11/2001 attack on the U.S. For so many it was a matter of duty, a measure of manhood, an obligation of the protector role that made them expendable for war in the first place. And there were the others—macho types ready for a fight, with that we'll-show-you-who-is-the-strongest-toughest-meanest bravado. In the end, by the time they were in combat, both the well-intended would-be protectors and the meanest macho men had become all the same.

Masculinity is constructed to become an instrument of state aggression. It expects men to fight for peace, or at least believe they are fighting for peace, risk their lives, not knowing whether they will return from a combat mission alive or in a casket. Failure to do so is failure to be a man. That is how violence and killing are embedded in the social expectations of masculinity. Of course, not all men are conditioned to violence, many choose paths of peace and resistance, refusing to kill. But they, unfortunately, do not represent the standard masculinity across cultures and around the globe. Encouraged toward violence in male dominated societies, that violence that men take into war will often explode against women in private.

In exploring the interiority of personalized violence of war and against women, I have found that remorselessness drives aggression. It is trained into soldiers by the military, reinforced in combat by the bravado of their buddies. It is required for them to be able and willing to bomb and kill. It gives rise to the kind of sociopathy we find among rapists, and men who abuse their partners, wives and children. And it is complete with satisfaction and glibness, joking about their kill or that house they just demolished, or that woman's body just invaded. Remorselessness is a failure of empathy that militaries count on in their soldiers who are engaged in state aggression.

By contrast, empathy for another's suffering, an individual rape victim, a battered wife, or a people such as Palestinians, Iraqis, Afghans who are occupied, can bring home to us the intolerable effects of state aggression. Empathy invokes action for peace. In writing *Unmaking War, Remaking Men* (2011), I found that I could not get close to realistic strategies for peace until I was able to empathize—not only with the innocent victims of war, but with the soldiers in combat too. Empathy made the differences between their intentions in enlisting and their actions in combat abundantly clear to me. From there I could begin to think of programs for security and peace. But any approach we take will require men divesting themselves of their conditioning to the masculinity of both war and violence against women.

Understanding the Myths
of War and Interventionism

Ryan Dawson

Ryan Dawson is the author of Welcome to the USSA: Corruption in the Government and Media *and producer of* War by Deception. *He is an ambassador of Good Will for Japan, a webmaster, radio host, and political filmmaker. He teaches Economics and Business English to Japanese professionals. Ryan is a graduate of the College of William & Mary, with degrees in History and Philosophy. He's also a professional Martial Arts instructor, father, social activist, and school teacher.*

I think when we are young (at least when I was younger, in the pre-internet days), many important questions about war and peace get framed under false linear dichotomies. Within these poorly framed questions come simplified opposing sides with troubling associations. As a young man, the position of peace was presented to me with associations to the naïve, to weaklings, to drugged-out hippies, to people who spit on soldiers and called them "baby-killers," and to parasitical groups of ungrateful people, who enjoyed the freedoms that others brought them through fighting, but who were unwilling to fight themselves.

Opposing war was seen as opposing "the troops," rather than merely opposing the government's decision to send them into battles. After all, they were brave and fighting supposedly on our nation's behalf. But people fighting and being brave isn't the question. The question is: should they be fighting at all, not how they are fighting. Opposing war is not opposing the troops, but getting that point across to cult-like followers of war can be quite a task.

War, on the other hand, was presented as a tragic but necessary thing. The world isn't always rational, and so force is needed to defeat force. It's not because we wanted it to be that way, but because it is that way. War was glorified. From GI Joe to historical figures, honor and reputation rests on heroic deeds of war. The shining example given of "good war" is WWII, because it supposedly ended the Holocaust. War was even said by some to be responsible for how the U.S. got out of the Great Depression, and a viable way to jump-start an economy in the future. We were in the middle of a Cold War with the U.S.S.R. and the picture was painted very clearly in black and white. We were good, they were bad and crazy; the only thing protecting us was support for the military, and military spending.

Missing from this rather flat analysis of war vs. peace were many things. First of all, the associations were misguided and irrelevant. The merit of an idea should rest in its philosophy and not on who is portrayed as accepting it. Secondly, the idea that all fighting is intrinsically about protecting or spreading the ideals of freedom—not polluted by economic motives, prejudice, deception, nationalist-ego, etc.—is a massive and foolish assumption. History shows that in war after war, one pretext is given to hide another less acceptable motive. But the press and government can control perception through deception.

[See http://www.rys2sense.com/anti-neocons/viewtopic.php?f=11&t=15034]

Painting war with a blanket brush, rather than looking at each case of each war individually, is another mistake. Assuming malicious intentions cannot or will not piggyback on top of more noble-sounding motivations is what is actually naive and not fitting with history. Even WWII, despite crushing fascist powers, must also be seen in its entirety. Millions of people were killed, not only by the Axis side but by the allies as well. Millions of people, even in the allies' own territory, were made to starve to death, because as a tactic it was determined to damage the enemies as well.

The overkill, once the writing was on the wall; the nuking of civilian cities; the unimaginable atrocities by the allied powers (and not just Stalin)... all this showed that the war between imperial powers, which had in the past killed off 20 percent of the earth's population, (in some cases, intending genocide), was not a war of good vs. evil, but of evil vs. evil. It wasn't the common soldier to blame, and there wasn't a uniform motive between the factions involved. There is so much deception and manipulation in war that a clear-cut label for who's malicious, who's was heroic, who's greedy or compassionate (or simply ignorant), can't be made in any broad, sweeping sense. It's much more complicated than that.

The idea that WWII is what ended the Depression is a horribly crass generalization, absent of any meaningful understanding of economics. But it tends to be ignorance, about economics and the industry of war, which obfuscates the more sinister facts about why and how wars get started and promoted. It seems every war has public and private layers. Private, for-profit motives are masked behind a more acceptable public pretext.

Sadly, there are many who will willingly accept whatever pretext they are fed. The propaganda doesn't have to be very sound, or even make sense. The official excuse for war can act as a moral high ground, no matter how transparent it is, to justify the acts of imperialism. A war-supporter may not be terribly interested is questioning whether or not the propaganda is based on evidence or sincerity. Prejudice; a vicarious sense of masculinity; primitive, base-level emotions of feeling powerful; conditioning, bigotry, party-affiliation, or psychological authoritarian personalities... all contribute to why a person will uncritically devote themselves to warmongering.

Of those, party-affiliation is the most baffling, because it ignores principles all together. There were those who passionately supported George W. Bush's wars, but opposed Bill Clinton's or Barak Obama's. Likewise, there were those who passionately opposed Bush's wars, but have looked the other way, or even made rationalizations for Obama, as he has continued the very same wars, and even started new ones. An action is wrong or right, based on what the act is and the effects it has, not on who is doing the act. For example, if poisoning children with depleted uranium was wrong when Bush did it –because of the horrible birth-defects it creates in newborns, or the slow, agonizing death it distributes randomly to innocents within its range—then the immorality of this act must certainly be the same under an Obama banner. The kids will still be dying in the same manner.

To go further, if purposely starving millions to death was wrong under Stalin during WWII, then why wasn't it also wrong under the British during the same war, as perpetuated in Bengal? Or how about the policies of the Internatoinal Monetary Fund (IMF), which intentionally creates debt for the profits of corporatism, even at the cost of pushing innocents into abject poverty and sometimes starvation? This ability to say to oneself, "it's not wrong when WE do it," is both mind-blowing and tragic.

Vast numbers of people are picking sides, not based on the situation at hand but on the beliefs they attribute to the side they oppose. Does the peace-advocate hate the particular war because of its gratuity, monetary and moral costs, or just because they associate the pro-war side with greedy "old white guys" and "Westernism"—to which they attribute some other ill, like racism or excessive wealth? Do they really have a problem with the war, or just with the characters currently in charge?

Meanwhile, do war-advocates really feel like the nation's security is threatened? Do they really hold deep concerns and beliefs that the military is 'liberating' people, and that it has nothing to do with financial interest and resources? Or do they just oppose the fashionable Western and white-man bashing that they associate with the "kooks" in the peace movement?

Or is it simply a case of being on the 'winning team?'

People are supporting and opposing wars for all the wrong reasons. They are supporting political candidates for all the same wrong reasons. It's become a contest of image over substance. Of course, I stand with the peace movement. I do so as an activist. My reasons are philosophical, and it doesn't make a dime's worth of difference to me which party or country is in charge of these unjust wars. A few eye-opening things have set me on this path. I remember them vividly and the impact they had on my thinking.

One was a passage from a Native American, who had witnessed a battle between French and Spanish forces in Florida. Then men just lined up and died, shooting at one another. The native man had never seen such total war. He had never seen it so large or deadly. He inquired to know what had happened to create such fighting. Learning the small differences between their takes on the same god did not clear up the matter at all. Learning that these men were strangers, but died trying to kill each other anyway, made the matter even more confusing. This was not personal; these were not families avenging some wrongdoing. These people were paid to try to kill one another, for the benefit of another whom they had also never met. And they were fighting over land that belonged to neither of them. (By 'them' I don't just mean France or Spain, I mean *them personally*.)

A similar eye-opener struck me after reading *All Quiet on the Western Front*. A German and French soldier injured one another inside a trench. They were both too damaged to finish the job, and so as time passed they began talking to one another. They discovered that they both had families and similar interests, and had the circumstances been that they had met in a bar instead of the trench, they would have been friends. Neither stood to gain much if anything from the war, nor held deep convictions for why they were fighting at all. "Throw the generals in a cage and let them duke it out," one of them thought. Now this sounds like hyperbole, but it is actually not far off. It's just something that sat with me in junior high, as a puzzle in the back of my mind. How could people risk their lives, trying to kill people they didn't hate, to award property to someone else they didn't even know?

Another spark was a conversation that took place in the film *JFK* by Oliver Stone. It was the discussion that took place outside between Jim Garrison (Kevin Costner's character) and Mr. X (Donald Southerland's character). This was my first peek into the industrial motives for a real war. He discussed Bell, the First Bank of Boston, General Dynamics, and so on, and the reasons to push for a medium to use the Helicopters and F-111 fighter jets, in order to procure profits for themselves, with the government acting as a giant ATM machine and the war acting as the stage. This was a case, though portrayed in an entertainment film, where the CIA was acting as a broker for transnational businesses. Meanwhile, back in reality, these companies were given lucrative contracts. The revolving doors among the CIA, DOD, elected government, and war industries have never stopped spinning. (President Eisenhower also warned about this in his farewell address.)

It is not listed as such because it is not categorized as such, but the U.S. military is the largest umbrella corporation in the world. The U.S. spends more on 'defense' than all of the rest of the countries in the world put together. Paying more for the machines doesn't make them any stronger just more expensive. An analysis of board of directors members for the largest defense contractors, and those of the parent companies of any of the major mass media outlets (ABCNBCBSFOX), reveals a disgusting degree of overlap. The press is a PR machine for the pentagon and big Pharma. This is because they own it, literally.

Political analysis is at sub-circus levels, with presumed adults screaming at each other to shut up, and trading name-calling and one-liners. It's the same garbage as the mindless factions of party tribalism, who can damn an action one minute and give it praise the next, once the same action is under their banner. The politicians are being marketed like brands, rather than evaluated based on their policies. They issue vague [fill in the blank with whatever is psychologically gratifying] remarks, like, "Yes we can," or simply "change," "hope," "believe"… They play on demographics; a veteran, a woman, a black guy, and whoever has more media attention wins. The people are choosing between the corporately preselected. Monetary policy and foreign policy remain the same, and about the only thing changing are the celebrity scandals and other non-news sensationalism used to fill up the airtime with nonsense.

This is why I became a writer, blogger, filmmaker, and all-around activist.

The key to bringing down this whole structure is breaking the media monopoly, and the way around the state-sponsored media is the internet. Truth can stand on its own. The only reasons my site and other grounded alternative media sites can exist, is because they tell the truth. They've stood the test of time, and told the truth while the mass media lied. People have prudence. Politicians can no longer lie about what they have said, without a worry that the news will call them out on it. Because of the internet, nearly anyone with a few minutes of time can post two videos side by side proving the liars' glaring contradictions.

In the old model, the politician could just lie about a position, and rely on people forgetting what was said, and simply denying it to those who don't forget. There are some comedy shows which have made a career out of filling the gaps the news media ought to be covering, but aren't. It's comical because the lies are so bad and so easy to detect and debunk. One wonders how anyone could be audacious. enough to pretend to have never done or said something, when we have them on tape doing and saying it! Yet it continues. The new anchors do the senseless adolescent junk and the comedians do the news analysis, albeit satirically. How strange.

Someone has to take it seriously. Why are the millions of people killed in the Vietnam, Korean, and Iraq Wars not considered holocaust-victims, like those from WWII? Because history books are written by the winners. Those families and those murdered or tortured by imperial hands died, not as victims but as "collateral damage." They are written off as a side-effect of the intended killing, but they are the bulk of the casualties. These were wars of choice and all were based on deceptions. But it's not terrorism when WE do it.

The excuse for the first two would be, the U.S. was fighting communism. That's what the Germans could say, too: they were fighting communist and international-finance corporatism (a special kind of communism for the upper class only, also known as crony capitalism). The excuse for the Iraq War changes with the seasons: nuclear threat, anthrax, WMDs, liberating Kurds, babies on incubators, 911, fighting Al Qaeda, getting rid of Saddam, an imminent threat on America or the UK… just about everything has been said, other that the actual reasons of the very men who actually created the lies that led to the war: the protection and interest of the State of Israel; and putting a U.S. military presence in the heart of the Middle East. The mission-name was even changed, from Operation Iraqi Liberation (OIL) to Operation Iraqi Freedom. A former AIPAC employee on CNN, Wolf Blitzer, wanted to coin the start of Shock and Awe as "A-Day." It sounded something like D-Day in the 'good' war, WWII. Apparently it didn't dawn on him that would also sound like "a day." Maybe he was too busy pontificating on the idea that people were sitting around, in sheer awe of how mighty his country's big bombs were.

Mass murder is mass murder. But no one is held accountable. The corporations pushing for war feel like their main moral obligation is to grow their company at any cost. It's growth for the sake of growth, the same ideology as a cancer cell. If someone in the cogs has a moral objection, they can quickly be replaced by someone who does not. It becomes a headless operation. Each person can rationalize that it is going to happen anyway, so why not let it be by their hands; at least that way, they're getting paid. It's like littering; very few single acts have a measurable effect. It's the collective process that makes it a danger.

Corporations are not intrinsically bad. They can be wonderful things that increase one's standard of living and provide beneficial technologies and products to those who desire them. Government is the problem. The signal greatest enabler of mal-capitalism is the government. And the largest enabler for that government is the Federal Reserve. This Banking, Government, Business *zaibatsu* is the greatest challenge of our day. There isn't a quick fix. But there is a solution. Key to bringing down the system is building a viable alternative media that rests on its reputation for telling the truth rather than on commercial strings.

If Thomas Paine had had the web, then "Common Sense" would have been on email, read over a viral youtube video, plastered on social networking sites, and originated on his personal website. Peace will not come by retreating into nature or some act of self-absorption. Peace comes when the propaganda for war has been rightly picked apart and exposed. That's what we do.

When you live outside the U.S. (like I do, in Japan, where the U.S. government dropped two nuclear bombs), and you see the school children at a kindergarten running around on a playground and moms watching the families, with all the same joys and problems as anywhere else, you wonder how the hell does it get to the point that these people are on fire? How are they at a point where they are being burned to death, by killing machines sent from across the ocean? How can people collectively punish whole populations for how a ruling class behaves? "They" didn't bomb Pearl Harbor, the Japanese military did, and Pearl Harbor was a U.S. military base not just some civilian city.

I don't want to get too deeply into the oil embargo, or the politics of the war. Japan was in a middle of a war with two U.S. allies, Stalin and Mao. The conflicts with China and Russia stretched back more than 50 years, with previous wars. Both countries neighbored Japan, and then the U.S. cut off 90 percent of Japan's oil. That is why Japan attacked U.S. bases in Hawaii and the Philippines. I have trouble discussing it dryly and academically. It's far simpler. Real people have been killed in unnecessary wars, and in more "legitimate" wars, real people are killed in the unnecessary overkill.

WWII is the best example for the pro-war mentality, yet even there, by some outrageous leap of logic, non-intervention is blamed for WWII, rather than Hitler's militarism. The conditions, economic and political, that allowed such a madman to gather such a following, are ignored. Germany was in a state of hyperinflation. The German public had ended WWI via munitions strikes. Germany had won the Eastern front, and then had a stalemate on the Western Front.

That was a war started by the allied powers, when the black-hand, a Serbian terrorist group, had assassinated Franz Ferdinand. Russia had sided with Serbia. The French central Banks had been financing the rapid industrialization of Russia. They had a vested interest in ensuring that Russia won the war and repaid their loans. England had been in a Naval Arms race with Germany, and all of them, including the newcomer Italy, had been politicking over dividing the "big African cake" among themselves.

It was a matter of time before colonial classic (the UK and France) took it to Germany. Once the Central Banking branch was created in America in 1913, the green light was on to ignite a massive war, but they underestimated the German industrial strength. In the aftermath of that war, the European powers had taken no mercy on the German economy. The German veterans had felt betrayed, and the general public had joined them in their ideologies, even as they ran out of bread. Madmen arise out of mad conditions. Everyone rightly condemns Hitler, but the quite similar imperial escapades and genocidal atrocities, committed by the allied powers in their own global colonial wars, get ignored.

Purposely brutalizing people financially is an act of aggression, accomplished through embargoes, the IMF, and the setting up of puppet governments through force or bribery by the CIA. These puppet governments then contract out their nation's wealth to U.S. state assisted corporations in exchange for personal wealth, or to simply avoid getting shot. The First World War was also an act of aggression not necessity. The blame should be placed on more than just the Germans. Interventionism needs to be recognized as having occurred long before the invasion of Poland. Violence begets violence.

It's the restrictions on trade, not just prejudice or greed and economic instability, that predicate wars. Freedom and Peace go hand in hand. Trading with people and working in collaboration with others is not isolationism, it's just not intervention. Restricting trade, and creating state-assisted monopolies to overtake an area's resources, is intervention and always harmful. Governments shouldn't be involved in enterprise at all, but exist only to uphold contracts through the courts and protect people from fraud; they should not be picking winners and losers in the market, or assisting their friends' business with the people's tax money.

When I was 15, my home in North Carolina was flooded by a hurricane; we moved to Virginia, where I finished high school. I had no trouble with my new school, or in making new friends. My trouble was after school, and it came not from criminals but rather from the police. I have no criminal record, because I have not committed a crime. But I was in court for something or other for six months in a row. Police pulled me over and searched my car, for no reason, on five different occasions. I protested and declared my rights. They simply ignored me.

I have always lived on an island, so I had no idea what a police state much of America was, and I had no idea what a prejudice towards youth existed there. I remember vividly my parents asking me why I was staying home one weekend, both Friday and Saturday nights. They wondered if I had adjusted to my new school. I had, but I didn't want to go into town. I'd been harassed by police six weekends in a row.

I had a cousin who played football at UVA, so I would go to his home games. But often after a game, you could see the police, in the parking lot or at the UVA "corner," beating the hell out of some teenager, or some drunk adult. A friend of mine was once stripped to his underwear and choked by three cops. They believed he had been drinking underage, because of his natural speech-impediment. They would not let him explain anything. They didn't let me explain anything, either.

One of the police officers even lied to me, and said they had film of both of us drinking from the parking lot camera and that we could go downtown. I said, "No! You don't have anything like that, because we were not drinking." I never had a drink until I was 22. My friend was a rather big guy for a high school student, and I believe the police enjoyed ganging up on him and humiliating him. (I foolishly called in and complained about what had happened. From that day on, I was hounded by police.)

There were drugs all over my high school. I was not a drug user, but I discovered one of the sources of the drugs was… from the school cops. Also, in my short time in Virginia our house was robbed. A good friend of mine had her head split open by a large rock, when she and two others were attacked by a gang. Instead of helping defend her from this group, I hesitated to act, because I was afraid of the trouble I would get in by the police. As a result, a 14-year-old girl needed surgical staples placed in her head.

The following year, I was assaulted the day before my prom. I didn't fight back; I was afraid of the trouble I would get in and that I would miss my prom. To this day, I don't know why the guy who hit me did so. The police did nothing to prevent any of these crimes, but the laws certainly prevented me from defending others and myself. I personally witnessed the police attacking unarmed people with excessive force more than a dozen times. It simply isn't reported. Nothing makes me feel less safe than seeing a cop. Nearly everyone has a story.

Just in 2009, the place where I taught martial arts was set on fire. It was clearly arson as the culprits moved no-trespassing signs from where they were in the parking lot up next to the building where the fire was. The police did nothing. They blamed the fire on a cigarette. I took pictures and made a video presentation about it. I had one detective talk to me on the phone about it, and they promised to come look at it. They never came. Nothing was ever done about it.

The arsonists were in all likelihood the kids who had been openly bragging about doing it, who were also spotted vandalizing some cars in the area the same night. Without a building, I was out of work. The economy of our Island was already decimated, because the government had shut down our beaches. The Park Service stood guard over a park they are Congressionally supposed to be providing access to; instead, they were blocking access to it.

It's abuse. But who do you go to, when it is your own government who is stealing the land? Who do you call, when it's the police themselves attacking people and selling drugs?

It was these events that helped me make my decision to leave the U.S.

again. I cannot imagine what a military occupation is like. But I do understand what it is like to be unable to step on the land you grew up on. I understand a little of what it might be like for Palestinians to get harassed by settlers, but not be able to fight back without a police force on top of them. Back in North Carolina, Blackwater was right in our backyard; the headquarters is close to my twin brother's house. I can tell you that even the worst cops would be the mildest of Blackwater grunts. These guys are holy-roller, jack-off-missile-Johnny, glass-parking-lot types, given high tech guns and virtually no oversight or accountability.

When our political leaders need helicopters and tens of thousands of armored police to protect their conventions from the public, something is wrong. When such a large percentage of the citizens have depression or some other mental illness, and kids are shooting up schools, something is wrong with the environment. Theft is right out in the open. Wall Street used fraud, in the form of false credit ratings and uninsured assets and non-collateralized bets, to swindle tens of billions of dollars. They were they bailed out via counterfeit money from Ben Bernanke, who passed the costs to the public in the form of inflation and a lower living standard.

Murder is out in the open. These recent wars have been based on lies. Civilians are killed as a matter of policies. Privacy is violated in the open. The TSA is taking naked pictures of people, while giving them radiation or fondling them in invasive, guilty-until-proven-innocent body searches. The government can search you home or your mail, without even telling you. It's theft, slavery, murder, invasion of property and person, and it's all done openly—in the name of protecting you. Intervention means loss of liberty at home and loss of peace abroad. It all hides behind the myth of the "good" war. The police and the military are given automatic honor. Some deserve it. Some certainly do not. It's wrong to automatically give honor to anyone, but we live in a world of black-and-white dichotomies.

We don't have an accounting problem, or a "they hate us for our freedoms" problem. We have a philosophical problem. Governments start wars by deception; that is easy enough to demonstrate. Having once lost my home, I can somewhat relate to those who have their homes bulldozed, or blown to bits, through no fault of their own. The difference is, wars and occupations are man-made. I fear for the U.S.: as the dollar declines and police brutality rises, secret prisons and torture continue to thrive, more nations are invaded for "humanitarian" reasons, the treasury is deep into the red, the cost of living is rising, unemployment continues to grow… and Washington just keeps doing more of the same. That's the definition of insanity.

All empires end the same way. We can either end the addiction to war and state-orchestrated money-junkie transfer of wealth from bottom to top, or we can have an economic collapse, and the intervention will end anyway, the hard way. What do we want to leave for future generations? What world do we want to live in when we are older? Do we want a world of torture and war, or one of peace and non-intervention? The choice is obvious to me.

War is Particularly Barbaric, and We Can Stop It

Robert Naiman

Robert Naiman is Policy Director at Just Foreign Policy. He edits the Just Foreign Policy daily news summary and writes on U.S. foreign policy at Huffington Post. *Robert has worked as a policy analyst and researcher at the Center for Economic and Policy Research and Public Citizen's Global Trade Watch. He has masters degrees in economics and mathematics from the University of Illinois and has studied and worked in the Middle East.*

Why peace? There are a lot of different forms of injustice and violence and unnecessary human suffering in the world, as we all know. But there are particular features of war as we know it that are particularly compelling, that give the issue of ending war a particular urgency, especially for those of us in the United States, whose government (as Martin Luther King said, and unfortunately it's still true) is the greatest purveyor of violence in the world today.

Total brutality

Modern war, as we know it, is total brutality. When a country is in a state of war, it's like a big neon sign telling people, "Forget everything you know about elementary human morality, everything you know from your upbringing, from your family, from your friends, from your knowledge of the world, from your religion, from your community, about basic standards for decent treatment of other people. Those rules are suspended and no longer relevant. Instead, you are now encouraged to treat other people in the cruelest way, either for the supposed cause, or your own benefit, or for sport." Everything bad that happens on earth in terms of people mistreating other people—genocide, murder, torture, rape, racism, massacres, driving people from their homes, destroying their livelihoods—is much more likely to happen in a state of war.

In high school, we had to read *Lord of the Flies*, a novel that describes children who are left on their own on an island and become beastly. At the time, I absolutely detested this book, because I understood the author to be saying, "People are just basically rotten, and if you remove the constraints of civilization, people will behave like cruel beasts, because that is the state of nature." I think this notion is very wrong, and very destructive. It suggests that we need to follow Authority, or else there will be brutal chaos. However, that notion misses the fact that it is often Authority which creates brutal chaos—for example, by promoting war—and we often need to resist Authority to make the brutal chaos stop.

But there is another way of reading the book, and that is that the author isn't describing humans in a state of "nature," but describing them in a state of

592

"war." And that story, I think, has a lot of truth to it. War is a tremendous engine for brutality, and creates a tremendous momentum for brutality. It's not just the direct violence ordered by the generals. That's for starters. It's also the "open season" created by the suspension of the ordinary rules of human morality. In every war, you see terrible atrocities that go well beyond the atrocities that the generals have explicitly authorized.

Consider Abu Ghraib, for example. It's obvious how something like this was quite predictable from the orders given by Cheney and Rumsfeld and others. And yet, of course, as far as we know, they never gave specific orders for those particular acts to be carried out, or for those acts to be photographed and the photographs to be spread around. Why would they? How did what happened at Abu Ghraib help the U.S. government achieve its objectives in Iraq, such as they were? It didn't.

To me that shows how there is a kind of genie of brutality that is unleashed in war. The leaders say: to achieve this objective, we need to unleash a certain amount of brutality—"get in touch with our dark side," as Cheney put it. But once the genie of brutality is unleashed, you can't contain it. You can't say, "you're allowed to be this much brutal, and no more," and make it stick, because it's a fundamentally a contradiction. Once you say it's okay to be brutal, then any constraint you try to impose seems arbitrary, legalistic, academic, bureaucratic. Any constraint you try to impose obviously doesn't come from basic human morality, because you've already thrown that in the trash. And that total brutality that is unleashed, in addition to the brutality directly ordered by the generals, is a fundamental reason to oppose war.

Most victims have no say

Not only is modern war total brutality, it's also an extreme violation of the most rudimentary values of self-determination and human freedom, because the overwhelming majority of victims of war never have any say in the decisions which lead to their victimization. When someone dies in a skydiving or mountain-climbing accident, that's a terrible tragedy. But at least, one presumes, the victim undertook the activity voluntarily, knowing that there was a certain risk. For the overwhelming majority of its victims, modern war isn't like that at all. The overwhelming majority of victims of war were never consulted in the decisions that led to them experiencing a state of war.

Recall the democracy and freedom story that was told before the U.S. invasion of Iraq in 2003. We were told that one of the key motivations of the war was to free the Iraqi people from the dictator Saddam Hussein and give them democracy and freedom.

In the abstract, divorced from context, it seems like a noble goal. If you could press a magic button, and thereby free millions of people from a brutal dictator and give them democracy and freedom, and if you were sure that pressing that magic button would have no cost to anyone, who wouldn't want to do so?

But of the course the reality isn't like that at all. Many hundreds of thousands of Iraqis lost their lives as a result of the U.S. decision to invade

Iraq. Would they—would their families—see this outcome as an acceptable trade-off? It seems doubtful that many would, but nobody bothered to try to find out. Of course, the idea that a small set of foreigners should make this decision about Iraq's future that cost hundreds of thousands of Iraqi lives and created millions of refugees, without consulting the people who would stand to pay the greatest cost, violates the most basic ideas of freedom and self-determination.

Wars, once started, are tremendously hard to stop

Modern wars have the property that, once started, they are tremendously hard to get out of. Protagonists of war frequently espouse the logic of losing gamblers: we have to keep going to recover our losses. Not all destructive human behaviors are like this. For example, sticking your finger in a pot of water on the stove is a dumb way to check to see how hot the water is. But at least it has the virtue that if the water is extremely hot, you will immediately withdraw your finger and limit the damage. Modern war is the opposite: the worse the war is going, the more we are told that we can't quit now, and indeed have to send more troops, drop more bombs, spend more money, be more ruthless.

Blowback and other long-term destructive consequences

Not only are wars hard to stop, but even after they end, their destruction doesn't stop. Civilians in Vietnam and Laos are still being killed by bombs the U.S. dropped during the Vietnam War. Veterans of wars that ended decades ago still suffer from combat injuries, from exposure to toxins, from post-traumatic stress.

Diversion of resources from human needs

War hurts civilians far from the field of battle, by stealing resources for destruction that should be used for meeting human needs. The U.S. is currently spending $100 billion a year for the war in Afghanistan, while the House has voted to cut funding for infant nutrition, supposedly as part of efforts to reduce the U.S. budget deficit. There are a lot of ways to waste money that could be spent on human needs, but war is a particularly expensive one.

Wars can be stopped

Some would have us believe that war is a permanent feature of the human condition that we can do nothing about. But the history of the last few decades shows that is not true. Wars can be stopped by concerted political action. Political pressure in Iraq and in the United States forced the Bush Administration in 2008 to accept a timetable for the withdrawal of U.S. forces from Iraq. International political pressure stopped the Israeli invasions of Lebanon in 2006, and of Gaza in 2009.

War is a uniquely evil force in human affairs, and it can be stopped. That is why I work for peace.

Building Blocks of a Global Campaign

Thomas Nash

Thomas Nash is Coordinator of the Cluster Munition Coalition.

Introduction

The international process to ban cluster munitions, often referred to as the "Oslo Process" after the city in which it was launched, is an example of a diplomatic initiative in which civil society played a highly involved role. States were of course the ultimate decision-makers, with a Norwegian-led core group of seven states launching the process in Oslo in February, 2007, and 108 states signing the Convention on Cluster Munitions in the same city in December, 2008. Civil society, though, organized under the banner of the Cluster Munition Coalition, was able to influence many of the decisions along the way, both at the national level and within the international negotiations. Because of this prominent partnership among states, civil society and international organizations, it is worthwhile looking more closely at some of the insights that can be drawn from the way non-governmental organizations approached the process to ban cluster bombs.

It is possible to draw many lessons learned from campaigns and coalition efforts in which one has been involved. Such insights will be different from different people's perspectives and it's impossible to present a definitive list. In this article, I have set out ten insights that have struck me as pertinent in relation to the civil-society effort to deal with the problem of cluster munition use, production and transfer by governments. They may or may not be applicable to other campaigning and coalition efforts, seeking to end other harmful government policies. There may also be other lessons learned from this campaign that are not captured here. By reflecting on these ten insights from the work of the non-governmental Cluster Munition Coalition, this article seeks to tell some of the story of how the movement against cluster bombs was able to achieve many of the goals it set for itself.

Global civil society coalitions, transnational advocacy networks

A lot has been written on the role of civil society in global politics, as well as on the phenomenon of global civil-society coalitions, or what are often called transnational advocacy networks.[1] There is also literature on the collaboration between these transnational advocacy

595

networks and middle power states. The process to ban cluster munitions has itself been the subject of such analysis.[2] This piece seeks to provide a contribution to this literature, by providing one concrete example of international civil society work.

Ten insights

The following ten points are drawn from my personal experience as Coordinator of the international non-governmental Cluster Munition Coalition (CMC), the central NGO partner throughout the process to ban cluster bombs.

1. Believe it's possible

The idea that you have to be convinced of something yourself before you can convince others is fairly obvious, but it assumes all the more importance when one is trying to rally a range of different NGOs with different interests and diverse cultures around a particular cause. This was certainly the case in the effort to prohibit cluster munitions. At the end of 2005—two years after the CMC was established—few people believed (or at least expressed a belief) that a ban on the weapon was possible. Indeed many observers stated that even a specific law restricting their use would be impossible. Three years later, in December of 2008, 94 governments signed a treaty prohibiting cluster munitions.

So even when critics and mainstream observers say the task is impossible, including perhaps some of your allies, it is crucial that a campaign have a leadership that genuinely believes the goal is achievable and necessary. Having a group of people who are somehow infected with the will to achieve what they believe is possible is a powerful unifying force: for the CMC, this group of individuals within the leadership kept each other motivated when the campaign faced setbacks and presented a united front to other campaigners and external partners including governments.

2. Be ready

When progress on the political front is difficult and it is impossible to get traction for advocacy efforts, a campaign can make good use of time to build the strength and reach of its network, to deepen the case behind the campaign and refine the intellectual framework underpinning it. It is worthwhile to consider the early period of the CMC, from its launch in November, 2003 to the Review Conference of the Convention on Certain Conventional Weapons in November, 2006.

During this period the CMC doubled the size of its NGO

membership, from around 90 when it was first established in 2003 to 180 at the end of 2006.[3] This period also saw the publication of a number of key reports on cluster munitions that began to present evidence, shape the debate and reframe the issue at hand. Brian Rappert, Richard Moyes and I published a number of reports and, with others, undertook a rather intensive process of discussions on the issue, with the aim of determining the best possible intellectual framework with which to pursue a prohibition on cluster munitions.

These reports included: "Out of Balance," which questioned the value of International Humanitarian Law (IHL) proportionality assessments in relation to cluster munitions given the UK government's failure to gather data on humanitarian harm; "Failure to Protect," which moved beyond IHL to set out a case for the prohibition of cluster munitions based on the pattern of harm and drawing on precautionary approaches; and "Foreseeable Harm," the first report on the use of cluster munitions during the conflict between Israel and Hezbollah in 2006.[4] Of course, during this period NGOs and other actors were undertaking a range of other work to document the problem and shape the discourse, including Human Rights Watch and other CMC members, the International Committee of the Red Cross (ICRC) and the United Nations (UN).[5]

Also during this period, a number of informal meetings took place between key players from NGOs, progressive states and international organizations. Two meetings were particularly significant in early 2006, the first hosted by the Geneva Forum and the second hosted by the Diana, Princess of Wales Memorial Fund. Both meetings brought together a relatively small group of key actors from states, civil society and international organizations to discuss strategy on a possible process to ban cluster munitions. These two gatherings were important in helping to develop and strengthen the strategic partnerships between for example Norway and the CMC. They were also important in helping to build a 'community of practice' on the cluster munitions issue, allowing key drivers of the process to feel a part of a group where they shared, were engaged in a shared enterprise, and could learn from each other and solve problems together.[6]

Of course, being ready means that once the foundations are in place, a campaign can take full advantage of opportunities when they arise. The CMC was faced with a number of such opportunities in 2006. When a close collaboration between Belgian civil society activists and progressive parliamentarians led to a process to prohibit the weapons in the national parliament in 2005 and 2006, the CMC had an early chance to mobilize and motivate its membership.

A December 14, 2005 email from Kasia Derlicka, asking CMC

campaigners to contact Belgian parliamentarians, urging them to support a draft bill banning cluster munitions stated that: "*If Belgium adopts the bill—it will be the first country to ban cluster munitions, which may have a domino effect on other countries, and hopefully can bring us to a global ban. Therefore, we believe it is very important if we can show international support for the current developments in Belgium.*"[7] On several other occasions during the draft law's eventually successful passage through parliament in early 2006, Belgian campaigners urged CMC members around the world to contact parliamentarians . This was the first major success for campaigners on cluster munitions.

The widespread use of cluster munitions in Lebanon in 2006 saw significant mobilization by a range of actors engaged on the issue. CMC member organization Human Rights Watch, together with UN personnel on the ground, confirmed that cluster munitions had been used. From that moment on, and as information on the scale of the use and contamination became available, the CMC issued regular updates to members based on communications with UN mine action staff in country.[8] States, independent researchers and in particular the global media were also heavily involved in the discussions on the use of cluster munitions. The CMC and such prominent members as Human Rights Watch in the U.S., Landmine Action in the U.K. and Handicap International in France regularly briefed the media on the issue to help shape and boost coverage.

3.   Move fast and make it inevitable

In order to take full advantage once an opportunity arises, an effective campaign can seek to move fast and maintain a sense of momentum and inevitability. Having an external deadline and a framework for the process can help keep up the pace and foster the sense that the outcome you seek is going to happen no matter what. The developments described above, together with other events in 2005 and 2006, provided the platform for the CMC to drive forward its ambition to prohibit cluster munitions and the campaign and its partners maintained a sense of urgency and intensity through to the signing of the treaty in December, 2008.

There was a genuine sense of humanitarian urgency throughout the process to ban cluster munitions. Not only were we dealing with continued casualties from unexploded cluster bombs dropped 40 years ago in southeast Asia, we had just seen the massive use in Lebanon and could envisage the devastation should the billions of submunitions stockpiled around the world ever be used. A common refrain from campaigners went something like this: "we are not going to spend years in negotiations, while people are being killed and injured on a daily basis and millions of cluster munitions sit in ammunition depots waiting to be used."

This sense of urgency was successful in pressing a remarkable pace in diplomatic terms: the period from the Lebanon conflict in July and August of 2006 to the adoption of the Convention on Cluster Munitions in Dublin in May, 2008 was less than two years. The seeds of this hectic pace were sown in the Oslo Declaration adopted at the initial meeting of likeminded states in Oslo in February, 2007. The key line of this political declaration stipulated a deadline of 2008, by which time states should "conclude" a legally binding instrument.[9] This was controversial and a number of states sought to remove the deadline. However, its value should not be underestimated and has not gone unnoticed in related circles: for example, the negotiating mandate adopted in 2009 for the Arms Trade Treaty included a deadline of 2012 for the conclusion of the instrument.

Once a campaign has momentum on its side and is able to control or at least regulate the tempo, it can help to foster a sense of inevitability of the outcome. If those involved in a process feel that events are moving fast and they are struggling to keep up with the schedule of meetings and the pace of developments, it can become easier for them to believe that the outcome being pursued by those driving the process is unavoidable. Once this change in attitude occurs, the political decision emerges as to whether it is better to get on board early and take a share in the credit or hold out and risk being dragged on board at the last minute perceived as a reluctant participant. In short, to use a sporting metaphor, a campaign with momentum behind it can stay on the front foot and keep opponents on the back foot.

4.   Dominate the data

Being able to command the information available on a particular issue is a very powerful asset to a campaign. The use of data was an important pillar of the campaign against cluster munitions.

Throughout the discussions on cluster munitions NGOs provided a lot of information on the humanitarian harm and on the global policy and practice with regard to cluster munitions.[10] In contrast states published very little information. This imbalance had a number of implications. States found themselves less effective at rebutting NGO claims about the impact of cluster munitions or the inadequacy of the IHL proportionality rule (given that they had gathered no data on humanitarian harm against which to balance the military advantage anticipated). States and others also failed to provide a case for the military necessity of cluster munitions. An ICRC meeting of experts from states, NGOs and the UN in Montreux provided a ready-made opportunity for pro-cluster munition military experts to set out the case in concrete terms as to why these weapons were essential. However, as the meeting's Irish rapporteur on military aspects noted, these experts did not deliver.[11] Instead, NGOs were able to come out of the meeting having presented data demonstrating a pattern of humanitarian harm over 40 years and—at least in the view of the NGO representatives at the meeting—having not received clear answers from the military experts from governments as to why cluster munitions were necessary and when they had ever been a battle winner.[12]

Through their use of data NGOs also became seen as authoritative. Government representatives from African and Latin American states and from states affected by cluster munitions, regularly came to CMC campaigners for advice in the negotiations. These government officials were often stretched covering a range of issues on the diplomatic agenda and many saw the CMC as a key resource. Their trust in and reliance on the CMC was in part possible because the CMC's interests were perceived as quite clearly humanitarian, rather than motivated by other factors, such as the military and commercial interests of producer and stockpiling states that were also providing briefings on the issue.[13]

It may not have been obvious to those involved on the NGO side at the time, but looking back, many campaigners may have overestimated the information and the expertise of those responsible for policy decisions. While a possible perception is that governments are all-powerful, well-resourced machines capable of outgunning campaigners, in the case of the CMC the NGO sector had at its disposal significantly more resources than probably any given government, in terms of the number of people with expert knowledge who were able to think about and research an issue when needed. So campaigners often know a lot more about the issues concerned than the people they are talking to in governments. This is likely to be true regardless of the field of work: environmental, human rights, and so on. A lesson here is that campaigners should never underestimate their strength with regard to the data and arguments at their disposal.

The CMC and many of its key members, such as Human Rights Watch, made a point of not overstating the case. This was considered essential in order to maintain credibility and on the issue of cluster munitions a highly conservative picture of the case was bad enough. There was a culture of scepticism and rigour within the CMC, and it was well understood that questionable use of data would only have given opponents an opening to criticize the campaign. It may also be considered that, in a situation where the legitimacy of NGOs can be difficult to establish, the use of data might be one of the only tangible metrics for NGO legitimacy—although this would rely on some objective criteria for monitoring the use of data by NGOs.[14]

5. Set the terms of the debate

Campaigns can win powerful advantages by framing the issue at hand in the way that suits them best, rather than struggling to win a debate whose terms have been set by those promoting the status quo. The CMC put a great deal of effort into framing the issue of cluster munitions as a humanitarian problem, where—based on an observed pattern of harm over many years—the starting position was that the weapon should be banned, and the burden of proof was on governments to argue that they should be permitted.

For several years, the prevailing wisdom was that cluster munitions were legitimate weapons that were not overly problematic if used in accordance with existing rules of international humanitarian law. Any concern over humanitarian harm caused by cluster munitions had to be balanced against the distinct military advantage they gave to armed forces. Rather than engage with this argument on the terms of military utility and the adequacy of international humanitarian law, the CMC worked to reframe the problem in a way that gave campaigners the upper hand. There were several approaches adopted here: scepticism, precautionary approaches and shifting the burden of proof.

The role of scepticism played an important part throughout the campaign, in particular in response to arguments focused on the essential military utility of the weapon. As noted above, the CMC regularly asked for specific examples of the military utility of cluster munitions, but users of the weapon were not able to provide any convincing material.[15] Precautionary approaches were also important. The CMC asked user governments what information they had on the humanitarian harm caused by the use of cluster munitions. In the case of the UK for example (and the UK was by no means an outlier), the answer was none.[16] On that basis, using the proportionality assessment to balance humanitarian harm against military advantage, how could they make a judgment on the permissibility of the weapon? The CMC also emphasised the need to move beyond a strictly legal approach based on IHL, and to shift the burden of proof onto governments arguing for the permissibility of cluster munitions. Given the demonstrated humanitarian harm over 40 years and on the basis of precautionary approaches, users were asked to justify the use of cluster munitions rather than NGOs having to justify their prohibition.[17] Crucially, the core group of states managing the negotiations on the text, in particular New Zealand, which was responsible for the definition of a cluster munition, was supportive of this approach.

6. Constant focus on the human impact

Another key element in reframing the debate was to emphasise the pattern of human suffering from cluster munitions as unacceptable.[18] The humanitarian evidence that member organizations of the coalition could gather through their fieldwork in areas affected by cluster munitions was important here.[19] This approach appealed to the moral sensibility of all those involved in the process. It was consistent with the notion of human security focused on protecting the lives of people and communities rather than traditional security focused on protecting the nation state.

The CMC maintained a human focus in all of its arguments, in its communications to the media and to governments, in its representatives to meetings (where survivors of cluster munitions played a prominent role), and in its audio-visual materials. Strong images of individuals and communities affected by cluster munitions were a regular feature at the regional and international meetings throughout the process. This unrelenting focus on the human impact helped the campaign to occupy the moral high ground, foster a sense of urgency, maintain pressure on delegates and keep the standard high during the negotiations, challenging others to reach it, rather than lowering the bar to allow others to meet it.

7. Leadership from those directly affected

Some of the most powerful advocates for a cause are those individuals, communities and states that are directly affected by the issue under discussion. Ensuring that campaigning and advocacy processes include these actors can be challenging for all involved, but it is vital in order to ensure legitimacy and relevance, and can be critical to the success of an initiative. Within the CMC individual survivors regularly participated in conferences and spoke out on behalf of the campaign. These campaigners—some of whom had lost limbs, lost their eyesight, or lost their children—not only influenced decision-makers in governments, but also helped to motivate people inside the campaign and to remind all involved why they were working on the issue.

Likewise the coalition actively engaged official representatives of affected states, in particular the Lao People's Democratic Republic (PDR) and Lebanon, to play prominent roles during the negotiations. An influential group of affected states emerged during this process, with a meeting for affected states held in Belgrade in October, 2007 and key interventions by affected states during the final negotiations in Dublin. Observers (Borrie, 2009) have noted the importance of the Belgrade Meeting of States Affected by Cluster Munitions and highlighted the role of affected states during the negotiating process in 2007 and 2008. There is little doubt that through their lobbying meetings and bilateral consultations, survivors and affected states helped to change minds and win arguments.

However, it is important to recognise the challenges in involving survivors. Above all, any initiative should be based on principles of dignity and respect. A sense of exploitation can easily emerge if campaigns simply bring in survivors to speak at a conference in a wealthy northern capital and then send them home again, where their home might be an impoverished village in Afghanistan or Lao PDR. Some kind of support network, peer-to-peer support structure or buddy system is vital, just so these individuals can get around and get through the day, let alone undertake lobbying activities. Individuals who have become involved in the campaign because they are survivors should be supported so that through their work they are seen primarily as campaigners rather than primarily as survivors.

This takes training and follow-up, including once these campaigners return to their homes. It can mean substantial commitments of funding and staff time. Handicap International ran a project throughout the Oslo Process to develop a group of 'Ban Advocates.' This initiative provided many of the positive elements required to make survivor inclusion in advocacy possible and also confronted many of the challenges outlined above.[20] As a result of intensive lobbying from the CMC, Article 5 of the Convention on Cluster Munitions includes an obligation to include victims in the development of policies and practice on victim assistance.[21] Implementing this obligation in practice will take some work, but it is an important articulation of the need for those making policy to be inclusive of those directly affected.

8. Build a powerful NGO coalition:

The CMC operated as a coalition of NGO members in around 100 countries. The significance and influence of these 'transnational advocacy networks' has been discussed from a range of perspectives, both theoretical and practical.[22] The global reach of these networks is a key aspect of their capacity to influence decision-making at the international level, and the CMC leadership put significant effort into developing and maintaining a network with global reach. Some of the aspects of this work are described below.

- *Coordination*: it was important to have a common message that all members were happy to promote, based on their own values and interests. The coalition leadership ensured that its messages to key partners and external audiences were carefully coordinated. This involved clear documentation translated into different languages and substantial time preparing for major conferences and global actions, including pre-meeting briefings.

- *Diversity*: the CMC was comprised of 400 organizations in around 100 countries, providing diversity across regions, linguistic groups, cultures, interest groups and worked hard to maintain a gender balance in its representative and decision-making work.

- *Inclusivity*: the campaign sought to listen to the voices of members and maintain a link between the broader membership of the coalition and the governance and leadership. The 'Steering Committee' was made up of thirteen organizations from the membership and took a hands-on approach to decision-making on policy, strategy and communications.

- *An affiliative approach*: NGO coalitions can be tricky to manage, given the diversity of actors involved. The coalition's leadership sought to foster a sense of belonging by understanding the interests, approaches and contexts of members and promoting shared interests, rather than laying down the approach all members must follow. The CMC did not experience—at least on a regular basis—conflict or competition amongst NGOs on policy, resources or profile, but where such tensions emerged the leadership sought to deal with them swiftly and openly (Borrie, 2009; pp. 274-275). Comprised of a centralized staff that did not represent one particular coalition member, the coordination team sought to promote the interests of the coalition as a whole.

- *Cooperation*: the coordination team sought to share the burden of work, using the skills of the different member organizations and individuals to undertake the tasks required. For example, during the final negotiations in Dublin, regional facilitators and thematic facilitators were appointed to coordinate advocacy work during the meeting. Based on a model adopted from the International Campaign to Ban Landmines (ICBL), internal workshops and campaign meetings were facilitated by campaigners themselves.[23]

9. **Foster strategic partnerships**

In addition to having its own wide-reaching network of NGO members, the CMC itself was part of a larger group working towards the same goal; the coalition leadership was included in a group of key individuals from states and international organizations very early on in the process. A particularly strong bond developed between the CMC,

Norway and the United Nations Development Programme (UNDP). This bond existed both institutionally and personally amongst the individuals involved. These interpersonal relationships were very tight, with information shared on a daily basis, ensuring a coordinated approach to problems and opportunities. Relationships also existed with key political leaders, which at times proved to be influential in encouraging those leaders to take risks in pursuit of the prohibition. There are concrete examples of these sorts of relationships, but it is difficult to provide them without exposing politicians and civil servants to claims that they may have been working against their own governments' instructions.

Strong partnerships were also forged with key regional players such as Zambia, Mexico, Indonesia, and New Zealand, as well as with cluster munition-affected countries like Lao PDR and Lebanon. By developing partnerships with parliamentarians, faith leaders, academics, journalists and other interest groups around the world, the CMC was able to take advantage of their existing networks of influence to promote change and apply pressure. Very importantly, the coalition recognised the importance of individuals as well as institutions. Although perhaps more difficult to document and analyse, it became apparent throughout the campaign that often the personalities of individuals and the relationships that they build with one another are more important than the policy positions and institutional interests of any one entity at any one time.

10. Do a lot with a little

The CMC thought carefully about where to place its resources and how to approach its advocacy and campaigning activities in order to get maximum impact. Throughout the Oslo Process, the coalition carved out a space for itself as a significant international campaign with the capacity to influence decision-makers in countries all over the world. The CMC was never a mass grassroots social movement that had the ability to mobilize millions of people around the world; it was a network of organizations, some professional, some voluntary, that could reach decision-makers directly. Although this raises questions of legitimacy and representativeness, which will be addressed below in the examination of some of the criticisms of the process, the success of the campaign suggests that a relatively small network can have significant impact.

For example, the CMC's experience was that one good contact with a strong relationship in a key country can be more important and have more of an impact than a major public campaign in that country. The value of a coalition is that all of these contacts can work together in the same direction. Similarly, strategic media work that targets decision-makers at key moments will amplify the significance of the campaign and make pressure felt where it counts. In the UK, a campaign by Landmine Action in 2007 targeted then Foreign Minister David Miliband with a large advertisement in Westminster tube station that read: "Cluster bombs: get them Milibanned." It is always difficult to assess the impact of such campaigns, but the following passage from a US Embassy cable published by Wikileaks is instructive. The passage refers to comments by senior UK Foreign and Commonwealth Office official Mariot Leslie:

> Leslie explained that [Her Majesty's Government] was experiencing much of the same public and political pressure to ban [cluster munitions] that the Norwegians felt. She noted [Foreign Secretary] Miliband had been targeted personally with posters saying "Cluster Munitions should be Milibanned!" [Her Majesty's Government], therefore, needed to be seen cooperating with the process and "could not just walk away."[24]

During the final negotiations for the prohibition in Dublin, the CMC undertook an advertising campaign aimed at fostering a sense amongst delegates that the issue that they were there to debate was the most important issue in town. Advertisements were placed in strategic locations along the routes that delegates were most likely to take, around their accommodations and outside the conference venue.[25]

The coalition's budget throughout the campaign was also relatively modest. There was only one fulltime member of staff until the beginning of 2007; at its peak, the coalition had five fulltime employees. The campaign never had a budget for mass public mobilization; rather it focused on supporting member organizations around the world (including through a small grants program) and maximizing strategic moments, in particular the key negotiating conferences, for which the coalition helped finance the participation of civil society.[26]

Global civil society coalitions can have an important role to play in bringing about positive change in international affairs. Each coalition may have to find its own way to deal with criticisms, but the experience of the CMC shows that a global campaign with long-lasting implications can be built on very little. Those involved with civil society activism—practitioners or observers—may need to accept that there will always be challenges related to NGO legitimacy and representativeness and criticisms over the role of middle-power civil society partnerships.

It will be important to keep addressing these challenges and criticisms, but it may also be time to move beyond some of these debates, which have been central elements of the literature on global civil society for the past decade. Emerging coalition work to address the impact of explosive weapons when used in populated areas and collective NGO work to promote a state obligation to record and recognise every casualty of armed violence may well provide further evidence on the importance and effectiveness of civil society coalitions at changing law and policy around the world.[27]

---

[1] Keck and Sikkink, Activists beyond Borders, pp 43-44, in Ahmed and Potter (eds); Finnemore and Sikkink, "International Norm Dynamics and Political Change," *International Organization* 52, 4, Autumn 1998, pp. 887–917.

[2] Matthew Bolton and Thomas Nash, "The Role of Middle Power-NGO Coalitions in Global Policy: The Case of the Cluster Munitions Ban," Global Policy, Vol. 1, Issue 2, May 2010, p.181.

[3] The membership doubled again from 2007-2008 during the key period of the treaty negotiations.

[4] See Rappert, B., 2005. "Out of balance: the UK Government's efforts to understand cluster munitions and international humanitarian law," London: Landmine Action; Rappert, B. and Moyes, R., 2006. "Failure to protect: a case for the prohibition of cluster munitions," London: Landmine Action; Nash, T., 2006, 'Foreseeable Harm: the use and impact of cluster munitions in Lebanon: 2006' London: Landmine Action.

[5] John Borrie discusses the early years of engagement on cluster munitions in *Unacceptable Harm: A History of How the Treaty to Ban Cluster Munitions was Won,* J. Borrie, December 2009, United Nations.

[6] Borrie, J. (2005) Rethinking multilateral negotiations: disarmament as humanitarian action. In: Borrie, J. and Martin Randin, V. (Eds.) *Alternative Approaches in Multilateral Decision Making: Disarmament as Humanitarian Action.* (Disarmament as Humanitarian Action) Vol. 1. Geneva: United Nations Institute for Disarmament Research, pp. 7-37.

[7] Email from Kasia Derlicka to the CMC international email distribution list, 14 December 2005.

[8] See emails from Thomas Nash to the CMC international email distribution list in July and August 2006, on file with author.

[9] See Oslo Conference on Cluster Munitions: Declaration, February 23 2007: accessed 30 August 2011 at:

http://www.regjeringen.no/upload/UD/Vedlegg/Oslo%20Declaration%20(final)%2023%20February%202007.pdf.

[10] For a list of relevant publications see the website of the Cluster Munition Coalition, accessed 30 August 2011 at: http://www.stopclustermunitions.org/campaign-resources/reports/.

[11] See ICRC, Humanitarian, Military, Technical and Legal Challenges of Cluster Munitions, Montreux, Switzerland, 18-20 April 2007 and in particular Lt. Col. Jim Burke's summary as rapporteur on military apects and possible alternatives, pp. 66-69. Accessed 30 August 2011 at: http://www.mineaction.org/downloads/1/ICRC%20expert%20meeting%20report.pdf.

[12] Author's notes from the Montreux Expert Meeting, April 2007.

[13] This respect for the CMC can be seen in the statements from a wide range of governments that praised the CMC during the closing debate at the Dublin Diplomatic Conference in May 2008 and during the Oslo Signing Conference in December 2008. In June 2011, the Lao Assistant Minister of Foreign Affairs referred to 'the great CMC' when introducing the CMC Director, Laura Cheeseman.

[14] Matthew Bolton and Thomas Nash, "The Role of Middle Power-NGO Coalitions in Global Policy: The Case of the Cluster Munitions Ban," Global Policy, Vol. 1, Issue 2, May 2010, p.181.

[15] For more discussion on the treatment of military utility in the negotiating process on the Convention on Cluster Munitions, see: Brian Rappert, "A convention beyond the Convention," Landmine Action, 2008, pp. 21-23; John Borrie, Unacceptable Harm, pp. 330-333.

[16] Brian Rappert, Out of Balance, Landmine Action 2005

[17] For an early discussion of this reframing, see Rappert and Moyes, "Failure to Protect," Landmine Action, 2006.

[18] While the campaign kept a focus on the human suffering from cluster munitions there was a recognition amongst many campaigners that, in line with interpretations of international humanitarian law, certain civilian deaths and injuries would happen. The key to the concept of "unacceptable harm to civilians," which underpinned the diplomatic negotiations, was that cluster munitions were exceptional in the harm they caused to civilians.

[19] See, for example, King, C., Dullum, O. and Østern, G., "M85: an analysis of reliability," Norwegian People's Aid, 2007.

[20] See the website of the Ban Advocates at http://www.banadvocates.org/, accessed 30 August 2011.

[21] See Article 5 of the Convention on Cluster Munitions: accessed 30 August at: http://www.clusterconvention.org/documents/full-text-enfres/.

[22] For a discussion on the practical aspects of coalition campaigning drawing on the experience from the CMC see Moyes and Nash: 'An introduction to global civil society coalition work', 2011 forthcoming; for an academic discussion on transnational advocacy networks see Keck and Sikkink 1998.

[23] Moyes and Nash: 'An introduction to global civil society coalition work,' 2011 forthcoming.

[24] Extract from 'INTERNATIONAL SECURITY DISCUSSIONS WITH HMG', Diplomatic Cable from the US Embassy in London, 6 March 2008, accessed 15 August 2011 at: http://www.telegraph.co.uk/news/wikileaks-files/london-wikileaks/8305077/INTERNATIONAL-SECURITY-DISCUSSIONS-WITH-HMG.html.

[25] More information on the media campaign during the negotiations in Dublin in May 2008 is available in the CMC's annual report for 2008, accessed on 15 August 2011: http://www.stopclustermunitions.org/wp/wp-content/uploads/2009/12/cmc-annual-report-2008.pdf.

[26] Moyes and Nash: 'A resource guide for global civil society coalitions', 2011 forthcoming.

[27] See the International Network on Explosive Weapons at: www.inew.org and the Every Casualty network www.everycasualty.org for more information on these two initiatives. Both websites accessed 30 August 2011.

References

Atwood, D., *et al.* (2009) "Learn, adapt, succeed: potential lessons from the Ottawa and Oslo processes for other disarmament and arms control challenges," *Disarmament Forum* (1 and 2), 19-25.

Matthew Bolton and Thomas Nash, "The Role of Middle Power-NGO Coalitions in Global Policy: The Case of the Cluster Munitions Ban," *Global Policy*, Vol. 1, Issue 2, May 2010, p.181.

John Borrie:

Unacceptable Harm: A History of How the Treaty to Ban Cluster Munitions was Won, J. Borrie, December 2009, United Nations

The Value of Diversity in Multilateral Disarmament Work, J. Borrie & A. Thornton, December 2008, United Nations

Thinking Outside the Box in Multilateral Disarmament and Arms Control Negotiations, J. Borrie & V. Martin Randin (eds), December 2006, United Nations

Disarmament as Humanitarian Action: From Perspective to Practice, J. Borrie & V. Martin Randin (eds), May 2006, United Nations

Nystuen and Casey-Maslen, *The Convention on Cluster Munitions: A Legal Commentary,* Oxford University Press, 2010

Margaret E. Keck and Kathryn Sikkink, Activists beyond Borders, 1998

Michael Edwards and John Gaventa, eds, Global Citizen Action, 2001

Ann M. Florini, ed, The Third Force: the rise of transnational civil society, 2001

Richard Price, "Reversing the Gun Sights: Transnational Civil Society Targets Landmines," *International Organization* 52, no. 3 (1998): 613-44.

Rappert, Brian and Moyes, Richard, A.N. Other (2011), "Statecrafting ignorance: Strategies for managing burdens, secrecy, and conflict," in Susan Maret (ed.) *Government Secrecy (Research in Social Problems and Public Policy, Volume 19)*, Emerald Group Publishing Limited, pp.301-324

Rappert, B. and R. Moyes. 2010. "Enhancing the Protection of Civilians from Armed Conflict: Precautionary Lessons," Medicine, Conflict & Survival 26(1), January-March: 24-47.

Rappert, B. and R. Moyes. 2009. "The Prohibition of Cluster Munitions: Setting International Precedents for Defining Inhumanity," in *Non-proliferation Review* 16(2): 237-256.

Sidney Tarrow, *Power in Movement: Social Movements and Contentious Politics,* 2nd Ed, 1998

Peter van Tuijl, and Lisa Jordan, "Political Responsibility in Transnational NGO Advocacy," October 1999, accessed 30 August 2011 at http://www.bicusa.org/en/Article.138.asp

CPSIA information can be obtained
at www.ICGtesting.com
Printed in the USA
LVOW12s1629270516

490234LV00005B/148/P

9 780984 980208